WINE

A comprehensive look
at the world's best wines

GRAMERCY

GRAMERCY BOOKS
New York

WINE
A comprehensive look at the world's best wines

© 2002 Rebo International b. v., Lisse, The Netherlands

This 2003 edition published by Gramercy Books, an imprint of Random House Value Publishing,
a division of Random House, Inc., New York, by arrangement with Rebo International b. v., Lisse, The Netherlands.

Gramercy is a registered trademark and the colophon is a trademark of Random House, Inc.

Printed in Slovenia

Random House

New York ● Toronto ● London ● Sydney ●Auckland

www.randomhouse.com

A catalog record for this title is avalaible from the Library of Congress.

ISBN 0-517-22165-9

987654321

Contents

Foreword

In this Great Wine Encyclopedia, I would like to take you on a fascinating journey around the world, visiting all the well-known and lesser-known wine-producing countries. The world of wine is constantly changing: new trends regularly emerge, and new countries and new names of wines are always being added. In this book you will come across many of these changes.

In this encyclopedia I hope to give you a clear picture of the latest developments related to wine. In addition to the well-known wine-producing countries of the past, such as France, Italy, Portugal, Spain, Greece, Germany, Switzerland and Austria, the countries of the former East Bloc and the Balkans are also working on a regeneration of quality in the world of wine, particularly Slovenia, Croatia, Hungary and to a lesser extent, Bulgaria and Romania. Some old, almost forgotten wine producing countries, such as Morocco, Algeria, Tunisia, Turkey, the Lebanon and Israel, are also joining in, although their contribution is in general still very modest. Of these countries, only the Lebanon has an important presence in the high quality wine market.

Lebanese wines, five thousand years of history

The important newcomers of the last ten to fifteen years include the Americas (Canada, the United States, Mexico, Bolivia, Brazil, Uruguay, Argentina and Chile) and South Africa, Australia and New Zealand. However, great attempts are also being made nowadays to catch up in Asia: Japan, China, Thailand and India are the most noticeable new wine-producing countries.

Countries such as Iran, Syria, Ireland and Zimbabwe and the Scandinavian countries, which are not yet very important with regard to wine production, have been left out of consideration here. The Scandinavian countries are experimenting with wine growing, and the vineyards in Jutland, Sweden, probably have the best chance. We may hear more of them in the future.

Bouchard wine cellars in Burgundy

Japanese wine, better and better, more and more serious

The journey we make in this encyclopedia is an invitation to devote more attention to the stories behind the different wines. Wine is not merely a nice drink, but also has a lot to say: about its background, its origins, its producer. All too often the consumer chooses wine as though it is just another brand name article. For example, he will buy a Bordeaux or Champagne. He buys a label, and forgets to listen to the story. In this book you will find some of the stories behind the labels, which will help to make drinking wine an even more enjoyable experience.

In the context of this book, I will devote attention to red, white and rosé wines, from dry wines to sweet wines, and also to various sparkling wines (including champagne, crémants, cava, spumanti) and so-called fortified or mutated wines (Manzanilla, port, Banyuls, and Maury, for example). However, we will not cover the different herbal aperitifs, such as vermouth.

In addition, there are some tips about serving wine, and for each wine you will find the sort of dish it can accompany. I wish you all the best in your reading, traveling and drinking.

Christian Callec

1

The history of wine and viticulture

ORIGINS OF THE VINE

European vines originate from the Indo-European Transcaucasian region (present-day Azerbaijan, Georgia and Armenia). This was revealed by discoveries made by botanists and archeologists. Wine was made there as long as 8,000 years ago. In this respect, biblical stories and reality come together. After all, according to local legend it was on Mount Ararat in Armenia that Noah's Ark came to rest after the Flood.

While the origins of the wine-producing vine, the *Vitis vinifera*, are in Transcaucasia, the *Vitis* family appears to be much older. There are fossils with the impressions of vine leaves sixty million years old. Spores, leaves and seeds of old *Vitis* species have also been found in Tertiary and Quaternary sediments. The vine managed to survive during the two Ice Ages in a number of sheltered areas, in particular, in North Africa, Spain, Italy, Greece, the Balkans and the above-mentioned

Healthy fruit of the *Vitis vinifera*

area of Transcaucasia. The vine was originally a climbing plant which liked to grow up deciduous trees to heights of ten to twenty meters, and thrived in areas with warm and wet summers. Other *Vitis* varieties flourished in different parts of the world. For example, there were no *Vitis vinifera* vines in North America, but there were hundreds of other descendants of the *Vitis* family. One of these, *Vitis labrusca* (also found in Europe), produced large grapes. This species is still used for wine nowadays, giving the wines a slightly tarry taste, the foxy quality which is so characteristic of the original Californian wines. Altogether, there are more than sixty *Vitis* species around the world. Only one of these, *Vitis vinifera*, is used to make quality wines nowadays.

Over the years, viticulture has become possible almost anywhere, as the result of the clever selection of varieties and the increasing skill of wine growers, even in relatively cold areas of Europe, such as Germany, the Netherlands and England. Viticulture has also become possible in rather humid climates of the Atlantic Ocean (Galicia, Portugal) and in the Mediterranean areas, which are really much too dry.

CLASSICAL ANTIQUITY

WINE AND VINES IN MYTHOLOGY

There is a story in the Bible about Noah planting a vine (Genesis IX, 23). It appears that he found his vines in earthly Paradise. After all, we know that after eating the forbidden fruit, Adam grabbed some vine leaves to cover the shame of his nakedness. The story in which Noah became drunk on his homemade wine is also a well-known passage. The Bible also tells how Moses and his followers came across many vineyards on their way to the promised land of Canaan. There are the scenes of the marriage feast at Cana, when the guests suddenly discovered in panic that the wine had run out! However, it was at the Last Supper that we reach the apotheosis, when Jesus spoke to his apostles and symbolized wine as the blood of Christ.

Wine was a divine beverage for the Phoenicians, the Greeks and the Romans. Dionysus and his Roman counterpart Bacchus were great lovers of wine. Wine was a central aspect of many religious and heathen ceremonies when it flowed freely.

Modern viticulture started when people actually started to grow and reproduce vines. The new plants were left as bushes or trained along natural supports. Barely a thousand years later, viticulture reached Egypt. From there it also went to Greece, probably thanks to the Phoenicians. In their turn, the Etruscans took the wine-growing skills to Italy, three thousand years ago. The Romans were responsible for the spread of vineyards all over Europe. Wherever the Roman legions marched, they planted vineyards. In this way, Roman soldiers never had to do without the divine drink of Bacchus, the god of wine.

TRANSCAUCASIA, MESOPOTAMIA, PERSIA AND SUMERIA

The oldest proof of the consumption of grapes as a type of fruit dates from the Neolithic age, a period when people often lived on the shores of big rivers and lakes. For example, grapes were already eaten around Lake Geneva (Lac Léman), in 12000 BC. Historians consider that it is quite likely that people were already drinking the fermented juice of grapes, (i.e., wine) in those days. However, at the moment, there is no proof that they did so. The oldest traces of viticulture have been found in Transcaucasia (Armenia, Georgia, Azerbaijan) and in the bordering region between the rivers (viz., the Tigris and the Euphrates), known as Mesopotamia, grapes were already being cultivated in 6000 years BC, probably also to produce wine. The vines probably grew there in bush form, low to the ground or as climbing plants on conifers, just as they do now in Cappadocia.

Recent archeological discoveries in Iran confirm that man was already making beer and wine there at least five thousand years before Christ. Recently, a complete Neolithic residence was discovered in Hajji Firuz Tepe, where six wine jugs were found, as well as a number of items of kitchenware and a bread oven. These discoveries date from 5400 to 5000 BC! Other archeological discoveries have revealed that the Neolithic civilization in the Middle East had developed some very sophisticated culinary practices. These people knew how to bake bread, and were able to ferment vegetables, produce wine and barley beer and use fresh herbs and spices with meat, prepare dishes with cereals and meat and store food and drink in earthenware pots and jugs. They were already doing this in 6000 BC! Spectrographic analysis has revealed that the jugs found in Hajji Firuz Tepe still contain traces of dried wine. It is also surprising that there were traces of turpentine resin. Botanists explained

this as follows: in those days the vines climbed up tall conifers, trees which are known to produce resin. However, it is still not known whether the turpentine resin was added to the wine (as the Egyptians, Greeks and Romans did later, also to protect the wine against going off and becoming vinegary), or whether the grapes themselves contained a high level of turpentine resin because they grew in the same soil as the conifers. Anyone who thought that Retsina was a Greek discovery must be disabused of this idea twice over, because the Egyptians were already adding resin to their wines before the Greeks, and the Mesopotamian wines dating from 6000-5000 BC already contained turpentine resin. In those days, people also knew how important it was to store wine in a cool place, and the jars were sealed with an earthenware stopper. The many discoveries in modern Iran (former Persia) and Iraq have shown us that there was a very lively trade in wine in ancient Sumeria and in Mesopotamia, at least 3500 BC, long before the Greeks, and even the Egyptians, learned to produce wine. Later, this heritage was spread further afield by the Phoenicians, to the distant shores of the Mediterranean Sea (including southern France, Spain and Tunisia).

EGYPT

Botanists have been surprised to discover that wine was being made in Egypt even before the time of the Greeks. After all, the vine was not indigenous in anci-

Egyptian wine

ent Egypt. However, historians have established that there was a flourishing trade between Ancient Egypt and the countries in the Middle East. This is probably how the first wines came to Egypt via Palestine. Traces of viticulture have been found dating back to at least 2700 BC. Hieroglyphs of nature (the grape vine) and the origin of the wines (including Saqqarah, Sile, Behbeit el Hagar and Memphis) have been found on the oblong Egyptian jars dating back to the third millennium BC. According to historians, these hieroglyphs are the first known versions of modern wine labels. The Egyptians also sealed their jars with earthenware stoppers.

The tomb of the Pharaoh Nakht was a rich source of information. Countless splendid murals show how popular viticulture was in ancient Egypt. The paintings reveal how the vines were trained along latticework in structures like pergolas, which are still occasionally found today. The grapes were collected in willow baskets and taken to the tub to be trampled. The Egyptians trod their grapes in these large open tubs. You can see how they had to hold on to a bar above them so that they did not slip. The must started to bubble and ferment in the heat. The fermenting must was then tran-

The wines of Samos are amongst the oldest in the world.

sferred to large earthenware jars, and the remaining pulp was wrapped up in a cloth, which was then knotted and battered with a stick to press out the last juices. Fermentation continued in the large jars sealed with a lid of mud and straw, and the carbon dioxide which was released escaped through a small hole in the lid. Because of the hot sun in the Nile valley the wines were very concentrated and contained a high level of alcohol and residual sugars, which meant that they could be kept for a reasonably long time in the large cool jars. This ancient wine-making technique was actually used in some parts of Spain until recently, for example, in Valdepeñas. In fact, the Spanish *tinajas* are not very different from the ancient Egyptian pointed jars, apart from their enormous size.

It is surprising that wine does not appear to have been a particularly popular drink with the Ancient Egyptians: they preferred to drink beer in daily life! Wine fulfilled a very paradoxical function. On the one hand, it was greatly appreciated by the pharaohs and high priests and was used in their sacrifices to the gods. Therefore wine was a popular drink in the afterlife; on the other hand, only slaves, servants and very poor people drank wine during their lifetime. The elite, who did drink wine during ceremonies, drank it from the most beautiful goblets; poor people drank it directly from the jar through a straw. The patron of vine growing, the god Osiris, was an inspiration in mythology for the Greek god Dionysus, and later the Roman god Bacchus.

GREECE

While the people of Transcaucasia were the first to engage in vine growing, and the Egyptians were the first to depict the techniques of viniculture and wine making, it was the Greeks who raised the making and, above all, the drinking of wine to an art form. Wine and everything related to wine was a very fruitful source of inspiration for Greek historians, philosophers, painters, sculptures and poets. The majority of the wines in ancient Greece came from the islands, and each island made a very specific wine. The wines from Chios, Samos and Lesbos in particular, soon became famous. A great deal of wine was also imported from the Middle East and from Egypt. As in Ancient Egypt, drinking wine was a great source of pleasure amongst the elite. The many Greek nations who spread their horizons to the coast of the Mediterranean Sea, took their vines and wine-growing techniques with them to almost everywhere they settled. For example, the Ionians/Phoenicians founded cities such as Massilia (Marseille), Nikaia (Nice), Antiopolis (Antibes) and Agathè (Aix-en-Provence), but they also occupied the south of Italy and Sicily. The wine-growing areas in these regions owe nearly everything to the Ancient Greeks. It has also become clear that the Greeks already had contacts with the Celts more than 600 years BC, and they too knew how to make wine.

In Classical Antiquity, vines were often grown up pergolas.

Before drinking it, all sorts of things were added to the wine.

CELTS

In the early days of viticulture, the grapes were simply harvested in the woods. For example, the priests of the Celtic gods and goddesses knew all about the cosmic and earthly magnetic forces, and knew how to determine the places where these various forces met, by means of performing secret measurements. There were often tall trees, usually oaks growing in these places. Two and a half thousand years ago, the Druids picked the berries of the climbing plants the *Vitis labrusca* which grew on these sacred oaks. They would also take some twigs of mistletoe along, which they placed on top of the grapes they had picked so as to keep this secret. The Druids produced a tonic from these freshly picked grapes, together with herbs and honey. They were already using wooden tubs and barrels for the fermentation and storage of the wine. Was this the secret of the magic drink made by the famous Gauls? Nowadays, fans of Asterix and Obelix as well as many others still believe that the village Druid climbed in the tall oak trees to pick mistletoe… However, a short study of the way in which mistletoe grows soon shows that it hardly ever grows on oak trees!

The techniques that were used soon changed: in order to ensure that the grapes were exposed to more sunlight, the leaves and trees around the more productive climbing plants were removed. Later on, the vines which had been removed from the forest were planted close to the village, next to existing trees. Productivity may have been reduced by pruning the vines, but the quality constantly improved.

ROMANS

Wine has been traded since time immemorial, usually between rich families who managed to keep viticulture going in this way. For centuries, wine was much sought after in trade. The Phoenicians, Greeks, Egyptians, Romans and others transported wine throughout Europe. Rome became the metropolis of the wine trade. Although the Celts and the Greeks played an important role in the development of European viticulture, we particularly owe a great deal to the unquenchable thirst of the Roman legions and to the great skills of the wine growers who settled everywhere. It was the Romans who revived the trade in wine. The production and drinking of wine was never promoted as much as it was under the Romans. In some cities, such as Pompeii, there were stalls selling wine on almost every street corner. In Roman times wine was also particularly

Sotanum

M. CM. XCVII

« Les vins de Vienne si renommés sous les Romains, se receuillaient à Seyssuel (...) Pline le naturaliste, Martial, Plutarque, &c. n'en parlent qu'avec éloges » (I).

« Le vin que produit le territoire de Seyssuel jouit d'une grande réputation : on peut en juger par ce passage extrait de l'ouvrage de M. Faujas de Saint-Fonds (II), p 183, (...) ; « Seyssuel est un village au nord de Vienne, qui en est éloigné d'une lieu ; la vigne y croit dans des collines seches et arides, formées des débris de schistes micacés granitoïdes Lyon en consome beaucoup, & l'on en fait des envois dans le nord du royaume » » (II).

« Un plant à raisin noir, appelé vitis Allobbrogica, cultivé sur le territoire de Vienne, donne trois crus : le Sotanum, le Taburnum, l'Helvicum suivant le terroir. Ce dernier est le plus recherché »(III).

Textes extraits de : (I) N.F Cochard Seyssuel et Chasse (1789) BM. Vienne A 8312 ;(II) Cet ouvrage est un mémoire sur les vins du Dauphiné; (III) N.F Cochard. Dictionnaire manuscrit du Dauphiné (1789), (III) Pline l'Ancien. Histoire naturelle, livre XIV, Belles Lettres (1958).

The Romans already appreciated the wines of the Rhône.

a drink for the elite. The best and rarest wines flowed freely at their banquets while the common people and the soldiers had to make do with vinegary wine which was watered down.

THE PRODUCTION OF WINE IN ANTIQUITY

In classical antiquity, technology was not very highly developed and voyages often took a very long time. The wines at that time were not or hardly treated: after a spontaneous process of fermentation, they were stored in large amphoras or jugs and then quickly consumed. On the other hand, the wines which were intended for trade often had to be processed in some way. For example, during the wine making, honey or currants were added to the juices to increase the alcohol content (alcohol is produced as a result of the conversion of sugars), so that the wines would not be adversely affec-

The wine was often pressed in the open air.

Wine played a major role in the liturgy.

ted by being transported. Sometimes they were also heated to concentrate them, or even smoked so that they would age faster. The wines obtained by this method were syrupy, heavy and very alcoholic. They had to be diluted with one or two parts of sea water before they could be drunk. Many wines were also given a special taste by adding different substances–nowadays we might prefer to say that the unpleasant taste was removed. Herbs and spices, pepper, resin, flowers, roots, leaves, bark and fruit juices were used for this purpose.

FROM ANTIQUITY TO THE MIDDLE AGES

When the Roman Empire collapsed as a result of the incursions of Germanic Barbarians from the north and Islamic Moors from the south, European viticulture was almost completely erased. Only occasional vineyards remained intact, particularly in the vicinity of large cities. Under Islamic domination there were harsh measures against wine growing almost everywhere. However, ironically one famous wine-growing area was ignored by the Shiite Muslims until the start the nineteenth century: the region of Shiraz, in modern Iran.

An uncertain hostile climate prevailed throughout Europe. The frequent wars led to a sense of unrest, hunger and poverty; under these circumstances, no one was interested in the wine trade. It was the Catholic Church which honored the tradition of the Last Supper (wine as the blood of Christ) that saved European viticulture from complete extinction. Priests and monks (re)planted the vines throughout Europe, not so much to produce high quality wines, but particular-

The Dordogne, an important artery in the history of viticulture in Aquitaine

ly to provide the wine for the mass. However, what started as a wine for the liturgy soon turned into a valuable trade.

THE MIDDLE AGES

THE DEVELOPMENT OF BORDEAUX AND THE SOUTHWEST

At the end of the Middle Ages a number of wine-growing areas became very well known: Anjou, Charentes (Cognac), Poitou, Cahors and Gascony in France, and the German areas around the Ahr, the Rhine and the Nahe, as well as Alsace. When the last strongholds of the Moorish rulers in Southern Europe had been removed, viticulture started to develop again very quickly, partly because of the work done by monks. Trade took place particularly along the Seine and the Rhine, but soon moved south to La Rochelle, Bergerac and Bordeaux. It was the Flemish and English who helped trade to flourish. In the thirteenth century wine growing developed very quickly around Bordeaux. Wealthy inhabitants of the city financed enormous deforestation projects on the less fertile soil along the Garonne and Dordogne rivers, and settled in new estates in the vineyards of Bordeaux. As the quality of the harvests could not always be guaranteed, although the demand increased very rapidly, there was a need for reserve wines for the Bordeaux region. Vineyards mushroomed everywhere along the Garonne, the Tarn and the Dordogne, even as far as Auvergne. Existing wine-growing areas such as Saint-Emilion, Bergerac, Cahors and Gail-

lac spread extensively. This came to an abrupt end during the wars between the French and English at the end of the thirteenth century and the beginning of the fourteenth century. Many vineyards were destroyed for military reasons.

The vineyards of Montravel (Bergerac) once belonged to the Bordeaux region.

Bergerac wines were extremely popular with the wealthy Flemish bourgeoisie.

GERMANY AND THE RHINE WINES

At the same time that the wines of Aquitaine became famous, the trade in Rhine wines also flourished, particularly in the city of Cologne. The collective term Rhine wines also included the wines from Alsace, Baden, Pfalz, Main, and Moselle. In Germany it was mainly white wines that were traded so that there was not any real competition with Aquitaine and the other French regions. In fact, they actually complemented each other. The emergence of breweries, a few very poor harvests, religious wars and some stagnation in demand unfortunately resulted in the golden age of German wine growing coming to an end in the seventeenth century. Wine growing areas lost ground everywhere and the fame of these once valued wines was limited to an ever-smaller circle.

OTHER WINE-GROWING AREAS

In other regions of Europe, but also in France itself, viticulture went through some dramatic times. In the Middle Ages, the Italian wines of Piedmont, Valtellina, Trentino-Alto Adige and South Tyrol became very famous, as well as those of present-day French Savoie (Apremont).

In France, the great southwest was flourishing. In addition to the wines of Bergerac, Gaillac and Cahors, the wines of Madiran and Marcillac were also doing very well. The wines in Burgundy only really had a breakthrough at the end of the fourteenth century, when Burgundy and Flanders became one large empire. However, as Burgundy wines could only be transported by road, they were confronted with the competition of the German wines (which could easily be transported on the Rhine), and the southern French wines (transported by sea). Nevertheless, because of their superior quality, they became more and more popular with wealthy Flemish families.

After the reconquest of the Moors (the Reconquista) in Spain, wine growing flourished once again. However, the vineyards had suffered extensively during the Moorish occupation and as a result the quality of the wine was so poor that the Spanish continued to import their wine from the southwest of France. Apart from the wines of Rioja and Navarra, which were still of a moderate quality in those days, there were a few acidic light wines such as the Basque Txakoli and wines from Galicia.

WINES FROM THE MEDITERRANEAN

The well-known wines from areas around the Mediterranean not only included Italian wines; Greek wines also went through a golden age, partly with the help of thirsty Italians. The traditional viticulture on many Greek Islands was revived by the Knights Templar. The Commondaria and Malvasia wines were so famous that they were soon copied everywhere, particularly by the Spanish (Malaga) and Portuguese (Madeira), but also by the Italians (for example, Recioto della Valpolicella, Malvasia and many Greek wines from southern Italy).

Spanish wines were transported in pigskins.

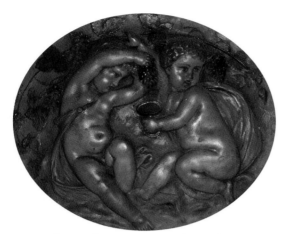

Sweet wines were extremely popular.

V.O.C. wine flask

THE SEVENTEENTH AND EIGHTEENTH CENTURIES

DUTCH BRANDIES

As the transport of wine was risky and, above all, an expensive business, the thrifty Dutch decided to modify the techniques that were used. The splendid Bordeaux wines and wines from the southwest were heated until their volume was considerably reduced. This meant that the wines could be transported and took up less space. These brandies were very popular in the Netherlands. They were drunk either neat or diluted with water. The same brandies were also used to cut the better wines from southern France. A significant proportion of brandy was added to these superior wines so that they would survive the journey better. As the Dutch started to dominate the trade in Bordeaux too successfully very much against the will of the French King Louis XIV and his minister, Colbert, this Dutch domination soon came to a halt. The fact that the Dutch were very proud of their republic was also a thorn in the French Kings side. The war between the Netherlands and France broke out in 1672. The most important consequence of this war from the point of view of this book was the sudden complete lack of interest of the Dutch in Bordeaux and the wines of the southwest, and the search for alternatives. New wine-growing areas were found in Portugal (Douro, famous for its port wines), the island of Madeira and Spain (Malaga, and especially Jerez de la Frontera). Following the Treaty of Nijmegen in 1678, the Dutch were able to return to the Bordeaux region under very advantageous conditions and they were received with open arms. It is surprising that the English, who fought on the French side during the Dutch-French conflict, were not afforded these favorable conditions. Frustrated, they ignored the French wines and in turn focused on Portugal (port) and Spain (sherry).

THE EMERGENCE OF NEW DRINKS

Beer had been popular for some time in Germany, the Netherlands and England, as had Scotch whiskey, Dutch jenever, English gin and various tropical distilled drinks such as rum and Curaçao triple sec. In those days it was much healthier to drink wine than water, or even milk. The quality of beer was not always particularly good either, and therefore relatively large quantities of wine were drunk. The competition for wine came from an unexpected corner, not from other alcoholic drinks, but from stimulating drinks such as tea, coffee and chocolate, which were brought back

Old champagne wine press

Champagne cellar in chalk

from the many voyages of discovery and which became increasingly popular. In England, there was a rage for coffee houses. In addition to serving coffee, tea and chocolate, these also served better and better wines, mainly fortified wines such as port, sherry, Malaga or Madeira. It was only at the beginning of the eighteenth century that the English once again showed an interest in French wines from Bordeaux, which had improved enormously in quality in the meantime. There was a steady growth in the trade of this French claret, but also in champagnes.

THE BREAKTHROUGH OF CHAMPAGNE AND OTHER HIGH QUALITY WINES

While the monks of the Champagne region preferred to make dry wines which were an improvement on the quality of other white wines, it was actually the English who became very fond of the mad wines, which bubbled so excitingly and naughtily in the glass. They showed the local monks how to bottle the wines in thick English bottles with a (Spanish) cork. The winemaker Dom Pérignon and his colleagues did not succeed in preventing spontaneous fermentation in the bottle despite many attempts at this, but as a result of their work, the quality of champagne wines improved enormously. They stopped fighting the bubbles, and

these sparkling champagnes soon became very popular.

In Burgundy it was above all the red wines which were known for their excellent quality. The white wines were drunk when they were still young and were often served as house wines. However, the preference of wealthy Parisians was for the fuller wines of the Rhône valley, particularly Cote Rôtie and Hermitage. In England these wines were never able to compete with the French claret.

THE SUPREMACY OF SWEET WINES

In the eighteenth century a number of other great sweet wines developed in addition to the already well-known Madeira, port, sherry, Malaga and sweet Greek wines. Marsala from Sicily and the Muscat du Languedoc, from Frontignan, were particularly popular. Nevertheless, the European courts became increasingly interested in the wines from the Hungarian region of Tokaj. Because of their surprising success, the famous wines of Tokaj were soon being imitated everywhere, not only in Germany, the French Jura and Northern Italy, but also in Monbazillac and Sauternes. The reputation of these wines grew in record time and the prices increased even faster. At the same time, people also became aware that some wines of exceptional quality were being imitated all too often with very different results. It was not only the techniques used and the skills of the winemaker that were important, but also their geographical origin, the terroir. Serious thought was given to ways of preventing the imitation of better wines. At the end of the eighteenth century, the first official legal protection was introduced for the names of the origin of wines. Together with the English, the wine makers from the Bordeaux region drew up a classification of the better wines (vins fins) from clearly defined regions (terroirs délimités). In addition, the better wines were being matured and stored in wood.

Old Burgundian wine press (Drouhin)

Tokaji wine, the real one!

Tools for the cellar

THE PROGRESS TOWARDS MODERN TIMES

While it was still mainly prosperous citizens who drank wine in the seventeenth and eighteenth centuries, more and more poor people were gradually also discovering the charms of wine. Wine became a popular

Old tools to combat oidium and Phylloxera

drink, particularly in Spain (Navarra and Rioja) and Italy. The southwest of France followed slightly later, but it was above all during the Industrial Revolution in the nineteenth century that the consumption of wine increased explosively. While the rich drank champagne, Burgundy and Bordeaux, the common people enjoyed wines from the Loire or Beaujolais.

Viticulture went through an extremely difficult time at the end of the nineteenth century when a voracious louse, the *Phylloxera vastatrix*, destroyed nearly all the vineyards of Europe. As the vineyards had already been significantly weakened shortly before this happened by an invasion of mildew, the consequences for European viticulture were disastrous. Fortunately, it was found that American vines were immune to this much-feared wine louse. Young European shoots were grafted onto American stocks so that all the vineyards could be replanted. However, the wine-growing area had been so badly affected that it never regained the extent that it had covered before the *Phylloxera* invasion.

THE TWENTIETH CENTURY

In the twentieth century, wine production went through a gigantic technical and scientific evolution, partly as a result of the introduction of mechanization and new scientific procedures which improved the health of the vineyards and of the wines themselves. Small independent wine growers joined together in powerful cooperations so that in this way they could have access to the most modern wine-making and maturing techniques.

Following a dubious period in the 1960s and 70s, when the wine industry focused on mass production on a large scale, there was a growing awareness of the enormous importance of quality and authenticity. This awareness is also increasing in the so-called new wine-growing countries (some of which actually started producing wine 500-600 years ago!). Now, in the twenty-first century, growers are more than ever prepared to adopt an approach focusing on quality in preference to a short-term, quantity-oriented policy. This is very reassuring!

The secrets of making wine

ESSENTIAL FACTORS

There is actually nothing mysterious about making wine. However, there are at least four factors which are essential for the final product: the soil, the grape variety, the climate and, of course, the wine grower.

SOIL

By soil we mean much more than the actual subsoil. Every bit as important are the geographical location (northern or southern hemisphere, country, region), and the topographical position (slope or valley, location in relation to the sun, proximity of a river, etc.).

GEOGRAPHICAL POSITION

As you discovered in the last chapter, vines naturally thrive best in areas where the summers are warm and humid. Anywhere outside these regions growing wine is only possible with human intervention. For example, viticulture has only been able to develop in countries which are too cold such as Germany, the Netherlands, Belgium and England or in regions which are too hot and dry such as Mediterranean regions, as a result of centuries of experience and searches for the most suitable varieties of grape for these climates. It may be said that in general the best results in wine growing are achieved between the 30th and 50th degree of latitude in the northern hemisphere and between the 30th and 40th degree of latitude in the southern hemisphere. However, these should certainly not be seen as absolu-

The soil is the key to (nearly) everything...

Vineyards on the gently undulating hills of Montravel (Bergerac)

tes: they are averages. For example, some pretty good vineyards can be found north of 50 degrees latitude in Germany, the Netherlands and England.

TOPOGRAPHICAL POSITION

The vine is an easy plant to grow which is quite satisfied if it has light, water and warmth. Therefore, looking for the ideal place for a vineyard, preference must be given to regions with many hours of sunlight. This could be on a slope, but could also be in a valley or on a plain.

However, too much sun is also harmful because the plants will dry out, particularly if there is little water in the area. Therefore a good vineyard will often be slightly higher up in very warm, dry areas (the higher it is, the cooler the air). In cold and often wet areas, for example in Germany, the vineyards will do best on the southern, eastern or western slopes. They receive most warmth there. Another advantage of slopes over valleys is that they are often less sensitive to frost.

In many northern wine-growing areas, the reflection of the sun in the water is also used. In the Swiss areas of Epesses and Dezaley, they even refer to the three suns: the sun in the sky, the sun in the lake, and the sun of

The best vineyards in the Rhône valley are roughly on the 45th degree of latitude.

The slopes of Côte Rôtie

Fall in the vineyards of Toul (Lotharingen)

In Wallis the heat of the sun is reflected
by the stone walls.

the many stone walls which capture the warmth in the daytime and then radiate it at night.

Another advantage of vineyards on a slope is that it is easier to drain the subsoil. Water is essential for vines and will have to be present in the subsoil, preferably at a depth of several meters, so that the vine roots better and is able to obtain more nutrients from the subsoil. Vineyards located in valleys must have good drainage, consisting, for example, of pebbles or rocks. This means that the soil can absorb a heavy shower of rain without any problems. In the very warm wine-growing areas of the southern hemisphere there is often insuffi-

cient underground water and there can be long periods without rain. These vineyards certainly have to be irrigated and watered. The watering is often done with extreme precision, sometimes even drip by drip. A completely computerized system can be used for this. In Europe, irrigation is prohibited everywhere as far as we know. Too much irrigation can make the vine very lazy. As in the case of large-scale, irresponsible fertilization, the roots of the plant no longer dig down into the depths, but remain on the surface. In Europe, many wine-growing areas are found along the banks of rivers. Large expanses of water in a cold environment provide

Pebbly soil for good drainage and temperature regulation.

Vineyards in Dezaleys (Switzerland)

In hot countries, water is even more important.

protection against cold frosts, while in hot regions, water provides the necessary cooling.

In addition to light, warmth and water, which are important parameters for the choice of the perfect location, it is also important to take the wind into account. The wind can have a positive influence by cooling the grapes down when it is extremely hot or by drying them after showers of rain. The wind may be cold or sometimes actually very warm. However, too much wind will always have a negative effect and can even have fatal consequences. In this case, a forest close by in the right spot may act as a very welcome wind screen.

THE SOIL AS A SOURCE OF NUTRIENTS

Vines obtain their nutrients from the soil through their roots. Here they will find all the minerals to ensure healthy growth and a good harvest in terms of quality and quantity, in particular nitrogen, phosp-

In Navarra, the wind in the open landscape has a cooling effect.

The soil as a source of nutrition
(Quinta das Heredias, Portugal)

The impressive soil of Quinta do Bomfim
(Portugal)

ORGANIC VITICULTURE

The organic movement had been warning against these consequences for decades but no one took any notice. For many wine growers, profits were the only thing that mattered. However, the organic wine growers were not always very convincing either. Many of these growers still seemed to be living a flower-power lifestyle, and with their romantic hippy views they were not always able to explain exactly what would be the best solution in practice. In the 1990s, many famous scientists became aware of the need for a more environmentally friendly approach to wine growing. At agricultural colleges the same alarm cry has been heard over and over again for a number of years: organic farming is no longer a mad dream, it has become a necessity! This resulted in a new generation of well-educated, skilled wine growers with an awareness of quality. They were not daydreamers or armchair philosophers, but hard-working fanatics with great charisma. In France, Nicolas Joly produced one of the best white wines in the country: the Savenniãres Coulée de Serrant – and produced it completely organically! In the Rhône valley, Michel Chapoutier (Tain-Le Hermitage) had changed over to organic wine growing years before. Countless great names throughout France, but also in Germany, Austria, Hungary, Spain, Italy and the United States have got the message by now. They are not concerned with an approach related to folklore but with the way to survive.

horous, potassium, magnesium, and calcium, but also sulfur, iron and zinc, as well as various trace elements.

The vine is able to absorb all the nutrients at a depth of several meters to more than fifteen meters through its root system. Suitable subsoils may be limestone, granite, or soil containing gravel and slate, covered with sediments, sand or clay.

Again it is very important that the plant is not given too much artificial fertilizer, because this means that it becomes lazy and works less hard. Experience has shown that overfertilizing can have a dramatic effect. Many nutrients were added to the soil after it had first been completely killed with countless chemical weedkillers, fungicides and insecticides, so that less work would be needed to obtain a bigger harvest. Unaware of the enormous consequences of their acts, many wine growers and larger firms used these simple and cheap techniques up to the 1980s. However, in the 1990s, scientists all over the world sounded the alarm: the soil was starting to reveal dramatic forms of mineralization everywhere. In other words, the soil was changing into rock!

The wines of Albet i Noya are good examples of modern ecological viticulture.

More and more famous wine makers are changing to organic wine growing.

With regard to organic wine growing, the key is the soil and the plants. In order to absorb the minerals in the soil, the vine needs special bacteria, just as humans need enzymes to digest their food. If the soil is killed with chemical weedkillers, as it was in the past, the plant is no longer able to absorb the minerals present in the soil, and the wines which are made with these vines lack all the characteristics of the terroir. Therefore these wines all become copies of each other, without any character.

Organic or biological-dynamic farming dates back to 1924, when the well-known scientist and philosopher, Rudolf Steiner introduced a method of farming in response to the anxiety of some farmers who were already aware that modern intensive agriculture was not good for the earth. The organic method is based on three aspects: respecting the value of the soil and the natural biotope, by using exclusively natural means (biology), in combination with the use of these means at very specific times of the yearly cycle of nature (dynamic), and the regular plowing and digging of the earth.

The aim of organic farming is to create a balance between the earth, the plant and the environment by working the soil regularly and in a thoughtful way. By providing an ideal environment, the quality of the soil is improved (more diversified bacteria and micro-organisms in the soil), the plant grows deeper and broader roots, and grows and flowers more healthily. In order to achieve these goals, specific materials are used, such as ordinary cow manure, but also manure which is stored under the earth in cow horns, as well as the powder of cow horns. Some special plant compounds are also used for plants to strengthen the vines. In organic agriculture there is a preference for creating an environment that is so healthy that the plant can provide its own defenses against fungi and diseases. In addition, care is taken to ensure that the balance is maintained between predators and prey in the animal kingdom. In principle, this is a rather fantastical theory, except that even organic wine growers occasionally resort to copper and sulfur, though in very small quantities. According to organic wine growers, this is permitted because sulfur and copper are also natural pro-

Respect is the essence of organic wine growing.

Organic wine growing is certainly not synonymous with careless wine growing!

Great wines of organic origin

ducts and can therefore be used. A number of oeneological research centers are experimenting with spraying fine clay onto the vines, sometimes with homeopathic quantities of copper, for protecting the vines against mildew and rot. These methods seem very promising, but are not yet applicable everywhere.

For the opponents of organic farming, who see this as a sort of modern quackery, the greatest stumbling block is the adoption of the astral calendar. Organic farmers observe a calendar based on the observations of Maria Thun, which incorporates the influence of the Earth, the sun and the planets on the vegetative cycle of the vine. Opponents consider this to be unscientific because it cannot be proved. Nevertheless, it has

often been shown that the radiation of the sun and moon certainly have an influence on earthly phenomena (just think of the tides!). Wine growers and farmers have always had to take the sun and the moon into account. Michel Chapoutier once summarized this for me as follows: "When the sun rises, plants have more light and the sap rises. When the sun sets the plants have less light and the sap recedes again. You really do not have to be a scientist to understand that it makes much more sense to prune your vines at night so that they do not lose any vital strength."

THE CLIMATE

Climatalogical factors also determine where vines flourish best. There are a number of important points in this respect: the winters have to be moderate and there should not be any lengthy night frosts while the vines are flowering. The spring must be moist and the summer warm enough to ensure that the grapes can fully ripen.

The profile of the weather (water-sun-temperature-wind) not only determines whether or not wine growing is possible, but also determine the quality and yield of the harvest to a large extent.

In general, a successful year requires an average of 1,800 to 2,000 hours of sunlight altogether for the grapes to fully ripen.

Some varieties of grapes require more and longer sunlight to ripen fully (late maturing grapes), while other varieties are ripe much more quickly (early maturing grapes) and can therefore be planted in places with fewer hours of sunlight. However, the sun is important for wine, because it ensures that there are many sugars in the grapes, sugars which will be converted into alcohol during the fermentation process. The more sun, the more sugars and the more potential alcohol. However,

The best vineyards are often situated on sunny slopes. (Tokaj, Hungary)

A young bunch of grapes

In hot countries the bunches hang under a protective
layer of leaves.

sun on its own (for example, in very hot, dry regions)
produces too much alcohol and little acid. This makes
the wines very heavy and dull. Therefore it is also
important to have enough rain; this ensures a good
level of acids and therefore a more balanced wine.

To flourish, the vine also needs water. To some
extent this water can come out of the ground, but the
plant does need a minimum of approximately 500 mil-
limeters (19.7 inches) rainfall per year. The vine certainly does not benefit from heavy showers which can
also result in the much feared wet feet if the drainage
is inadequate. Even when the drainage is adequate, the
damage to the buds and young fruit can be irreparab-
le if there is too much rain at a time, and certainly
when there are hail storms! A balanced distribution
of rainfall is important for perfect growth.

In addition to the necessary hours of sunlight and
rainfall, the average annual temperature is also very
important for viticulture. It should not really fall below
9 °C (48 °F), and certainly not rise above 21 °C (70 °F),
because the vine cannot cope with this. In climatological areas where the average annual temperature is rather low (for example, in Germany), the wines produced are mainly white wines, while in warmer zones
(such as the Mediterranean areas) red wines are usually in the majority.

Vines can survive weeks of severe winter frost.
However, night frosts in spring, particularly when the
vines are flowering, are extremely harmful. During
this period, the wine growers are extremely alert to
protecting the vines at the first sign of night frost.

Finally the wind is also an extremely important
climatological factor. Strong winds or gusts of wind
can cause great damage, particularly in spring when all
the vegetation is still very soft and vulnerable. Cold
northerly winds usually have a harmful effect, but in
areas which are too hot they can actually cool the
vines down and in wet areas they can blow away the
surplus moisture. In hot areas, warm winds entail a risk
of the vines drying out, but in cool moist areas, they
create an ideal climate for the benign *Botrytis cinerea*
fungus, which is essential for liquorous wines such as
Sauternes.

Humid sea winds in the Vinho Verde region (Portugal) force the wine growers to train their vines at
a height of two to three meters (6.5–9.8 ft) to protect
them against the destructive gray rot. The sea winds
may also be salty, and in high concentrations this salt
can be harmful for the leaves and grapes.

THE GRAPES

It is certainly no coincidence that the wines produced
in Alsace and Germany are mainly white wines or that
some wine-growing regions have sworn by the same
varieties of grapes for centuries. After countless
successful and less successful experiments, experience
shows which grapes thrive in which climatological,
geographical and topographical conditions. In Europe
there is a great attachment to the concept of the terroir, while most wine growers in countries in the so-
called new wine world are generally not very interested in this… For them it is more important to get the
most out of the grape itself than to find a particular
combination of grape and soil. Of course there are
a few exceptions, but in most cases the French wine
grower will produce a typical Chablis or Médoc, while

Young grapes are very sensitive to frost.

Humidity, heat and a drying wind, the secret
of the noble Botrytis

his colleague in Australia or California prefers to produce the best Chardonnay or Cabernet Sauvignon.

THE VINE

The vine belongs to the immense *Vitis* family, and botanists know of thousands of different varieties. Only about two hundred of these are suitable for wine growing to various extents, and provided they are used in their natural environment. All European varieties of grapes have developed from the *Vitis vinifera* (wine-bearing vine). Although this family includes almost four thousand descendants, the average wine drinker will not recognize more than twenty. An experienced wine importer or oenologist will find it difficult to recognize forty or fifty varieties.

The variety of grapes, the climate
and the soil must suit each other
(Laroppe, Auxerrois, Toul).

VARIETIES OF GRAPES (CEPAGES OR VARIETALS)

Some varieties of grapes are very well known in particular areas, such as the Hungarian kadarka, or the picolit and fresa from Northern Italy. Others are cultivated all over the world, sometimes because they are truly noble grapes, sometimes because the name is well-known and attractive for commercial reasons. For example, in the 1980s, chardonnay, cabernet sauvignon, pinot noir, merlot, syrah, shiraz, and sauvignon wines were produced everywhere, to the great irritation of the French, as well as the local purists. In the 1990s, the concept of terroir also became established in many countries in the New Wine World, and more and more wines are being produced with their own identity, such as the Argentinean Torrontés, the Chilean Carmenāre, the Uruguayan Tannat, and the Californian Zinfandel. Obviously it is impossible for some countries, where the vines were introduced by European immigrants not that long ago, to use their own grapes. But while many Chilean wines were cheap copies of Spanish or even French wines for years, wine growers in New Zealand managed to give their wine a totally individual character.

A list of some of the well-known varieties of grapes and their characteristics follows below. This list is not

Nowadays, there are made-to-measure clones (*V.C.R. Friuli*).

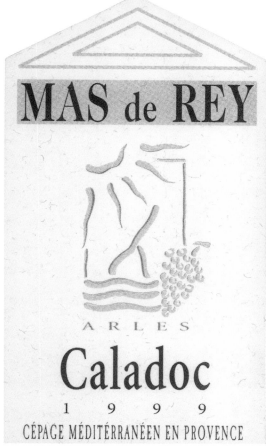

The caladoc (grenache x malbec) is the most promising of the new varieties of grapes.

Aglianico del Vulture (*V.C.R Friuli*)

complete, but you will come across countless other varieties of grapes in other places in this encyclopedia.

RED GRAPES

AGLIANICO
The aglianico, a famous grape from the south of Italy produces fairly heavy, full, robust wines which are very concentrated.

ALEATICO
A quality grape from the south of Italy related to the muscat; it is mainly used to produce full, heavy and aromatic sweet wines.

BARBERA
The barbera is found in many regions of Italy, but is mainly a special grape from Piedmont. Depending on the origin of the grapes (for example, the barbera of Alba and Asti are particularly famous), the wine will be supple, light and fruity, or robust and extremely aromatic. Plums, cherries and redcurrants are very common barbera aromas.

CABERNET FRANC
The cabernet franc is also often used in Bordeaux to supplement the cabernet sauvignon and merlot varieties. Originally this grape was not found in Bordeaux but it was introduced when the vineyards were replanted after the *Phylloxera* invasion, usually to replace the carmenère grape. The purest cabernet franc wines come from the Loire, particularly from Bourgueil, Chi-

non and Saumur-Champigny, where this grape sometimes achieves an astonishingly high quality.

The cabernet franc is slightly softer and less rich in tannin than the cabernet sauvignon, but much fuller than the merlot, and can mainly be identified by its highly fruity quality (strawberries, blackcurrants) and the aroma of freshly cut green paprika.

CABERNET SAUVIGNON
This grape was originally used in the French Médoc, Graves, and Bordeaux wines, and nowadays also in wines from California, Chile and Australia – actually almost everywhere.

The cabernet sauvignon produces wines rich in tannin with a lot of taste and a distinctive aroma, which are very suitable for maturing in wood (for

Barbera (*V.C.R. Friuli*)

Cabernet sauvignon (*V.C.R. Friuli*)

Freisa (*V.C.R. Friuli*)

a long time). The taste and aroma often includes a hint of blackcurrants (cassis), pansies, cigar boxes (cedarwood), and tobacco.

CANAILO NERO
One of the four basic grapes for Chianti wines.

CARIGNAN
Carignan is the French name of a Mediterranean variety of grape. Cariñena and carignano are the Spanish and Italian names. Carignan is a grape which wholly relies on the sun. The characteristic qualities of carignan wines are their dark color and specific aromas such an ink, plums and pepper. The carignan is sometimes used as the only variety of grape, but usually this grape is blended with other Mediterranean grapes such as grenache, cinsault and syrah.

Dolcetto (*V.C.R. Friuli*)

CINSAULT/CINSAUT
Wines made of 100% cinsault are becoming rare. In general, cinsault is used in blends, for example, with grenache, syrah and carignan. Cinsault provides the body and meaty quality to the wines. In South Africa, the cinsault is also called hermitage (also see Pinotage).

CORVINA
This is the basic grape for Valpolicella and Amarone wines. They vary greatly in quality, from lighter wines to wonderful classic wines.

DOLCETTO
This widespread Italian grape mainly produces interesting, juicy and fruity wines in the north (Piedmont), reminiscent of the Primitivo/Zinfandel.

FREISA
Typical indigenous grape from Piedmont. It produces fascinating meaty wines with surprising aromas of strawberries and raspberries. It is made as a dry or sweet wine.

GAMAY
The gamay has become world famous because of the Beaujolais wines, but a great deal of gamay is also produced in the Loire, particularly in the Touraine.

A gamay wine should be fruity through and through: raspberries, (wild) strawberries, redcurrants, cherries... In the better crus of Beaujolais wines you will also recognize many floral aromas. The simpler the wines, the lighter and more cheerful they are and the better, fuller and more generous they become.

GRENACHE
The grenache is particularly well known in France (Rhône, Tavel rosé, Languedoc, Roussillon) and

Merlot *(V.C.R. Friuli)*

Montepulciano *(V.C.R. Friuli)*

Spain (Rioja, Navarra, Penedés), and is sometimes found in California and Australia.

Grenache wines are usually very sturdy and strong, but they also stay fruity and supple. They can mainly be identified by the combination of peppers, herbs and fruit (usually blackberries).

MERLOT

This grape is also well known in the Bordeaux region, particularly in Saint-Emilion and Pomerol. The merlot is also found in several Balkan countries, Italy, Chile, California and Australia.

The merlot is slightly softer, rounder, and especially less rich in tannin than the cabernet sauvignon. The grapes are often combined to supplement their respective qualities. In the aroma and taste you will recognize a good merlot by red fruit (usually cherries, sometimes red currants).

MONTEPULCIANO

The montepulciano grape is found almost all over Italy, though it is mainly a specialty of the central part of the country. Many supple generous and extremely tasty Italian wines owe their charm to this montepulciano, a grape which unlike many other Italian grapes produces wines which can be drunk when they are young, also because of the soft tannin.

MOURVEDRE

A less well-known, but essential grape from the southern Rhône valley, particularly Bandol. It produces strong, powerful wines, which age well.

NEBBIOLO

This is one of the best grapes in the world! However, to a great extent it is geographically limited to the north of Italy, where the nebbiolo is used for Barolo, Barbaresco and Gattinara wines. These wines are always very rich in tannin, almost opaque, and certainly have to mature for a few years before they can be drunk. A good nebbiolo wine smells and tastes of laurel (licorice), stewed prunes, truffles, brushwood, mushrooms and sometimes cocoa or tar.

PINOTAGE

The oenologist from KWV, Abraham Perold, crossed the cinsault (known as hermitage in South Africa) and the pinot noir in 1927, producing the pinotage wines which now determine the face of South Africa. For years, the pinotage grape was planted only in South Africa; now the grape is also cultivated in Australia and New Zealand, amongst other places. Wines produced with the pinotage differ in character, depending on their origin.

Nebbliolo *(V.C.R. Friuli)*

Pinot Noir (*V.C.R. Friuli*)

The best pinotage wines are full-bodied (particularly the wines which are thoroughly matured in wood) and are slightly herbal, but always with (ripe) fruit, and finally have a hint of pepper in the aftertaste.

Poorer pinotage wines sometimes have a characteristic smell somewhere in between the smell of acetone and old bicycle tires (rubber).

PINOT NOIR

The pinot noir is the ultimate red grape for Burgundy wines but is also used for red Sancerre and the pinot noir from Alsace. Good results have also been achieved with this grape in Italy, the Balkans, Hungary, South America, California and Oregon.

In general, wines made with the pinot noir grape are more elegant and generous than heavy. They can be identified by an earthy undertone, between the smell of a good stable and manure... After this initial shock, you will discover a great deal of fruit in a good

Tempranillo/cencibel

Sangiovese (*V.C.R. Friuli*)

glass of pinot noir, mainly redcurrants, (wild) strawberries and sometimes cherries.

PRIMITIVO

A very popular grape in Italy. Also see Zinfandel.

SANGIOVESE

The sangiovese grape is the key to the best Tuscan wines, such as Chianti, Vino Nobile di Montepulciano and Brunello di Montalcino. Good wines made with sangiovese are rich in tannin, powerful, and with a fairly full-bodied taste. You will often discover blackberries, cherries or plums with a hint of herbs and spices, and in the great wines, tobacco and vanilla.

SYRAH (SHIRAZ)

Syrah is the only grape permitted for the northern wines from the Rhône area (Hermitage, Crozes-Hermitage, Saint-Joseph, Côte Rôtie, Cornas). In addition, the syrah is also largely responsible for the characteristics of the southern Rhône wines (such as Chateauneuf-du-Pape and Gigondas). Nowadays, syrah wines, known in English as shiraz wines, are still made in South Africa, Australia and the USA.

Syrah wines have a deep and very powerful color. They have a full-bodied, strong taste which requires a few years to mature in the bottle. A good syrah is often easy to recognize from the characteristic, herbal, peppery aroma and taste, the sun-ripened fruit and the almost animal-like undertones. This could be reminiscent of a warm saddle after a long horse ride.

TEMPRANILLO/CENCIBEL

The tempranillo is the perfect grape for the better Spanish wines from Rioja, but also from Navarra and Ribera del Duero. As its Spanish name suggests, this tempranillo is a grape which ripens early. Although it

Zinfandel/primitivo *(V.C.R. Friuli)*

is often blended with other grapes, the tempranillo can produce some astonishing results on its own, as in Navarra. Young wines made with the tempranillo, which have not been matured in the barrel, are light, fruity (strawberries, plums) and can be drunk quickly. After maturing in wood for some time, they acquire a characteristic herbal taste with undertones of vanilla and tobacco and hints of dried prunes or homemade jam.

ZINFANDEL
This grape was taken to the USA a long time ago, probably by a Hungarian immigrant. The Hungarian name zirfandli was used by mistake for what was subsequently shown to be an Italian variety of grape, the primitivo, with the help of a DNA examination. In California, the zin was extremely successful but the number of zin fans is also steadily growing in Europe. The zinfandel can produce good rosés (dry or slightly sweet) as well as full-bodied herbal red wines. Both types taste and smell of ripe fruit amongst other things (blackberries, blueberries and blackcurrants) with a herbal undertone and a characteristic peppery taste.

WHITE GRAPES

AIRÉN
Many people have never heard of this grape and yet it is (was?) the most widely planted variety of grape in the world! The airén certainly does not owe this popularity to its intrinsic characteristics with regard to aroma and taste, but to the fact that the very thick skin protects the grape against extreme heat. Because of this, the grape is extremely suitable for hot, dry Spanish areas such as La Mancha and Valdepeñas. Airén wines do not really have a pronounced taste, at most there is some green apple and a handful of almonds in the taste and aroma and they do not mature.

ALVARINHO/ALBARINO
This is a very common variety of grape in the north of Portugal (Vinho Verde region) and the neighboring region of Galicia in Spain. The grape is often used in blends, but the best wines are made with 100% alvarinho/albarino grapes. These wines are often very aromatic and have a tempting taste.

ALIGOTÉ
The French are familiar with the aligoté grape from the eponymous tart wine from the Burgundy. At best, the aligoté (for example from Bouzeron) produces a cheerful, fruity wine for an aperitif or with oily dishes. More surprising (though certainly not in a positive sense) are the wines made with the aligoté grape in the countries of the former East Bloc. In these countries the aligoté is particularly rated for its high acid content. Occasionally the wine is drunk when it is still young, for example, with fatty leg of lamb when the acids and the fats neutralize each other, but aligoté wines are also drunk after a period of maturing for more than ten years. In this case, the wines have completely oxidized and the acids have broken down. The result is comparable to a very old dry sherry. In Moldavia, Hungary, and some other countries, older people are very fond of this wine, but young people prefer more modern wines.

AUXERROIS
This is a confusing name for the pinot auxerrois, a member of both the pinot blanc and the chardonnay family. This variety of grape is widely used for Edelzwicker blends, but also to supplement or even replace the pinot blanc.

CHARDONNAY
The chardonnay is very well known from top burgundy and champagne wines. Nowadays, the chardonnay grape is truly cultivated everywhere, not

Chardonnay *(V.C.R. Friuli)*

always because it is a top grape although it certainly is but particularly because the grape sells well.

Chardonnay wines are often fresh and pleasant when they have not matured in wood. After maturing in wood for a long time they change into full creamy wines with a characteristic taste and aroma, which is most reminiscent of a piece of still warm, toasted bread, spread with a large lump of creamy butter. Some wine growers have not yet mastered the art of achieving a balance between the wood and the fruit and produce wines which are dominated by a sensual, almost sickly vanilla aroma, and taste of (American) oak. This is a pity because a well-made chardonnay wine should also have a generous aroma in which it is possible to identify exotic fruits, peaches, melon, pineapple and citrus fruits. Mature burgundy wines also contain a hint of nuts, usually hazelnut or walnut.

Chenin blanc

This is another world-famous grape, particularly because of the fantastic wines of the Loire from Vouvray, Saumur, Anjou, Bonnezeaux, Coteaux du Layon, and Quart-de-Chaumes. The grape is also harvested in South Africa, where it is often known by its local name.

The chenin blanc grape is blessed by its fresh acids, which are not only valued in dry wines, but also in sparkling wines. In fact, it is precisely in sweet wines that these delicate acids provide extra strength and balance, as well as - and this is also important - a long life. A Coteaux du Layon from a top year can therefore be kept for more than thirty years. The sweet wines from the Loire should also rest for at least ten years to reach their peak. But this will provide you with a wonderful cocktail of honey, peaches and apricots, scented flowers, hazelnuts and much more depending on the soil in which the grapes were cultivated.

Clairette

The clairette is mainly found in the Rhône valley and in Languedoc Roussillon, but also in South Africa. The clairette is mainly used to make sparkling wines which are not too dry, of a reasonable or good quality. The taste and aroma of clairette are fairly soft, ranging from neutral to subtle and are never exuberant.

Gewürztraminer

This is a well-known variety of grape from Alsace. This grape is also known simply as the traminer in Germany and Italy. The wines made with this grape can be dry or sweet. In Alsace you will also find two types of gewürztraminer wines: the lighter type which is fairly dry and should be drunk when it is still young, and the rather fuller, heavier type which usually still contains a little bit of sugar. In addition, there are also the extremely sweet wines of grapes harvested later on, sometimes even by hand: in this case each grape is individually selected.

Gewürztraminer wines are often described as being extremely herbal. Personally, I have never yet had

Gewürztraminer (*V.C.R. Friuli*)

a single herbal Traminer, though I have had heavy, full-bodied and enormously concentrated wines with a dominating perfumed aroma and taste which are more reminiscent of flowers and overripe fruit (mangos and tropical fruits) than herbs. Some wines also have an inexplicable hint of the skins of muscat grapes.

Maccabeo/viura

In Rioja and Navarra, this variety of grape is known as viura; in other places in Spain (and in French Catalonia) the grape is called maccabeo. In general, the viura produces a fairly fragile, light, fresh fruity wine which does not mature very well. Although some of the wines made with 100% viura can have a reasonable quality, the preference of connoisseurs, particular-

Malvasia aromatica (*V.C.R. Friuli*)

Muscat blanc (*V.C.R. Friuli*)

Pinot bianco/pinot blanc (*V.C.R. Friuli*)

ly in Navarra , is for a ratio of two-thirds viura to one-third chardonnay, which gives the wines more of a backbone and rondeur.

MALVASIA

This famous ancient Mediterranean variety of grape is the basis for many legendary sweet wines from the distant past and in the present. There are many varieties of malvasia which can produce very different wines, from aromatic dry wines to strong, extremely sweet dessert wines.

MARSANNE

This high quality grape from the Rhône valley forms the basis of the greatest white wines from the Rhône valley, together with the Roussanne. The marsanne is also cultivated in Longuedoc-Roussillon.

MUSCADELLE

In Europe, this grape is rarely used on its own. It is very aromatic and familiar from the blends with sauvignon and sémillon, for example, in Sauternes and Bergerac. In Australia, the muscadelle is used to made liqueur wines, mistakenly called Tokay by the locals. How long will they continue to do this?

MUSCADET/MELON DE BOURGOGNE

A well-known variety of grape from the banks of the Loire, particularly in the region around Nantes, where Muscadet wines are made. Although these are not pedigree wines, they are usually fresh and subtle, and sometimes surprisingly good, with a salty mineral taste.

MUSCAT

If there is one grape which is almost immediately recognizable it is the muscat grape. A well-made Muscat wine smells and tastes of ripe, freshly picked muscat grapes, slightly exotic with an occasional hint of flowers. Muscat wines can be dry (Alsace, Tunisia, Samos, Navarra,

Latium) or sweet (Italy, France) or even very sweet (Navarra, Samos, Beaumes-de-Venise, Frontignan, Hungary, Australia). They are always sensual wines with a great deal of charm. Although we only refer to one Muscat there are actually different varieties: muscat ottonel (Austria, Germany, Alsace, South Africa), muscat/petits grains (Alsace) and the less well-known, often rather coarser muscat d'Alexandrie (South Africa).

PALOMINO

This is the perfect grape for fino sherry and manzanilla. It thrives best in a chalky soil (albarizas) and produces tart, elegant and subtle wines. Recently, ordinary, non-fortified and non-oxidized wines made with the palomino can also be found in the bodegas of Jerez. These are not great wines, but they are excellent when accompanying shellfish, amongst other things.

PEDRO XIMÉNEZ/PX

While the palomino is the grape for dry sherry, PX is the perfect grape for the sweetest sherry. Wines made with a hundred per cent PX are rare, but they are always a real experience. However, the Pedro Ximénez is also often used for delicate blends of less sweet sherries.

PICOLIT

This fairly recently rediscovered variety of grape from Friuli is quite unique. What happens to other grapes only in bad years, happens every year for the picolit: the bunches spontaneously lose the majority of their fruit (*abortus fructalis*) and retain only a small quantity of healthy grapes. Provided they are of a good stock and have been cultivated in the right soil, these grapes produce a delicious sweet wine with a sufficient level of acidity to achieve a perfect balance. By itself, Picolit does not provide any guarantee of a good wine: occasionally it produces a very poor wine, but the best wines are certainly some of the greatest in the world!

Pinot grigio/pinot gris (*V.C.R. Friuli*)

However, the price of these top wines is really rather high.

PINOT BLANC

The pinot blanc is very well known in Alsace, but also in Italy and the Balkans. In Alsace and in Italy rather neutral, pleasant, fruity wines with low acidity are made with the pinot blanc grape.

In Slovenia, winemakers have made exceptional wines with the pinot blanc (beli pinot). In the area of Ormoz, the pinot blanc is sometimes harvested very late, which gives the grape a great complexity and potential for maturing. In 1997, I tasted a beli pinot which was 26 years old, made by the firm Jeruzalem Ormoz, and it was still surprisingly fresh!

PINOT GRIS

The pinot gris is fairly common in Northern Italy, Hungary, Austria, Germany, Switzerland and many other countries, but does not achieve the quality that it does in Alsace, anywhere else. The taste and aroma depend entirely on the origin, as does the structure of the wine. Pinot gris wines can be light, subtle, dry and softly aromatic, for example, in Northern Italy, but they can also be very powerful, full of aroma and slightly sweet, or even very sweet in Hungary and Germany, and of course in Alsace.

RIBOLLA/ROBOLA

This grape, which is unfortunately still underestimated, often produces fascinating wines in Northern Italy and Greece (Cephalonia), usually with tempting aromas of citrus fruit and a hint of honey.

RIESLING

For connoisseurs this is one of the best grapes in the world. The riesling originally came from Germany (including Alsace, originally a province of Germany), but is now cultivated all over the world.

Most Riesling wines are fresh and fruity and are reminiscent of flowers and herbs. Mature riesling wines develop a very characteristic aroma which is comparable to the odor of old-fashioned Kerosene stoves. Young Riesling wines also reveal a hint of fresh apples, citrus fruit and sometimes passionfruit. Older wines tend to honey and luxuriant flowers. In Germany, the riesling often grows on volcanic or mineral soil. This can certainly be tasted in the wine, at least when it is well made. There are actually two main varieties of riesling: the famous and very aromatic Rhine riesling and the less pronounced Italian riesling or wälsch riesling.

ROUSANNE

Together with the marsanne, this is a very important variety of grape for the white wines from the Rhône valley. The roussanne produces rich, full-bodied wines, often with an exotic aroma. The grape is well known, for example, in the Hermitage and Chateauneuf du Pape blanc.

SAUVIGNON BLANC

This is a very well-known grape, which produces top wines both in the Bordeaux and Bergerac regions and in the Loire. In South Africa the grape is sometimes called blanc fumé; in America and Mexico, fumé blanc. However, more and more people are using the name sauvignon on the label. Good Sauvignon wines can be found nearly everywhere in the world nowadays.

Depending where the sauvignon grape is harvested, the aroma and taste of the grape have different characteristics. The wine always remains fresh, spicy, aromatic and fruity. A sauvignon wine from Bordeaux or Bergerac often smells and tastes of green apples (Granny Smith), freshly mown grass, or even box or basil. (In the trade, these last two characteristics are sometimes referred to disrespectfully as cat's piss...) In

Riesling Italico (*V.C.R. Friuli*)

Sauvignon blanc *(V.C.R. Friuli)*

Trebbiano romagnono *(V.C.R. Friuli)*

the Loire, Sancerre or Pouilly-Fumé, you will some-times identify (green) asparagus, or occasionally fen-nel or aniseed and a hint of licorice. However, the most expressive sauvignon wines are found in New Zealand, where you will be treated to an explosion of tropical fruits, grapefruit and gooseberries. Sauvignon wines are best when they are young.

Sémillon

A pure sémillon wine is certainly not to be disparaged. However, the problem is that this grape does not con-tain enough acid, so it is often blended with another grape. In Europe, this is almost always a sauvignon (Bor-deaux, Bergerac); in Australia, the sémillon is often combined with chardonnay, which makes the wine even more luxurious. In France, the best sweet wines are made with the sémillon, particularly when the grape is affected by the benign fungus, *Botrytis cinerea*, which causes the grapes to shrivel up, making the taste, aroma and sugars more concentrated. Typical examples of wines produced with this method of noble rotting (pourriture noble) are Sauternes, Barsac, Monbazillac, and Saussignac.

A sémillon wine can generally be recognized by the taste and aroma of juicy fruits such as peach, apricot, or mango. The wine also has a pronounced undertone of honey, with the occasional hint of warm butter.

Sylvaner

In Germany this is also spelled silvaner. It is well known in Alsace and in Germany, where the grape produces soft, light, elegant wines with a clearly recog-nizable bouquet of delicate flowers and a hint of herbs.

Trebbiano/ugni blanc

In Italy, the trebbiano on its own produces acceptable or good wines, but few great wines. In France, the ugni blanc is mainly used for distillation (cognac, armangnac), but also for the usually rather simple wines in Gascony, or in blends in Provence, the Rhône valley and Languedoc-Roussillon. The charm of the trebbiano/ugni blanc lies mainly in the fresh acids, and, particularly in the Italian wines, the aromas of green apple and citrus fruit initial-ly, and the shades of bitter almonds in the aftertaste.

Verdejo

This is a very popular grape in Spain (Rueda), and pro-duces light, delicate fruity wines with aromas of green apples, nuts and a slight hint of mint.

Verdelho

This is a famous grape, which produces dry, sophisti-cated white wines in Madeira.

Verdicchio *(V.C.R. Friuli)*

Vermentino (*V.C.R. Friuli*)

VERDICHIO

This is a very popular variety of grape in Italy. It is used on its own or in blends, in still or sparkling wines. The wines of the verdicchio are usually dry, fresh and delicately fruity.

VERMONTINO

This is a popular grape in Italy, particularly in Liguria and on Siciliy and Sardinia, but also in Corsica. The wines made of the vermentino grape are fresh and delicately aromatic.

VIOGNIER

Twenty years ago, few people had heard of the viognier grape: only a few connoisseurs of the older wines produced around the city of Condrieu in the French Rhône valley had heard of this variety of grape. When a few young winegrowers gave a new lease of life to the legendary viognier wine, which had almost disappeared, and

convinced the world of the quality of this grape, it was cultivated in other regions as well. The grape produces very good results in Languedoc-Roussillon and in the Ardêche, but also, for example, in Australia, the United States and even Canada. Well-made viognier wines have an unbelievably rich aroma and taste of juicy peaches and apricots combined with the soft delicate bouquet of meadow flowers and honey.

THE HUMAN FACTOR

If the soil is suitable, the weather permits, and the grapes have been well selected, a good winemaker must be able to produce a good wine. Nevertheless, it is unfortunately not always that simple. Small-scale winegrowers who do not have the necessary financial means to invest in new equipment are eventually forced to produce wines of a lesser quality which can be sold quickly, but at a lower price. In order to avoid the problems of liquidity, even potentially good winegrowers often opt for this desperate solution all too easily. However, for less affluent winegrowers there is almost always an acceptable way out: cooperation. Not every winegrower concentrates on viticulture full time. For example, many French winegrowers are first and foremost ordinary farmers who happen to have a few vineyards, in addition to cultivating corn and wheat and keeping cows and other livestock. They often manage their vineyards without much motivation, and all too often resort to radical methods as soon as some disease affects the vines.

There are also special cases, as in the former East Bloc countries. In the past, these often produced very acceptable wines. However, this situation changed as a result of the Russian domination. Quality was replaced by quantity, and sophistication by large amounts of alcohol to help the Russians to quench their thirst. When the Russian troops left and large-scale social changes took place, the winegrowers were left with an enormous hangover. The equipment was hopelessly out of date, and all the money was gone, although the

At V.C.R in Friuli there are constant experiments with new clones for customers all over the world.

A good example of how things should not be done (ex-combination, Villány, Hungary).

A successful example of foreign investment (Disnókö, Tokaj, Hungary)

knowledge and skill, as well as obviously the perfect topographical and climatological conditions were and still are present. This was an unfortunate situation, particularly as the local governments often reserved the agricultural subsidies for other crops which attracted foreign currencies to the countries concerned more quickly. Fortunately, many foreign businesses have now recognized the positive aspects of investment, and viticulture is once again flourishing in many of the former East Bloc countries.

Terroir and tradition are important in the established wine countries

3 Wine making

THE GRAPE AS A RAW MATERIAL

The last chapter showed how important, the grapes, the soil and the weather are to make a good wine. If the wine maker is also skilled and well equipped, there is hardly anything that can go wrong. The methods for the preparation of wine depends on a number of factors:

– the type of wine (young, to be drunk quickly or to be kept)
– the color of the wine to be made (white, red or rosé)
– the sort of wine (still, sparkling or fortified)
– the winegrowers requirements (taste preference, ethical considerations, etc.)
– the consumer requirements (trends)
– the economic situation (recession or economic growth)
– the target group (for example, the Dutch often drink different wines from the French or Spanish).

In the context of this book we will restrict ourselves to the different methods of wine making for:
– white, red and rosé wines
– sparkling wines
– fortified wines

For these three wine-making methods, it is important that the raw material (the grapes) is healthy and of good quality. The formula for the success of a good wine usually lies in the grapes.

The colorants responsible for the differences in the color of red, white and rosé wines are in the skins of the grapes. With a few exceptions, the juice of black and white grapes is always colorless. This means that it is also possible to make white wine with black grapes! However, it is not possible to make red wine with only white grapes. The color of red wine is produced as follows: the alcohol present in the fermenting juices dis-

The grape as a raw material

36

The terroir and the grape are inextricable linked

solves the colorants (anthocyanids) in the skins, which have also fermented. For rosé wines, this does not take very long at all and the color remains light. For white wines, the winemaker removes the skins and only the juices are fermented.

The various components which produce the aroma and the taste of the wine are in the skin and just below the skin of the grapes. The deeper the roots go into the soil, the more nutrients and therefore flavor is taken from the soil.

The tannins which are particularly important for red wines are in the skin, as well as the pips and stalks (which

are usually removed nowadays). The more tannin, the longer the wine can be kept (provided there are also enough other acids and alcohol in the wine). Tannin is actually a natural preserving agent. This substance gives the wines a familiar rough taste when young, which makes them very unpopular with most consumers. It is like biting into an old tea bag: bitter, sour and acidic. Tannin is also known as lye, and this is also clearly present in tea. In the better wines that are stored, tannin is a blessing. However, the buyer must have the patience to leave the wine to rest for a few years so that it can fully mature. Unfortunately many wines rich in tannin are sold and drunk when they are still too young.

The skins of grapes contain a whole range of yeast cells which have found their way onto them with the help of the wind or different insects. In the past, these natural yeast cells were entirely responsible for the process of fermentation. However, nowadays, this is assisted by specially selected cultures which are added to the grape at the start of the wine-making process. In this way, the wine grower can be more in control of the process of fermentation.

The juices contain two components which determine the success of any wine: the sugars which are converted into alcohol by the yeast cells during the alcoholic fermentation and the acids which are so important for the freshness and life of the wines. Grapes with too many acids (and therefore too few sugars/alcohol) are not very popular, while grapes with too few acids (i.e., with too many sugars/alcohol) are not very good either.

Obviously the pulp also contains the most important component of the wine that is to be made: water.

Tannin-rich wines have to mature extra long.

Natural yeast cells on overripe grapes
(Switzerland)

Grapes from extremely hot countries generally
contain fewer acids.

THE PREPARATION

Before moving onto a detailed description of the different methods of wine making, a few terms are explained below.

DESTALKING

The grapes are usually harvested in bunches with their stalks. As the stalks contain many tannins, they are often removed immediately upon arrival at the winery. This can be done manually (only for the better wines), or with machines. In years when the skins contain few tannins, some of the stalks are retained. This is better than crushing the pips because these give the wine an unpleasant bitter taste.

ALCOHOLIC FERMENTATION

This first fermentation is the conversion of the sugars that are present in the grapes (including glucose and fructose) into alcohol, and carbon dioxide. The natural and/or added yeast cells are responsible for this process. The carbon dioxide escapes during the process of fermentation, except in sparkling wines, when it is deliberately retained. The escape of carbon dioxide is accompanied by a great deal of movement in the must: it looks as though the must is boiling.

When they arrive, the grapes are taken
to the destalking machine.

The juice comes out on one side...

...the stalks on the other side

Bubbling during the alcoholic fermentation

During the fermentation the temperature must be constantly checked.

The conversion of sugars into alcohol takes place in accordance with a set pattern. As soon as it is clear how much sugar there is in the grapes, it is easy to calculate how much alcohol the wine will eventually contain. For this reason, winegrowers pick a few grapes just before the harvest to analyze the juice of the crushed grapes in a small machine. With the help of a complicated technique involving the interruption of light, it is possible to measure the quantity of sugars. The fermentation automatically stops when all the sugars that are present have been fermented, or when an alcohol percentage of approximately 17% has been achieved (however, in practice, this is often 15%). There are also ways of stopping the process of fermentation prematurely, for example, if some residual sugars are to be left in the wine. Usually, the must is thoroughly cooled and the yeast cells are then removed by a filtering or centrifugal process. A great deal of heat is also released during the fermentation. Therefore it is very important to keep a close eye on the temperature. With modern methods of wine making in particular, the temperature is completely regulated by computer. During the fermentation of red wines the temperature does not usually exceed 30 °C (86 °F), but the ideal temperature for better wines is between 18 and 26 °C (64.4 and 78.8 °F). For white wines, a temperature of approximately 20 °C is considered the maximum temperature, but in practice the temperature fluctuates between 6 and 18 °C (42.8 and 64.4 °F).

MALOLACTIC FERMENTATION

Young wines contain a great deal of sharp acids, so-called malic acid or *acide malique* in French. In spring, when the temperature in the cellars rises, this apple acid is converted into the rather softer lactic acid (*acide lactique*). This second fermentation, also known as malolactic fermentation, is a very gradual process during which the wines clearly improve in taste, aroma and rondeur. It is always used with red wines, but is sometimes inhibited in white wines which do not contain enough acids, as can be the case in some very hot coun-

tries. In this case, the winemaker passes the white wine through a series of filters or even through a centrifuge to eliminate the bacteria which cause this second fermentation. A second commonly used way of compensating for the lack of acids is to add tartaric acid (*acide tartrique*). This perfectly legal process is used in many very hot countries (e.g., in Australia).

CARBONIC MACERATION

This complicated term is best explained as soaking in carbon dioxide under pressure. This special fermentation technique is often used for wines which are drunk when young, which should be particularly fruity, with little tannin. The most typical example of this is the Beaujolais primeur or nouveau, but the technique is also used, for example, for young commercial wines from the South of France or Bordeaux. The technique is also widely used outside France. Wines produces by this method cannot be kept very long but they are not intended for keeping.

The principle is simple: the whole bunches of grapes first go through an internal fermentation process in a hermetically sealed fermentation tank filled with carbon dioxide, and the sugars are converted into alcohol and

Malolactic fermentation in the barrel (sur lie)

carbon dioxide in the grapes. This process takes place at a fairly low temperature and has the advantage that the wine retains a great deal of the fruity aroma and a lot of its color. After a while, the grapes burst open under the pressure of their own weight and the pressure of the carbon dioxide. The rest of the process of wine making takes place as normal.

PELLICURAL MACERATION

This method of soaking is used for white and rosé wines. Normally the skins of the grapes are removed straightway when white wines are made. However, by allowing them to soak in the juices for a little while, the wines are injected with aromas and tastes which are just below the skin. As long as the method is used properly and not as a camouflage technique, wines produced by this method have an added value. This applies both for dry and for sweet white wines.

SUR LIE

Wines which have not been filtered still contain come impurities such as microscopic particles of grape skin and leaves, and particularly dead yeast cells. Gravity causes these to sink to the bottom of the barrel or tub. This sediment is known in French as lie. Originally, white wines were only left to rest sur lie (on the sediment) as they matured in the Muscadet region, but nowadays this practice occurs in many wine-growing areas. The wine is filtered only at the bottling stage. Because of the lengthy contact with the sediment, the wines gain in aroma, taste and complexity. When they are drunk young, these wines also have a pleasant gaseous taste which slightly stimulates the tip of the tongue and makes the wine more elegant and fresh.

MICRO-OXYGENATION (HOMEOPATHIC ADDITION OF OXYGEN)

This process, also known as micro-bullage, was developed fairly recently, and is currently being practiced in many places. During the early 1990s, the method was discovered by the Frenchman, Partrick Ducourneau, based on a study by Pontalier (Chateaux Margaux) on the importance of oxidation (the influence of oxygen) for better wines. Partrick Ducourneau, from Chapelle L'Enclos in Madiran, discovered the micro-bulleure, and since then winegrowers have experimented with this method all over France and in many places outside France with tremendous success. In 1996 the process was approved by the European Community.

What exactly does this process entail? A minimal quantity of oxygen enters the wine through the slats of a wooden barrel. In combination with the colorants (anthocyanids for red and flavonoids for white) and the tannins, the oxygen gives the wines added complexity and character. The micro-bullage technique consists of adding pure oxygen to the wine by an almost homeopathic method: evenly and in very low doses. This takes place during the winemaking process while it matures in wood. The process is used particularly for wines made with cabernet sauvignon and sémillon grapes, and to a lesser extent for those made with merlot and sauvignon blanc. The result is astonishing: more fruit, very pure aromas, more body, more fatty tannins, a better balance – in short, a fuller wine. Nowadays, micro-bullage is used by almost a thousand of the better winegrowers in Madiran, Bergerac and Bordeaux, but also in Burgundy, Languedoc and the Loire region. In other countries there are also about a hundred wineries which are experimenting with this method, including wineries in Spain, Portugal, Switzerland, Italy, England, Canada, Chile, Argentina, Australia and the United States.

CHAPTALIZATION

This process, which was discovered by the Frenchman Chaptal, means that sugars (or extra-concentrated sweet must) are added to the young must before the alcoholic fermentation so that more alcohol can eventually be converted from these extra sugars. This legal process is often used when there have been disastrously cold summers in which the grapes were not able to ripen fully. Unfortunately it is also sometimes misused by people who prefer not to take any risks, and want to make money quickly. In this case, the grapes are actually harvested too early, and this is compensated for by adding sugars.

SULFUR

Sulfur is an efficient disinfectant and preserving agent which is widely used in wine cellars. The sulfur is added to the grapes as a powder or in liquid form when they arrive at the winery. This prevents premature fermentation and above all eliminates any malignant bacteria which could cause the grapes to rot. The addition of sulfur occurs mainly in hot countries or in places where the distance between the vineyards and the presses is more than one hour. When the grapes are not harvested very carefully, the addition of sulfur can also prevent problems. In principle this should not be necessary if only the healthy grapes were harvested, if the grapes are pressed in the vineyards, or certainly within one hour of being harvested, or if the grapes were transported in cooler conditions. For example, in South Africa grapes are often harvested at night to ensure that the temperature is kept at an acceptable level. However, in practice the addition of sulfur is unfortunately still very often a necessary evil. In particular, if it starts to rain just before or after the harvest, and there is a great danger of the grapes rotting, there is no way round this practice. Sulfur is also used in the cellars: in tablet form to disinfect the barrels. In this case, a tablet of sulfur is lit in the barrel, and the fumes then ensure that the barrel is wholly free of bacteria.

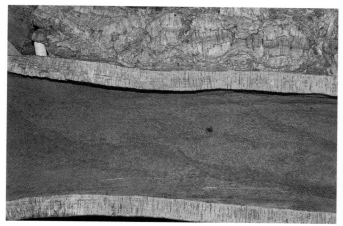

Cork comes from the bark of the cork oak.

Cork is mechanically extracted from the bark.

Finally, sulfur gas is sometimes added to the wine, either before or during the bottling stage, particularly with sweeter wines, for example to prevent a second fermentation from occurring in the bottle. As long as this is done properly, it is a completely harmless process. However, some wineries sometimes take extra precautions and add an extra portion of sulfur gas to the wines which are not top wines, usually sweet wines, with all the attendant unfortunate consequences this entails.

WINE-MAKING FOR DIFFERENT SORTS OF WINE

THE WINE-MAKING PROCESS FOR RED WINES

The most important difference between the process for making white and rosé and red wines is that the skins are not removed for red wines. These actually contain the colorants which determine the color of the wine once they are dissolved in alcohol. The fermentation of red wine takes place in barrels. In the past, the fermentation always took place in open barrels, usually made of wood though also made of cement, concrete, granite or synthetic resin. A sort of crust, known in French as *a chapeau* (hat), forms on these open barrels on top of the fermenting must. This crust consists to a large extent of fermenting grape skins. As carbon dioxide is released upwards during the alcoholic fermentation, all the particles are constantly drawn up. The crust is broken up from time to time and pushed under, so that the must constantly remains in contact with the colorants in the grape skins. This also prevents bacterial infections in the must: the heat could easily cause millions of harmful micro-organisms to collect if the crust were not broken up. By constantly submerging the crust in the must, the bacteria are killed off by the alcohol that has formed.

In many countries and in most large-scale wineries, the wine-making process now takes place in sealed barrels, or even in fermentation tanks. The advantage of

THE CORK

The Romans were probably already familiar with the secret of sealing amphoras with a cork. Nevertheless, the use of cork only became widespread in the sixteenth century. The cork comes from the bark of the cork oak, usually from Spain, Portugal or North Africa. It takes nine or ten years before the bark grows to the desired thickness. The layer of cork is removed with sharp axes and the cork is treated with hot steam (against insects) and fungicides (against fungi and bacteria), dried and then processed to produce the familiar corks. Longer, better corks for wines which are laid down can last for more than fifty years. Shorter corks are used for wines which are drunk quickly, and compressed cork is used for everyday wines. Although it is not particularly pleasing from an aesthetic point of view, using a screw-top is preferable to a compressed cork for these everyday wines, because these are often of inferior quality. Unfortunately, the average consumer still intuitively opts for the poor cork in preference to these very functional and hygienic screw-tops.

Open wooden fermentation vats are still used occasionally. (Guelbenzu, Navarra)

When treading the grapes, the *chapeau* of skins is also constantly submerged (Quinta do Noval).

Stainless steel provides extra cooling.

these barrels or tanks, usually made of stainless steel, is that they allow for better-computer monitored temperature regulation. One disadvantage is that it is difficult to get to the fermenting must and that the winemaker is completely dependent on technology. If anything goes wrong it is difficult to intervene. There is a system in these stainless steel barrels or tanks which constantly pushes the crust down. To ensure an even better absorption of color there is a very effective technique that is sometimes used: a large quantity of the must is siphoned off from the bottom of the barrel, and this is passed back up through tubes and then forcefully dropped back on the crust (remontée du chapeau).

During fermentation it is important that the sugars in the must are completely fermented to prevent any undesired fermentation later on. Extra sulfur is often added to red wines which contain a residue of sugar to prevent this later fermentation, or sugar is artificially added to these wines in a sterile environment after the wine has been filtered and any yeast cells have been removed.

The fermentation of red wines lasts approximately two weeks, after which the young wines can go to the press. The wine obtained before they are actually pres-

sed (these are more or less siphoned off) known as vin de goutte; wine which is obtained after pressing, is vin de presse (pressed wine). The latter have a coarse taste and structure and contain more tannin. Depending on the quality and the type of wine, none little, or all the pressed wine will be added to the vin de goutte at a later stage.

After pressing, the young wine is stored. Again the desired type of wine determines how and how long wine is kept. For better wines (which can be stored) there is a preference for it to mature in oak barrels. Wines which are to be drunk quickly and are very fruity, are not or are hardly matured in wood.

The second fermentation takes place when the wine is stored: the malolactic fermentation or lactic acid (second) fermentation. Then the stored wines will often be siphoned off to aerate them and separate them from the sediment very gently. At the end of this stage, the wine is filtered and/or cleared: some lightly beaten protein or product containing proteins such as fish glue or bentanite powder (a fine type of earth) is added to the wine. This creates a sort of layer which gradually sinks to the bottom, taking all the floating impurities with it. The storage in wood varies from a few months

Old Burgundian wine press (Drouhin)

Modern wine presses (Navarra)

Better red wines are matured in wooden barrels.

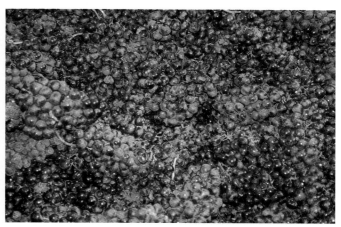

No matter how good the technology, you can never make great wines with rotting grapes!

to two years for better wines for keeping. The wines are then bottled.

In order to make fresh, fruity red wines, rich in color, the maceration carbonique process is often used. This means that the juice of the grapes is fermented inside the skins, not outside, in the usual way.

At the moment wine makers are experimenting with new techniques all over the world. All these techniques have a common denominator in that they are aimed at producing rounder, fuller and fruitier wines which mature fully more quickly. The emphasis is on aroma and taste of the wine rather than on its keeping properties. Without wishing to enter into the debate, I would like to make a distinction between two different sorts of techniques:

– in my view, the product and consumer-oriented techniques, such as the micro-oxygenation process discussed above, improve the quality of the wine enormously, and make the wines accessible more quickly (and therefore ultimately cheaper) for the consumer without any loss of quality. Therefore these techniques are a positive development particularly as they are often more environmentally friendly.

– the profit-oriented techniques, such as the addition of wood shavings or socks filled with sawdust, and the use of special wine barrels made of synthetic materials with recesses for wooden planks, are aimed at producing wines with a certain character more quickly and cheaply. In some countries these techniques are used for quality wines, while in other countries they are only permitted to improve vins de pays. As long as the consumer will not accept that there is a price to pay for quality and authenticity, these practices will unfortunately continue to gain ground.

THE PROCESS OF MAKING ROSÉ WINES

There are actually three ways of producing rosé wines:

– mixing red and white wines, which is prohibited in most countries nowadays. In France, this method is

A good rosé has a wonderful taste.

only used to produce rosé champagne, for which a small amount of still red wine from the Champagne region is added to the sparkling white wine;

— tapping off the red wine after a short period of contact with the grape skins (between one night to two whole days). In France, this technique is sometimes known as saignée or bleeding. It is also possible to allow a whole barrel of black grapes to ferment with their skins and to filter the must as soon as the desired color has been achieved. After filtering or siphoning off the rosé wines, they are processed like white wine;

— the use of black grapes with naturally colored juices such as the poulsard.

THE PROCESS OF MAKING WHITE WINES

To make white wines, only the juice of white or black grapes is used, or a blend of both (this is possible in theory). As the grapes have already been pressed before fermentation, the juices contain few or no solid particles; therefore the fermentation usually occurs in barrels. White wines not only have a different color but also a different taste to red wine. This is because of the lower tannin content of white wine and because of the use of different grapes which also grow in different soil.

White wine can be dry (sec in French) with little residual sugar, medium dry (demi-sec), sweet (doux), full and very sweet (moelleux) or even like a liqueur (liquoreux). In dry white wines, virtually all the sugars have been fermented in the must. After pressing, lesser quality wines are often treated with a hefty dose of sulfur, killing all the 'spontaneous' yeast cells and bacteria. Sometimes they are also centrifuged so that a lower dose of sulfur can be used. Then selected yeast cells are added to the must. For good quality wines, natural yeast cells are used and the must ferments for a longer time at a lower temperature with the addition of very little sulfur. Increasingly the wines are matured on their sediment (sur lie) until they are bottled. The stage of maturing white wine is comparable to that for red wine. More and more French wine makers are opting to ferment the top white wines in oak barrels. This leads to exceptional results, particularly in Burgundy, Bordeaux, Bergerac and in the southwest. However, too much wood is always damaging to white wine. Therefore the secret lies in craftsmanship and moderation. The storage of white wines in oak barrels is also a controversial subject. Personally, I consider that only wines with sufficient structure and potential for maturing should be matured in wood. Wood should add something to the wine and not camouflage its defects or drive out all the other components of taste by dominating too much.

The process is different for sweet wines. In this case the sugars are not all allowed to ferment. For cheap sweet wines, sulfur is added to the must to stop the fermentation prematurely, after a very rapid fermentation. This is done when the wine has reached the desired level of alcohol and residual sugars. When the wine has been siphoned off, filtered, or cleared, quite a lot of sulfur remains in the wine to prevent a disastrous second fermentation in the bottle. Some wineries prefer to use centrifugation or rapid cooling of the must rather than adding sulfuric acid to stop the fermentation. However, even then, sulfur is also added to the wine. As there are not always sufficient natural sugars in the must, some concentrated must is sometimes added to the juices or in some cases, even ordinary sugar, out of sight of any potential witnesses.

For the better sweet wines (Sauternes, Monbazillac, Saussignac), the process is different. The grapes remain on the vines for much longer and are affected by the benign Botrytis cinerea fungus, which shrivels up the grapes, actually increasing the concentration of sugars in the grapes themselves. The must therefore contains a very high level of natural sugars. The yeast cells are killed off when the fatal alcohol level of 14.5 to 15% is reached. The fermentation of the better sweet wines is slow in contrast with that of cheaper wines. After fermentation, even high quality sweet wines are treated with sulfur.

THE PROCESS OF MAKING FORTIFIED WINES

This heading includes various wines from Jerez de la Frontera (sherry) Sanlucar de Barrameda (manzanilla), Huelva, Montilla-Moriles, Malaga, Madeira, Marsala and port, as well as the Vins Doux Naturels of France, such as the Muscat de Beaumes de Venise, Mireval,

The fermentation of Tokaji Aszú occurs very slowly, at a low temperature.

Great port wines, such as the Nacional vintage, rest in wood for two years before being bottled.

Nothing can beat real champagne!

Rivesalts, Lunel, Saint-Jean and the Grenache, Maury and Banyuls.

For fortified wines the fermentation process is interrupted by adding (wine) alcohol to the must. This is usually aimed at producing a very sweet and fruity wine, but the addition of alcohol can also have the aim of killing off the veil of yeast in dry, very sophisticated Manzanilla, Fino or Amontillado wines.

Stopping the fermentation by adding sulfur gas or wine alcohol is known in French as *muter*. After this intervention it is possible to opt for various different methods to mature the wine: either storing it in wood or not, for a short time or a very long time, etc. Most fortified wines, whether dry or sweet, contain between 15.5 and 22% alcohol.

THE PROCESS OF MAKING SPARKLING WINES

For the sake of simplicity, we use the term sparkling for all the wines which contain dissolved carbon dioxide. When the bottle is opened, the wine bubbles cause a refreshing, slight tingling on the tongue. Sparkling wines are made in different ways. The best-known method which produces the best quality is the *méthode champenoise* from the French Champagne region. Although this method was already used almost everywhere in France a long time ago, the monks of *Champagne*, and later the powerful Champagne houses, managed to patent the name. Champagne and the *méthode champenoise* have therefore become one, which means that the wines which can have this name must come exclusively from the Champagne region. Other regions have to be satisfied with the term, *méthode traditionnelle*. In Spain, these wines are also called cava.

This widely applied method entails starting in the first instance with still wines which have been produced separately. After extensive tests and tasting, the cellar master will blend various fermented wines in accordance with secret proportions (known as *assemblage* in French).

A sort of liqueur (liqueur de tirage), consisting of a syrup made of cane sugar and strictly selected yeast cells, is then added to the blended wines. A second induced alcoholic fermentation then takes place in the bottle so that the carbon dioxide cannot escape. This process lasts between ten days and three months. Then the wines have to rest for months, or sometimes years, while the bottles are regularly turned neck down, either by hand or mechanically, so that the sediment

Spanish Cava

The pre-selection of still basic wines
to blend champagne

Still wines are blended in large tanks

goes to the neck of the bottle. By rapidly freezing the necks in a solution of brine, this sediment (dead yeast cells and unfermented sugars) forms a plug of ice under the cork. The bottles are then quickly turned upside down and the (temporary) cork is removed so that the plug of ice shoots out of the neck of the bottle (*dégorgement*) as a result of the large internal pressure of the carbon dioxide trapped in the bottle. The wines are now pure and clear.

Depending on the desired taste (from very dry to sweet), the bottle is filled up with the same wine, or with wine to which different quantities of cane sugar have been added (liqueur de dosage). The wines are sealed again, this time with a real cork, and are provided with their final labels and samples (habillage). Champagnes or wines made by the *méthode traditionelle* containing rather less carbon dioxide, either deliberately or as a result of geographical factors, are also known as *crémants*.

A much cheaper way of retaining the carbon dioxide in the wine is to use the sealed tank method, also known as the *méthode charmat*, or cuve close. Wines

which are made by this method can also be of an extremely good quality. The principle is almost the same as that of the *méthode champenoise/traditionelle*, though in this case the second induced fermentation does not occur in the bottle, but in a sealed tank. The wine is then filtered very quickly and bottled. This method is successfully used in Italy (spumante) and Germany (sekt).

There is another method, which is unfortunately still used, which we would merely like to note here without going into it in any detail, the *méthode gazéifiée*. This simple, and above all, ultra-cheap method is more closely related to the soft drinks industry than to the

Young sparkling wines resting on pupitres

Dégorgement

Some basic wines for champagne are first (partly) matured in wood.

External storage tanks in Pazmand, Hungary

production of wine. A quantity of (coarse) carbon dioxide is simply injected into the fermented wines. The names perlante and vin perlé, describe these lemonade-like wines.

Finally, there are also some (real) wines which contain a small quantity of carbon dioxide, even though they are not sparkling wines (mousseaux). These wines have a tingling effect on the tongue and are fresh and pleasant. The usual names for these wines are: frizzante, pétillant or spritzig.

4 Wine tasting

PROFESSIONAL WINE TASTING

There are several ways of tasting wine. Depending on the purpose, tasting wine can be a very technical matter or could actually be a way of relaxing, a delicious moment.

The cellar master is the first to taste the wine: the grapes, the juice, the unfermented must, the fermented must, the young opaque wine and later the wine itself as it develops, at regular intervals. Tasting young wine is certainly not very pleasant. Because of the strong acidity of some wines, the enamel on your teeth

can be spontaneously removed! Heavy, still rather woody tannins cause the mouth to contract, the teeth to go black, the tongue to feel rough. This wine-tasting method, which is purely technical, is mainly intended to control the wine and gain an idea of how the wine will develop.

After the cellar master and often the owner of the vineyard, journalists and wine makers come to taste the wine. This usually takes place in the cellars of the house of the winegrower concerned. The young wine is tasted under the direction of the cellar master, if necessary with appropriate comments. The first opinion

By means of regular tastings, the cellar master can follow the development of his wine.

on the quality and future prospects of the wine is established in this way. Obviously the taster should have done his homework on this in advance.

Some wine buyers use agents who pre-taste and select the wines when they are very young. On the other hand, others will be present at the first tasting and select the wines themselves. In both cases the wine is tasted again after maturing for several months. If it should be to the wine buyer's taste, a few samples are taken which can then be regularly tasted at the winery. Again this is a clinical tasting which is carried out in a clinical way. The wine is analyzed in terms of its acids, alcohol, tannins, fruit and residual sugars. If the wine seems to be promising and the price is right, an order is placed, and when it arrives, the wine is compared with the remaining samples which were taken by way of control.

Semi-professional tasting area for sales purposes (Henri Maire, Jura)

CRITICAL TASTING

What is wine? Wine is the result of a complex interrelationship of particular varieties of grapes, soil and climate linked to the know-how and individual style of the wine maker with a rich tradition of wine growing as a guideline.

Wine tasting is a true experience but also a technique which you can only master with lots of practice. A knowledge of wines cannot be simply found in a wine glass. In order to taste as a connoisseur, you need a great deal of experience, and you need to have tasted thousands of wines, as well as having a great deal of information about them. In principle, anyone can learn to taste except for the odd person who should avoid wine tasting for medical reasons. Although wine tasting is traditionally mainly carried out by men, women can taste just as well as men; in fact, their sense of smell is even better than that of men! Wine tasting is an examination, an analysis and a sensory experience. There is no computer which can replace us to do this.

THE WINE-TASTING ENVIRONMENT

For professional tastings, there is a preference for a neutral (usually white) environment. Background colors actually have a very strong influence on our perceptions. For example, did you know that the color red reinforces our perception of sugars? Or that green appears to make a wine taste fresher (more acidic), while the color blue makes the wine taste more bitter, and yellow makes it taste more salty? Inexperienced tasters are sometimes misled in this way…

In addition, the tasting area should be clearly lit and ventilated, but also as quiet as possible. Sunlight is preferable to artificial lighting, because sunlight emphasizes the shades of color of the wine more effectively. Smoking before or during the tasting, perfumes and aftershave are obviously out of the question because these leave such strong and overwhelming odors and dominate the subtle aroma of the wine.

THE MOOD OF THE TASTER

Tasting wine requires a great deal of attention and concentration. If you do not feel well or you are tired and stressed or slightly despondent, it is better to postpone a serious tasting. Worries, pain or an hormonal imbalance will also have a negative affect on our concentration and on our perception of sensory stimuli. Heavy smoking is another inhibiting factor, as well as the consumption of strong or sweet drinks before the tasting. Smokers do not always taste less than non-smokers, but it does take much longer before they can taste the same things. The taste buds become tired as a result of the use of tobacco, alcohol or sugar, and they respond less promptly. Therefore the time of the tasting must be chosen very carefully to restrict these effects to a minimum. Usually people opt for the end of the morning, at about 11 o'clock, when most people still feel quite fresh. It is best not to engage in a wine tasting after lunch or after the evening meal. At that time the taste buds are too saturated, while the start of digestion means that the attention is easily distracted.

THE RIGHT GLASS FOR TASTING WINE

A good wine-tasting glass should be transparent, completely clear and colorless from the foot to the rim. This means that the color can be perceived more clearly. The cup of the glass should be broad and round at the bottom, tapering up slightly to the top like a tulip. This is important for the various aromas and the bouquet to be released. As the wine should not be warmed by your hands, the glass should have a very long stem. The glass is only one third filled; this is to achieve the right color concentration, but also so that there is enough room to swirl the wine and release the aromas. In France, there is an official tasting glass which is approved by the controlling institute for the names of the origins of wines, the Afnor-Inao glass.

Afnor/Inao glass

THE TEMPERATURE FOR WINE TASTING

The best temperature for tasting wine fluctuates between 8 and 16 °C (46.4 and 60.8 °F), and depends on the sort of wine being tasted. As the ambient temperature is often about 18 to 20 °C (64.4 to 68 °F), it is always better to taste a wine too cold than too warm. The wine will gain a few degrees extra. Wines which are very rich in tannin become more pleasant when they are tasted at a temperature of 16–18 °C (60.8–64.4 °F); young, fresh and fruity red wines are better tasted cooler. For white wines, the temperature has a big influence on our perception of the acids: the higher the temperature, the more unpleasant the acids. Finally, the temperature also has an influence on our perception of aromas, sugars and alcohol. The higher the temperature, the better you perceive the aromas and the bouquet. The wine also appears to be sweeter and to contain more alcohol as the temperature rises, while the tannins become softer.

THE CORRECT ORDER OF WINE TASTING

Opinions are very divided about the correct order for wine tasting. Professional tasters prefer to start with the red wines and then go on to white wines. However, in my opinion, most tasters prefer the more logical order from white to red. Nearly everyone also agrees about tasting young wines before old, as well as dry wines before sweet.

SENSORY PECEPTION

All over the world, tasters start by judging the color (eye); then the aroma (nose), the taste (mouth + tongue + nose) and finally the aftertaste. Personally, I would also like to add the sense of hearing to the list of senses to be used. It may sound rather strange, but there are all sorts of wonderful things to be heard in your glass, particularly with sparkling wines…. Just try it, and listen to the softly tingling bubbles in a glass of champagne and compare this to the coarse bubbling of a glass of vin perlé. The glugging sound of the wine when it is poured also has a charm of its own, although this does not say anything about the quality of the wine.

COLOR

The visual aspect of food is very important, as is smell. Our brain quickly responds to signals from the visual and olfactory nerves and prepares for the digestive process. An unpleasant color or smell is repellant. A dull or opaque wine is not inviting.

The color actually refers to more than just the color of the wine. A visual examination includes an examination of the color, but also of the clarity, the density and structure of the wine. How does the wine respond to being swirled round in the glass? Does it stick to the sides of the glass, and is it syrupy and slow, or does it waltz like water? Is the surface of the wine quite smooth or are there a few small bubbles of carbon dioxide?

It is best to look at the color of the wine against a white background. Hold the glass at an angle so that

The color…

it is possible to distinguish the various shades of color more accurately.

In general, the color of white wines, varying from pale, (almost colorless) to golden yellow, says something about the age and concentration of the wine. The darker the color, the more extract. Nuances of orange or golden brown can indicate age or even in young wines oxidation (in this case the wine smells and tastes of old sherry or port). Finally, a hint of green in the glass often indicates a young wine. In red wines, the red color evolves with age. Young wines have a familiar purplish color, while wines which have matured in wood tend towards a more reddish-brown color. In turn, older wines reveal beautiful nuances between the red of roof tiles and dark brown. The descriptions of color which are often heard (from light to dark) include the following:

- **for white wines**
  pale, light green, lemon yellow, straw-colored, golden yellow, amber;
- **for rosé wines**
  raspberry, strawberry, redcurrant, salmon or tile-colored shades, onion skin, orange or brown;
- **for red wines**
  purple, purplish-red, pomegranate red, cherry red, ruby red, chestnut, brown.

The wines must be clear, i.e., transparent and pure, without any floating particles or opacity. To check this, it is best to hold the wine in front of a lit candle for a moment.

AROMA

During this second stage of the tasting, you study the various aromas in the wine, whether pleasant or unpleasant. You will certainly not want to taste a wine which has an unpleasant, musty, old chemical or vinegary smell. In fact, there is a big chance that there is something wrong with the wine. In everyday life, we do not really realize how important our sense of smell is. Our taste buds can only distinguish four tastes: sweet, sour, salt and bitter. We can also assess the temperatu-

Taking a sip...

re and density of the wine. However our nose is ten thousand times more sensitive than our sense of taste! No doubt you have had a bad cold, which made everything taste less pleasant. However, it did not really taste any less; you were simply unable to smell it, so it seemed less tasty! Our sense of smell can distinguish thousands of specific odors, even if they are combined and camouflaged.

In order to assess the aroma of a wine accurately, you should smell it three times: with the nose itself, first with a still glass, then after swirling the wine in the glass, and finally through the back of the mouth. To do this, take a sip of wine, suck some air into the mouth and then allow the air to escape through the nostrils (retro-olfactory perception). In this way, the olfactory nerves are stimulated as much as possible.

The aroma...

Retro-olfactory analysis...

Three sorts of aromas can be distinguished:

- *the primary aromas* come directly from the grape and are immediately released in the still glass. This includes all the fruity aromas (red fruit, blackcurrants, peach, apricot, pineapple, grapefruit, gooseberry), floral aromas (rose, peony, pansies, acacia) and vegetable aromas (grass, box, hay, aniseed, fennel, asparagus).
- *the secondary aromas* are the result of the process of fermentation, and can be discerned particularly after rotating the glass or by retro-olfactory perception. For example, this includes dairy odors (yogurt, in the case of macération carbonique), typical wine aromas, alcohol (banana, in the case of macération carbonique), acids, etc.;
- *the tertiary aromas* are the result of maturation. These are perceived after rotating the glass or by retro-olfactory perception. In contact with oxygen, these aromas form the bouquet. Typical tertiary aromas include the various hints of wood (vanilla) but also all the herbal undertones such as pepper, nutmeg and cloves as well as heavy aromas such as tobacco, tar, leather, coffee and cocoa.

In addition to the (positive) aromas, there may also be (negative) odors in the wine: musty, old damp wood (of wines which have been kept in old barrels in a very damp environment), and earthy peasant tastes such as concrete, cement or clay, which suggests that mistakes were made in the preparation of the wine, or that it was badly stored. Cork also belongs in this list, as well as all the strong chemical odors, such as sulfur, aggressive acids and the smell of a chemists shop.

TASTE

Our sense of taste is formed by the tongue, and particularly the taste buds. The tongue as a whole should really be seen as a sort of receptor with specific functions. As far as taste is concerned, we can in the first instance distinguish four different zones of perception:

- The tip of the tongue is sensitive to sweet tastes. This means that not only can you taste sugars with it (fructose, glucose and sucrose), but also the various carbohydrates which are responsible for a sweet or soft taste in the wine (e.g., alcohol and glycerin). A wine is characterized as a dry wine if it contains less than 4 g of sugar per liter (0.14 oz per 34 fl oz), or a maximum of 9 g (0.3 oz) with a tartaric level of acidity of 2 g per liter (0.07 oz per 34 fl oz); it is medium dry if it contains 18 g of sugar per liter (0.63 oz per 34 fl oz); medium sweet if it contains 18 to 45 g (0.63 oz to 1.6 oz) and sweet if it contains more than 45 g of sugar per liter (1.6 oz per 34 fl oz). The quantity of sugar on its own does not always determine the taste of the wine. A lack of acid to counter this can make a wine heavy, cumbersome and unbalanced, while the same wine seems much

A taste: great concentration...

less sweet when it has a higher level of acid! In Hungary, I tasted a Tokaji Aszú Eszencia with no less than 400 g of sugar per liter (14 oz per 34 fl oz), which seemed fresher because of the 21 g (0.7 oz) level of acidity than many syrupy Graves Supérieures sold by a lot of wine merchants.

- The sides and the bottom of the tongue taste acids. In wine, these can be malic acid, lactic acid, citric acid, tartaric acid and succinic acid. Some acids are produced by the grapes themselves (tartaric acid, citric acid and malic acid) and are linked to other components in the wine. On the other hand, other acids are volatile acids which are a result of the fermentation (acetic acid, lactic acid and succinic acid). The presence of acids is very important for the vitality of the wine (degree of freshness and excitement), as well as for the life of the wine. However, too many acids will make the wine taste very green and aggressive.

- Salt is also tasted by the sides of the tongue, though further in. You may wonder whether there can be any salt in wine, but this is certainly possible. Some Swiss wines, as well as a few Muscadet and Vinho Verde wines, contain traces of sea salt which are derived from the soil! In addition to kitchen salt, there may also be some sulfur salts or carbon salts in the wines.

- We taste bitter tastes with the middle of the tongue at the back. Various components may produce a bitter taste; everyone knows that tannins can be very bitter like other acids, but a surfeit of alcohol can also produce a bitter taste as can the anthocyanids and polyphenols (colorants for respectively red and white wines).

In addition to these four taste zones, there is a fifth zone which is not directly linked to taste, but rather to the sense of touch. Right in the middle of the tongue we are able to gain an impression of the warmth of the wine. This does not refer only to how warm or cold the wine really is, but rather to a number of very subtle sensations of pseudo warmth. You can try this out for yourself. A wine with quite a few acids will make a fresh impression, while a strongly alcoholic wine produces a warm sometimes even a burning effect. This touch center on the tongue also allows us to experience the density of the wine. If the wine is thin, it may feel like water, or it may be rich and full-bodied, so that you can almost bite into it. This is related to the amount of extract, or the body of the wine.

Up to now, we have dealt with aspects such as salt, sour, bitter, sweet, warm, fresh, full and thin. However, when you drink wine you will also become aware of other aspects, for example, what about the taste of fruit, flowers or herbs which can be discovered in many wines? The answer is not as simple as you might expect.

You know that the taste of the wine is always determined by its aroma. For example, once we have smelled and tasted a banana, these perceptions remain stored in the brain. Every time we smell something which reminds us of a banana, the brain is stimulated and the new smell and taste are immediately associated with a banana. If you smell banana in your wine, this does not mean you have gone mad, but I can assure you that no banana was involved in making the wine. What we smell and what we taste is a familiar acid (amino acid) and/or alcohol, which both smell of banana. There are also acids which smell of honey, butter, vinegar or caramel, carbon compounds which are reminiscent of hawthorn, bitter almonds, lilac, cherries, cinnamon, hyacinths and oils, which emit the smell of hay, grass, licorice, roses, geraniums etc. As it passes through your mouth, the wine is slightly heated, so that these volatile smells are released (in the form of gases) and disappear in the presence of the olfactory nerves. This means that we perceive all the nuances which are not sweet, salt, bitter or sour. All these originally natural components are artificially imitated every day for all sorts of purposes, in air fresheners, for example, and in special aerosols which spread the smell of freshly baked bread. In some countries these sprays are actually used to make people feel hungry when they are doing the shopping, even though no bread is actually being baked.

To return to wine: when you are tasting wine, the sweet, soft sensations are perceived first. We feel whether the wine is thin or full and quickly gain an impression of the temperature of the wine (fresh or alcoholic). The other perceptions soon follow: sour, salt, bitter. Sometimes they can camouflage each other. For example, a wine with many tannins is softer when it contains

Excellent aftertaste, excellent wine!

residual sugars, as in some former East Bloc countries. On the other hand, a great deal of alcohol softens the taste of the sugars and strengthens the perception of the acids. This is one of the reasons why you always have to taste the wine with a great deal of concentration. Tasting it too quickly can give the wrong impression of the wine, so take your time. Finally, it should be noted that experience is very important in this respect. The more often you taste, the sooner you will unveil the secrets of the wine.

THE AFTERTASTE

During professional tastings, the wine is spat out into special receptacles when it has been tasted. This is necessary because the alcohol would eventually start to affect our judgment. After spitting out the wine though sometimes people do secretly take a small sip when tasting the better wines – the taster should note how long the wine remains in his mouth. Sometimes it is gone very quickly, while other times the taste lingers for a long time. If this is a positive experience, it is described as a long aftertaste. In some cases a strong, unpleasant taste remains in the mouth after spitting out or swallowing the wine. In this case there is simply a bad aftertaste.

Professional tasters often give points for the various aspects. In general, the judgment is determined for 10–15% by the color, 30% by the aroma and 55 to 60% by the taste. There are countless systems of awarding points, but we will not go into these in any further detail in this book.

INFORMAL WINE TASTING

A relaxed informal tasting is often not really intended to judge the quality of the wine, for not everyone is able to do this, but rather to try out a wine or simply pass a pleasant evening with a few friends. In that case the emphasis is unfortunately often placed more on enjoying the wine than on its quality. In my opinion, these two aspects can be very satisfactorily combined, provided there is enough information made available about the wines being tasted. Here is a typical example which I have experienced several times during consumer tastings: for a Chablis tasting I had collected seven real Chablis which were each extremely beautiful and elegant. A good Chablis has a pale, lemony color with a hint of green, and contains strong acids not everyone is able to appreciate a true Chablis. In addition, I had bought a fake Chablis at a department store for half of the price of all the other wines. This wine was a dark yellow, almost golden color with few acids, and worse still, it actually contained some residual sugar! When I tasted it blindfold, I immediately rejected this wine as being quite untypical. The consumers who had tasted wine before and all regularly bought wine actually thought this was the best wine! A similar judgment also takes place with so-called consumer panels, for example, organized by consumer organizations or television programs. The wine is tasted, people either like it or not, and then judge whether the price is acceptable. They do not say a word about the quality or the properties of the wine! Tests have been carried out in various countries with prohibited, completely artificially made wines: water with some acids, sugar, alcohol, artificial flavoring etc. Not a grape nor a wine grower was involved in making it. Most of the consumers did not realize this, and considered the wines very acceptable, even delicious. Therefore the results of these types of consumer tests should always be taken with a pinch of salt.

You can organize various tastings at home. For example, these could be based on a theme such as spring wines, or cool summer wines, or wild wines. Tasting random samples can also be interesting: Bordeaux, the South West, the Midi, etc. It can be fascinating to taste particular varieties of grapes: compare a vin de pays Sauvignon with similar wines from Bordeaux, the Loire, California, New Zealand or Australia. You can also start by tasting the wine and then drinking it again with your meal. This often results in all sorts of surprises.

For an informal relaxed tasting, you need only a few things: a light wall as a background (preferably white), a white tablecloth, so that the color of the wine can be seen more clearly, a few candles to determine the clarity, water so that the tasters can swill out their mouths between two wines, a sufficient number of glasses (all the same), writing materials, wine and …. good friends. Do not fill the glasses too full (one third full is enough) and take your time.

The best thing is not to swallow the wine during the first stage of the tasting, but to spit it out onto the floor (or a cool bucket) for this purpose. In this way you

Some tastings leave unforgettable memories.

will be able to really taste six or eight wines in one evening. If you really think that it is wasteful to spit out the wine (although professionals always do so!), do not taste more than four wines one after another. After that, your perceptions will become slightly unreliable as a result of the alcohol …after four glasses you will like anything! It is also important to rinse out your mouth with water between two wines. However, eating bread or nuts is certainly not advisable, as this will have a negative affect on your taste.

When you taste the wine make a note of what you experience. Do not hesitate to use your own words to do this. You are always right, because it is your own perception. Tasting is a matter of the moment. You taste with your experience and with your own material for comparison. If you have never smelt or tasted a truffle you will have to make do with terms such as a mushroom odor, kindling, ammonia, wet leaves, autumn these are all correct. After tasting each wine, discuss your impressions with the other tasters. This is not only interesting, but it can also be good fun. Finally, draw up a sort of synthesis of the taste experiences for yourself and for everyone together. Is it a good wine? Do you like the wine? What do the others think that the wine costs? If you regularly taste wine with a circle of good friends, you will notice that you improve. It is also enjoyable to develop your taste by devoting a great deal of attention to what you eat or drink. In an age when taste is often sacrificed for the sake of efficiency and price, it is good to reflect occasionally on what Mother Nature has provided for us.

5 Buying and laying down wine

LAYING DOWN WINE

Wine is often bought on impulse. When a particular wine is on offer (sometimes the price is only a few pennies different from the normal price), people often buy six or even twelve bottles at a time. This is not really very sensible. Never buy so many bottles of wine when you haven't tasted it first. In addition, it may be more fun for you, the people you live with and your guests, to drink a different bottle occasionally. Be adventurous, regularly try new wines and make a note of your conclusions. It is also good fun to organize wine-tasting evenings and invite a number of good (wine) friends. For this sort of evening, look for a number of attractive wines which can be tasted by everyone on that evening. Keep a note of the results (you could keep the labels), as well as the place where you bought the wines and how much you paid for them. This will give you a standard for every occasion. You will never have disappointed guests with the look in their eyes which may be familiar to you, and which appears to say: And I thought you knew about wine….

There are still a disconcerting number of people who think that any wine improves as it becomes older. Nothing could be further from the truth! Most wines (certainly more than three quarters of the annual world production) are intended to be consumed within three or a maximum of five years. Only a very small percen-

Professional storage of wine (Robbers & v/d Hoogen, Arnhem)

Attractive wine cellar in Navarra, for a great thirst!

Watch the temperature fluctuations
in your cellar carefully.

tage of wines benefit from being laid down for a long time. This must be done in good circumstances, because otherwise it is waste of the wine, time and money. Great wines which are laid down in good conditions can develop to unknown heights.

In red wines the color gradually changes from a purple color to orange. Depending on the original intensity of the color of a young wine, the color of an old wine will vary from orange-brown to reddish-brown. On the other hand, white wines always gain color with age and tend towards a gold, golden brown or amber color. If you buy better and therefore more expensive wines to lay down for a long time, you should regularly check how they are developing. Consulting a good wine magazine may be very useful in this respect. Sometimes wines develop surprisingly well or badly. Wines from a year that was originally considered inferior may develop better as a result of the whims of nature than wines from a year which was originally considered to be a good one. Therefore it is worth keeping a note of this. Regularly open a bottle to follow the development of the wines you have laid down. If you buy wine with several people, which is a very good idea, invite them to take turns to open a bottle together of the respective cellars. Keep a logbook of these tastings.

Not every place in the home is suitable for laying down wine for a long time. It is important that the place is not too dry or damp, and there should certainly not be a draft, but it must be dark and free from vibrations.

Storage temperature

In a good wine cellar the ideal temperature is between 10 and 12 °C (50 and 53.6 °F). This concerns an average, slightly higher or lower is also possible but there should not be any abrupt temperature fluctuations. You must make sure that the temperature never falls below 0 °C (32 °F) or rises above 25 °C (50–53.6 °F). This can have fatal consequences for the wine.

If the temperature is too high, the wine will start to expand slightly which means that the cork has a tendency to be forced out of the bottleneck. This can result in

fatal oxidizing effects. Wines which are constantly kept too warm (but not above 25 °C/77 °F), will develop more quickly in the best cases, but they will never achieve the complexity which they would have achieved otherwise. Furthermore, a wine which develops (too) quickly will pass its peak more quickly and then rapidly deteriorate.

If the temperatures are too low, the wines will also develop less satisfactorily. At low temperatures some white wines will be affected by deposits of tartaric acid. In fact, this quite harmless phenomenon also means that the wine is less fresh. In addition, it means that the wines cannot be stored as long.

Humidity

It is extremely important to lay the bottles down so that the cork does not dry out. This would result in oxidation and eventually in a loss of quality of the wine. The ambient air should not be too dry because this means that the wine will evaporate through the cork, which also results in oxidation. Nor should the air be too damp, in connection with the possible development of fungi. In that case the musty odor will quickly penetrate the cork with fatal consequences. The effect damp has on the labels is also unfortunate; they tend to become unstuck, and then you can no longer be sure which wine is in the bottle!

You can influence the humidity by placing some gravel or sand on the floor. There are also special damp resistant coatings available to put on the wall.

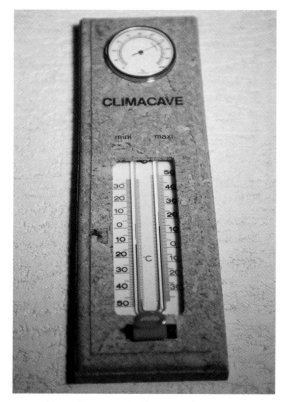

Use a thermometer for your wine cellar.

Gravel on the floor will make sure that the cellar remains humid.

to rest. It is only then that the wine can really develop. Great and particularly old wines are very sensitive to vibration. Therefore it is best not to lay down any expensive wines next to a busy road or railway! However, they should not be laid down under the staircase either, particularly when there are children thundering up and down the stairs several times a day. This is also important for ordinary wines which you take with you from your holiday home. A long car journey, particularly in summer or winter can really mistreat your wine. Allow it to rest for a few weeks before you open it.

DRAFTS

A draft is quite different from ventilation. A good storage place must be well ventilated. However, wines which are in a draft tend not to develop very well. You could say that the wine catches cold and is no longer able to recover. The same thing often happens in (bad) restaurants: wines which are stored in large racks are often placed between the front door (cold, drafts) and the kitchen (warm, damp). In these circumstances any wine will deteriorate.

VIBRATIONS

Wines which are laid down for a long time must be able

Slats keep the bottle stable.

LIGHT

Light can be dangerous for wine, but also for beer or (olive) oil. The effects of UV radiation can change the chemical composition of the wine. Light (whether sunlight or artificial light) particularly influences the polyphenols and anthocyanids which determine the color of the wine. These can break down and the color will change, which also has a negative influence on the taste. The wine acquires a taste of light. Take a careful note of the lighting in the shop. Never buy a bottle which was right underneath a neon tube or a spotlight (light and heat!). Always choose a bottle which was lying in the dark. Worst of all are the bottles which have been left in the window of some liquor stores for three weeks at a stretch, so that the sunlight could have a field day and where temperatures can go well above 30 °C (86 °F), which is a terrible shame.

ODORS

This aspect is all too often ignored. I have visited fantastic cellars which met all the norms. However, the owners would also keep their potatoes and onions in the same cellar, just below some of the grand cru wines from the Bordeaux region. It is hardly surprising that these wines exhibited strange earthy undertones when they were opened! A similar thing happened when a famous restaurateur thought he could cleverly save money by not moving the wine cellar when his restaurant was

Keep your bottles in a cool dark place.

Blocks of lava stone for the wine cellar.

renovated. For a few weeks the building was like a playground for the painters, who painted the restaurant a bright new color. When the customers all started to complain about the wines after the restaurant was reopened, the restaurateur realized how stupid he had been. All the wines, from good table wines to extremely expensive grand crus, tasted of paint!

A WINE CELLAR OR A WINE CUPBOARD?

Few of us are privileged enough to have a good wine cellar. Of course, it is quite ideal to have such a cellar full of bottles, preferably one where you can stand up, with stone niches and racks, sand and gravel on the floor, soft, (candle) lighting… Unfortunately this ideal is no more than a dream for most of us. In modern houses, no attention is devoted to the wine cellars. Large fitted cupboards are also a thing of the past. These were also often suitable for storing a real collection of wine if the inside and the doors were well insulated and a thick layer of sand or gravel was placed on the floor. The modern alternatives are to stack together separate building blocks of lava stone. These blocks are good at regulating humidity and temperature and they are very stable. They are certainly not particularly cheap, but a house with an old-fashioned cellar is even more expensive.

If you wish to lay down a store of good wines, but do not wish to leave them for ten years, a cupboard with a regulated temperature can be a solution. These are rather like a refrigerator with a glass or a sealed door. They are chic, elegant and fit in any interior. The advantage of these cupboards is that not only can the wines be kept at the right temperature for storage but

they can also be set to the serving temperature. This means that your wine is always at the right temperature. They are rather expensive, but for anyone who wishes to have a good cellar but lives in a small home, this is a fantastic solution.

Anyone who cannot or does not wish to spend so much money will have to be creative. However, remember that the longer you wish to lay down the (better) wines, the better the conditions must be. An old cupboard a dresser or a sideboard can be very useful. Nowadays it is also possible to buy foam cellars in which not only can you transport the wines, but can also store them. The wine remains protected from temperature fluctuations and excessive humidity. If you merely want to store wine, but not for a long time, you can simply

Use one of the better temperature-regulated cupboards.

stack the bottles in strong wine boxes. As you see, with a bit of creativity, there are many possibilities.

BUYING WINE

Before writing about the ideal wine store, I would like to make some notes about offers of cheap wines. Cheap wines can sometimes be quite good, but they will never be great wines. If you come across a Bordeaux for about 12 Euros (2001 consumer price), never be tempted to buy it. You will NEVER buy a good Bordeaux for that price. Some wines simply cannot be made cheaply without taking all sorts of underhand short cuts. If you cannot afford a grand cru from the Bordeaux region (and who can, nowadays, with the ridiculously high prices there are!), buy a top wine from the Bergerac region (for example, from David Fourtour, Luc de Conti, or a Dauzan Lavergne of the Mallard family that are a guarantee of good quality)! If you wish to buy an excellent wine, remember that there is more between heaven and earth than the most expensive Bordeaux and Burgundies. You could try a wonderful Madiran from Alain Brumont (Château Montus/Boucassé), Irouléguy of the Brana family, Cahors of the Baldès family (for example, Triguedina Prince Probus) and you will be astonished!

Make sure that you buy a variety, not only wines which will be drunk in ten or fifteen years time. You will probably be thirsty in the meantime! Buy wines for daily use and wines for special occasions. When you buy wine it is important to think about when you expect to drink it. What are you drinking it with, and whether you prefer French, Italian or Chinese food? Try to think in advance which wine you will need to go with these meals. Also think about the preferences of your guests. Do not buy only whole bottles (0.75 cl/25.3 fl oz), but also some half-bottles (0.375 cl/12.7 fl oz). If you are buying a wine which you would like to drink, for example, eighteen years after the birth of your son or daughter, buy it in Magnum bottles (1.5 l/50.7 fl oz, or even larger). These will last longer than small bottles.

WHERE DO YOU BUY THE WINE?

Buying wine from an ordinary liquor store is certainly not the best choice. Many liquor stores simply do not know enough about wine to be able to give you any good advice. It is perfectly all right to buy a daily table wine there, or a good wine for a party, but this is not the place to buy the wine you are going to lay down.

In France and Belgium a consumer can buy all sorts of wines in a big supermarket, from liters of table wine to the grand crus from the Bordeaux region! More and more of these large shops have a special corner for the better wines where you can also consult a specialist salesman.

In Europe most wine these days is sold in supermarkets, probably for the sake of convenience. The quality of supermarket wines has improved enormously in the last few years. However, the problem is the presentation and storage of wine in the supermarkets themselves. The personnel are not properly instructed and cannot help you make the right choice of wine. Fortunately, more and more big groceries now realize the importance of providing adequate information and have responded to this need. It is still a very impersonal way of finding out about wine to read all the information on a tiny sticker on the racks or on the back of a label of the bottle, but at least this is something. The publications of these grocery chains can also be very informative.

In general, the level of shops which specialize in wine is much better. For example, oenologists (literally: wine connoisseurs) from the Wine Academy have a much higher level of tasting skills than people in liquor stores. A good oenologist must keep up with his trade and make sure he does not rest on his laurels. The world of wine is constantly changing, and customers are becoming increasingly interested in wines. Every year they are becoming more wine wise and demanding. Simply go on looking for a wine merchant if you are not satisfied with the one you have at the moment. There are enough excellent professionals with a great love for their profession, who will be happy to serve you.

The large chain wine merchants are not always very well informed of what is happening in the world of wine. In fact, the standard of some chain wine merchants is quite deplorable. Fortunately, there are also some very good ones who can certainly compete with traditional wine merchants in terms of their range, and who are also improving all the time in terms of expertise. Again and again, buyers are able to find new jewels all over the world. However, the danger of

Extra large bottles for special occasions.

Buy your wine from a better wine store
(Robbers & v/d Hoogen, Arnhem)

Of course, you can also buy from the producer himself
(Henri Maire Jura).

this formula is that the customer looking for some support eventually becomes tired of constantly being confronted with new wines. For the adventurers and travelers amongst us, this sort of liquor store is a true wine paradise!

You can also buy wine from private wine merchants. For anyone who is looking for very high quality wines, this is the most obvious place. These family businesses have several generations of knowledge about wine and experience of buying wine at their disposal. Choose a well-known house and you will never be disappointed. Make an appointment and taste the wines before you buy. In many cases, you can also buy the great wines from Bordeaux or Burgundy by signing in advance (en primeur), and these can often be fully developed for years in the sometimes monumental cellars of these wine houses for no charge or for a very low price. The range of wines of these private wine houses is often rather limited, and even slightly old-fashioned. However, for connoisseurs of great French wines this is certainly no obstacle. The price is usually slightly higher than at the ordinary liquor store, but you will have more professional help, better advice, understanding and above all, love for the wine.

Finally, there are countless businesses, from very good to very poor, which sell wines by mail order. Again, it is wise to be cautious. Read the small print extremely carefully. Only buy wine with a guarantee that you get your money back if it is not good. Some companies tempt their customers with very cheap offers of great wines, but also sell ordinary wines accompanied by a good story and proportionately staggering profits. For example, in some cases, the top wine of a certain château is described in a catalogue, but you will receive the second wine from that house upon delivery. Watch out for this, and remember that your rights as a consumer apply here as well.

One fairly new phenomenon is the sale of wine over the Internet. For consumers this is a very positive deve-

lopment. It avoids many (expensive) intermediaries. The customer reads about a wine, the house and the tasting notes of a well-known and respected wine taster, and orders what appeals to him/her directly from the wine grower. This then arrives within a few days with a return guarantee. We also see that more and more traditional wine merchants and importers are using the Internet to promote their wines, and even offer them for sale. In the long term this may mean the loss of a few jobs, but the consumer will certainly benefit.

THE CHOICE OF WINE

In order to give you an idea of what you could buy, we have subdivided the wines into different types on the basis of an idea of Oz Clarke, the well-known wine writer. It is important that you try to discover your own taste on the basis of experience. In doing this, take into account the meals you often eat, the preferences of your friends and guests, the celebrations and birthdays coming up, etc. For each type of wine we give you some examples. No matter how impressive, this list is certainly not exhaustive, but should give you some ideas for choosing a particular type of wine.

RED WINE

Light and fruity (juicy, few tannins, drink young)
- Beaujolais nouveau (France)
- Tempranillo sin crianza (Rioja, Navarra, Spain)
- Vino joven (Rioja, Navarra, Ribera del Duero, Spain)
- Gamay Beaujolais (Niagara Peninsula, Ontario, Canada)

Young with few tannins (slightly more structure than the last wine, fresh and fruity, also drink young)
- Beaujolais villages, crus du Beaujolais, Bourgogne

Saint-Pourçain

Irouléguy

Hungarian Cabernet Sauvignon

passe-tout-grain, Bourgogne grand ordinaire, Gamay de Touraine, Gamay de Haut Poitou, vins de pays Gamay, Côtes du Forez, Châteaumeillant, Cheverny, Coteaux du Giennois, Coteaux du Loire, Chinon, Bourgueil, Sancerre rouge, Béarn, Côtes du Lubéron, Côtes du Ventoux, Tricastin, Costières de Nîmes (France)
- Valpolicella, Classico Superiore, Bardolino, Alto Adige (Italy)
- Navarra, La Mancha, Valdepeñas (Spain)
- Dôle (Switzerland) and Egri Bikavér (Hungary)

Medium body from a temperate climate (attractive elegant wines)
- Anjou, Pinot Noir d'Alsace, better Chinon and Bourgueil, Côtes de Nuits villages, Côtes de Beaune villages, Arbois, Bordeaux, Bergerac, Pécharmant, Haut-Médoc, Tursan (France)
- Ghemme, Gattinara, Dolcetto (Italy)
- Spätburgunder (Assmannhaüser, Germany)
- Pinot Noir (Valans, Switzerland)
- better Penedés, Navarra, Rioja and Ribera del Duero (Spain)
- Australian red (Australia)

- Oregon Pinot Noir, Californian Merlot, Cabernet Sauvignon, or Pinot Noir (USA)
- better Cabernet Sauvignon and Cabernet Franc (Hungary)

Medium body from a warm climate (slightly more herbs and sometimes more of a peasant taste than the previous wines, always fascinating)
- Côtes du Roussillon villages (Caramany), Fitou, Collioure, Irouléguy, Cahors, Madiran, Côtes du Rhône villages, crus des Côtes du Rhône, Provence, Bandol, Corsican wines (France)
- Chianti Classico Riserva, Brunello di Montalcino (Italy)
- Bairrada, Dao, Douro (Portugal)
- top Navarra, top Penedés (Spain)
- Naoussa, Nemea, Château Carras (Greece)
- top Cabernet Sauvignon, Merlot, Pinot Noir, Pinotage (South Africa)
- top Chilean, Californian and Australian

Herbal and powerful taste (full-bodied wines with a lot of character)
- crus des Côtes du Rhône (Hermitage, Côte-Rôtie, Châteauneuf-du-Pape, Saint-Joseph, Cornas, Gigondas), Madiran Château Montus, Irouléguy Domaine Brana (France)
- Barabaresco, Barolo, Taurasi (Italy)
- Priorato (Spain)
- Château Musar, Château Ksara (Lebanon)
- Petite Syrah and Shiraz wines from California, Mexico, South Africa and Australia

Excellent, elegant and full-bodied
- Côte-Rôtie or (H)Ermitage, great Bordeaux and Bourgogne, Pomerol, Saint-Emilion, Cahors Prince Probus Triguédina (France)
- Tignanello, Lapparita, Solaia, Boscarelli, Sassicaia, and all Vino da Tavola top wines from Tuscany, Vino Nobile di Montepulciano, Brunello di Montalcino, top Barolos, top Chiantis (Italy)
- great wines from Penedes (Torres Mas de la Plana), Ribera del Duero (Vega Sicilia)
- great wines from California and Oregon (United States)
- great wines from South Africa (Rust en Vrede, Hamilton Russel, Meerlust Rubicon), Chile (Casa Lapostolle Cuvée Alexandre, for example) or Australia (Penfolds Grange)

Only for the real connoisseurs, a few sweet red wines outside the categories
- Imiglyko (Greece)
- Austrian, German sweet red wines

I would like to mention one high quality, sweet red wine separately, the Recioto della Valpolicella (amongst others, the wine from Masi is absolutely wonderful, but it is very expensive).

WHITE WINES

Fresh and neutral, not matured in wood (drink young)
- Sylvaner (Alsace), Chenin blanc from the Loire,

Barolo

Côte-Rôtie

Brunello di Montalcino

Châteauneuf-du-Pape

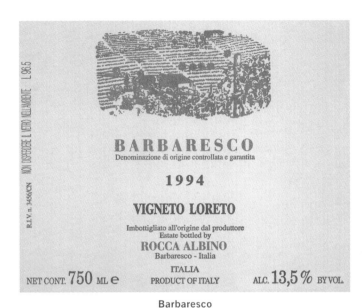

Barbaresco

Pinot bianco from Friuli

Rueda Viura/Sauvignon blanc

Chilean Sauvignon blanc

Anjou blanc sec, Cheverny, Muscadet, Gros Plant du Pays Nantais, dry white wines of the Savoie, Abymes, Apremont, Crépy, Corsican wine, Corbières, Languedoc, Picpoul du Pinet, Gascogne, vins de pays (France)

Fresh and fruity, not matured in wood (drink young)
– Savennières, Vouvray sec, Anjou, Saumur, Haut Poitou Chardonnay, Jurançon, Viognier vin de pays, Seyssel, Condrieu, Macon blanc, Beaujolais blanc, Saint-Véran, Rully, Montagny, Mercurey, Chablis, Bourgogne Aligoté, Alsace Pinot Blanc, Edelzwicker, Arbois (France)

Very aromatic and with a herbal taste, not matured in wood (mainly sauvignon)
– Sancerre (smells of asparagus or licorice), Sauvignon Haut Poitou (grass, sparking), Bordeaux (grass, cats piss = box tree) (France)

– Sauvignon from Spain (grass, fennel)
– Sauvignon from California (grass, melon, fig), Chile (grass, melon, sometimes citrus fruit), Australia (exotic fruit, grass), New Zealand (extremely fruity, sparkling, tropical, gooseberries) or South Africa (gooseberries, fresh fruit, fig, melon, flint)

Very aromatic, not matured in wood.
– vin de pays Marsanne or Viognier, Riesling, Pinot gris from Alsace, Jura and Arbois blanc, Pacherenc du Vic-Bilh (France)
– Grauburgunder/Pinot Gris or Riesling (Germany)
– Grüner Veltliner, Riesling (Austria)
– Ermitage (=Marsanne!) or Petite Arvine and Amigne du Valais (Switzerland)
– Pinot Grigio from Collio and Isonzo, Tocaï Friulano, Trebbiano d'Abruzzo (Italy)
– Galicia, Rías Baixas (Spain)
– Pinot Gris Zölt Veltelini (Hungary)

Grüner Veltliner

- Pinot Gris from Oregon (USA)
- Riesling, Viognier (Canada)
- Riesling, (New Zealand)
- Riesling, (Australia)

Elegant and dry, matured in wood
- vins de pays Chardonnay, Bourgogne Chardonnay, Chablis premier cru, Chablis grand cru, Condrieu, Hermitage blanc, better Jurançon, Graves blanc sec, better Bordeaux blanc sec (France)
- Alto Adige, Collio, Isonzo Chardonnay (Italy)
- Chardonnay from Penedés (Spain)
- Chardonnay from California, Chile, Australia, New Zealand, South Africa or Niagara Peninsula (Ontario, Canada)

Penedés Chardonnay

Full-bodied and dry, matured in wood
- great Chardonnay wines from Burgundy (for example, Chassagne-Montrachet), but also wines such as Pacherenc du Vic-Bilh sec of Château Montus from Madiran (France)
- great Chardonnay from Penedés (Jean Leon, Torres Milmanda) or from Navarra (Chivite) (Spain), great Chardonnay from California, Australia (Penfold's, Tyrell's) or South Africa.

Very aromatic and full-bodied, reasonably dry, sometimes matured in wood
- Muscat and Gewürztraminer from Alsace, vin de pays
- Dry Muscat (France)
- Traminer (Germany)
- Moscatel secco (Spain)
- Gewürztraminer from California or Oregon (United States)
- (Gewürz)traminer (Australia)
- Torrontes (Argentina)

Vins de pays Chardonnay

Penedés Milmanda

65

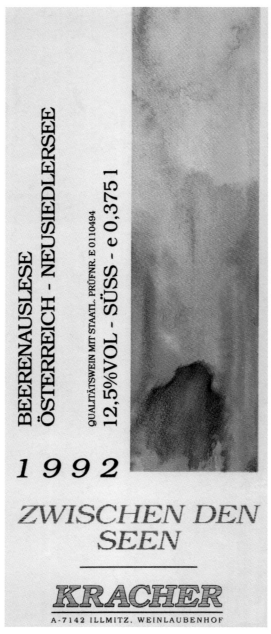

Beerenauslese

Loupiac

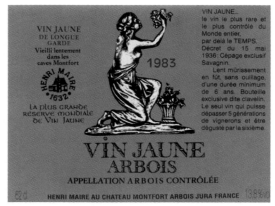

Vin jaune

Semi-sweet, sometimes matured in wood (very broad category with a great variation in quality)
– Vouvray demi-sec or moëlleux, Montlouis demi-sec or moëlleux, Coteaux du Layon, Bonnezeaux, Jurançon moëlleux, Pacherenc du Vic Bilh moëlleux, Cadillac, Cérons, Loupiac, Saussignac, Rosette, Côtes de Montravel, Haut-Montravel, Alsace vendanges tardives (France)
– Moscato d'Asti, Orvieto Classico abboccato (Italy)
– Spätlese Auslese from Germany or Austria
– American or Australian Late Harvest

Full-bodied sweet, with noble rot (pourriture noble/*Botrytis cinerea*) usually matured in wood
(only made in top years!)
– Vouvray, Bonnezeaux, Coteaux du Layon, Quarts de Chaume, Alsace vendanges tardives, Château de Cérons, Jurançon moëlleux, Quintessence van Domaine Cauhapé, for example, the very rare botrytized Condrieu of Yves Cuilleron, Sauternes (France)
– German Beerenauslese (certainly that of Muskat Ottonel!), Austrian Beerenauslese or Ausbruch, South African Special Late Harvest, Australian Botrytis or Noble wines, Tokaji Aszú

Full-bodied sweet, without noble rot, sometimes matured in wood
– Vin de Paille from the Arbois, Alsace, Ardèche (Chapoutier!) or Auvergne (Claude Sauvat), Pacherenc du Vic-Bilh vendanges tardives, Jurançon vendanges tardives (France)
– Sweet wine from Navarra (Spain)
– Vin Santo, Recioto di Soave, Moscato Passito (Italy)
– Amigne du Valais (Switzerland)
– Muscat de Patras, Samos Muscat (Greece),
– Ice wine (Canada)
– South African Muscat wines (for example, Vin de Constance from the Klein Constantia Estate)

Vin de pays Muscat sec

Vin fou from the Jura

Specific white wines, outside the categories

- Vins jaunes, Château Châlon, L'Etoile from the French Jura (which develop flora, but are not fortified)
- Tokaji Szamorodni Száraz (dry) or Edes (sweet) from Hungary
- Retsina from Greece (dry white wine, aromatized with resin)

ROSÉ WINES

Dry

- Rosé des Riceys (excellent high quality rosé from the Champagne region), Marsannay (excellent rosé from the Bourgogne), Tavel, Lirac (from the Rhône region, including the especially nice Bandol rosé), Coteaux d'Aix-en-Provence, Rosé du Béarn, Rosé de Loire, vin de pays rosé (France)
- Rosé from Navarra (for example, Ochoa Rosado de Lágrima, Chivite Gran Feudo or Castillo de Javier from Las Campanas), Penedes (Torres) or Rioja (Marqués de Caceres, amongst others) (Spain)
- Gris de Boulaouane or Gris de Chellah (Chantebled); simple, but pleasant full rosé from Morocco

(Medium) sweet

- Rosé or Cabernet d'Anjou (do choose a good one they are never very sweet or you will have a hangover before you have even had a drink)
- Portuguese rosé
- Blush wines (Grenache blanc or Zinfandel) from California

SPARKLING WINES

White, light, dry

- Clairette de Die brut, Seyssel (from Savoie), crémant de Bourgogne, d'Alsace, de Loire, Saumur, Vouvray, Champagne brut without a year (France)
- crémant du Luxembourg, cava (Spain), sekt (Germany), English, Australian and South African sparkling wine, Prosecco (Italy)

White, medium-full, dry

- crémant de Limoux, blanquette de Limoux, champagne (Bollinger, Krug, Deutz, Mumm, Pol Roger, Roederer, Ruinart, Tattinger) (France)
- better cavas (Spain), spumante (amongst others, the excellent Franciacorta (DOCG) from Italy, South African, American and Australian top sparkling wines

White, medium-sweet or sweet

- demi-sec champagne (France) or Asti spumante (Italy)

Rosé, dry

- Saumur rosé, champagne rosé (France)
- Californian sparkling rosé, sparkling wine (Mumm, Cuvée Napa, for example) (USA)

Rosé from Marmande

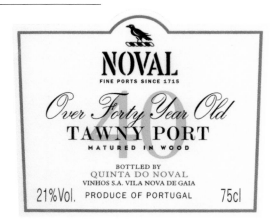

There should be a good rosé champagne.

Rosé, medium-sweet or sweet
– rosé or champagne rosé demi-sec (France)

Red, dry
– red Saumur of Bouvet-Ladubay, Rubis Excellence (France)
– outstanding Australian sparkling wines made with the shiraz grape (such as Seppelt)
– Lambrusco secco de Sorbara (no screw top, but a real cork and much more expensive than ordinary sweet Lambrusco) (Italy)

Red, medium-sweet or sweet
– red Saumur mousseux, Cuvée Cardinal of Gratien & Meyer (France)
– Lambrusco (some better Lambruscos can be really delicious. The cheaper varieties are usually more like fizzy lemonade)
– Russian Krimski sekt

FORTIFIED WINES

Dry elegant and light
– Manzanilla (Pasada Solear Barbadillo, Principe Manzanilla Barbadillo (Spain)
– Fino secco Jerez/sherry (La Ina Domecq, Tio Pepe, Gonzalez Byass (Spain)
– Madeira Sercial from the Portuguese island on the African coast, Madeira
– Crispy dry white port (Portugal)

It is not only vintage port that deserves a good cellar!

Dry and full-bodied
– Amontillado del Duque, Gonzalez Byass, Palo Cortado Sibarita Domecq or Manzanilla Pasada Barbadillo (Spain)

Dry and heavy
– Oloroso secco (Spain)
– Marsala Vergine (Italy)

Sweet and medium-heavy
– Banyuls, Rivesaltes rancio, 15-year-old Maury (Mas Amiel) (France)
– Madeira Bual, Late Bottled Vintage Port, Vintage Character Port (Portugal)
– Moscatel (Spain)
– Mavrodaphne (Greece)

Sweet and heavy
– Vintage port, Moscatel de Setúbal, Malmsey Madeira (Portugal)
– Malaga Pedro Ximénes, Priorato Dolç de l'Obac, Pedro Ximénes Xeres (Spain)
– Marsala (Italy)
– Muscat de Mireval, de Rivesaltes, de Saint-Jean de Minervois, du Cap Corse, Beaumes-de-Venise; Maury Vintage (Mas Amiel) (France)
– South African KWV Vintage (Limited Release), Australian liqueur wines made with muscat or muscadelle

THE LANGUAGE OF LABELS

The label is the proof of the wine's identity. You could see it as a label which in most cases provides all the relevant information about the wine concerned. However, just like a place of origin, the label does not say anything at all about the quality of a wine!

All wine-producing countries are working very hard to make their own systems of control more or less watertight. However, this can only be really successful if there was an agent posted by every barrel for 24 hours a day, 365 days a year - an impossible dream. Don't allow yourself to be taken in by what the label says. How-ever, from a legal point of view, it is certainly important to be able to trace the culprit when you

Some labels, no matter how beautiful, do not say
enough about the wine,
therefore the label on the back is compulsory.

N.B.: The term 'table wine' is often used for very good
(and by no means cheap) wines!

come across a particularly bad wine. For this purpose code numbers are often used on labels. I always have doubts about people who wish to be mentioned anonymously on a bottle. If the wine is good, you ought to be proud of it and want your signature to be shown on your cherished product.

Look carefully at changes on the label. It is possible that the wine grower still has an enormous supply of labels from the previous year (which did not sell very well), and that he decided to cross out the old year and show a new year on the labels because he thinks it is a shame to throw all the old labels away. The percentage of alcohol can also sometimes vary from one batch to another, but a difference of more than 1 or 2% is usually more likely to be the result of tax evasion than because of any differences between the batches of wines.

It is better to buy wines from a well-known house. This certainly does not have to be a big house, so long as it can be traced. Nowadays there are sufficient guides available to find good and reliable addresses (for

example, the *Guide Hachette)*. If you don't know where to start, consult a good wine merchant. He will be pleased to help you.

REGULATIONS ON LABELLING

What should a label say? Depending on the country of origin (inside or outside the European Union), and the indication of quality, the label should always show the following information.

Compulsory information for all wines of EU origin
– nominal volume (how much wine is there in the bottle?)
– name or code of the bottler
– member state of origin
– actual alcohol percentage per volume
– product identification number (so that the batch can be traced)

An AOC label

Chinese wine label

In addition, the label should indicate:
– the word table wine (vin de table) for table wines with no geographical indication which do come from the EU
– the word vin de pays for vin de pays with a geographical indication of EU origin.
– an indication of the region
– the indication VQPRD (=Vin de Qualité Produit dans un Region Déterminée), AOC (=Appellation d'Origine Contrôlée), VDQS (=Vin Délimité de Qualité Supérieure) or, for example, QbA (=Qualitätswein bestimmter Anbaugebiete) etc. for quality wines of EU origin

Compulsory information for wines from third countries
– nominal volume
– name or code of the importer or bottler in the European Union
– country of origin
– actual alcohol percentage per volume
– product identification number

Depending on the quality requirements of the country concerned, the label should also indicate:
– the word wine (vin, vino, wein, wine, etc.) for wines without a geographical indication
– the geographical area (defined wine region) for wines with a geographical indication.

As you see, a label could actually be quite simple. Any embellishments and additional information often only serve to confuse the consumer unnecessarily. It would be better to provide bottles with a label on the back giving all the additional information; this would make the bottles easier to identify for consumers (and for people stacking them on the shelves!)

South American vine label

6 Drinking wine

THE WINE GLASS

Now that you have acquired the necessary theoretical knowledge in the first few chapters, we come to the best part of wine, i.e., drinking it! However, there is still some theory to be examined if you want to enjoy your glass of wine to the full. Let us start by considering the most important friend of wine: the glass.

In Spain and southern France an attractive custom has survived: drinking wine from an earthenware or glass flask with a spout. This is very old-fashioned and particularly funny for onlookers. Villagers often slyly try to take tourists for a ride in this way. This sort of spout is not very easy to deal with. City dwellers have become used to drinking wine from a glass or beaker, usually without making too much of a mess.

However, did you know that the shape of the glass certainly has an affect on our perception of wine? If you are skeptical about this, try it yourself: pour the same wine into a straight glass, a round glass (ballon) and in a tapering glass (tulip) and taste the differences ... you will be astonished! It is not surprising that every region uses its own glass. Admittedly, this is also a matter of tradition, but scientists have proved with countless tests that the shape of the glass has a direct influence on the way in which molecules are released in the wine. In other words, depending on the shape of the glass, you will smell or taste more with the same wine if you use the correct glass. If you want to take wine seriously, you must take this into account for your own enjoyment.

SHAPE

The bowl is particularly important when you are choosing a good glass. However, the stem should also comply with a number of requirements. The stem should certainly not be too short. You should be able to hold the wine glass easily without having to touch the bowl. Picking up the glass by the cup is definitely bad form.

Mold for a guild glass from Leerdam

Not only will this make the glass dirty so that you can no longer appreciate the clarity and color of the wine, but you will also warm up the wine and it does not look very elegant either. There is only one important factor as regards the foot of the glass, and that is stability. However, it should not be too heavy: the whole thing must be practical. The perfect glass has the following qualities:
- completely colorless
- transparent
- no decoration
- made of thin glass, preferably crystal
- a cut and polished rim
- an oval (tapering) or rounded cup (depending on the type of wine)
- a (long) stem

INFLUENCE OF THE SHAPE AND SIZE

The aromas of a wine can only fully develop at a particular temperature. When the wine is poured (assuming that you pour the wine at the right temperature), some of the aromas immediately start to evaporate and fill the glass. Measurements have shown that the aromas can be divided into three main types. The lighter aromas (fruit, flowers) quickly rise to the rim of the glass and are perceived first. Vegetal and mineral aromas are slightly heavier and remain halfway up the glass. Finally, there are the heavy aromas of alcohol and wood which remain at the bottom of the glass. When you rotate the glass, the walls become wet and the thin layer of wine evaporates more quickly, which produces more and more intense aromas. Surprisingly, these aromas do not intermingle, but remain hanging in the same horizontal layers. If you take different glasses you will see that the width and intensity of these layers of aromas depend entirely on the shape (wide, round, oval, tapering) and size of the glass. In some very open glasses, the fruit and flowers disappear very quickly, while the heavier aromas actually gain in strength. In closed glasses the aromas of fruit and flowers remain trapped longer. Red wines, particularly those with a lot of character, require a larger glass than white wines. For fortified wines, it is advisable to use smaller glasses so that the fruit rises more, rather than the alcohol.

The shape of the glass clearly also has an influence on the way in which you hold the glass when you are drinking. You can try this out: take a glass with a wide open bowl and make a note of how you drink from it. Your head goes down and you take small sips of the wine. Then drink from a glass with a more closed bowl. In order to take a sip, your head moves back slightly so that the wine flows onto the back of your tongue. Have you ever noticed that in this way you are stimulating different centers of taste and touch, and that this is probably not a pure coincidence? The more slowly you drink the wine, the more sensations of taste and smell you will perceive.

Every wine has a story to tell, whether this is a long or short story, about the soil, the climate, the grapes,

Riedel glasses, a different glass for every type of wine.

and perhaps even about the wine grower. All aromas are complex chemical compounds which we can poetically refer to as fruit, acids, minerals, tannin or alcohol. When you are choosing the right glass, make sure that the wine can reveal its story to you through all these chemical compounds. A glass is not just a glass!

RIEDEL GLASSES

The perfect glass exists, there is no doubt about it! The German glassmakers of Riedel have been looking for the best and most beautiful glasses for generations, not only for wine, but also for beer and for distilled drinks. In 1973, they launched a magnificent series of glasses, the Sommeliers. Even the greatest skeptics had to throw their doubts overboard … After a long search for perfection, every glass was designed for a particular type of wine, and allows the wine to tell its own story as it really is. There is no beating about the bush, just straightforward perceptions from the heart of the glass. This means that the specific characteristics of a particular wine are sublimated. Thus there are glasses for various types of red, white, sparkling and rosé wines. For connoisseurs of great wines, these handmade glasses are an absolute must: after all, it would be a terrible shame to miss part of the story told by the wine. A nobleman from the Bordeaux region simply does not speak the same language as a powerful estate owner from Piedmont! However, remember that these sublime glasses with their infinite love of wine can be just as merciless if the wine is no good … or if a wine is poured into the wrong glass. For example, an old patriarch from Burgundy will feel like a young farm laborer when it is poured into a Bordeaux glass.

Anyone who does not drink grand cru wines from Bordeaux or Burgundy on a daily basis, but would like to have an excellent glass for his good wines, could buy

Riedel glasses, the better wines deserve the best!

Excellent (champagne) glasses can be found at the Cristalleries d'Arques.

Riedels second line, the Vinum series. Although these glasses are machine-made, they have almost the same qualities as the Sommelier glasses. There is slightly less choice, but the price is lower.

In addition to Riedel glasses, a number of other glasses are also very suitable for the enjoyment of your daily glass of wine. However, you will not discover the same range of aromas in your wine although they are perfectly good for ordinary wines. First, there is the so-called Afnor glass (formerly known as the Inao glass) from France, which is widely used in professional tastings. The shape and dimensions of these glasses have now been thoroughly standardized, and they are used by various producers such as Verreries & Cristalleries D'Arques in northern France. In the Netherlands, we recommend the guild glasses from the glass factory in Leerdam.

LOOKING AFTER YOUR GLASSES

Apart from finding the most suitable glass it is also important to know how you can look after your glasses best. If you are to believe the advertisements on television, most dishwashers are quite safe for your glasses, provided you use the tablets which are made to prevent deposits of limestone. However, these tablets do not remove the specific odor of a dishwasher. Personally, I always prefer old-fashioned washing up for my glasses. Use a moderate amount of soft washing up liquid, particularly if the glasses are rather greasy. However, it is better to work with soda dissolved in hot water. Most washing up liquids have a fresh, lemony odor which may benefit a coarse white wine, but would certainly not suit

a great wine. In any case, always rinse your glasses thoroughly in hot water. Also always use a clean tea-towel to dry your glasses, and make sure it does not leave any fluff. Tea-towels which have been left in the cupboard too long can absorb strange smells, so smell the tea-towel first. Place your glasses in a closed cupboard which is dust-free and grease-free. As glasses quickly tend to absorb the odor of the environment, it is certainly not advisable to store the glasses bowl down. This means they will soon start to smell musty or of wood. Before you use the glass, check it for strange smells and make it is clean. If necessary, shine it up by holding it above some steam (the kettle or an open pan) and then polishing it softly with a clean glass cloth. This means you will get the most from your glasses, and therefore also from your wines.

OPENING THE WINE
WHEN AND HOW?

Some wines deserve more attention when they are served than others. The older the wine, the more care you should take. However, young wines can also benefit from a bit of extra attention.

OLDER WINES

For wines which have been laid down for a while there is a choice of two different methods. In Bordeaux, the moment when a great wine is to be drunk is anticipated. The bottle lying down is helped into a vertical position one or two days beforehand. The wine is then given the time to rest at the temperature of the cellar and the lees can sink to the bottom. If you use this method, it will be simple to serve the wine. You simply leave a bit of wine in the bottom of the bottle where the lees remain. The other method is used for example in Burgundy. Apparently they are slightly less formal there than in the Bordeaux region. Family members, friends and acquaintances are always welcome, and a good friend always deserves a good wine. Visiting the cellar always produces a good bottle. The bottle which is still lying down at cellar temperature is carefully placed into a basket for pouring, so that it can be drunk straight-away. Once it is in the living room, the wine only needs a few minutes to acclimatize and get used to the ambient temperature. The wine is then carefully poured, and this stops as soon as a veil of the lees becomes visible.

DECANTING

After a while, the colorant breaks down in the wine. This means that it is no longer dissolved in the liquid mass but assumes a solid form and sinks to the bottom. Another type of sediment is found in top wines, which are often not filtered on principle and are bottled in a state that is as natural as possible. These wines can form a slight sediment at a very young age, consisting of miniscule particles of vegetable matter, colorants and tannins. In itself, this sediment does not have an influence on the taste of the wine but anyone who has

The famous 'duck' carafe for decanting and aerating wine

ever accidentally ingested a sip of the lees (dépot), knows how unpleasant this is. In addition, the sediment makes the color of the wine rather cloudy.

One efficient way of separating the wine from its dépot is to decant it. Literally, this originally French word means that the wine is separated from its sediment. Only unfiltered or old wines which have formed a dépot are decanted. This is done as follows: pour the content of the standing bottle (Bordeaux method) or horizontal bottle (Burgundy method) carefully into a wide carafe, keeping a soft source of light (candle) by the neck of the bottle and continue pouring until you see the first veils of sediment. In this way, the cloudy wine and sediment remain in the bottle. Do not throw it away but filter it carefully through a linen cloth or cheesecloth and use the remainder for a delicious sauce.

ODORS

Airing a wine is similar to decanting it, although the reasons for this are different. When the wine is aired it is not a matter of separating it from the lees, but bringing it into contact with oxygen, which will certainly benefit young wines. Apart from most young wines with a great deal of structure, robust and forceful wines (for example from the southwest of France or northern Italy) will also benefit from being transferred to a wide carafe before drinking it. This increases the surface area of the wine so that it can come into contact with more oxygen. If there is a vestige of CO_2 gas remaining in the wine, airing and transferring the wine is also a good idea. Young wines should be transferred between thirty minutes to two hours before they are drunk. For robust wines, particularly those from northern Italy, it is better to transfer the bottle hours beforehand (between four and twelve hours). If you think that only red wines benefit from this, you are wrong. Some great white wines also deserve a stretch (a short while for a Dauzan Lavergne Montravel of the Mallard family, but a long time – 24 hours! – for a Coulée de Serrant Savenniãres of Nicolas Joly).

Old decanting set

REMOVING THE CAPSULE

The majority of bottles are still sealed with an aluminum or plastic capsule, which may or may not be transparent. Some bottles which contain cheap (and often also sparkling) wine are very user-friendly. The capsules have a pull-back strip, which is very useful for opening the bottle. However, for most wines you first have to cut through the capsule with the knife of the corkscrew or a separate capsule cutter. It is best to do this below the ring of the neck. Occasionally, you will still come across a bottle with a wax seal. Most sommeliers loathe this. It is better to cut or break up the wax with a sharp knife than to break it, even softly. It takes slightly longer, but it is better for the wine. With a clean cloth, clean the neck and top of the cork after removing the wax or capsule. This means that the wine cannot come into contact with the wax, the plastic or aluminum. Fortunately we no longer have to be afraid of lead poisoning as the use of lead capsules has now been prohibited. (In the past, you would spill quite a lot of wine over these old-fashioned capsules and then it would make you ill…)

UNCORKING

There are different sorts of corks. The quality of modern corks is definitely worse than in the past. Old-fashioned corkscrews were intended to remove the strong, long cork from the neck of the bottle with a great deal of force. Nowadays, corkscrews look slightly more civilized.

Extra long corks are found virtually only in the very great wines that are laid down. The better wines now have medium corks, because these wines are not laid down for so long. Pre-war wines could sometimes be kept for twenty or fifty years (or even longer). The present generation of wine drinkers wish to enjoy their wines sooner, and most wine growers simply cannot permit themselves to rest their wines in cellars for years. Shorter corks are often used for everyday wines, sometimes made of compressed or glued cork waste. The wine cannot breathe through these corks, and the question is how long this practice will continue. Tests with odorless and tasteless synthetic materials (in the shape of a cork) produce very satisfactory results. Screw tops with a thin layer of cork on the inside work very well, but are still not accepted by the general public. It is strange that almost everyone is quite happy to drink sherry from a bottle with a screw top, but will not accept this in wine. It is a complete mystery to me why this should be. A visit to Switzerland convinced me that it is better for the wine to use a screw top than a compressed cork, and it is actually cheaper! In Switzerland, even very good white wines are bottled with a screw top. As they should be drunk within a few years, a screw top is an excellent solution for these wines. Complaints about cork should definitely be

Old corkscrews

a thing of the past. The corks made of better synthetic materials are also of an excellent quality and ideal for wines which should be drunk within five years. A real cork is only useful if the wine can improve from being laid down for a long time.

IDEAL CORKSCREWS

Many years ago, there were still many bad corkscrews on the market, usually with closed spirals (rather like fret drills). They may have been traditional and elegant with their curving vine handle or simply made with a sawn-off broomstick, but these corkscrews disappeared into a drawer of the sideboard quite anonymously. The bottle would usually be opened in the kitchen, away from any disapproving looks. Corkscrews based on a lever principle were easier to use and our modern tools are based on these.

A good corkscrew should not have a tight spiral, but one that it is compared by the French to a pigtail, an open spiral you can pass a matchstick through. The better spirals are now covered with a layer of Teflon, which does even less damage to the cork. Unfortunately this Teflon layer will only survive pulling about six hundred corks.

There are all sorts of corkscrews, from cheap ones to extremely expensive ones. For example, the sommelier corkscrew is comfortable in the hand (except for the cheap, very thin models), and it is strong, with a small knife (which may be serrated) to cut the capsules, and a medium length or long open spiral. This corkscrew is very useful for anyone who has to open

The Pulltaps, one of the best sommelier knives

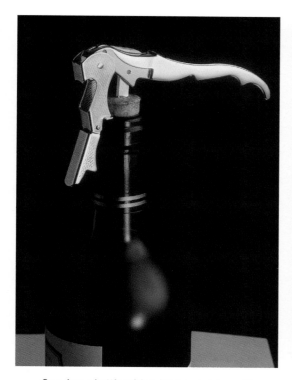

Opening a bottle with a long cork (stage 1)

Opening a bottle with a long cork (stage 2)

many bottles quickly one after the other. There is also a waiter's version with a built-in (crown cork) bottle opener for bottle tops.

For better wines it is a good idea to use better cork-screws, such as the Screwpull or Boomerang. The former is a corkscrew based on the lever principle with an extra long spiral, and is eminently suitable for top wines with long corks. To cut the foil, you use the separate capsule cutter, the Foil cutter. The Boomerang is an improved Sommelier corkscrew with a built-in capsule cutter. It is extremely easy and quick to use. Finally, there is also the Pulltaps from Spain, a very elegant, practical and ingenious corkscrew with a double lever for extra long corks. It is ideal for use in the home and in the catering industry.

The Laguiole (pronounced: layole) corkscrew deserves a special mention. Originally, this corkscrew was made in the village of Laguiole in southern France. Nowadays, the production of this world-famous knife has moved to the town of Thiers. Nevertheless, there are still a few firms which make the Laguiole knives and corkscrews as a craft in the village itself. For an individual person who does not open an expensive bottle of wine very often, the beautiful Châteaux Laguiole can be thoroughly recommended.

However, if you want to use your Laguiole very often, it is better to choose a stronger version from the Forges de Laguiole. Although Laguile knives were originally made with a cow horn shaft, there are all sorts of models available nowadays, from olive wood to mahogany or other sorts of wood.

Châteaux Laguiole

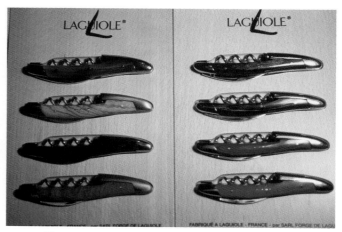

There are many different models of Laguiole knives

TEMPERATURE

Every type of wine feels best at a particular temperature. The wine will be able to tell you its story only at that ideal temperature. Wines which are too warm will sleepily end their stories much too early, while wines which are too cold will be quite speechless. The ideal temperature at which to serve the wine depends on a number of factors: the type and age of the wine, but also, and this is often forgotten, the ambient temperature or the temperature in the room. In winter, you will generally want to drink your wines less cold than in summer.

In a warm room or on a sunny terrace, the temperature of the wine will rise fairly quickly in the glass. Therefore it is always better to pour the wine slightly too cold than slightly too warm. After all, red wine simply should not be served as warm soup. However, make sure that you do not pour white wine too cold in summer, because in very hot weather a wine which is served at 10 °C (50 °F) will feel icy cold! This will not do the enamel on your teeth any good. In this case, serve (dry) white wine at around 12 °C (53.6 °F), or even 14 °C (57.2 °F) for better white wine.

Wines which are served before a meal as an aperitif are usually served slightly colder than with the meal itself. Red wines are served at room temperature (NB: 16–18 °C/60.8–64.4 °F!) and certainly never above 20 °C (68 °F). In southern regions I often ask for a cooling bucket with my red wine.

Young wines certainly taste better at a lower temperature of about 12 °C (53.6 °F), particularly when they are very fruity. On the other hand, older wines prefer temperatures around 17 or 18 °C (62.6 or 64.4 °F).

The temperatures indicated here are guidelines. As people feel the cold and warmth in different ways, the ideal temperature may be one or two degrees higher or lower for each individual.

WINE AND FOOD

For some connoisseurs there are ideal marriages between wines are particular meals, although connoisseurs do not agree entirely about the best combinations. Taste is

Champagne, preferably in a cooling bucket

a very personal thing. All too often, the person is ignored as a catalyst for a particular combination. For me, the perfect combination is also the combination in which the wine can tell its story fluently, the meal also has something to say and where you are prepared to join in as an attentive listener. If you have no time or do not feel like it, a combination between a delicate elegant Alsace wine and a sophisticated culinary meal of sea bass is simply a waste of time for you! For example, at that moment, you may feel more like a soft scrambled egg with a glass of rosé vins de pays. In winter, when you have just come back from skating for the afternoon, a steaming plate of winter stew with a glass of heart-warming red Navarra will probably be more attractive than a dozen perfect oysters and a glass of Chablis grand cru! Taste is, and always will be a personal matter, but it is also determined by a particular moment. It would not occur to anyone to order a glass of extra heavy red Châteauneuf-du-Pape in the middle of summer, sitting out on a terrace in the heat of the day. A cool fresh Muscadet would be much more suitable in that particular situation.

Nevertheless, there are a number of rules which cannot be denied. These are not only based on positive experiences, but actually particularly on negative experiences. For example, we know that it is better not to drink a French Pinot Noir or a Gamay with a ripe camembert or brie, because this will usually produce an unpleasant metallic taste in your mouth. In fact, the same also applies for raw ham and most wines, and smoked salmon or eel with many white wines. On the other hand, there are also rules which have started to live a life of their own. For example, the myth that red wine does not go with fish. This is nonsense! However, you must find the right combinations. Delicate fish with

IDEAL SERVING TEMPERATURES		
– Great red Bordeaux, top Cabernet Sauvignon:	16–18 °C	(60.8–64.4 °F)
– Great red Burgundy, American, South African, Pinot Noir:	15–16 °C	(59–60.8 °F)
– Other red wines:	14–16 °C	(57.2–60.8 °F)
– Great dry white wines (Burgundy, Loire):	12–14 °C	(53.6–57.2 °F)
– Young, fruity red wines (Beaujolais):	12 °C	(53.6 °F)
– Everyday red wines (vins de pays):	10–12 °C	(50–53.6 °F)
– Other good white wines (Bordeaux, Alsace):	10–12 °C	(50–53.6 °F)
– Rosé wines:	10–12 °C	(50–53.6 °F)
– Everyday white wines (vins de pays):	8–10 °C	(46.4–50 °F)
– Champagne, sparkling wines:	8 °C	(46.4 °F)
– Sweet wines:	6 °C	(42.8 °F)

a very light taste should not really be accompanied by a heavy red wine. Of course, you can drink this if you hate fish and wish to remove the taste of the fish as quickly as possible, but this combination is not really very balanced. A freshly caught gurnard which has just come out of the sea and is being grilled with its scales, and is served with only some freshly ground salt and pepper, will be very grateful for a glass of lightly cooled red wine from the Roussillon, particularly from Collioure. There are countless other combinations of fish and red wine. With regard to red meat it is also possible to deviate from the rule (red with red). Some people do not like red wine and are ashamed to drink white wine with their red meat. However, if you choose a full-bodied white wine rich in extracts and do not drink it too cold, you can really enjoy the combination. For example, choose a Pinot Gris from Alsace from a warm year or a white Châteauneuf-du-Pape, and success is guaranteed.

THE ART OF COMBINING

All sorts of combinations are possible, depending on who is present. A meal can be so strong and have such a pronounced taste that there is virtually no wine which can equal it. In this case, opt for a pleasant thirst-quenching wine without too many pretensions. Examples could be a Thai meal with French rosé, Indonesian food with Pinot Blanc, and Chinese meals with a simple Riesling or Sauvignon. The wines accompany the meal.

A wine which is so full-bodied and strong in taste that no meal can match it is best drunk in the evening with friends and some cubes of mature cheese, or at the table with some sort of gratin. In this case, the food accompanies the wine.

For a fairly neutral meal you can choose a fairly neutral wine such as asparagus with a Pinot Blanc from Alsace. The wine and the meal respect each other, but are not indispensable to each other.

A delicate meal requires a delicate elegant fresh wine. These are made for each other and will live together happily ever after. Their life will be harmonious and interesting, but there will be no question of any real passion.

A sturdy meal with a strong character with a full-bodied heavy wine will certainly enjoy their marriage in the late hours. You could certainly call this passion, but it does not say much about good table manners.

Finally, a very pronounced meal with a very pronounced wine with completely contrasting characteristics such as a salty, creamy, slightly bitter Roquefort with a full-bodied, sweet, almost overwhelming Sauternes is the peak of culinary passion. This can be overwhelmingly sensual! It is a true clash of the titans, and both parties make themselves heard and felt. It will soon become apparent that there will be no victor, and that both parties provide value for money. They will give anything they have to the very last, and finally make peace. It is the guest who wins.

WINE AND FOOD COMBINATIONS

Below you will see which wines accompany which dishes or courses of a meal.

Champagne or sparkling wines
    Manzanilla or sherry fino secco
    Dry white wines
    Young fruity red wines

Shell fish and crustaceans
    Dry white wines
    Dry rosé

Smoked salmon
    Aromatic dry white wines (Sancerre, Pouilly-Fumé, Quincy)
    Dry sherry (Manzanilla, Fino Secco).

Fried fish
    Dry white wines
    Dry rosé
    Light red (slightly cooled)

Poached fish in sauce
    Dry white wines
    Dry rosé
    Light red wines (slightly chilled)

BASIC RULES

- The best combination is always the combination which you enjoy most.
- An ideal combination of wine and a meal is a combination in which both parties emphasize or complement each other.
- Always drink young or light wines before older or heavier wines.
- Drink dry white wines before sweet white wines. If this is not possible (for example, after Sauternes and foie gras), it is best to neutralize the sweet taste, for example, with a clear, savory bouillon, before you go on to the other wines.
- It is best to serve wines of increasingly good quality. After a top wine, lesser quality wines will soon disappoint. In the case of wines of the same quality level, always start with the younger wines and then go onto the older wines.
- If possible, pour the wine at the right temperature to avoid disappointment.
- Do not serve a top wine with meals which overwhelm the wine, such as meals with a high level of acidity (lemon, orange or vinegar), meals with chocolate, or very spicy Asian meals.
- Some combinations are not necessarily the very best, but may add a festive character to a particular occasion (a birthday, wedding or anniversary) (for example, champagne with the whole meal).

Champagne, the ideal aperitif

Delicious with shellfish

Patés, ham and cold meats
Dry white wines
Dry rosé
Light red wines

Goose or duck liver
Sweet white wines
Mature champagne with a lot of body

White meat or poultry
Dry white wines
Dry rosé
Light red wines
Champagne
Sparkling wines

Grilled red meat
Light red wines
Full-bodied red wines

Braised red meat
Light red wines
Full-bodied red wines

Fowl
Light red wines
Full-bodied red wines

Game
Light red wines
Full-bodied red wines

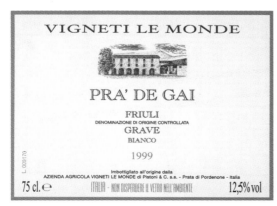

Fish in sauce with a good white wine

Delicious Spanish cold meats with a glass of Rosado
or a light Tinto which has not matured in wood

Chicory with ham and cheese baked
in the oven should be accompanied by
a full-bodied white wine.

Surprisingly refreshing: Saumur rosé brut with fresh
strawberries with... pepper!

Exotic cuisine

Chinese: dry fruity, fresh white wine with character (Muscat d'Alsace, Gewürztraminer) with dishes
that are not too spicy
Indonesian, Thai dishes: dry, fruity rosé with
character

Soft cheeses

Dry white wines
Dry rosé

Creamy risotto with carrots, veal in a cream sauce
with mushrooms: serve with a full-bodied white wine
or not too heavy red wine.

Medium-dry rosé
Light red wines

Strong cheeses

Full-bodied red wines

Fruit deserts

Saumur brut rosé
Sweet white wines
Medium-dry rosé
Sweet dessert wines, (including Muscat wines,
Banyuls, Maury, Rasteau)

Pastry

Champagne brut or demi-sec, depending on taste

Chocolate

Banyuls, Pedro Ximénez

Ice cream

Preferably no wine!

7 Europe

FRANCE

For centuries, France was the country for quality wine. There seemed to be only two things to say about the wine trade: All French wines are good, and All good wines come from France. Obviously these views were never justified because countries such as Italy, Spain, Germany, Hungary and Greece have also made top wines for a long time. However, the French managed to convince the world of the sublime quality of French wines by means of clever marketing and by linking wine to other aspects of the rich French culture.

The history of France seems to be inextricably bound up with that of viticulture. Frenchmen have always been attached to their daily drink of glorified grape juice, from the common gros rouge (a simple table wine) to the very best wines. Sharing a glass of wine was always synonymous with contentment, socializing and sharing the good things in life, particularly in the family circle, but also with friends, and even at work. Wine was the soul of the French nation, a soul which the French have always managed to cherish, despite the many invasions which have confronted France.

Unfortunately this seems to be changing. Because of the many anti-alcohol campaigns conducted by the government, and also, and above all because of the leveling off of the quality and the globalization of the French cuisine, people are drinking less and less wine. They are increasingly drinking water, soft drinks or beer with their meals. For an aperitif they increasingly pre-

Historic wine cellar in Burgundy

There will always be a market for luxury wines.

fer a glass of whiskey or pastis rather than a glass of good dry white wine, whether this is sparkling or not. In this respect, things are also going rapidly downhill. Because of the steadily growing popularity of fast food chains that have come over from America, as well as their French counterparts, and because of the increasing amount of junk food available in local hypermarkets, the average Frenchman (and this applies particularly to younger people) takes neither the time nor the trouble to open a good bottle of wine. French wine consumption is falling dramatically. More and more French wine firms feel forced to survive by exporting the majority of their products. However, this requires, knowledge, time, energy and extra money, which many people are unable to find.

THE HISTORY OF FRENCH VITICULTURE

The Celtic Druids were familiar with the secrets of the lambrusque (*Vitis labrusca*), the wild vine which grew up oak trees. The French predilection for wine dates back to those days. Wine was made in oak casks for magical and medicinal purposes. Even then, the Druids knew that wine should be kept in oak barrels. And yet there is little about this custom in most history books. Wine was made in Gaul even before the first seafaring invaders set foot on Celtic soil.

In the thirteenth century BC, the Phocaens were the first people to explore Gaul. We now know that they had vineyards themselves and their certainly brought some of the cultivated varieties with them from the Middle East. They were followed shortly afterwards by the Phocaens who come from modern-day Turkey. The

Phocaens practiced viticulture on the banks of the rivers and on the shores of the seas of southern Gaul. When their own country, Phoenicia, fell into Greek hands, Gaul was overrun with Greek merchants, sailors and wine growers. Looking for suitable land for viticulture, more and more Greeks traveled up the Rhône towards the north. This is how the Greeks and the Celts who had planted the first vineyards in Burgundy conducted their trade. Trade flourished along the coast in the Greek ports of Massalia (Marseille), Nikaìa (Nice), Antipolis (Antibes) and Monoìkos (Monaco). While the Greeks spread viticulture in southern Gaul (as well as Italy, for example) along the coast, other people entered Europe from the Caucasian mountains. They introduced viticulture to central and northern Europe, particularly via the Danube and its tributaries. Viticulture also entered Alsace and the Jura via the Rhine, and vineyards also spread throughout Burgundy in this way.

When the Romans invaded Gaul they came across extensive vineyards. The history books are too generous to the Romans when they say that they were at the very start of French viticulture. During the four hundred years of their occupation, the Romans only managed the vineyards that were already present and well looked after, which had been planted by their predecessors. Obviously a few new vineyards were also planted occasionally when troops were moved about. During the bloody Gallic war, Julius Caesar had enormous areas along the riverbanks deforested in about 50 BC and planted with vines so that he could quench the thirst of his legions.

For a while, it looked as though things would get exciting for viticulture in Gaul when Rome had an

The church played an important role in French viticulture (Kirchberg, Alsace, *ES*)

Frenchmen are often (quite justifiably) very proud
of their wine!

enormous surfeit of Italian wines and Emperor Domiti-
an ordered all the vineyards in Gaul to be destroyed for
protectionist reasons. Fortunately these orders did not
extend beyond Provence. In 210 AD, the Gauls were
allowed to grow their vines again. Following the fall of
the Roman Empire (313 AD), the influence of Chris-
tianity increased. French viticulture owes a lot to the
priests and believers in those days who considered wine
a sacred drink. After all, wine was seen as the blood of
Christ! Therefore wine was needed for the mass and
new vineyards were planted all over the country.

For centuries this liquid gospel was spread from
France. In the eighteenth century, during the French

Revolution, the vineyards changed owners. The church
retained a few vineyards here and there for their own
use, but the majority went to the rich families of the
new French bourgeoisie. During the Industrial Revolution in the nineteenth century many vineyards
were bought up by businesses.

French viticulture flourished. However, fate inter-
vened and was merciless in the form of a small voracious wine louse, the famous *Phylloxera vastatrix*. At the
end of the nineteenth century, the French (and later all
the European) vineyards were completely destroyed in
no time at all by this plague which had spread from
America. Even the most drastic measures did not help.
As the disastrous louse had come from America, and
the vines there proved to be immune to this plague, it
was decided to replant all the vineyards with American
stock. The existing European varieties were then grafted onto these, and French viticulture was saved.

AN IDEAL WINE COUNTRY

In order to understand why France is still the most
famous wine country in the world, it is probably appropriate to look at the conditions for viticulture.

The French climate is ideal for quality viticulture:
the winters are not too severe, the summers are not too
dry and there is a lot of rain and sun. The enormous
diversity of different types of soils also helps to explain
the success of French viticulture over the centuries:
thick layers of chalk in the Champagne, sedimentary
layers with many shells in the Auxerrois (Chablis),
marl, clay, gravel and pebbles in the Médoc, blue and
gray slate in the Muscadet, tufa in Anjou Saumur, slate
slopes in Collioure and Banyuls, and the warm rocks of
the southern Rhône. Furthermore, there is enough

Hoar frost and snow in Alsace (*ES*)

A good soil is vitally important for viticulture!
(Alsace, *ES*)

Some splendid sweet wines fall outside the law and have to be sold as 'partly fermented must'!

water everywhere in France, either indirectly by the sea, or even directly from the many rivers and subterranean reserves of water.

FRENCH LEGISLATION

As there are very many sorts of wine produced in France, strict laws are very important. Obviously it is impossible for the tax man and other controlling authorities to check every wine barrel, but in general, the strict rules are carefully observed. However, no system is absolutely watertight. There will always be scoundrels who exploit the most naive amongst us… and there will always be people who want to have a front seat for a few pennies and play into the hands of malevolent wine merchants. It is sad but inevitable. However, the many controls on quality and authenticity are a great incentive for bona fide wineries, which fortunately still account for the majority of wine production.

Although European legislation recognizes only two categories of wines: viz., table wines (vin de table) and quality wines produced in a defined area (VQPRD, Vins de Qualité Produits dans une Région Determinée), France adopts a more detailed system. The French system is based on the names of the origin and production or on wine-making requirements. In theory, the quality of the wines should coincide with the stricter requirements, but this is not always the case. The name of an origin says a great deal about the region where the wine was made, about the methods of wine making used there and the yield per hectare but nothing at all about the quality of the wines! Therefore it is possible that some excellent wine houses deliberately fail to observe the demanding and often outdated local practices and start to experiment. The wines produced in this case are not made according to the book, and may not be sold as recognized regional wines (AOC) and are then declassified as simple table wines. However, some of these wines are of such a good quality that they are much more expensive that the real wines of the region.

CATEGORIES OF WINE

VINS DE TABLE

In principle, the vins de table are fairly simple daily wines with a constant taste which are usually produced by blending. This category also covers a number of very specific wines which do not comply with the strict requirements of the local names referring the place of origin, but are of an excellent quality. In this case the price can be much more than that of known AOC wines from the region.

VINS DE PAYS

Vins de pays are currently experiencing an enormous increase in popularity. This is not surprising, because the quality of these reliable superior table wines has improved enormously in recent years.

Vins de pays come from a strictly defined wine-growing region and represent the soul of a particular terroir, linked to specific characteristics of one or more varieties of grapes. More and more, consumers recognize these wines and the clear language on the label and the bottle. Some vins de pays are

Vin de table (table wine)

made so well and reflect so much love on the part of the wine growers that they wholly transcend the characterless AOC wines of large anonymous merchants in quality as well as price. Modern wine drinkers demand quality for their money, and therefore they increasingly opt for vin de pays rather than the characterless pretentious wines which shamelessly hide behind a meaningless label with a well-known name.

APPELLATION D'ORIGINE – VINS DÉLIMITÉS DE QUALITÉ SUPÉRIEURE

The quality of this category of wines is certainly no less than that of AOC wines. In fact, the selection criteria are often stricter than those of most AOC wines. The VDQS wines are the only wines which have to be tasted every year if they are to be eligible for this predicate. VDQS wine is therefore always approved by a panel of experts before being released. You can put your faith in these wines blindly.

APPELLATION D'ORIGINE CONTROLÉE

Wines with an AOC originate from clearly defined regions, and the soil, climate, varieties of grapes and various legally imposed obligations (minimum alcohol content, maximum yield per hectare, pruning methods, production and winemaking conditions, etc.) are a guarantee of the origin and authenticity. However, this is not a guarantee of quality, because the wines are certainly not tasted every year, and some wines certainly do not deserve this description. Nevertheless, these AOC wines are at the top of the French wine classification.

Vin de pays

ADDITIONAL INFORMATION ON THE LABEL

This is not a reference to the meaningless cheap expressions such as vin supérieur de la cave du patron or cuvée réservée du sommelier, and other meaningless comments, but rather additions such as cru classé or grand cru classé for Bordeaux wines. In 1855, a classification of the better Bordeaux wines was drawn up at a world fair on the basis of the quality criteria used at the time (fami-

Vin de pays monocepage (made with one variety of grape)

AOVDQS

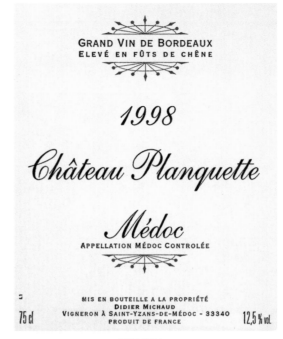

AOC Médoc

liarity, notations of the trading price and so on). This only concerned wines from the Médoc and Sauternes, as well as one wine from Graves. In 1959, the latter was also given its own classification. Other regions with a similar grand cru classification are Saint-Émilion (since 1955) and the Côtes de Provence (since 1955).

The indication cru bourgeois has also been used in the Médoc since 1932. In Burgundy indications such as premier cru or grand cru are part of the official reference to the origin. These indications will be described in more detail with the wine regions concerned.

We will take a clockwise tour through the French vineyards, starting with the Champagne region. We will start by visiting vineyards in the northeast and go on to the southeast, the southwest and the northwest of France.

The splendor of a champagne house (Taittinger)

NORTHEAST FRANCE

Champagne

Champagne, the ultimate symbol of sparkling merriment may only be produced in one region in the world, viz., the Champagne region in France. No other wine, no matter where it is made, in or outside France, and in whatever way it is made, may use the prestigious name of Champagne. Champagne is undeniably an unparalleled wine.

THE REGION

The historic heart of the region, Rheims, is about 94 miles northeast of Paris, while Epernay, which is slightly further south, is the geographical heart of the region. Champagne is subdivided into four large regions: the montagne de Rheims (slopes to the south of Rheims), the Vallée de la Marne (the Marne valley from Châteaux-Thierry to Chalon-sur-Marne), the Côte des Blancs (hillside south of Epernay) and finally the Côte de Bar in the département of the Aube, between Bar-sur-Seine and Bar-sur-Aube. Each of these regions has its own geographical identity. This is because of the differences in location, hours of sunlight, relief and soil, and finally because of the different grapes that are planted. This means that each piece of the gigantic puzzle is unique, with its own character and potential. In the Champagne there are more than three hundred different ter-

Besserat de Bellefon

Perrier-Jouet

roirs, known as *crus*, which are all equally unique and reflect the soul of the countless villages.

CHAMPAGNE HOUSES

Most Champagne houses are located in the larger towns, particularly in Rheims and Epernay. They all have their own story to tell and have become part of the history of the region. For centuries these houses were ambassadors of the Champagne region and of France. Therefore they are now so proud to welcome you to their own cellars. When you enter these cellars you will discover a world of passion and magic. It is a prestigious world with a certain class and experience of life, but above all a world of *joie de vivre*.

CHAMPAGNE WINES

Wild vines were already growing in the Champagne region centuries before Christ, as is revealed by the many fossilized remains found deep in the chalky soil. The long history and the preparation of wine that has been perfected in the smallest details, combined with an enormous passion for the final product and extremely strict regulations for protecting the quality, together guarantee the high quality champagnes that we know. The chalky soil of the gently undulating hills in this region is covered with a thin layer of loam. The vines penetrate very deep down into the chalk rocks (sometimes 16 ft deep) looking for the necessary nutrients and water. In addition to regulating the water, the chalk rock also regulates the temperature.

Only three different varieties of grapes are permitted in the Champagne. All three give champagne wines their own character (in combination with the soil). The pinot noir particularly provides the backbone to the wine and a full-bodied quality. The chardonnay is responsible for the elegant acids and sophisticated taste.

Champagne, an unparalleled wine!

Cellars hewn out of chalk

Tasting still wines (vins clairs)

The pinot meunier gives the wines a fresh and lively character.

In the Champagne region the vineyards are always supervised. The uncertain northern climate, the vagaries of nature and the extremely strict regulations mean that there is a great deal of extra work to do. The vineyards are looked after with a great deal of care and attention. This is still often done by hand (whether or not this is required by law). The pruning and picking are subject to countless regulations, all aimed at controlling the yield, and therefore quality control.

The grapes are pressed at a very high rate each variety and cru separately in the nearby pressing houses. 4,000 kilos (8,818 pounds) of grapes may only produce 2,666 liters (704 gallons) of juice. However, for the better cuvées, only the first press is used, about 2,050 liters (542 gallons). The last 616 liters (163 gallons), known here as *tailles* are used only for inferior wines. The remaining juice and *marc* (the cake of skins and pips) is used to make *marc de champagnee*, a poor man's alcohol.

The must of the pressed grapes is siphoned over into enormous tubs and allowed to rest. In this way the majority of impurities such as bits of skin, leaves and earth which were still present in the juices, sink to the bottom. Following this resting period of approximately twelve hours, the must is transported to the yeast barrels or tanks. The first (alcoholic) fermentation takes place here. This takes several weeks. The wine is then cleared. This young wine will be thoroughly tasted by the cellar master throughout the winter.

MAKING CHAMPAGNE

In the first instance, clear wines (*vins clairs*) are used in order to make sparkling champagne. These are always the wines of a single variety of grape and for the better *cuvées*, from just one vineyard. Following countless tastings, the most suitable wines are blended. This results in the *cuvée*. The characteristics of each *cuvée* vary for each type of wine, but also for every house. Some houses produce a strong champagne with a lot of pinot, while others make very elegant champagnes with a great deal of finesse, based on chardonnay. Most cuvées are made using both green and black grapes.

In addition to the luxury vintage *cuvées* (showing the year), there are also ordinary *cuvées* (without a year). These may contain wines of several different years. These constant and balanced wines are often the visiting cards of the house. For a rosé, a white and a red still wine from the Champagne are blended, usually from Bouzy or Cumières.

When the final *cuvée* has been blended, the winemaker adds a siqueur de tirage. This is a combination of indigenous yeast cells and a small quantity of cane sugar. In this way, a second fermentation can take place in the bottle. The bottles which have a provisional top are stacked on slats in cool cellars. During the second fermentation, the sugar present in the wine is converted into alcohol and carbon dioxide by the yeast cells. This produces the fine bubbles which give Champagne wines their charm.

The wine matures for an average of three more years in the dark cellars, after this second fermentation. As there is some sediment during the second fermentation, the bottles are placed upside down in pupitres or in large rotating pallets (*giropallettes*). If they are placed in pupitres, the bottles are turned through 90° by hand at regular intervals by a remueur. In this way the sediment is gradually worked towards the neck. With the *giropallette* method, a forklift truck regularly moves the bottles. Obviously this last method is much faster than doing it by hand, but make no mistake, a professional remueur can easily turn 4,000 bottles per day!

At the end of the remuage period, all the sediment has gone down to the bottom of the cap. The bung that has collected must be removed from the neck. This *dégorgemente* is achieved by submerging the bottles upside down in an icy bath of brine. The sediment under the cork

One of the best cuvées from Champagne

Ready for the finishing touch

Removing the cork for the *dégorgement*

freezes and the bottle is then quickly turned the other way round and opened. The lump of ice shoots out with a loud pop. This leaves the wine completely clear. The last step of preparing the wine is to add the *liqueur de dosage*. In order to compensate for the loss of champagne in the bottle, the content is made up with a blend of older champagne and cane sugar. The more cane sugar is added, the sweeter the champagne. The bottles are then corked with a real cork, a *muselet* of wire thread (like a muzzle), a capsule, a label on the neck and a label. The champagne is finally ready for a new and festive occasion.

OPENING AND DRINKING CHAMPAGNE

You can always drink champagne anywhere. As an aperitif, to accompany a meal of delicate poultry or fish, or simply to be convivial. Champagne should preferably be drunk chilled, at 6–8 °C (42.8–46.4 °F). Using a shallow open goblet is definitely not right. This allows the elegant and lively bubbles to escape. The most suitable glass is a slender flute.

When you open the bottle, never allow the cork to explode into the room. This is extremely dangerous: at a pressure of 6 atmospheres the cork will fly out at more than 56 miles per hour. This can cause harm. Furthermore, it is a great waste of the champagne, because a lot of the valuable liquid is lost when it is uncorked in this way.

So how should it be done? After undoing the wire, the bottle should be held at a slight angle. For a firmer grip, you can use a cloth. Try not to remove the cork from the bottle forcefully, but hold it firmly and turn the bottle round gently. In this way you more or less unscrew the bottle from the cork. If it is uncorked properly, this ends in a hiss. Allow the pressure of the bottle to do the work. If the cork remains stuck you can also use special champagne tongs to hold the cork more firmly.

STORING CHAMPAGNE

In principle, the wines which leave the cellars are perfect for drinking. The ordinary *cuvées* (without a year) will no longer improve in quality. Therefore they should be drunk in the year you buy them or are given them. However, the better *cuvées* can be stored for a long time. Ask your wine merchant about this.

TYPES OF CHAMPAGNE

Some labels contain the indication *grand cru* or *premier cru*. However, these indications are certainly no guarantee of the quality of the champagne. They only refer to the quality of the raw material – the grapes. The best *terroir* of the Champagne, where the best grapes should theoretically originate, are indexed at 100% on the quality scale. This means that the wine growers who cultivate grapes in these vineyards can ask the full price that is determined for their grapes. These 100% *terroirs* can use the indication *grand cru*. For slightly lower quality *premiers crus terroir*, the wine maker may only ask 90 to 99% of the set price. For all the other *terroirs*, they may only ask for a maximum of 89% of the price. However, even with excellent raw materials, the moderate wine maker will make only moderate champagne.

CHAMPAGNE EXTRA BRUT / BRUT SAUVAGE

These wines are extremely dry. After the *dégorgement*, these extra brut varieties are filled with only the same wine and therefore they contain no residual sugars (max. 0.6% vol.). Few people like this sort of extremely dry champagne, and it is widely found.

CHAMPAGNE BRUT (WITHOUT A YEAR)

This is the most commonly drunk type of champagne. It is dry but not too dry: these visiting cards for the Champagne houses contain a maximum of 1.5% vol. of residual sugars. The brut wines consist of a blend of the three classical grapes, the chardonnay, pinot noir, and pinot meunier. They generally come from different parts of the Champagne region and different years. A young, fresh and exciting brut will loosen most tongues. It has a pale yellow color, sometimes with shades of rosé. Depending on the blend, a young brut smells of white fruit (almonds, green apple), or red fruit (grapes, raspberries), with a hint of warm white bread. It is an extremely suitable aperitif, but can also accompany most light starters, particularly poultry or shellfish.

A mature brut (older then three years) is slightly less fresh with a full-bodied spicier taste. The color is a darker yellow with shades of orange, and the aroma is reminiscent of ripe apples, dried fruit, spices or sometimes black cherries or blackcurrants (a great deal of pinot noir). The taste and aroma no longer has any hints of white bread, but rather of luxury rolls or a French brioche. This wine is excellent in combination with a main course of fish or white meat (delicious with veal!).

The mature bruts (older than five years) have rather exuberant carbon dioxide, but have a full-bodied, complex and very rich, almost creamy taste. The color is a dark yellow with hints of brown. The aroma is reminiscent of toasted nuts and dried fruits with occasional tertiary aromas of coffee and sometimes even some old leather… The luxury roll is now toasted and spread with a thick layer of fresh creamy butter. It is best to drink these wines on their own, with good friends, a good book or your partner, when you are in a romantic mood.

Brut without a year

CHAMPAGNE BRUT MILLÉSIMÉ (WITH YEAR)

This brut, with a year, actually has the same characteristics as the ordinary brut, but is only made in top years.

CHAMPAGNE BRUT BLANC DE BLANCS

Blanc de blancs champagnes are made exclusively with chardonnay grapes. Therefore they are white wines made with white grapes. They can be marketed with or without the year. They are usually fresh fruity wines with very delicate acids. They are a pale yellow color with a hint of green when they are young, increasingly tending to yellow and a golden yellow as they age.

A young brut blanc de blancs has tempting aromas of citrus fruits, fresh mint, spring flowers and an almost unashamed freshness.

A mature brut blanc de blancs tends more towards the aromas of a bouquet of freshly cut summer meadow flowers and a hint of lime blossom. Although it is still very fresh, this

Brut with a year (millésimé)

wine has more *rondeur* and strength than in its youth. The taste is much fuller and more balanced. An old brut blanc de blancs is a dish full of exotic fruit with hints of freshly milled pepper and spices.

CHAMPAGNE BRUT BLANC DE NOIR

This is extremely rare in the Champagne. It is a strong, very tasty, full white wine, made with black pinot noir and pinot meunier grapes.

CHAMPAGNE EXTRA DRY/EXTRA SEC

These wines are mainly intended for the English and American markets. With the motto call them dry, make them sweet, these extra dry champagnes still contain 1.2 to 2% residual sugars.

CHAMPAGNE SEC

The name is confusing. For this wine the same comment applies as above: these wines are not really dry and even contain between 1.7 and 3.5% residual sugars.

CHAMPAGNE DEMI-SEC

This is a gentle, slightly sweet wine with 3.3 to 5% residual sugars.

CHAMPAGNE DOUX

The sweetest of all, with a minimum of 5% residual sugars. Some people, usually older people, are crazy about it. Younger generations prefer types which are less sweet.

CHAMPAGNE ROSÉ

Champagne rosé or rosé champagne is made by adding still red wines (Cumiãres, Bouzy) from the Champagne region to the *cuvée*. Rosé champagne is marked as ordinary *brut*, *brut millésimé* and *brut demi-sec*. The color varies from a pale pink or salmon color to a raspberry or even light cherry-red. Rosé champagnes are truly tempting, excellent aperitifs, but also, and above all, the perfect accompaniment for any romantic occasion.

With a meal this rosé is particularly suitable with cold meat and poultry, but it certainly wont go amiss with a delicious suckling lamb!

OTHER WINES FROM THE CHAMPAGNE

In addition to sparkling wines, the Champagne region also has a number of still wines.

Rare blanc de blancs-cuvée with the year

COTEAUX CHAMPENOIS

(AOC since 1974), produced as white, red and rosé wine. These are all extremely rare wines, vestiges of a long ago past. The best known red wines are named after their village: Bouzy, Cumières and Ambonnay. The Coteaux Champenois are best drunk young. Red wines are served cooled (approximately 10 °C).

ROSÉ DES RICEYS

This is also extremely rare, and without any doubt, one of the best French rosé wines. A simple Rosé des Riceys should be drunk young and cooled. Wines matured in wood can be left to mature much longer (ten years or more). Serve this wine less cool (10–12 °C/50–53.6 °F) with the meal.

Rosé brut

THE NORTHEAST

Viticulture once flourished in Lorraine. At the end of the nineteenth century, the vineyards covered an area of no less than 72,000 and the French Moselle wines were extremely well known, both in France and far beyond. The *Phylloxera* invasion, followed by economic instability and the disastrous First World War put an end to the aspirations of local wine growers. It was only after the Second World War that a new generation of wine growers started to replant the vineyards. Their attempts were finally rewarded in 1951 when the government definitively recognized the wine regions around Toul and the French Moselle.

Coteaux Champenois Cumières

Rosé des Riceys

VINS DE MOSELLE

The small vineyards are situated along the gently undulating slopes of the valley of the French Moselle (mother of the Luxembourg Moselle and the German Moselle) on soil consisting of sediment. There are nineteen villages which can produce these Vins de Moselle, but the majority of production takes place in the neighborhood of Metz. Little is

produced here, partly because the vineyards are too far apart. The wines produced here are mainly fresh white wines with a lot of fruit and finesse, made with the pinot blanc or auxerrois. The rarer wines made with the pinot gris grape are of an excellent quality for a very reasonable price. The red wines, made with the pinot noir and gamay, are pleasant and fruity, but lack the finesse of the white wines.

CÔTES DE TOUL

The vineyards of the Côtes de Toul lie slightly further south than those of the Vins de Moselle, west of the town of Toul, on the banks of a characteristic bend in the river Moselle. The vineyards are spread out over eight municipalities on a soil of sediment, clay and chalky rocks. The good drainage, the perfect position in relation to the sun and the climate make this wine-producing region one of the most interesting in France. Virtually the entire production of this still rather unknown region, which is too small for large-scale exports, is consumed locally at home or in one of the many restaurants of Lorraine.

The specialty of Toul is undoubtedly the light colored, fresh elegant, round and generous rosé, Gris de Toul, made with the gamay grape. This wine is an excellent accompaniment to the local specialty, consisting of pork, and especially with the famous suckling pigs of Lorraine (Thionville), and is also surprisingly good with a real Quiche Lorraine. In addition to this special rosé, fresh, pleasant and elegant white wines are also made with the auxerrois grape, as well as delicious, confident red wines made with the pinot noir. Finally, there are some wonderful sparkling wines produced here though

Côtes de Toul

on a small scale including an excellent méthode traditionelle. The wines of the Côtes de Toul are certainly underrated and deserve to be reinstated.

ALSACE

Although people in ancient times were aware of the charms of the fermented juice of wild vines, it was the Romans who were considered responsible for the cultivation of wines in Alsace. In the sixteenth century, Rhine wines (including those of modern-day Alsace) were very famous. In those days, traminer, muscat and riesling were the best-known varieties of grapes. After the Thirty Years War, Alsace experienced some very turbulent times. Economic interests meant that increasingly poor quality grapes were planted because of the higher yields. Despite attempts by the government to put an end to this practice, this impoverishment of viti-culture in Alsace continued. It was partly because of the poor quality of the wines that were produced and because of the German influences, that people drank more and more beer. At the end of the nineteenth century, the *Phylloxera* louse destroyed virtually all the vineyards. The situation further deteriorated as a result of the Franco-Prussian conflict from 1870 up to and including World War II (Alsace was passed to and fro between France and Germany). After the World War I, there was a renaissance of viticulture in Alsace. The poor vineyards of the valleys were destroyed and viticulture concentrated on the slopes, where quality grapes were replanted. Unfortunately there are

There are many artistic, quality Champagne cuvées for collectors.

still some large corporations today which adamantly continue to work the bottom of the market (in the sense of drink a lot and enjoy little). Nevertheless, the good name and quality of Alsace wines have been secured for good by the efforts and passion of the new generation of wine growers.

IDEAL WINE-GROWING CONDITIONS

Although the region is fairly northerly, Alsace is characterized by an exceptionally favorable climate. The Vosges act as an enormous natural protection from westerly winds and the rain. As a result, Colmar has the same low rainfall as Perpignan in the extreme south. The summers are warm, and the winters are not extremely cold. The spring is soft and wet, while the fall is often warm and dry. As most of the vineyards face south or southeast, this guarantees excellent conditions for high quality wine growing.

Anyone looking at the vineyards in Alsace from the air may feel they are flying over endless allotments. Most vineyards are of a modest size, partly because of the division of land resulting from inheritances, but particularly because of the nature of the soil in Alsace. Once upon a time the Vosges and the Black Forest (Schwarzwald) formed one mountain range, part of the large mountainous area which covered two thirds of French territory. This mountain was torn in two approximately fifty million years ago. The break and erosion formed the valley of the Rhine. There are different types of soil here, unevenly spread throughout the valley and the slopes: clay, marl, chalk, granite, gneiss (deposits of rock consisting of mica, quartz and feldspar), and even volcanic rock. Each of the seven varieties of grape used in Alsace flourishes best in a different soil. This explains the many small vineyards.

THE SEVEN ALSACE GRAPES

For most French wines, the name of the origin is the most important information shown on the label. In

Vineyard in Kirchberg, Ribeauvillé *(ES)*

Spring in a vineyard in Alsace *(ES)*

Alsace, a mosaic of allotments *(ES)*

Alsace, all wines are called Appellation Alsace Contrôlée, but they are mainly identified by the variety of grape. For example, a Riesling, a Sylvaner, a Gewürztraminer, a Pinot Blanc, a Pinot Noir or a Pinot gris can be ordered anywhere in France and everyone knows

Riesling with a good origin (Kirchberg grand cru, *ES*)

straightaway that it is an Alsace wine. It is only for a Muscat that the name of the region is also stated, because there are many different types of Muscat in France (including the sweet wines from the south). This does not apply for any other region in France.

SYLVANER

Wines made with the sylvaner grape are pleasant, light, fresh thirst-quenching wines which make friends very quickly. It is an ideal aperitif and goes well with light starters, cold meats, shellfish, fish terrines, Japanese dishes of raw fish (sushi) and savory pies (quiches).

PINOT BLANC

This is one of the most widely planted grapes in Alsace. The wines are fresh and supple, usually with a taste that is not particularly pronounced. This means that they can be drunk with almost anything.

Another member of the pinot blanc family, the auxerrois, is often sold under its own name. The pinot blanc is also sometimes found under the old local name, clevner or klevner. (In fact, there is also a Klevener de Heiligenstein, which has nothing to do with the pinot blanc. See under: Other grape varieties. Pinot blanc wine goes well with most light starters, cold meats, shell fish, savory pies, (quiches), soft vegetables (such as asparagus), white meat and poultry, soft fish and fresh cheese (with a mild taste).

MUSCAT D'ALSACE

Muscat wines can be recognized straightaway from their sultry, extremely aromatic quality, which is reminiscent of ripe Muscat grapes. In Alsace, the Muscat is always prepared dry, in contrast with most southern Muscat wines. No other wine manages to retain the essence of the odor and taste of the fresh grapes as successfully as Muscat wines. It is delicious as an aperitif, excellent with asparagus, but can also be drunk just like that, when you want to share a glass of wine with friends.

Pinot Blanc

RIESLING

The riesling is known as a noble grape all over the world. In Alsace riesling achieves excellent quality. The wines are elegant, fresh and delicate. Depending on the soil, there may be hints of fruit, flowers or even minerals. The better Rieslings have a lot of character and are at the same time quite sophisticated. They are excellent wines to accompany a meal. They go very well with shellfish, fish terrines, raw fish (sushi), fish dishes, poultry, goats cheese and young mild cheeses.

GEWÜRZTRAMINER

Anyone who thinks of Alsace, thinks of gewürztraminer (in German the name of this grape is written with an umlaut on the u; in Alsace, without an umlaut). The gewürztraminer is able to bridge the French-German border better than any other grape. Wines made with this grape have a great deal of character, a full color, an intense and almost exotic aroma of tropical fruit (lichees, grapefruit) and indigenous fruits (quince), flowers (acacia, roses), and spices (cinnamon, pepper, cloves) as well as a full generous round structure. The lighter Gewürztraminer wines are real charmers and are greatly appreciated as an aperitif. The heavier varieties are perfect for long winter evenings, but are just as suitable for accompanying pronounced dishes of the exotic cuisine (especially with sweet and sour or sweet and salt combinations), foie gras (try one of the vendanges tardives!), a not too ripe Munster cheese, or slightly sweet desserts and pastry (Kugelhopf, cheese cake or damson cake, for example).

Riesling grand cru, Kanzlerberg, Bergheim

PINOT GRIS

The pinot gris is sometimes mistakenly referred to as tokay-pinot gris, but the name tokay is misleading. The pinot gris grape, known in Germany under the name gray Burgundy allegedly originates from Hungary. There the grape is known as gray monk or szürkebarat. When the Austrians conquered the Turks, the Hungarians marched into Europe with thousands of barrels of Tokaji wine, to Alsace, amongst other places. Later the Hungarians themselves sent vines from Tokaj to Alsace. In former Yugoslavia and in northern Italy the pinot gris is also sometimes mistakenly called tocai. (In Friuli there is also a tocai Friulano, but this is a different variety of grape, the sauvignonasse or sauvignon vert). Obviously Alsatian wine growers radically reject these stories. The present generation of wine growers in Alsace would do well to omit this incorrect indication.

In any case, the Pinot Gris wines from Alsace deserve a great deal of praise. The wines are dark in color and have a very expres-

Pinot Gris, a particularly sensual aperitif!

Gewürztraminer grand cru Altenberg de Bergheim

sive aroma, dominated above all by spices, and both the aroma and the taste are powerful, full and intensely complex. Because of these strong qualities this is one of the few white wines which are quite at ease with a delicious piece of meat. A good Pinot Gris is an excellent accompaniment to foie gras, fish with herbs, roast pork or veal, wildfowl, or even game. For connoisseurs, a glass of Pinot Gris d'Alsace is an extremely sensual aperitif.

PINOT NOIR

In addition to the six white grapes, there is just one red grape in Alsace. In fact, there are three sorts of Pinot Noir wines. First of all, there are the generous, fresh and friendly rosé wines (N.B.: some are very tempting, but can be extremely deceptive, particularly in summer… enjoy, but drink in moderation!). The light red Pinot Noir wines are one step further up on the wine scale. These are most like a simple Burgundy, with a typical aroma and taste of red fruit (cherries). Finally, there are the better red Pinot Noir wines, for which juice is constantly taken from the bottom of the fermentation tanks or barrels during the wine-making process and then added back on top of the *chapeau* of skins. This strengthens the colorants and taste so that the wines are much fuller. These Pinot Noir vinifiés en rouge are usually matured in large oak barrels. The top selections come from the oldest vineyards and are described on the label as Cuvée Vielles Vignes. This wine is often used as an aperitif, as a rosé, served not too cold. It is also an excellent accompaniment for all meat dishes. This pinot noir is produced as a red wine and accompanies all sorts of meat, poultry and light game very well. It is also delicious with medium hard cheeses.

Pinot Gris

OTHER VARIETIES OF GRAPES

In addition to the above-mentioned grapes, there are two other grapes that should be mentioned. The first, the chardonnay grape, is planted in Alsace, but is only used for sparkling wines. The second, the klevener de Heiligenstein is a very old Alsace grape, better known as a traminer or savagnin in the neighboring region of the Jura. It was once a commonly used variety of grape, but was gradually replaced by its much more aromatic brother, the gewürztraminer. However, the klevener is extremely suitable for drinking with a good meal and is highly valued.

NAMES DENOTING ORIGIN

There are three recognized names denoting origins in Alsace.

Pinot Noir

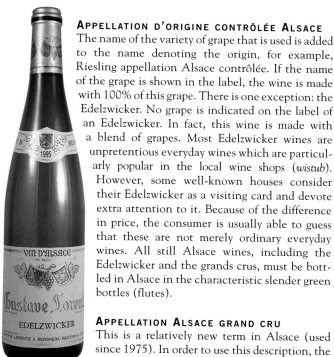

Edelzwicker

APPELLATION D'ORIGINE CONTRÔLÉE ALSACE

The name of the variety of grape that is used is added to the name denoting the origin, for example, Riesling appellation Alsace contrôlée. If the name of the grape is shown in the label, the wine is made with 100% of this grape. There is one exception: the Edelzwicker. No grape is indicated on the label of an Edelzwicker. In fact, this wine is made with a blend of grapes. Most Edelzwicker wines are unpretentious everyday wines which are particularly popular in the local wine shops (*wistub*). However, some well-known houses consider their Edelzwicker as a visiting card and devote extra attention to it. Because of the difference in price, the consumer is usually able to guess that these are not merely ordinary everyday wines. All still Alsace wines, including the Edelzwicker and the grands crus, must be bottled in Alsace in the characteristic slender green bottles (flutes).

APPELLATION ALSACE GRAND CRU

This is a relatively new term in Alsace (used since 1975). In order to use this description, the wines must come from one of the fifty permitted and strictly defined areas which were chosen for their special geological and microclimatological qualities. The name of these selected crus must be shown on the label. In addition, these wines must be made exclusively of the following grapes: riesling, gewürztraminer, pinot gris or muscat. One detail which is important to the consumer is that these wines must also always be approved in a professional wine tasting. In this way an attempt is made to guarantee the qualities and authenticity of these wines. They are all unique wines of exceptional quality. However, the price is also on the high side, though compared with top wines from Burgundy, these prices are completely justified in view of the quality on offer.

The fifty grands crus d'Alsace (the village from which they come and the type of soil are shown between brackets).

- Altenberg (Bergbieten, marl + chalk + limestone)
- Altenberg (Bergbieten, marl + limestone)
- Altenberg (Wolxheim, marl + limestone)
- Brand (Turckheim, granite)
- Bruderthal (Molsheim, marl + limestone)
- Eichberg (Eguisheim, marl + limestone)
- Engelberg (Dahlenheim/Scharrachbergheim, marl + limestone)
- Florimont (Ingersheim/Katzenthal, marl + limestone)
- Frankstein (Dambach-la-Ville, granite)
- Froehn (Zellenberg, clay and marl)
- Furstentum (Kietzheim/Sigolsheim, limestone)
- Geisberg (Ribeauvillé, marl + limestone + sandstone)
- Gloeckelberg (Rodern/Saint-Hippolyte, granite + clay)
- Goldert (Gueberschwihr, marl + limestone)
- Hatschbourg (Hattstat/Voegtlinshoffen, marl + limestone + loess
- Hengst (Wintzenheim, marl + limestone + sandstone)
- Kanzlerberg (Bergheim, clay + marl + chalk)
- Kastelberg (Andlau, slate)
- Kessler (Guebwiller, sand + clay)
- Kirchberg (Barr, marl + limestone)
- Kirchberg (Ribeauvillé, marl + limestone + sandstone)
- Kittlerlé (Guebwiller, sandstone + volcanic rock)
- Mambourg (Sigolsheim, marl + limestone)
- Mandelberg (Mittelwihr/Beblenheim, marl + limestone)
- Marckrain (Bennwiht/Sigolsheim, marl + limestone)
- Moenchberg (Andlau/Eichhoffen, marl + limestone + eroded rock from hilltops)
- Muenchberg (Nothalten, sandstone + volcanic rock + stone)
- Ollwiller (Wuenheim, sand + clay)
- Osterberg (Ribeauvillé, marl)
- Pfersigberg (Eguisheim/Wettolsheim, limestone + sandstone)
- Pfingstberg (Orschwihr, marl + limestone + sandstone)
- Praelatenberg (Kintzheim, granite + gneiss)
- Rangen (Thann/Vieux-Thann, volcanic rock)
- Rosacker (Humawihr, dolomite limestone)
- Saering (Guebwiller, marl + limestone + sandstone)
- Schlossberg (Kientzheim, granite)
- Schoenenbourg (Riquewihr/Zellenberg, marl + sandstone + chalk
- Sommerberg (Niedermoschwihr/Katzenthal, granite)
- Sonnenglanz (Beblenheim, marl + limestone)
- Spiegel (Bergholtz/Guebwiller, marl + sandstone)
- Sporen (Riquewihr, clay + marl + stone)

Grand cru Kirchberg, Ribeauvillé, *(ES)*

**Crémant
d'Alsace**

– Steinert (Pfaffenheim/Westhalten,
limestone)
– Steingrubler (Wettolsheim, marl
+ limestone + sandstone)
– Steinklotz (Marlenheim, limestone)
– Vorbourg (Rouffach/Westhalten,
limestone + sandstone)
– Wiebelsberg (Andlau, sand
+ sandstone)
– Wineck-Schlossberg (Kat-
zenthal/Ammerschwihr, granite)
– Winzenberg (Blienschwiller,
granite)
– Zinnkoepflé
(Soulzmatt/Westhalten,
limestone + sandstone)
– Zotzenberg (Mittelbergheim,
marl + limestone)

APPELLATION CRÉMANT D'ALSACE

These sparkling wines are obtained by the traditional method
which is used for Champagne
wines. The basic grape to be used
is mainly the pinot blanc, but the
riesling, the pinot gris, and occasionally the chardonnay grape also produce excellent results. There is also
a rare blanc de noir, white wine made with black grapes using the pinot noir. Obviously a crémant d'Alsace
is an excellent aperitif or a wine for a celebration (birthday, anniversary, wedding, examination, etc.), but it is
also a very refreshing accompaniment with pastry that
is not too sweet (Kugelhopf).

VENDANGES TARDIVES

Sometimes the label includes the indication vendanges
tardives. This addition may apply either for ordinary
Alsace wines or for the grands crus, and refers to the
time of the harvest. Vendange tardives wines are made
with overripe grapes which were harvested late, as the
name suggests (comparable to the German Spätlese). However, here the wines can only be made with
the gewürztraminer, pinot gris, riesling and muscat
d'Alsace. Wines made with the first two varieties of
grape have a particularly high alcohol percentage,
sometimes above 14%. They are very concentrated
wines with a great deal of power and character and
a large range of aromas.

SELECTION DE GRAINS NOBLES

This name is the counterpart of the German Trockenbeerenauslese. As the name suggests, the grapes
are often individually selected for this wine and only
the overripe grapes affected by noble rot (*Botrytris
cinerea*) are eligible for these wines. The grapes affected by this benign fungus lose their water content over
the weeks, resulting in an enormous concentration of
aroma and tastes. The wines obtained in this way are
extremely full-bodied, powerful and intensely aromatic. They are masterworks of mother nature, each and
every one. Because of the very low yield, the price of
these wines is extremely high. Therefore the wine is
also sold in half bottles. This is not a problem, because just one sip is enough to take you into seventh
heaven.

Wine cellars in Bergheim

Great Alsace wines can mature very well *(ES)*

VIN DE GLACE

Following the success of the German Eiswein, there are
a small number of experimental eisweins in Alsace
made with overripe grapes which remain on the vine
up to the first night frost. These wines are extra concentrated, extremely sweet, but lack the finesse and aromatic strength of a good selection de grains nobles.

THE FRENCH JURA

With its rich history, many castles and museums, subtle gastronomy, compté en vacherin cheeses and exceptional wines, the Jura soon manages to charm everyone. Once you have discovered the local wines, you will never forget these extremely special individual wines. There are countless jewels growing in this idyllic region which produce white, rosé or red wines, the most well known of which are known as vin jaune and vin de paille.

The best Jura wines mature in these cellars

THE REGION

The département of the Jura is in the east of France, in Franche-Comté, between the Burgundian Côte d'Or and Switzerland. This narrow strip of vineyards in the Jura Bon Pays (good land) or Revermont (the back of the hill) stretches in a gradual curve over approximately 62 miles along a north-south axis. The vineyards are situated on the gently undulating hillsides (revermont) of the limestone plateau of the Jura, at a height of 820 to 1,574 ft, with soil consisting of marl and occasionally some broken down chalk rocks. The climate is semi-continental with typically severe winters and very warm summers, an early soft spring and a warm fall ideal conditions for growing grapes.

HISTORY

The wine-growing area of the Jura is one of the oldest in France: going back at least five thousand years, according to archeologists. Clear traces of trade in local wines have even been found dating from the sixth century BC! The Greeks who traveled to the Jura from Massilia and Nikeia (present-day Marseille and Nice) via the Rhône, always took some wine with them on their journey back. The Romans were also very keen on the wines of Séquanie (as the Jura were known at the time). The great wines of Arbois, L'Étoile and Château Chalon have been praised by writers and poets, as well as politicians and kings, for more than a thousand years. Of all the names linked to wine growing in the Jura, there is one which cannot be left out of the story of success: the name of the genius, Louis Pasteur, born as a Franc-Comtois, who invented modern oenology amongst other things, and once owned a vineyard that still exists today. Louis Pasteur played a key role in the development of modern oenology. Amongst other things, he was the first to reveal the secret of how yeast cells worked during the process of alcoholic fermentation.

Viticulture reached its peak in the Jura during Pasteurs time. The *Phylloxera* plague, which destroyed the vines, two wars and one economic crisis after another, were very harmful for wine growing in the Jura. Of the 48,000 acres/75 squared miles of vineyards which existed at the end of the nineteenth century, only 4,920 acres/7.6 squared miles have survived, including 3,960 acres/6.2 squared miles which have AOC classification. However, more than ever before, it is the enthusiasm and love of wine growing which can now be clearly experienced in the wine growers who remain.

THE FIVE VARIETIES OF GRAPE

Only five varieties of grape are permitted here for the production of the AOC wines (with a guarantee of their origin).

CHARDONNAY

The chardonnay, which was imported from neighboring Burgundy in about the fourteenth century, represents about 45% of all the grapes that are planted. It is an easy grape which usually ripens without any problems in about mid-September. It contains a high level of sugars (therefore potentially a lot of alcohol) and produces very floral wines, fruity and generous.

SAVAGNIN

The savagnin (15% of the grapes planted) is also very popular here. This indigenous grape, which has existed since time immemorial, is a local variation of the traminer and produces the best wines from the Jura (the famous vins jaunes). This grape ripens late and is often the last to be harvested at the end of October.

Arbois Chardonnay

PINOT NOIR

The pinot noir also comes from Burgundy and was brought to the Jura as long ago as the fifteenth century. It ripens quickly and has a great deal of taste. This grape is hardly ever used on its own here, but is blended with the poulsard grape, giving it additional color and backbone.

TROUSSEAU

The trousseau (5%) is also an indigenous grape which flourishes on the warm sandy soils in the north of the wine region. It flowers fairly late, and provides very colorful and concentrated juices. The wine of the trousseau reaches an unparalleled peak after being allowed to rest for about ten years in a good cellar. Unfortunately, this wine is fairly rare and is not yet very well known. If you have an occasion to taste it, you should certainly do so; the poulsard (20%) is an indigenous grape which has a beautiful pale red color, a lot of fruit and gives the wine all sorts of wild aromas. The poulsard is used for light red wines, but also for rosé, such as the famous Pupillin rosé.

NAMES OF ORIGIN

The Jura has four regional names denoting origin: Château-Chalon, L'Étoile, Arbois, and Côtes du Jura.

CHÂTEAU-CHALON

The village of Château-Chalon literally and figuratively dominates the whole region. It is situated at 1,476 ft, in the middle of the Jura region, and is the cradle of the king of all Jura wines, the vins jaunes, which are made exclusively with savagnin grapes. Vins jaunes can be made throughout the Jura. However, the best ones come from the village of Château-Chalon. The wines obtained here are of an extremely high quality and are not made every year. The process of preparing this wine is the same as that for the other vins jaunes, with the difference that

there is one extra control of its quality. This giant in the range of French wines should be consumed with a traditional dish: coq au vin jaune (stewed chicken in wine sauce) or better still, veal chops with morels and yellow wine sauce…a guaranteed culinary delight!

The vins jaunes, including those from Château--Chalon, are bottled in a special bottle with a thick base and a different content of 62 cl (21 fl oz), known as clavelin. Why only 62 cl (21 fl oz)? This is because 62 cl (21 fl oz) is what remains of one liter of young wine after maturing in the barrel for six years and three months. The clavelin of Château-Chalon is the only one to have a decorative seal around its neck.

L'ÉTOILE

No one can be certain where this village got its name (étoile means star in French). Perhaps it is because of

Arbois Pupillin in red and rosé

Château Chalon

Arbois Savagnin + Chardonnay

the five surrounding hills, which together seem to form a star, or because of the five splendid castles in the immediate vicinity. Or perhaps the name is related to the many discoveries of shellfish and starfish found in the chalky soil of the vineyards. Very high quality white and sparkling wines are made in approximately 92 acres. They all have the characteristic taste of the terroir of Le Étoile: flint and … hazelnut!

Try an Étoile with a chicken stew with hazelnuts, or with veal with field mushrooms.

ARBOIS

The vineyards around the attractive town of Arbois produce the largest quantity of wines of the Jura. The fact that wines of a special quality with a very individual character are produced in these 1,920 acres is apparent from the fact that the wines of Arbois were the first in France to be given an appellation d'origine contrôlée. Mostly white and red wines are made here, as well as a small quantity of rosé (Pupillin).

The red wines are firm and full-bodied. They are an ideal accompaniment to all sorts of fowl, as well as hare.

The rosé wines are full-bodied and elegant with a great deal of finesse. They go well with poultry and with meals made with pork. They are also delicious with cold meats.

White Arbois wines have a great deal of structure and a very sophisticated taste. They are ideal with any sort of fish, particularly trout and pike.

CÔTES DU JURA

This name covers a colorful collection of white, red, sparkling and rosé wines, vins jaunes and vins de paille, which are not covered by the first three wines in which the origin is indicated. It is almost incredible that so many and so many different quality wines can be made in such a small area.

The white wines of pure chardonnay have a pale yellow color and smell of fresh grapes in their youth. After two or three years of maturing in casks, they acquire their characteristic flinty aroma. Wines made with chardonnay and savagnin have an even stronger taste and aroma of the terroir. Wines made with pure savagnin are particularly delicate and aromatic. The white Côtes du Jura are dry and meaty, and are excellent with fish dishes, cheese dishes (for example, with comté or French emmental) or with poached poultry.

The rosé wines made with poulsard are elegant and subtle. They often have the color of coral and are extremely juicy and full-bodied. They go well with cold meats, fish dishes and poultry.

The red wines are also very typical. They are made with the poulsard grape and are often similar to the rosé, although these really are red wines. The taste and aroma are reminiscent of brushwood and wild forest fruits. On the other hand, the wines made with the trousseau are warm, rich in tannin, round and full-bodied with aro-

Vin Jaune

mas of red fruits. They often contain a lot of alcohol, and age well.

Both types of wine are excellent with delicate dishes of game, particularly with venison, although they can also be combined very well with red meat and roast pork or veal.

NAMES DENOTING ORIGINS WHICH ARE NOT GEOGRAPHICALLY DETERMINED

In addition to these four names denoting origins, there are a few non-geographical names denoting origins in the Jura.

VIN JAUNE

According to the people of the Jura, these yellow wines are only found in the Jura region. Nevertheless, it seems appropriate to compare these wines to the Finos and Manzanillas of Jerez. In the Jura a layer of yeast cells also develops spontaneously on the wines, a sort of veil (*voile*) as it is known to the French. This protects the wine from rapid oxidation because the yeast cells feed on oxygen. These yellow wines (*vins jaunes*) are matured in the barrel for six years and three months. This gives them the characteristic taste and aroma of walnuts, hazelnuts and green almonds, which the French call *goût de jaune*. These *vins jaunes* can easily be kept for a hundred years or more. They are certainly not light wines, partly because of their characteristic taste, but also, and particularly because of the alcohol content: at least 13%, but some wines even reach 15%!

When you think of *vins jaunes*, you think of morels in addition to ceps, the most delicious mushrooms in the world. Poultry (chicken, guinea foul, pheasant) or fish (pike) braised in yellow wine, with mushrooms and a finishing touch of fresh cream is an excellent dish to eat with these individual yellow wines. Finally, a piece of comté will go very well with any *vin jaune*.

Vin de paille

Clos des Mouches, one of the most famous vineyards in Burgundy

VIN DE PAILLE

These straw wines are made with very healthy bunches of grapes which are carefully harvested by hand. The bunches are then placed on straw in small boxes or are suspended one by one from the large beams of the attic in a dry and above all, extremely well-ventilated area. The grapes are pressed around Christmas. By that time they have thoroughly dried out and have become wrinkly, with a high sugar content and a great deal of aromas and taste. During the fermentation, the conversion of sugars into alcohol will not exceed 15 or 16% of alcohol. Therefore there will always be residual sugars remaining in the wine. After maturing in the barrel for at least two but often three of four years a liqueur-like white wine is produced of a very rare quality. This valuable wine is bottled in special 37.5cl bottles.

Many books of recipes will tell you that dessert wines should accompany extremely sweet desserts. Like many other gastronomes, I do not agree with this at all! Sweet with sweet is too much of a good thing: it paralyses the taste buds and all you taste is the different sorts of sugars. Thus this is not particularly interesting. With this gift from Bacchus you should try a fresh and tart piece of French apple pie

or a sophisticated and not too sweet almond pastry. Of course, it is also possible to simply enjoy this full-bodied sweet wine, for example, in the middle of winter by the open fire. Time will stand still for you.

THE SPARKLING WINES OF THE JURA

The mousseux and crémant mainly come from the vineyards of l' Étoile and the Vernois. They are produced as brut, sec or demi-sec, white or rosé, and are made according to the méthode traditionnelle with a second fermentation in the bottle. These are all playful wines, suitable for any occasion: perfect as a spontaneous aperitif, daring with light starters, exciting with a fruit dessert, sensual with pastry, jovial with a group of friends, romantic and sometimes slightly mischievous at a wedding... there is always a suitable occasion for a glass of Jura mousseux.

BURGUNDY

The Celtic Druids were familiar with the secret of the wild vines long before the time of Christ. A drink was also made using fermented grape juice in Burgundy. The first traces of organized viticulture take us back six centuries BC, when the Celts returned from their conquests

Sparkling wine from the Jura

There are many AOC wines from Burgundy

in Italy, loaded with the gnarled, cultivated *Vitis* shrubs. These distant ancestors of present wine growers were responsible for the first vineyards in Burgundy. The Greeks were the first to be introduced to these wines. However, it was the Roman occupiers who traded them for the first time. Following a black period after the fall of Rome and the many barbarian invasions, the Burgundian gospel was propagated all over the known world by monks from Cluny and Citeaux. For centuries, Burgundian wines were the greatest in all Christendom. When the powerful Duchy of Burgundy even extended to the Low Countries, the exuberant lifestyle of the various dukes became famous far over the borders of Burgundy. After the French Revolution, the vineyards fell back into the hands of the wine growers themselves, which resulted in great fragmentation.

THE REGION

Burgundy is a terroir, a soil consisting of limestone and marl, clay and gravel, with occasional deposits of iron.

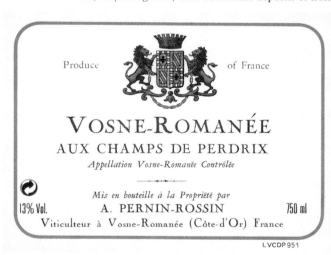

Vosne-Romanée, appellation communale

Some famous premiers crus and grands crus

Chambertin and Clos Vougeot grand cru

The severe winters and warm summers, together with the soil, produce an individual character and personality. The pinot noir, chardonnay, aligoté and gamay all grow here. Some sauvignon also grows near Saint-Bris in the Auxerrois. Burgundy is a complicated patchwork of vineyards (known here as climat), villages, clos and crus, subdivided into four names denoting origin.

APPELLATION REGIONALE (22)
The ordinary Burgundy, Bourgogne Grand Ordinaire and Bourgogne passetout-grain come from all over the region. The rather better burgundy comes from a strictly defined area (e.g., Côtes de Nuits and Côtes de Beaune).

APPELLATION
These wines have the names of a municipality such as Chablis, Nuits-Saint-Georges, Vosne-Romanée or Vougeot.

APPELLATION PREMIER
These wines can add the name of a plot (*climat*) to the compulsory indication of the municipality of origin. In terms of organization, these *premier cru* wines fall in the category *appellation communale/villages*. The climats must be of an exceptional quality if they are to be included in the premier cru elite. Some examples include: Chablis premier cru Montmains, Chambolle-Musigny Amoureuses, Puligny-Montrachet Folatiāres, Beaune Clos des Mouches and Beaune Grāves.

GRAND CRUS (33)
Because of their consistent quality, these climats have become very famous over the centuries. The label of these wines can show only the name of the climat. Some examples include Chablis grand cru Vaudésir, Echezeaux, Charmes-Chambertin, Clos de Vougeot, Bonnes Mares, Romanée Saint-Vivant, Corton and Montrachet.

THE DIFFERENT WINE REGIONS

Chablis

Burgundy is subdivided into nine geographical areas: Chablis, Auxerrois, Côte de Nuits, Côte de Beaune, Côte Chalonnaise, Maconnais, Beaujolais villages and Beaujolais en Coteaux du Lyonnais. In practice, the last three fall under the Beaujolais, while the Auxerrois fall under the Chablis. The Beaujolais will be dealt with separately.

Chablis

PETIT CHABLIS

Drink these light, fruity, fresh wines young, preferably with a good paté. It is also delicious with shellfish.

CHABLIS

True Chablis ages extremely well, but is already deliciously fruity in the first year. They are only fully developed after three years. The wine is a light golden color with a hint of green. A Chablis has pronounced fruity and vegetable aromas of grapefruit, coriander, ferns, privet, (green) asparagus and even artichoke. The taste is literally and metaphorically bone dry, but also fruity with occasionally a mineral undertone and sometimes a hint of iodine.

Young Chablis with oysters is a classical combination. In fact Chablis is sometimes described as oyster wine because there any many oyster shells in the chalky Chablis soil, as silent witnesses to a very distant past. However, local wine growers prefer a simple cheese roll (gougāre) with their Chablis, or a small andouille or andouillette (sausage made with intestines, a French specialty), or a fresh goats cheese.

CHABLIS PREMIER CRU

The Chablis premier cru achieve their peak after three to five years. They are not as profound as the grands crus, but are ready to be consumed sooner which is useful for anyone who is impatient. A Chablis premier cru has a golden color with obvious hints of green. The aroma is fruity, above all with a vegetal aroma: lemon balm, ferns and a hint of coriander. The taste is dry and is reminiscent of chalk, occasionally with a hint of iodine.

Chablis grand cru Vaudésir, Chablis premier cru
Montmains and Chablis

These Chablis are excellent with shellfish (oysters), river fish (pike), or poultry (chicken, guinea foul). They are also excellent with goats cheese, particularly when it has first been warmed up.

CHABLIS PREMIER CRU (GROUPED BY GEOGRAPHICAL REGION)

The subsidiary regions of every main climat are indicated between brackets. They can also be shown on the label, together with the name of the main climat.

- Les Beauregards (Côte de Cuissy)
- Beauroy (Côte de Savant)
- Berdiot
- Chaume de Talvat
- Côte de Jouan
- Côte de Lechet
- Côte de Vaubarousse
- Fourchaume (Vaupulent, Côte de Fontenay, l' Homme Mort, Vaulorent)
- Les Fourneaux (Morein, Côte des Près Girots)
- Mont de Milieu
- Montée de Tonnerre (Chapelot, Pied d' Aloup, Cote de Brechain)
- Montmains (Foret, Butteaux)
- Vaillons (Chatains, Secher, Beugnons, Les Lys, Melinots, Roncieres, Les Epinottes)
- Vaucoupin
- Vau de Vey (Vaux Ragons)
- Vau Ligneau
- Vosgros (Vaugiraut)

Chablis grand cru
Les Clos

CHABLIS GRAND CRU

These wines should rest for at least five years after being bottled, and can certainly age for twenty years. They are rare wines, very dry with a good balance between strength and finesse. The color is very pure, pale yellow with the tiniest hint of green. The aroma is even more reminiscent of ferns and coriander than the Chablis premier cru, with occasionally some candied citrus fruits. The taste particularly reflects the chalky soil with an even more pronounced undertone of iodine than the premier cru. The candied citrus fruits again emerge in the aftertaste.

A Chablis grand cru is excellent in combination with shellfish (lobster, langoustine) and with crustaceans (coquilles St. Jacques), but also with braised veal in a creamy sauce or with goats cheese.

CHABLIS GRAND CRU

Officially there are seven Chablis grand cru:
- Blanchots
- Bougros
- Les Clos
- Les Grenouilles
- Les Preuses

Crémant de
Bourgogne

– Valmur
– Vaudésir

However, there is an eighth Chablis grand cru which is not officially recognized as an AOC, though it is universally considered to be equivalent, viz., La Moutonne.

Auxerrois

SAUVIGNON DE SAINT-BRIS (VDQS)

These are very fresh and fruity white wines, ideal as an aperitif, but also excellent with (green) asparagus.

IRANCY

Since 1999, Irancy has been sold under its own AOC name, while it was formerly sold as Bourgogne Irancy. The basic grape used is the pinot noir, occasionally supplemented with an ancient indigenous variety of grape, the césar. Red Irancy wines are usually very fruity, but sometimes also strong and rich in tannin. They are excellent in combination with chicken or other poultry, or even with veal in a red wine sauce. There is also a rosé version which goes well with peasant dishes.

CRÉMANT DE BOURGOGNE

Most crémants de Bourgogne are made with grapes from the Auxerrois. These are very fresh, generous and cheerful wines which can simply be used at any time of the day or year.

Côte de Nuits

The Côte de Nuits is world famous for its red wines and encompasses a large range of terroirs and styles. It begins in Marsannay and ends in Corgoloin. The soil is chalky with a lower layer of marl and clay.

MARSANNAY

The red wines are rather firm and harsh in their youth. After a few years of maturing, the tannins become softer and the wine is slightly rounder and meatier with aromas of red fruits, particularly cherries, blackcurrants and redcurrants, or sometimes with a hint of prunes, licorice, cocoa or coffee. They are perfect wines for poultry or beef, stewed in red wine.

The rosé de Bourgogne is the best known of the Marsannay wines. The wine has a light rosé color with shades of orange. The aroma is very fresh and pleasant and the taste is reminiscent of red fruit. It is an excellent rosé which goes well with cold meats, white meat, and poultry, starters and main courses, but also, for example with rabbit.

The white wines are very fresh, full and exciting. After resting for a while they become rounder and more supple. They are intense in color with a typical chardonnay aroma, of exotic fruits such as grapefruit and pineapple, and have a full-bodied taste.

FIXIN

This is mainly known for it red wines. They are usually powerful meaty wines with quite a high level of tannins in their youth which means that they keep extremely well. They are ruby red in color with an aroma of red fruits (cherries, strawberry, raspberry) when they are young, and plums or even leather as they mature.

Fixin goes very well with any type of meat, particularly with boeuf bourgignon.

GEVREY-CHAMBERTIN

These are a beautiful ruby red color and are extremely pure and clear. They have the characteristic aroma of black cherries, blackberries and other small fruits, occasionally with a hint of licorice. As they are matured in wood, the wine acquires a bouquet of herbs and spices (nutmeg) as well as leather. When it reaches a respectable age, this bouquet changes into earthy tones such as brushwood, wet leaves and mushrooms. The tannins are powerful but never intrusive, partly because of the natural oiliness of the wine. The taste is full bodied and very fruity. This wine is delicious with any red meat, game, poultry (preferably stewed in red wine), mushrooms and soft mature cheeses. It can be stored for ten to twenty years after the harvest. Gevrey-Chambertin premier cru Les Cazetiers is particularly highly recommended!

Gevrey-Chambertin

CHAMBERTIN GRAND CRU

This is one of the top wines from Burgundy, but also one of the most difficult wines to make because of the unpredictable microclimate. The color is clear, pure and a deep ruby red of extreme intensity. A young Chambertin has an aroma of black cherries and sometimes plain chocolate. After a few years in the bottle, nuances of licorice, truffles and wood develop; at a later age the aroma tends towards leather and other animal odors as well as aromas of candied fruit. The tannins are strong and harmonize will with the rounded, full, almost oily taste of the wine and the elegant delicate acids. In the taste you will encounter ripe fruit, such as black cherry jam with a hint of liquorice.

This wine is too complex to accompany a simple dish. It is best served with game in rich sauces or with beef in a strongly reduced red wine sauce. If you feel daring you can also serve the wine with a strong mature cheese rich in bacteria such as L'Ami du Chambertin a delight for anyone who enjoys sensual experiences!

Gevrey-Chambertin Combottes

Charmes-Chambertin grand cru

CHAMBERTIN CLOS DE BÈZE GRAND CRU

This wine, which dates back to the seventh century, has a wonderful deep, dark red color, aromas of fruit (raspberry) and hints of wood and herbs, sometimes roasted almonds. It has a full-bodied, powerful taste, oily and with a good structure. It is certainly a wine that can be stored.

It is extremely suitable for drinking with heavy, rich stews and also with game.

LATRICIÉRES-CHAMBERTIN GRAND CRU

This has slightly less structure and is fuller than a Chambertin Clos de Bèze. This wine sometimes has a slight aroma of spicy cake (spices) with an occasional hint of candied orange peel. It is certainly an extremely elegant wine which goes well with poultry and rabbit.

CHAPELLE-CHAMBERTIN GRAND CRU

These wines are powerful, complex, and have a very good structure. Again, there are hints of spicy cake and orange. They are excellent wines which remain velvety soft, despite their intrinsic strength. Try Chapelle-Chambertin grand cru with wood pigeon breasts in red wine sauce!

CHARMES-CHAMBERTIN GRAND CRU

This wine has a beautiful color with a tempting aroma of strawberries, black cherries or raspberries and an occasional hint of apricot stone, lime blossom or licorice. Sometimes, particularly when it is young, the wood is still too dominant, particularly in the aroma. When you swirl the wine in the glass for a while, the fruits return. The aftertaste is a real experience: candied fruits (cherries), exotic wood, herbs and spices. It is a very classical, powerful and complex wine, which still has enough fruit and elegance to be a real charmer.

This is an excellent wine with roast leg of lamb, any boeuf bourgignon and game. It is delicious with dishes containing morels and/or truffles. This wine should certainly not be drunk too warm (max. 18 °C/64.4 °F).

Griotte-Chambertin grand cru

GRIOTTE-CHAMBERTIN GRAND CRU

The aromas of a Griotte-Chambertin are complex and extremely subtle. You will identify hints of cherry liqueur and candied cherries, a trace of leather and a soupçon of nutmeg. In more mature wines, there are additional hints of truffle and animal aromas, (the French describe this as an odor of game, because it is reminiscent of the smell of game that has been well hung). The tannins are soft but clearly present, and the high alcohol percentage ensures a velvety, almost soft wine. The sensations of the aromas are reflected in the taste, although they are slightly softer and accompanied by elegant nuances of wood.

A good Griotte-Chambertin has incredible class, and a rich complex character. In its youth (after four or five years) it is excellent with rich casseroles, roasted or grilled beef or game. Once it has matured (between eight and fifteen years), a Griotte-Chambertin is more at home with sophisticated dishes which are not too heavy.

MAZIS-CHAMBERTIN GRAND CRU

This is a rare wine from Chambertin, powerful and supple at the same time, with a good structure, complex and yet elegant and subtle.

It is a fascinating wine which is excellent when it accompanies any casserole, roasted or grilled poultry, or simply with chicken in a red wine sauce.

MAZOYÈRS-CHAMBERTIN

This is an elegant charming red wine with an average structure. It not particularly complex or powerful, but is very fruity.

Do not drink it when it is too old, but consume it for example with fowl.

MOREY-SAINT-DENIS

The wines from Morey-Saint-Denis deserve greater recognition. They have been rather forgotten amongst the powerful wines of Chambertin with their strong character, as well as the delicate tempters from Chambolle-Musigny. They are an extremely bright red color with an aroma full of fruit (morels/cherries) and hints of wood, herbs, spices, brushwood and leather, with a full-bodied, velvety and very balanced taste. Further more these wines are excellent for keeping for a long time. In short, Morey-Saint-Denis is a wine for the true connoisseur who prefers to pay a reasonable price for an excellent, though rather unknown Burgundy, than an absurdly high price for one of its famous brothers (which may not necessarily be that much better!).

Therefore this wine has a twofold attraction, particularly with rabbit, pheasant or other meats.

(Also recommended: the premier cru, Les Ruchots).

Morey-Saint-Denis

Morey-Saint-Denis Clos Sorbet

CLOS DE LA ROCHE GRAND CRU

This wine has a very deep ruby red color. The aroma again contains black cherries, sometimes with a hint of animal odors (musk) and almost always shades of cedar wood (cigar boxes). It is a great harmonious wine with powerful tannins, but also a velvety structure. It remains in the mouth for a long time.

This is an exceptional wine which asks for a robust meal, such as roast game or beef with lots of fried mushrooms. It also goes surprisingly well with red bacterial cheeses which should not be too ripe.

Chambolle Musigny

CLOS SAINT-DENIS GRAND CRU

This wine has an attractive ruby red color with touches of garnet. It has a surprising and complex aroma containing black-currants, blackberries, prunes, occasionally a hint of musk, herbs, spices, coffee and sometimes pansies or other flowers. Try this wine with an old-fashioned sweetbread deliciously fried.

CLOS DE TART GRAND CRU

This wine has a very dark ruby red color, a tempting aroma of spicy cake and hints of coffee or cocoa. It is powerful and sophisticated at the same time.

This full-bodied, slightly oily wine matures extremely well and is excellent with robust meats which are not too lean, such as goose, preferably in red wine sauce.

CLOS DES LAMBRAYS GRAND CRU

This is a rather shy wine which is often forgotten. It is a classical Burgundy with a lot of fruit (black cherries) and hints of flowers and animals (leather, musk). It is a full-bodied, round wine with a great deal of elegance. This wine goes with simple meals but will not object to a few truffles…

CHAMBOLLE-MUSIGNY

These are feminine, almost tender red wines with a pure ruby red color, an aroma full of fruit (raspberry and cherry) when they are young, and later tending towards mushrooms, brushwood or even animal undertones (of game). They are elegant and refined wines, mild and aromatic.

Bonnes Mares grand cru

Musigny grand cru and Chambolle

The better wines come from the premier cru climats, in particular from Les Amoureuses a name and a wine to fall in love with! The color is sometimes rather inclined towards a cherry red and the aromas vary from raspberry to cherry liqueur with hints of truffle, mushrooms and brushwood. In some years, the wine also has rather more animal aromas such as musk. These are very tempting wines which steal the head and heart of many connoisseurs without leading them to behave too badly. They are full of feminine charms.

These are excellent wines for refined dishes in which game can play a major role. They are also delicious combined with mild creamy and delicate cheeses. Do not drink this wine too warm, preferable at 17 °C (62.6 °F).

Musigny les Baudes

BONNES MARES GRAND CRU

This is a classical pedigree Burgundy with a beautiful ruby red color, extremely intense and clear. It is enormously aromatic: with an aroma of black cherries, raspberries, tobacco, cherry wood and even truffles and musk when it matures. It is a pleasant, full-bodied soft wine, with a powerful but elegant structure. The taste remains in the mouth for a long time.

This wine just asks for roast beef or game, but is also quite satisfied with good mature cheese.

MUSIGNY GRAND CRU

This wine is one of the pearls of Burgundy. It has a very pure deep ruby red color. In its youth it develops the aromas of pansies and cherry stones. After a few years of maturing in the bottle the bouquet become extremely complex and rich: humus, brushwood, autumn leaves, moss, and some animal odors such as leather or even noble game. As a counterpart to these powerful aromas the wine becomes extremely gentle and round in structure at a later age, velvety, fresh and elegant. The taste remains in the mouth for a long time. Finally you will rediscover the cherry stones combined with exotic wood.

This extremely fascinating wine requires an equally exciting though certainly not too heavy dish. It could accompany red meat or light game (hare/water fowl). This subtle Burgundy is also excellent for accompanying mature, soft creamy cheeses.

Clos de Vougeot

VOUGEOT

Some great wines are made in this tiny village. Although they are almost exclusively red wines, the extremely rare Clos Blanc de Vougeot certainly deserves a mention.

The Vougeot premier cru wines are elegant, fruity (blackcurrants) with occasional hints of pansies and licorice. It is a typical wine for accompanying game such as venison.

CLOS DE VOUGEOT GRAND CRU

No fewer than seventy owners share this vineyard, which covers an area of 50 hectares! The wines are world famous and the price is relatively attractive. Whether this is quite justified is an open question. However, as a buyer, you will find that a glass of this very good wine has a fascinating story to tell you, about the monks of Burgundy who once surrounded the vineyards with a symbolic wall. Did they know the success their wine would have? I doubt it. The beautiful castle of Vougeot is also important for the reputation of this wine. It is still the head office of the famous Burgundian wine brotherhood, Les Chevaliers du Tastevin.

There is no denying that most Clos de Vougeot grand cru wines are of an excellent quality. When they are young, the wines have a magnificent ruby red color, which tends towards a warm reddish and orange color later on. The aromas also evolve with age. At first, you will identify raspberry and wild cherries; later the aroma is more inclined to brushwood, truffles and candied fruit. The wine has a firm structure, and above all it is elegant. The taste is slightly oily, round and fresh at the same time: a very good balance.

The aftertaste is extremely long and delicious. In fact, the name Clos Vougeot on the label is the same as that of Clos de Vougeot.

This wine deserves the very best cuisine you can prepare, for example a tournedos in a red wine sauce, game (venison or boar) or even fowl. If there is any wine left over, drink this with your best cheese.

Echezeaux

Grand Echezeaux grand cru

ECHEZEAUX GRAND CRU

This wine has an intense bright red color, with aromas of fruit (blackcurrants, blackberries, cherries, raspberries), the pips of fruit, cocoa and cedar wood (cigar box). They are very juicy wines, fresh and with a good structure, velvety with a final taste of plain chocolate. The taste remains in the mouth for a long time.

This wine is excellent with more daring combinations such as guinea fowl or duck with peaches, but also with traditionally roasted poultry or even lamb. It is also good with creamy cheeses which do not have a very pronounced taste.

GRANDS-ECHEZEAUX GRAND CRU

These wines have an extremely deep, but very pure, clear garnet color. When the wine is young, the fruit aromas dominate (cherries), with hints of the burnt aroma of cocoa or plain chocolate. After maturing in the bottle for some time, the bouquet changes and it is possible to identify brushwood, truffles and leather, with a hint of cedar wood and tobacco. It is a very elegant classical burgundy with delicate tannins a velvet structure and it is fresh and extremely harmonious. The aftertaste is very long.

A Grands-Echezeaux should accompany meats which do not have a particularly pronounced taste, light game or soft cheese, but is also excellent with lightly cooked lamb with spring vegetable and a sweet and sour onion sauce (*sauce soubise*).

Vosne-Romanée Beaumonts

VOSNE-ROMANÉE

These wines have a beautiful clear color with fascinating reflections and an intriguing aroma of wild cherries, redcurrants, raspberry, cocoa, nutmeg, leather and various vegetable undertones. When it matures it often develops a clear aroma of black truffles. These are extremely rich sophisticated complex wines with a velvety structure and a long aftertaste.

Vosne-Romanée

Richebourg

They go well with hunting scenes, preferably with a still life of mushrooms, but are also easily combined with a delicious piece of cheese.

Do not drink a Vosne-Romanée until it is seven or eight years old.

The premiers crus of Vosne-Romanée are even more refined and rich than the ordinary Vosne-Romanée, but the grands crus from this village are the wines which really steal the show. You will find the most expensive Burgundy wines in Vosne-Romanée, but each and every one is of excellent quality.

RICHEBOURG GRAND CRU

These are fascinating, dark ruby red wines with strong aromas of plums or prunes, black cherries, red fruit (redcurrant) and a hint of cocoa, burnt vanilla, herbs and animal odors. The wine has an extremely powerful taste, very concentrated with great potential for aging. These are real wines to lay down.

Rich dishes accompany this wine very well: meat with rich creamy sauces, for example, or combine the wine with a mature, creamy Époisses: this will bring out the animal in you and in the wine…

LA ROMANÉE GRAND CRU

This is one of the smallest vineyards in France, but what a vineyard! The wines have a very intense ruby red color, with fiery reflections. The aroma is reminiscent of red fruit, cherry liqueur and candied fruit. They are extremely concentrated wines, velvety and generous.

This is an excellent choice with roast veal, which may be stuffed with mincemeat and mushrooms.

LA ROMANÉE-CONTI GRAND CRU

The same applies here as for the wines of La Romanée, except that these wines are possibly even finer and more elegant, with a clear expression of the terroir. This is a sublime wine for the happy few, one of the most impressive experiences in the life of a wine lover.

Romanée-Saint-Vivant

This jewel requires a real jewel of the French cuisine, a typical game casserole with a red wine sauce and lots of mushrooms.

ROMANÉE-SAINT-VIVANT GRAND CRU

Like the other grands crus from Romanée, this wine has a deep, intense ruby red color. The youthful aromas of red fruit, blackberries, raspberries, black cherries, candied fruit and fruit liqueur are replaced for a more vegetable bouquet with nuances of moss, brushwood, truffles and noble game. The structure is full-bodied and robust, the taste fresh, elegant and juicy. You will rediscover the ripe fruit in the aftertaste, this time with a hint of exotic spices.

With this wine, serve dishes of game or roast beef with sophisticated sauces. Or you could confront the wine with a mature cheese: a powerful but loving end to a festive meal. Lay these wines down for at least ten to fifteen years.

LA GRANDE RUE GRAND CRU

This wine is less well know and less complex than its grandparents from Vosne-Romanée. It was given the name to denote its origin fairly recently (1992) and must still prove that it is an acquisition for this region.

Côte de Nuits villages

LESS WELL-KNOWN WINES

In addition to the great wines described above, there are countless less well-known wines, though they are certainly no less interesting. We will focus on some of these here.

CÔTES DE NUITS

These wines cannot wait to be discovered and accompany a good entrecote in a red wine sauce.

CÔTES DE NUITS VILLAGES

This wine is possibly more characteristic than the ordinary Côtes de Nuits, with slightly more terroir. It has a ruby red color, pure and clear, with tempting aromas of cherries and other small red and black forest fruit, with a hint of herbs and spices in the aroma and taste. After maturing in the bottle for a few years, it also develops a bouquet of mushrooms and brushwood. These wines are still slightly rough and restless in their youth, but become soft and supple after a few years.

Drink these wonderful and relatively cheap wines at a temperature of 16–18 °C (60.8–64.4 °F) with roast or grilled meat, hare or other game and then drink it with your cheese.

Nuits-Saint-Georges

Aloxe-Corton

NUITS-SAINT-GEORGES

These wines are a garnet red color and have intense but very sophisticated aromas of cherries, wood and herbs which change as the wine matures to the characteristic aroma of noble game. The taste is stubborn, meaty, juicy and velvety at the same time. In the aftertaste you will discover a great concentration of ripe fruit with occasional spices. Do not drink these wines too young, and certainly not before their tenth birthday, and make sure they are not too warm (16–17 °C/60.8–62.6 °F).

A Nuit-Saint-Georges combines perfectly with game, boeuf bourgignon garnished with delicious potatoes, chestnuts and mushrooms, but is also excellent with a ripe Burgundian cheese.

Côte de Beaune

Côte de Beaune, between Ladoix-Serrigny and Maranges, is particularly known for its white wines.

LADOIX

Ladoix (pronounced: 'ladwah') is another example of a wine still far too unknown. Yet here we are right next door to the world-famous Corton vineyards. Ladoix wines have a ruby-red color with amber tints. An enticing bouquet, in which spices, leather and brushwood predominate. The taste is soft and fruity with a long aftertaste. Drink these Ladoix wines at a temperature of about 16 °C (60.8 °F). Open them a little beforehand to let them breathe.

Excellent with all kinds of meat, poultry or game. Try them some time with a traditional dish of duck with cherry sauce or rabbit with mustard sauce.

Some white Ladoix is also made; they are dry, and the nose has a vegetable connotation with a hint of hazelnuts and dried fruits. Charming, concentrated wines.

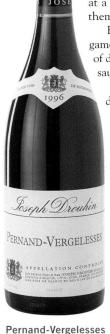

Pernand-Vergelesses

ALOXE-CORTON

Robust, concentrated wines that travel well. The color is sometimes a little odd, full and deep, varying from ochre to rust-colored! This is from the presence of iron in the soil. In the nose you meet all kinds of red and ripe fruits from cherries and plums to raspberries, blackberries and blackcurrants. Splendid wines, full and powerful, with traces of spices and wood in the long aftertaste.

A classic Aloxe Corton 'shouts' for game, roast beef… or a ripe Burgundian cheese.

PERNAND-VERGELESSES

The white Pernand-Vergelesses are scarcer and less well known than the reds. They have a lovely golden color, typically Chardonnay, with a light hint of green. In the better years the nose is reminiscent of honey, honeysuckle, citrus fruits and an explosion of tropical fruits. At the start the wood may still be a little too dominant, but that changes after a year's maturing in bottle. The taste is rich and full, with great tenderness and charm.

An ideal accompaniment to freshwater fish (pike) poached in white wine. Or be wicked and serve a plump lobster or crab with it. Various kinds of white meat and rabbit also go well with a Pernand-Vergelesses, as does lightly roasted guinea-fowl breast with a creamy crayfish sauce.

The red wines have a ruby-red color and a remarkable nose, where wild sloes accompany Russian fur, hazelnuts, blackcurrants, spices and chocolate. A fabulous taste, both full and fat, velvety-soft and powerful, with a very long aftertaste.

In Burgundy they like to drink red Pernand-Vergelesses with veal kidneys fried pink and served with mustard sauce, but a good veal or pork roast with the same sauce will also go well with it.

CORTON GRAND CRU

Another very well-known wine, not because it is better than other Burgundies, but mainly because thanks to its structure it can travel well anywhere in Europe and even to Africa and America without losing its quality.

The wine has a very intense red color, powerful aromas of crystallized fruits, plums, musk and brushwood as it ages, with a dash of pepper and spices. These full, powerful, fat and tannin-rich wines must be allowed extra maturing in bottle; it will greatly enhance the taste. The wine has a very long and full aftertaste.

Corton-Bressandes Grand Cru
A few great white wines, including Corton-Charlemagne, Montrachet and Chevalier-Montrachet.

Corton-Bressandes grand cru

**Savigny-lès-Beaune
Premier Cru**

This wine is very suitable to drink at table with good friends, in the winter, by an open fire. Serve it with rich meat-dishes, roast game, or ripe Burgundian cheeses.

CORTON-CHARLEMAGNE GRAND CRU

The vineyards for these magnificent white wines are said to have been planted on the orders of the great emperor Charlemagne, famous for his vanity. He was fond of red wine, but spilt so much of it down his splendid white beard that he had – reluctantly – to change to white. But at least to a good one!

These white wines are very pure and clear, with a typical Chardonnay nose in which warm butter, toast, grilled almonds and hazelnuts are recognizable, with here and there a hint of honey and minerals; very full, almost thick wines, capable of presenting themselves as perfect ambassadors of good Burgundian living.

Take care not to drink them too cold (12–14 °C/54–57 °F) and serve them with a lightly seasoned chicken dish with, for instance, a creamy tarragon sauce.

SAVIGNY-LÈS-BEAUNE

Magnificent white wines with a wide variety of fruity, floral and even mineral aromas. Full and elegant, with sometimes a plump aftertaste. Extremely full of taste with suggestions of white fruits (apples, pears or peaches) and a hint of fresh toasted bread with melting butter.

Thinking of plumpness, toast and melting butter, you may associate the wine with *foie gras*. However, on a weekday these wines will be very happy with a fricassee of white meat or poultry.

Perhaps better known are the red wines of Savigny. They have a beautiful ruby-red color and aromas of wild fruits with a touch of pepper, very characteristic of the region.

Delicious, delicate and supple wines, which would embellish any hunting scene.

Chorey-lès-Beaune

**Beaune (du Château)
Premier Cru**

The better *premier-cru* wines demand better cuts of meat, a serving of pink-roasted lamb or a sirloin steak, for instance.

CHOREY-LÈS-BEAUNE

A splendid wine to look at, with its pure, clear, and decorative cherry-red color. The wine has very intense, predominantly fruity aromas (raspberries, pomegranate, blackberries and cherries) which later change into classic flavors such as crystallized fruit, brushwood and game. This not really complicated wine has a good structure and a full, supple and velvety-soft taste.

Chorey-lès Beaune will actually go with any good meat or poultry dish. It also goes very well with not too ripe cheeses.

Beaune Grèves

BEAUNE

The very old vineyards round Beaune produce numerous excellent red wines. The strength of this wine-growing area lies in the *premier-cru* plots, of which those of Les Grèves are the best known and probably the best.

The wines are very rich in color, deep and clear. The youthful aromas of red fruits and spices, with here and there a hint of blackcurrants, soon make way for more robust aromas, often reminiscent of smoke and tobacco. Very concentrated wines, robust and complex, which become a little softer after a few years maturing in bottle.

Excellent wines with grilled beef and a red wine gravy.

**Beaune Clos des
Mouches Blanc**

**Beaune Clos des
Mouches Rouge**

Volnay Chevrôt | Volnay Santenots | Volnay

Another well-known *premier cru* is that of Clos des Mouches, available in white or red. The white wines are a light golden color, very clear. The nose is reminiscent of butter, honey, almonds and lemon balm; later of hazelnuts and grilled dried fruits.

Serve these wines not too cold (13–14°C/ 55–57°F) with freshwater fish, crustaceans (lobster, crab) or shells (scallops) or with white meat or poultry in rich sauces. A good alternative for people who do not favor a sweet wine with their *foie gras*.

The red Clos des Mouches have a light ruby-red color, and aromas of ripe cherries, spices and some smoky scents. They are full, elegant, yet powerful wines which go well with red meat and fine cheeses. Don't serve them too warm (16–18 °C/61–64 °F).

CÔTES DE BEAUNE

Uncommon red wines. In general they are fairly rich in tannin. A substantial Burgundian casserole goes very well with these wines.

CÔTES DE BEAUNE VILLAGES

First-class red wines from the vineyards of some sixteen villages, which the locals prefer to drink young, within three to five years after the harvest.

Drink these wines at a temperature of about 17°C (63 °F) with local casseroles and not too ripe cheeses.

Côtes de Beaune
Villages

POMMARD

Beyond any doubt Pommard is the best known Burgundian appellation in the world. The sound of the name is like the taste of the wine: a thunderclap on a warm fall evening.

A highly captivating red color, very powerful smell (black cherries, spices, leather) and taste. Full, fat wine, both powerful and harmonious: a more traditional Burgundy is hard to find.

Excellent with red meat, grilled game and poultry, robust Burgundian casseroles and strong-tasting cheeses.

Pommard has several *premiers crus*, of which the most famous and best are Rugiens and Epenots.

VOLNAY

These red wines seem, oddly enough, to be better known and more popular among painters, sculptors and authors than among gourmets. Perhaps for their almost artistic, tender and feminine side – Volnay is certainly no macho wine!

The wines have a clear red color, very pure. When they are young, they have aromas of violets and black-currants or sloes; later they acquire a more complex bouquet with a variety of fruits, flowers, spices and mushrooms.

These round, velvety wines – all sensuality – are excellent companions for tender (white) meat dishes, rabbit or poultry.

Here, too, the better wines come from the *premier cru* vineyards. These wines deserve rather more sophisticated dishes. Serve them, for example, with pink-fried lamb or red meat with elegant sauces.

MONTHÉLIE

For some unknown reason Monthélie has still not really been discovered. However, some very pleasant white and red wines are made locally, which can certainly hold their own among those of neighboring Volnay. These are wines for wily customers who want quality at

Pommard Rugiens | Pommard | Pommard Epenots

a lower price. The question is how long this will last. One day the world will be ashamed at not having discovered Monthélie earlier, if only because of its (still) extremely favorable price/quality ratio!

The white wines are the weaker of the two brothers. They are classic Burgundian Chardonnays, full of butter and (sometimes too much) wood in the nose, and a soft, full taste. The better white Monthélie wines also have the specific suggestions of toast, white flowers and honey, with here and there some blonde tobacco.

Auxey-Duresses

A white Monthélie accompanies rather richer starters without difficulty.

The red Monthélie wines have an attractive, clear and pleasant red color. The nose is very fruity when they are young (blackberries, bilberries, blackcurrants) with sometimes some hints of flowers (violets). At a later age the wines acquire the classic smells of brushwood and mushrooms, while the fruit becomes more reminiscent of traditional home-made jam. They are rich, supple, generous and friendly wines, which only give all they have got after a few years maturing in bottle.

Drink them with sophisticated meat dishes. Try some sweet-and-sour sauces in which fruit (blackcurrants, cherries, blackberries) and a drop of liqueur from the same fruit has been used.

AUXEY-DURESSES

The two sides of the hill are very different. On one side red wine is made; white on the other.

The white Auxey-Duresses are light-yellow in color, very aromatic (fruity and mineral) with sometimes a dash of exotic fruit (mango). The taste is warm, open and generous. A wine that puts on no airs, and among other things goes surprisingly well with creamy vegetable dishes. This is the wine for the gastronomically-inclined vegetarian! And still affordable, too!

The red Auxey-Duresses steal the show. But be sure not to drink them too young, because they can still be quite rough. The color often tends towards garnet red, and the aromas are reminiscent of ripe fruit. Warm, full wines with plenty of structure.

Drink them with rather richer local stews. The better *premier cru* wines, once they have reached a respectable age, are a good match for truffles.

SAINT-ROMAIN

Although very acceptable red wines are also made, it is the white wines that are most rewarding here. They are very typical Chardonnay wines, light-golden colored, sometimes with a trace of green and with sophisticated aromas of white flowers and white fruits (pears, mirabelles, peaches). In smell and taste you will detect plenty of butter, hazelnuts, almonds and sometimes toasted dried fruits.

Rich and complex wines which will go well with roast veal and pork.

MEURSAULT

Meursault wines are famous all over the world for their lovely yellow-gold color and their intensive aromas of butter, honey, hazelnuts and lime blossom, sometimes with surprising hints of wildflowers (may) and gingerbread. Soft as silk, full and generous with a lingering aftertaste.

Meursault Charmes

Meursault Les Criots

Enjoy a young Meursault as an aperitif or with light starters. A rather more mature Meursault is excellent with freshwater fish, veal fricassée or creamy poultry dishes, for instance, garnished with white asparagus or tender vegetables. Don't drink Meursault at less than 12 °C (54 °F).

The rather better *premier cru* Meursault wines can easily be matched with a creamy *foie gras*, but they are happier in the company of a plump lobster or a crisply

Puligny-Montrachet

Puligny-Montrachet Les Folatières

fried sweetbread. A fresh or half-ripe goat's cheese to finish with will make it curl up with pleasure.

There is also a red Meursault, fruity and pleasant, but this wine is never really convincing.

BLAGNY

Elegant red wines, with a great deal of feminine charm. No high-fliers. Drink these wines with traditional casseroles or with an improvised lunch.

PULIGNY-MONTRACHET

The 'ordinary' Puligny-Montrachet are standard examples of sophistication and complexity. Light golden in color, with aromas of white flowers and fruit, sometimes with honey, grilled dried fruits, almonds and quinces. In the better years they also develop aromas of tropical fruits. Very fine wines, fresh and soft as silk, with an enormous variety of flowers and fruits in the taste and the lingering aftertaste.

Drink Puligny-Montrachet wines young as an aperitif before a special meal, or when a little more mature with freshwater fish (trout, salmon, bass) or scallops. They also go marvelously well with fresh goat's cheese.

The *premier cru* wines (such as Folatières and Clos de la Garenne) are more complex in their aromas: freshly cut hay, honey, fresh almonds, dried fruits, spices…

These wines should really be kept for some years (at least five) before you can enjoy all their qualities with, for instance, a helping of *foie gras*, fish (turbot) in a rich sauce, lobster, scallops, or simply a creamy white fish dish. Don't drink them too cold, about 13 °C (55 °F).

Montrachet Grand Cru Marquis de Laguiche

MONTRACHET GRAND CRU

This Montrachet (pronounce mon-rah-chay) is one of the pillars upholding the good name of Burgundy wines in and outside France.

A fabulous light-golden color. These wines need a considerable number of years to let the aroma trapped in the wine come to its full development. Anyone drinking this wine too young will be disappointed, because its nose is still rather blocked. So be patient. After about five years an almost unimaginable bouquet develops in which the youthful exotic fruit combines with

Le Montrachet: one of the best vineyards in the world

the scents of exotic wood, citrus fruit, spices, flowers (such as lilies of the valley), white fruit (peaches) and almonds… Some vineyards add a light mineral undertone as well. The wines are fresh and round, full and elegant, sophisticated and tempting. The aftertaste lingers on. Drink this rare and costly wine at a temperature of 13 °C or even 14° C (55–57 °F).

There is little choice in the dishes which can accompany Montrachet wines: your best *foie gras* or lobster with a creamy cheese sauce (Mornay sauce), for example, or perhaps scallops or a fresh turbot would thank you for such an honor.

Bienvenues-Bâtard-Montrachet Grand Cru

CHEVALIER-MONTRACHET

Gold-colored, with very tempting aromas of butter, toast and vegetable undertones, here and there with hints of minerals. Full, warm, generous and succulent wines, very aromatic in taste.

These well-balanced and elegant wines go well with all kinds of freshwater fish.

BÂTARD-MONTRACHET

Another scion of the Montrachet family which should be left in peace for the first few years to be enjoyed fully. The color is then a clear, pure golden yellow, and the aromas fly out of the glass: exotic fruit, luxury rolls with warm butter, exotic wood, almonds, honey… Fresh and silken-soft taste with a hint of tannins and a lingering aftertaste.

Drink these wines at a temperature of about 13 °C (55 °F) with gently fried duck's liver, fine shellfish, crayfish or crisply fried veal sweetbreads.

BIENVENUES-BÂTARD-MONTRACHET

Golden yellow with a hint of green. Very fruity aromas and a little toast, butter, citrus fruits, and sometimes a typical flint undertone.

This full, fresh and fruity wine calls for crustaceans or shellfish.

CRIOTS-BÂTARD-MONTRACHET GRAND CRU

Very rare white wine. Similar in many ways to that of Bienvenues-Bâtard-Montrachet, particularly in respect of the typical flint smell and taste.

This elegant fruity wine is happy with a few crayfish.

CHASSAGNE-MONTRACHET

Once only red wines were made here. Now the whites and the reds balance each other.

The white Chassagne-Montrachets are light gold in color and have a very intense nose in which you can recognize luxury bread rolls or butter croissants, as well as flowers, citrus fruits and later on grilled almonds and spices. In some wines a mineral smell and taste is also detectable. In general the white Chassagne-Montrachet wines are fresh, full of character, succulent and very sophisticated.

Drink them with *foie gras*, freshwater fish, crustaceans or shellfish and all kinds of white meat.

The red Chassagne-Montrachets have a dark red color, aromas of ripe cherries, blackcurrants and other forest fruits, with a hint of licorice. Most of the wines are well structured, full and fat.

Serve them with an oven-roasted leg of lamb (above all, don't forget the garlic!) or with duck meat and young vegetables.

SAINT-AUBIN

Although red wines are made here, too, it is predominantly its white wines which uphold the honor of Saint-Aubin.

The color of this wine is a pale golden-yellow and the nose is reminiscent of flowers (such as acacia), yellow plums and almonds. Later the smell changes to

Chassagne-Montrachet
Blanc

Chassagne-Montrachet
Rouge

Santenay

Santenay Premier Cru
Beaurepaire

dried fruits and honey. They are fine wines, fresh and generous, with sometimes some plumpness and a mineral undertone. A very aromatic taste and aftertaste.

Get to know these less well-known Burgundies over a light starter of shellfish, or just as an aperitif.

Maranges Premier Cru

SANTENAY

Ruby-red wines with aromas of red fruit and forest fruit (blackberries, bilberries). When they are young the tannins can still be fairly rough. This changes after a few years maturing in bottle. Once mature, a good Santenay develops fascinating wild aromas of brushwood and truffles.

These still too often underestimated wines appreciate something with character. Serve them with wildfowl or robust Burgundian casseroles.

The white wines are in general not highfliers. Choose one from a *premier-cru* vineyard, because they are really worth the effort. They are full, fruity wines with a clearly recognizable Chardonnay character: butter, luxury rolls, toast, hazelnuts, citrus fruits and white flowers.

Again an excellent wine for our vegetarian readers. It goes extremely well with fried field mushrooms, but a white Santenay will never turn down a freshwater fish or a chicken dish.

White Burgundy   Red Burgundy

MARANGES

Less well-known wine region where white and red wines are made.

The white wines (preferably choose one from a *premier cru* vineyard) are fruity (apricot, almonds) and fresh, with a slightly fat taste, full of tenderness and elegance.

Excellent as an aperitif on Sundays or with light starters.

The red Maranges (and certainly the *premier cru* wines) are of outstanding quality. The best have a high concentration of color, smell and taste.

These very aromatic wines, with hints of ripe red fruit and black cherries, licorice and spices, require robust opponents, such as wildfowl or even venison (roe deer).

Generic Burgundies

Before we move south, a few general wines are reviewed here.

BOURGOGNE

The white Bourgogne AOC (Chardonnay) are aromatic, fresh white wines which do well as aperitifs or with fish or white meat starters. Drink them at nearly 11 °C (52 °F), preferably within two years of the harvest.

The red Bourgogne AOC (Pinot Noir) are ruby-red in color and smell of red fruits and forest fruits (raspberries, blackcurrants, blackberries and redcurrants).

Drink these wines at a temperature of about 16 °C (61 °F), within five years of the harvest.

These supple, generous and friendly wines should go particularly well with cold meats, white meat, poultry or cheeses, but also with vegetable dishes with cheese sauce and pasta *au gratin*.

Also in this category come Bourgogne Villages or Bourgogne AOC with the addition of a more narrowly defined place of origin. Examples are: Bourgogne, with the addition of Chitry, Coulanges-La-Vineuse, Epineuil, Côtes-Saint-Jacques, Montrecul, Le Chapitre, Chapelle Notre Dame, Côtes d'Auxerre, Vezelay, Côtes du Couchois and Bourgogne-Côte Châlonnaise.

BOURGOGNE PASSE-TOUT-GRAIN

The red wines are made of at least one-third Pinot Noir grapes, to which Gamay grapes are added. However, the better wines are made with a predominance of Pinot Noir. They are light, cheerful and generous wines which should be drunk young.

In Burgundy they are often served with the local *jambon persillé* (spiced ham in aspic) but they also go well with ham served hot on the bone or light starters and with most kinds of cheese that are not too strong.

For the record: there is also a rare rosé variety.

The white Rully wines have a very pure and clear white golden color, very tempting aromas (broom, almond, citrus fruit) and a fresh and elegant taste with hints of fruit and flowers.

This wine combines very well with fish and shellfish, but can also serve very well as an aperitif, with a few cheese puffs, or as a luncheon wine, perhaps with a fresh goat's cheese.

When young the ruby-red Rully smells of red fruits (blackberries, blackcurrants, red-currants) and later evolves into wines with tastes of riper fruits, dashes of tobacco and wet autumn undergrowth. The taste is typical of Burgundy, fat and fresh, with elegant tannins and plenty of fruit, particularly in the aftertaste.

Such wines go excellently with poultry and rabbit cooked with mushrooms. Or make a rather more adventurous choice: roast pork with blackcurrant sauce. A red Rully served

Mercurey

Bouchard's historic maturing cellars (15th century)

BOURGOGNE GRAND ORDINAIRE

You will no longer meet this appellation very often. It sounds too 'ordinary' for a Burgundy. Yet in this category you will often find very acceptable white, red or rosé wine at a very reasonable price.

BOURGOGNE ALIGOTÉ

Very popular in Burgundy and far beyond. These very fresh wines with often marked acidity possess many aromas of green apples, lemon and white flowers (hawthorn) with occasionally a hint of flint.

Drink them neat, as an aperitif, with or without a few cheese puffs (*gougères*). However, you can also mix them with a little blackcurrant liqueur (Crème de Cassis), as Canon Kir, who has meanwhile become famous, used to do. His name is now associated across the world with this refreshing drink: Kir.

Côte Châlonnaise

Between Chagny, Montagny and Couches, the Côte Châlonnaise will surprise many visitors.

RULLY

The soil of limestone and stones gives these white and red wines a great deal of aromatic subtlety.

Givry premier cru

cool in fact goes surprisingly well with freshwater fish in a red wine sauce.

MERCUREY

Most white Mercureys (pronounced: mer-cu-ray) are light, friendly and above all uncomplicated aperitif wines.

The red Mercurey have a lovely ruby-red color and fruity aromas (blackcurrants, redcurrants and cherries) often with a touch of spices.

This and their fruity taste (cherries!) make them good accompaniments to duck breast fillets with a sweet-and-sour cherry sauce, but they also soon adapt themselves to all kinds of red meat or a cheese board.

Rully Blanc

Givry

GIVRY

Just like their neighbors in Montagny, the white wines of Givry are completely underrated wines from the Chardonnay grape, and they are therefore also extremely favorably priced for the quality they offer. There are a few very good white Givry wines with delightful aromas of acacia, hawthorn, apple, almond and sometimes lime blossom and lilac as well. These full, fat white wines can be found in the extremely reliable Guide Hachette. Drink a white Givry with freshwater fish.

The red Givrys are very rich in color and intensely aromatic (redcurrants, blackcurrants) with a spicy undertone as they grow older. Meaty wines with great subtlety and a pleasant fruity taste. They really go with almost anything: white or red meat, poultry, roasts, light game or cheese.

MONTAGNY

The best Montagnys have a light and nondescript color, but a very rich variety of aromas: apple, citrus fruit, fresh almonds, fern, hazelnuts and butter. The taste is supple, elegant, fresh and rounded.

Drink a Montagny as an aperitif or at a meal with freshwater fish, shellfish or a light starter. A Montagny is also an excellent choice if you are looking for a smart picnic or luncheon wine.

BOURGOGNE ALIGOTÉ DE BOUZERON

This is a step up from the ordinary Aligoté AOC. Extremely pleasant, fresh wines with a tempting nose of flowers (roses, peonies) and white fruits, here and there accompanied by some spices (cinnamon).

This wine is very suitable as an aperitif, but don't mix this Bourgogne Aligoté with Crème de Cassis: that would be a waste.

Mâconnais

The Mâconnais, between Senecey-le-grand and Saint-Vérand, is pre-eminently the domain of 'fast' charmers.

MÂCON, MÂCON SUPÉRIEUR, MÂCON VILLAGES

With a few exceptions, the ordinary white Mâcons are uncomplicated, excellent wines which you don't have to think about for long.

Drink these friendly, fruity Chardonnays young, as an aperitif, at lunch or with a light starter.

Their red opposite numbers are of rather better quality. They are made of Pinot Noir and Gamay. The more Gamay

included in the wine, the friendlier, more generous and often fruitier the wines are. However, some Mâcon with a lot of Pinot Noir can be powerful and tannic, with a great deal of structure, especially if it has been raised on wood.

Pouilly Fuissé

Serve red Mâcon with beef casseroles or just drink the wine when you happen to feel like it.

The better wines from the Mâconnais – and there are some – are labeled with their own appellations.

POUILLY-FUISSÉ

Chardonnay always does well on lime soil, and that is clearly noticeable from the wines. Pouilly-Fuissé has a very clear, light golden-yellow color, aromas of fresh grapes and almonds and a succulent fresh taste with much elegance. The wines, which are raised on oak, also develop the characteristic aromas of vanilla, toast, hazelnuts and grilled almonds.

The wines are excellent companions to all poultry dishes, fish, shellfish or cold meats.

POUILLY-VINZELLES, POUILLY-LOCHÉ, VIRÉ-CLESSÉ

Less well known and in general rather lighter than the wines of Pouilly-Fuissé. They are often elegant, very aromatic wines (butter, lemon, flowers, grapefruit) which always do well as an aperitif or with freshwater fish in a cream sauce.

Mâcon Villages

St-Véran

Burgundian wine cellars in Beaune

SAINT-VÉRAN

The name of these exceptional wines from the region bordering the Beaujolais is spelt without a final 'd'; the name of the village of Saint-Vérand has a 'd'.

Saint-Véran wines are light, elegant and fruity, eminently suitable for an aperitif, but they also go well with pork or cold meats. Try a Saint-Véran with soft cheeses.

BEAUJOLAIS

Although the Beaujolais region is officially part of Burgundy, it is usually treated as an independent unit. This is done because the wines from the Beaujolais have an identity of their own, to some extent reinforced by the very active publicity campaigns for this precocious little brother of Burgundy. Obviously the best known

Beaujolais is still Beaujolais Primeur, perhaps better known as Beaujolais Nouveau, which is marketed year by year with a great fanfare. There is, however, much more to discover in the Beaujolais region. There are at least twelve different local appellations.

HISTORY

The name of this region is derived from the lords of Beaujeu, who were lord and master of it in the ninth, tenth and eleventh centuries. Not until the fourteenth century did the Beaujeu lands pass to the French crown, after a well-calculated marriage. In 1514 the town of Villefranche, founded by Humbert III in 1140, became the official capital of the Beaujolais region. From the seventeenth century onwards Villefranche developed into an industrial center, based mainly on the leather and textile industries. These activities were substantially enlarged in the nineteenth century. Today the region has three major activities: trade and industry, the wine trade, and farming and forestry.

THE REGION

The Beaujolais region starts some $6^1/2$ miles below Mâcon in the department of the Rhone. It is a relatively small region: 40 miles long by $7^1/2$ miles wide. It extends over the hilly ridges bordering the valley of the Saône.

The region is divided into two sub-regions. The better wines, the ten *crus* and the Beaujolais Villages are made in the north (Haut Beaujolais). The soil here consists chiefly of granite and quartz fragments on a bed of slate.

The southern section (Bas Beaujolais) has a soil consisting of a mixture of clay and limestone. Here is where most of the ordinary Beaujolais wines are made: white, rosé and red.

The king of Beaujolais, Georges Duboeuf and his son Franck

The 'hameau du vin' (wine hamlet) in Beaujolais: museum and temple

THE VINEYARDS

Only about 2 % of the vineyards are planted with chardonnay grapes. A very rare white Beaujolais is made from these. The remainder of the vineyards are planted with gamay. This is used to make a little rosé, but mainly red wines.

THE MANUFACTURE OF BEAUJOLAIS

In recent decades the winegrowers of the Beaujolais region have realized that a better and above all more environmentally-conscious protection of their vineyards, together with an improvement of their plant and more hygiene in their cellars, would greatly benefit the quality of their wines. Regrettably there are also wine producers in the Beaujolais who seem only interested in making a quick profit. This is unfair to the hard-working winegrowers who put quality before quantity and do their best to improve the quality of their wines. Nor are the consumers entirely innocent. Anyone buying Beaujolais Nouveau for less than three Euros is conniving at the theft of the good name of Beaujolais!

CARBONIC MACERATION

When we talk of Beaujolais, we talk of carbonic maceration. This vinification technique, used throughout the region, works as follows: the gamay grapes are collected as quickly as possible after the harvest in large vats (wood, cement or stainless steel). The bunches of grapes are left intact on their stalks. The grapes at the bottom are gently crushed by the actual weight of the bunches. In the juice this produces (10 to 30 % of the total volume of the vat) fermentation starts slowly. The sugars in the juice are converted by the fermentation into alcohol and carbon dioxide. The carbon dioxide rises and pushes up the 'head' of the bunches. During this soak in carbon dioxide the alcohol breaks down the coloring and the tannins, which in their turn are taken up in the fermenting liquid. The concentration of carbon dioxide is greatest at the top of the vat. Under the great pressure the grapes themselves are metabolized. They ferment, as it were, from inside outwards. Alcohol is produced and the content of malic acid drastically reduced. But just as important and characteristic of this method of vinification is that the absence of oxygen guarantees the preservation of an abundant fruitiness in smell and taste.

After this soaking in carbon dioxide, which lasts from four to ten days, depending on the type of wine you want to make, the *vin de goutte* (seepage wine) is tapped. The remaining mass of grapes is then gently pressed and the *vin de presse* (pressed wine) produced in this way is added to the tapped wine. For some *cuvées* only seepage wine is sometimes used. These wines are often recognizable by the celestial appellation on the label: 'Paradis'. This is what they call the sweet, very fruity and aromatic seepage wine in France.

When the alcoholic fermentation is finished, the second fermentation (malolactic fermentation) follows, in which the hard malic acids are converted into soft lactic acids. The young wines are then ready for immediate consumption (Beaujolais Primeur or Nouveau) or for further processing (Beaujolais, Beaujolais Villages, Crus du Beaujolais).

BEAUJOLAIS PRIMEUR

Faithful to tradition, these young, extremely fruity wines are sold from the third Thursday of November onwards. Seasoned wine tasters see these young wines merely as a forecast of what the results of the vintage may be and don't make a meal of it. In their view the arrival of Beaujolais Primeur (or Nouveau) is more a custom than a fashion, and for them exaggerated folkloric fuss around it is unnecessary. In any event, it is up to you if you choose to buy it or not, but avoid the cheaper specimens which have really nothing to offer but a stomach ache and a hangover. Always drink the better Beaujolais Primeur (if possible a Beaujolais Villages Primeur) cool, at about 10 °C (50 °F).

The terms Beaujolais Primeur and Beaujolais Nouveau are often used as alternatives, even by the French themselves. Originally 'Beaujolais Nouveau' meant no more than the 'young wine of the year', but these days the producers no longer differentiate between the two terms.

A Beaujolais Primeur is specially vinified (a short four-day soaking) so that it can be drunk within six months of the harvest. The wine is then at its best in terms of fruitiness. After these six months nothing much happens to the wine, and certainly nothing happens suddenly, as some people fear. The wine slowly loses its fruit and then tastes more like an ordinary rather flat table wine. Still fine for cooking, but no longer really pleasant to drink. However, the better Beaujolais Villages Primeur can be drunk for up to a year after the harvest, without a problem.

The traditional 'pot', a half-liter bottle for ordinary Beaujolais

BEAUJOLAIS

This ordinary Beaujolais comes in white, rosé and red. On more than 25,000 acres/39 squared miles of mainly lime soil, light fruity wines

Beaujolais Blanc

Beaujolais

are made which go particularly well with the local *charcuterie* (cold meats), but also with various cheeses without too pronounced a taste, and all kinds of local dishes. Drink these wines at a temperature of around 11 °C (52 °F) whenever you feel like it. A Beaujolais is very adaptable to whatever you want.

Since the existence of the most southerly Burgundian appellation for white wines, Saint-Véran, the production of white Beaujolais has sharply declined. Beaujolais Blanc is made of Chardonnay (with sometimes a little Aligoté). The wine smells and tastes fresh and fruity. Here, too, the experienced taster can detect a hint of hazelnuts, mint, butter and sometimes some green vegetables, such as paprika.

The wines are preeminently suitable for aperitifs, but can accompany any fish or chicken.

Graceful 'major' flagon for Beaujolais Villages   Beaujolais Villages

BEAUJOLAIS VILLAGES

There are thirty-nine communes that can carry the label AOC Beaujolais Villages. These are soft, generous wines with a splendid cherry-red color and plenty of fruit in the smell and taste (blackcurrants, strawberries).

Drink a Beaujolais Villages at a temperature of 11–12°C (52–54°F).

THE TEN CRUS

Côtes de Brouilly

The local 'wine wisdom' tells us that Easter must be over before these better wines are at their best: '*Les Crus du Beaujolais doivent faire leurs Pâques*' (The Beaujolais Crus must make their Easter Communion). So you will not usually find them in the shops any earlier. Only after a few months rest do the ten *crus* develop fully into mature wines.

CÔTE DE BROUILLY

Round the 485 m (1600 ft) high hill of Brouilly, on a granite and slate soil, are two of the ten Beaujolais *crus*. You find the 750 acres of the Côte de Brouilly vineyard on the sunny side of the volcanic hill.

The wine has a purple-red color and a very sophisticated and elegant nose of fresh grapes and irises. Leave a Côte de Brouilly to rest for some time before you open it.

Drink the wine at about 13 °C (55 °F) with cold meats, or perhaps rabbit chasseur or a grilled steak.

BROUILLY

Here the vineyards are rather larger, some 3,000 acres (4.7 squared miles). The soil is mainly granite and sand. The wines have a ruby-red color and a fruity nose in which red fruit, plums and sometimes peaches are clearly detectable. In the better Brouillys you can also sometimes detect a hint of minerals. They are full, dark wines with a robust taste. Drink them at about 12 °C (54 °F) with game, red meat or stews. The local combination of this wine with a casserole of freshwater fish in red wine is very striking.

Régnié

RÉGNIÉ

These 1,300 acres (2 squared miles) of vineyards were only recognized as a Beaujolais Cru in 1988. The ground is gently sloping and moderately high (average 1,000 ft. Here rather supple wines are made, elegant and tempting. The color is a pure cherry-red and the aromas reminiscent of red fruits (raspberries, redcurrants, blackberries) with here and there a hint of flowers. The fruit in this wine is best when you drink it young, within two years of the harvest.

Serve the wine at a temperature of about 12 °C (54 °F) with cold meats, patés and terrines, white meat, poultry or light starters with a creamy sauce.

CHIROUBLES

The vineyards lie round the village of Chiroubles on a granite soil at a height of around 400 m (1,300 ft). On such acid and poor subsoil only vines will grow; other crops are not

Brouilly

Chiroubles

at home there. The subtle, sophisticated, light-colored wines are very tempting and can almost be called feminine. The smell is reminiscent of a complex bouquet of wildflowers, in which violets, peonies and lilies of the valley predominate.

Morgon

Serve Chiroubles at 12 °C (54 °F) with cold meats, poultry, white meat or starters, particularly with salads containing slightly bitter vegetables, such as artichoke hearts or green asparagus.

MORGON

Morgon is mentioned in the local wine records as long ago as the tenth century. The Morgon vineyards, of 2,700 acres (4.2 squared miles), lie on a soil of granite and schistose slate. The Morgon wines are full-bodied, powerful and generous and can age well. They possess a great aromatic variety reminiscent mainly of stone fruit, such as cherries, peaches, apricots and plums. A Morgon which has reached a respectable age may also acquire an undertone of cherry brandy or kirsch, and starts increasingly to resemble Burgundy.

Drink a Morgon at 13 °C (55 °F). Good with casseroles, red meat with rich gravy, or even game.

Fleurie

FLEURIE

In a 2,000 acre (3.1 squared miles) vineyard, at the foot of the Black Madonna, one of the fruitiest, but also – the name says it already – the most floral *cru* of the Beaujolais is produced. Igneous and granite rocks give the wines of Fleurie something special; a rare sophistication and feminine charm and, above all, powerful aromas of, for example, irises, violets and roses. The color is a pure ruby-red with marvelous reflections; the taste is velvety soft and at the same time fleshy. A good Fleurie from a top year can become reasonably old, ten years or more.

Drink a Fleurie at a temperature of about 13 °C (55 °F) with pink-roasted leg of lamb, chicken or other poultry, or with white meat.

MOULIN-À-VENT

This famous *cru* derives its name from the finely restored wind-driven flour mill in Romanèche-

Moulin-à-Vent, with and without cask-maturing

Thorins. The soil of the 1,600 acres (2.5 squared miles) of vineyards consists of a pink granite subsoil and manganese. This gives the wine its dark, very concentrated ruby-red color in which, when the wine is still young, purple and dark red shades play hide and seek. The nose is most reminiscent of noble flowers, such as roses, with a hint of raspberries. The taste is powerful and fairly rich in tannin. Because of its robust structure, Moulin-à-Vent can age very well (sometimes as much as fifteen years). As it gets older this powerful wine becomes very like a Burgundy.

Leave a Morgon to mature quietly for a few years and then serve it at about 14 °C (57 °F) with red meat, goose, game birds, or the stronger kinds of cheese.

Chénas

CHÉNAS

This wine is, completely undeservedly, almost unknown outside its own region. This very elegant wine, with its sophisticated aromas of peonies and roses with here and there a touch of wood or spices, is grown on 650 acres (1 squared mile) of granite soil. The taste is soft, generous and friendly.

Serve these wines at about 14 °C (57 °F) with meat and red wine gravy or strong kinds of cheese. Chénas can also age well.

JULIÉNAS

This is the most northerly located *cru* of the Beaujolais, on the border with the Mâconnais. This deep-colored ruby-red wine with its powerful, full taste is produced on 1,400 acres (2.1 squared miles) of stone and clay strata, covered with sediment. The aromas are mainly fruity (wild wood strawberries, redcurrants, raspberries) with a floral undertone (peonies and roses). A good Juliénas can age for several years.

Juliénas

Serve this wine at about 13 °C (55 °F) with the famous *coq au vin*, lamb, game birds or poultry in rich sauces.

SAINT-AMOUR

The last of these northern *crus*. The vineyards are 700 acres (1 squared mile) and lie on the border between the lime-rich Mâconnais (Chardonnay) and the granite hills of the Beaujolais (Gamay). The soil is a mixture of clay, boulders, granite and sandstone. The wines have a splendid ruby-red color and a very aromatic nose of peonies, raspberries, redcurrants, apricots and sometimes a dash of cherry brandy or kirsch. The taste is very tempting, velvety soft and full, with hints of spices.

St-Amour

Serve these lovely wines at about 13 °C (55 °F) with poultry, game birds, or crisply fried veal sweetbreads.

Although most *crus* from the Beaujolais go very well with all kinds of meat, particularly with Charolais beef, we warmly recommend the somewhat less obvious combination of a young *cru* with a fresh goat's cheese from the western valleys of the Beaujolais.

THE SATELLITES OF THE BEAUJOLAIS

Although they are not actually in the Beaujolais, we list here three wines which in character and taste approach the Beaujolais wines. All three are made from the Gamay grape.

COTEAUX DU LYONNAIS

These very old vineyards have become the victim of the expansion of the town of Lyons. The wines made here are friendly, light but generous, with pronounced fruity aromas.

Drink these wines well cooled, about 12 °C (54 °F). They go very well with all kinds of cold meats, or simply with a fresh goat's cheese. There is also a white version, made from the Chardonnay and Aligoté grape.

Coteaux du Lyonnais

Côte Roannaise

CÔTE ROANNAISE

Very clear ruby-red wines with a great deal of fruit and a light, very pleasant, taste.

Preferably drink a Côte Roannaise cool at 12 °C (54 °F) with cold meats or a terrine of chicken livers.

CÔTE DU FOREZ

Light, generous wines with lots of fruit. The rosé wines are perfect accompaniments to informal lunches or picnics, but a grilled freshwater fish and a glass of Forez Rosé would also be a happy combination. The red Côtes de Forez wines are an obvious choice for warm summer evenings, for instance with a cold buffet. Drink both wines at about 12 °C (54 °F).

Côtes du Forez

AUVERGNE

The Auvergne is a separate wine region, poised between the Loire (Sancerre, Quincy, Reuilly, and so on) and Burgundy. The region is divided into two sub-regions, Saint-Pourçain and Côtes d'Auvergne.

SAINT-POURÇAIN

To the south-east of the town of Moulins lies the small town of Saint-Pourçain, on the river Sioule. The Saint-Pourçain wine region covers nineteen communes with a total surface area of around 1,200 acres (1.8 squared miles). The vineyards are located on hills and flat expanses of limestone and/or gravel soils. Once the white wines of the local Tressallier grapes enjoyed a high reputation. Now red Gamay grapes and Pinot-Noir are in the majority, but attempts by the local cooperative to replant the traditional white wine grapes have had some success.

The wine growers of Saint-Pourçain now offer a rich range of white, rosé and red wines of excellent quality. Admittedly, in the past there have been difficulties with the quality of these wines, but the younger generation of hardworking and enthusiastic winegrowers deserve all your trust.

The white Saint-Pourçain wines are made of a combination of Tressalier, Chardonnay and Sauvignon. The combination of calcareous clay or sandy soils, a favorable aspect for the sun, and these three grape varieties produce wines with special characteristics. Depending upon the percentages of

St-Pourçain Blanc

Tressallier, Sauvignon and Chardonnay the wines take on totally different characteristics. Wines in which Tressallier and Chardonnay dominate are good for laying down, while wines of the Tressallier-Sauvignon type are fresh and fruity, suitable for early consumption. In wines in which Chardonnay and Sauvignon dominate, freshness, richness and subtlety are combined. Finally there are the fat and fully aromatic wines of Chardonnay, Tressallier, Sauvignon and Aligoté. As you see, there is something for every taste.

Drink these white wines with dishes from the local regional cuisine, such as freshwater fish dishes or the rather richer casseroles. Drinking temperature: 8 °C (47 °F) (Sauvignon-Tressallier) or 12 °C (54 °F) (Chardonnay).

The rosé and *vin gris* of Saint-Pourçain are made of 100 % Gamay. These are fresh, elegant and fruity wines which do very well with the excellent Auvergne cold meats, but also with tender vegetables, such as carrots and leeks. Drinking temperature: 10–12 °C (50–54 °F).

Finally the red Saint-Pourçain, made from Gamay and Pinot Noir. Depending on the percentages of each used and the style of vinification, the wines are fresh, fruity and easy to drink (100 % Gamay), full and complete

St-Pourçain

St-Pourçain Rouge

(80 % Gamay, 20 % Pinot Noir) or harmonious, complex, rich and delicate (50 % of each). The type of *terroir* also determines the eventual richness and complexity of the wines. The red wines from calcareous soils are in general more elegant and more complex than those of the gravely sandy soils. However, these last are fuller and richer in taste.

Drink these wines with chicken dishes in which you have poured a good measure of red Saint-Pourçain, or with local dishes of duck, small game, game birds or lamb. A red Saint-Pourçain combines excellently with green lentils, but also, for example, with turnips, beet or kohlrabi. Drinking temperature: 12–14 °C (54–57 °F).

CÔTES D'AUVERGNE AOVDQS

For more than 2000 years grapevines have grown on the slopes of the extinct volcanoes of the Auvergne. After a lengthy 'dark age' resulting from the *Phylloxera* invasion, World War I, the economic crisis of 1929, and World War II after it, wine-making began to flourish again in the Auvergne.

After a generation of growers who put quantity before quality, a new generation of quality-conscious wine-makers has arisen. Not only are these young winegrowers better educated and more professional, they are also, above all, proud of their trade, their *terroir* and their wines. And you can taste that!

The soil of the Côtes d'Auvergne wine region is very varied. Round the town of Clermont Ferrand you will meet two kinds of soil: the volcanic substratum and the calciferous layer of marl, both resulting from the great volcanic eruptions of the quaternary era. The landscape here is very hilly and makes a visit to the area all the more interesting.

The vineyard acreage covers a surface area of some 1,200 acres (1.8 squared miles), from the north of Riom to the south of Issoire. The vineyards are at a height of 900–1,500 ft, between the extinct volcanoes of the Chaine des Puys and the river Allier. The rainfall is comparable to that of the Sancerrois.

About 90 % of the grapes planted are Gamay. Pinot Noir and Chardonnay account for the remaining 10 %.

The appellation Côtes d'Auvergne contains mostly generic wines, but since 1977 the region has also had five *crus*, each with its own character. The generic wines can be white, rosé or red. They may come from anywhere in the region.

The white Côtes d'Auvergnes are made of the Chardonnay grape and are very fruity, elegant and fresh. The wines which have been raised on wood can age very well, the best for more than ten years!

Drink these white wines as aperitifs or at meals with fish or poultry or with one of the gorgeous oven dishes (of potatoes, dumplings and/or vegetables) in which cheeses from the Auvergne (such as Cantal or Salers) have been added. Drinking temperature 9–11 °C (48–52 °F).

The rosé Côtes d'Auvergne are made of the Gamay grape and are fresh, very fruity, generous and easy to drink. They are excellent thirst quenchers in summer, but they are mature enough to accompany cold meats and light starters throughout the year. In the winter they also taste excellent with the rather rich local specialties, such as stuffed cabbage or tripe. Drinking temperature 10–12 °C (50–54 °F).

The red Côtes d'Auvergne can be made of Gamay, Pinot Noir or a combination of them. These wines, too, are surprisingly fruity and fresh, supple and fleshy at the same time.

Drink these wines with local dishes based on pork or lamb or with casseroles, peasant terrines or patés. Drinking temperature 12–14 °C (54–57 °F).

Côtes d'Auvergne

CRUS

The *crus* from north to south are:
– Madargue (above Riom) produces red and rosé wines. Both are characterized by their very deep color, tempting fruitiness (raspberries and redcurrants) and full, rounded taste with soft tannins. Drinking temperature 14–16 °C (57–61 °F).
– Chateaugay (between Riom and Clermont-Ferrand) makes white, red and rosé wines. The red wines are the most interesting, with their dark, ruby-red color and very typical aromas of spices such as cinnamon and nutmeg. The taste is elegant and well balanced. Drinking temperature 14–15 °C (57–59 °F).

Vineyards in Châteaugay (Rougeyron)

– Chanturgue (above Clermont-Ferrand) produces only red wines. These are also dark ruby-red in color and very aromatic: red fruit, raspberries and cherries. The taste is fresh and fruity. Drinking temperature 13–15 °C (55–59 °F).

– Corent (between Clermont-Ferrand and Issoire) is the domain of the rosé wines. With their marvelous aromas of citrus fruits, hazelnuts, cherries, apricots, peonies and fresh butter, these outstanding wines should immediately convince all skeptics. The structure of the wines is full, broad, and almost fat and the aftertaste lasts for ages. Choose the best of them, such as those from Jean Pierre and Marc Pradier. There is no need to stint yourself at the price. Drinking temperature 10–12 °C (50–54 °F). Of course, good white and red wines are also made in Corent, but these are not as exceptional as the rosé.

– Boudes (below Issoire) produces white, red and rosé wines. At the lower end these wines are interesting and well made, but not exactly fascinating. The top wines of Boudes, on the other hand, are real treasures. Consider the white and red wines of Claude and Annie Sauvat, who have achieved miracles in this small wine region. The white wines of Chardonnay can without difficulty compete with those of their distant cousins from Burgundy. The red wines from Gamay are deep and dark colored, with wonderful aromas of raspberries, redcurrants, strawberries, spices, vanilla and pepper. The Pinot Noir wines smell more of plums, cherries, leather, licorice, wood, coffee and toast. Don't expect any elegant, feminine wines here: these red Boudes possess robust but vola-

Côtes d'Auvergne
Rosé Corent

Vineyards in Boudes (Sauvat)

tile tannins and a full, fat and complex taste. Drinking temperature: 14–16 °C (57–61 °F).

SOUTH-EAST FRANCE

The Rhône Valley

Between Vienne and Avignon, in the Rhône valley, wine has been made for more than 2000 years. Gauls, Greeks and Romans laid the foundations for one of the best known wine regions of France, the Côtes du Rhône. The issue of the marriage between river and vineyard, the new-born infant soon gained the blessing of the seven popes who were based in Avignon. The very extensive wine region, with its very diverse *terroirs* and microclimates, developed into a unity.

A COOL WIND

As early as the seventeenth century the wines around Uzès in the *département* du Gard enjoyed such a reputation that they were soon copied. To preserve their origin and quality they were officially recognized in 1650 and their territory clearly defined. Age-long struggles for recognition were finally rewarded in 1937 when the AOC Côtes du Rhône became official.

In 1956 the dreaded mistral blew for three weeks at speeds of more than 100 km (60 miles) an hour over the

Côte Rôtie, one of the most prestigious wine regions in the world

kers, these wines have an enormous variety of aromas, and are in general generous and friendly wines.

The red wines are well structured, full of bouquet and taste, and well rounded. They can be drunk young, but can also be kept for a time.

The rosé wines come from the southern part of the region. These wines with their raspberry to salmon-pink color are always fruity and supple.

The white wines are dry, balanced, well structured, very aromatic and thirst-quenching.

whole Rhône Valley and the mercury stayed below freezing at about -15 °C (5 °F).

To crown the disaster, all the olive trees froze to death. Because the vines had survived this ice-cold winter, the ruined peasants decided to devote themselves to viniculture. This marked the beginning of the gigantic growth of Côtes du Rhône.

GRAPE VARIETIES

Throughout the region, there are at least twenty-three different kinds of grapes used (plus the *Muscat à petit grain* for the naturally sweet wine of Beaumes de Venise). In the northern part only Syrah is used for red wines and Viognier, Roussanne and Marsanne for the white wines; in the southern part Grenache, Mourvèdre, Cinsault and Carignan are used for the reds, in addition to Syrah, and Grenache blanc, Clairette and Bourboulenc for the whites.

CÔTES DU RHÔNE VILLAGES AOC

In the southern Rhône there are seventy-seven communes which can carry the description Côtes du Rhône Villages. Sixteen of these can put their own name on

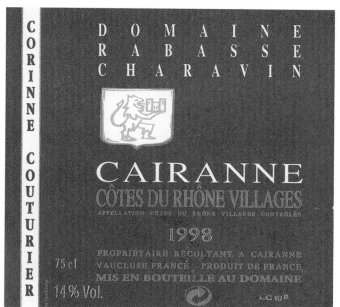
Côtes du Rhône Villages Cairanne

APPELLATIONS

The wines of the Rhône are divided into four categories: the generic wines with the appellation Côtes du Rhône Régionale, the better Côtes du Rhône Villages, the *crus* and the satellites, which are part of the region geographically, but lead their own lives (Clairette de Die, Crémant de Die, Vins du Diois, Coteaux du Tricastin, Côtes du Ventoux and Costières de Nimes).

CÔTES DU RHÔNE

The generic Côtes du Rhône accounts for 80 % of the production. Because they represent so many *terroirs*, microclimates and winema-

Côtes du Rhône Rouge   Côtes du Rhône Blanc

the label. For white, red and rosé wines strict rules apply covering planting, cultivation, production and vinification.

Some of the best known Côtes du Rhône Villages are:
- Beaumes-de-Venise (red and rosé)
- Cairanne (red, rosé and white)
- Chusclan (red and rosé)
- Laudun (red, rosé and white)
- Rasteau (red, rosé and white)
- Rochegude (red, rosé and white)
- Séguret (red, rosé and white)

Côtes du Rhône Villages Valréas   Côtes du Rhône Villages Rasteau

– Valréas (red, rosé and white)
– Vinsobres (red, rosé and white)
– Visan (red, rosé and white)

All these wines are excellent companions to the Provençal cuisine. A few special combinations are:
– Red Laudun and game
– white Laudun and shellfish
– white Rochegude and grilled fish with fresh herbs
– white Séguret and fresh goat's cheese
– white, rosé and red Visan with the local specialty – fresh truffles.

Drink the red wines at a temperature of about 16 °C (61 °F), the rosé at about 14 °C (57 °F), and the whites at about 12 °C (54 °F).

CRUS FROM THE CÔTES DU RHÔNE

These thirteen great wines each have their own very individual character. They are often legendary wines: they offer the taster an introduction to the district, the soil and the grape varieties, and invite a personal meeting with the winemaker. On the steep, rugged hills round Tain-l'Hermitage the substratum is granite and the climate is a mild continental one. In the southern part of the Rhône the soil is calcareous, here and there covered with silts. The climate is warmer and dryer because it is so close to the Mediterranean.

Côtes du Rhône
Villages Vinsobres

CÔTE RÔTIE

The exclusively red Côte Rôtie comes from two very steep granite hills, the Côte Blonde and the Côte Brune. According to legend, the domain of Lord Mangiron was in the Middle Ages divided between his two daughters – one was blonde, the other a brunette. This is said to be the origin of the hills' names.

Côte Rôtie wines have a deep red color and aromas of raspberries and spices, with a hint of violets. At a later age vanilla and a typical bouquet of apricot or peach stones takes over. The wines have much body, strong but rounded tannins, an enormous wealth of taste and a very long aftertaste.

They are a perfect complement to all kinds of fine meats, and also wildfowl. Put a few truffles in the sauce and the wine will indulge all your senses. Open the bottle well beforehand and decant it.

CONDRIEU

These white wines also come from steep granite hills, which make mechanization impossible. They are made from the Viognier grape and have a light-golden color, a powerful bouquet

Côte Rôtie

of meadow flowers, irises, violets and apricots, and much strength and roundness. Since 1990 there have once again been a number of rare Condrieu *vendages tardives* from, among others, Yves Cuilleron.

Condrieu wines are perfect accompaniments to fish dishes, but they will really surprise you with *foie gras*.

CHÂTEAU-GRILLET

This wine region of just over 8 acres (0.01 squared mile) and 10,000 bottles a year is one of the smallest appellations, and produces one of the best white wines in France. You should try these wines locally, if you have the opportunity.

Condrieu

The color is clear yellow and tends towards straw-colored as it ages. The nose is often rather closed and only 'gives itself up' after a while. Again it is apricots and (white) peaches which predominate. The taste is full, fat, very rich and complex.

Drink this rare wine with freshwater fish in sophisticated sauces. Don't forget to open the bottle a few hours in advance.

SAINT-JOSEPH

The dark-red wines, with a subtle scent of blackcurrants and raspberries, later changing into hints of leather and licorice, are very fine, harmonious and elegant.

Drink a Saint-Joseph lightly cooled, at about 15 °C (59 °F). Nice with a good piece of meat or chicken. You should definitely not serve too heavy sauces with it.

The white wines have a sunny yellow color with a trace of green and a bouquet of meadow flowers, acacia and honey. They are fresh wines, with lots of depth.

Drink them well cooled at about 12 °C (54 °F) with sophisticated dishes from the modern cuisine.

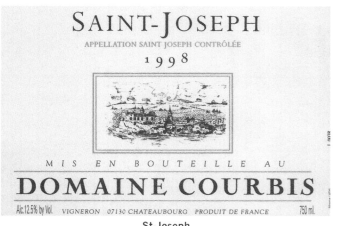

St-Joseph

CROZES-HERMITAGE

In volume this is the largest of the northern *crus*. Although they are of rather lower quality than their cousins, in their characteristic bouquet and taste Crozes-Hermitages do come close to the Hermitage wines.

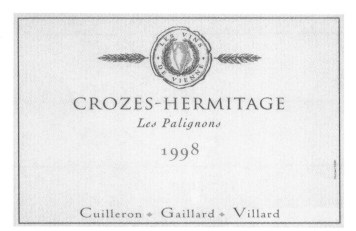

Yves Cuilleron and partners' Crozes-Hermitage

The whites have a clear yellow color, a very floral nose and a full, fat taste. They are good companions to freshwater fish and grain-fed free-range chickens. Drink at around 12 °C (54 °F).

The red wines are dark red in color, very intense. The nose is reminiscent of red fruits, leather and spices. The taste is elegant in spite of the presence of discreet tannins.

Serve these red wines lightly cooled, at around 15 °C (59 °F) with your better chicken or other poultry dishes.

HERMITAGE

The red Hermitage wines are rather strong when they are young, and require several years rest – five, ten or even twenty years, depending on the quality. If you have the patience, you will be rewarded with a very great wine, with a sensual bouquet in which leather, red and white fruits and wildflowers are dominant. The taste throughout is of crystallized fruit. Hermitage wines are excellent companions for red meat and game. Serve them at a temperature of 16–18 °C (61–64 °F).

Red Hermitage

Chapoutier's well-known red Hermitage

White Crozes--Hermitage

Red Crozes--Hermitage

Chapoutier's famous white Hermitage

Hermitage vin de paille, rare but sublime!

White Hermitage

The white wines are ready to drink rather earlier, but can also age very well. The bouquet reminds of a sea of flowers, with here and there a few touches of vanilla and toasted almonds. They are powerful, well-rounded wines with great aromatic potency.

Drink these wines at a temperature of about 12 °C (54 °F) with freshwater fish or white meat.

Near Tain-l'Hermitage, too, a very rare wine is produced – regrettably in increasingly small quantities – (H)Ermitage *vin de paille*. This wine is made in the same way as its namesake in the Jura. Healthy grapes are carefully selected by hand, placed in boxes in a layer of straw and left like that for a few months. The grapes begin to shrivel, the water evaporates, so that the juices are extremely concentrated and very sweet. After fermentation there is still some residual sugar in the wine in spite of the high alcohol content of about 15 %.

CORNAS

Cornas

These red wines have a dark color and a very fascinating nose with, among others, red fruits, freshly ground peppers, licorice, crystallized fruits and even truffles.

Cornas has an almost animal undertone and goes very well with all game and red meat dishes.

SAINT-PERAY

This is the only appellation which also makes sparkling wines. These wines are not always so interesting.

Drink them young in the company of friends and with not too rich nibbles.

GIGONDAS

Gigondas is made of Grenache grapes, supplemented mainly by Syrah and Mourvèdre.

The red wines have a splendid color and a nose full of red fruit when they are young, developing into animal overtones and brushwood as they age. They are full, powerful and well-balanced wines, which are

St-Péray

rather harsh in their youth. They need several years rest. Red Gigondas is wonderful with lamb, red meat or game.

The rosé wines are fresh and cheerful with plenty of concentration. Drink them young.

Gigondas

VACQEYRAS

Drink the white and rosé wines young, when and where you feel like it.

The red, with a recognizable nose of ripe red fruit, cherries, and a dash of licorice, has more strength. However, they are unpretentious wines which feel good anywhere. Drink them at about 17 °C (63 °F).

CHÂTEAUNEUF-DU-PAPE

Although thirteen varieties of grape are permitted, the red wines are mainly made of Grenache, Cinsault, Mourvèdre, Syrah, Muscardin and Counoise, and the whites of Clairette and Bourboulenc.

The red wines are very complex in smell (red fruit, leather, aniseed, licorice, spices) and in taste (rounded, balmy, powerful, with a very long aftertaste). Drink the reds only from the fifth year after the harvest and the whites while still young. These wines go very well with all kinds of red meat, particularly when they include garlic and sun-dried tomatoes.

World renowned Châteauneuf-du-Pape

Châteauneuf-du-Pape Rouge

Châteauneuf-du-Pape Blanc

The whites are very aromatic and rounded, with a nose of floral undertones, such as honeysuckle and daffodils. Ideal as a sensual aperitif, with all grilled fish and also surprisingly good with *tapenade*.

The bottles of the genuine Châteauneuf-du-Pape, estate-bottled, display the arms of the town of Avignon on the bottle itself – the papal crown and St Peter's two crossed keys. The keys of Paradise?

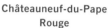

LIRAC

The wines of Lirac are also gaining ground. Bottle for bottle, good wine for relatively little money.

The rosé is a very good accompaniment to the Mediterranean cuisine, while the white livens up all sea fish, and the generous and full red wines add pleasure to red meat and game.

Red Lirac

TAVEL

Tavel is one of the most wonderful rosé wines in France. The rosé color often tends towards a roof tile-colored red or even orange. In the nose you will find hints of apricots, peaches and roasted almonds.

Tavel is the perfect accompaniment for the Mediterranean cuisine, but also goes extremely well with Chinese or Thai cooking. Drink the wine at a temperature of about 13 °C (55 °F).

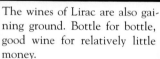

Tavel Rosé

THE SATELLITES OF THE RHONE

These so-called satellites are wine districts which are geographically within the Rhône region, but lead their own separate lives (Clairette de Die, Crémant de Die, vins du Diois, Coteaux de Tricastin, Côtes de Ventoux and Costières de Nimes).

CLAIRETTE DE DIE

The Clairette de Die is a very old wine which was already known in Roman times (Pliny the Elder, 77 BC). It was then called Aigleucos and was made by the local Gauls. They used to plunge the barrels in which the wine had just begun to ferment into the ice-cold mountain streams. In this way the fermentation was prematurely stopped and the wine retained its bubbles.

Up to World War II this Clairette de Die was only intended to be drunk from the wood as a young, still fermenting wine. It was a little wine for friends and parties. Only in 1950, when the Cave Coopérative Clairette de Die was established, did the situation change radically. The vineyards were expanded and techniques enormously improved. While retaining respect for tradition, a new drive was given to this almost lost popular drink.

Clairette de Die is made from Muscat and Clairette grapes. Before the wine has completely finished fermenting, it is bottled without any addition. The carbon dioxide produced during the fermentation then stays trapped in the bottle as natural bubbles. This age-old method is officially called the *méthode*

Clairette de Die méthode ancestrale (sweet)

Dioise ancestrale. The taste of these traditional Clairettes de Die is especially fruity (Muscat), mild and delicious.

Because of the low alcohol content (7 %) this drink is a sensual aperitif, but it can also be served at meals, with chicken or rabbit casseroles, in which a good dollop of this wine has been added. Surprisingly good!

CRÉMANT DE DIE

Since 1993 this dry (*brut*) version, made only from Clairette grapes by the traditional method, has been called Crémant de Die. The smell brings to mind apple and other white and green fruit, with, as it ages, hints of dried fruits and almonds.

With its fine *mousse* (foaming bubbles) this *crémant* is a very elegant and festive wine, ideal for aperitifs.

CHATILLON-EN-DIOIS

Below the first foothills of the Alps lies this appellation. Châtillon Gamay red and rosé are fruity and supple wines with a great deal of bouquet. Drink them young. The only

Rosé and red Châtillon-en-Diois

Apart from these generic wines there are also various *domaine* wines of outstanding quality. But be quick, because demand exceeds the supply.

Crémant de Die (dry)

Anonymous but delicious Chardonnay!

exception is the special *cuvée* aged in wood, which can age for some time. Delicious with cold meats, grilled meat or even cheese (goat's cheese).

Châtillon Aligoté is an elegant, fresh, dry white wine with aromas of wild herbs. Drink young, for instance as an aperitif, with goat's cheese, starters or fish.

Châtillon Chardonnay is a fuller, more serious white wine which improves after a year's maturing in bottle. Serve it with fish or chicken dishes.

COTEAUX DU TRICASTIN

These wines actually differ very little from the Côtes du Rhône wines. For rather obscure reasons, however, they do not belong to the elite Rhône group. From the same vine stocks and on almost identical types of soil, white, red and rosé wines are produced here.

These assertive and very characteristic wines go excellently with all dishes in the Provençal cuisine.

Coteaux
du Tricastin

COTES DU VENTOUX

The climate here is rather colder than that along the Rhône, so the wines contain less alcohol than the average Rhône wines. These mainly red wines are fresh and elegant and should be drunk fairly young.

For some years the AOC Côtes du Ventoux have been doing well. The quality is steadily improving and the wines are finding an eager market. Here, too, people have realized that quality rather than quantity is the only solution for a long-term policy. To raise the level even higher, the winegrowers and the local and regional institutions are exploring the possible creation of a higher status AOC Côtes du Ventoux Villages.

COTES DU LUBÉRON

This appellation for white, red and rosé wines has only been in existence since 1988. Here, too, the climate is rather cooler, which explains the relatively high percentage of white wines. In general these are fairly cheap, good quality wines which are gaining increasing popularity. We suspect that this region will develop further in the new century. Keep a sharp eye on these wines! In taste there is little difference from the other Rhône wines, except perhaps that the Lubérons can be a little less full and structured.

Côtes du Lubéron wines are excellent companions to the dishes of the Provençal cuisine.

Val Joanis, a Lubéron of great class

COTES DU VIVARAIS

On calcareous soil mainly red wines are produced here, based on Grenache and Syrah grapes, sometimes supplemented by Cinsault or Carignan. The wines should consist of a maximum of 90 % Grenache (minimum 40 %) and Syrah (minimum 30 %).

The local fresh rosé is also extremely pleasant. This is made from at least two of the three grape varieties, Grenache, Syrah and Cinsault, with no single grape variety making up more that 80 % of it, and the wine containing at least 25 % Syrah.

The white wines must consist of two of the three grape varieties Clairette, Grenache Blanc and Marsanne, with no single variety representing more than 75 %.

An ideal wine for informal meals with friends or for barbecue parties or cold buffets in summer. The wine is always of first-class quality and offers the wine lover 'much pleasure for little money'. Drink the red wines lightly cooled between 14–16 °C (57–61 °F) and the rosé and white wines at 10–12 °C (50–54 °F).

White or rosé, the quality of this Lubéron
surprises everyone

NATURALLY SWEET WINES

Two communes in the Rhône region make very high-quality sweet wines based on the Muscat grape: Beaumes de Venise and Rasteau. In Beaumes de Venise a full strong white wine with an enormously aromatic potential is produced in a totally natural way. This white wine smells and tastes of fresh Muscat grapes, peaches, apricots and here and there freshly picked meadow flowers. Drink these wines very well cooled at 5–8 °C (41–47 °F), for instance, with fresh fruit desserts or perhaps after a meal, with a piece of cheese.

In Rasteau, on the other hand, a fortified red wine is produced. The fermentation is stopped by adding wine alcohol to the still fermenting must. The wines produced in this way are still very sweet, very fruity and a little like port. In France these wines are served as aperitifs, or in the evening after dinner with some good friends. Serve the wine a little below room temperature.

Fresh and very aromatic Muscat de Beaumes de Venise

SAVOY AND BUGEY

The vineyards of Savoy are not so extensive, some 5,000 acres, but they are spread over a much larger region. Starting at the Lake of Geneva in the north, the wine region stretches to the foot of the Alps in the east and as far as the Isère valley, past Chambery, some 60 miles south of the Lake of Geneva.

It is a great pity that the wines from Savoy are so little known. The mainly white wines are particularly fresh and full of taste. Because the vineyards are widely scattered and the hilly nature of the ground makes them difficult to work, the price of a good wine from Savoy cannot be on the low side.

Savoy wines are subtle, elegant and characteristic, and tell the story of their *terroir* better than any other. That cannot always be said of the many show-off, hyper-commercialized and characterless kinds of Chardonnay that fill the shelves of our supermarkets. Anyone who takes the time to explore the wines of Savoy will not be disappointed.

Savoy wines

HISTORY

Here, too, it was the Gauls (Allobroges) who planted the first vineyards. Savoy lay at a very strategic crossroads for the Roman legions, who were able to maintain and improve the viniculture. The wines of Savoy were soon called after the villages from which they came, with Crépy as the first to set the pattern officially, closely followed by Apremont. Only in 1957 did Savoy wines receive their certificates for *vin delimité de qualité supérieur*, and in September 1973 the crown of their work, the *appellation d'origine controlée*.

THE REGION

The vineyards of Savoy are like a long string of small regions, in the shape of a half moon. The districts lie on the east and south-east. The following subdivision can be made (from north to south):
- vineyards on the Lake of Geneva (Ripaille, Marignan, Marin, Crépy)
- vineyards in the Arve valley (Ayze) and Usses valley (Frangy)
- vineyards in the valley of the Rhône (Chautagne, Marestel, Monthoux, Jongieux), and Lake Bourget (Charpignat and Brison) and in the valley of the Isère (Abymes, Apremont).

The climate is essentially continental, but is softened by the presence of the great lakes and rivers. On the west the Jura mountains help to protect the vineyards from the rain-bearing west winds. An extremely important point is the large number of hours of sunshine (average 1600 per annum).

The vineyards lie at a height of 1,000–1,500 ft. The soil is made up of a mixture of lime, marl and grit from the old Alpine glaciers.

WINEGROWING

The most important appellation is *Vin de Savoie* (still, sparkling and lightly sparkling wines). There are eighteen *crus* which may mention their names on the label. The appellation *roussette de Savoie* (made only from the local Altesse grape) also has four *crus*.

As a winegrowing region Savoy is certainly worth a special visit, if only to discover its four unique native grape varieties: the white Jacquère, Altesse (also

Savoy: mainly white wines

called Roussette) and Gringet, and the red Mondeuse.

In addition to these local grapes other kinds of grape are also used: Aligoté, Chasselas, Chardonnay and Molette for the white wines, and Gamay, Persan, Joubertin and Pinot Noir for the red and rosé wines.

SAVOY WINES

VINS DE SAVOIE BLANC

Apremont

These white wines are all made from the Jacquère grape. They are fresh, very aromatic wines. Depending on their *terroir* the strength of their color, aromas and taste will vary from pale yellow, light and generous with floral undertones (honeysuckle), often with a light sparkle on the tongue, to light yellow, full and fruity. Drink these wines well cooled at 8 °C (47 °F) and young, for example, as aperitifs, or as table wines with *fruits de mer*, fish, meat, or cheese dishes (such as Savoy fondue and *raclette*).

These white wines owe their characteristics to the Chasselas grape (well known from the top Swiss wines). The color

Ripaille

is light yellow and the bouquet is reminiscent of ripe fruit, sometimes even of dried fruit. The taste is fresh and full. Some wines, particularly Crépy, have a very pleasant sparkle. It is said that a good Crépy should 'crackle', or: 'Le Crépy crépite'.

Crépy

Excellent wines for an aperitif, but also suitable companions for fish or shellfish. A first-class wine for a cheese dish, too!

CHIGNIN-BERGERON

These outstanding white wines based on the Roussanne grape deserve a special mention. They are very complex wines with hints of roasted nuts and toast, dried fruits and here and there a dash of aniseed or fennel. Surprisingly elegant and fresh, with a full taste which lasts a long time.

Chignin-Bergeron is a wine for special occasions, as a chic aperitif or at meals with noble freshwater fish in

Chignin

St-Joire-Prieuré

Jongieux

Montmélian

Chautagne

Abymes

Chignin-Bergeron

Roussette de Savoie (generic)

Seyssel (still or lightly sparkling)

sophisticated sauces. Don't drink these wines too cold. A temperature of about 12 °C (54 °F) is fine.

ROUSSETTE DE SAVOIE AND SEYSSEL

Roussette de Savoie wines are subdivided into:
- Frangy
- Marestel
- Monthoux
- Monterminod

These white wines (all Roussette de Savoie wines and Seyssel) are made from the Altesse grape (Roussette).

Roussette de Savoie Frangy

Roussette de Savoie Monthoux

This noble grape variety appears once to have been brought back from distant Cyprus by a local princess during a crusade.

The color of these wines is light yellow with a few fine bubbles when they are young. These disappear in the course of time. The nose is like an immense bouquet of flowers from forest and field, such as violets and irises, with a sprinkling of almonds. The taste is full and round. These wines sometimes still contain a little residual sugar, which makes them even more pleasant.

Delicious as an aperitif, particularly on a dreary fall evening.

Roussete de Savoie Monterminod

VINS DE SAVOIE ROUGE

This covers three different types of wine: Gamay wines, Mondeuse wines and Pinot Noir wines. The Gamay wines are very typical and characteristic of their *terroir*. Their color is cheerful and fresh, which also applies to their aromatic taste.

Drink these wines cool, at about 12 °C (54 °F). Good with cold meats, white meat or vegetable dishes.

The Mondeuse wines are much darker in color, with purple glints. The aromas and the taste are more complex than those of the Gamay wines. You can smell and taste a mixture of red fruit, pepper and spices.

Arbin, red Savoy wine

St-Jean-de-la-Porte

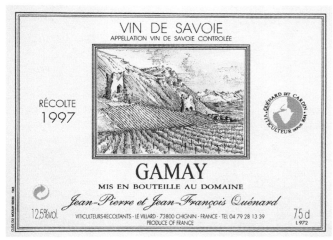

Savoy Gamay

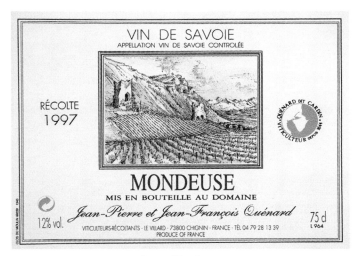

Savoy Mondeuse

The presence of tannin can sometimes be quite harsh in young wines, but later becomes softer. Good Mondeuse wines can be kept a long time.

These are excellent accompaniments to red meat and game. Serve them at 14 °C (57 °F).

The Pinot Noir wines are rather scarce. They have a lovely ruby-red color and complex aromas and taste.

Serve this type of wine lightly cooled at about 14 °C (57 °F). First class with cold meats, white meat, poultry or rabbit.

SPARKLING SAVOY WINES

Savoy Pinot Noir

Ayze
Seyssel

Ayze is made from the Gringet grape, while Seyssel owes its charm to the Molette and Altesse. They are both outstanding (light) sparkling white wines with great elegance.

Essentially festive wines, but also suitable for 'ordinary' occasions. Drink them at about 10 °C (50 °F).

TIP

Excellent cheeses are made in Savoy, which go very well with the local wines. Although the Abondance, Beaufort, Reblochon, Chevrotin des Aravis, Tamié and Tomme de Savoie also go very well with red wines, it is certainly worthwhile trying them with the fresh white wines of Savoy too. In this way you will get to know the heart and soul of the region.

Ayre, lightly sparkling white wine

Bugey

The Bugey vineyards lie to the west of Savoy, in the department of Ain (O1). The VDQS wines produced there are relatively unknown and regrettably also often unloved, because of their very fresh acidity.

The Bugey wine region was once very large. Today the small vineyards are spread over a large area, mostly on a soil of fragmented limestone. Thanks to the enthusiastic efforts of a new generation of winegrowers the region seems to have had new life breathed into it.

The grapes used are largely the same as those in neighboring Savoy (Mondeuse, Pinot Noir, Gamay, Jacquère, Altesse, Molette, Chardonnay and Aligoté). For the sparkling wines a little Poulsard (see the grape varieties listed in the paragraph on the 'French Jura') is also used. A peculiarity of the Bugey wines is that they are always 'monocépage', in other words, wines made from a single variety of grape.

BUGEY BLANC

White Bugey is always a still wine, in contrast to the Roussette du Bugey or Bugey Brut. The wines can be made of the Jacquère or Chardonnay grapes. Bugey Blanc Chardonnay is the most popular. Depending on the vinification selected, the wines will display another aspect. When the malolactic fermentation is not or only partly carried out, the wines still have plenty of freshness, with sometimes quite lively acidity. These tough Bugey Blancs are mildly fruity and go well with green salads, starters and even shellfish. When it is allowed to carry on to a second or malolactic fermentation the hard green acids become much softer. This gives the wines a fatter structure and a rather richer aromatic strength. The Bugey Blanc Chardonnay then gets warm aromas of ripe fruit, luxury bread rolls, hazelnut, snakeweed or lime blossom. Such wines go very well with the local hard cheeses, and also with those from the neighboring county of Jura.

BUGEY MANICLE BLANC

This *cru* is produced on the soil of the Cheignieu la Balme commune. Here the Chardonnay thrives, so that this is the only grape variety from which Manicle Blanc is made. They are full, powerful wines with a fat structure and complex aromas, which often yield nothing to their neighbors from the Mâconnais.

Delicious wines to serve with freshwater fish (pike, perch) in a soft creamy sauce. Don't drink too cold, 10–12 °C (50–54 °F) is fine.

ROUSSETTE DU BUGEY

This is the still version of the Roussette, made of Altesse grapes (also called Roussette grapes). Roussette du Bugey is usually full, rich and elegant, particularly that of the local *crus* from Montagnieu and Visieu-le-Grand. In contrast to many white wines you can keep a Roussette du Bugey very well for five to ten years. The bouquet of a Roussette du Bugey evolves with age. When the wine is still young, the aromas of ripe fruit (peach, apricot) are dominant. After five to eight years sensual aromas of honey and beeswax appear. The strength and essence of a Roussette du Bugey only develop after the necessary years of ageing.

A young wine is certainly good to drink, for instance as an aperitif, but the combination of a mature Roussette du Bugey with creamy freshwater fish dishes is not to be scorned! Also delicious with cheese dishes and with a ripe local Reblochon cheese. You can drink the young wine a little cooler, at about 10 °C (50 °F); mature wine should certainly be served at about 12 °C (54 °F).

BUGEY ROUGE

Bugey Rouge can be made from Gamay or Pinot Noir. Both are generous, fresh, fruity and with little tannin. They are easy wines intended mainly for everyday consumption. Because of their wide versatility they are very popular with the local restaurant trade. Drink the ordinary wines within three years; the better ones (particularly those from the older vineyards, *vieilles vignes*) can age rather longer.

BUGEY ROUGE MONDEUSE

The Mondeuse grape gives this noble Bugey Rouge a very individual character, quite recognizable from its darker color with splendid purple-blue glints. Bouquet and taste are quite strong, headed by blackcurrants and peppers. Although you can also drink Bugey Rouge young, it is advisable to keep the wine at least five years. The best wines can even age for up to ten years.

Serve a Bugey Rouge Mondeuse with spicy beef casseroles or with roast or grilled game.

BUGEY MANICLE ROUGE

Like its white namesake, the red Manicle is made from grapes harvested in the commune of Cheignieu la Balme. Manicle Rouge is always made from Pinot grapes, which thrive in this area. Conspicuous in Manicle Rouge is the powerful bouquet and taste (ripe fruity accents and spices).

These are ideal wines for roast red meat or small game.

BUGEY BRUT AND MONTAGNIEU BRUT

Both sparkling wines are made by the traditional method familiar from other wines, including champagne. A number of suitable basic wines are selected which can come from different vineyards and are made of various grape varieties. The second fermentation takes place in bottle, with the bottles laid down on racks for a period of at least nine months. Soon afterwards the bottles are turned over quickly to bring the sediment into the neck. By local freezing of the neck the sediment is caught in a plug of ice. By quickly turning round and opening the bottle, the plug of ice is removed from the bottle. Before

Cerdon, very special and good!

the bottles are finally corked, they are filled up with the same wine and a small quantity of sugar until the desired taste is achieved, either *brut* (dry) or *demi-sec* (medium sweet).

CERDON

This is an exceptional wine, made by a very old method, also known from wines such as Blanquette de Limoux Ancestrale and Clairette de Die Ancestrale. Unlike Champagne and other sparkling wines where the second fermentation takes place in the bottle with the object of capturing the mature aromas, the wines made by the *méthode ancestrale* are distinguished by their sublimation of the primary (grape) and secondary (alcoholic fermentation) aromas. In other words, in these wines you taste the essence of the grapes themselves. Not all varieties of grapes are suitable for this 'ancestral method', only the very aromatic grape varieties.

Once jars or bottles were filled with the still fermenting must, and cooled in the water of the local river. The process has now been modernized a little, but the principle is still the same. The grapes for the manufacture of these Cerdons are still picked by hand on the steep hills, and only when they are fully ripe. This gives the wine a deeper rosé to red color and extra aromatic richness. During transport the grapes are lightly crushed to get more color and aromas from the skins. After careful pressing, the must is cooled to 5–10 °C (41–50 °F) in good years to stabilize the juices, which ensures extra aromatic strength. The first (alcoholic) fermentation takes place very slowly at low temperatures (1–9 °C/34–48 °F) and is only initiated spontaneously by the grape's own inherent yeast cells (*Saccharomyces uvarum*). After reaching the desired density the still fermenting must is cooled to -2 °C (28 °F) for 48 to 72 hours. After filtering the wine is bottled without any added sugar or yeast cells. The second fermentation happens in the bottle of its own accord by the action of the surviving residual sugars and the small number of yeast cells which have survived the gentle filtering. After eight days extra carbon dioxide starts to form through the conversion of the residual sugars in the yeast cells present, producing carbon dioxide and alcohol. After this second fermentation it is again gently filtered and the bottles are given their final corks. The result is quite amazing: extremely fruity (strawberries, blackberries, raspberries), full of taste, but light in structure (little alcohol), slightly sweet, but fresh enough to be well balanced. Not a wine to philosophize over, but rather one you can just sit back with and enjoy. Serve cool, between 6 and 8 °C (43–47 °F).

PROVENCE

Historically Provence is the oldest wine region in France. Of course, the Gauls had already enjoyed the noble grape, but it was the Greeks who planted the first organized vineyards in the immediate vicinity of their colonies in Southern France (Nice, Marseilles, Antibes).

After the Greeks the Romans made the region better known. The local monks improved the vineyards and vinification techniques. After the French revolution the wines of Provence fell out of favor somewhat. Only in the second half of the twentieth century did these wines become popular again, particularly the cheerful, generous and juicy rosé wines associated by everyone with holidays and the Mediterranean Sea. Partly thanks to the preference of film stars and directors for the picturesque coast of the Riviera and its many small fishing ports (Saint-Tropez, Antibes, Saint-Raphael) the popularity of the Provençal cuisine and wines grew enormously. A whole generation was brought up on the pastis and rosé of Provence.

THE IMAGE OF ROSÉ

In the 1990s consumers became increasingly interested in wine and gastronomy. They also became increasingly more knowledgeable and demanding. Consumers were given more and better information about wine. Moreover, the range available was expanded. Yet rosé lagged behind in this development. Only since 1998 have there been signs of rosé making an effective comeback.

So rosé is 'in' again. Yet it still remains to be seen whether this revival will extend beyond the summer months. People still associate rosé with the sun, sitting outside a café, lunch and holidays. In the sunny south of France gallons of rosé are drunk each year by tourists on the campsites, but once back home in a rather cooler

Even a simple rosé can be nice

climate, nobody is interested in it any more. A pity, because rosé deserves better!

For instance, rosé can be drunk all through the year with Indian, Indonesian, Chinese and particularly Thai dishes. But also with crustaceans and shellfish (cooked quickly with finely chopped shallots, parsley and garlic) it is lovely to drink a glass of Rosé de Provence, even on a cold winter's day. Did you know that a good Rosé de Provence, particularly the better *crus*, combines very well with salmon cooked *à la minute*? And other kinds of fish too, preferably grilled, with a garnish of tomatoes, basil, thyme, garlic and olive oil, demand an enjoyable Rosé de Provence.

TIP

In choosing a Rosé de Provence, pay attention to the color. In general the light-colored rosé wines are suitable for aperitifs or with light starters. The darker colored wines go better with main courses.

THE REGION

The Provençal wine region extends over an enormous area, from Nice to Arles. No wonder that the wines here differ so much in color, bouquet and taste. The vineyards are often a long way from each other, which involves much extra work. Most winegrowers are therefore members of a cooperative to keep down costs and work. However, the top wines come mostly from the smaller independent estates which do their own bottling. Obviously the price of these wines will always be rather higher than that of the cooperative wines, but the difference in quality justifies these higher prices.

THE GRAPE VARIETIES

Like anywhere else in the south of France, in Provençe, too, a large number of grape varieties are used, about twenty in all. Most wines here are made from several varieties.

For red and rosé wines a choice is made from Carignan, Cinsault, Grenache, Mourvèdre, Cabernet Sauvignon, Syrah and the less well know Tibouren, Calitor, Braquet, Folle Noire (Fuella) and Barbaroux.

The best wines can be found in small estates
(Château Revelette, Peter Fischer)

For the white wines the varieties used are Ugni Blanc, Clairette, Rolle and Sémillon, with here and there additions of Chardonnay, Grenache Blanc, Picpoul, Sauvignon Blanc and Muscat.

THE WINES

Provence has nine AOC wine regions. We start with the northernmost region and then travel along the coast from Nice to Arles.

Coteaux de Pierrevert

This region lies on both sides of the river Durance, around and to the north of the town of Manosque. The fresh white, red and rosé wines are full of character and are relatively low in alcohol.

The white wines are made from the following grape varieties: Grenache Blanc, Vermentino, Ugni Blanc, Clairette, Roussanne, Marsanne and Piquepoul (Picpoul), with up to the 2006 harvest at least 25 % Grenache Blanc and Vermentino, and after that date at least 50 %. No more than 70 % of the assembled grapes in the wine may be of any one variety.

The red wines must consist of at least two grape varieties, Grenache Noir and Syrah, which together must make up at least 70 % of the mix, which can be topped up if desired by Carignan, Cinsault or Mourvèdre, provided the relative grape varieties had been planted before 1998. The rosé wines consist of at least two of Grenache Noir, Syrah, Carignan and Cinsault, with at least 50 % Grenache Noir and 20 % Syrah. The wine may also have up to 20 % of the white grape varieties listed above.

Coteaux de Pierrevert are excellent wines for lunch, picnics or beach parties and usually provide a great deal of pleasant drinking at a relatively low price.

Bellet

In 1995 the brand-new owner of the local Château de Crémat declared that Bellet would become 'not the largest, but the best'… He still has a little way to go. The region is indeed small; about 80 acres. Excellent wines are made on the steep hills around Nice, but alas, most of it is sold locally.

BELLET ROUGE

Very characteristic wines of Folle Noire, Grenache, Cinsault and sometimes Braquet. A clear, cardinal-red color, very fruity aromas of blackcurrants and raspberries, with a hint of wood. The taste is velvety soft, full and round. These wines can age for some years.

Drink a Bellet Rouge lightly cooled with typical casseroles from the Provençal cuisine, such as *pot-au-feu*, *daube à la Provençale*, or *estouffade*.

BELLET-ROSÉ

Made of Braquet, Grenache and Cinsault, these rosé wines are fresh and soft as silk. The color tends towards pastel pink, the bouquet is fresh and inviting, with floral notes. The taste is soft, generous and friendly.

Drink the wine cool at 10–12 °C (50–54 °F) with the local pizza topped with plenty of tomatoes, onion and anchovy (*pisssaladière*) or egg dishes with paprikas and tomatoes.

Bellet, tiny, but it does have
a real château!

BELLET BLANC

Here it is Rolle and increasingly often Chardonnay which determine the taste of this wine. The wine has a pure and clear color, an elegant nose of toasted almonds with a whiff of white flowers and a fresh elegant taste, very well balanced, with a clear, but not too tight structure.

Côtes de Provence

In volume this is the most important AOC in Provence. The region is subdivided into five *terroirs*:
- the hills of the Haut Pays: around Draguignon, in the north of the region – limestone hills;
- La Vallée Intérieure: more to the south, in the interior between Fréjus and Toulon, to the north of the Maures range. The ground consists of ferruginous soil of clay and sand;
- the maritime border: along the coast, from Cannes to Toulon, at the foot of the Maures range. Soil of igneous rocks, schist and granite;
- the Beauset basin: rather jammed between the AOC Cassis and Bandol. Limestone soil;
- La Sainte-Victoire: around the imposing Sainte-Victoire mountain range, below Aix-en-Provence. Soil of clay and schist.

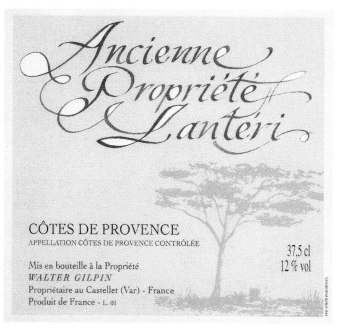

Côtes de Provence in the coastal region of Beausset

CÔTES DE PROVENCE ROSÉ

The color of this rosé depends on the vinification technique chosen, and the length of time the juice is in contact with the skins. The longer the contact time, the darker the wine. This Provençal rosé is dry, fruity and elegant. The color is always beautifully clear and sparkling.

The ever-smiling Guy Négrel in his vineyards at the foot
of Mont Ste-Victoire

Drink this wine at about 10 °C (50 °F) with fish, crustaceans and shellfish, vegetables or even white meat, poultry or lamb, cooked with onion, garlic, tomatoes, paprikas, basil, thyme, rosemary, oregano, olives and olive oil: the more of these ingredients, the tastier the combination.

CÔTES DE PROVENCE ROUGE

Outstanding wines, made traditionally with the help of the most modern technology. In these red wines there is a very great variety of color, bouquet and taste, from the differences in *terroir*, the grape variety used and the method of vinification. Some wines are light and fruity, with hints of flowers. Others – mostly wines which have been raised on wood – are rather more robust and fuller, and need to be kept for several years. Be that as it may, a fruity wine or one for laying down, a Côtes de Provence Rouge is able to please everyone.

Serve the fruity types, which are lighter in color, cooled (around 14 °C/ 57 °F) at lunch or a picnic. Also pleasant with light meat dishes. The heavier types are

Côtes de Provence rosé and red

best served a little less cool (around 16 °C/61 °F) with red meat, wildfowl or even a good cheeseboard.

CÔTES DE PROVENCE BLANC

Rather rare wines of high quality, always made only from white grapes (*blanc de blancs*). Here, too, the grape variety used and the *terroir* determine what type of wine is produced: fresh and supple or rounded and full. A wine you really ought to discover and which will teach you about another aspect of Provence.

Drink a Côtes de Provence Blanc cool, at 10–12 °C

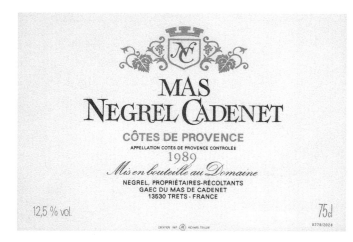

Take particular note of the special *cuvées* of the smaller estates!

(50–54 °F)), with everything good the sea has to offer. Also pleasant with a fresh goat's cheese.

Coteaux Varois

To the north of Bandol, wedged, as it were, between the *terroirs* of La Sainte-Victoire and of La Vallée Intérieure, are the vineyards of a relatively recent wine region. Only since 1993 have the Coteaux du Varois been officially recognized as a member of the AC family. In the center of the department of Var, around the picturesque Provençal town of Brignòles, pleasant, fruity and full wines are made (60 % rosé, 35 % red and 5 % white). They are very similar to the Côtes de Provence wines (see there for recommended dishes).

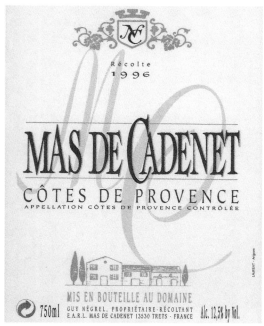

Mas de Cadenet Rouge, impressive and still very affordable

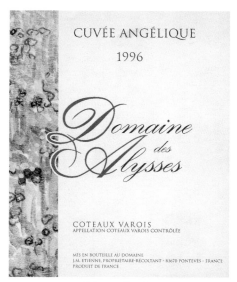

Coteaux Varois

Bandol

The vineyards of Bandol are planted on terraces (*restanques*) of poor, lime-rich, gravely soil, protected by an amphitheater of wooded mountains (Massif de Sainte-Beaume, 3,500 ft). Here the sun shines as much as 3,000 hours per year! Fortunately the easterly and south--easterly breezes supply the necessary rain showers and the south winds from the Mediterranean soften the extremely warm climate.

Generations of hard-working winegrowers have built and maintained these terraces by hand. On the dry soil of the steep slopes a perpetual struggle has gone on for centuries against destructive erosion. It is never quiet in the vineyards here. A great deal still has to be done by hand, because the terraced structure does not everywhere allow mechanization. This has obviously influenced the price of a good Bandol.

Also important for the price is the yield. The legally prescribed maximum yield of 40 hl per hectare (45.5 US bushels per acre) is barely reached here. The average is about 35 hl per hectare (39.75 US bushels per acre). The total area of the vineyards is just under 2,500 acres.

The local winegrowers are perfectionists; they are constantly searching for the best sites, the best grapes, the best vats, and so on. The result speaks for itself. Bandol wines belong to the elite club of great French wines.

A good Bandol is among the elite of French wines

BANDOL ROUGE

Red Bandol has to be made from at least 50 % Mourvèdre, which may be made up to 90 % with Grenache and/or Cinsault. The remaining 10 % may come from Syrah and Carignan, so the Mourvèdre determines the character of red Bandol. Where other grape varieties might produce scorched aromas caused by the large amount of sunlight, Mourvèdre retains its fruity aromas which makes the grape particularly suitable for the hot Bandol vineyards.

A red Bandol is very tannic when it is young, after at least eighteen months on oak. Many people think that a red Bandol is too expensive and the wines too hard. These people have not had the patience to keep the wines for at least six, but preferably ten years. Only then is a red Bandol at its best... The bouquet is a sublime combination of red and black fruits (wild cherries), peonies, brushwood and heliotrope (a Mediterranean plant with pleasantly scented purple-blue flowers, a little like borage). When the wine is a little older (more than ten years) the classic aromas develop of truffles, pepper, vanilla, licorice, cinnamon and musk. A red Bandol of a good year can certainly be kept for twenty years. If you then look back after ten or twenty years at what you paid for it, you will agree with me that it was more than reasonable in the light of the quality it offers.

So don't drink your Bandol Rouge too young, but at a mature age. It is good with red meat dishes and all kinds of game. Serve the wine at 16–18 °C (61–64 °F).

You will always get value for money with a Bandol

BANDOL ROSÉ

Here, too, the same strict proportions apply for the grape varieties. A Bandol rosé combines the essential elements of Mourvèdre (wild cherry, red and black fruits, peonies, heliotrope, pepper) with a charm, strength, freshness and depth of its own.

Serve Bandol rosé at 10–12 °C (50–54 °F), as an aperitif, or with dishes in which olive oil, olives, garlic and Provençal herbs are noticeably present. Also excellent with grilled sea fish.

Bandol Rosé

BANDOL BLANC

These white wines are extremely fresh, lively and impudent. They are made from Clairette, Ugni Blanc and Bourboulenc. In the nose you will usually recognize citrus fruits (grapefruit, lemon) and flowers. The taste is full, fleshy and playful at the same time.

A Bandol Blanc is an excellent accompaniment to sea fish, crustaceans and shellfish, and all dishes with grilled paprikas, garlic and olive oil. Don't serve a Bandol Blanc too cold (10–12 °C/ 50–54 °F).

Cassis

Cassis is the name of an idyllic small port on the Mediterranean. The harbor is surrounded by imposing rock faces which offer protection to the vineyards of one of the finest white wines of France. Of a total 440 acres, 300 acres are devoted to white wines.

Rosé and red are also made at Cassis, both strikingly fruity, supple and pleasant. Delicious with dishes containing olives and anchovies.

CASSIS BLANC

You will not easily find a good Cassis Blanc outside the region where it is produced. Local demand virtually exceeds production. The wine smells of beeswax, honey, ripe fruits, cedar wood, flowers (may, lilac), almonds and hazelnuts. The taste is very fresh and full-bodied. The obvious presence of acids ensures a good structure.

Drink this wine with the local *bouillabaisse* (fish soup). Above all, don't forget the *aioli* (garlic-mayonnaise) and the *rouille* (sauce with hot peppers and saffron). Try it some time with aubergines or courgettes scented with anchovy butter, or a robust *tapenade* (a paste of olives and anchovy). Drink this white Cassis at 10–12 °C (50–54 °F).

Palette

Palette is a tiny wine region near Aix-en-Provence. The vineyards lie on a soil of fragmented limestone, protected from the burning sun and the harsh winds by a circle of woods. Palette wines (red, rosé and white) are appreciated by connoisseurs all over the world. Because of their high price they are, alas, only for the 'happy few'.

PALETTE ROUGE

Very elegant and sophisticated wines, ruby-red in color, with subtle aromas of red fruits and violets, and a pene-

Cassis Blanc,
tremendous with sea food!

Château Simone (Palette), the dream of many
a sommelier!

trating bouquet of musk, vanilla and pine trees. The taste is complex, rounded and full, with plenty of structure. This powerful and well-balanced wine deserves to be kept for several years.

Drink the wine at about 16 °C (61 °F), with wildfowl, rabbit or other kinds of meat, with a sauce containing olives.

PALETTE ROSÉ

Light ruby-red in color with amber glints. The nose is very fruity and the taste fresh and full, with much elegance and finesse.

Drink Palette Rosé at 10–12 °C (50–54 °F) with, for example, grilled sea fish, crustaceans and shellfish or grilled paprikas. Anchovy goes well with them, too.

PALETTE BLANC

According to connoisseurs, quite the best of the three Palette wines. A white Palette does not give itself up at once. Allow it time to breathe, if necessary decant it first. After a little while it will reveal its secret: aromas of flowers, brushwood, young wood combined with quince jelly, ripe fruits and, above all, much power and elegance in the luxurious taste. These wines can age very well, and they take on a splendid old-gold tint. The bouquet of a mature white Palette is overwhelming, almost intoxicating. Sommeliers who have had the opportunity to try such a great wine, wax lyrical – or are speechless – years later when the name Château Simone is mentioned. Without doubt one of the finest white wines from France and far beyond!

Rare, not cheap, but really sublime

Drink a Palette Blanc at about 12 °C (54 °F) with grilled sea fish, such as gurnard or sea bream, or with grilled Provençal vegetables with good olive oil, garlic and fresh herbs. An unforgettable experience.

Coteaux d'Aix-en-Provence

This extensive region lies to the south of the river Durance and stretches to the Mediterranean Sea in the south and to the Rhône in the west. The soil consists of limestone and the landscape is characterized by an alternating scene of small hills and alluvial valleys. The hills run parallel to the coast and are covered with low shrubs, wild herbs (*garrigue*) and coniferous forest. The valleys consist of a substratum of friable stone and siliceous earth with here and there calcareous sandstone and schist and is covered by a mixture of sand, gravel and alluvial deposits. The region is quite large, some 8,500 acres.

Until the 1970s mainly red wines were made here, but the production of rosé has expanded explosively since then. Currently 70 % of production is rosé wines. The grapes most used for rosé and red are Grenache and Cinsault, supplemented by Syrah and Cabernet Sauvignon.

COTEAUX D'AIX-EN-PROVENCE ROSÉ

These wines are light, fruity and very pleasant. The better Coteaux d'Aix-en-Provence rosés are full and powerful with a floral dominance. Drink these wines young, at a temperature of 10–12 °C (50–54 °F).

Good with Provençal dishes such as grand aioli (vegetables, fish and potatoes with garlic mayonnaise), ratatouille, grilled fish or grilled vegetables (eggplants, courgettes, paprikas, tomatoes, artichokes, fennel).

Coteaux d'Aix en Provence Rosé

COTEAUX D'AIX-EN-PROVENCE ROUGE

Fascinating wines which can still sometimes be a little coarse. So not too much elegance or subtlety, but *terroir*, fruit, power and sensual notes of leather, pepper, spices and herbs. The tannin is soft, so that the wines can be drunk when still young. However, the better wines are only at their best after two or three years.

Drink these wines at 14–16 °C (57–61 °F) with roast meat (a joint of lamb!), Provençal vegetables (tomato, eggplant, courgette) stuffed with a well-spiced lamb mince. Mature wines will also serve well with a not too heavy dish of game.

COTEAUX D'AIX-EN-PROVENCE BLANC

These rather uncommon white wines from Grenache Blanc, Bourboulenc, Clairette, Grolle, Sauvignon and Ugni Blanc are often full, charming and elegant at the same time. They smell of flowers (may) and/or shrubs (privet, box) and the taste is fresh, full, very aromatic and full of character.

Served at 10–12 °C (50–54 °F) these wines are perfect companions for fruits-de-mer, but they also combine excellently with (fish) dishes made with saffron, olive oil, tomato and garlic.

Coteaux d'Aix en Provence Rouge

Coteaux d'Aix en Provence Blanc

Baux de Provence

This region is really part of the Coteaux d'Aix-en-Provence, but since 1995 it has had its own AOC. The scene here is dominated by the wild and picturesque Alpilles hills, with vineyards alternating with olive groves. The region acquired its own appellation thanks to the local microclimate and its rather stricter product standards. Only the red and rosé wines, which are produced on an area of 750 acres around the town of Baux de Provence may carry this AOC.

BAUX-DE-PROVENCE ROSÉ

The color strikes you first: a splendid salmon pink. The bouquet is reminiscent of redcurrants, strawberries and other red fruits. The taste is fresh, fruity (grapefruit, cherries) and very pleasant. This rosé is capable of charming everyone.

Drink a Baux-de-Provence Rosé cool (10–12 °C/50–54 °F) as an aperitif or with Provençal dishes.

BAUX-DE-PROVENCE ROUGE

The color of these red wines is a rather, deep ruby-red. The nose is complex and powerful, with shades of wood, vanilla, licorice, plum jam, caramel, coffee, cocoa, brushwood and sometimes cherry brandy. Because of the robust youthful tannins, the taste in the first years is quite rough, but after a few years in bottle it becomes rounder, full and powerful. Certainly no charmer at first sight, rather a civilized heavy-weight.

Drink this rouge at 16–18 °C (61–64 °F) with roast meats, game or robust hard or semi-hard cheeses.

CORSICA

HISTORY

For a long time Corsica was known as a treasure island to all sea-going peoples. Phoenicians, Greeks, Romans and Moors were frequent visitors. It was in all probability the Greeks who first cultivated vines on the island, long before our era. But there were wild vine stocks growing there as long ago as 6000 BC.

Clos Mireille of the legendary Domaines d'Ott (Provence) produces one of the finest French white wines

When the Greeks established their colony of Massalia (Marseilles) around 600 BC, Corsica was a wild mountain in the Mediterranean. The island was inhabited only by shepherds and swineherds. The Greeks quickly realized the strategic importance of the island and built a naval base in Alalia, surrounded by cultivated vineyards. During the Roman occupation the island acquired a slightly more civilized and better organized existence. Small harbors became towns, small-scale vineyards and fields were turned into rather larger agricultural enterprises.

After the fall of the Roman Empire the island was brutally assaulted by a variety of peoples. Agriculture went into decline. In spite of the Saracen occupation and the invasions of barbarian pirates, the brave monks from small Christian settlements kept up the vineyards.

From the eleventh century until 1285 Corsica came under the rule of Pisa. After Pisa was defeated by Genoa, Corsica changed ownership. It remained Italian until 1755.

In 1755 the island was bought by the French for a song. Until World War II it was mainly Corsica's sweet liqueur wines which sold well. Not until 1957 was the world of wine put to rights in Corsica. Viticultural legislation was tightened, while planting vines on the most suitable soil was strongly encouraged by the authorities.

Following the Algerian struggle for independence, when the French hastily had to abandon their former colony, the refugee French winegrowers found second homes in Languedoc-Roussillon, the Rhône valley and in Corsica. At least 17,000 of them settled in Corsica, which gave an enormous boost to Corsican winegrowing. This injection was, however, more quantitative than qualitative in nature. Used as they were in Algeria to the large-scale production of wines for blending, the newcomers for years went to work in the same way in Corsica. Because the price of the wine was often based on its alcohol content, tons of sugar (chaptalization) went into these 'foster brother' wines, which were designed to help their weaker brothers in Languedoc-Roussillon to keep going.

Since 1976 these blending wines have no longer been so popular. French technology has improved to the point that almost all French wine regions can support themselves, without any addition of imported wines being necessary. Since that time Corsica has made a gigantic U-turn. The younger generation of winegrowers have radically changed course. Where masses of moderate wine were once produced, now old traditional vines, such as nielluccio, sciaccarello and vermentinu (vermentino) have been replanted. Quality now comes first.

TWO VIEWS

Vins de table, vins de pays, vins de cépage, and no less than nine AOC wines are produced on the island of Corsica. There are really two Corsican wine-growing zones: the north, east and south coasts, which are the traditionally oriented wine regions that include all the small-scale AOCs; and the east coast, where there is more interest in manufacturing generic Corsican wines, vins de pays and vins de cépage. For the first eight AOCs the traditional grape varieties are used (nielluccio, sciaccarello and vermentinu), while the generic AOC Vins de Corse are based on vermentinu, nielluccio, sciaccarello and grenache. In the vins de pays and vins de cépage cabernet, merlot and chardonnay dominate.

Corsica is also divided into two parts in respect of terroir. The north (Bastia, Calvi, Corte, Aléria) has a complex soil of clay and lime around Bastia (AOC Patrimonio) and blue schist on the east coast, while the south (Porto, Ajaccio, Sartene, Bonifacio and Porto-Vecchio consists of igneous rock and granite. This dividing line is, of course, largely academic, since over the whole island there are countless mini terroirs and microclimates to be found.

GRAPE VARIETIES

Corsica's 'own' three grape varieties cannot actually be called native. The names just sound a little different from anywhere else, though two of the three are familiar.

VERMENTINO

The white vermentino is also called 'Corsican malvoisie' and is a typical Mediterranean grape. This grape, also cultivated in Italy, Spain and Portugal, delivers white wines of high quantity, very floral, mostly high in alcohol, full and rich in taste and with a recognizable aftertaste of bitter almonds and apple. As happens more frequently in Italian wines, vermentino is sometimes added to red grapes, making splendid rosé wines. The taste of red wines is also enriched by it.

NIELLUCCIO

This is a world-famous grape which we know better under the name 'Jupiter's blood' or sangiovese (Tuscany). The wines from this grape are recognizable from their aromas of red fruits, violets, spices and sometimes apricots. As they get older, characteristic hints of game, fur and licorice develop. The taste is luxurious, fat and supple. Nielluccio is mainly used for the Patrimonio wines.

SCIACCARELLO

In Corsica also called 'sciaccarellu', which means something like 'crisp'. This variety of grape does particularly well on granite soils, for instance, in Ajaccio. The wines from sciaccarello are very sophisticated and can be recognized particularly from their typical peppery bouquet and taste.

THE NINE AOCs

COTEAUX-DU-CAP-CORSE

With only 75 acres of AOC vineyards, this is a tiny region, lying on mountainous slopes to the north of the town of Bastia. Here red and rosé, but mainly white wines are made. The white wines, based on vermentino, are excellent and very sophisticated.

MUSCAT-DU-CAP-CORSE

These wines are made in the same mountainous region as the Coteaux du Cap Corse and also in the Patrimonio region. This appellation was only officially recognized in 1993, but the local Muscat wines have enjoyed international fame for centuries. They are fine and very aromatic. The best Muscat wines are made from late-harvested grapes which, placed in small boxes, continue to ripen and shrink under the hot sun. In this way full, very aromatic, fat and powerful wines, which age well, are produced. Drink them well cooled, at around 8 °C (47 °F).

When they are young and fruity these wines go well with fruit salads or fruit cake. Rather older and wiser, they can be a match for a *foie gras* or even strong blue cheeses (Roquefort or Gorgonzola).

PATRIMONIO

One of the best known, and often also the best wines of Corsica. Red and rosé wines are made from niellucciu grapes. Vermentinu also guarantees splendid white wines here.

– Patrimonio Blanc: light yellow wines with a green glint. Floral aromas (hawthorn and white flowers), fresh and fruity taste, round and full, with occasionally a light sparkle. Drink these elegant wines at about 10 °C (50 °F) as an aperitif or with fish dishes, crustaceans and shellfish, poultry and white meat. Excellent with the local fresh goat's cheese, but any other goat's cheese will go well with them.

– Patrimonio Rosé: light clear pink color. Aromas of red fruit (cherries, redcurrants) and sometimes exotic fruits. Drink this fresh and fruity rosé at about 10 °C (50 °F) with cold meats, fish dishes, salads with fish, meat, or vegetables, and cheese without too pronounced a taste.

– Patrimonio Rouge: these wines are made in two versions: a lighter version and a robust traditional one. The lighter Patrimonio Rouge wines are usually ruby-red in color, very fruity (blackcurrants, blackberries), velvety soft – in spite of the presence of tannins – and very well-balanced. As the wine gets older, the fruity aromas evolve into earthy shades, such as brushwood. Drink this type of wine at about 16 °C (61 °F) with red meat, game, casseroles and strong cheeses.

The traditional rather more robust Patrimonio are darker in color and have more tannin than their lighter cousins. As they age, their fruity bouquet and taste change into more complex aromas of overripe or crystallized fruits, leather and licorice.

Serve these heavy-weights at 16–18 °C (61–64 °F) with robust red meat dishes, game, casseroles and

Muscat-du-Cap-Corse

Patrimonio

Calvi

sheep's cheese. Both types of Patrimonio will benefit from being decanted a few hours before the meal.

VIN-DE-CORSE-CALVI

On a very irregular soil of rough stones, boulders and gravel very fruity red wines, fascinating, sophisticated and aromatic rosé wines and very pale, generous and easy white wines are produced from the nielluccio, grenache, cinsault, sciaccarello and vermentino grape varieties.

Lightly cooled, they all combine well with dishes from the Mediterranean cuisine.

AJACCIO

This wine region, situated on uneven rocky hills, is proud of its 'permanent resident', the sciaccarello grape, which here produces great wines with recognizable aromas of toasted almonds and red fruits (raspberries). These traditional wines can age well. Very rewarding too are the white wines for laying down from malvoisie (vermentino).

VIN-DE-CORSE-SARTÈNE

The sciaccarello, grenache and cinsault grapes, which produce full red and fresh rosé wines, are here cultivated on steep hills. These wines are mainly drunk by the local population. You will rarely meet them outside the island.

VIN-DE-CORSE-FIGARI

This is the most southerly wine region of France, to the north of the town of Bonifacio. Here they make robust red, white and rosé wines.

Ajaccio Rouge

VIN-DE-CORSE-PORTO-VECCHIO

In the south-east of the island elegant, full and rounded red wines and fresh, sophisticated and very aromatic rosé wines are produced from the nielluccio and sciaccarello grapes, together with grenache. Very dry and intensely fruity white wines are made from vermentino.

VIN-DE-CORSE

In the – by Corsican standards – immense wine region round Aléria and below Bastia (3,800 acres), generic wines are made. This is a relatively recent appellation, but the first results are extremely promising. After centuries of neglect the vineyards are being replanted in places where once the Greeks and Romans made their better wines, at the foot of the 3,600 ft rock face. Here all types of wine are made, including excellent *vins de pays*. As well as very traditional wine-growing businesses, there are also hypermodern cooperatives, which are becoming increasingly known in and outside France for their less traditional, but very correct wines. In *vin de pays*, too, the tendency seems to be towards quality. The market for the AOC is growing, as is that of the better *vins de pays* and *vins de cépage*. For this reason in Corsica, too, fewer mediocre wines are made and quality is becoming more and more important.

Vin de Corse Blanc Vermentino and Ajaccio Rosé

This extremely tragic passage in the history of Languedoc-Roussillon is still kept alive today by the native population. The proud and pure character of the Cathars appeals to people. The inhabitants of Languedoc-Roussillon are very attached to their *terroir* and their ancestors.

This respect for tradition, certainly among the younger generation, you will also find in their wines. A miracle has occurred in Languedoc-Roussillon: the proud blood of the Cathars has flowed back into the vines, and that is what makes the wines so full of character.

Between the Rhône and Languedoc

COSTIÈRES-DE-NÎMES

The region lies geographically between the Rhône valley and Languedoc-Roussillon, but is not in fact accepted by either region as a legitimate descendant. You will often come across Costières-de-Nîmes as a maverick among the Languedoc wines. It is not wrong to list it here, but it is simply the author's choice.

Costières-de-Nîmes wines are produced in white, rosé and red, in a very picturesque region between the town of Nîmes and the Camargue. The total area of the AOC vineyards has grown enormously in recent decades (now 30,000 acres) and it is expected to expand

LANGUEDOC-ROUSSILLON

A third of all French wine comes from Languedoc-Roussillon. However, most of this wine falls into the category of *vins de pays* or even *vins de table*. Languedoc-Roussillon produces at least 75 % of the French *vins de pays*. These wines are of a higher quality than the ordinary table wines, but do not in general reach the level of a well made AOC wine. Of course, there are many exceptions to this rule. Many *vins de pays* are in fact sold under the name of the grape variety, as *vins de cépage*.

The history of Languedoc-Roussillon has always been linked with wine and wine-growing. Greek and Roman ruins, castles, abbeys and churches are the silent witnesses of a turbulent past. In Languedoc-Roussillon bloody battles took place, particularly to silence the Albigensian Cathars. The region has always been of great strategic importance to the kings of France and their arch-rivals from Aragon to the south. At that time the Cathars controlled the important passes from their castles built like true eagle's nests. Because the Cathars were anathema to the Catholic Church, a monstrous alliance was made between the king of France and the Church to eradicate the members of this heretical sect. Under the flag of the fearsome Inquisition, the inhabitants of the region were completely 'cleansed'. The Cathar fortresses were overcome with a great show of strength, and burnt. Thousands of Cathars were cruelly murdered, without any form of trial.

Many of the French *vins de pays* come from Languedoc-Roussillon

Excellent white *vins de pays* come from neighboring Ardèche

Ever more famous wine houses are established in Languedoc-Roussillon (Baroness Philippine de Rothschild and Pierre Mirc of Aimery, partners for excellent *vins de pays*)

further. The ground of Costières-de-Nîmes is hilly and contains a lot of gravel and boulders.

The white wines are often made with the most modern technology. They are fresh, very aromatic (flowers, exotic fruits, peaches) and are extremely pleasant. Drink them as aperitifs or with crustaceans, shellfish and sea fish, at around 10 °C (50 °F).

The rosé wines are dry and full-bodied, with a great deal of fruit (red fruits, peaches). The taste is fresh and rounded with a good balance between acidity and roundness. Such a rosé wine is a first-class accompaniment to cold meats. Serve the wine at 10–12 °C (50–54 °F).

The red wines are fruity, full and full-bodied. The nose is reminiscent of freshly picked blackberries, redcurrants and blackcurrants, with sometimes a whiff of vanilla (pod) and tobacco.

Drink these red wines at 14–16 °C (57–61 °F) with red meat, preferably barbecued.

CLAIRETTE DE BELLEGARDE

For the sake of completeness, we also mention this small wine region within the boundaries of the Costières-de--Nîmes; only white wines are produced there. They are very fascinating, partly because of their characteristic intense aromas of white flowers and citrus fruit. Delicious as a fresh aperitif, or at a meal with all kinds of delicacies from the sea. Drink at a temperature of 10–12 °C (50–54 °F).

Languedoc

HISTORY

Wine has been grown here from time immemorial, but only in the seventeenth century did it start to play an important

Costières-de-Nîmes

Costières-de-Nîmes Rouge

role in the economic life of the region. At that time the Dutch were searching everywhere for sourish wines for the production of their brandies. The main markets were in Bordeaux and Bergerac. After the completion of the navigable link between the Mediterranean and the Atlantic via the Canal du Midi, it was possible for the winegrowers from Languedoc to transport their wines to Bordeaux.

In the nineteenth century the industrial revolution reached the continent of Europe. The large cities – particularly Paris – had a great need for manpower, and there was a major exodus from the French countryside. The work was heavy and badly paid. There was little time for recreation, so many sought refuge in the local cafés and bars. This meant that wine consumption soon increased enormously. The winegrowers of Languedoc found themselves with an unexpected new market. Whole cargoes of cheap wine were carried to Paris by train. Languedoc enjoyed a golden age. But quite soon competition from Algeria, Italy and Spain became greater and more fatal. Revolts by furious farmers did not help; the struggle was an unequal one and lost in advance.

A complete restructuring was necessary to breathe new life into the region. For decades they worked with might and man for a comeback, in which quality and variety were the keywords. In less than twenty years Languedoc has developed from one of the most recent to one of the largest wine regions; today with its more than 75,000 acres of AOC wines it is the third largest in France. Shortsighted mass production has given way to quality and authenticity, with respect for tradition, but with the help of the most modern technology.

THE REGION

The success of this comeback is, of course, largely due to the work of the winegrowers and of the local authorities, who had the nerve to start again right from the beginning. But Mother Nature lent a hand, too. Languedoc is a very extensive region with many aspects: the wide sandy beaches of the Mediterranean, countless small lakes in the interior, the steep slopes of the Cévennes, soils of lime, schist, gravel and pebbles – a true mosaic of *terroirs* and vineyards.

In the last twenty years the vineyards of Languedoc have been completely renewed, with the emphasis being placed on the Mediterranean grape varieties of Grenache, Mourvèdre and Syrah. In addition research is being done into the possibilities for restoring the reputation of the various local grape varieties, and

Nowadays excellent wines are produced in Languedoc-Roussillon

improving them. As a rule, wines in Languedoc are vinified separately by grape variety and mixed after fermentation.

APPELLATIONS FROM EAST TO WEST:

COTEAUX DU LANGUEDOC

In a region of 20,000 acres between Nîmes and Narbonne various white, red and rosé wines are made. Some of these wines (Saint-Chinian and Faugères among the red and Clairette du Languedoc among the white) can carry their own AOC. The others carry the AOC Coteaux du Languedoc, coupled with the name of their *terroir*, or just Coteaux du Languedoc. All the *terroirs* have an added value of their own, but characteristic of all the Coteaux du Languedoc are their freshness, their suppleness, and their pleasant, attractive taste.

THE TERROIRS

Above Lunel and Montpellier:
Coteaux de Saint-Christol
Coteaux de Vérargues
Saint-Drézery
Pic Saint-Loup
Coteaux de la Méjanelle
Saint-Georges-d'Orques

Above Clermont-l'Hérault:
Saint-Saturnin
Montpeyroux

Above Sète:
Cabrières
Picpoul-de-Pinet (blanc)

Below Narbonne:
La Clape (rouge & blanc)
Quatourze

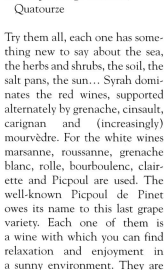

Unfiltered wine

Try them all, each one has something new to say about the sea, the herbs and shrubs, the soil, the salt pans, the sun… Syrah dominates the red wines, supported alternately by grenache, cinsault, carignan and (increasingly) mourvèdre. For the white wines marsanne, roussanne, grenache blanc, rolle, bourboulenc, clairette and Picpoul are used. The well-known Picpoul de Pinet owes its name to this last grape variety. Each one of them is a wine with which you can find relaxation and enjoyment in a sunny environment. They are

not wines to philosophize over for hours, but just to enjoy, for instance, at lunch, a picnic, an *al fresco* meal, a barbecue (with grilled fish and meat) or for an intimate evening with your best friends. There is a Coteaux du Languedoc for every occasion. The white wines of La Clape and Picpoul are also excellent companions to fish and *fruits de mer*. Drinking temperatures: white wines 10 °C (50 °F), rosé 12 °C (54 °F) and red 14–16 °C (57–61 °F).

MUSCAT DE LUNEL

La Clape

A very small appellation (750 acres) of extremely fruity Muscat wines, which fall under the category of *vin doux naturel* (naturally sweet wines). The soil consists of boulders on a substratum of red clay. The vineyards lie on hilly ridges round the small towns of Lunel, between Nîmes and Montpellier. Here the only grape variety used is the very scented Muscat à petits grains. Characteristic of a Muscat de Lunel are the aromas of citrus fruits and flowers, rounded off with hints of honey, crystallized fruit and raisins. The better Muscat de Lunel sometimes also have a pleasant bitter and peppery aftertaste.

Drink them by themselves or with blue cheeses (Roquefort, Bleu d'Auvergne). For a wine lover a fresh fruit salad (for instance of apple, orange, grapefruit, papaya, mango, pineapple and passion fruit) softens the sweetness of the wine. Also good with the local delicacies of

Picpoul-de-Pinet

Try the better organic wines from Languedoc some time

marzipan garnished with pinecone seeds. Drink at a temperature of 6 °C (43 °F).

CLAIRETTE DU LANGUEDOC

The white clairette grape is one of the oldest varieties of grape and Clairette du Languedoc one of the oldest (and smallest) appellations in Languedoc. The vineyards lie on the hills of the Hérault valley, to the south of the small town of Lodève, some 30 km (20 miles) from the sea.

This fresh, full, rounded wine goes especially well with fish dishes, particularly oven-cooked ones, but a Clairette du Languedoc is also a first-class luncheon wine, to accompany egg dishes, such as omelets. Drink at a temperature of 10–12 °C (50–54 °F).

MUSCAT DE MIREVAL

Vins doux naturel from Mireval, between Montpellier and Sète. The vineyards lie on the southern flanks of the Gardiole, a mountain dominating the inland lake of Vic. The soil is limy with here and there some alluvial deposits and rock. Here, too, only Muscat à petits grains is used. The wines are plump, fruity and rather like liqueurs. The charm of a Muscat de Mireval lies in its subtle aromas, both floral (jasmine, lime blossom, snakeweed, roses) and fruity (citrus, raisins).

Drink them by themselves in the evening after a meal or with French fritters, in which a little orange-blossom water and aniseed liqueur has been used. Also nice with elderflower fritters! Drinking temperature: 6 °C (43 °F).

MUSCAT DE FRONTIGNAN

The Frontignan vineyards lie rather more to the south than those of Mireval, just above Sète. The Muscat wines they produce are more robust than the last two and tend more towards liqueur. The nose is a little less aromatic than the other Muscats, rather rougher (though there are exceptions). There are recognizable aromas of citrus fruits and overripe muscat grapes up to and including raisins. The best Muscat de Frontignan wines develop outstanding aromas of exotic fruits (passion fruit!) and peaches, and are very elegant.

They are pleasant to drink by themselves with a few pretzels, or with a fresh fruit salad (passion fruit, peach, orange). Drinking temperature: 6 °C (43 °F).

FAUGÈRES

A little to the north of Béziers lie the vineyards of Faugères on soft hilly ridges of schist. The region is wild, uneven, but at the same time welcoming and intimate. In the small villages supple, silky-soft red wines are made which smell and taste of ripe fruits and licorice. After a few years extra maturing, the wines tend towards spicy aromas and notes of leather.

An ideal wine for small game birds, but also for red meat, white meat and poultry. Drinking temperature 14–16 °C (57–61 °F).

Faugères also produces a little rosé, which combines the velvety and fruity character of the red wines with a soft freshness.

Good with grilled fish, cold meats and chicken or other poultry. Drinking temperature: 12 °C (54 °F).

Muscat de Frontignan

SAINT-CHINIAN

At the foot of the Montagne Noire, north-east of Béziers, the red and rosé wines of Saint-Chinian are made. There are two types of Saint-Chinian: a light, playful one that is supple and generous, with lots of fruit, and a heavier type, full of character and powerful, with aromas of ripe fruit, bay and flint.

Drink the first type while the wine is still young, preferably cooled (12–14 °C/54–57 °F) with light kinds of meat and chicken or other poultry.

The second type is better left to mature for several years and then served at 14–16 °C (57–61 °F) with casseroles, stuffed vegetables, grilled meat or even game. Excellent with duck.

Drink a Saint-Chinian Rosé at lunch, with fish, crustaceans or shellfish or with chicken. Drinking temperature: 12 °C (54 °F).

MUSCAT DE SAINT-JEAN-DE--MINERVOIS

At a height of 600 ft, among the wild undergrowth and Provençal herbs, lie the vineyards of Saint--Jean-de-Minervois. The soil is a mixture of lime and schist on a substratum of red clay. Here, too, only muscat à petits grains is used. In this tiny region of 390 acres, outstanding, very aromatic wines are produced. Characteristic of a Muscat de Saint-Jean-de-Minervois are the intense aromas of citrus fruits, fresh muscat grapes, exotic fruits and ... menthol!

In spite of their liqueur-like character, these Muscat wines are still extremely fresh. Try them with

It pays to look for the better cuvées

a fresh fruit salad of oranges, orange-blossom water, honey and... peppermint leaves. If you dare, you can also add a thin trickle of fruity olive oil to the dish. Drinking temperature: 6 °C (43 °F).

MINERVOIS

The vineyards of Minervois lie in the triangle Carcassonne, Narbonne, Béziers, and are characterized by their many terraces. Mainly red wine is made there, but if you search hard you will sometimes find a rosé, or even more rarely, a white Minervois. The red wines are fruity, sophisticated, elegant and well balanced. There are as

St-Chinian

Muscat de St-Jean-de-Minervois

Minervois

many types of Minervois as there are types of *terroir*. Here in the Minervois you are given a free lesson in geology with your wine... Gneiss, limestone, schist, lignite and alluvial deposits mingle in the soil and give each wine a character of its own.

Drink the rosé wines cooled (12 °C/54 °F) with cold meats, and the red wines with the local cassoulet (a dish of beans stewed with goose fat), or with light game dishes (hare). Drinking temperature: 14–16 °C (57–61 °F).

MINERVOIS-LA-LIVINIÈRE

Even in the Languedoc itself by no means everyone is aware of this new, tiny AOC. And yet, for a long time something special has been happening there. It began in the 1960s, when Jacques Tallavignes planted the first syrah stocks on the land of his Château de Paulignan. At a time, when the region produced mainly thin, insignificant wines, he nonetheless saw a gol-

den future for Languedoc. He soon managed to persuade his neighbors to plant syrah stocks too. This marked the beginning of a kind of cultural revolution in the Minervois.

In the 1970s two men attended the birth of the present-day success of La-Livinière: Roger Piquet, a wine merchant, convinced of the good quality of the local vineyards, and Maurice Piccinini, president of the local Cave Coopérative (cooperative cellars). They worked like two fanatics for the delivery of a *grand cru* from Languedoc. They were supported in this by several other growers, among them Daniel Domergue (Clos Centeilles), Michel Escande (Borie de Maurel) and Robert Eden (Château Maris), a congenial Brit.

In 1989 the Syndicat du Cru La-Livinière was set up. Its fight for recognition of quality was just before the new millennium crowned with the award of its own AOC.

From the 1998 harvest onwards, the wines made here may display Minervois-La-Livinière AOC on their label.

Real gems sometimes hide behind insignificant labels

LA-LIVINIÈRE

La-Livinière is the name of a picturesque village already known for its wines in Roman times, as witness its old Latin name of *Cela Vinaria*. The *terroir* of La-Livinière resembles a miniature version of the Minervois, with limestone rocks and marl as the dominant types of soil. The best vineyards lie on the sunny slopes of the hills. But more perhaps than the type of soil it is the microclimate of La-Livinière, which is of great importance. Jammed in between the Oupia mountains and the hills of Laure-Minervois, this is a very dry region, particularly in summer. The daytime summer temperature can run up very high. This is, however, compensated for at night by the cool air from the mountains, which ensures more complexity and aromatic strength in the wine.

Minervois-La-Livinière, a new AOC

SYRAH

Besides soil and climate the individual character of the local wines is mainly determined by the choice of the syrah grape. In many parts of Languedoc nowadays the familiar Atlantic grape varieties: cabernet sauvignon, merlot and so on, are preferred. Only in Cabardès and Malepère does syrah play a modest role. However, in La-Livinière syrah is the leading variety for the production of quality wines. According to Jean-Christophe Piccinini, La-Livinière forms the definitive western limit for this Mediterranean variety of grape. Besides syrah, mourvèdre and grenache are also used: in total at least 60 % of the wine must be made from these three grapes. Other permitted varieties are carignan, cinsault, terret, piquepoul and aspiran. To be able to carry the AOC, the wines must be raised in barrels or vats for at least fifteen months.

The best wines are very complex and characteristic: aromas of blackcurrants, wild Provençal herbs, flowers, black olives and leather. They are full, rounded and robust wines which will happily keep for five or even ten years. The price/quality/pleasure equation is really exceptional.

These are tremendous wines for roast or grilled red meat, small game or even wild boar on the spit. Drinking temperature: 16–17 °C (61–63 °F).

CABARDÈS

The Cabardès *terroir* is characterized mainly by its shape, an amphitheater with softly sloping sides at the foot of the Montagne Noire, hanging above the historic town of Carcassonne. The location of the amphitheater is perfect: all the vineyards face south and enjoy the full sun. The soil of limestone rock, and a little higher of granite, schist and gneiss, is warmed by the sun and reflects that warmth back at night. The flanks of the amphitheater are provided with sufficient water by as many as six streams. The wind, too, is of great importance here, mild, cool and wet west winds, alternating with warm east winds off the Mediterranean. The vineyards lie at an average height of 300–1,000 ft.

Like the climate, the types of grape planted locally are a mixture of Atlantic and Mediterranean influences. At least 40 % of planting must consist of Atlantic grape varieties (merlot, cabernet sauvignon, cabernet franc), at least 40 % of Mediterranean ones (syrah, grenache) and the remaining possible maximum of 20 % may only consist of cot/malbec/auxerrois, fer

Syrah gives its power to the Minervois-La-Livinière

servadou and cinsault. The grape varieties are vinified separately with a long fermentation process at a low temperature, and are only assembled in the spring.

The rather unique character of these red wines lies in the balance between the freshness, fruitiness and elegance of the Atlantic grape varieties and the sultriness, warmth, richness and sensuality of the Mediterranean ones. Although the rosé wines are also excellent, the strength of the region is in its red wines. The structure and taste of the wines varies, depending on their composition and the dominance of Atlantic or Mediterranean grapes.

Serve the best wines with an oven-roast or grilled joint of beef or lamb. Drinking temperature: 14–16 °C (57–61 °F).

CÔTES-DE-LA-MALEPÈRE AOVDQS

This is the most westerly appellation of Languedoc, situated in the triangle of Carcassonne, Limoux and Castelnaudary.

The red and rosé wines here are very light and fruity, and go well with the everyday Mediterranean cuisine, but specially with the local cassoulet (a dish of beans from the oven, prepared with goose fat). Drinking temperature: rosé 12 °C (54 °F), red 14–16 °C (57–61 °F).

Limoux

In the forty-one communes round Limoux, still and sparkling white wines are produced. The climate of this area is clearly influenced by the Mediterranean, but is somewhat tempered by influences from the Atlantic. It

Cabardès has recently been promoted from AOVDQS to AOC

is much greener here than elsewhere in Languedoc, but despite the apparent coolness the local wines are full of temperament.

Various Roman writers emphasized the quality of the still wines of Limoux as long as 2000 years ago. Not until the sixteenth century, in 1531, did a Benedictine monk discover the natural conversion of still into sparkling wine. The first *brut* in the world first saw the light in Saint-Hilaire, near Limoux.

BLANQUETTE DE LIMOUX

This fresh, sparkling wine must consist of at least 90 % Mauzac. Only chardonnay and chenin blanc are

Limoux makes splendid light-sparkling wines

allowed to be added to this. After a first fermentation and production of the basic wine, the *tirage de liqueur* is added to the mix. This causes a second fermentation in bottle, from which the wine gets its sparkle. After at least nine months storage in bottle the sediment is removed by *dégorgement*. Depending on the taste desired (*brut* or *demi-sec*) either none at all, a little, or more fortifying liqueur is added to the wine before bottling. Blanquette de Limoux wines are light yellow in color, with a tinge of green, and have a fine, long-lasting sparkle, fine aromas of green apple and spring blossom and a floral, fresh and fruity taste.

These wines are most suitable as an aperitif with lightly salted toasts. They can also grace any festive meal. Drinking temperature 6–8 °C (43–47 °F).

CRÉMANT DE LIMOUX

This is actually Blanquette de Limoux's little brother. The only differences are the proportions of the grape varieties – for the Crémant at least 60 % mauzac (instead of 90 %) and at most 20 % chardonnay and 20 % chenin – and a mandatory maturing

Blanquette de Limoux

time of twelve months instead of nine. The color is light gold, the smell very aromatic, with hints of white flowers and toast, and the taste is complex, fruity, light and fresh. A Crémant typically always has a lighter and finer sparkle, making it very delicate and elegant.

Extremely suitable for a chic aperitif. Drinking temperature: 6–8 °C (43–47 °F).

There are numerous luxury *cuvées* of both the Blanquette and the Crémant. They may not have the finesse of a top champagne, but do have the warmth and generosity of the Mediterranean and the South of France… and the price is exceptionally favorable.

BLANQUETTE MÉTHODE ANCESTRALE

Crémant de Limoux

These Blanquettes are produced by a very old method in which the wines of 100 % mauzac grapes ferment naturally until only 100 grams per liter is left. The fermentation is stopped by drawing off the must and filtering it. The incompletely fermented must is then bottled and heat produces a second fermentation in the bottle. When a perfect balance between alcohol (5 to 7 % vol.), sugars (approx. 70 grams/ /liter) and specific gravity is achieved, the fermentation is abruptly stopped by cooling the bottles severely. The color of these wines is straw-yellow and is not always equally clear. Because this is a traditional and natural process, with modern technology kept to a minimum, the wines can still contain some sediment (unfermented sugars and dead yeast cells). The nose is reminiscent of a ripe golden rennet apple, and the taste is fresh, thanks to the 4.5 gram per liter level of acidity and the carbon dioxide, but also fruity and soft, partly due to the residual sugar. Because these wines are low in alcohol (maximum 7 %), they can be used as an enjoyable refreshment at any time of the day.

Luxurious cuvée Crémant de Limoux

In the warm south these wines made by the ancestral method serve mainly as a sensual aperitif or as a decadent companion to desserts. Drinking temperature: 6 °C (43 °F).

LIMOUX

Besides the familiar sparkling wines, excellent still wines are also produced here. They must contain at least 15 % mauzac, which can be supplemented with chardonnay and chenin. The local Cave des Sieurs d'Arques knows how to raise these still Limoux wines to unprecedented heights. They produce four different wines, each from a specific *terroir*.

–Terroir Méditerranéen: round, harmonious and supple wines with a great deal of fruit. Wine/food combination: aperitif. Drinking temperature 12 °C (54 °F).

– Terroir Océanique: rather lighter in color than the other three; splendid aromas of citrus fruits, fine and elegant. The taste is fruity, with a dash of iodine. Very fresh and elegant. Wine/food combination: aperitif; *fruits de mer* and fish. Drinking temperature: 12–14 °C (54–57 °F)

– Terroir d'Autan: yellow with golden glints; intense aromas with a finish of crystallized fruits; broad, rounded and fruity taste. Wine/food combination: *foie gras*, fish, white meat. Drinking temperature 12–14 °C (54–57 °F).

– Terroir Haute Vallée: yellow with golden glints, delicate aromas of white flowers. Very harmonious taste: rounded and fresh, at the same time both subtle and complex. Wine/food combination: fish, white meat, poultry, fresh goat's cheese. Drinking temperature 12–14 °C (54–57 °F).

Blanquette de Limoux méthode ancestrale

Limoux terroir Méditerranéen   **Limoux Terroir Océanique**   **Limoux Terroir d'Autan**

The Cave Coopérative des Sieurs d'Arques also produces good *vins de pays* and *vins de cépage*.

Limoux wines, ideal for gourmets

Vin de pays d'Oc Blanc   **Limoux terroir Haute-Vallée**

Vin de pays d'Oc Rouge

Corbières, a somber past, golden future?

CORBIÈRES

The Corbières district is so hilly and sometimes so inhospitable that no other form of agriculture than growing vines would be imaginable. The vineyards are spread across 57,000 acres amidst numerous silent witnesses of their turbulent past. The ruins of the old Cathar fortresses sound haunted and shake on their foundations in the harsh winds…

In the high Corbières the soil consists of limestone and slate; few trees grow there apart from a few proud cypresses that perforce bow their heads before the savage winds. The rather milder coastal strip of Sigean consists of calcareous hills, while central Corbières consists mainly of gravel and pebbles. The Corbière district is a real patchwork of different soils and microclimates, subdivided into eleven *terroirs*: Sigean, Durban, Quéribus, Termenès, Saint-Victor, Fontfroide, Lagrasse, Serviès, Montagne d'Alaric, Lézignan and Boutenac, so it is almost impossible to give a general idea of the characteristic properties of a Corbières wine.

The white wines are fine and fresh, with floral aromas. The acids and the roundness are in perfect balance. The wines of Lagrasse smell of exotic fruits, wood and something smoky; those of Quéribus of pears and pineapples, with a finish of white flowers. The wines of Lézignan bring to mind snakeweed and aniseed.

Excellent accompaniments to fish, *fruits de mer*, white meat, poultry and a preferably fresh Pélardon (a goat's cheese). Drinking temperature: 10–12 °C (50–54 °F).

The rosé wines are fresh and very pleasant, sometimes light and fruity (Durban), sometimes full and velvety (Alaric), but mostly very aromatic (fruits, flowers, spices) and sophisticated. Excellent with fish (particularly grilled tuna) or meats. Drinking temperature 12 °C (54 °F).

The red wines are intense, broad and rounded with typical aromas of red fruits, spices and a little pepper to finish. They have good and soft tannins and can age for several years. In Sigean the mourvèdre gives some extra elegance to the wines, in Serviès it is the syrah.

The velvety, full and complex wines of Quéribus often develop aromas of cocoa, coffee or other roasted flavors.

Those from Alaric are very fruity (wild berries) with a vegetable or spicy undertone. The wines of Termenès evolve as they age into classic aromas of brushwood and truffles. Those of Lézignan are very fruity (overripe or even crystallized fruits), with shades reminiscent of the Provençal *garrigue*, the typical landscape of low shrubs and strongly scented herbs. Sometimes you can taste some cloves in them. The wines of Boutenac bring to mind Provençal herbs: thyme, rosemary and bay, with here and there some licorice and vanilla. The variety in Corbières is endless!

Depending on the type of wine, you can serve a red Corbières with grilled red meat, poultry, all types of game, or stews and casseroles. Drinking temperature: 14–16 °C (57–61 °F).

Corbières Blanc and Rosé

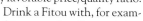

Corbières Rouge

FITOU

This is the oldest AOC wine region of Languedoc for red wines. There is a clear difference between the Fitou wines which are made along the coastal strip and those from the interior. In a region of 6,000 acres, situated halfway between Narbonne and Perpignan, splendid full and powerful red wines are produced. In smell and taste the best Fitou wines remind you of Provençal herbs (bay, thyme, rosemary), sometimes with a touch of cloves, and flint. The best Fitou wines enjoy a lengthy raising on wood and can age extremely well. In England and France people are very keen on these wines; elsewhere these friendly heavy-weights still await discovery; it is certainly worth trying them, if only for the very favorable price/quality ratio.

Drink a Fitou with, for example, casseroles of red or white meat (veal) containing Provençal herbs, garlic and olives. Drinking temperature: 16 °C (61 °F).

Since 2000 there has also been a white Fitou with AOC. Fitou Blanc is a mixture of grenache blanc, macabeu and a small quantity of muscat de Frontignan and muscat d'Alexandrie. The fermentation of the white Fitou is on wood; the young wine is then still kept in vat for several months before it is sold.

First-class wines that do well with fried sea fish. Drinking temperature: 12 °C (54 °F).

Roussillon

To the south of Corbières, at the foot of the Pyrenees, lie the vineyards of Roussillon, in a part of Catalonia that has been French since 1642. The vineyards extend from the sea far inland, over various kinds of soil and landscapes under the dry heat of the Mediterranean sun. The coastal strip from Fitou to Argelès-sur-Mer is an oasis of peace for nature lovers and sun worshippers. Below Argelès and up to the Spanish frontier, the contours are rougher and hillier, with only the picturesque bay of Collioure offering a peaceful break. The fertile valleys of the interior provide scope for plenty of agricultural activities besides winegrowing, which form the economic strength of the region. The best peaches and apricots in France grow here, fully profiting from the hot sun and mild winters. Other fruits (kiwis!) and vegetables do very well here, too.

Fitou is too often underestimated

MAURY

One of France's loveliest wines is produced around the town of Maury: the Maury red *vin doux naturel*. On a rocky soil the low-growing blue grenache wines thrive under the hot sun, producing very few grapes, but those very rich in juice. Young Maury wines are garnet red, older ones tend towards a mahogany red. A good Maury is very aromatic. A young Maury develops mainly fruity aromas (red fruits); at a later age it is mainly hints of cocoa, coffee and crystallized fruits that dominate. Although the cheapest Maury wines can be very pleasant, you will always do better to choose the more expensive ones, because you will get real value for your money. One estate deserves a special recommendation for its velvety soft wines with unprecedentedly fascinating aromas of spiced gingerbread, licorice, plums and cocoa: the Domaine du Mas Amiel.

You can drink Maury as an aperitif or with dessert, but it is best enjoyed by itself, after a good meal. Drinking temperature 16–18 °C (61–64 °F).

RIVESALTES

This is the largest appellation of the *vins doux naturels* 27,000 acres. Once mediocre sweet wines were made here of the red and white grenache. Since 1996, however, all this has changed.

The planted areas have been cut back heavily, the yield per hectare has fallen and the winegrowers seem to have become more aware of the potential quality of their wines. Various grape varieties are used for these *vins doux naturels*: white and red grenache, macabeu, malvoisie and muscat.

Maury vintage   Maury cuvée spéciale

There are two kinds of Rivesaltes: the amber-colored wines from white grapes and the roof tile-red wines from at least 50 % grenache noir. The better *cuvées* (Rivesaltes *hors d'âge*) are aged for at least five years.

Drink the young, simple Rivesaltes as aperitifs, at about 12 °C (54 °F). The better, older Rivesaltes taste wonderful with a dessert (not too sweet!) or after a meal. Drinking temperature: 14–16 °C (57–61 °F).

MUSCAT DE RIVESALTES

The appellations Maury, Rivesaltes and Banyuls, in all 11,200 acres, are planted with muscat d'Alexandrie and muscat à petits grains. The muscat d'Alexandrie gives 'breadth' to Muscat de Rivesaltes, as well as aromas of ripe fruits, raisins and roses, while the Muscat à petits grains is responsible for the sensual aromas of exotic fruit and citrus fruits, with a dash of menthol. These Muscat de Rivesaltes have the best fruit when they are still quite young.

Serve them with fresh fruit desserts (such as lemon or strawberry tarts and fruit salads) or cakes made with nuts or almond pastry. Striking with Roquefort. Drinking temperature: 8–10 °C (47–50 °F).

CÔTES-DU-ROUSSILLON

In the Pyrénées Orientales département 118 communes (11,800 acres) produce red (80 %, rosé (15 %), and white (5 %) Côtes-du-Roussillon.

Besides the traditional grape varieties (grenache noir, carignan, cinsault, iladoner pelut, grenache blanc, maccabeo and malvoisie du roussillon), increasingly Mediterranean varieties are used (syrah, mourvèdre, roussanne, marsanne and vermentino). Syrah in particular seems to be gaining much ground, whereas mourvèdre cannot really adapt itself to the local climate. The soil of the vineyards is very complex and varied (lime, clay, schist, gneiss, granite

Muscat de Rivesaltes in the well-known bottle

Muscat de Rivesaltes' top cuvee

and alluvial deposits) which explains the great diversity of types and tastes of the Roussillon wines.

There are four major production zones in the Roussillon: the valleys of the Agly in the north, the Têt in the middle, the Tech in the south and the Salanques in the east, near the sea. The climate is extremely hot in summer and mild in winter, but rain is irregular throughout the year. A whole vineyard can be completely destroyed by a cloudburst. In recent decades the wine industry of the Roussillon has undergone enormous changes; in particular control of the temperature before and during the fermentation has been drastically improved.

The white Côtes-du-Roussillon are light, fresh and fruity. Serve them as aperitifs or with fish dishes, such as grilled tuna steaks or gurnet. Also good with mussels. Drinking temperature 10–12 °C (50–54 °F).

The rosé wines are vinified by the *saignée* method, in which the young wines are tapped prematurely and are vinified further as white wine. Because they are tapped so soon, the skins have had just enough time to give the wines a splendid pink color without making the wine tannic.

These rosé wines are very fruity and go with most kinds of cold meats, crustaceans, shellfish, fish, poultry or white meat with olives and Provençal herbs. They also have a secret passion for anchovy… Drinking temperature: 12 °C (54 °F).

Two types of red wine are available. The light red wines, often produced by the addition of carbon dioxide (*macération carbonique*), are fruity, a little spicy, and very pleasant indeed.

Serve these red Côtes-du--Roussillon young at parties, barbecues or *al fresco* meals, or with grilled kebabs or cheese. Drinking temperature: 12–14 °C (54–57 °F).

Outstanding *vin de pays* from Roussillon

Côtes-du-Roussillon Blanc

Côtes-du-Roussillon Blanc Taichat

Côtes-du-Roussillon Rosé

The traditionally made red wines are rather more robust and rounder. The aromas tend more towards red cherries, plums, crystallized fruits and spices. By being raised in wood they can age for several years and then happily accompany red meat, grilled poultry and cheese. Delicious in combination with garlic! Drinking temperature: 14–16 °C (57–61 °F).

**Cask-aged Côtes-
-du-Roussillon
Rouge**

**Côtes-du-
-Roussillon
rouge**

CÔTES-DU-ROUSSILLON-
-VILLAGES

These red wines distinguish themselves from their cousins through their specific *terroirs*, usually located on the flanks of hills or terraces of schist, limestone and granite. The grape varieties used are the same as those in the ordinary Côtes-du-Roussillon, but the yield per hectare is much lower. In a total area of 5,000 acres in the north of the *département*, thirty-two communes may carry the appellation Côtes-du-Roussillon-Villages. The wines are more robust, more powerful and more complex than the ordinary Côtes-du-Roussillon, and can age rather longer.

They are ideal wines for red meat, all kinds of game, casseroles and the rich specialties of Catalan country cuisine. Drinking temperature: 16 °C (61 °F).

Of the thirty-two communes which can carry the appellation Côtes-du-Roussillon-Villages, there are four which may also put their name on the label, as a kind of recognition of their superior quality.

**Côtes-du-
-Roussillon-
-Villages**

**Traditionally
vinified wine
from grapes still
on their stalks**

CÔTES-DU-ROUSSILLON-VILLAGES-
-LATOUR-DE-FRANCE

On 430 acres round the village of Latour de France, and on a few parcels of land in the surrounding communes of Cassagnes, Estagel, Montner and Planèzes, wines are produced that are very characteristic of their soil of brown schist. The wines of Latour de France were the first to be allowed to put their name on the label.

CÔTES-DU-ROUSSILLON-VILLAGE
CARAMANY

Here it is the gneiss soil that makes the difference. This wine may be made in the commune of Caramany (Agly valley) and some parcels of land in Belesta and Cassagnes.

CÔTE-DU-ROUSSILLON-VILLAGES-
-LESQUERDE

This wine is produced on an area of 47 acres in the commune of Lesquerde Latour de France. A tiny appellation on a granite soil, where Syrah and Mourvèdre are better represented than in other parts of the Roussillon Villages district.

Latour-de-France

Caramany

CÔTES-DU-ROUSSILLON-VILLAGES-TAUTAVEL

This is the most recent of the Roussillon Villages appellations to be allowed to put the commune's name on the label (1997). On 200 acres of clay and lime-rich soil, full, rich and robust wines for laying down are made from grenache and iladoner pelut.

COLLIOURE

This rather small appellation (800 acres) extends over the soil of four communes: Collioure, Port-Vendres, Banyuls-sur-Mer and Cerbère. Collioure wines, in rosé or red, are made from grenache, mourvèdre and syrah.

The red wines are very harmonious, full, warm and fleshy, with aromas of ripe fruits, minerals and exotic hints (pepper, vanilla, oriental spices).

There are also special *cuvées* which are made in old vineyards where the soil consists of rough and igneous rocks. These *cuvées vignes rocheuses* are extra concentrated.

Red Collioure wines can be drunk in two ways: young and cool (12 °C/54 °F) with grilled sea fish, tomatoes stuffed with anchovy and olives, or grilled meatballs prepared with small pieces of anchovy and olives; or mature and at a higher temperature (16 °C/61 °F) with Mediterranean specialties, grilled meat, grilled paprikas or with Catalan chicken and rice dishes. Red Collioure wines are among the top wines of France.

The rather rarer rosé wines are fresh, full-bodied and extremely rich. Drink them at about 12 °C (54 °F) with any of the delicacies from the Mediterranean.

Tautavel

BANYULS

The vineyards of this *vin doux naturel* lie on terraces of schist along the coastal strip. In 3,600 acres, mainly grenache noir grows, accompanied by carignan, cinsault, syrah and mourvèdre. The rich, warm and powerful character of Banyuls is accounted for by 50 to 75 % of Grenache Noir. The ground here is extremely poor and rocky with a thin layer of top soil that slides away with every heavy thunderstorm. It is hard work here and much of it still has to be done by hand. The strong sun ripens the grapes very well and by the time they are harvested they contain an enormous quantity of sugars.

Alcohol is often added to the must (*mutage*) at a very early stage, when the grapes have not yet even been pressed. As in Maury, the oxidation of the wines is Banyuls' secret. By only partly filling the wooden vats or allowing the wines to evaporate in large glass jars in wicker baskets under the sun, contact with oxygen is reinforced.

A number of different *cuvées* are made up by the cellar master depending on the type of wine desired. Some Banyuls (*rimages*) are not exposed to the forced oxidizing processes, but are just vinified, retaining their fruity aromas. The *rimages* are rather like vintage port in style; the traditional Banyuls like tawnies and *colheitas*.

Depending on the type, Banyuls wines can be very fruity (red fruits, cherries) or have burnt aromas (cocoa, coffee) and aromas of crystallized (raisins) and dried fruits (almonds, nuts, prunes, figs).

Drink young, fruity Banyuls (*rimages*) as an aperitif at about 12 °C (54 °F). Mature to very old (*hors d'âge*) Banyuls are better drunk less cool, at 14–18 °C (57–64 °F). These older Banyuls are so good that they are the only wines capable of accompanying chocolate

Banyuls

Collioure

Full, robust and fiery Collioure

Collioure Vignes Rocheuses

Banyuls tradition

Banyuls hors-d'âge

Banyuls hors-d'âge special cuvée

desserts, but they also go very well with almond pastry, figs and semi-soft strong cheeses. Some famous gourmets are very keen on decadent combinations such as a plump crayfish, with a rich Banyuls sauce, and Banyuls to drink with it... Why not, if you like it, but for most people a duet with chocolate is more to their taste.

BANYULS GRAND CRU

These wonderful treasures are only produced in top years. They distill and sublimate all the good qualities of Banyuls. Although these wines can grace a sweet biscuit or almond pastry, with perhaps a few chocolates, the enjoyment of a glass of Banyuls Grand Cru is a matter of great moment which should not be disrupted by anything or anybody. A sip of these rich, intense wines is a foretaste of paradise on earth.

Between Languedoc-Roussillon and Auvergne

CÔTES-DE-MILLAU-AOVDQS

Although the wines of Millau are officially classed as wines of south-west France, it is more logical, in the light of their geographical location between Languedoc and the Auvergne, to include this region in the south-east. Only since 1994 have the white, red and rosé wines of Millau and its surroundings had the right to a AOVDQS recognition. In the idyllic frame of the Tarn narrows, the vineyards of the Côtes de Millau are spread over a length of 50 miles with a total area of only 125 acres.

The white wines are made from chenin and mauzac. The body and aromatic strength of mauzac compensates for the lively acidity of the chenin and give the wine a fresh, pleasant character that goes well in combination with fruits de mer. Drinking temperature: 10–12 °C (50–54 °F).

The red and rosé wines are of better quality. syrah and gamay noir are here supported by cabernet sauvignon and fer servadou. The rosé wines are fresh and fruity (strawberries) and demand a tasty dry sausage. Drinking temperature 12 °C (54 °F).

The red wines are more mature, with aromas of crystallized fruits and spices, and a good balance between fruit, alcohol, acidity and tannins. First-class wines for all dishes from the local cuisine, but also for a grilled sirloin steak followed by a plate of hard or half-hard sheep's cheese. Drinking temperature 14–16 °C (57–61 °F).

SOUTHWEST FRANCE

The French *Sud-Ouest* (the area between Bordeaux and Languedoc-Roussillon) is a large region covering about a quarter of France. As a winegrowing area its boundaries are not so easy to define. Great social and economic interests have persuaded some of the wine regions in the geographical south-west to associate themselves with their older cousins in Bordeaux. Geographically, regions such as Bergerac and Côtes-de--Duras should be part of the south-west, but socially they are closer to the capital of Aquitaine (Bordeaux) than to that of the southwest (Toulouse). Because these regions also use the same grape varieties as Bordeaux, the link is easy to understand. In the context of this book, however, we have for convenience kept to the geographical divisions, counting Duras and Bergerac as part of Aquitaine.

The Aveyron (Rouergue)

ENTRAYGUES AND LE FEL VDQS

This tiny region in the heart of the Lot valley, between the Rouergue and Auvergne, is one of the most picturesque wine regions of France. The vineyards lie on the steep hills round the town of Entraygues and the village of Le Fel, on a total area of some 50 acres. In Entraygues the soil consists of fragmented granite and in Le Fel of brown schist. In this cold wine region both types of soil ensure good drainage and control of heat by their stony substrata. The wines of Entraygues, Le Fel and neighboring Marcillac were once well known and popular throughout France. After the *Phylloxera* plague and the exodus from the French countryside, it was not until the 1960s that these wine regions achieved their recovery.

The white wines are made of the old chenin grape, which produces fresh wines with aromas of flowers, citrus fruits and box. These are full-bodied wines that go well with cold meats, fish and *fruits de mer*, but also extremely well with Le Fel's fresh goat's cheese. Drinking temperature: 10 °C (50 °F).

The rosé wines are fresh and full-bodied in their acidity. They are first class with cold meats or an *al fresco* lunch. Drinking temperature: 12 °C (54 °F).

The red wines are, like the rosé, aromatic and fresh, but their taste is rather fuller and rounder. These wines, made from fer servadou (mansoi) and cabernet franc, seem to have been invented for the rich country cuisine of the Auvergne and Rouergue. Also excellent with Laguiole cheese. Drinking temperature 16 °C (61 °F).

ESTAING AOVDQS

The long-established Estaing vineyards lie quite near the town of Rodez on hills of schist and limy clay.

The white wines are made from the old chenin stock, sometimes with some help from mauzac and rousselou. These grape varieties thrive on Estaing's stony soil and

Entraygues & du-Fel Rosé

give fresh, fruity wines with a hint of flint in the aftertaste. Excellent wines for fish and *fruits de mer*, and also for white meat and poultry. Drinking temperature: 10 °C (50 °F).

The rosé wines are sophisticated and easy to drink, which makes them very popular with the many tourists who visit the area in the summer. Delicious with lunch or cold meats. Drinking temperature: 12 °C (54 °F).

MARCILLAC

This wine region near Rodez produced one of the classic wines of France before the *Phylloxera* plague. The 330 acres of vineyard lie on a typical soil of red clay near the limestone plateaus.

Mansoi (the local name for fer servadou) is the dominant grape variety for this AOC, which was only authorized in 1990. This grape and the typical soil ensure the very original character of Marcillac rosé and red, between rusticity and modern fruitiness. The better Marcillacs are true gems for lovers of wines with character, in which you can still taste the terroir. Aromas of fruits (raspberry, black-currants, blueberries, blackberries), vegetables (green paprika), spices (green pepper) and often also hints of cocoa, ensure a very complex whole. Spicy and rounded tannins reinforce the individual character of these wines.

A Marcillac soon makes friends with all dishes from the local cuisine, but also with, for example, grilled leg of lamb. One particular combination can be thoroughly recommended: a red Marcillac from a good year, four to five years old, with a well-matured Laguiole cheese from Rouergue. Drinking temperature: 16 °C (61 °F).

Entraygues & Le Fel Rouge

Marcillac, at the foot of the limestone plateau

Quercy

CAHORS

The vineyards of Cahors are among the oldest in France. These wines were already famous in the fifth century. Because the wines were robust, complex and very concentrated, they could be shipped without difficulty anywhere in the world, without travel affecting the quality. Cahors wines were consequently in great demand, not only in America, but also, and particularly, in Czarist Russia. After the *Phylloxera* invasion all went quiet for decades round Cahors. The vineyards deteriorated, the wines were hardly more than everyday quaffing wines. After World War II a halt was called to this decline. The efforts of a generation of hardworking winegrowers were rewarded when in 1951 Cahors wines were admitted to the AOVDQS family, and in 1971 could be awarded the highly--coveted AOC recognition.

Marcillac wines, once renowned worldwide

IDEAL CONDITIONS

The vineyards lie between the 44th and 45th parallel, which in the northern hemisphere is a guarantee of splendid, full wines. The location of the vineyards, half-way between the Atlantic and the Mediterranean, is also very favorable. This means that they do not suffer from the moist influence of the west-winds and the often rainy falls of the Mediterranean climate. So, ideal conditions, headed by a dry, hot fall, ensure that the grapes have every opportunity to ripen in peace.

Cahors has two types of soil: the Lot valley with a substratum of limestone and a top soil of alluvial deposits with here and there pebbles and erosion residue, and the calcareous higher levels (here called *causses*), with a fairly shallow top layer of stones and marl.

THE GRAPES

Only red wines are made in Cahors. They are based on the auxerrois grape (elsewhere also called 'cot noir'). For the right to the Cahors AOC this must make up at least 70 % of the total planting. The auxerrois gives the wines backbone, robust tannins, color and aging potential. For the traditional Cahors wines, pure auxerrois is used, or auxerrois with tannat (familiar from the Madiran and Irouléguy districts), a variety of grape closely related in its characteristics to the auxerrois. The rather more modern wines often contain a good dose of merlot, which makes them rather rounder, plumper and more aromatic.

Traditional Cahors

THE WINES

The modern Cahors are better drunk young. Their tannins make them the perfect accompaniment to local dishes of goose or duck, usually braised in their own fat. They can also accompany any kind of red meat or even game birds. Drinking temperature: 14 °C (57 °F).

The traditional Cahors are much broader and more complex. If you drink them too young the tannins are too dominant. Preferably wait five or even ten years for the better Cahors. The wine then becomes rounder, velvety soft, full and powerful, and the aromas will be more sophisticated.

Serve a mature Cahors with dishes from the better southern-French cuisine, and bear in mind red meat, truffles and wild mushrooms. Game is also a possibility. If you like powerful, contrasting and fascinating combinations of food and wine, try a rich Roquefort or a Bleu des Causses with a little Cahors. You will surely hear the sheep bleat! Drinking temperature 16 °C (61 °F).

GAILLAC

The wines of Gaillac were known as early as the fifth century, particularly in ecclesiastical circles. With the arrival of the Benedictine monks in the tenth century, Gaillac developed into one of the best wine regions of France. Official quality standards for Gaillac wines were laid down by the thirteenth century. In 1938 white Gaillac wines acquired their AOC recognition; the reds and rosé had to wait until 1970.

Wine is grown on 6,000 acres on both sides of the river Tarn, from the town of Albi to above Toulouse. The left bank of the Tarn has a poor soil of rock and gravel, ideal for red wine. The right bank is rather more complex and varied: granite, lime and sandstone form the major part of it. Here white, but also red and rosé wines are produced. Today 60 % of Gaillac production consists of red wine.

White Gaillac is made of the Mauzac grape which is also used in Languedoc

Cahors top cuvée

(Limoix) and in various small wine regions in the south-west. Here the Mauzac is supported by the Len de l'el grape, which gives it subtlety and aromatic strength. The Len de l'el is also used in French and Spanish Catalonia. The wines on the right bank are well balanced, have rich, fruity and floral aromas and are very fresh. The white wines made by modern techniques are rather less broad, less supple and don't have such a long aftertaste as the traditional wines from Mauzac and Len de l'el. On the left bank fruity, juicy and warm white wines are made.

Drink a dry white Gaillac with fish dishes or shellfish, as an aperitif or with fresh cheeses, such as the Cabecou de Rocamadour. Drinking temperature: 10 °C (50 °F).

Sweet white Gaillac is a good accompaniment to duck or goose liver, but also goes very well with blue cheeses, such as Bleu des Causses, Roquefort and Bleu d'Auvergne. Drinking temperature: 8 °C (47 °F).

There is also a sparkling white Gaillac, obtainable in two versions. The *méthode artisanale* is produced without the addition of liqueur. The gas bubbles come from the fermentation in bottle from the wine's own sugars. These Gaillac *méthode artisanale* wines are very fruity and full of character. The Gaillac *méthode traditionnelle* is obtained by a second fermentation in bottle, after the addition of a dose of liqueur. These sparkling wines are perhaps a little fresher, but less complex and above all less fruity. Drink them as aperitifs at around 8 °C (47 °F).

The rosé Gaillacs are mostly obtained in a modern way by the *saignée* method: drawing off a little red wine early while it is steeping, and processing it like a white wine. These rosé wines are friendly, easy to drink and very light. Very good with a light lunch, a picnic, cold meats or a plate of light fresh cheeses. Drinking temperature: 10–12 °C (50–54 °F).

Red Gaillacs are made from the duras, an old grape which was rediscovered about twenty years ago, supported by the local braucol (or brocol, the local name for the fer servadou or mansoi). The duras gives the wines color, backbone and sophistication. The braucol gives it color, fleshiness and a rustic charm, with excellent aromas of red fruits (blackcurrants, raspberries). The red wines from the lime-rich soil, made in the modern way, are light, aromatic and easy to drink. They are the closest to their

A playful name for a white Gaillac from the Mauzac grape

rosé cousins. On the granite soil of the hills warm, robust, but supple red wines are made with many fruity aromas (crystallized fruit, red- and blackcurrants). These wines can age well. The red wines of the left bank have a rather deeper color and are richer in taste, with aromas of crystallized fruit, spices and blackcurrants. These robust and tannic wines demand several years maturing in bottle.

Drink modern red Gaillac with a more substantial lunch or a light evening meal, or after a meal with cheese in hand. Drinking temperature 14–16 °C (57–61 °F). Serve the traditional, robust, red Gaillac with roast red meats, grilled poultry or hard or half-hard cheeses. Drinking temperature: 16 °C (61 °F).

CÔTES-DU-FRONTONNAIS

The Frontonnais, famous since the fourth century, enjoyed a golden age in the eighteenth and nineteenth centuries. However, the voracious *Phylloxera* brought this history of renown to an abrupt end. After World War II every effort was made to polish up the blazon of the Frontonnais again. Generations of hard work and struggling against the vested interests of Bordeaux were in the end successful; in 1975 the wines of the Côtes-du-Frontonnais gained the highly-coveted AOC recognition. Today's Frontonnais wine district is a combination of two older wine regions in the hinterland of Toulouse: Fronton and Villaudric.

The Côtes-du-Frontonnais region, between Toulouse and Montauban, is about 4,950 acres in area. Here the soil is very poor and dry with a great deal of stone and gravel, resulting in many fruity and floral aromas in the wines. In the not too distant future the total area of vineyards will increase by about a third.

A very exceptional feature in the Côtes-du-Frontonnais is the use (only in rosé and red) of the old native grape variety négrette, which accounts for between 50 and 70 % of the planting. This grape gives the wines a characteristic refinement and much fruitiness. cabernet franc, cabernet sauvignon, syrah, fer servadou, cot (here called merille), and to a lesser degree gamay and cinsault, are all used here in addition to Negrette.

The Négrette grape

The rosé wines of the Frontonnais are very light in color and very aromatic. They are very dry and fine in taste. Drink a rosé Frontonnais young, with fish dishes or cold meats, or as a unique wine at a summer picnic or lunch. Drinking temperature: 10 °C (50 °F).

Red Frontonnais comes in two types. The modern wines are light, elegant, supple and fruity, often with a smell of blackcurrants and plums.

Serve these boisterous young wines with grilled or roast red meat or sheep's cheese from the nearby Pyrenees. Drinking temperature: 14 °C (57 °F).

The traditional red Frontonnais are more complex, more robust and fuller. The aromas are a little less boisterous and the taste a little steadier. Drink these wines after a few years maturing in bottle with dishes from the south-western country cuisine, such as beans with goose (cassoulet) or duck or goose cooked in its own fat. These wines also feel very much at home with grilled or roast red meat or small game. Drinking temperature: 16 °C (61 °F).

LAVILLEDIEU AOVDQS

The vineyards of Lavilledieu are to the north of those of Frontonnais, west of the town of Montauban. The wine region, which is divided over thirteen communes, acquired its AOVDQS certificate as early as 1947. The name 'Lavilledieu' is a memory of the old religious wars which made the district so unsafe. Once the town was called La Ville Dieu du Temple, and the population was Protestant (Huguenots, many of whom emigrated).

The soil of Lavilledieu consists mainly of a mixture of pebbles and alluvial deposits on a substratum of stone and hard ferruginous brown sandstone. The grape varieties used for these exclusively red wines vary: négrette, cabernet franc and Tannat could be called local, imported syrah and gamay rather less so. The mix is carefully calculated and nevertheless produces pleasant, very fruity wines: round, velvety soft and well-balanced.

Côtes-du--Frontonnais Rosé

Côtes-du--Frontonnais Rouge

Gaillac Rouge

Serve these wines with chicken and other poultry, with casseroles, or with soft cheese. Drinking temperature: 12–14 °C (54–57 °F).

Traditional Côtes-du-Frontonnais

CÔTES-DU-BRULHOIS AOVDQS

Another old acquaintance, already known to the Romans. The fame of these wines grew until the late nineteenth century. After the *Phylloxera* plague the Brulhois vineyards went on producing second-rate wines until long after World War II. The generation of winegrowers born after the war has, however, taken up the torch again – and how! In 1984 the growers were rewarded for their efforts: their wines acquired the AOVDQS appellation.

On sloping hills of stone and gravel, rich, full, dark-colored red wines are made which can age well. They have a large range of powerful and subtle aromas. The grapes used are the typically south-western varieties, tannat, cot and fer servadou, together with cabernet franc, cabernet sauvignon and merlot.

The red Côtes-du-Brulhois are certainly no elegant, sophisticated, feminine wines, but rather macho in type and very true to their *terroir*. Serve them preferably with local dishes, stews, grilled red meat or crisp cheeses. Drinking temperature: 14–16 °C (57–61 °F).

BUZET

The vineyards of this 4,200 acres wine region lie in the heart of Gascony, to the south of the small town of Buzet, on the left bank of the Garonne. Almost the whole production of Buzet is controlled by the local cooperative of the Vignerons du Buzet. The Buzet vine-yards are very old and were known before the Christi-an era. For centuries Buzet wines were exported to the Low Countries, England, Prussia, the West Indies and the United States (Louisiana, Mississippi). Buzet has an exceptional position in the south-west: unlike all the other wine regions it was not taken out of circula-tion for a long time by the *Phylloxera* louse. Even in those difficult times the area of its vineyards grew. In 1953 Buzet became a AOVDQS, and thanks to the obstinate and united efforts of the winegrowers

association the wines obtained a definitive AOC recognition.

The region has two types of soil, producing different types of wine. The wines produced on the stony and sandy substratum of the terraces are elegant and delicate; those from the richer substratum of clay and alluvial deposits, with here and there some protruding sandstone, are fuller, heavier and more aromatic.

Red wines make up most of Buzet. They are made from a mixture of merlot, cabernet franc and cabernet Sauvignon. The color is ruby red and the aromas are reminiscent of red fruits, vanilla and crystallized fruits. The best Buzet wines can age for several years. Young and cheaper red Buzets are pleasant accompaniments throughout a meal and are not choosy. Drinking temperature: 12–14 °C (54–57 °F).

The better red Buzets (Château or Domaine) have more body and tannins. They can be kept for ten to fifteen years. The aromas are more complex and often tend towards brushwood, strawberry jam, tobacco, cedar wood and occasionally a whiff of game.

These wines can accompany all meat and game dishes of the traditional as well as the modern cuisine. Drinking temperature: 14–17 °C (57–63 °F).

CÔTES-DU-MARMANDAIS

The AOC Côtes-du-Marmandais region 4,500 acres lies on the right bank of the Garonne, on softly sloping hills with a soil of gravel and pebbles, alternated with limy sandstone and calcareous clay. The Marmande wines were already known to the Romans, and later the English were important consumers of these Haut--Garonne wines. After the *Phylloxera* invasion in the late nineteenth century, viniculture in the Marmandais would have completely disappeared if a group of hard-

Buzet: good, and inexpensive

working farmers had not linked forces and set up the local cooperative. By 1955 the Côtes-du-Marmandais were granted AOVDQS status and in 1990 reached the top of the AOC ladder. In the Marmandais too, quality and *terroir* are increasingly becoming more important than quantity.

The white Côtes-du-Marmandais, made of sémillon, sauvignon, muscadelle and ugni blanc, are quite dry, fresh and fruity, with aromas of white flowers and sometimes almonds.

Traditional red Buzet

Drink these very acceptable white wines with sea fish and fruits de mer, at al fresco meals, quick lunches or as an aperitif. Drinking temperature: 10–12 °C (50–54 °F).

The rosé wines are fresh, fruity and fairly light. They are pleasant wines which should cheer up any lunch or picnic. Also nice with sea fish and fruits de mer. Drinking temperature: 12 °C (54 °F).

The red Côtes-du-Marmandais are made from the Bordeaux grapes cabernet sauvignon, cabernet franc, merlot and malbec, supplemented by the local abouriou and fer servadou, and where necessary a little Gamay or Syrah.

Drink these aromatic, supple and rounded red wines with grilled red meat, lamb or small game. Because there is very little difference in price, you should buy the better cuvées, which are more than worth the money (for instance, Richard Premies, Tap de Perbos, or La Vieille Eglise). Drinking temperature: 14–16 °C (57–61 °F).

CÔTES-DE-SAINT-MONT AOVDQS

This wine region in Gascony was already known to the Romans. Benedictine monks were behind its success,

which lasted until the *Phylloxera* plague. In the early twentieth century the local vineyards were in decline.

Sunny vineyards in the Marmandais

Not until the 1950s did this change; partly through the enormous efforts of the local cooperative the winegrowers succeeded in reviving the region. In 1981 the Côtes-de-Saint-Mont were granted AOVDQS. For the red and rosé wines tannat and fer servadou are used, supplemented where necessary by cabernet sauvignon and cabernet franc to give more roundness and subtlety. The white wines are often made of a mixture of the typical local grape varieties gros manseng, arrufiac, petit manseng and petit courbu, with here and there some clairette.

The eastern and southern hills are the domain of the red wines and have two types of soil. The pebbly soil produces light red wines, which are vinified in the modern way. They are pleasing, generous wines without pretension. Drink them young and well-cooled, at about 12 °C (54 °F). The rather heavier clay soil produces full, rounded and fleshy wines which can age well. When they are young, they can be served with grilled or roast red meat and poultry at 12–14 °C (54–57 °F); the rather older wines go well with richer dishes from the local cuisine, casseroles, or even strong cheeses. Drinking temperature: 16 °C (61 °F).

The rosé wines are soft, very pleasant and aromatic. Their taste is fruity and fresh. They are ideal companions to cold meats, starters, *al fresco* buffets, picnics and lunches. Drinking temperature: 12 °C (54 °F).

Choose the better red Marmandais wines

The western hills, with a soil of lime and clay, produce very subtle, elegant white wines. The aromatic strength of their youth soon changes into a complex bouquet. Serve these fresh wines with fish and *fruits de mer*. Drinking temperature: 10–12 °C (50–54 °F).

TURSAN AOVDQS

Tursan wines also have a rich history. They are alleged to have been served in the days of the later Roman emperors. Their fame, in France and outside it, was very great. In the twelfth and thirteenth centuries Tursan wines were welcome guests at many European courts from Spain to the Low Countries and England. Alas, the vineyards were completely destroyed by the *Phylloxera* louse. Only in the early 1950s did a fresh breeze blow through the vineyards. A new generation of winegrowers continued the age-old tradition of winemaking. In 1958 the Tursan wines (white, rosé and red) were received with open arms into the AOVDQS family.

The Tursan vineyards lie on the edge of the Landes, an extensive piece of land now planted with pine trees, but once a place of swamps and sand dunes. Their other neighbors are Gascony and Béarn. The soil of the 1,250 acres region consists of a mixture of clay and sand, with here and there some lime and sandstone. The best vineyards are on hills of fragmented limestone blocks. About half the production consists of white wines, the other half of red and rosé wines.

White Tursan is made from the baroque grape, which may be supplemented by not more than 10 % gros manseng and sauvignon. The wines are fresh, fruity, very aromatic and have a pleasant taste.

Serve a white Tursan with fish, shellfish or fruits de mer. Also good with all light starters. In their native district these white wines are served with foie gras. There is nothing against this, but personally I prefer a Jurançon or Pacherenc du Vic-Bilh Moelleux with duck or goose liver. Drinking temperature: 8–10 °C (47–50 °F).

The rosé wines are light, fresh, dry and quite delicious. They are made of cabernet sauvignon and cabernet franc.

These rosé wines are ideal for lunch, picnics, cold meats, white meat, poultry, mealtime salads, starters and with cheese. In short, a wine for almost every occasion. Drinking temperature: 10–12 °C (50–54 °F).

Finally the red wines, made of cabernet sauvignon and cabernet franc (at least 60 %) topped up with no more than 40 % tannat. These wines are full and generous, with much subtlety, charm and great aromatic strength.

A red Tursan wine does extremely well as a companion to the rural cuisine of the south-west, and to casseroled wood pigeons and other game birds, goose or duck. If you don't happen to have any duck or goose handy, don't panic – a grilled sirloin steak will also taste

Côtes de St-Mont Rouge

good with it. The southern cheeses from the Pyrenees, too, make a good combination with a red Tursan. Drinking temperature: 16 °C (61 °F).

Modern Tursan wines

MADIRAN

Madiran wines were known at least a century before the Christian era. Here, too, Benedictine monks contributed to the success of the local viniculture.

THE REBIRTH OF MADIRAN

After a very somber period in which it looked as if Madiran had been wiped right off the map, rescue appeared in the form of Alain Brumont, the modest, obstinate, ambitious, but charming and friendly son of a local winegrower. At that time the same principle applied in viniculture as in all other branches of agriculture: the more was produced, the more money came in. High yields and tons of fertilizer ensured the desired result. When Alain Brumont first gave voice to his revolutionary ideas in 1979, he was laughed out of court by most people. His own father even showed him the door! However, Alain went ahead with his plans. He bought the abandoned Montas wine *domaine* and replanted the vineyards with the traditional Tannat grapes, which had once formed the charm of Madiran wines. The quality of the vineyards and the wine stocks was closely watched over, very high quality standards were imposed, and the yield kept extremely low. Particularly this last factor was considered wrong by many older wine-

Traditional red Tursan

growers. However, when they tasted the results, they all offered him their apologies, some with tears in their eyes… Alain Brumont's efforts had led to the rebirth of the real Madiran! This 'fighter' had in less than five years made Madiran one of the best known red wines in France – a tremendous performance. With his success Alain Brumont brought a new generation of French winegrowers to the top: Patrick Ducournau (Chapelle Lenclos), Jean-Marc Laffitte (Château Laffitte-Teston), François Laplace (Château d'Aydie), Didier Barré (Domaine Berthoumieu) and recently, among others, Guy Capmartin (Domaine Capmartin) and the only lady in this celebrated company, Christine Dupuy (Domaine Labranche-Laffont).

A rather older Madiran has a bouquet of toast, coffee, cocoa, spices, vanilla, crystallized fruit, licorice and much more. Discover these great wines with wildfowl and small game, grilled red meat or mature sheep's cheese from the Pyrenees. Drinking temperature: 16–17 °C (61–63 °F).

PACHERENC-DU-VIC-BILH

The Vic-Bilh wine region is the same as the Madiran. In one and the same region red wines are made (Madiran) and dry, semi-sweet to sweet wines (Pacherenc-du-Vic-Bilh). The name 'Pacherenc' is said to have been derived from the Basque word for 'berry' or 'grape', but other sources maintain that the word is of Gascon origin and refers to the many posts which are set in rows in the vineyards.

The ideal soil for these white wines is a mixture of clay and sandstone. The grape varieties used are the local arrufiac, petit manseng, gros manseng, courbu, and for the more modern wines also a little Sauvignon and Sémillon.

The dry Pacherenc-du-Vic-Bilh are very aromatic, with hints of flowers and citrus fruits and a full taste of

WINEGROWING IN MADIRAN

The Madiran vineyards, in total 2,700 acres, are on a soil of calcareous clay with here and there an island of poorer, very pebbly, ground. For the Madiran wines tannat grapes are used, if necessary supplemented with fer servadou, cabernet sauvignon and cabernet franc, to soften the more robust aspects of the tannat.

Madiran is a very tannic wine which needs several years maturing in bottle (at least two to four years, ten for the better wines) to develop all its charms. A top Madiran can certainly last twenty to thirty years. A Madiran is the stereotype of a masculine wine: powerful, full, robust, sensual and fleshy.

If you drink a Madiran young (after at least two years), it is very fruity, but the tannins can sometimes be rather dominant. To neutralize this somewhat your best choice would be for rich dishes, such as goose or duck stewed in their own fat. A grilled duck breast (still pink) is also good with it. Drinking temperature: 14 °C (57 °F).

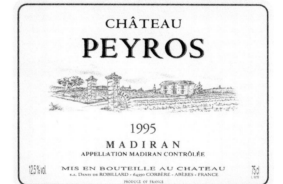

Madiran, masculine wines

ripe and overripe fruits. Serve these wines as an aperitif or with chicken, fish or *fruits de mer*. Drinking temperature: 10–12 °C (50–54 °F).

Domaine Capmartin: excellent for the price

Young Madiran is still rather rough

The semi-sweet or sweet Pacherenc-du-Vic-Bilh has the same aromatic strength as the dry types (citrus fruits, crystallized fruits, dried fruits and flowers) with a little honey, toast and exotic fruits as well. The structure and the taste are fuller, fatter, fleshier and juicier.

Serve these stunning wines with duck or goose liver, or simply after a meal, purely for enjoyment. The less sweet wines can be served at meals with fish in sauce. Lastly, most ladies and many men with a sweet tooth will also appreciate a glass of sweet or semi-sweet Pacherenc as a – slightly decadent – aperitif. Drinking temperature: 8–10 °C (47–50 °F).

Here, too, the excellent quality of the local *vin de pays des Côtes-de-Gascogne*, and the many *vins de cépages* should be noted. The Côtes-de-Gascogne *vin de pays* from colombard, gros manseng and sauvignon (white) and from Jurançon rouge, egiodola, tannat and cabernet sauvignon deserve a separate honorable mention here.

Château Montus: the most famous Madiran

JURANÇON

This wine region, below the town of Pau and close to the French Pyrenees, is rather less old than the regions just described. The first traces of viniculture here date from the late tenth century. But the Jurançon wines soon gained a high reputation thanks to the French king Henry IV. He came from French Navarre, the province which includes Pau. To be crowned as king of France he had to abandon his Protestant faith in 1593

Pacherenc-du-Vic-Bilh sec

and have himself baptized as a Catholic. To make the bitter pill easier to swallow, the king had the baptismal water replaced by… Jurançon wine! Needless to say, the christening ceremony went very well.

In 1936 Jurançon became one of the first AOCs in France, and in 1975 the dry Jurançon wines received their own recognition.

The region is little more than 600 ha (1,500 acres) and the vineyards are very scattered over the whole area. Over a distance of 40 km (25 miles), they lie like small islands among the other vegetation. The better wines are produced on the hills, about 300 m (1,000 ft) high, of mixed soil (clay, sandstone and pebbles). The climate combines the high, but regular rainfall from the Atlantic and the harsh winters of the Pyrenees. However, the area seems to be blessed with warm Indian summers and warm, dry, southerly winds to produce overripe grapes, as is necessary for making great sweet wines. In the Jurançon the local grape varieties are used: gros manseng, petit manseng, courbu, camaralet and lauzet.

Jurançon Sec is quite dry and freshly acid with vegetable (broom, acacia) and fruity aromas (passion fruits, white peaches, citrus fruits). As they age they develop more complex aromas of almonds, nuts, dried fruits and very occasionally truffles!

Jurançon Sec is an excellent aperitif, but is mainly served with crustaceans and shellfish, fish (try locally the famous salmon of the Adour river, and the mountain trout,

Sweet Pacherenc from late--harvested overripe grapes

cooked *à la minute* with small Espelette peppers and bacon). You can also serve this wine with cold meats or young cheeses. Drinking temperature: 8–10 °C (47–50 °F).

The Jurançons Doux and Moelleux are little gems. The color hovers between gold and amber, the aromas are rich and complex, varying from honey, vanilla, toast and overripe fruits to the most subtle aromas of white flowers, lime flowers, chamomile, pineapple and citrus fruits. The taste is full and round and the high sugar content is held in perfect balance by the fresh acids. These sweet wines can age well.

Serve these delicious wines with the many variants of duck and goose liver, with blue cheese (Roquefort, Bleu des Causses) or with a mature sheep's cheese from Ossau-Iraty or Laruns. Striking, too, is the rather unusual combination with the fine oriental cuisine of China, Thailand and Japan. For lovers of pure liquid enjoyment the *vendanges tardives* of the Manseng can be recommended. Drinking temperature: 10–12 °C (50–54 °F).

BÉARN-BELLOCQ

The Romans already realized that good wines could be made in Béarn. During the French religious wars it is estimated that hundreds of thousands of people from central and southwest France moved to the Netherlands, England, North and South America. This great company of émigré Huguenots (and their thirst) saw to it that the trade in wines from the southwest would flourish. As it did in Béarn. The Béarn wines were classed as AOVDQS as early as 1951; AOC recognition did not come until 1975. In 1990 the best wines gained their own AOC of Béarn-Bellocq.

The Béarn soil is very hilly and lies at the foot of the Pyrenees. Béarn benefits from an ideal microclimate, combining the moisture of the Atlantic with a harsh mountain climate.

White Béarn is rather rare and is produced around Bellocq. These white wines from Raffiat and Manseng grapes are fresh and fruity with an undertone of floral aromas (broom, acacia). Like a Jurançon Sec, a white Béarn is the perfect companion for freshly caught and quickly cooked mountain trout and of salmon from the

Jurançon sec

Adour. Also good with a fresh goat's cheese. Drinking temperature: 10–12 °C (50–54 °F).

The rather more ordinary Béarn Rosé owes its charm to the combination of tannat with cabernet sauvignon and cabernet franc (here better known as bouchy). These rosé wines are velvety soft, full, rounded and very fruity.

You can serve this rosé on any summer occasion, but also in winter with, for example, filled omelets or other egg dishes, or even with a traditional bubble-and-squeak type of meal. Drinking temperature: 10–12 °C (50–54 °F).

The simple red Béarn wines are sprightly, generous and easy to drink. In their bouquet and taste you can recognize the Cabernet Franc rather than the Tannat. Serve them whenever you feel like it: they adapt themselves easily. Drinking temperature: 12 °C (54 °F).

The better red Béarn-Bellocqs are more robust, fuller, more full-bodied, and fleshier. Here it is plainly the Tannat which has the upper hand. These wines require a robust grill or casserole. You can also serve them with game. Drinking temperature: 14–16 °C (57–61 °F).

IROULÉGUY

This wine region in the heart of the French Basque country was already well known in the time of Charlemagne. The small village of Irouléguy was then already a center for the sale of these Basque wines. After the *Phylloxera* invasion, wine-growing there fell virtually into oblivion. Only in the early 1950s did a few wine-growers decide to pick up the thread again. A cooperative was set up under the leadership of Alexandre Bergouignan. The vineyards of once famous Irouléguy were restored and replanted.

Enormous investments were made to improve the quality of the wines. So much effort and goodwill was rewarded in 1953 with AOVDQS recognition, and in 1970 the Irouléguy wines at last gained their AOC. More hard work followed in the 1980s to raise the level even higher. New vineyards were planted, mainly on terraces. In addition to the efforts of the local cooperative, various private initiatives developed, such as that of Etienne Brana, whose business is today world famous. Meanwhile winegrowing in Irouléguy has been improved so much that it can be said without qualification that the area has become one of the top wine regions in France. Of course, the winegrowers still have to work on making their products better known: the limited quantities of wine they produce do not help, the more so since

Medium sweet Jurançon

White Béarn

An excellent Béarn in rosé and red

a major part of their production is exported to the USA, to slake the thirst of hundreds of thousands of émigré Basques for Basque wine and for their native land. Yet meanwhile the quality of these wines is unanimously acknowledged by all connoisseurs, and certainly the wines of the Brana family, who are ranked as members of the elite club of the best winemakers in the world. Their brandies, too, are among the very best in France.

WINEGROWING

The Irouléguy vineyards are near Saint-Jean Pied de Port and Saint-Etienne de Baigorry, mostly on terraces on a soil of red sandstone, clay and schist, with here and there some limestone. This produces splendid, picturesque contrasts, with the green of the vineyards against the red of the iron-oxide-containing sandstone. The climate is a compromise between the mildness of the oceanic climate and the harshness of the continental and mountain ones. The winters are quite mild, with snow and rain. The spring is wet, with sometimes dangerous frosts. The summer is hot and dry; the greatest danger to the vineyards then comes from the heavy thunderstorms, sometimes accompanied by hail, with all its consequences. Finally, the falls are often very hot and dry, which is ideal for harvesting ripe, healthy grapes. Because of their difficult environment and the often bad accessibility of the vineyards the yield here is quite low.

Irouléguy, a vineyard reborn

THE WINES

About two-thirds of Irouléguy production is red. The character of red Irouléguy comes from the tannat grape (maximum 50 %), cabernet franc (axeria) and cabernet

Brana, the leading estate in Irouléguy

sauvignon. There are three categories of these red wines: in ascending order of quality they are the ordinary Irouléguy, the *cuvée*, and the *domaine* bottled. The simplest Irouléguys are robust, rich in tannins, fruity (blackberries) and spicy. The better *cuvées* possess slightly more body, have enjoyed a rather longer raising on wood, and have the advantage of several years bottle age. The top *domaines* (Brana, Ilarria, Iturritxe and Mignaberry) are outstanding wines, with powerful aromas of spices and black fruits (blackberries, plums) and a dash of vanilla. The taste is complex, rich, full and round with a perfect balance between the fresh acidity, fruitiness, alcohol, body and the robust but rounded tannins.

Like Collioure, the ordinary red Irouléguy, provided it is served young and cool, can be combined with all kinds of grilled fish dishes, particularly when these are served garnished with grilled paprikas. Drinking temperature: 14–16 °C (57–61 °F).

The *cuvées* and *domaine* wines deserve more important dishes: wood pigeon, wildfowl, small game, roast or grilled red meat or lamb. All dishes in which a little Espelette pepper is included will make red Irouléguy sing! An exceptional and enticing combination is that of mature or even old sheep's cheese from Ossau-Iraty or Laruns, served with sweet-and-sour morello cherry or plum jam and a glass of your best red Iroul é guy! Drinking temperature: 16–18 °C (61–64 °F).

The rosé wines are fresh and quite dry. It was on these that the good name of Irouléguy wines was originally based. Here, too, we have a combination of tannat, cabernet franc and cabernet sauvignon. The color resembles that of redcurrants, the bouquet is delicate and fruity (cherries, redcurrants) and the taste is fresh and fruity.

One dish goes with this wine better than anything else: Basque *piperade*, a simple but delicious dish of grilled paprikas, sometimes accompanied by a fried slice of Bayonne ham and scrambled eggs. But cold meats and grilled fish will also be happy with a rosé Irouléguy.

Terraced vineyard in Irouléguy

It is interesting in combination with Serrano or Iberico raw Spanish ham. Drinking temperature: 10–12 °C (50–54 °F).

The rare white Irouléguy from the grape varieties xuri ixiriota (manseng) and xuri cerrabia (petit courbu) are richer and fuller than their Béarn cousins. These very classy white wines possess characteristic aromas of white flowers, white peaches, citrus fruits, butter, hazelnuts and almonds, supported by a whiff of vanilla and a mineral undertone.

White Irouléguys can accompany any freshwater or sea fish, and also crustaceans, shellfish and other *fruits de mer* (squid). Drinking temperature: 9–10 °C (48–50 °F).

Duras and Bergerac

As we said earlier, the wines from Duras and Bergerac occupy a separate place between those of Bordeaux and those of the true southwest. Socially and economically both regions are attracted more to the capital of Aquitaine (Bordeaux) than to the capital of the southwest (Toulouse). The great commercial involvement of Bordeaux and the economic interests of Duras and Bergerac play an important role in this.

Classic red Irouléguy

A young red Irouléguy combines well with grilled sea fish, among other things

CÔTES-DE-DURAS

The Duras wine region seems to be squeezed between the vineyards of Bordeaux in the west, Bergerac in the north and east, and of the Marmandais in the southwest. The wine region is not really large, only some 5,000 acres. Centuries of experience makes this a special region with outstanding wines.

Although the people here are proud of their wines, they do not promote them actively. The native population of Duras prefer to work quietly and concentrate on their products. Duras wines (AOC since 1937) are intended for real wine lovers, not for 'label drinkers'. Only people who take the trouble to go and search for quality and the joy of wine without frills, will derive pleasure from these splendid wines. In spite of the age-old links with the many émigré Huguenots originally from Duras, Duras wines are still rather undervalued outside France. A pity, because it is there that their remarkable price/quality ratio could prove very attractive. Or are they all just 'label drinkers' outside France?

The Duras vineyards lie at the top (white wines) and on the south flank (red wines) of softly sloping hills. The substratum is very varied, but at the top of the hills the soil is lime-rich sandstone, while the soil on the flanks is formed by a mixture of compact clay and limestone full of fossil shells. The climate here is comparable to that of Bordeaux, with the difference that in Duras it is generally a little warmer and there is rather less rain. For the white wines mainly sauvignon,

White Irouléguy is still rare

sémillon and muscadelle are used (with occasional traces of ugni blanc, mauzac, ondenc and chenin blanc) and for the red and rosé wines merlot, cabernet sauvignon, cabernet franc and a very small quantity of Cot (Malbec). Most of the production (54 %) consists of red wine and dry white wine (42 %), with 2.5 % sweet white wine and 1.5 % rosé.

The Côtes-de-Duras Sec are light, fresh, elegant and fruity dry white wines with a splendid color, clear, pale yellow with green glints. These wines, in which sauvignon dominates, are without qualification among the better Aquitaine Sauvignons.

The Côtes-de-Duras Sec are outstanding accompaniments to any freshwater or sea fish, but also shellfish and crustaceans. They are also first-class aperitifs. Drinking temperature: 8–10 °C (47–50 °F).

The Côtes-de-Duras Moelleux are rare, sweet white wines in which Sémillon dominates. They are harmonious, fully sweet wines with aromas of honey, vanilla, toast, apricots, peaches, overripe fruits, almonds, walnuts, hazelnuts and figs. The structure is fat, almost balmy, and the taste lasts a long time.

The French like to drink these wines as aperitifs, with a few slices of goose or duck liver paté. There is nothing against this – it is delicious, even! But what do you drink afterwards? Only a great wine can stand up to such an onslaught on the taste buds. If this is not

Duras vineyards

within your budget, it would be better to opt for the classic combination with Roquefort, Bleu d'Auvergne or Bleu des Causses, or for the less well known but very pleasant combination with fresh strawberries or peaches. Drinking temperature: 6–8 °C (43–47 °F).

Côtes-de-Duras rosé wines, produced by the *saignée* method, are fresh, fruity and very aromatic (blackcurrants, fruit gums). Ideal companions for all summer dishes or, all through the year, for cold meats, paté or meat salads. Drinking temperature: 10–12 °C (50–54 °F).

The Côtes-de-Duras Rouge can be very pleasant, supple, elegant and fruity, when made by steeping in carbon dioxide (macération carbonique). These days, however, most wines are made by the traditional vinification method, which makes the wine rather fuller and more fleshy, without affecting its fruitiness.

Always drink the first category (macération carbonique) young and cool (12 °C/ 54 °F). The second category – the traditional wines – can be kept for at least five to ten years. Serve a mature Côtes-de-Duras rouge with red meat, preferably grilled or roast, or with any stews or oven dishes from the local cuisine, and hard or semi-soft cheeses. Drinking temperature: 14–16 °C (57–61 °F).

Bergerac

WINEGROWING

Bergerac is full of surprises and offers every visitor the pleasure of a splendid environment, the commitment

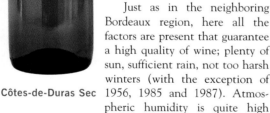

Côtes-de-Duras Sec

and passion of its winegrowers, the universally prized truffles, mushrooms, goose liver and wild boar of Périgord, and the emotions irreversibly released by each sip of wine. The soil of this wine district is formed mainly by a mixture of loam and limestone, loam and granite sand on the plateaus, Périgord granite sand, and washed-down sediments and pebbles. On the right bank of the Dordogne you will find many terraces with a poor substratum and a top layer of sediments. The southern slopes are strewn with pebbles. On the left bank the ground is very calcareous, particularly on the slopes of the hills, with here and there some loam.

Just as in the neighboring Bordeaux region, here all the factors are present that guarantee a high quality of wine; plenty of sun, sufficient rain, not too harsh winters (with the exception of 1956, 1985 and 1987). Atmospheric humidity is quite high because of the vicinity of the Atlantic and the good supply of water from the Dordogne and its many tributaries.

However good the *terroir* may be, it does not make wine! In Bergerac the profession of wine-grower has been in existence for two millennia. The enthusiasm and experience of generations of winegrowers have raised winemaking almost to an art. These days most young winegrowers make a compromise between age-old traditions of winemaking and the most modern vinification techniques. With the interactive combinations of the various *terroirs* and the grapes planted on them, an enormous diversity of types and tastes of wine, including thirteen AOCs, is to be found on only 27,000 acres.

Côtes-de-Duras Rouge

The grapes used for the red wines are cabernet sauvignon (robustness, tannins, color; bouquet of blackcurrants and cedar wood), cabernet franc (a great deal of bouquet – strawberries and fresh-sliced green pepper – and quick to mature) and Merlot (a bouquet of cherries, red berries and plums, and a velvety soft body).

The white wines are made of sémillon (susceptible to noble rot; a bouquet of honey, apricot, peach or mango; good balance between sweet and sour), sauvignon (subtlety, aromas of green apples, gooseberries, fresh-mown grass) and muscadelle (intense scent of honeysuckle and acacia). A well known winemaker from the district has been experimenting for several years with chardonnay grapes, which also give excellent results here. However, his wines have to be sold as *vin de pays*, as the use of chardonnay is completely taboo in Bergerac.

THE WINES

BERGERAC ROUGE

The red wines come mostly from the hillsides and the highland plateaus. They are mainly fruity, fine wines with a bouquet and aroma of strawberries, blackcurrants and other small red fruit.

Bergerac vineyards

These wines are at their best when drunk young, for example with roast white meat, patés and terrines, mushroom omelets and all kinds of 'one-pan dishes'. Drinking temperature: 12–14 °C (54–57 °F).

CÔTES-DE-BERGERAC ROUGE

The better selections of red Bergerac come into this category. They are wines with intense color and plenty of structure. They are extremely complex, with aromas of crystallized fruits (plums, prunes). These wines are often rich in alcohol and tannins, so they can age well.

Serve a Côtes-de-Bergerac Rouge with local dishes of goose, duck, poultry, wildfowl etc. Drinking temperature:14–16 °C (57–61 °F).

PÉCHARMANT

The vineyards for the top red wines of Pécharmant have a very favorable location in an amphitheater of hills. The soil is a decisive factor for the quality of these wines. Sand and gravel from the erosion of granite rocks have in the course of centuries often been 'washed' by the sea and rivers. It is this hard top layer, impenetrable to water, which gives the wines their typical taste of the *terroir*. Pécharmant wines are in general dark in color and very concentrated. They contain a great deal of tannin and are therefore often very bitter and undrinkable in their first youth. They are good wines for laying down. Once they are more mature, they have a broad palette of scents and tastes and become fuller.

These wines are ideal companions to game, roast meat and semi-soft cheeses. The combination with a casserole of fresh eel or chicken is superb, but replace the water in it by a red Bergerac! Drinking temperature: 16–17 °C (61–63 °F).

MONTRAVEL ROUGE

Since the harvest of 2000, the red wines from Montravel may also be sold under their own AOC. Previously they disappeared under the generic name of Côtes-de-Bergerac Rouge. Red Montravel wines must be made of at least 50 % Merlot with possible additions of both kinds of cabernet and cot (malbec). Before they reach the market, the wines must have been kept for at least eighteen months. Depending on the method chosen (only in bottle, partly on wood, or completely in vats) the wines will turn out different, from elegant, light and fruity to mature, fleshy and powerful.

Serve a Montravel Rouge with fried, roast or grilled red

Bergerac Rouge

These wines are a match for a great Bordeaux!

meat. Drinking temperature: 16 °C (61 °F) for the lighter wines, 17–18 °C (63–64 °F) for the heavier ones.

BERGERAC ROSÉ

The Bergerac Rosé wines are mostly very good, but not particularly complex. Whether they are made by the *saignée* method or by a short maceration, they are always fresh, 'friendly', salmon-colored wines, with a great deal of fruity aromas.

Three top wines from Côtes-de-Bergerac

For quality at an acceptable price Bergerac is a good choice

Ideal as a summer aperitif, with an informal lunch or an *al fresco* meal, and also with a barbecue or picnic. Drinking temperature: 12 °C (54 °F).

Pécharmant

Jean Rebeyrolle (La Ressaudie) is one of the driving forces behind the new Montravel Rouge AOC

BERGERAC BLANC SEC

The vineyards for Bergerac Blanc Sec are distributed over both banks of the Dordogne, mainly on the plateaus and hills. Modern vinification methods (including pellicular maceration) are used more and more often; they give these wines, which are not naturally really spectacular, rather more scent and taste.

A Bergerac Blanc Sec is a good accompaniment for crustaceans and shellfish, and for all kinds of fish. Because of its high acidity this wine goes well with the fresh sauces often served with fish (lemon sauce, sorrel sauce, and so on). Also delicious as an aperitif. Drinking temperature: 10–12 °C (50–54 °F).

MONTRAVEL

The splendid dry white Montravels are made in the extreme west of the Dordogne *département*. Here, too, modern vinification produces very aromatic wines, soft as velvet in the mouth. The ordinary Montravel can be drunk still young in all its fruitiness, but can also be kept for a few years. The better Montravel, which has been soundly raised on wood, should be laid down a little longer.

Montravel wines do very well as an aperitif, or at meals with fine freshwater fish, white meat and poultry (turkey). Drinking temperature: 10–12 °C (50–54 °F).

CÔTES-DE-MONTRAVEL

The semi-sweet white Côtes-de-Montravel form a smooth transition between the dry white Montravels and the sweeter Haut-Montravel whites.

Although this wine is often served locally as an aperitif with goose liver on toast, a freshwater fish or white meat might be preferable. A perfect combination is a Côtes-de-Montravel with white meat (fillet of pork or veal) stuffed with goose or duck liver and truffles. Drinking temperature: 10–12 °C (50–54 °F).

HAUT-MONTRAVEL

These wines come mainly from the banks of the river. The wines are mostly really plump, with a high sugar and alcohol content, but they have enough acidity to be well balanced and they can age well.

These fine, splendidly sweet white wines do well in combination with melon, fish in sauce, or ... blue cheese! Very striking, too, is the combination

Montravel (La Ressaudie) vineyards

Bergerac rosé

with a sweet-and-sour plum tart or plum mousse. Drinking temperature: 8–10 °C (47–50 °F).

CÔTES-DE-BERGERAC

The Côtes-de-Bergerac Moelleux, mainly made of sémillon, may come from anywhere in the district. They are darker in color than their dry opposite numbers, and often have more bouquet, more subtlety and more body. The quality of the end product is in part dependent on the soil, the grape variety used, and the method of vinification. These wines can be drunk after four or five years, but can also mature longer.

Haut-Montravel

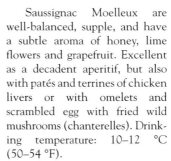

Bergerac
Blanc Sec

Excellent as an accompaniment to duck and goose liver, but also with turkey or guinea fowl fillets poached in white wine with a sweet-and-sour wine-grape sauce. Drinking temperature: 8–10 °C (47–50 °F).

ROSETTE

You will not often come across Rosette Moelleux, from the sunny slopes to the north of the town of Bergerac, outside the district itself. This is a pity, because a good Rosette is a true masterpiece. The wine is a light straw-yellow color with an overwhelming bouquet and a taste of flowers and fruit. There is a perfect balance between its elegant softness and its fine acidity.

Montravel AOC,
always dry

You will get most enjoyment from a glass of Rosette if you opt for a combination with lightly cooked mushrooms (chanterelles, *pieds de mouton*, *trompettes de la mort*), and a delicious sauce containing Rosette and truffles. A really magnificent combination! Drinking temperature: 9–10 °C (48–50 °F).

SAUSSIGNAC

Saussignac is a tiny district: just one small valley between the vineyards of Monbazillac and the first Bordeaux vineyards. Most of the wines of this district come from old vineyards.

Saussignac Moelleux are well-balanced, supple, and have a subtle aroma of honey, lime flowers and grapefruit. Excellent as a decadent aperitif, but also with patés and terrines of chicken livers or with omelets and scrambled egg with fried wild mushrooms (chanterelles). Drinking temperature: 10–12 °C (50–54 °F).

Saussignac Liquoreux are generous, rounded, broad and fat wines with aromas of acacia and peaches. Like the Moelleux, these wines should be kept for at least five to ten years before they can be drunk. They are true gems.

Drink them as they come, with your best friends or your partner, relaxed. Drinking temperature: 9–10 °C (48–50 °F).

Côtes-de-Bergerac
Moelleux

MONBAZILLAC

The very sweet, liqueur like Monbazillac Liquoreux comes from the south bank of the Dordogne. The vineyards lie at a height of 150–550 ft on the north-facing slopes, opposite the town of Bergerac. Thanks to their favorable location and their microclimate, the vineyards have plenty of moisture and warmth in the fall, so that the *Botrytis cinerea* mold, which is essential for the production of great liqueur-type wines, can develop well. Monbazillac should certainly not be drunk too cold: 6–8 °C (43–47 °F) for the lighter types; 10–12 °C (50–54 °F) for the richer ones. This will bring out the luxurious bouquet of acacia and honey properly. The wide checkerboard of tastes will then also develop better.

Some of the regional gourmets swear by a combination of Monbazillac and the local *foie gras*; others would rather eat white meat or poultry with it. A combination with

Rosette Moelleux

melon, fresh strawberries or fruit salad, perhaps accompanied by a soft almond pastry, possibly filled with almond paste, will almost certainly go down well. On a cold winter evening you can also serve a glass of Monbazillac with a platter of exclusively blue cheeses (Roquefort, Bleu des Causses, Bleu d'Avergne) with some walnuts and almonds.

BORDEAUX

No wine is so well-known across the world, and no wine region in the world produces so many top wines, as Bordeaux. All over the world the names Mouton--Rothschild, Lafite-Rothschild, Pétrus and Yquem sound like the almost unattainable dreams of youth. The top Bordeaux wines enjoy a separate status, far above the

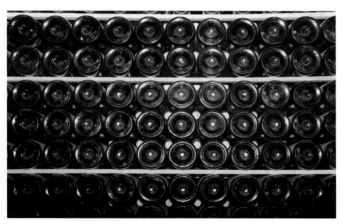

Pure gold liqueur wines from the Bergerac region

rest, but increasingly often elevated far above reality. It is, however, still arguable how justified this is in all cases.

Since 1855 there has been virtually no change in the classification of the *grand crus* of Médoc (and Sauternes). Many of the *grand crus* perform below their level, others far above it. Many a *cru* which was not on the 1855 list by now certainly deserves the label '*grand cru*'. And yet the classification has never changed. How can that be? Because very great economic (and political) interests are involved. A purely qualitative assessment based on soil and microclimate would in the Médoc cause a real revolution and would shake the whole world of marketing. Bordeaux has become one of the most successful brand names in the world, a synonym for quality and luxury. Of course, superb wines are made in Bordeaux, but the speculation in the top wines has put them out of the reach of ordinary people, and so made them a desirable object for the wealthy of this world. Trade is booming in Bordeaux – but how long will it last?

HISTORY

Wine has been grown in Bordeaux for at least 2000 years. The well-known fourth-century Roman poet

and wine lover Ausonius had a luxurious villa built in the Libournais, partly so that he could enjoy the local wines (the forerunners of Saint-Émilion). But it is above all the English who made Bordeaux famous and spread its reputation. By the marriage of Eleanor of Aquitaine to Henry Plantagenet, Bordeaux and the whole of Aquitaine came under English rule for three centuries (1154–1453). The great preference of the English for Bordeaux wines stems from that time. Because the color of these red wines was lighter than those from Spain or Portugal, the English called them *clairet* (*clair* being 'light' in French); they still use the name 'claret' for red Bordeaux wines, and so do the Americans.

It was the Dutch, who in the seventeenth and eighteenth centuries were the authors of a gigantic breakthrough. Teams

Monbazillac

of Dutch water engineers helped the French to drain and reclaim the great swampy region of the Médoc. At a stroke the winegrowing area expanded to unprecedented dimensions. Many wealthy wine aristocrats from the town of Bordeaux and far beyond had large country houses built there, each more eccentric and larger than the last. Because some of these buildings had a splendid appearance, from stately mansions to imposing palaces, they were dubbed 'castles' (*châteaux*), a term that soon spread to cover the estate and its wines. Thanks to the influential aristocracy of Bordeaux, and the increasing number of *nouveaux riches* from the worlds of industry and banking, the fame of Bordeaux wines spread out over the whole world. Demand was so great that the winegrowers of Bordeaux had to enlist the help of people from the surrounding wine regions (Bergerac, Duras, Cahors) to produce enough wine. The easy navigability of the Garonne, the Dordogne and the Lot, coupled with the fact that the Gironde and the port of Bordeaux were easily accessible, ensured the wider distribution of the new French clarets. The door to England and, later, to the other side of the Atlantic stood wide open.

However, the success of the Bordeaux region would never have been so great without the enormous speculation in the wines. Bordeaux has become a prestige object; a Château Pétrus is more often traded than drunk. Eccentrics in England, America and across the world keep this artificiality in place: never change a winning team. For some years, however, a growing number of protests have been heard against the ridiculous high prices which are the result of this speculation and which no longer have any relationship to the quality of the wines. Increasingly more buyers are seeking alternatives, looking for wines which still

Will such great wines be made
a hundred years from now?

BORDEAUX AOCs

The Bordeaux region has a great variety of appellations. The system is a simple one. It starts at the bottom with the so-called 'branded wine', standard wines from several *terroirs* of constant quality year in, year out. This is really the wine merchant's visiting card. The better the wine merchant, the better his branded wine.

A step up the ladder are the wines from one or more *terroirs* in the whole region. Where branded wines carry only the name of the wine merchant (Cordier, Ginestet, Yvon Mau, Dourthe and many others) and the description Bordeaux, the four categories Bordeaux, Bordeaux Supérieur, Bordeaux Clairet and Bordeaux Rosé are sold under the names of their châteaux.

A further step up, you will find the wines from a single defined region within the Bordeaux wine area. This can be a whole district (Entre-Deux-Mers, Graves, Médoc, Haut-Médoc, Côte-de-Bourg) or a single village (Saint-Émilion, Pomerol, Sauternes).

At the top of the ladder are the appellations referring to a commune in the Haut-Médoc. These bear the name of their village: Saint-Estèphe, Pauillac, Saint-Julien, Listrac, Moulis and Margaux. These exceptional communes from the Haut-Médoc produce the famous Médoc *grand crus*.

As a rule we can accept that the more restricted the appellation, the higher should be the quality of the wine. But there are many exceptions to this rule.

THE BORDEAUX CRUS

In addition to the well-known appellations, the Bordeaux region also has a number of its own classifications. The better wines are here called 'grand crus' (literally 'great growths'). But there are also numerous lesser *crus*.

GRANDS CRUS CLASSÉS
There are three official *grand cru* classifications in the Bordeaux region:
– the 1855 classification for Médoc wines (including one red Graves). The better wines of Sauternes and Barsac are also listed in the same classification;
– the classification of Graves wines (1953–1959);
– the classification of Saint-Émilion (1955).

The first two classifications are not really reliable, because they have not been subjected to a regular revision. In this respect the third is more reliable: it is revised every ten years. A classification without promotion or relegation is actually not so much a classification as a cross-sectional snapshot. That the wines of Saint-Émilion and Pomerol were not included in the 1855 classification is purely the result of local government administration. Saint-Émilion and Pomerol came under the authority of Libourne, while Médoc and Graves came under Bordeaux. The *grand-cru* list of 1855 was made on the occasion of the Bordeaux international exhibition by the *courtiers* (wine brokers) of Bordeaux. The wines of the Libournais fell outside their responsibility, so they did not

have a link with their *terroir*, for wine growers who still have calluses on their hands and dirt under their fingernails, and don't wear white gloves... He who seeks shall find top wines, even outside the Bordeaux district. Wines which surpass the quality of many an expensive *grand cru*, but are still very affordable. It seems as if the whole south-west of France has suddenly woken up and become conscious of the unjustified hegemony of the lords of Bordeaux. These are very interesting developments for consumers.

WINEGROWING

The Bordeaux vineyards lie in the French *département* of Gironde, which owes its name to the estuary of the rivers Garonne and Dordogne. However, the wine area does not cover the whole of the *département*, though officially this would be possible. After all, not all terrains are suitable for growing vines (woods, built-up areas, fields of maize and tobacco). The climate of Bordeaux is quite mild, thanks to the volume of the water in the rivers, including the Gironde, and the proximity of the Atlantic. In general Bordeaux has a mild winter, an early and wet spring, a hot and mostly dry summer, and a mild, often sunny, fall, so that the vine stocks have perfect quantities of sun and water. That things don't always go to this plan was proved by the exceptionally cold winter of 1956 (virtually all the vines were frozen) and the many floods of the Garonne and the Dordogne.

classify them. Surprisingly, the 1855 list did not actually include a classification. All the *crus* were just listed. Only in 1862 were the wines subdivided into the familiar five categories. Since then nothing in the list has been altered except in 1973, when Château Mouton-Rothschild was promoted from the second to the first category of *grand cru classés*. Altogether sixty châteaux from the Médoc and one from Graves are included in the lists: five first *crus*, fourteen second *crus*, fourteen third *crus*, ten fourth *crus*, and eighteen fifth *crus*.

CRUS BOURGEOIS

The '*bourgeoisie*' of Bordeaux dates from the twelfth century. When Aquitaine was under English rule, a number of prosperous merchants managed to gain the same privileges for themselves as the ruling aristocracy had, such as being allowed to bear arms in public. More important for us is that they were also allowed to own land, which until then had been reserved for the nobility. These bourgeois families from Bordeaux played an enormously stimulating role in the development of the Bordeaux wine trade. The concept of '*cru bourgeois*' had long been lurking in the wings of the wine theatre, but became official only in 1932. The family of these *crus bourgeois* then accounted for 444 'offspring'. The after-effects of the economic crisis of 1929 and the destructive World War II were fatal to many of them. In the 1960s a trade association of Crus Bourgeois was set up. In 1976 (although it was not mandatory) the description 'Cru Bourgeois' on the label was authorized by the European Commission. Today there are some 420 Crus Bourgeois in the Médoc, accounting for about half of Médoc's total production. Many businesses on the original 1932 list have vanished and been replaced by worthy successors.

The criteria for recognition as a Cru Bourgeois are: at least 17 acres of vineyards; the wine must come from one of the eight Médoc AOCs and the owner must vinify and raise the wine himself. The quality of the wines is closely monitored and every so often there is a competition between all the Crus Bourgeois. Since 1985 there has been a Coupe des Cru Bourgeois de Médoc, a great competition in which 300 professional tasters (sommeliers, chefs, merchants, wine scientists, journalists) have the rewarding task of choosing the best Cru Bourgeois of the year.

In January 2001, after lengthy preparation, new guidelines were published for the classification of Cru Bourgeois, to be put into effect in 2002, replacing the 1972 ones. Like the wines of Saint-Émilion, the Médoc Cru Bourgeois will be subjected to an investigation in depth every ten years. A new classification will then be made based on the results. The list of important criteria for deciding this classification are the quality and state of maintenance of the vineyards and the *domaine*, the quality of the cellar installations, the image of the business, market prices and, of course, a comprehensive organoleptic check (tasting for taste and smell) on the integrity and the qualities (trueness to type) of the wines. All the wines have to be vinified on the *domaine* itself. The Cru Bourgeois then has to be subdivided again into three quality categories: Cru Bourgeois, Cru Bourgeois Exceptionnel and Cru Bourgeois Supérieur. However, the argument still continues on whether these terms should appear on the label. This is what the French institutions want, but the European Union had earlier rejected a similar plan. No list of Cru Bourgeois is included in this book, because the current list is not representative and the new list has not yet appeared.

CRUS ARTISANS

Since 1994 the European Commission has allowed the description 'Cru Artisan' on the label of a Médoc wine. The term Cru Artisan has in fact been in existence for more than 150 years. Although more than 330 *domaines* (11 % of the total Médoc production) have the right to this description, there are only a few more than a hundred businesses which actually use the name.

A Cru Artisan is a wine made by an independent winegrower, who keeps everything under his own control. He does the work himself, with his family or a few employees. The businesses are small in scale, roughly 1 to 5 ha (2.5 to 12 acres) each. Because the grower is himself responsible for the end product, the Cru Artisan label offers the consumer a guarantee of quality, genuineness and being true to type. This guarantee is endorsed by a jury of wine scientists, winemakers, wine merchants and winegrowers, who taste the wines each year and decide whether they justify the description Cru Artisan.

THE GENERIC AOCS

We start our journey through the Bordeaux area in the south of the region. But before we deal with the provincial or commune appellations, we first take a trip round the generic ones. These wines may be produced anywhere in the Bordeaux region.

BORDEAUX SEC

It may come as a surprise to many people that two centuries ago ten times as much white wine was produced in the Bordeaux region as red, but the story does not mention that much of this wine was destined for the Dutch brandy stills. Since then the quality of dry white Bordeaux has improved enormously. This is partly thanks to the complete renovation of most of the wine-producing plant, and also to the cooperatives that pro-

A Grand Cru Classé from Médoc

Cru Bourgeois, will they soon all be
as reliable as these two?

duce most by volume. Dry white Bordeaux are made
from sauvignon, sémillon and muscadelle. The better
wines are matured in wooden casks, which makes them
fuller and more elegant. In general this Bordeaux Blanc
Sec is very scented: grass, box, acacia, lemon, peaches
and grapefruit are discernible in the bouquet. The taste
is fresh and delicate.

These wines make an elegant aperitif. If you like,
serve them with savory canapés. A Bordeaux Blanc Sec
is a first-class accompaniment for oysters, crustaceans
and shellfish, fish, poultry and white meat in a creamy
sauce. Also good with soft fresh goat's cheese. Drinking
temperature: 9–10 °C (48–50 °F).

BORDEAUX ROSÉ, BORDEAUX CLAIRET

The difference between Bordeaux Rosé and Bordeaux
Clairet is simple: the skins for the Bordeaux Clairet are
steeped in the juice rather longer than those for the
rosé wines (24–36 hours as opposed to 12–18 hours).
This gives the rosé wines a light pink color and the
clairet a deep pink one. Otherwise both wines after
steeping are treated in the same way as white wines.
Both are made of Cabernet Sauvignon, Cabernet Franc
and Merlot; they are light and very fruity (raspberries,
redcurrants, cherries, strawberries) with a whiff of
flowers (irises, violets).

A rosé or clairet is best drunk young, for instance
with cold meats, terrines, patés, warm or cold salads
with meat or poultry, and starters, tasty pies containing
chicken, turkey or white meat, light lunches, summer
meals and the more upmarket barbecues (excellent
with any kind of kebab!). Also nice with fish. Try

a fresh salmon steak cooked *à la minute* some time, with
a glass of Bordeaux Rosé. Drinking temperature: 10 °C
(50 °F).

BORDEAUX, BORDEAUX SUPÉRIEUR

Welcome to the largest vineyard in France (about
150,000 acres). Bordeaux and Bordeaux Supérieur
together account for more than half the total
production of Bordeaux. Profiting from the good
reputation of their bigger brothers from the Médoc,
Saint-Émilion, Pomerol and Sauternes, both Bordeaux
and Bordeaux Supérieur have quickly conquered the
hearts of French and foreign consumers. An important
reason for their success – apart from the recognizable
name – is the outstanding ratio between quality, price
and enjoyment. Unfortunately, in European supermarkets there are also plenty of bad Bordeaux which do
no honor to their origins. As soon as a product starts to
be successful, the counterfeit trade strikes. Fortunately
there is nothing wrong with the quality of most Bordeaux and Bordeaux Supérieur, but anyone buying
a Bordeaux for the price of a house wine is often the
victim of his own stinginess (particularly the morning
after!).

It is difficult to give a detailed description of these
wines, which are made by so many different people
(independent growers, cooperatives and commercial
firms) on totally different types of soil. Add the
influence of numerous microclimates and the different
percentages of the grape varieties used in each wine,
and you will understand that here we have an enormous
variety of types of wine and of tastes.

Bordeaux Blanc Sec

BORDEAUX ROUGE

These wines are made from the familiar cabernet sauvignon, cabernet franc and merlot. The acreage of these red Bordeaux is about 94,000 acres. The wines are a beautiful red color and have an attractive range of aromas (wood, vanilla, violets, blackcurrants, cherries, peppermint). The structure is rich and soft, with a full flavor. The wines will vary in strength depending on the year.

Wines of lighter years are better drunk young, with a variety of dishes, such as omelettes, pastas, cold meats and mild cheeses. Drinking temperature: 14–15 °C (57–59 °F).

Wines from better years can be served with all dishes from the modern cuisine, particularly with cold meat platters, patés or terrines, omelettes (with fried mushrooms), au gratin pasta dishes, or mature cheeses. Drinking temperature: 16 °C (61 °F).

Bordeaux Rosé

BORDEAUX SUPÉRIEUR ROUGE

The acreage of red Bordeaux Supérieur is much smaller than that for red Bordeaux: some 20,000 acres. A Bordeaux Supérieur has a rather higher percentage of alcohol, a lower yield per acre, and may only be sold after being kept for twelve months. Most of these wines are very typical of their district and can age well.

A red Bordeaux Supérieur can be served on any formal or informal occasion. Success is guaranteed when you serve it with roast veal, chicken and pork, red meat with a red wine sauce and/or fried mushrooms, game birds and cheese. Drinking temperature: 16 °C (61 °F).

BORDEAUX BLANC, BORDEAUX SUPÉRIEUR BLANC

These wines are always sweet or sweetish (*doux* or *moelleux*). Production of them is modest (only 2 % of sales), but it is very surprising how many of these rare wines there are in the supermarkets. The 'real' Bordeaux Blanc Moelleux are splendid, almost balmy wines, with aromas of flowers, peaches, apricots and pineapples.

You can serve these wines from sauvignon, sémillon and muscadelle grapes as aperitifs, but they do better as companions to meat or chicken salads and starters, or simply with some toast with blue cheese, avocado or peaches. Drinking temperature: 8 °C (47 °F).

CRÉMANT DE BORDEAUX

This appellation for sparkling wines from Bordeaux is quite recent (1990), but their history began back in the nineteenth century. The excellent Crémants de Bordeaux are made by the traditional method. The combination of typical Bordeaux grapes and champagne-type vinification produces a remarkable result. The white and rosé Crémants de Bordeaux are mainly known for their freshness, elegance, *mousse* (foam) and pleasant fruitiness.

Drink these wines as a smart aperitif or at meals with fish, crustaceans, *fruits de mer* or fresh cheeses. Also nice with sweet desserts. To drink a dry (sparkling) wine with a sweet dessert is refreshing and surprisingly good. Drinking temperature: 6–8 °C (43–47 °F).

GRAVES

The Graves region extends southwest of Bordeaux from just below the village of Saint-Pierre de Mons to Blanquefort. It is subdivided into three large wine-growing regions. Graves (Graves Rouge, Graves Blanc Sec, Graves Supérieures Moelleux and Liquoreux), Pessac-Léognan (Rouge and Blanc Sec), the enclave of sweet-wine producing areas, Sauternes, Barsac and Cérons. The whole area is 30 miles long and contains forty-three communes.

Graves is the only French appellation to bear the name of the specific soil on the label. Graves is the French word for gravelly soils, where winegrowing flourished best in the days of English rule

Bordeaux Supérieur

(Médoc was then a swampy area only later drained and reclaimed by Dutch water engineers). Out of respect for the generosity of the soil, the name Graves became indissolubly linked with its wines. It is really these wines which created the great reputation of Bordeaux, and certainly not the Médoc wines. These only came along much later, half-way through the eighteenth century, and profited from the reputation of the Graves wines.

Bordeaux Blanc
Moelleux

WINEGROWING

In Graves, too, the great diversity of *terroirs* is very striking. In general the soil consists of terraces of gravelly clay and sand, with plenty of pebbles. Here the quality of the soil determines the ultimate quality of the wines. The wine acreage of Graves has been put under severe pressure in the twentieth century. Some 7,000 ha (17,000 acres) have disappeared through the expansion of the town of Bordeaux. This process was accelerated still further by the economic crisis before the World War II, the war itself, and the extremely cold winter of 1956. Particularly the vineyards in the suburbs of Bordeaux suffered heavily. For outsiders is often seems extraordinary that top châteaux, such as Haut-Brion and La Mission Haut-Brion, should both literally and figuratively be permanently under the pall of Bordeaux's smoke.

On Graves' 7,500 acres, 53 % of the wines produced are red, and 47 % white. The better wines (including all the Graves *grand crus classés*) have had an appellation of their own, Pessac-Léognan, since 1987. Merlot, cabernet franc and cabernet sauvignon are used for the red wines, possibly supplemented by malbec and petit verdot. The white wines are made from sémillon, sauvignon and muscadelle.

Graves, a good and affordable quality

GRAVES ROUGE

From an historical point of view, the red Graves wines are the great wines of Bordeaux. The vineyards were planted by the Romans and the wines were very popular at imperial banquets in Rome. Thanks to the English they became world famous, and the French kings were also very keen on them. AOC recognition came as early as 1937.

Depending on their *terroir* red Graves can be light and elegant or quite full, powerful, fat, fleshy and full of tannins. Particularly these last wines can age well. Very characteristic of these red Graves is the light smoky undertone in bouquet and taste, which comes from the soil. Other recognizable aromas are vanilla, ripe fruits, strawberries, blackcurrants, orange peel, toast, green paprika and some cinnamon, coffee, cocoa and brushwood as they age.

A red Graves is happiest with grilled or roast red meat, or calf's liver cooked pink with a bordelaise sauce (shallots, red wine, herbs and beef marrow). Fried mushrooms (don't forget the garlic and the shallots!), grilled poultry, game birds and small game are good alternatives. Drinking temperature: 16–17 °C (61–63 °F).

GRAVES BLANC SEC

These dry white Graves are always fresh, fruity and very aromatic (box, bay, peaches, apricots, citrus fruits, ivy, mint, vanilla, toast, almonds).

Drunk young, Graves Blanc Sec is full-bodied in its acidity, which makes it an excellent aperitif, but they are also first-class companions to mussels and oysters. You can serve a rather older Graves Blanc Sec with fish (if you have no sturgeon, serve some pike with a mousseline or hollandaise sauce) or with white meat. Drinking temperature: 10–12 °C (50–54 °F).

GRAVES SUPÉRIEUR

We will say nothing here of the frightful, characterless and syrupy wines which are available in the supermarkets at knock-down prices; these wines are more like alcoholic lemonades and hardly deserve to be called wines. These cheap Graves, which are far from 'superior', have nothing to offer but liquid, alcohol and a large amount of sugar. True Graves Supérieures are excellent, but not cheap. These sweet (*moelleux*) to liqueurlike (*liquoreux*) wines are very aromatic (hazelnuts, vanilla, toast, honey, peaches, apricots) and velvet soft. The presence of fresh acids makes these wines well-balanced.

A good Graves Supérieurs can face the confrontation with goose and duck liver without problems, as it can blue cheese. The *moelleux* goes well with rich fish dishes, lobster or exotic dishes too. Drinking temperature: 6–8 °C (43–47 °F).

PESSAC-LÉOGNAN

Since 1987 the communes of Cadaujac, Canéjan, Gradignan, Léognan, Martillac, Mérignac, Pessac, Saint-Médard d'Eyrans, Talence and Villenave d'Ornon have been able to carry the AOC Pessac-Léognan. All the *grands crus classés* of Graves (1959) came under this appellation, including Château Haut-Brion. In all, fifty-five *domaines* and châteaux carry the appellation Pessac-Léognan. The wines produced here are of higher quality than most Graves. This is partly thanks to the soil of Pessac-Léognan, which is very poor and hilly, and a perfect location, with good drainage and sufficient water in the substratum.

Graves Rouge

The total wine acreage of Pessac-Léognan covers 3,500 acres. Almost half of this has been replanted since 1970. Wine growing in Pessac-Léognan then threatened to be smothered under the smoke of the expanding town of Bordeaux. The survival instincts of the remaining winegrowers (almost all of them *grand crus classés*) resulted in AOC recognition in 1987. Since then wine-growing has been well protected against further expansion of the town. As the wines of Pessac-Léognan do very well in export markets (75 % of the total production is exported) and the region badly needs money, there is reason to be optimistic about the future of winegrowing in Pessac-Léognan, particularly in view of the excellent price-quality ratio of these wines. They are top quality and yet affordable.

Pessac-Léognan Blanc is always dry. Sauvignon dominates in these wines, assisted sometimes by sémillon. The color is clear, pale yellow to straw yellow. The bouquet is extremely enticing; you can discern vanilla, toast, lime blossom, broom, citrus fruits (grapefruit), apricots, peaches, quince, exotic fruits (mango, lychee), butter and almonds. The taste is fresh, fruity, fat and rounded.

Serve these splendid wines with your best fish dishes, such as lamprey, monkfish or turbot, or with fillets of poultry breast (guinea fowl) with a soft mousseline or hollandaise sauce. Drinking temperature: 12 °C (54 °F).

The Pessac-Léognan Rouge are of exceptional quality. The color is dark purple to carmine red – deep and fascinating. In their youth these wines develop aromas of ripe fruits (blackcurrants, plums), vanilla, toast, almonds and their typical smoky aroma. These aromas later change into mature undertones of brushwood, prunes, game and truffles. Most wines have cabernet sauvignon as their main grape, topped up with some merlot and cabernet franc, so the wines keep well.

Serve Pessac-Léognan Rouge with grilled or roast red meat and lamb, or with game birds and small game. Drinking temperature: 16–17 °C (61–63 °F).

Pessac Léognan Blanc

Pessac Léognan Rouge

SAUTERNES, BARSAC AND CÉRONS

Like everywhere else where sweet or liqueur-like wines are made from late-harvested grapes, whether or not affected by noble rot, here in this sweet wine region you will hear strange tales about the historic origin of this manner of winemaking. It may seem a curious coincidence that some landowners in, for example, Hungary, Austria, Alsace, Sauternes and Bergerac were all at about the same time 'accidentally' prevented from harvesting their grapes, and only completed getting their harvest in several weeks later. Just as accidentally all these grapes were affected by the same mould, *Botrytis cinerea*, and after pressing all produced exceptional wines…

Late harvesting is a common phenomenon throughout Europe, including all the countries round the Mediterranean. The process was known to the Greeks and Romans long before a drop of wine flowed over the soil of Sauternes. After all, it is a natural process which can only occur in places where the climate is warm and humid. *Botrytis* is, however, an awkward, unreliable mould, which does not turn up tidily in the same place and in the same way every year. Sometimes it does not appear at all. Making good sweet wine is very labor-intensive and extremely painstaking work, and above all demands a great deal of luck. The winemaker counts his blessings when the *Botrytis* takes the overripe grapes under its wing. The water in the grapes is sucked away by the mould and evaporates in the warm air. In the shriveled grapes the concentration of aromas and sugars rises. The resulting wines are very aromatic, full, plump, powerful and high in alcohol.

SAUTERNES

The wine acreage of Sauternes covers just over 4,000 acres. There are many varieties of soil; limestone, calcareous clay and gravelly clay account for most of it. To produce this divine nectar Sémillon (70–80 %) and Sauvignon (20–30 %) are used, with sometimes a little muscadelle. The sémillon gives the wine charm, lushness, plumpness and splendid aromas of honey, apricot, peach, quince, orange, mandarin, pineapple and so on. The Sauvignon gives the wine freshness and balance. A good Sauternes is plump, fat and velvety soft, but also fresh, sophisticated and elegant.

A slightly less expensive Sauternes can be drunk young. Well cooled (6–8 °C/ 43–47 °F), this is an original and sophisticated aperitif to go with a few toasts with duck or goose liver. A young Sauternes is also a striking partner for salmon, turbot, monkfish, poultry, or medaillons of veal with a soft Sauternes mousseline sauce.

1953 CLASSIFICATION (1959): GRAVES CRUS CLASSÉS

Château Bouscaut (red and white)
Château Carbonnieux (red and white)
Domaine de Chevalier (red and white)
Château Couhins (only white)
Château Couhins-Lurton (only white)
Château de Fieuzal (only red)
Château Haut-Bailly (only red)
Château Haut-Brion (only red)
Château Laville-Haut-Brion (only white)
Château Malartic-Lagravière (red and white)
Château La Mission-Haut-Brion (only red)
Château Olivier (red and white)
Château Pape-Clément (only red)
Château Smith-Haut-Lafitte (only red)
Château Latour-Haut-Brion (only red)
Château Lat Tour-Martillac (red and white)

Don't drink a great Sauternes (Yquem, Rieussec, Sigalas-Rabaud, Clos-Haut-Peyraguey, Doisy-Daene, Doisy-Védrines, Fargues, Guiraud, Lafaurie-Peyraguey, Lagnet La Carrière, Les Justices, Malle, Rayne-Vigneau, Roumieu, Suduiraut) as an aperitif, and certainly not young! Let this marriage of dew and honey ripen for some years. A top Sauternes can be at least 20 to 30 years old. After a few years maturing in bottle a luxurious and fascinating bouquet develops in which honey, quince, crystallized fruits, orange marmalade and hazelnuts provide the dominant notes. Drink these wines with your best friends. Serve a few slices of *foie gras* or a good Roquefort (Papillon Carte Noire) at room temperature with them. In the battle between these two giants of the world of sweetness and savory both will give of their best, in the end bringing the taster to a culinary peak in a fond embrace. Drinking temperature: 8–9 °C (47–48 °F).

BARSAC

The wines produced in the Barsac commune have a luxury identity problem: they may be sold under their own appellation of Barsac, but also that of Sauternes! The difference is that Barsac wines may be a little lighter and less like a liqueur than their partners from Sauternes. Otherwise these wines are as like Sauternes as two drops of water. The price/quality ratio is, however, often more favorable.

Like Sauternes, you can serve these fruity and luxurious wines with *foie gras* or blue cheese. Drinking temperature: 8–9 °C (47–48 °F).

CÉRONS

Cérons wines are perhaps a little lighter still then those of Barsac and Sauternes. They form a golden road midway between the better liqueur-type wines and the better sweet wines of Graves Supérieures. The Cérons wines are, however, extremely sophisticated, with aromas of flowers, honey and fruits (peaches, apricots). The taste is full, round, harmonious and juicy. Cérons are characterized by the remarkable ratio between their price, quality and… enjoyment.

Try these wines some time with freshwater crayfish or lobster with a creamy sweet wine sauce. Drinking temperature: 9–10 °C (48–50 °F).

Sauternes, great classic wines

1855 CLASSIFICATION: SAUTERNE CRUS CLASSÉS

PREMIER CRU SUPÉRIEUR
– Château d'Yquem

PREMIERS CRU
– Château Climens
– Château Coutet
– Château Guiraud
– Château Lafaurie-Peyraguey
– Château Haut-Peyraguey
– Château Rayne-Vigneau
– Château Rabaud-Promis
– Château Sigalas-Rabaud
– Château Rieussec
– Château Suduiraut
– Château La Tour Blanche

SECOND CRUS
– Château d'Arche
– Château Broustet
– Château Nairac
– Château Caillou
– Château Doisy-Daene
– Château Doisy-Dubroca
– Château Doisy-Védrines
– Château Filhot
– Château Lamothe (Despujols)
– Château Lamothe (Guignard)
– Château de Malle
– Château Myrat
– Château Romer
– Château Romer-Du-Hayot
– Château Suau

Entre-Deux-Mers: between Garonne and Dordogne

We leave the left bank of the Garonne and continue our journey via the triangular piece of land between the two 'seas', the Garonne and the Dordogne. Anyone who has experienced these two rivers in flood will realize what people here mean by 'Entre-Deux-Mers'. The Entre-Deux-Mers district is a large, high plateau, crisscrossed by numerous small valleys and streams which meander along the softly sloping hills. It is quite a large region, mainly covered by the AOC of the dry, white Entre-Deux-Mers. Other appellations are Côtes-de-Bordeaux Saint-Macaire, Sainte-Croix-du--Mont, Loupiac and Cadillac (all sweet liqueur-type white wines), Graves de Vayres (red, dry and sweet white wines), Premières Côtes-de-Bordeaux and Sainte-Foy Bordeaux (both red and sweet or liqueur-like white wines). Apart from the wines listed, a great deal of Bordeaux and Bordeaux Supérieure (red and rosé wines and dry or sweet white wines) are produced throughout the Entre-Deux-Mers region.

Cérons, excellent value for money

ELDORADO OF SWEET WINES

Straight opposite the Sauternes, Barsac and Cérons (discussed earlier) is a second goldmine of sweet liqueurlike wines.

CÔTES-DE-BORDEAUX-SAINT-MACAIRE

The area of these Côtes-de-Bordeaux-Saint-Macaire wines, officially part of the Premières Côtes-de-Bordeaux, was once known for its exceptional sweet white wines, but because of the changing patterns of wine consumption (much less sweet wine is being drunk) and the cut-throat competition of its neighbors, more and more red wine which may carry the appellation Bordeaux or Bordeaux Superieur is being made here. However, the sweet white wines that have a right to the appellation AOC Côtes-de-Bordeaux Saint-Macaire are still produced in a region of barely 60 ha (150 acres).

These full, rich and very aromatic wines (honey, toast, crystallized fruits) can, of course, be served with *foie gras* or blue cheese, but also just by themselves, after a meal, purely for pleasure. Drinking temperature: 8–9 °C (47–48 °F).

SAINTE-CROIX-DU-MONT

Sadly the superb wines of Sainte-Croix do not enjoy the reputation that their exceptional quality deserves. The Sainte-Croix-du-Mont vineyards lie just opposite those of Sauternes on an excellent soil of limestone and gravelly earth. In Sainte-Croix-du-Mont, too, the microclimate conditions favor the arrival of the *Botrytis* mould. In short, the same grapes, excellent soil, the same favorable microclimate, the same methods of vinification, near enough the same quality… but a much lower price! It is unbelievable that people outside France have hardly discovered it yet.

These rich, full, fat wines with their aromas of honey, citrus fruits, peaches, quinces, pears, crystallized fruits, spices, gingerbread, white flowers and so on can be served in the same way as a Sauternes, but a Sainte-Croix-du-Mont goes equally well with rich patés and terrines of poultry, and is delicious with freshwater fish or calf's liver in a creamy wine sauce. Drinking temperature: 8–9 °C (47–48 °F).

LOUPIAC

The wines of Sainte-Croix-du-Mont tend in general to be more like liqueurs than this. The wines of Loupiac to the north-west are plumper in type. Loupiac is an old wine region, already known in the thirteenth century. Compared with the wines of Sainte-Croix-du-Mont those of Loupiac have rather more freshness, certainly in their aromas of citrus fruits (oranges!), peaches, acacia, broom and quince, besides honey, crystallized fruits and almonds. The wines are juicy, fat, rich and powerful, with a good balance between the full sweetness and the fresh acids.

Loupiac wines are good companions for poultry and white meat in creamy sauces, but also for not too sweet desserts, such as *millas Girondin* (egg custard with almonds). Drinking temperature: 8–9 °C (47–48 °F).

CADILLAC

The name of the familiar motorcar from Detroit is alleged to have come from the little village of Cadillac in the Gironde. Whether this deluxe American car was

Ste-Croix-du-Mont

given the name of the village as a mark of respect for the local Marquis de Cadillac or for the Cadillac wines is not quite clear.

The sweet Cadillac wines, which acquired their AOC recognition only in 1980, are of exceptional quality. The better Cadillac wines are full, fat, and well-balanced. They, too, tend to be plump rather than syrupy. The bouquet is luxurious, with aromas of crystallized citrus fruits, toast, almonds, peaches, honey and here and there a hint of beeswax. The taste is rich and full with a good balance between sour and sweet.

Enjoy these lovely wines with rich freshwater fish dishes (pike) or with not too sweet desserts. Drinking temperature: 8–9 °C (47–48 °F).

PREMIÈRES-CÔTES-DE-BORDEAUX

This wine region on the right bank of the Garonne is some 40 miles long, from the suburbs of Bordeaux to the border with Côtes-de-Bordeaux Saint-Macaire. The landscape is hilly and offers splendid views of the river and the Graves vineyards. The soil is very varied, with mainly limestone and gravel on the hills, and the sediments of the Garonne. Predominantly red wines are made there, and a few plump to syrupy white wines (in the south-east corner, near Cadillac, Loupiac and Sainte-Croix-du-Mont). However, many white wines vanish, more or less anonymously, in the great mass of sweet Bordeaux wines.

Loupiac: a great price/quality ratio

The rare sweet white Premières Côtes-de-Bordeaux are in general of excellent quality. They are fairly complex, fat, broad and soft, but also possess a certain finesse and elegance. The rich aromas of honey, toast, orange, crystallized fruits, gingerbread and overripe grapes (whether or not with a touch of *Botrytis*) will tempt many.

Drink these charmers with scrambled eggs, plump omelettes or fish. Drinking temperature: 8–10 °C (47–50 °F).

Cadillac

Red wines are in the majority. These Premières Côtes-de-Bordeaux Rouge are always an agreeable surprise and very pleasant to drink. They are deep in color, quite full and crisp, full-bodied with aromas of ripe red fruits, plums, toast, vanilla and spices with sometimes a hint of burnt coffee and leather. In the young wines the presence of tannins is clear, but after a few years ageing they become rather rounder and softer.

Drink these excellent red wines with red meat, grilled poultry, wildfowl or game. Drinking temperature: 16 °C (61 °F).

ENTRE-DEUX-MERS

The AOC Entre-Deux-Mers does not cover the whole Entre-Deux-Mers region. Although Entre-Deux-Mers was once known for its sweet white wines, today's AOC is exclusively reserved for dry ones. The wines are mainly made of the sauvignon grape and are crisp and fresh (especially in their youth) and very aromatic: citrus fruits, almonds and exotic fruits are discernible in them. The better wines, however, are made of a mixture of sémillon, sauvignon and muscadelle, and are a little fuller and broader. The aromas listed above are then supplemented by splendid floral perfumes and the scent of white fruits (peaches).

Drink the sauvignon types of wine young, as an aperitif or perhaps with *fruits de mer* or sea fish. The fuller wines of sauvignon, sémillon and muscadelle are excellent accompaniments to freshwater fish, poultry, white meat (veal!) or soft offal, such as sweetbreads. However, they also go well with egg and vegetable dishes. Drinking temperature: 10–12 °C (50–54 °F).

Premières-Côtes--de-Bordeaux

ENTRE-DEUX-MERS-HAUT-BENAUGE

The wines of this small AOC may only come from nine specific communes in the extreme south-east tip of Entre-Deux-Mers. No one understands why this should be so, or what this separate AOC has to offer that an 'ordinary' Entre-Deux-Mers does not have: Haut--Benauge wines are as like as two peas in a pod to their neighbors from the land between the rivers. Who can say? Even the winegrowers of these nine communes don't know why. In any case, this appellation exists, and so has to be mentioned. For the description see under 'Entre-Deux-Mers'.

GRAVES-DE-VAYRES

A little to the south of the Dordogne and the town of Libourne is the small wine region of Graves-de-Vayres (1,300 acres). Mainly red wines are made here, and a little dry white. Most of the Graves-de-Vayres seen in the shops will be white, which was the original strength of the region. Here, too, changes in drinking practices have meant increasing plantings of red grape stocks. Many of the red wines produced will go through life as ordinary Bordeaux or Bordeaux Supérieur; only the best will bear the AOC Graves de Vayres.

Entre-Deux-Mers

The dry white wines are fresh and fruity, with aromas of citrus fruits and sometimes a recognizable *terroir* aroma of flint.

Excellent as a refreshing aperitif, but also a good accompaniment for fish (stewed eels), *fruits de mer* and egg dishes. Drinking temperature: 10–12 °C (50–54 °F).

The red wines are sometimes rich in tannins and a little harsh when they are young, but always pleasantly fruity (blackberries, raspberries, blackcurrants, cherries, plums). The taste is soft, full, supple, round and fruity, with a spicy finish.

These red wines, too, go very well with egg dishes, particularly with omelettes filled with fried mushrooms. However, they are at their best with poultry, white meat, red meat or small game. Drinking temperature: 16 °C (61 °F).

SAINTE-FOY-BORDEAUX

This wine region lies to the south of Bergerac. The little town of Sainte-Foy seems to consist of two parts: on the right bank of the Dordogne and hence in Bergerac, is Port Sainte-Foy, and on the left bank and so in Bordeaux, is Sainte-Foy-la-Grande.

The soil of Sainte-Foy varies from deposits of red loam to white calcareous soils. The substratum is pebbly, sandy or calcareous clay. This explains the diversity in types and tastes of the Sainte-Foy wines.

The majority of the wines are red and are made from merlot, cabernet sauvignon and cabernet franc. Most of the wines are quite dark in color, very fruity, with aromas of red fruits and vanilla, which as they age develop into more complex bouquets such as leather, brushwood, coffee and spices.

These wines go very well with all kinds of meat, but are at their best with game birds. Drinking temperature: 16 °C (61 °F).

The dry white Sainte-Foy wines are fresh and quite full-bodied. They are made mainly from sauvignon, sometimes topped up with some sémillon and muscadelle and are quite aromatic: exotic fruits, flowers, white fruits, yellow fruits and vanilla (when raised on wood).

First class as an aperitif, excellent as accompaniments to *fruits de mer* and sea fish. Drinking temperature: 10–12 °C (50–54 °F).

The sweet white Sainte-Foy-Bordeaux are classic wines of good quality. They are only made in top years. They are light, fresh, fruity, with the typical sémillon aromas of honey, ripe (muscat) grapes, lime blossom, beeswax and apricots. When the overripe sémillon grapes have also been honored by a visit from *Botrytis*, the wines are full, rich and extra powerful.

Drink these luxurious wines as aperitifs or just for pleasure. You can also marry them with a terrine of poultry or a few toasts liberally spread with *foie gras*. Drinking temperature: 8–9 °C (47–48 °F).

Libournais, Merlot country

Round the town of Libourne, on the right bank of the river Dordogne, you will find the Libournais vineyards. Here you encounter famous names: Saint-Emilion, Pomerol, Canon Fronsac and Fronsac. Although these wine regions are not so far from Bordeaux, it is a quite different landscape. No large, tidy, bleak *domaines* as in the Médoc, but much smaller, friendlier estates and country houses. Where in Médoc the cabernet is lord and master, here the merlot grape rules. The Libournais wines do not, therefore, keep as long as their distant relatives from the Médoc, but they are much more approachable. Because their character is less 'hard', these wines will adapt more easily to your culinary wishes.

CÔTES-DE-CASTILLON

The little town of Castillon-la-Bataille occupies an extremely important place in the history of the whole Bordeaux region. In 1453, during the Hundred Years War, there was a decisive battle here between the English troops of John Talbot, earl of Shrewbury, and those of the king of France. Talbot was killed, and the English lost the battle and with it their rule over Aquitaine. Every year this battle is replayed in an imposing manner in Castillon, to the great enjoyment of countless grateful tourists, but above all of the local population themselves.

Since 1989 the Côtes-de-Castillon wines may mention the AOC on their labels. Before that they were part of the anonymous family of Bordeaux and Bordeaux Supérieurs. In organoleptic tests these Côtes-de-Castillon do not differ so much from the ordinary Bordeaux; the difference lies mainly in the lower yields, and hence in the higher level of complexity and concentration. The aromas are fairly representative of all the Bordeaux region: cherries, blackcurrants, plums, toast, vanilla, pepper, menthol, spices and, at a later age, game, cocoa, coffee, cinnamon, dried fruits and so on. Depending upon the style of the maker, these wines will be elegant and almost feminine or, conversely, quite masculine, powerful, fleshy and full. The wine deserves an extra recommendation for its usually very favorable ratio between quality, price and enjoyment.

These red Côtes-de-Castillon feel at home with all types of cuisine, but particularly with grilled meat or small game. Drinking temperature: 16–17 °C (61–63 °F).

BORDEAUX-CÔTES-DE-FRANC

Very acceptable white and red wines are produced on some 1,200 acres between Saint-Émilion and Bergerac. The 'côtes' here are fairly high hills of marl and lime-rich clay.

The dry white wines, made from sauvignon, sémillon and muscadelle are sophisticated, sensual and very aromatic: flowers, vanilla, dried fruits (almonds) and ripe white and yellow fruits (peach). This lushness of aromas and the fattiness of the sémillon are kept in good balance by the freshness of the sauvignon.

These Côtes-de-Franc not only do well as aperitifs, but also as an accompaniment to meat or poultry patés, terrines and salads. Drinking temperature: 10–12 °C (50–54 °F).

The red Côtes-de-Franc are deep in color and have rich aromas of red fruits (raspberries, cherries, blackcurrants), vanilla and rather more earthy smells, such as Russian fur, leather and wood. The taste is full, broad, fat and powerful. Because they are raised on wood, most of the wines are quite harsh in their early years, but this changes after two or three years bottle age.

Ideal accompaniments for red meat and small game. Surprisingly but certainly pleasant is the local custom of drinking these red wines with sweet and sour desserts containing red wine. Drinking temperature: 16 °C (61 °F).

SAINT-ÉMILION

The Saint-Émilion vineyards lie round the picturesque village of the same name. The Romans were already convinced of the quality of the local vineyards, as confirmed by the celebrated poet and consul Ausonius. The vineyards round Saint Émilion lie in a plain of limy soil and on hills of calcareous loam or clay. To the west of Saint-Émilion, however, the ground is gravelly. That is the area of the great wines. Most of the Saint-Émilion wines, however, come from the sandy deposits and fer-ruginous sandstone country which stretches to the Dor-dogne. The dominant grape variety here is merlot, sup-ported by cabernet franc (locally also called *bouchet*), cabernet sauvignon and malbec or cot.

An attractive, serious, and original factor is the quite recent classification which is not only strictly checked, but is also revised every ten years, which acts as an extra stimulant for quality. For it is not the types of soil or the landowners that are being checked and weighed up, but the wines, and that over a period of ten years. A system of promotion or relegation keeps everyone on their toes and the consumer profits accordingly.

We can be quite brief about the quality of the Saint-Émilion wines – most of them are exceptional. These dark red wines are generous, round and easily approachable. Their aromatic palette contains mostly ripe fruits (blackberries, cherries, strawberries), dried fruits (apricots), herbs and spices (bay, cinnamon), vegetable scents (ivy), leather and earthy smells (wood, brushwood, truffles). The better wines possess the necessary tannins and require several years maturing in bottle. The structure is broad and supple in spite of the presence of the tannins. A good Saint-Émilion gives the taster a warm, sensual and juicy impression that lingers quite a long time in the mouth and the memory.

When it is still young, a Saint-Émilion feels very happy next to a piece of grilled beef (entrecote à la Bordelaise, for instance), but also with lamprey, monkfish or other robust fish in a red wine sauce. Mature wines prefer softer and juicier kinds of meat, such as a joint of lamb, roast pink. But they will not object to a roast game bird either. In fact you can eat almost anything with a red Saint-Émilion, except that a pungent blue cheese will not suit the wines. Drinking temperature: 16 °C (61 °F).

SAINT-ÉMILION (PREMIER) GRAND CRU CLASSÉ

The classified wines of Saint-Émilion are perhaps a little better and come from better types of soil. Most of the *crus classés* are concentrated in the direct surroundings of the village of Saint-Émilion. The standards for quality, yield and minimum price are strictly controlled. In general this results in rather more assertiveness, backbone, tannins and therefore potential for ageing, and clearly more complexity.

Generic St-Émilion

These better wines are happy with any dish, but if you can, choose roast game birds to partner them. Drinking temperature: 16–17 °C (61–63 °F).

THE SATELLITES OF SAINT-ÉMILION

To the north of the Saint-Émilion wine region there are four communes that can add their name to the appellation Saint-Émilion. Or is it actually the other way round? Whatever the answer, the wines of these four communes are in general rather more rustic and less refined in structure and taste than their brothers from Saint-Émilion, but they are certainly worth trying, particularly for their more than favorable price/quality relationship.

SAINT-GEORGES-SAINT--ÉMILION
A robust wine which goes well with grilled or roast poultry or game birds.

MONTAGNE SAINT-ÉMILION
A full, rich and robust wine which is happiest in the company of casseroled poultry or game birds in a red wine sauce.

PUISSEGUIN SAINT--ÉMILION
These wines are perhaps a little more elegant than their neighbors. Appetizing with roast poultry or game birds, possibly

Two famous St-Émilion Grand Crus

There are often pleasant surprises among the less well-known *grands crus*.

stuffed with liver, grapes, truffles and Armagnac or Fine de Bordeaux…

1955 CLASSIFICATION, REVISED IN 1996: SAINT-ÉMILION GRANDS CRUS

PREMIERS GRANDS CRUS CLASSÉS

A
- Château Ausone
- Château Cheval Blanc

B
- Château Angelus
- Château Beau-Séjour (Bécot)
- Château Beauséjour (Duffau-Lagarosse)
- Château Belair
- Château Canon
- Château Clos Fourtet
- Château Figeac
- Château La Gaffelière
- Château Magdelaine
- Château Pavie
- Château Trottevieille

GRANDS CRUS CLASSÉS
- Château Balestard La Tonnelle
- Château Bellevue
- Château Bergat
- Château Berliquet
- Château Cadet-Bon
- Château Cadet-Piolat
- Château Canon-La Gaffelière
- Château Cap de Mourlin
- Château Chauvin
- Clos des Jacobins
- Clos de l'Oratoire
- Clos Saint-Martin
- Château Corbin
- Château Corbin-Michotte
- Château Couvent des Jacobins
- Château Curé Bon La Madeleine
- Château Dassault
- Château Faurie de Souchard
- Château Fonplégade
- Château Fonroque
- Château Franc-Mayne
- Château Grandes Murailles
- Château Grand Mayne
- Château Grand Pontet
- Château Guadet Saint-Julien
- Château Haut-Corbin
- Château Haut Sarpe
- Château La Clotte
- Château La Clusiâre
- Château La Couspaude
- Château La Dominique
- Château La Marzelle
- Château Laniote
- Château Larcis-Ducasse
- Château Larmande
- Château Laroque
- Château Laroze
- Château l'Arrosée
- Château La Serre
- Château La Tour du Pin-Figeac (Giraud-Belivier)
- Château La Tour du Pin-Figeac (Moueix)
- Château La Tour Figeac
- Château Le Prieuré
- Château Matras
- Château Moulin du Cadet
- Château Pavie-Decesse
- Château Pavie-Macquin
- Château Petit-Faurie--de-Soutard
- Château Ripeau
- Château Saint-Georges Côte Pavie
- Château Soutard
- Château Tertre Daugay
- Château Troplong-Mondot
- Château Villemaurine
- Château Yon-Figeac

LUSSAC SAINT-ÉMILION

This is the softest of the four, perhaps even the most feminine. But appearances can be misleading… Serve this wine with pink-roasted lamb and flageolets.

POMEROL

What a big name for such a small wine region of only 2,000 acres! Wine is grown here on a small plain with a special kind of soil, very rich in iron oxide. The contrast with the aristocratic estates of Médoc is striking. Here everything seems to have more 'normal' proportions, as if they know much better how to enjoy life, even in the smallest everyday details. No misplaced fuss, but a friendly welcome;

Yet here, too, very great wines are made, such as the world renowned Pétrus, Trotanoy, Vieux Château Certan and Le Bon Pasteur, to mention just a few. But it looks as if all the Pomerol wines, large or small, belong to the same close and loving family.

The soil is very varied, the main types being sandy soils near Libourne,

St-Georges-St-Émilion

gravelly sand and clay soils in the west, gravelly clay in the center and gravelly sand in the north. In spite of this diversity in types of soil, the Pomerols are all clearly scions of the same family.

Pomerols are full, powerful and supple. They are very fruity: blackberries, cherries, raspberries and plums, which in top years sometimes tend towards dried fruits, dominate. Other recognizable aromas of top Pomerols are violets, irises, vanilla, spices, toast, game, leather, tobacco, cocoa or coffee, licorice, sometimes also cinnamon (Pétrus!) and truffles. Pomerol wines are exceptionally sensual, fat and creamy, fleshy and round, with often a mineral undertone in the aftertaste. Never drink them too young, in any

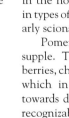

Montagne-St-Émilion

case never before they are four or five years old (ordinary Pomerol) and six or seven years (the better Pomerols).

A Pomerol is easy to fit into a menu, because these wines, like their makers, have not put on any airs, despite their quality or price. They take just as much pleasure in an entrecote grilled on vine twigs as in finer dishes from a three-star cuisine. If you like sensual combinations, why not try a roast snipe with a red wine

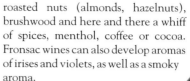

sauce with your best Pomerol. Other game bird dishes will also please any Pomerol. Drinking temperature: 16–17 °C (61–63 °F).

LALANDE-DE-POMEROL

To the north of Pomerol is the wine region of Lalande-de-Pomerol. This is much larger than the Pomerol region. The exclusively red wines of this AOC are, like their big brothers in Pomerol, rich in color and aromas, full, powerful, fleshy and fat. In the nose you recognize plums, licorice, ripe fruits, vanilla, spices (nutmeg, for example), cocoa and coffee, and sometimes a hint of menthol. The top *domaines* of Lalande-de-Pomerol can match those of Pomerol or Saint-Émilion without a problem.

A Libournais specialty is lampreys, here prepared in a tasty red wine sauce.

Generic Pomerol

Traditionally you would drink a Saint-Émilion or Lalande-de-Pomerol with this dish.

You can replace the lamprey, which is not always easy to get, with monkfish, Victoria bass, hake or red snapper. If you prefer not to eat fish with your red wine, then opt for poultry, preferably game (wood pigeon), with or without a red wine sauce. Drinking temperature: 16–17 °C (61–63 °F).

FRONSAC AND CANON-FRONSAC

This Libournais district is characterized by rather steep slopes, reaching the astronomical height of 200 ft, guaranteeing a magnificent view of their surroundings. The soil of this wine region of just over 2,500 acres consists of calcareous clay. The hills contain more limestone and only the wine from them may carry the AOC Canon-Fronsac.

Both wines are red, elegant and refined, and at the same time full and lively. There are clearly recognizable aromas in the nose of ripe red fruits (cherries), vanilla, toast, leather,

A famous Pomerol, now renamed Château Hosanna

roasted nuts (almonds, hazelnuts), brushwood and here and there a whiff of spices, menthol, coffee or cocoa. Fronsac wines can also develop aromas of irises and violets, as well as a smoky aroma.

A Canon-Fronsac demands one of the richer kinds of meat, such as goose or duck. A Fronsac, on the other hand, is fond of small game (hare) or wild rabbit. Drinking temperature: 16–17 °C (61–63 °F).

Blayais and Bourgeais

To the south of Charentes Maritimes (the home of the famous cognac distillates) there are two more Bordeaux regions: the rather larger Côtes-de-Blaye (including Premières Côtes-de-Blaye) and the small Côtes-de-Bourg, both on the right bank of the Gironde estuary.

The area produces red wines (in the south) and dry white wines (in the north).

Lalande-de--Pomerol

Pomerol

CÔTES-DE-BOURG

This 9,000 acres wine district is sometimes called 'the Switzerland of Bordeaux' because of its many sloping green hills. Red and white wines are produced here. The latter are very rare exceptions – not of the best quality.

These white wines from the sauvignon grape are just fresh and pleasant and are at their best as an aperitif. You can, however, also put them aside for an everyday fish dish. Drinking temperature: 9–10 °C (48–50 °F).

The red wines are a beautiful deep red color and quite aromatic. In their youth they are sometimes quite harsh, but a few years ageing in bottle softens the hard tannins. The taste is then round, full and often even seductive. The better wines have great class, sophistication and elegance.

Drink them with egg dishes (such as poached eggs in a red

Canon-Fronsac

wine sauce), roast veal or pork, beef or small game. Drinking temperature: 16 °C (61 °F).

CÔTES-DE-BLAYE

These white wines were once intended for the manufacture of cognac. These days much of the acidic, mediocre white wines of this district are still used as the raw material for Fine de Bordeaux, the locally distilled bran-

Côtes-de-Bourg

dy, which is actually very good!. The better wines bear the appellation Côtes-de-Blaye and are all quite dry. They are reasonably aromatic (citrus fruits, pineapples), fresh and broad.

Serve these wines as refreshing aperitifs or as companions to *fruits de mer* if you have really have nothing else to hand. Drinking temperature: 10–12 °C (50–54 °F).

PREMIÈRES-CÔTES-
-DE BLAYE

Most of these wines are red, but there is also a small minority of dry white wines. These are fresh, elegant and typically sauvignon with their aromas of citrus fruits (mainly grapefruit) and vegetal undertones (box and broom).

Excellent wines as an aperitif or with a plate of fresh oysters. Drinking temperature: 10–12 °C (50–54 °F).

The red Premières-Côtes-de--Blaye are mostly quite light in structure, but the better ones are more complex and fuller. In general red Côtes-de-Blaye are

Côtes-de-Bourg, often surprisingly good

flinty wines with some vegetal undertones. Choose a top *domaine* if you can – the relatively low price makes this possible. You will certainly get value for money. These better wines are often surprisingly powerful, with almost atypical aromas of game and leather, without this making them too 'rustic'.

Drink the simple wines young and lightly cooled (14 °C/57 °F) with egg dishes, fried mushrooms, patés or terrines. The better and fuller wines demand more attention: red meat, small game (rabbit or hare, perhaps) or even a rather more mature hard cheese. Drinking temperature: 16–17 °C (61–63 °F).

Since 1990 an additional quality indication has been created by the local winegrowers association on the model of the Médoc: the Crus Bourgeois des Premières Côtes-de-Blaye. These wines from twelve *domaines* must satisfy strict criteria relating to origin and qualities, and each year are strictly checked and tasted before they can carry the description on their label. An extra guarantee of quality and authenticity.

The Médoc

We leave the right bank and end our tour through the Bordeaux region in the Médoc, on the left bank of the Gironde. The Médoc is a kind of peninsula of vineyards, bordered by the waters of the Gironde in the north, the Atlantic in the north-west, the town of Bordeaux in the south-east, and the extensive wooded area of the Landes on the southwest.

HISTORY

The name of the district comes from Latin, but etymologists are not entirely sure of its exact origin. Might it have been *In Media Aqua* (in the middle of water) or *Pagus Medulorum* (the country of the Meduli)? The Romans from neighboring Burdigala (Bordeaux) came to hunt and fish in this swampy region, inhabited by the Meduli, a tribe of Gauls. In the seventeenth century the region was drained by Dutch water engineers and reclaimed. The swamps were soon replaced by wheat fields and wide meadows. In the late seventeenth century more and more magistrates and nouveaux riches bourgeoisie of Bordeaux settled in this area. It was soon realized that the gravely soil of the Médoc lent itself admirably to winegrowing. After many years of experimenting the definitive breakthrough of these new Bordeaux wines came in the early eighteenth century.

**Premières-Côtes-
-de-Blaye**

Vinification techniques were improved and the better wines carefully selected and stored in large cellars to mature further. It was also in the eighteenth century that the concepts of *grand cru* and *château* acquired their present-day interpretation.

In the late nineteenth century the *Phylloxera* louse destroyed all the Médoc vineyards. The grapes all had to be replanted using American root stocks. In addition, the economic crisis after the notorious 1929 stock market crash was fatal for many firms. After World War II, winegrowing in Bordeaux was again hit by a disaster. In the winter of 1956 most of the vines were frosted and had to be replaced. However, in the 1960s much money and fertilizer began to be invested to make the Médoc a great and healthy wine region again. The above ground stores and the vinification cellars in particular were taken in hand and completely renovated. A great deal of money was needed for this. Many *domaines* changed hands. Banks, insurance companies and many multinationals took over old family businesses. The image of the Médoc was enormously changed by this. Fortunately some of the small-scale producers were able to keep not only their family property, but also their own standards and values; they went on making their own wines with heads unbowed.

SOIL AND CLIMATE

Smaller independent estates often offer good value for money

The sand and gravel strip about 3 to 7 miles wide offers a great variety of *terroirs* and microclimates. What is here called *graves* is a complex mixture of clay, pebbles and sand. The pebbles are carried down by the rivers; some of them came originally from the Pyrenees (quartz and eroded material from the glaciers) carried down by the Garonne. Others came from the volcanic hills of the Massif Central (quartz, flint, sandstone, eroded volcanic material, sand and clay), and were carried first by the Cère and then by the Dordogne. Occasionally layers of calcareous clay interrupt the pebbles. Moreover, the Médoc plain is crisscrossed by numerous small valleys which not only make a pleasant change in the landscape, but also, and most importantly, provide excellent drainage. Altogether it forms excellent soil for winegrowing. The soil is so poor that the vines have to give of their best to obtain the necessary nourishment and water. This improves the quality of the grapes they produce. No wonder that the most famous wines of France are born on this soil.

The climate is quite mild, influenced by their favorable location on the 45th parallel, the presence of the Atlantic and the accumulated waters of the Gironde, the Garonne and the Dordogne, so that the vineyards not only get sufficient warmth and sunlight, but also sufficient moisture. The vines are reasonably protected by the west winds from spring night frosts and from mold infections. Although in principle this situation is very favorable for winegrowing, it does not guarantee a constant quantity and quality for the harvest. No great wines are made in years when the summer stays wet and cold. The fickleness of the climate makes the Médoc all the more fascinating for lovers of wine.

GRAPE VARIETIES

According to the well-informed specialists of the Conseil des Vins de Médoc only one variety of grape need actually be considered here, the original biturica (biture, vidure) from the *Vitis* family, which the Romans first brought here. All the modern grape varieties in the Médoc would have stemmed from this. Names such as cabernet, malbec and verdot first appeared in the eighteenth century, and merlot popped up more than a century later. What is surprising is the almost complete disappearance of an extremely interesting grape variety which in those days helped to lay the foundations of the success and quality of the Médoc wines – carmenère. Only after a prolonged search will you find this grape in the Médoc, and then only in minimal quantities. The wines made from them are of outstanding quality. However, the yield compared to other Médoc grapes is so low that growers have gone over in large numbers to cabernet franc, a variety which does not originate in Médoc, but on the western Loire, where it has acquired the nickname 'Breton'.

Cabernet savignon is a real Médoc discovery. No other grape in the world has been exported so much as cabernet sauvignon. You meet it in South America, California, Australia, the Balkans, Spain, Italy and Greece. People were so convinced of the quality of Bordeaux wines (possibly the price had something to do with it!) that all over the world they planted cabernet sauvignon and merlot in the hope of being able to produce sham-Bordeaux as quickly as possible, and to sell it at lower prices. They were not successful, because it is not only the grape that is important, but also the soil. And that is much more difficult to import or to copy.

In addition to cabernet sauvignon, which gives the wines backbone and fruity aromas, use is also made of merlot (which matures faster and is more approachable) to soften the cabernet sauvignon, cabernet franc (splendid aromas), petit verdot (color, power and body) and malbec (tannins, color, finesse and aromas).

MÉDOC AOC

Although the whole geographical Médoc district (including therefore Haut-Médoc and the six communal AOCs) has the right to carry the appellation Médoc, most Médoc AOC wines come from the north of the peninsula, between the villages of Saint-Vivien de Médoc and Saint-Germain d'Esteuil. The northern Médoc vineyards are generally rather newer than those of Haut-Médoc. Here and there, however, there are a few older wine *domaines*.

The *domaines* of the Médoc AOC are mostly small in area. Many of them have joined up in cooperatives in order to work more efficiently, and often just to be able to survive. The soil is typical of Médoc, with various kinds of gravel and sporadically some calcareous clay.

Because of the variety of *terroirs* and the large number of small estates, the Médoc AOCs are very diverse in style and taste. However, two main types can be distinguished:

- light, elegant, refined, subtle and enticingly aromatic wines which need to be drunk young. You can serve them safely with all patés, terrines, cold meats, and meat and poultry dishes. These light Médoc wines are also good companions to not too sharp, half-hard cheeses. Drinking temperature: 16 °C (61 °F).
- full, robust and tannin-rich wines which benefit from several years maturing in bottle. These are best served with roast or grilled meat, poultry or game, if possible garnished with fried mushrooms and a red wine sauce. Drinking temperature: 16–17 °C (61–63 °F).

HAUT-MÉDOC AOC

Southern Médoc or Haut-Médoc ('Haut' here refers to its location higher up the river and has nothing to do with contour heights) stretches some 40 miles from the village of Saint-Seurin-de-Cadourne to Blanquefort. The division of north and south Médoc dates officially from 1935, but has in fact been in general use since the early nineteenth century. In the south of Haut Médoc many winegrowers were faced with the expansion of the town of Bordeaux, and many vineyards (and some *domaines*) disappeared for ever. Every possible method is being used to try to bring this to a halt, but it is a hard fight.

Here, too, the great variety of *terroirs* lies behind the diversity in taste and type of the wines. However the resemblances between the wines of this great family are also plain: the Haut-Médoc produces wines of an

Médoc

intense color, fresh and elegant, rich but not too powerful, with superb aromas of ripe fruits (plums, raspberries, blackcurrants, cherries), vanilla, toast, cedar wood (cigar boxes) and sometimes some menthol, spices, tobacco, coffee or cocoa. These wines deserve to be kept for several years; the bouquet will then reveal itself better.

Haut-Médoc wines can accompany all kinds of red meat and small game, but they are also surprisingly good with pork or veal roasts and with poultry. Young Haut-Médoc served cool also tastes excellent with freshwater or sea fish in red wine sauce. Drinking temperature: 16–17 °C (61–63 °F).

CRUS OF THE MÉDOC

Five of the sixty-one *grands crus classés* of Médoc come under the appellation Haut-Médoc: Château La Lagune (*3e grand cru classé*), La Tour-Carnet (*4e grand cru classé*), Belgrave, Camensac and Cantemerle (*5e grand cru classé*). The other Médoc *crus* may in fact be produced in the geographic area of Haut-Médoc, but come officially under one of the four smaller communal AOCs of Saint-Estèphe, Pauillac, Saint-Julien and Margaux. Haut-Médoc also has two more small independent communal appellations which do not, however, produce any grand crus, but do produce excellent wines: Moulis and Listrac.

SAINT-ESTÈPHE

This is the most northern of the six communal appellations. The Saint-Estèphe vineyards lie around the commune of that name and cover some 3,000 acres. Because of their northerly location, the relative height of the hills, (a dizzying 120 ft!, the rather heavier gravely sand and clay soil and the typical limestone substratum these wines are different from the rest of Haut-Médoc. They are deeper in color, more robust in structure, the bouquet and taste are more clearly typical of the *terroir* and the tannins are very powerful. This makes Saint-Estèphe wines excellent for laying down. It also means that they retain their freshness and youthful fruit for surprisingly long. The characteristic aromas of Saint-Estèphe are red fruits, vanilla, wood, toast, smoke, spices, cocoa, brushwood and licorice.

Haut-Médoc Cru Bourgeois

Drink these robust wines with perhaps game (hare, wild boar), roast or stewed in red wine. Drinking temperature: 17–18 °C (63–64 °F).

PAUILLAC

The small town of Pauillac (the administrative center of Médoc) is a pleasant place to stop on the wine route past the great estates of Haut-Médoc. Once Pauillac was an important port, now it has become a picturesque fishing port and yachting harbor, with a good shopping center and plenty of restaurants on the quay beside the moorings. In the local eating places you can enjoy freshly caught shrimps and flat fish from the Gironde, together with numerous local specialties: *lamproie* (lamprey), *alose* (shad), or *lotte* (monkfish) *à la Bordelaise*, or if you prefer meat or poultry: chicken, guinea fowl, duck, veal, lamb or beef in red wine sauce with mushrooms. You can also have all kinds of game dishes. Obviously, you will drink a rosé (Château Clarke or Rosé Saint-Martin) or a red wine with it.

However, Pauillac is more than just an attractive tourist town. Some of the finest French wines are made in its immediate surroundings: Lafite-Rothschild, Mouton-Rothschild and Latour to mention only a few.

The Pauillac vineyards lie to the west of the town, parallel to the Gironde. The northern vineyards are on a rather higher and more hilly stretch than the southern ones. Both have a soil of lean, very gravely ground: in the south the stones are rather larger (pebbles) than in the north. The whole area has a well-drained substratum.

The wines of Pauillac have their own individual characteristics which they owe to their soil. They are very full in color (purple red/ garnet red), robust, powerful, with plenty of backbone and tannins, but at the same time juicy, very sophisticated and elegant. It is recommended that they should be kept at least five and preferably ten years before they are opened. Some characteristic aromas: blackcurrants, cherries, plums, strawberries, raspberries, violets, roses, irises, cedar wood (cigar boxes), vanilla, menthol, spices, cocoa, coffee, licorice, leather and toast.

These robust wines, with great finesse and elegance, seem to be afraid of nothing. They are just as happy with a simple, but oh so good leg of lamb from the oven (with mushrooms) as with a tournedos Rossini (with real goose liver and truffles). Considering the price of most of the wines, you may prefer rather more exclusive combinations, but even the most conventional *grands crus* have been, and sometimes need to be, drunk without

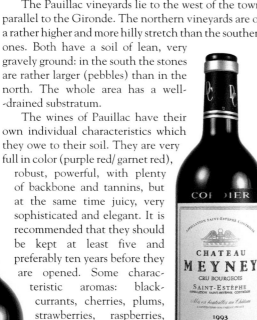

Meney, a well-known and always reliable St-Estèphe Cru Bourgeois

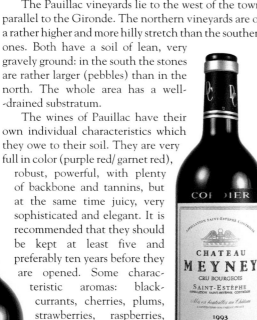

St-Estèphe Grand Cru Classé

RECOMMENDED WINES FROM SAINT-ESTÈPHE

- Château Calon-Ségur (3e grand cru classé)
- Château Chambert-Marbuzet cru bourgeois
- Château Cos-d'Estournel (2e grand cru classé)
- Château Haut-Marbuzet cru bourgeois
- Château Meyney cru bourgeois
- Château Montrose (2e grand cru classé)
- Château La Peyre cru artisan
- Château Phélan-Ségur cru bourgeois

- Tradition du Marquis (from the excellent Saint-Estèphe cooperative)

frills with the old-fashioned local fare Mother Nature has to offer. Drinking temperature: 17–18 °C (63–64 °F).

SAINT-JULIEN

A little to the south of Pauillac are the vineyards of Saint-Julien, concentrated round the two centers of Saint-Julien and Beychevelle. Here you will find few small *domaines*; almost all the chateaux are owned by big businesses. The Saint-Julien area is more or less in the center of Haut-Médoc and is subdivided into two smaller areas: that of Saint-Julien Beychevelle in the north and that of Beychevelle in the south. The soil of both is heavy and gravely with here and there large pebbles. The greatest differences between the *terroirs* of Saint-Julien are related to their distance from the river. The closer to the river, the milder the microclimate. The many small hilly ridges protect the Saint-Julien vineyards well from any possible flooding of the Gironde.

The wines of Saint-Julien are a little less robust and powerful than their northern neighbors in Saint-Estèphe. They are a beautiful color (ruby red), very aromatic, juicy, well-balanced, full, round, rich and elegant. In short, they are true charmers, who are very popular worldwide. Unfortunately this has great influence on their price, which seems to be constantly rising. A few characteristic aromas of these wines are cherries, blackcurrants, pepper, freshly cut paprika, spices, animal scents, leather, vanilla, toast, (hazel)nuts and menthol.

Serve these charming wines with rather softer and more delicate kinds of meat, such as calf's liver or veal kidneys, possibly in a red wine sauce. Drinking temperature: 17–18 °C (63–64 °F).

Pauillac Grand Cru Classé

RECOMMENDED PAUILLAC WINES

- Château Cordeillan-Bages cru Bourgois
- Château Haut-Batailley (5e grand cru classé)
- Château Lafite-Rothschild (1er grand cru classé)
- Château Latour (1er grand cru classé)
- Château Lynch-Bages (5e grand cru classé)
- Château Mouton-Rothschild (1er grand cru classé)
- Château Pichon-Longueville-Baron (2e grand cru classé)
- Château Pichon-Longueville-Comtesse de Lalande (2e grand cru classé)

- Les Forts de Latour (Château Latour's second wine)

MARGAUX

Of course, everyone knows Château Margaux, the flagship of this appellation. The Margaux AOC covers the communes of Margaux, Arsac, Cantenac, Labarde and Soussans.

The very poor soil of the Margaux area is gravely with rather larger pebbles. The microclimate makes this region different from the others. First of all, Margaux lies more to the south than the other *grand cru* areas, which means it is warmer and the grapes ripen quicker. Equally important, however, is the role of the islands and sand banks in the Gironde in front of Margaux. These protect this small region against the cold winds from the north. Ideal conditions therefore for making great wines.

Obviously the wines of Margaux are also excellent wines for laying down, but their charm lies more in their subtlety and elegance than in the power of their tannins. Margaux are perhaps the most feminine wines of the Médoc: soft, delicate, subtle, sensual and seductive. A few characteristic aromas of these wines are ripe red fruits: cherries, plums, spices, resin, vanilla, toast, gingerbread, coffee and newly baked bread rolls. Drink these juicy wines with classic meat dishes, such as tournedos, châteaubriand or sirloin, or with tender game birds or duck. Drinking temperature: 17–18 °C (63–64 °F).

Mouton-Rothschild, probably the world's most famous top wine

RECOMMENDED SAINT-JULIEN WINES

- Château Beychevelle (4e grand cru classé)
- Château Branaire-Duluc-Ducru (4e grand cru classé)
- Château Ducru-Beaucaillou (2e grand cru classé)
- Château Gruaud-Larose (2e grand cru classé)
- Château Lagrange (3e grand cru classé)
- Château Léoville Poyférré (2e grand cru classé)
- Château Léoville Barton (2e grand cru classé)

LISTRAC-MÉDOC

This small appellation has no *grand cru classé*, but is distinguished by the quality of its wines. With its 130 ft high hills Listrac is the Médoc's 'roof'. The soil here is a combination of gravel and calcareous earth, providing good natural drainage. Through the presence of numerous woods and under the influence of the cold north winds, the grapes ripen rather more slowly then in the earlier named communal AOCs. The wines are full, round and fleshy, velvety soft and broad. Their tannins make them age well.

Serve a Listrac-Médoc with grilled poultry or game birds (snipe). Drinking temperature: 17–18 °C (63–64 °F).

MOULIS

About midway between Margaux and Saint-Julien, in the interior of Haut Médoc, the Moulis vineyards lie on a mixed terrain of gravel and limy soils.

Anyone who has tasted a top Moulis will immediately be inclined to plead for a revision of the 1855 *grand cru* classification. The color of the wine is deep ruby red. The wines have an enormous range of aromas and their taste is full, complex and powerful. Moulis have plenty of tannins to enable them to age well. An exceptional quality, price and enjoyment ratio.

Moulis can be warmly recommended to accompany lamb, fried mushrooms or robust dishes of beef, poultry or game birds. Drinking temperature: 17–18 °C (63–64 °F).

NB While this encyclopedia is being written, attempts are being made by the winegrowers organizations in Moulis and Listrac to have the two appellations merged in a single AOC Moulis-Listrac.

Gruaud-Larose, very reliable, even in off years

RECOMMENDED MARGAUX WINES

- Château La Berlande
- Château Brane-Cantenac (2e grand cru classé)
- Château Cantenac-Brown (3e grand cru classé)
- Château Ferrière (3e grand cru classé)
- Château Malescot-Saint-Exupéry (3e grand cru classé)
- Château Margaux (1e grand cru classé)
- Château Marquis du Terme (4e grand cru classé)
- Château Palmer (3e grand cru classé)
- Château Rauzan-Ségla (2e grand cru classé)
- Château Vincent cru bourgeois

- Pavillon Rouge (second wine of Chateaux Margaux)

1855 CLASSIFICATION (REVISED IN 1973*): GRANDS CRUS DU MÉDOC

PREMIERS CRUS
- Château Lafite-Rothschild (Pauillac)
- Château Latour (Pauillac)
- Château Margaux (Margaux)
- Château Mouton-Rothschild (Pauillac)*
- Château Haut-Brion (Graves)

SECONDS CRUS
- Château Brane-Cantenac (Margaux)
- Château Cos-D'Estournel (Saint-Estèphe)
- Château Ducru-Beaucaillou (Saint-Julien)
- Château Dufort-Vivens (Margaux)
- Château Gruaud-Larose (Saint-Julien)
- Château Lascombes (Margaux)
- Château Léoville-Las-Cases (Saint-Julien)
- Château Léoville-Poyferré (Saint-Julien)
- Château Montrose (Saint-Estèphe)
- Château Pichon-Longueville-Baron (Pauillac)
- Château Pichon-Longueville-Comtesse-de-Lalande (Pauillac)
- Château Rauzan-Ségla (Margaux)
- Château Rauzan-Gassies (Margaux)

TROISIÈME CRUS
- Château Boyd-Cantenac (Margaux)
- Château Cantenac-Brown (Margaux)
- Château Calon-Ségur (Saint-Estèphe)
- Château Desmirail (Margaux)
- Château Ferrière (Margaux)
- Château Giscours (Margaux)
- Château d'Issan (Margaux)
- Château Kirwan (Margaux)
- Château Lagrange (Saint-Julien)
- Château La Lagune (Haut-Médoc)
- Château Langoa (Saint-Julien)
- Château Malescot-Saint-Exupéry (Margaux)
- Château Marquis d'Alesmes-Becker (Margaux)
- Château Palmer (Margaux)

QUATRIÈMES CRUS
- Château Beychevelle (Saint-Julien)
- Château Branaire-Ducru (Saint-Julien)
- Château Duhart-Milon-Rothschild (Pauillac)
- Château Lafon-Rochet (Saint-Estèphe)
- Château Marquis-de-Terme (Margaux)
- Château Pouget (Margaux)
- Château Prieuré-Lichine (Margaux)
- Château Saint-Pierre (Saint-Julien)
- Château Talbot (Saint-Julien)
- Château La Tour-Carnet (Haut-Médoc)

CINQUIÈMES CRUS
- Château d'Armailhac (Pauillac)
- Château Batailley (Pauillac)
- Château Belgrave (Haut-Médoc)
- Château Camensac (Haut-Médoc)
- Château Cantemerle (Haut-Médoc)
- Château Clerc-Milon (Pauillac)
- Château Cos-Labory (Saint-Estèphe)
- Château Croizet-Bages (Pauillac)
- Château Dauzac (Margaux)
- Château Grand-Puy-Ducasse (Pauillac)
- Château Grand-Puy-Lacoste (Pauillac)
- Château Haut-Bages-Libéral (Pauillac)
- Château Haut-Batailley (Pauillac)
- Château Lynch-Bages (Pauillac)
- Château Lynch-Moussas (Pauillac)
- Château Pédesclaux (Pauillac)
- Château Pontet-Canet (Pauillac)
- Château du Tertre (Margaux)

NB The names given are the current (1998) names. Some of these wines have changed their name in the course of time.

NorthWest France

The Loire Valley

The longest river in France, the Loire (630 miles long) rises in the Ardèche *département*. The turbulent mountain stream flows first in a northerly direction as far as Orleans, from where, with a wide curve to the left, as a majestic river it makes its way peacefully to the sea.

The valley of the Loire displays a very changing picture: vineyards, forests and all forms of agriculture are spread over the flat banks and gently sloping hills. This area, thanks to its agrarian wealth and colorful beds of flowers, has earned the name *Le Jardin de la France* (the garden of France).

Listrac, good value for money

A few recommendations:

- Château Clarke Cru Bourgeois (here they also make an excellent rosé!)
- Château Fourcas-Dumont
- Château Fourcas-Dupré Cru Bourgeois
- Château Fourcas-Hosten Cru Bourgeois
- Château Fourcas-Loubaney Cru Bourgeois
- Château L'Ermitage Cru Bourgeois

History

For centuries the kings of France chose the peace and richness of the Loire valley and held their courts there. The Loire was then the lifeblood of France. Kings and nobles had numerous chateaux built along it, and immense gardens laid out. In 1492 the then French king

Some top Moulis wines

- Château Chasse-Spleen cru bourgeois exceptionnel
- Château Poujeaux cru bourgeois exceptionnel (both of these are genuinely of a *grand cru classé* level)
- Château Brillette cru bourgeois
- Château Maucaillou cru bourgeois

Charles VIII expressed the wish to make his birthplace, the forbidding fortress of Amboise, into an idyllic residence. For this he invited twenty-two famous Italian craftsmen. He had no idea how great the influence of these Italians would be on France. They were to produce a true renaissance in the world of architecture. Today the magnificent designs by Leonardo da Vinci and his colleagues are admired everywhere. Nowhere in Europe will you find such a concentration of architectural masterpieces as along the Loire. The abundance and extravagance of all these châteaux make a journey to the Loire something special, something grand – a journey through the heart of France.

Moulis, surprisingly good and not really expensive

Winegrowing

The Loire vineyards are spread along the whole valley in varying concentrations. Some of them are as far as 50 miles from the river. In total more than a hundred different wines are made in the Loire valley.

Pays Nantais

The area around the town of Nantes is known mainly for its Muscadets, which can be of outstanding quality. Depending upon their geographical location, these wines are divided into four AOCs: Muscadet, Muscadet Coteaux de la Loire, Muscadet Côtes de Grand-Lieu and Muscadet de Sèvre et Maine.

The soil of the Muscadet region consists mainly of schist (blue or gray), gneiss, and ancient alluvial

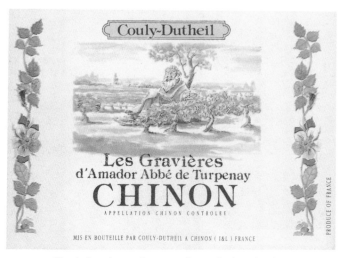

The Loire vineyards are a pleasant place to stay

deposits, some of volcanic origin. The substratum of igneous rock and granite is crisscrossed by countless small valleys which ensure good drainage. That is in fact very necessary, given the proximity of the Atlantic. The climate here is temperate oceanic, with mild winters and hot, often wet, summers.

MUSCADET

These wines may also be made outside the three regions defined below.

MUSCADET-DES-COTEAUX-DE-LA-LOIRE

– are produced round the small town of Ancenis, on the banks of the Loire.

MUSCADET-CÔTES-DE-GRAND-LIEU

– quality wines which come from the hills round the lake of Grand Lieu south of the town of Nantes. Only since 1994 have these Muscadets acquired the right to be sold under their own appellation.

Tremendous wines and a warm welcome
(François Chidaine, Montlouis)

MUSCADET-DE-SÈVRE-ET-MAINE

Accounts for 80–85 % of production. This is where the best Muscadets come from. The vineyards cover twenty-three communes on the banks of the two small rivers, the Sèvre Nantaise and the Petite Maine. The country is rather more hilly than the rest of the area. This AOC was granted in 1936.

All Muscadets are made from the unique Muscadet or Melon de Bourgogne grape, a variety completely forgotten in its native Burgundy, but worshipped here. The better Muscadets are vinified and bottled on their lees, sur lie. This method guarantees great freshness and enhances the fine taste and bouquet of the wines. Unfortunately it often also raises the price… Muscadets are dry and have a lovely fresh nose.

Their freshness and delicate taste makes Muscadets ideal aperitifs and companions for fish, shellfish and crustaceans. They also soon make friends with a few slices of French sausage. Drinking temperature 8–10 °C (47–50 °F).

GROS-PLANT AOVDQS

Gros plant is the local name for the folle blanche, a grape variety from Charentes. Wines from the of folle blanche are thin and fairly acidic and are used in Charentes as the raw material for the distillation of Cognac. In the neighborhood of Nantes this grape produces quite lively wines with a high acid content and a typical, slightly rural, character.

A Gros-Plant-du-Pays Nantais is always very dry and harsh, and therefore not popular with everyone. Yet a good Gros Plant is a perfect accompaniment for fresh oysters. The match is a little more pronounced, but much more genuine than that with a glass of Chablis! Other shellfish, too, such as mussels, cockles or other clams, will benefit from this marriage of sea and land. If you dislike *fruits de mer*, you can resort to cold meats, terrines and patés. Drinking temperature: 8–9 °C (47–48 °F).

FIEFS VENDÉENS AOVDQS

This small region of about 950 acres was only recognized as AOVDQS in 1984. Within a broad triangle between Les Sables-d'Olonne, La Roche--sur-Yon and Fontenay-le--Comte exceptionally fruity, fresh and attractive red and rosé wines are produced from gamay, cabernet franc and pinot noir. The white Fiefs Vendéens are made of chenin

Superior Muscadet-de-Sèvre-et-Maine from an independent estate

Vieilles vignes are usually more concentrated

and a few supplementary grape varieties, such as grolleau gris, colombard, melon de Bourgogne and sauvignon. These wines are light, fruity and very refreshing. The best wines come from the communes of Brem, Mareuil, Pissotte and Vix.

Drink the white wines with *fruits de mer* or fish, the rosé with chicken or poultry, and the red wines with red meat or game. Drinking temperature: white 8–10 °C (47–50 °F); rosé 9–10 °C (48–50°F) and red 14–16 °C (57–61 °F).

COTEAUX-D'ANCENIS AOVDQS

Like a kind of transitional region, the 750 acres of the Coteaux d'Ancenis vineyards lie between those of Nantes and Anjou--Saumur. Four types of wine are made round the small town of Ancenis: two reds from gamay and cabernet franc, and two whites, from chenin and malvoisie (the local name for pinot gris). Gamay accounts for 80 % of the production.

Drink the fresh, fruity, dry rosé or red wines from gamay grapes (and from cabernet) with light starters, meat salads and light meat dishes. Drinking temperature: 12–16 °C (54–61 °F).

The white wines are light and refreshing. Drink them as an aperitif or with fish, *fruits de mer* or poultry. Drinking temperature: 8–10 °C (47–50 °F).

Anjou-Saumur

Great wines have been made here for more than fifteen centuries. With its twenty-seven appellations the Anjou-Saumur area offers something for everyone. This is truly a region for a voyage of discovery, where both novices and great connoisseurs will find enjoyment. Unfortunately the name of this beautiful region is still linked to the enormous lakes of sweet and almost undrinkable rosé d'Anjou that used to be exported to other European countries. Because too many concessions were made on price, the quality of these wines was not reliable: they caused countless hangovers, particularly in academic circles. Even wines that would normally have been sent to the vinegar factories, were acceptable to some dealers, on condition that they were sweetened. Ignorance and greed led to lorry-loads of undrinkable plonk being dumped in some supermarkets. A disgrace, since a good rosé, even from Anjou, is excellent. However, their high price does not match the image that a Loire rosé has in some countries, though fortunately this is beginning to change.

The soil of Anjou is very complex. However, a broad distinction can be made between two principal types of soil: 'Blue Anjou' with a soil of blue schist and fragmented volcanic rock from the Massif Central, and 'white Anjou' (Saumur, Vouvray, Montlouis) with a soil of limestone and tufa.

The most commonly used grapes are the chenin blanc (pineau de la Loire) for the white wines, and both cabernets for the red wines. Here and there it is also possible to see plantings of chardonnay and sauvignon for the white wines and gamay for the red.

ANJOU BLANC

In general dry, sometimes semi-sweet. This wine is made of chenin grapes, sometimes with the addition of some chardonnay or sauvignon. Some characteristic aromas are apple, pear, grape fruit, pineapple and exotic fruits.

An Anjou Blanc is a good accompaniment for freshwater fish and *fruits de mer*. A surprisingly good and daring combination is with grilled lamb kebabs. Drinking temperature: 9–10 °C (48–50 °F).

ANJOU-GAMAY

A fairly simple red wine, fresh and light. If you drink an Anjou-Gamay young, it has a lovely purple color and a soft nose and taste (with a hint of redcurrants and other red fruits).

Served cool, this wine will go with almost anything, from poultry to fish and even sweet-and-sour Chinese dishes (but don't put your expectations too high!). Drinking temperature: 12–14 °C (54–57 °F).

ANJOU ROUGE AND ANJOU-VILLAGES

These ruby-red wines are made from both cabernet varieties. They have a luxurious bouquet of, for example, raspberries and blackcurrants. You can sometimes also detect a hint of freshly cut paprika and a smoky aroma. In general these are quite light wines which should be drunk young.

Cooled, they are good accompaniments to grilled meat, cold meats and light cheeses. Anjou-Villages can also age a little and should then be drunk slightly less cool. Drinking temperature: 14–15 °C (57–59 °F).

ROSÉ-D'ANJOU AND CABERNET-D'ANJOU

Both rosé wines are semi-sweet. A Rosé d'Anjou, made of grolleau, cabernet franc and gamay, is usually light and playful. They are best drunk young, when still full of fruit. The Cabernet d'Anjou, on the other hand, has rather more backbone and in top years shows surprisingly good aging potential. It is generally rather more elegant and fuller than the ordinary Rosé d'Anjou.

Serve these wines cooled with starters, savory pies and oriental dishes (Thai cuisine). Also good with fresh goat's cheese and strawberries and/or raspberries, sprinkled with a little ground pepper.

But remember, a good Rosé d'Anjou or Cabernet d'Anjou is never cheap. Ignore the cheap colored wine lemonades with a flavor of dirty old floor cloths and choose the real wines (such as Domaine de Bablut). Drinking temperature: 10–12 °C (50–54 °F).

ROSÉ-DE-LOIRE

This rosé is also made from cabernet, gamay and grolleau, but it is a dry rosé, fresh, generous and very pleasant.

This wine is best drunk young and cooled, with starters, cold meats, poultry and crustaceans. It also acts as a first-class fire extinguisher with hot oriental food, and is an outstanding wine for picnics and luncheons. Drinking temperature: 10–12 °C (50–54 °F).

Anjou Blanc

COTEAUX-DE-L'AUBANCE

White, semi-sweet or sweet wines. These are real wines for laying down, made of the chenin grape. The wines are extremely aromatic, with hints of minerals.

These very harmonious wines do very well as aperitifs, with noble meat dishes and terrines of poultry, *foie gras*, veal or the better kinds of fish. Drinking temperature: 9–10 °C (48–50 °F).

Rosé d'Anjou

ANJOU-COTEAUX-DE-LA-LOIRE

Wines from the pinot de la Loire, golden-colored, with superb aromas of overripe fruit and a lively character. They are characterized by great sophistication, freshness and elegance.

Serve an Anjou Coteaux de la Loire with starters, grilled or oven-cooked freshwater fish, or just as an aperitif. Drinking temperature: 9–10 °C (48–50 °F).

Anjou Rouge Villages

SAVENNIÈRES

These predominantly dry, robust white wines are among the best white wines of France. This is chenin at its best, due to the typical *terroir* of steep, rocky hills, here and there studded with schist and sand. The location, facing south/south-east, is also ideal.

Two especially good wine regions may carry their own names on their labels: the *crus* Savennières Coulée de Serrant and Savennières Roche aux Moines. The first is an exceptional wine region owned by only one wine producer, Nicolas Joly, the guru of French dynamic-biological viniculture.

Savennières wines are fantastic companions to crustaceans and shellfish, freshwater fish (salmon, pike and pickerel), sushi and sashimi. Drinking temperature: 10–12 °C (50–54 °F).

A small quantity of special Savennières are semi-sweet to fully sweet wines. Serve these as aperitifs or to accompany your better fish and poultry dishes, if possible with a soft, creamy and fruity sauce.

COTEAUX-DU-LAYON

This fully sweet white wine is a true wine for laying down, very fruity and delicate. With a few years maturity it becomes a very complex, subtle, aromatic wine.

A Coteaux du Layon is a perfect companion for *foie gras*, fish or poultry in sauce, blue cheeses, not too sweet desserts and fresh (exotic) fruit salads. Drinking temperature: 8–10 °C (47–50 °F).

CHAUME

Since 2001 the wines formerly produced under the name Coteaux de Layon Chaume have been sold as AOC Chaume. In exchange for this privilege none of the Loire wines may use imaginative descriptions such as *grand cru* on their labels.

BONNEZEAUX

This sweet or even syrupy white wine is a really big classic one. The chenin grape is harvested overripe and so gives the wine an extremely full taste and aroma of redcurrants, apricots, mango, lemon, pineapple and grape fruit, as well as hawthorn and acacia. A real experience.

You can serve this liquid gold with *foie gras*, fish in sauce, blue cheeses, desserts based on pears or almonds, or fresh fruit salads. Drinking temperature: 9–11 °C (48–52 °F).

Coteaux de l'Aubance

QUARTS-DE-CHAUME

A superior Coteaux-du-Layon, made of overripe grapes. This golden-colored wine has an overwhelming bouquet of honey, spices and ripe fruit. Ideal with *foie gras* and blue cheese, but also with fish or white meat in a creamy sauce, with good company or a romantic evening… Drinking temperature: 8–10 °C (47–50 °F).

CRÉMANT DE LOIRE

White or rosé, the Crémants de Loire are good, sparkling wines, fresh and very aromatic.

Ideal as an aperitif or with a not too sweet dessert. Drinking temperature: 8–10 °C (47–50 °F).

Medium sweet to fully sweet Savennières

Savennières

SAUMUR BRUT

After Champagne, the Saumur region is the second sparkling wine producer in France. The white or rosé Saumur Brut are very fine, elegant sparkling wines made by the traditional method. The wines are *brut* or *demi-sec*.

These wines, too, are ideal as aperitifs or as a festive ending to a meal. Drinking temperature: 8–10 °C (47–50 °F).

Coteaux-du-Layon

SAUMUR BLANC

Dry white wine, made of chenin blanc, sometimes in combination with chardonnay and sauvignon. Served cold, these subtle and fruity wines go very well with crustaceans and freshwater fish. Drinking temperature: 8–10 °C (47–50 °F).

If you don't want to spent time searching and only want to taste one white Saumur – and then the best – you should go to Souzay-Champigny. That is where the very traditional Château de Villeneuve Saumur Blanc Sec is made. It is difficult to find such power and grandeur in a white wine anywhere else on the Loire (or for that matter, in France).

Coteaux du Layon Villages Beaulieu

SAUMUR ROUGE

These very aromatic, generous red wines are made of cabernet franc and/or cabernet sauvignon. A young Saumur Rouge is still very rich in tannins, so it needs to be drunk cool with, for instance, red meat dishes and various cheeses. A Saumur Rouge can also without any problem accompany freshwater fish stewed in red wine. Drinking temperature: 12–14 °C (54–57 °F).

Bonnezeaux from the famous Château de Fesles

Nicolas Joly's very refined organic wines

After a few years maturing, red Saumurs are rather fuller in taste and fleshier and can be served rather less cool. Serve them with red meat, chicken, turkey, roast game birds or small game. Drinking temperature: 15 °C (59 °F).

CABERNET-DE-SAUMUR

A tiny appellation for dry rosé wines made from cabernet franc on calcareous soil. Splendid salmon-colored rosé wines with plenty of freshness and fruit (raspberry, redcurrant).

Drink these wines with meat or poultry terrines, or with poultry casseroles. Drinking temperature: 10–12 °C (50–54 °F).

COTEAUX-DE-SAUMUR

Superb full, sweet wines from chenin blanc from a tufa soil. These are wines with a rich, full taste, an excess of floral and fruity (pear, citrus fruits) aromas with a hint of toast and rich warm bread rolls.

A Coteaux-de-Saumur is very good drunk by itself, just for enjoyment. At meals, however, they are a good 'sparring partner' for fish and poultry in rich sauces. Drinking temperature: 8–10 °C (47–50 °F).

SAUMUR-CHAMPIGNY

It is above all the chalky substratum that distinguishes these wines. Here both Cabernet varieties develop rich

aromas of red fruits and spices. The wines are at their best after several years maturing.

A Saumur-Champigny goes very well with game birds, duck, small game, pork, grilled meat and cheese. Drinking temperature: young 12 °C (54 °F); a little older 15 °C (59 °F).

A classic example of a traditional, old-fashioned, delicious and powerful Saumur-Champigny can be found in the Chevalier family's Château de Villeneuve (Souzay-Champigny).

A rather less classic, but excellent and very seductive Saumur-Champigny is the Vatan family's grandiose Château de Hureau (Dampierre-sur-Loire).

Touraine

There are nine appellations round the picturesque town of Tours. The wines are made of the same grapes as those of Anjou-Saumur. The climate is quite mild and tem-

Cabernet-de-Saumur

perate. The soil consists mainly of tufa, but in some valleys you will also come across calcareous clay and sand, with traces of flint.

TOURAINE

Dry, white Touraine is in our opinion the most interesting. They are fresh and fruity, with plenty of bouquet and much character. Unlike most white wines in the region, Touraines are made of the sauvignon grape. Excellent as an aperitif, with (fried) freshwater fish or with fresh goat's cheese. Drinking temperature: 9–10 °C (48–50 °F).

The red wines from Gamay (Pineau d'Aunis) are light, supple and fresh. These wines can accompany any meal you like, but have perhaps a slight preference for poultry or cold meats. Like their opposite numbers in the Beaujolais, the Gamay Touraine wines are not afraid

A high-quality Saumur Blanc

Saumur-Champigny from a top estate

Finally, for the sake of completeness, mention must also be made here of the sparkling Touraine, which can be vinified to be fully sparkling or slightly so: *pétillant* or *mousseux*. They are made by the traditional method in white and rosé, and are elegant, fresh, floral and fruity. Excellent as an aperitif. Drinking temperature: 8–10 °C (47–50 °F).

TOURAINE-AMBOISE

These white, red and rosé wines are of higher quality. The better wines can age well.

Drink a white Touraine-Amboise preferably with stews and casseroles of fish, eel or poultry. Drinking temperature: 8–10 °C (47–50 °F).

A rosé Touraine-Amboise tastes best with rather more robust, richer dishes from the local cuisine. Drinking temperature: 10–12 °C (50–54 °F).

A red Touraine-Amboise is usually a keen companion of grilled or roast pork, particularly when accompanied by some prunes or tender spring vegetables. Drinking temperature: 12–14 °C (54–57 °F).

TOURAINE-AZAY-LE-RIDEAU

Excellent white wine, with fresh acidity, an ideal companion for fish or for vegetable dishes containing potatoes, leeks, onions and possibly white beans. Drinking temperature: 8–10 °C (47–50 °F).

There is also a fresh rosé for drinking with lunch, cold meats, patés and terrines, but also with offal such as sweetbreads, kidneys or chicken livers. Drinking temperature: 10–12 °C (50–54 °F).

Touraine Blanc from the Sauvignon grape

of the odd pickled gherkin. Drinking temperature: 12–14 °C (54–57 °F).

There is also a dry, fresh rosé which does very well with cold meats and grilled fish, but also with omelets and other egg dishes. Drinking temperature: 10–12 °C (50–54 °F).

Relaxed wine tasting in the Château de Villeneuve wine cellars

TOURAINE-MESLAND

These are white, rosé and red wines, all fresh and fruity, which should be drunk young.

Touraine-Mesland Rouge goes successfully with all meat dishes, particularly if some of the wine is included in the sauce. Drinking temperature: 12–14 °C (54–57 °F).

Touraine-Mesland Blanc combines well with freshwater fish, fish or chicken casseroles, or stewed eel in chervil sauce. Drinking temperature: 8–10 °C (47–50 °F).

Touraine-Mesland Rosé is not so choosy. Drink it with cold meats, sausages (hot or cold) or liver dishes. Drinking temperature: 10–12 °C (50–54 °F).

TOURAINE-NOBLE-JOUÉ

Since the spring of 2001 a few villages in Touraine (Chambray-les-Tours, Esvres, Joué-les-Tours, Larçay and St Avertin) have been able to market their wine as AOC Touraine Noble Joué, sometimes with the addition 'Val de Loire'. This is only for rosé and *vin gris* made from pinot meunier, pinot gris and pinot noir.

BOURGUEIL

There are two types of red Bourgueil. First the wines from the lighter soils. These are light in structure and are better drunk still young, while still fruity. The wines from the rather heavier soils have more aging potential. They usually also have more body and roundness. A few characteristic aromas are fresh-cut green paprika, wild strawberries, raspberries and redcurrants.

Drink the lighter Bourgueil reds with freshwater fish, hare or poultry in red wine sauce, casseroled poultry or rabbit. Try them some time combined with fresh goat's cheese or freshly picked strawberries. Drinking temperature: 12–14 °C (54–57 °F).

You can serve the heavier red Bourgueil with duck, game birds, hare, or even venison. A mature Bourgueil from a top year could even face a wild boar steak. Drinking temperature: 14–16 °C (57–61 °F).

There is also a light, fresh and fruity Bourgueil Rosé. Drink it with cold meats, patés, terrines, roast chicken or veal or – why not – with fresh goat's cheese and strawberries. Drinking temperature: 10–12 °C (50–54 °F).

SAINT-NICOLAS-DE-BOURGUEIL

These light red wines are very similar to their elder brother from Bourgueil. Serve them with casseroles of rabbit, veal or poultry. Don't forget the mushrooms and bacon! Drinking temperature: 12–14 °C (54–57 °F).

CHINON

Cabernet franc here produces full wines with aromas of red fruits (redcurrants, wild strawberries and raspberries), freshly cut green paprika and violets. Red Chinon wines can be drunk very young (less than a year old) or not until they are considerably older (after three to five years). In the intervening period of two to three years the wines are often fully closed with rather less taste.

A young red Chinon goes very well with eggs and meat or chicken dishes, but is also an excellent accompaniment to desserts containing strawberries or peaches and red Loire wine. With the local goat's cheese (especially those rolled in ash) this red Chinon does very well, too. Drinking temperature: 12–14 °C (54–57 °F).

Rosé Chinon is very fresh and fruity and combines well with cold meats, patés, terrines and roast pork or veal, but also with (fried) fish and tender vegetables (for instance, asparagus) with a sharp, seasoned sauce. Also good with fresh goat's cheese and strawberries or pea-

Bourgueil Rouge

ches in red wine. Drinking temperature: 10–12 °C (50–54 °F).

White Chinon is quite rare. It is a fresh and pleasant wine which goes well with fresh goat's cheese, but also with freshwater fish. Drinking temperature: 10–12 °C (50–54 °F).

MONTLOUIS

This wine is usually made semi-sweet. Sometimes, in top years, a fully sweet Montlouis is made as well. There are also dry Montlouis. The better wines can age very well. The still Montlouis are elegant, sophisticated and fruity.

Drink the dry Montlouis (*sec*) with fish (salmon, pike) with a creamy butter sauce. Drinking temperature: 8–10 °C (47–50 °F).

The semi-sweet or fully sweet Montlouis (*moelleux*) is usually served with sharpish desserts such as fruit salads (melon, pear, strawberries) or plum tart. Drinking temperature: 8–10 °C (47–50 °F).

There are also a couple of sparkling Montlouis (*mousseux* and *pétillant*). Both make excellent aperitifs. The *pétillant* has a lower carbon dioxide content. Drinking temperature: 8–10 °C (47–50 °F).

VOUVRAY

Vouvray, too, is mostly vinified to be semi-sweet. In a good Vouvray you will recognize a wide range of ripe fruits (plums, quinces) and honey. Fully sweet and dry Vouvrays are sometimes also made. A good Vouvray can last a very long time.

A dry Vouvray (*sec*) quite likes something rather rich. In Vouvray itself this wine is served with black pudding or tripe with a Vouvray sauce. If this does not suit you, you can opt for a freshwater fish in a white wine butter sauce. Vouvray Sec is, of course, also very suitable as an aperitif. Drinking temperature: 8–10 °C (47–50 °F).

Chinon

Semi-sweet to fully sweet Vouvray (*moelleux*) is excellent with poultry casseroles. Use a Vouvray wine for the sauce. You can also try them with fresh goat's cheese, or rather more daringingly a blue cheese from the high Auvergne: Fourme d'Ambert. A mellow Vouvray Moelleux is also good with dessert, preferably sharpish desserts, or with almond pastries or cream cake. Drinking temperature: 8–10 °C (47–50 °F).

The dry, sparkling Vouvray Mousseux Brut is an exceptional aperitif. Its semi-sweet brother Vouvray Mousseux Demi-Sec can also be served as an aperitif, but is more of an after dinner wine to have with a good book, good conversation, or an exciting game. Drinking temperature: 7–9 °C (45–48 °F).

COTEAUX-DU-LOIR

No, this is not a spelling mistake: the Loir is a river which just below Angers joins the Loire with the Mayenne, the Authion and the Sarthe. The hills on both banks of the Loir produce white, red and rosé wines.

The white wines are made from the chenin blanc (pineau blanc de la Loire) and are very fruity (apricots, bananas, peaches, exotic fruits) with sometimes a little smokiness.

Montlouis: also light sparkling wines

Very well-balanced wines, which taste very pleasant as an aperitif or at meals with cold meats, poultry terrines, white meat, poultry and fish. Drinking temperature: 8–10 °C (47–50 °F).

The scarce rosé wines are fresh and fruity with typical spicy aromas. Drink these sophisticated wines at meals with chicken or other poultry or perhaps hot ham on the bone. Drinking temperature: 10–12 °C (50–54 °F).

The red Coteaux-du-Loir are made from the pineau d'Aunis, gamay or cabernet franc. They are light, fruity, with a trace of spice, and go very well with anything, whether it be poultry, veal or pork. The choice is yours. Drinking temperature: 12–14 °C (54–57 °F).

JASNIÈRES

This wine region, 2 ½ miles long and a few hundred yards wide, is located on the hills by the river Loir. Here, on a soil of tufa, a very small quantity of rare white wines are produced which are among the best wines of France. Made from pineau de la Loire (chenin blanc) these wines have a great deal of subtlety. Characteristic aromas are citrus fruits, almonds, quince, apricots, peaches and sometimes some hints of flowers (roses) or herbs (thyme, mint). Depending on the style and the year, these wines can be either dry or just semi-sweet.

Montlouis, from dry to sweet

Vouvray, dry and sweet

Jasnières wines combine very well with white meat, poultry or fish. Drinking temperature: 10–12 °C (50–54 °F).

COTEAUX-DU-VENDÔMOIS AOVDQS

A small appellation between Montoire and Vendôme, on the banks of the Loir. On hills of tufa, white, red and rosé wines are produced.

The white wines from chenin blanc are very similar to those of Jasnières and the Coteaux-de-Loir. They are fresh, fruity and pleasant. Ideal as an aperitif, but also at meals with, for instance, white meat and fish. Drinking temperature: 8–10 °C (47–50 °F).

The red wines are made of a mixture of pineau d'Aunis, gamay, pinot noir and cabernet franc, in various proportions depending on the style. Red Coteaux-du--Vendômois are rich and fruity and can be surprisingly rich in tannins in their youth.
A first-class wine with red meat, roast poultry or game birds. Drinking temperature: 12–14 °C (54–57 °F).

L'ORLÉANAIS AOVDQS

Once these wines had a very high reputation, particularly in the Middle Ages, when they regularly appeared on the table of the kings of France. Although they have long been almost forgotten, the vineyards of the Orléanais are still kept going by a few fanatic winegrowers who are trying to recover their old fame. On the gentle levels of the banks of the Loire round the town of Orléans mainly red and rosé wines are produced, together with a very small quantity of white.

The rare white wines are made from auvernat blanc (chardonnay). They are fresh and fruity (citrus fruits, almonds).
Drink them as an aperitif or at meals with white meat or poultry. Drinking temperature: 10–12 °C (50–54 °F).

The red wines are made of auvernat rouge (pinot noir), pinot meunier and breton (cabernet franc). They are supple, aromatic and fresh. However, some wines display fairly strong tannins in their youth, but these soon become softer.
Drink these wines with red meat, game birds or roast poultry. Drinking temperature: 12–14 °C (54–57 °F).

The rosé wines are perhaps the best of the Orléanais wines, thanks to their characteristic and assertive pinot meunier (gris meunier). The wines are full of color, fresh and very fruity (including red- and blackcurrants).
First-class accompaniments to dishes of game birds, and also of meat and poultry terrines and fresh goat's cheeses. Drinking temperature: 10–12 °C (50–54 °F).

CHEVERNY

White Cheverny is made from sauvignon, sometimes topped up with chardonnay. The wines are fresh and elegant and have splendid floral aromas. In the taste it is mainly the fruity shades of gooseberries and exotic fruits that dominate.
Drink these white Cheverny as an aperitif or with freshwater fish dishes (such as eel). Drinking temperature: 10–12 °C (50–54 °F).

The rather scarce rosé Chevernys are made from Gamay and are fresh and fruity. These dry rosé wines should preferably be drunk with cold meats (potted rabbit). Drinking temperature: 10–12 °C (50–54 °F).

The red Chevernys are made mostly from Gamay and Pinot Noir and in their youth are fairly fresh and fruity. After a few years maturing in bottle the Pinot Noir takes over and the wines acquire a rather animal (gamy) aroma.
Drink a red Cheverny with red meat or perhaps small game (hare) or game birds. Drinking temperature: 14 °C (57 °F).

COUR-CHEVERNY

An extremely rare white wine made in the immediate neighborhood of Chambord, exclusively from the old native grape variety romorantin; this grape is characterized by powerful aromas of honey and acacia. Since 1993 Cour-Cheverny wines have been able to put AOC on their label.
Drink these Cour-Cheverny with creamy fish, poultry or white meat dishes. Drinking temperature: 10–12 °C (50–54 °F).

VALENÇAY AOVDQS

The vineyards of this wine region are halfway between Châteauroux and Romorantin. They lie on a soil of calcareous clay with some traces of alluvial deposits. The region is better known for its remarkable pyramid-shaped fresh goat's cheeses than for its wines. Yet Valençay is certainly worth exploring.

White Valençay is made of the sauvignon grape, sometimes with the addition of some chardonnay. They are fresh, generous and very pleasant.
Good as an aperitif or with a Valençay goat's cheese. Drinking temperature: 10–12 °C (50–54 °F).

Cheverny

Rosé Valençay, from pineau d'Aunis and gamay, are light and fruity.

Ideal with cold meats, patés and terrines. Drinking temperature: 10–12 °C (50–54 °F).

Red Valençay, from gamay, malbec (cot), cabernet franc (breton) or pinot noir are very fruity (cherries). In their youth they can be a little harsh from the tannins, but that soon passes.

Although they also taste surprisingly good with the local goat's cheeses, these red Valençay wines combine very well with red meat, poultry, small game and game birds. Drinking temperature: 12–14 °C (54–57 °F).

Poitou

There is no doubt that this region is part of the Loire area, but because it never really seems to be at home there, it is given separate listing. This is an honor for a region which a few years ago was on the verge of bankruptcy. The takeover of the local cooperative by the ever-enterprising Georges Duboeuf meant not only its rescue from certain death, but a second life, more dynamic then ever before.

The Neuville-de-Poitou cooperative guarantees about 85 % of the production of Haut-Poitou. The soil of limestone and marl is extremely suitable, particularly for white wines made from Sauvignon and Chardonnay.

The white Chardonnay wines are elegant and subtle, with typical aromas of white fruits and citrus fruits. The taste is fresh and harmonious. First class as aperitifs, but also to accompany fish, crustaceans or white meat. The better *cuvées*, such as La Surprenante, are more complex and offer enticing aromas of privet, acacia, vanilla, toast and hazelnut.

Drink these full wines with fish or *fruits de mer*, possibly served with a very creamy butter sauce. for example, with scallops in a mousseline sauce. Drinking temperature: 10–12 °C (50–54 °F).

The white sauvignon wines are fresh and elegant, with a typical flinty aroma. Drink them as aperitifs or at meals, with *fruits de mer* or fish in a fresh sorrel or lemon sauce. Drinking temperature: 8–10 °C (47–50 °F).

The red wines can be made of several grape varieties. The best come from the cabernet franc and cabernet sauvignon vineyards on limy and flinty clay soils. They have characteristic aromas of red fruits and violets, with a whiff of tufa.

Drink a red Haut-Poitou with grilled or roast chicken, game birds, Easter lamb or fresh, not too assertive cheeses. Drinking temperature: 12–14 °C (54–57 °F).

The Center

The wine regions of 'the Center' of France consist of two wine-growing islands: the Sancerrois (Gien, Sancerre, Bourges and Vierzon) and Châteaumeillant (above Montluçon).

The Sancerrois consists of the AOCs Pouilly-sur-Loire, Pouilly Fumé, Sancerre, Menetou-Salon, Quincy and Reuilly, and the AOVDQS Coteaux du Giennois.

COTEAUX-DE-GIENNOIS

On both banks of the Loire, from Gien up to just above Pouilly--sur-Loire, are the Coteaux-du-Giennois vineyards on the best gravely and calcareous hills. Three traditional grape varieties grow here:

White Haut-Poitou

Surprisingly good Chardonnay from Haut-Poitou
(la Suprenante means 'the surprising one')

sauvignon for the white wines, and gamay and pinot noir for the red and rosé wines. Although as this book is being written the wines produced here are still classed as AOVDQS, Coteaux du Giennois are expected to be promoted to the AOC elite.

The white Coteaux-du-Giennois are fresh, easy to drink wines with generous aromas of citrus fruits, white fruits, gooseberries and blackcurrants, quinces, pineapples, white flowers, and hints of light vegetable scents.

Drink these uncommon wines as aperitifs or with freshwater fish (shad, pickerel); crustaceans and shellfish are also warmly recommended. Drinking temperature: 8–10 °C (47–50 °F).

Red Haut-Poitou

Rosé Coteaux-du-Giennois are light and fresh, fruity and supple. Drink them with stews and casseroles of fish, veal or poultry. Drinking temperature 10–12 °C (54–57 °F).

The red Coteaux-du-Giennois combine the aromatic sophistication of pinot noir with the playful generosity of gamay. The nose is seductive, with aromas of fresh fruits such as cherries, blackberries, strawberries, blackcurrants and bilberries. The taste is very soft.

No shortage of good Sancerrois (Sylvain Bailly)

You will generally not meet robust, tannin-rich wines, but rather fresh elegant ones which at meals go well with red meat or lamb, but also with rabbit, poultry or veal with a light mustard sauce. Try them some time with tender vegetables (courgette, aubergine, potatoes) stuffed with lightly seasoned mince, and cooked au gratin in the oven. Drinking temperature: 12–14 °C (54–57 °F).

POUILLY-SUR-LOIRE

Pouilly-sur-Loire is a small town on the Loire, east of the well-known Sancerre vineyards. Two wines are made here, the famous Pouilly-Fumé (see below) and Pouilly-sur-Loire. Both are white, and come from the same type of calcareous soil. The difference is in the grapes used. While Pouilly-Fumé may only be made from sauvignon, Pouilly sur Loire is made from chasselas. Anyone who has the idea that Chasselas is an inferior grape (and there are plenty who do) should take a trip to Pouilly-sur-Loire to taste these magnificent wines.

The Pouilly-sur-Loire wines are very fresh and aromatic with characteristic aromas of hazelnuts, dried fruits, white flowers, citrus fruits, exotic fruits and sometimes a whiff of menthol or aniseed. In the mouth the wine leaves a pleasant, fresh impression reminiscent of ripe Spanish or Moroccan oranges.

Excellent aperitif wines, but also at meals with crustaceans and shellfish (scallops with a light saffron and orange sauce!). Drinking temperature: 8–9 °C (47–48 °F) as aperitifs; 10 °C (50 °F) with meals.

POUILLY-FUMÉ

The term *fumé* (smoked) does not, as many people think, refer to a smoky undertone in the wine, but to the dull gray film usually visible here on the grapes, making them look as if they were covered in ashes. These sauvignon white wines are very fresh and aromatic. In aroma and taste you will recognize shades of green asparagus, box (cat's piss), blackcurrants, broom, white flowers (roses), acacia, white peaches and aniseed. In short, splendid wines with a rich and powerful taste.

Ideal as aperitif, but also at meals with *fruits de mer*, fish and poultry. One special recommendation – chicken with tarragon sauce! Drinking temperature: 8–10 °C (47–50 °F)

SANCERRE

Sancerre is one of the best known wine regions of the Loire and probably even of France. Since the first beginnings of the AOC classification, in 1936, the white Sancerre wines have been members of the elite corps of French viniculture. The rosé and red Sancerre did not get their AOC recognition until 1959. The vineyards for the white, rosé and red Sancerre (approximately 5,000 acres) lie on the land of eleven communes, of which Sancerre, Chavignol and Bué are the best known. The region is characterized by a beautiful landscape of softly sloping hills with calcareous or gravely soils. The grapes used here are sauvignon for the white wines and pinot noir for the red and rosé wines.

White Sancerres are fresh, lively and very aromatic. A few characteristic aromas are citrus fruits, white peaches, broom, acacia, jasmine, exotic fruits, white flowers, green ferns, (green) asparagus and fresh wood. The taste is fresh, rich and full. The traditional accompaniment for these wines is the equally famous local goat's cheese, Crottin de Chavignol, but a good Sancerre tastes just as nice with fish or crustaceans – perhaps with a mild lemon sauce – or with white meat, rabbit or poultry. Drinking temperature: 10–12 °C (50–54 °F).

Pouilly fumé

Rosé Sancerres are pleasing, generous and subtle with fruity aromas of apricots, redcurrants or even grape fruit, and hints of peppermint.

Although Sancerre rosé is often recommended to accompany oriental dishes – particularly curries – it is better with the rather more traditional local cuisine. Think of it with light starters, tender meat, poultry or fish salads, delicate patés and terrines (rabbit),

casseroles of white meat and poultry... Drinking temperature: 10–12 °C (50–54 °F).

Red Sancerre is clearly typical of pinot noir. In top years the red Sancerre is of outstanding quality. In lesser years it is best ignored, because the ratio of price to quality is then right out of balance. A good Sancerre Rouge (for instance, from Paul Prieur & Fils, Sylvain Bailly) is light, delicate and very aromatic (cherries, morellos, blackberries, licorice). In exceptional years it can get a little fuller and rounder.

In many restaurants the wine waiter will recommend the combination of a red Sancerre with casseroles of poultry – classical, but not really exciting. Just try a well-cooled red Sancerre with a fat carp, or rather less cooled with game birds or wildfowl. Drinking temperature: with fish 12 °C (54 °F) (take a young Sancerre for this) and 15–16 °C (59–61 °F) in other cases.

MENETOU-SALON

Another completely underrated wine, white, but also rosé and red. Menetou-Salon is near the town of Bourges on a soil of limestone and alluvial deposits. In total this appellation covers just more than 330 ha (800 acres).

Château-de-Sancerre, the region's figurehead

The white wines, from sauvignon, are fresh and fruity, with recognizable aromas of citrus fruits, box, peppermint and white flowers, with soft hints of spices and musk. The taste is full and round, supple and friendly.

Chavignol, a famous village for wine and cheese

Three top wines from Sancerre

Sancerre castle really exists

Nice as an aperitif, but also excellent at meals with fish, white meat and poultry. Drinking temperature: 9–10 °C (48–50°F)'

The Menetou-Salon Rosé wines are made from pinot noir. These wines are mostly fresh and fruity, with delicate aromas of white and red fruits.

Drink a Menetou-Salon Rosé with meat, poultry or fish salads, at lunch, with light starters or with omelets or other egg dishes. Drinking temperature: 10–12 °C (50–54 °F).

The red Menetou-Salon wines surprise the taster by their superb ruby-red color and their fruit: plums, cherries and morello cherries.

Drink these sophisticated and harmonious wines with country patés or terrines, small game birds, wildfowl or even game (wild rabbits) and, if you dare, lightly cooled with freshwater fish. Drinking temperature: 12 °C (54 °F) with fish, otherwise 14 °C (57 °F).

QUINCY

On the other side of Bourges, in the direction of Vierzon, is the small wine-growing region of Quincy. Quincy's wines were recognized as AOC as early as 1936. Quincy wines have been among France's elite for more than sixty years, but unfortunately they are not often found outside their own area. This wine region in the center of France, to the west of the Loire and on the left bank of the Cher, was already well-known in the Middle Ages. The wine acreage covers only two towns, Brinay and Quincy, a total of around 180 ha (445 acres). The plains on which the vines grow are covered with a mixture of sand and ancient pebbles. The subsoil consists of calcareous clay. The unique Sauvignon grape thrives particularly well on this poor soil.

A Quincy is very much like a better Sancerre blanc. Quincy wines are fresh and surprisingly aromatic: white flowers, citrus fruits (lime, orange) and plant undertones of box, broom or (green) asparagus. The flavor is fresh, elegant, succulent and particularly pleasant.

Menetou-Salon

You can serve these white wines as an excellent aperitif, and just as easily with meals of white meat and poultry. A good Quincy has one other great love: asparagus, preferably green. Try a warm salad of fresh asparagus with a young goat's cheese, crayfish *al dente* and a few pine nuts. Drinking temperature: 9–10 °C (48–50 °F).

REUILLY

All too often the mistake is made of confusing Reuilly and Rully. Rully is also white but comes from Burgundy. An error of this kind is also often made with Pouilly fumé (Loire) and Pouilly fuissé (Bourgogne Mâconnais). The 320 acre designation of origin Reuilly is slightly to the west of Quincy. The vines grow on softly glowing hills of calcareous loam soil and on plains of siliceous sandy soils. By contrast with its neighbors from Quincy, this area produces not only white, but also red and rosé wines.

The white Reuillys, made from the sauvignon blanc, are prime examples of Sauvignon wines from the Loire. The bouquet is enough to make you turn lyrical and bucolic: asparagus beds, still half asleep under a thin blanket of morning dew, are gently awakened by the first rays of the sun… You can also smell white meadow flowers, grass, clover and white fruits in them, with nuances of menthol and lemon or lime.

Drink these subtle, elegant and refined wines with mild (starter) dishes of seafood or crustaceans, or with poached poultry or fish. Drinking temperature: 10–12 °C (50–54 °F).

The Reuilly rosé is always particularly fruity and fresh. In top years (with a lot of sun) the better wines may be slightly stronger and more full-bodied. Most of the rosé wines are made from pinot noir, but besides these there are also some subtle traditional rosé wines to be found made from pinot gris! Some characteristic aromas of the Pinot Noir rosé are strawberries, raspberries, white peaches and peppermint.

Drink these hearty rosé wines with rustic dishes of rabbit, pork or veal, with terrines and patés, or with an omelette with fried forest mushrooms. Drinking temperature: 10–12 °C (50–54 °F).

The red Reuilly is made from pinot noir and is rich in color, but quite light in texture and flavor. These wines are a veritable explosion of fruity aromas: cherries, plums, blackberries, wild strawberries, red and white currants, blackcurrants… All this is often supplemented by the typical pinot noir aromas of leather and game, with a dash of pepper as a finishing touch.

Drink these red wines with rustic casseroles of beef, veal, hare or game birds. Drinking temperature: 14 °C (57 °F).

Reuilly

Quincy

**Châteaumeillant
gris**

CHÂTEAUMEILLANT AOVDQS

The wines of the 200 acre wine region were accorded the designation AOVDQS in 1965. Yet in a short time these wines have become quite well known, principally in the better circles and in the local catering industry. The area's secret is its special rosé wines (vin gris), made from gamay, and the good relation of price to quality. The soil of Châteaumeillant is a combination of siliceous sand and clay. The varieties of grapes used are pinot noir, pinot gris and gamay.

Châteaumeillant's vin gris is fresh, lively and very seductive. It has rich aromas of white fruits (peaches) with a herby undertone and sometimes a few floral nuances. The flavor is fresh, but also supple and hearty.

Drink this vin gris with good quality (meat) barbecues, with lunch or – all year long – with cold meat starters, patés and terrines. Drinking temperature: 10–12 °C (50–54 °F).

The less well-known red Châteaumeillants can also be surprisingly good. The wines are very fruity, with aromas of ripe red fruits, mainly blackcurrants, and nuances of menthol and licorice. They are the ideal accompaniment to casseroles of chicken or other poultry in red wine sauce, but these red wines are equally at home with rustic dishes of green cabbage or leeks with potatoes and beef sausages. Drinking temperature: 12–14 °C (54–57 °F).

N.B. For wines from the Auvergne see Burgundy/Beaujolais.

**Châteaumeillant
rouge**

New vines in full bloom

SPAIN

Spain is a fairly large country with an enormous variety of landscape, climate and culture. The Iberian Peninsula, formed by Spain and Portugal, is separated from France and Andorra in the north by the Pyrenees and otherwise surrounded by water on all sides. The mountain ranges in the interior divide the country into large natural regions and determine the climate. Around three quarters of Spain consists of huge plains called *mesetas*. The different microclimates make Spain an extremely exciting country.

The Meseta has a semi-continental climate with severe winters and hot summers. In the north-western coastal strip the climate is influenced by the Bay of Biscay (Atlantic Ocean). The climate there is moderately oceanic and proportionately quite humid. The winters are mild and the summers pleasantly warm. The eastern Costa has a typically Mediterranean climate. The summers are fairly warm and dry and the winters mild and damp. Finally, in Andalucía in the south the climate is half continental and half Mediterranean, with very hot and dry summers and particularly mild winters.

WINE-GROWING

The total area of vineyards in Spain fluctuates around 3 million acres. This is extremely large, being 1$^1/_2$ million larger than the wine acreage of either France or Italy. Yet there is less wine produced than in both those countries. The difference in production figures from the two other European wine-growing leaders can be partly explained by the large proportion taken up by the Denominación de Origen wines. In Spain, relatively speaking there is less vino de mesa, vino comarcal (table wine) and vino de la tierra (regional wine/vin de pays) made than in France or Italy. The bulk of Spanish production comes from Cataluña (Catalonia), Valencia and La Mancha. Zones like La Rioja, Aragón, de Levante and Andalucía do indeed produce quality wines, but the total yield is on the low side. This is also partly due to the particularly warm, dry climate of, among other places, the south of Spain. Because the weather conditions are so extreme the vines have to be kept very low and this means the crop is not much more than a few bunches per vine.

Spain was once a rather inhospitable area of huge dry plains (mesetas) and thickly wooded mountain ranges. The oldest known inhabitants of the Iberian Peninsula probably came from North Africa and lived as nomads. Traces of these Iberians take us back to 3000 BC. They owe their name to the area where they settled, around the river Ebro. The Iberians soon took possession of southern and eastern Spain. About three centuries BC they interbred with the northern Celtic peoples. We now know that the Celtic druids had already mastered the art of wine-making. At the same time as these druids from the north were happily sipping the fruits of the *Vitis labrusca*, the Phoenicians were settling in the south, near the trading port of Gadir (now better known as Cádiz). In around 1000 BC they began to reconnoiter the interior of southern Spain and built the small town of Xera (Xéres, Jerez). They estab-

The Spanish Meseta, a huge plain (Valdepeñas)

Spanish wines: popular gifts for relations

Little yield per vine
(Valdepeñas)

lished Spain's first vineyards on the surrounding hills. The warm climate enabled them to make outstanding sweet wines that soon became known all over the Mediterranean region. This was the beginning of a series of attempts at colonization.

After the Phoenicians came the Greeks, the Celts and the Carthaginians. They also sought out the nicest spots to settle and cultivate. The Romans were the next uninvited guests. They conquered all the other ethnic minorities and gave the Iberian Peninsula the name Hispania, the latest province of Rome. Wine-growing was already flourishing in the time of the Romans and was further extended by the West Gothic Christians, who played a large role in spreading the Gospel. In 711 the West Gothic realm was defeated and completely dismantled by the Moors, who had crossed over from North Africa. Even at the time of Moorish domination (which lasted, believe it or not, until 1492) grape-growing was continued and extended, though, apart from a few exceptions, the intention was not to make wine from the grapes, but fine grape juice.

Even though Moorish domination was a blessing for Spain on a cultural, social and economic level, the wine industry was given a low profile. Only after Spain was conquered by the Christians (the Reconquista) did the wine trade prosper again. In the sixteenth century the English also discovered the charms of Spanish wines, even if it was often after having won a bloody battle with the Spanish fleet. In peacetime thousands of barrels of wine were sent to The Netherlands and England. Spanish wine-making experienced glorious times. When the French vineyards were destroyed at the end of the nineteenth century by *Phylloxera vastatrix*, many French people emigrated to, among other places, the Rioja and Navarra and brought their grape varieties, such as cabernet sauvignon and merlot, with them. Spanish

wine-making flourished as never before. Unfortunately an abrupt end was brought to this when the greedy louse let rip on the Spanish wine acreage. Once all the vineyards had been re-planted using immune American root stock, the Spanish wine trade was amazingly quickly restored. But unfortunately, although Spain was spared in the World War I, the Spanish Civil War again hit wine-making very hard, followed by the turbulent times of the World War II. Not until the beginning of the 1950s did Spanish wine-making appear to stabilize again, albeit with cheap bulk wines. Since the 1990s Spain has its own profile again, thanks to the quality and authenticity of Spanish wines in spite of the relatively low price.

Not long ago wine-making in Spain was still hopelessly old-fashioned. You can still see all around the unhygienic concrete, artificial resin or even pottery

Este vino ha sido elegido tras una cuidadosa cata entre la clientela de esta casa

Selección de Bodegas Victorianas

Spanish wine is usually delicious and not expensive

(*tinajas*) barrels that made it impossible to produce fresh, fruity wines, because there was no adequate temperature control. The wines also very frequently – unintentionally – came into contact with oxygen and were old before they left the bodega. These heavy, ponderous wines are still sporadically found in Spain, but most *bodegas* have since gone over to easier to handle (and cheaper to use) stainless steel barrels. Vinification techniques have also improved. For example, more attention is paid to the transport of the grapes. The best bodegas take various measures to keep the harvested grapes as cold as possible, reducing the addition of sulfur to a minimum. The cellars are increasingly being automated, leading to enormous improvements, especially in the fermentation process. Because a constant eye is kept on the temperature and it can be precisely set, it is possible to obtain any type of wine desired.

Ancient underground tinajas in Valdepeñas

By harvesting early the grapes are kept cool

In the best bodegas you can also see that more thought has been given to storage in wood. At one time old casks used were not always as fresh-smelling as they might have been, which made the wine musty and completely dominated by wood. Even so-called top wines had to contend with this problem. For several years now wood has been treated with greater care. It was realized that many wines in no way benefited from cask-maturing and in fact tasted much nicer if they came straight from the stainless steel tanks. Especially the white and rosé wines have therefore since become much fresher and fruitier. But the change is clearly noticeable with the red wines too. At one time all kinds of wood were used indiscriminately. Now a distinction is made between American (Tennessee), French (Limouisin, Allier, Tronçais, Nivernais) and Slovenian oak. The latter is used in particular for simple wines, because it is cheaper. American and French oak is mostly used for the better wines.

American oak produces faster oxidation because the pores of the wood are slightly larger. It also gives the wines a strong, rather sweetish vanilla flavor in a shorter time. The use of this type of wood with light, delicate red wines would have fatal consequences, because the wines would be completely dominated by wood and vanilla. So these American casks are used for robust, full red wines, which are ready to drink sooner.

French Limousin oak has smaller pores and produces far less vanilla flavor and aroma. The aging process is far slower and the wines develop more delicate and refined aromas. Limousin casks are often used to further refine the better wines just before bottling. This type of wood has a great influence on the quality and finesse of the wine, but never dominates.

French Allier oak has even smaller pores and is even more neutral in aroma and flavor. These casks are primarily used for the top wines, which are vinified in the cask.

The use of American wood would make the wines so sickly as to be almost undrinkable. Both types of French oak are very expensive, however, not only to

Many bodegas use both American and French barrels

acquire, but also because the wines age far more slowly due to the small pores and therefore cannot be sold anywhere near as soon! And storage is not cheap.

Spanish legislation concerning the official maturity specification of the wines is fairly similar to that of the Italians. Here too things used to be chaotic. Words such as *crianza*, *reserva*, or *gran reserva* were used, whether relevant or not, and the criteria varied enormously from region to region. This has been brought more into line in the last few years.

The quality of the casks is decisive for the final result

This tinto cosecha 1996 is not a crianza, but was matured in wood

The tinto cosecha 1995 is a crianza, however

VINO JOVEN

These young wines are also well-known as *Vino del Año*, wine of the year. At one time you would see the negative slogan *sin crianza* (not cask-matured) on the bottles, but this is now a thing of the past. This expression was too confusing, because some wines were not cask-matured, but did remain for six years or so in the wine cellars before they were allowed to be sold! The vinos jóvenes are usually fresh and fruity wines that do not benefit from ageing, as they then lose the charm of their fruitiness. This type of wine is by far the favorite among the Spanish themselves, whereas the wines that have been cask-matured are hailed by wine connoisseurs all over the world. But with the Spanish it is not just a question of taste: the difference in price also plays a part.

Vino joven, not cask-matured

VINO DE CRIANZA

This 'cask-matured' wine must be a minimum of two years old and have been cask-matured for at least six months. In practice, however, a minimum of twelve months is assumed in the Rioja, Ribera del Duero and Navarra! The white and rosé crianza must be at least one year old and have been kept in the wood for six months.

RESERVA

This needs a minimum of three years maturing in the bodega, including at least one year in the wood. The white and rosé reserva must be at least two years old and have been kept in the wood for a minimum of six months.

GRAN RESERVA

These great wines are produced only in top years and may not be sold until their sixth year, with a minimum of two years in the wood and a minimum of three years in the

Crianza

Reserva

bottle. You will not find very many white or rosé gran reserva. These little gems may not be sold until their sixth year either, after a minimum of six months in the wood and a minimum of four years in the bottle.

As a consumer you actually have only one thing to remember. A Spanish cellar master works differently from a French cellar master. In Spain some wines

Gran Reserva

are also sold quickly, for example thanks to the use of American oak or simply by not storing the wines in the wood. But in general the Spanish cellar master keeps the wines in his cellar as long as possible, so as to be able to sell only those wines that are perfect for drinking. This brings in proportionately more money, but there is a greater risk. French cellar masters go for quicker sale of wines that are not yet ready to drink and have to mature for several more years in the cellars of end-consumers. In this way they are sure of their cash flow and they need less storage space. Spanish cellars are often huge and conceal great hordes of wine. In short, you, as consumer, are lucky if you have a bottle of Spanish wine, as you do not have to wait years to open it! However, that does not mean that you have to drink the bottles within a year. Remember: the shorter the cask-maturing, the less time the wines can be kept. It is better to drink a vino joven within two years of harvesting, a crianza within five years, a reserva within six to seven years and a gran reserva within ten to fifteen years. If you wait too long these wines will often be sluggish and tired. Some top wines from La Rioja, Ribera del Duero, Penedés or Navarra can be left until they are far older.

DESIGNATIONS OF ORIGIN

Spain, like all the other European countries, has a designation of origin classification system, sub-divided into the two main categories of table wine and quality wine (VQPRD.)

TABLE WINE

To this category belong French vin de table and vin de pays/vin de cépage, Italian vino da tavola and indicazione geografica tipica and German Tafelwein and Landwein.

The Spanish have the vino de mesa (table wine), vino comarcal (local wine) and vino de la tierra (regional wine). Few demands are made of the vinos de mesa. They can be made anywhere in Spain, originate from different regions and carry no other geographical indication or year number.

You can keep the best wines slightly longer without any worries

The vinos camarcales are vinos de mesa from a particular district, provided with a year number. This category is actually completely superfluous and is only used to give the wines a little more class. Within the scope of European wine legislation this category will supposedly soon disappear, but you will still come across this designation in the shops.

The vinos de la tierra originate from distinctly demarcated regions, known for their quality and their individual characteristics. Many of these wines may in principle be promoted in future to the designations of origin.

In anticipation of possible promotion the serious candidates for a Denominación de Origen may give a temporary classification on the label, the Denominación Especifica (Provisional) or (provisional) specific designation of origin. This can only be used if the entire district is on the way to DO recognition. If, rather than the entire district, just some top bodegas are applying for promotion, the Spanish employ the special designation of origin Denominación de Origen Provisional, or provisional designation of origin.

Vino de la tierra

This is all meticulously kept up to date by the umbrella organization for Spanish wines, the INDO (Instituto Nacional de Denominaciones de Origen), which delegates local powers to the local Consejos Reguladores (administrative councils). All very democratic and decentralized, but this begs the question of whether such a fragmented body is not rather old-fashioned in the European context, at least if Spain wants to continue in the same innovative way.

QUALITY WINE

Spanish wine-growing has two designations of origin for quality wines: the Denominación de Origen (DO) and the Denominación de Origen Calificada (DOC). The DO applies to most quality wines and corresponds to both the French VDQS and AOC, while the DOC applies only to the top wines and is comparable to the Italian DOCG. Since the introduction of the DOC in 1988 only one region in Spain has been allowed to bear the highly sought-after designation and that is La Rioja. To become DOC a whole series of agreements have to be made about matters such as the price of the grapes, bodega bottling and strict production and checking measures, including regular tastings and sample research.

Denominacion de Origen (DO)

REGIONAL DIVISION

In this book we use the classical regional distinctions used by the official Spanish wine authorities. We distinguish the following regions with the local DO(C)s in brackets:

- the northwest: Galicia (Rías Baixas, Ribeira Sacra, Ribeiro, Valdeorras, Valle de Monterrei), the north of the País Vasco (Txakoli de Getaria, Txakoli de Bizkaia), the north of Castilla y Léon (Bierzo), Asturias and Cantabria;
- the high Ebro valley: the south of the País Vasco (Rioja), La Rioja (Rioja), Navarra (Navarra, Rioja) and Aragón (Cariñena, Campo de Borja, Catalayud, Somontano);
- the Duero valley: the south of Castilla y Léon (Cigales, Ribera del Duero, Rueda and Toro);
- Catalonia and the Balearics: Cataluña (Alella, Ampurdán-Costa Brava, Cataluña, Conca de Barberà, Costers del Segre, Penedés, Priorato, Tarragona, Terra Alta) and the Balearics (Binissalem);
- the Levante: the east of Castilla-La Mancha (Almansa), Valencia (Alicante, Utiel-Requena, Valencia) and Murcia (Bullas, Jumilla and Yecla);
- the Meseta plain: Madrid (Vinos de Madrid), the middle and west of Castilla-La Mancha (La Mancha, Méntrida, and Valdepeñas) and Extremadura (Ribera del Guadiana);
- Andalucía and the Canary Islands: Andalucía (Condado de Huelva, Málaga, Montilla-Moriles, Jerez, Manzanilla de Sanlúcar de Barrameda) and Canarias (Abona, El Hierro, Lanzarote, La Palma, Tacaronte-Acentejo, Valle de Güimar, Valle de la Orotava and Ycoden-Daute-Isora).

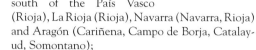

Denominacion de Origen Calificada (D.O.Ca.)

This makes a total of fifty-two regional designations of origin, but there is also a fifty-third DO, Cava. These sparkling wines, made according to the *méthode traditionelle*, may be made in the south of the País Vasco, in La Rioja, Navarra, Aragón and Cataluña.

CHAMPAGNE AND CAVA

It is a shame that almost everything containing bubbles is called Champagne. After all, there are top *méthode traditionelle* Cavas, which are of a far higher level than the lowest Champagne varieties. So it would not be doing these wines justice to call them Champagne. Neither would it be correct, because – as with all the other great sparkling wines – the Spanish Cavas have their own story to tell: about the varieties of grapes used, the soil and the weather conditions, which are actually quite different from those in Champagne. This Spanish version of the *méthode traditionelle* has been made since the end of the nineteenth century. Cava was born in 1872 in the province of Barcelona, simply because the local catering industry managers could not satisfy the increasing demand for good sparkling wines. Instead of importing consistently expensive Champagnes or cheap *Blanquette de Limoux*, the Catalans decided to start producing sparkling wines themselves. These wines are made in precisely the same way as the other *méthode traditionelle* wines, but they have their own flavor and character, determined by the use of different grapes and by a different idea of what a good sparkling wine should taste like.

The grapes destined for Cava production are selected and harvested with the greatest of care. The best grapes for Cava come from highly calcareous soils, at a height of 650–1470 ft. In the interior the vineyards are lower lying than in the province of Barcelona. The warm Mediterranean climate of Barcelona is compensated by the high position of the vineyards, because the height provides wind and thus a cooling effect. The best vineyards for Cava are around the village of Sant Sadurni d'Anoia, in the province of Barcelona.

The following grapes are used for the base wines: macabeo (fruity and fresh), parellada (floral aromas) and xarello (acidity and alcohol). Now and then Chardonnay is also added to this list. Garnacha, Tempranillo and Monastrell are used for Cava Rosada Cariñena. The inland Cavas are usually made from viura (macabeo). As it can be quite warm in Spain, the grapes for Cavas are usually harvested early in the morning. As soon as they have been brought in the grapes are gently pressed. The juice is siphoned into stainless steel tanks,

Good Cava is just as good as an average class Champagne

where fermentation takes place at a constantly controlled low temperature. After fermentation the wine rests for a while and is continually tested by the cellar master. The best cuvées are selected and blending takes place in the greatest secrecy. After this blending the wine is bottled and stored on its side in huge cellars for a minimum of nine months (often longer). During this period the second fermentation takes place in the bottle. As in Champagne, Saumur or Limoux, a texture of fine bubbles emerges. The bottles, on racks or in giro pallets (girasoles), are shaken by hand or mechanically so that the floating particles of non-fermentable sugars and dead yeast cells sink to the neck of the bottle. The neck of the bottles is immersed in a salt solution bath to freeze the sediment. When the bottles are opened the wedge of sediment is removed from the bottle under the pressure created. The wines, which are now clear, are then filled up with the same wine or with a liqueur (see: sparkling wines) and given a cork and wire cage. The wine is then ready for distribution to satisfied customers.

More than 90% of Cava production comes from Catalonia, principally from the Penedés. Two gigantic wine merchants between them account for 90% of the market. Freixenet (also owner of Segura Viudas and Castell Blanch) is the undisputed leader on the export market. In Spain itself Codorniu is the leader.

Cavas are usually slightly less dry than French sparkling wines and they have just that little bit of Spanish temperament as an extra. The price of the top Cavas is particularly low in relation to the quality. But be careful: some cheating goes on, particularly with the obligatory maturing time of a minimum of nine months. Court cases have been going on for years against brands that do not abide by those nine months and therefore do not deserve the designation Cava. Officially there are only two varieties of Cava, the white and the rosé. The white Cava is sub-divided into various flavor categories.

CAVA ROSADO BRUT

Particularly elegant Cava with a glittering color. Splendid floral and fruity aromas. Full, dry, fresh and fruity. Great as an aperitif, especially with delicious fishy snacks (salmon!), but also with food for celebratory meals.

CAVA EXTRA BRUT

This is the driest (least sweet) of all the Cavas. The sugar content in this wine is less than 6 g/liter ($^1/_8$ oz//pint). They make excellent aperitifs, but they also go particularly well with oysters or other shellfish.

CAVA BRUT

This wine is slightly less dry than the former, but still very dry (though less than a French champagne). The Cava brut is by far the favorite among non-Spanish consumers. Sugar content: 6–15 g//liter ($^1/_8$–$^1/_4$ oz/pint).

Cava rosado brut

CAVA EXTRA SECO

Sugar content 12–20 g/liter ($^1/_4$–$^3/_8$ oz/pint).

CAVA SECO

Although this Cava is called 'dry', the Cava seco is really slightly sweet, but still reasonably fresh and very pleasant. Sugar content: 17–35 g/liter ($^1/_4$–$^3/_8$ oz/pint).

CAVA SEMI-SECO

This Cava begins to taste really sweet, but not too much so. The Spanish still choose this sweeter sparkling wine over the extra seco or brut. Sugar content: 35–50 g/liter ($^3/_8$–$^7/_8$ oz/pint).

Cava extra brut

Cava brut

CAVA DULCE

For lovers of the really sweet! Sugar content above 50 g/liter ($^7/_8$ oz/ /pint).

ESPUMOSOS

As well as Cavas a number of other sparkling wines are made in Spain that can make no claims on the DO Cava.

MÉTODO RADICIONAL

These sparkling wines are made in the same way as Cavas, but in districts that do not come under the DO Cava. The quality is never really amazing, though some can be quite pleasant. You will not often find them outside the production district.

GRANVÁS

Granvás is the Spanish name for *méthode charmat* or *méthode cuve close*. The principle is simple. Instead of in the bottle, the second fermentation takes place in large tanks (*grandes envases*), which are hermetically sealed. After fermentation the wine is clarified and bottled. Here too the flavor is determined by the sugar content. Distinguished from dry to sweet are:

- extra brut [less than 6 g/liter ($^1/_8$ oz/pint)]
- brut [0–15 g/liter (0–$^1/_4$ oz/pint)]
- extra seco [12–20 g/liter ($^1/_4$–$^3/_8$ oz/pint)]
- seco [17–35 g/liter ($^1/_4$–$^3/_4$ oz/pint)]
- semi-seco [35–50 g/liter ($^3/_4$–$^7/_8$ oz/pint)]
- dulce [above 50 g/liter ($^7/_8$ oz/pint)]

THE NORTHWEST

In the northwest of Spain are the following autonomiás: Galicia, the north of the País Vasco and the north of Castilla y Léon, Asturias and Cantabria. The latter two autonomiás produce only vinos de mesa. We shall split the other regions into DO wine-growing regions.

The climate in the north-west of Spain is distinctly influenced by the Bay of Biscay and the Atlantic Ocean. The weather conditions are colder, wetter and more windy that in the rest of the country. Daily life is emphatically marked by the sea and fishing. Culturally speaking, the district does not give the impression of being truly Spanish: its features are more Celtic and Basque than Castilian and the Moorish invasion has left few traces here. The local cuisine is based on the fruits of the sea: fish, crustaceans and shellfish. The local wines are in general white, dry, fresh and light, apart from a few light, fresh red wines.

GALICIA

Galicia seems to have found a place on the wine map of Spain at last. Just over a decade ago the excellent wines were still reserved only for local wine bars and eating places. At that time there were few tourists in green Galicia, the forgotten corner above the border with Portugal, though every year thousands of pious pilgrims came past on their way to the famous Santiago de Compostello. Local wine-growing has an enormous wealth of old grapes, which give Galician wines their charm. Had anyone heard of Albariño, Godello or Treixadura fifteen years ago? Unfortunately, unenlightened wine buyers for years gave preference to the fashionable wines from La Rioja, Navarra, Penedés, La Mancha and Valdepeñas, ignoring this district. Galician wines were considered too light, too thin, too sour and too rough and oxidized far too quickly. In France the same thing happened with wines like the Gros Plant du Pays Nantais and in Portugal with the Vinho Verde. Many winegrowers were so bowed down by the criticism that they began to plant easier and better-selling foreign grape varieties. The wines they made from these were of such poor quality, however, that the new generation of winegrowers reinstated the old grapes. Production was less, but better. The best combinations of grape, microclimate and soil were sought. The results speak for themselves. Galician wines are greatly on the up, the quality is excellent and the fame of these little gems is fast increasing internationally.

Galicia, as you can see from the name, has a distinctly Celtic background, but its present-day culture is largely determined by Portuguese influences. Both influences can be clearly traced in the naming of the districts and wines. For instance, in Galego (the local language, also written as 'Gallego' in Spanish) different articles are used from the Spanish: 'o' and 'a' instead of 'el' and 'la' respectively. An 'x' is pronounced here as 'sh' and not as 'ks'. However, for export most of the labels have Castilian spelling.

RÍAS BAIXAS

Rías Baixas (pronounced 'rias baishas') is by far the most famous – but as far as quality is concerned not the only – DO in Galicia. It is principally the white wines made from albariño that enjoy justifiable recognition. Galicia is characterized by a beautiful coastline interspersed with large bays (the 'low rivers' or 'rías baixas'), reminiscent of the Scandinavian fjords. The rest of the country consists of green valleys with the coolest and wettest vineyards in Spain. There are three types of soil in the Rías Baixas: alluvial deposits, a subsoil of granite with an upper stratum of alluvial deposits and a subsoil of granite with an upper stratum of sand. The average height of the vineyards is about 1,479 ft.

The wines are principally white and made from about 90% albariño grapes. The albariño is supposed to be a twin of the riesling and was at one time brought to Santiago de Compostella by German monks. A few wines are also made from treixadura and loureira blanca, and unusual red wines from the brancellao and caiño.

The white Albariño wines have to be made from 100% abariño. They are stern, fresh and crisp wines with a great deal of class and a delicate flavor, with the dominant tone provided by fruits and flowers.

Drink these wines with mussels that have been marinated in Albariño wine and cooked *au gratin* in the oven ('vieras al albariño'), spider crab *au gratin*, ('centollo/changurro relleno', monkfish with grated cheese ('rape al queso'), hake with fennel ('merluza al hinojo') or with young rabbit in a shallot and wine sauce ('lamprea a la gallega'). You can also choose to combine it with a fresh, sour Galician cheese, such as tetilla or ulloa. Drinking temperature: 8–10 °C (46–50 °F).

RIBEIRO

The district of Ribeiro is inland and is the continuation of Rías Baixas in the province of Orense. Ribeiro used to be a famous export center for Galician wines. However, while the rest of Europe was improving its wine-making techniques Ribeiro fell behind and to some extent descended into oblivion. The quality of the wines produced here left a great deal to be desired and came nowhere near that of the Rías Baixas. However, there have been changes since internal and foreign investors started to become interested in this district. The wine-making equipment has been enormously improved and large bodegas, with more of a Spanish feel, have been built to meet the great expectations. Ribeiro is on the up and the wines will soon be on sale in other countries too. The white and red wines of Ribeiro are great for everyday use and here and there you will discover one or two magnificent wines. The white wines are made from treixadura, possibly supplemented with, among others, palomino, torrontés, albariño, loureira, godello or macabeo. The better quality wines are mainly produced from the Albariño. Drink these dry, fresh and fruity wines with crustaceans or shellfish (*mariscos*) or fishcakes (*xouba empenada*). Drinking temperature: 8–10 °C (46–50 °F).

Rias Baixas Albariño

Most of the red wines, made from caiño, supplemented with, among others, garnacha and mencía, are light but quite rich in tannin. The better wines are made from garnacha and are somewhat fuller.

Drink these red wines with hearty Galician dishes such as tripe with spicy vegetables (*callos a la gallega*), pork tenderloin pasties (*raxo empenada*) or duck casseroles (*pato al estilo de Ribadeo*). Drinking temperature: 12–15 °C (54–59 °F), depending on the quality. The better the

quality, the less cold.

The rosé wines are fresh, fruity and light. Drink them with the local *mariscos* or with the main course fish soup *caldeirada gallega*. Drinking temperature: 10–12 °C (50–54 °F).

RIBEIRA SACRA

Ribeiro blanco

The vineyards of this region are situated on terraces in the picturesque landscape of the provinces of Lugo and Orense. The white wines made here from, among others, albariño, treixadura, godello, loureira, torrrontés and palomino are very similar to those of Ribeiro, but often seem less fresh. The red wines are made from, among others, mencía, alicante, caiño, sousón and garnacha and are of acceptable quality. As here too much can be invested to replace or improve the vineyards, the wine-making equipment and the storage rooms, the potential quality can very quickly go sky-high. The white wines combine excellently with the fresh, sour Galician cheeses San Simón and cebreiro. Drinking temperature: 8–10 °C (46–50 °F) for the white and 12–14 °C (54–57 °F) for the red wines.

MONTERREI

This DO still has to make a name for itself. The quality produced so far is moderate to acceptable, and yet this district has been granted its own DO. The wines are primarily made from the white grapes palomino, godello (here also called verdelho) and boña blanca and the red grapes alicante and mencía. The best white and red wines are fresh and fruity and have a relatively low alcohol percentage.

VALDEORRAS

This wine-growing region is the furthest inland, on the border of Castilla y Léon. Most of the vineyards are in the Sil valley. Not so very long ago heavy, dark wines were made here, which have disappeared into the anonymity of the local bars. The grape varieties Godello (white) and Mencía (red), once regarded as local, have been reinstated little by little and more and more quality wines are being made. The wine equipment has been improved enormously and preparation of the wine has become more 'hygienic'. The result was inevitable. The white wines are typically Galician: light, fresh and crisply dry. You can drink them with *mariscos* and with most fish dishes. They would certainly go down well on a warm summer day as an aperitif and are equally delicious with the Galician cheeses tetilla, cebreiro, San Simón and ulloa. Drinking temperature: 10–12 °C (50–54 °F).

The red wines, way in the minority, are, in my opinion, even more worthwhile than the white. Most of them are light and fruity, but the better crianza wines have wonderful aromas of blackberries, plums and licorice, a beautiful cherry-red color and a soft, rich and very pleasant flavor. Drink these wines with grilled or fried red meat, leg of lamb roasted pink in the oven or on the spit or simply with a tasty piece of cheese. Drinking temperature: 12–14 °C (54–57 °F).

CASTILLA Y LÉON

Castilla y Léon is a huge wine-growing area where many table and regional wines of outstanding quality are made (including Cebreros, Valdevimbre-Los Oreros, Tierra del Vino de Zamora) and in the districts of Bierzo, Cigales, Ribera del Duero, Toro and Rueda first-rate DO wines are also produced. The four latter wine-growing regions are situated around the town of Valladolid and the river Duero and will be dealt with in another chapter. The DO of Bierzo is an outsider situated in the extreme north-west of Castilla y Léon. As far as the climate is concerned, Bierzo (Léon) belongs more with the other wine-growing regions of this chapter than with its four neighbors from Castilla.

BIERZO

This DO has officially existed since 1989 but only since 1991 have the grapes for the Bierzo wines been permitted to come exclusively from its own district. This latter measure has been the principal reason for the improvement in quality. The present wine-growing area is about 13,600 acres. As the only DO in Castilla y Léon, Bierzo is not in the immediate vicinity of the Duero, but on the border of Galicia. Bierzo is regarded as a transition area between the wine-growing of Galicia, especially that of neighboring Valdeorras, and the wine-growing of the Duero valley. The Bierzo district lies in a valley, well protected by the surrounding mountains of the Cordillera Cantábrica and the Montes de Léon aga-

Valdeorras

inst extreme effects of weather. The climate is still distinctly influenced by the Atlantic Ocean (damp, wind) but has more hours of sunshine than Galicia. The vineyards lie on the sides of the hills of granite and clay and produce good white wines from doña blanca and godello, and also red and rosé wines from mencía and now and then a little garnacha. Unfortunately you still come across white wines made from the poorer quality palomino grape. The white wines are slightly less pronounced in flavor than the Galician ones, but are delicious, light and freshly dry. They make very good aperitifs and go well with the many local fish dishes of Léon, principally trout and cod or hake. Drinking temperature: 8–10 °C (46–50 °F).

The rosé wines made from granacha are of a first-rate standard, particularly if they have been cask-matured for a while. They are full, aromatic and powerful. They go perfectly with Léon's many meat specialties. Try these rosados for example with smoked spicy chorizo, *morcilla* (onion black pudding), *cecina* (air-dried beef) or even with the famous *botillo*. This excellent *botillo* used to be a poor people's meal, but now this dish of tripe stuffed with herbed pork, served with new potatoes and vegetables, is very popular. Drinking temperature: 10–12 °C (50–54 °F).

The red wines from Bierzo are, in my opinion, the best in the area. Most of them are made to be drunk young and are light, fresh and fruity with slight floral undertones. The better wines, however, are cask-matured and come on to the market as reserva. They are fuller, stronger and more adult. Finally there are the gran reservas which are full of promise for, hopefully, a not too distant future, Most of the red Bierzo wines have recognizable aromas of red fruits, plums, dates or raisins, sometimes with a touch of licorice and celery or fennel. Keep an eye on these wines – we shall hear more of them!

Drink the better red Bierzo (for the money you certainly can allow yourself this) with casseroles of beef with haricot beans (preferably from La Bañeza!) and tomato sauce, with lentil dishes with *morcilla* or with roast or fried lamb. Try this red Bierzo sometime with a stew made with rib of beef! It's best to keep the gran reservas for roast or fried beef, pork or lamb or for game (e.g. hare). Definitely serve a glass of your best Bierzo with a chunk of zamorano or ibérico cheese. Drinking temperature: 12–16 °C (54–61 °F), 16 °C (61 °F) for the gran reservas.

Bierzo

PAÍS VASCO

The Basque country actually has three aspects: the picturesque coastal strip with countless beaches and fishing ports, the large industrial towns and the beautiful green landscape of the interior. The Basque country has its own culture, its own language – probably one of Europe's original languages – and above all, its own character.

The Spanish part of the Basque country still has close ties with the French part (País Vasco, Gascony) and on both sides of the border the Basque country is very much in the hearts of the native people. In this chapter we shall restrict ourselves to the north of the País Vasco, in particular to the districts of Bizkaya (Vizcaya) and Getaria (Guetaria). We will use the Basque spelling with the Castilian in brackets.

GETARIAKO TXAKOLINA (CHACOLÍ DE GUETARIA)

You will not often encounter Txakolí (pronounced 'chakolí') outside the Basque country. A shame, because it is a particularly delicious wine to drink with fresh crustaceans and shellfish and is also a fresh, smooth aperitif. On little more than 99 acres around the towns of Zarautz, Getaria and Aia primarily white wines and a few red wines are produced. Owing to the rather heavy soil of clay and alluvial sediments and the cold, damp and windy climate you cannot expect too much finesse from these wines. Under these circumstances the native white hondarrabi zuri or black hondarrabi beltza never fully ripen. And yet the white, rosé and red Txakolí are very pleasantly fresh, often with a slight tingle of carbon dioxide on the tip of the tongue.

The quality is generally not very high, but they are great wines to enjoy with a few Basque friends – soon made in the local cafés – with a few *pinchos*, with *chiquiteos* (Basque tapas) of with some young idiazábal. Drinking temperature: 8–10 °C (46–50 °F) (blanco), 10–12 °C (50–54 °F) (rosado) and 12–13 °C (54–55 °F) (tinto).

BISKAIAKO TXAKOLINA (CHACOLÍ DE VIZKAYA)

This is the youngest scion of the Txakolí family. The vineyards for this Biskaiako Txakolina are situated around the city of Bilbao on approximately 148 acres of clay soil with alluvial sediments. Here too the climate is windy, cold and damp – nevertheless ideal for wine-growing. The grapes for this Txakolí are the same as those of the Getariako Txakolina: hondarrabi zuri for the white wines and hondarrabi beltza for the red and rosé wines. Drink these fresh, strictly dry, white, red and rosé wines in the local wine bars and harbor restaurants as an aperitif or as an accompaniment to seafood and fish or some nata cantabria cheese. Drinking temperature: 8–10 °C (46–50 °F) (blanco), 10–12 °C (50–54 °F) (rosado) and 12–13 °C (54–55 °F) (tinto).

THE HIGH EBRO VALLEY

In this high valley are situated the south of the País Vasco, Navarra, la Rioja and Aragón. All regions produce DO wines, apart from La Rioja, which makes Spain's only DOC, the Rioja. Rioja wines can also be produced, though, in part of Navarra and in the south of the Basque country (País Vasco).

The climate in this valley is much warmer than in the northwest of Spain, where the influences of the Atlantic Ocean and the Bay of Biscay make themselves felt. The climate is primarily continental, although the south of the Basque country is still influenced to a certain extent by the cold, damp air of the Atlantic Ocean. In the high Ebro valley the winters are cold and the summers warm, while the fall and spring are mild and slightly humid. Navarra and La Rioja have for years set their sights on the French market, including the Bordeaux district. A typical example of this is found in Rioja in the Enrique Forner (Marques de Caceres) bodega, which has enjoyed great renown in France under the name of Henri Forner. So it is no wonder that the style of these wines is influenced by its northern neighbor. Many of these wines are more like French or European wines, which does nothing to diminish their quality. The traditional white wines of the Ebro valley were often heavy and robust and went with the Basque cuisine (sea and river fish specialties). The traditional red wines were also sturdy and combined well, for example, with barbecued or spit-roast lamb and beef. Today the white wines are becoming increasingly fresher and lighter and the reds more aromatic, fruitier and finer in flavor. To make things clearer we are dealing with the Rioja wines under a single title and not per region.

RIOJA DOC

Rioja wines are made in three regions: the southern Basque country, Navarra and La Rioja (only the district has an article for Rioja, not the wines). La Rioja and Rioja wines owe their name to the small river Rio Oja, which joins the Ebro close to Haro. The Rioja district is subdivided into three regions: the northwest highlands of Rioja Alta, the northern vineyards of the Rioja Alavesa in the province of Alava and the lowlands of the Rioja Baja in Navarra and La Rioja. The entire region is protected from the cold north winds by the northern mountains of the Sierra Cantabria. The river Ebro, which has its source in the Cantabrian mountains, flows towards the Mediterranean.

Wine has been made in the Rioja district for more than 2,000 years, but the breakthrough in today's Rioja wines did not take place until the end of the nineteenth century. Previously mainly tempranillo grapes had been grown in the Rioja district. Only a few well-off aristocrats owned cabernet and merlot vineyards, because at that time it was fashionable to plant French grapes everywhere. When first the oidium and soon afterwards the *Phylloxera* destroyed the French vineyards, French winemakers were forced to travel to Spain to buy young cabernet sauvignon and merlot wines. They discovered the charms of the tempranillo wines and helped the Spanish to improve their methods of wine-making. This did not always go down well, as the local winegrowers did not really appreciate the know-all attitude of their northern neighbors. In addition most of the Spanish could not see the sense in expensive equipment and hygienic conditions. Fortunately there were some people with foresight, such as the famous Marqués de Riscal. Thanks to these people the Rioja district has developed into one of the most famous wine-growing regions in the world. The first Rioja wines to receive any kind of recognition were made from 100% Cabernet Sauvignon. Although Rioja wines were given the official DO recognition in 1926, it was still a long time before they came on to the European market under their

Atmospheric wine cellars in the Rioja

own name. The English still call these wines Spanish Claret or Spanish Burgundy, while the French imported gallons of Rioja into France in bulk for a song to boost sick Bordeaux wines. The Bordeaux wines therefore owe their good name largely to Spain, though the gentlemen of the French wine capital prefer not to be reminded of this. Rioja is now associated worldwide with quality and the name is mentioned in the same breath as Bordeaux and Burgundy.

The soil of the Rioja district consists mainly of a mixture of calcareous and iron-rich clay. By the banks of the Ebro alluvial soil also occurs, while the soil of the Rioja Baya also contains some sand. The better vineyards are situated at a height of 980–1640 ft, preferably in the northwestern part of the Rioja Alavesa (País Vasco) and Rioja Alta (La Rioja + a small enclave in the province of Burgos). Owing to the heavier soil and the lesser height (max. 300 m/980 ft), which means there is less cooling effect, the wines of the Rioja Baya are less refined and delicate than those of the other two Rioja regions. On the other hand, they are fuller and

ready to drink sooner and therefore easier to buy, especially in view of their relatively lower price.

In the high lands (Alavesa + Rioja Alta) the tail end of the westerly winds from the Atlantic Ocean cools the warm vineyards. In the north the strong winds from the Pyrenees are filtered through the Cantabrian mountains. This results in a cold winter, a mild, sunny spring, a warm summer and a mild fall with cool night breezes. While the highlands have a typically continental climate, in the Rioja Baya there is more of a Mediterranean climate with warm and dry summers with far more hours of sunshine.

The wines of the Rioja come in white, rosé and red. For the white wines the main grape used is the viura (elsewhere also known as macabeo or macabeu), which gives the wines its fine acidity. Malvasía is used as a supplementary grape. This is responsible for the fresh bouquet and the fine acids. A certain amount of garnacha blanca is also added to give the wines more roundness and alcohol. The rosé wines are often made from garnacha, sometimes with the addition of tempranillo and even white viura. However, more and more modern rosados are being made from the tempranillo. The red wines, finally, are principally made from tempranillo, often mixed with garnacha, mazuelo and/or graciano. The once so popular cabernet sauvignon is no longer planted and is disappearing from today's cuvees.

Rioja wines are categorized according to the year of harvest and type of maturing. The classification is given on the label, on the back label or sometimes on the sealing band. Rioja – without additions – indicates that the wine was bottled in its first year (vino joven) and should be drunk young. 'Crianza' means that the wine has been cask-matured for at least one year (red wines) or six months (white and rosé) in small barricas and the rest of the time has been matured in the bottle. These wines may not leave the bodega until their second year (white and rosé) or even third year (red wines). 'Reserva' is used for red wines that have been cask-matured for at least one year in oak barricas and then for at least one year in the bottle. White and rosé wines should be matured for at least six months in the wood and may not leave the bodega before their third year. 'Gran reservas' are special wines that are made only in top years. They have to be matured for at least two years in barricas and at least three years in the bottle. The wines (usually red) may not leave the bodega before their sixth year.

White (joven) Rioja wines are excellent, fresh and fruity. They make good aperitifs, but are also good with meals, for example with espárragos (asparagus), menestras

Rioja, a classic among the world's great wines

(mixed vegetable dishes), *merluza* (hake), *rodaballo* (turbot) or even with fatty, spicy sausage dishes, such as *chorizo a la brasa* (whole grilled chorizo sausage). Drinking temperature: 8–10 °C (46–50 °F).

White Rioja crianza/reserva/gran reserva are often rounded, full, succulent wines with varying aromas from citrus fruits to white fruits, flowers and wild herbs. Depending on the house style, they can be very fresh or actually very ponderous. Old-fashioned white Rioja wines are often dominated by the wood, while the modern wines put more emphasis on the fruitiness of, among others, the viura grape.

Drink these wines at mealtimes with fish dishes. As a basic rule, remember that the modern Rioja wines go with modern or light dishes, such as *menestras* (vegetable dishes) – choose, for example, *cardo,* a vegetable that looks like white celery, but tastes like artichoke – and with fish dishes of *rape* (monkfish), *merluza* (hake) or *rodaballo* (turbot) with fresh sauces. You can also go for crustaceans such as *cigala* (lobster) or *langosta* (crawfish). The rather old-fashioned, ponderous, heavily wooded Rioja wines come into their own more with heavier or more spicy fish dishes, for example with a lot of garlic, but also with vegetable dishes or soups with garlic as a main ingredient. Combinations of a traditional white Rioja with *revueltos de ajos* (a dish of scrambled eggs cooked with mild young cloves of garlic) or *bacalao a la Riojana* (heavily spiced hake with olive oil, onions, garlic and strips of pepper) are excellent. Drinking temperature: 10–12 °C (50–54 °F).

The rosado that has not been cask-matured is fresh and fruity. It makes a great accompaniment to *mariscos* (seafood), *menestras* (vegetable dishes, preferably with spicy chorizo) and *tortillas* (omelettes – choose *tortilla de patata*, a sturdy rustic omelette with potatoes). The crianza or reserva rosado need tasty fish dishes, for example *salmón* (salmon) or *trucha* (trout). Drinking temperature: 10–12 °C (50–54 °F).

The red Rioja wines that have not been cask-matured (joven) are mainly made from tempranillo. It is recommended to drink these wines young, while they are still fresh and contain seductive fruit. Great

combinations with a Rioja tinto joven are, for example, with *callos* (tripe with a Rioja Baya), *morcilla* (slightly sweet black pudding), chorizo or *menestras* (vegetable dishes, preferably *alubias al chorizo*, a wonderful combination of green beans, chorizo and a lot of garlic). Drinking temperature: 12–14 °C (54–57 °F).

The better Rioja tinto reserva and gran reserva deserve better dishes. The wines are full, elegant and sophisticated, with a distinct nuance of wood reminiscent of vanilla. Traditional Rioja wines often contain a touch of citrus fruits in bouquet and flavor, and fine acids. You will still find old-fashioned, ponderous Rioja wines on the market, but they are being made less and less. Just as well, as these wines were completed dominated, not to say contaminated, by the enormous amount of wood and they were often a tiny bit musty and oxidized. The modern top Rioja wines can compete with the best French or Italian wines, as regards price too.

Rioja blanco

Young Rioja

Cask-matured Rioja blanca

Drink your best Rioja tinto reserva or gran reserva with grilled or fried meat, such as *chuletas de cordero* (barbecued lamb cutlets), *cordero lechal asado* (sucking lamb roasted on the spit), *cabrito asado* (roast young goat), *asado de buey* (roast beef) or *cochinillo asado* (roast sucking pig). Reserve a little wine for

Rioja rosado

Cask-matured Rioja tinto

Rioja tinto gran reserva

a portion of idiazábal or zamorano cheese. Drinking temperature: 16–18 °C (61–64 °F).

NAVARRA

The district of Navarra is home to two designations of origin: the Navarra DO and the Rioja DOC (for Rioja see previous section). The landscape of Navarra is quite hilly. The Pyrenees form the natural border with France in the north. In the south the river Ebro divides Navarra from La Rioja. Navarra's western and eastern neighbors are the Basque country and Aragón respectively.

From 1234 to 1512 Navarra was part of France and the bonds with the Counts of Champagne were particularly close, as witnessed by the many historical monuments to be found in Navarra (including in Monjardín). It was the Counts of Champagne (Thibault I and II) who brought the vines to Navarra. According to reports the early-ripening tempranillo grape is supposed to originate from the old pinot noir, which was brought from Champagne. In 1512 the southern part of Navarra was annexed by the Spanish king Ferdinand the Catholic. The northern part above the Pyrenees remained French. Spanish Navarra flourished as never before thanks to its healthy agricultural activities, including wine-growing. Navarra is still of very great importance for Spanish agriculture. When the vineyards of Bordeaux were destroyed by the *Phylloxera*, the desperate French winegrowers came to buy their wines in Navarra and Rioja. This golden age did not last long, though, because the vineyards of Navarra were in turn reached and ravaged by the greedy louse. At the beginning of the twentieth century more than 98% of the vineyards had to be re-planted, this time on American root stock.

For years producers in Navarra were more concerned with making wines that were easy to sell than with establishing their own identity and strengths. When drinking rosé wines became fashionable, the bodegas of Navarra made an attempt to make a full, rounded and, above all, delicious rosé from the local Garnacho (Garnacha). Because there were few other rosados in Spain at the time, this rosado de Navarra

Bodega Guelbenzu in colonial style

soon become well-known. Unfortunately this fame had a flip side. When Navarra tried to give itself a profile as a region for good red wines this was not taken seriously. Navarra is still unjustly associated by many Spaniards (even by Spanish sommeliers and respected restaurant owners!) with the country of the rosado. Navarra deserves better.

It was also difficult for Navarra to work its way out from under the shadow of Rioja. Thanks to the enormous exertions of the local umbrella organization Evena (Estación de Viticultura y Enología de Navarra) and substantial subsidies from the government and from the EU, in the 1990s, Navarra managed to develop into a respected and renowned wine-growing region. As well as the previously mentioned authorities, the efforts of a number of very impassioned people was of importance in this, including the late Julián Chivite and Señorío de Sarria.

Navarra is now more interested in its own identity, its own terrain, even the many cooperatives. Some cooperative bodegas (as in Cascante) are still behind because European subsidies are coming in in dribs and drabs and essential modernization can only be carried out gradually.

The future of Navarra in any case looks very rosy. Within ten years Navarra will, by its own estimation, equal the standard of the Rioja and Ribera del Duero. Top companies like Chivite, Güelbenzu, Ochoa, Magaña and Virgen Blanca have already reached that standard, now it remains for the rest to follow. Navarra can grow only by gambling on quality and authenticity.

Bodega Castillo de Monjardin

Navarra: more than just rosé!

Maybe this will eventually bring the much sought after DOC?

Navarra's soil consists of well-draining soils of limestone and pebbles with a brown loamy upper stratum in the north (Valdizarbe, Tierra Estella, Baja Montaña and Ribera Alta) and a dry, sandy soil in the far south (Ribera Baja). In general the height of the vineyards varies from 790 to 1,770 ft.

In the north (Valdizarbe, Baja Montaña and Tierra Estella) there is a (semi-)continental climate. The further south you go, the warmer and drier the climate becomes. In Ribera Baja you come across almost desert-like scenarios. In the west (Estella) the tail end of the oceanic climate can be felt (slightly more rainfall and cooling west winds by the Ebro) and in Ribera Alta and Ribera Baja influences are more Mediterranean.

THE WINES

Just like the other Spanish wine-growing regions, Navarra uses age classification for the wines. The ordinary Navarra (vino joven) has not been cask-matured and is intended to be drunk young. The crianza wines have matured for at least six months in *barricas* and the rest of the time in the bottle. They may not leave the bodega before their third year. The reserva wines must have matured for at least a year in barricas and a year in the bottle. They cannot be sold before their fourth year. The gran reserva, finally, must be matured for at least two years in barricas and at least three years in the bottle. They may not leave the bodega until their sixth year.

Navarra also produces a little white wine made from Viura, sometimes supplemented by 30% Chardonnay. The wines of 100% Viura are very austere in their acidity and do not have the same roundness as the combined wines of Viura and Chardonnay. Both – pure or combined – taste fresh and slightly spicy and are pleasant aperitif wines or accompaniments to fish and shellfish. You can also drink them with *menestras de verdures del tiempo* (seasonal vegetable dishes), *caracoles a la corellana* (escargots stewed with garlic and herbs), *caracolillas de Navarra* (oven-cooked small escargots with a spicy tomato sauce) or *habas de Tudela* (fresh garden beans

Magnificent wine from the old vineyards of Julian Chivite

Probably the most famous rosado in Navarra

with, among other things, eggs and artichokes), Only a few wines of 100% viura reach a more than reasonable level. Gran Fuedo blanco from chivite is a must. Drink this superior wine for example with *cardo a la Navarra* (cardoon dish with béchamel sauce and ham) or *tortilla de Tudela con espárragos* (asparagus omelette). Drinking temperature: 9–10 °C (48–50 °F).

The better, more unusual white wines made from chardonnay can be of unprecedented quality, such as the first-rate 100% Chardonnay, Coleccion 125, from the same Chivite! The more common Chardonnay can be served with *espárragos de Tudela* (boiled asparagus, usually with a creamy mayonnaise) or *truchas con jamón* (mountain trout with strips of fried ham). The better Chardonnays can easily be combined with the excellent goose liver from Navarra, and also with all the better types of fish, for example *lubina* (wolf fish), *rape* (monkfish) or *rodaballo* (turbot) and other sea delicacies. 12 °C (54 °F).

Very rare and a class apart are the dry wines made from moscatel. These very aromatic wines are best offered as aperitifs, but they also combine particularly well with the local *espárragos* (asparagus). Drinking temperature: 10–12 °C (50–54 °F).

The rosé wines are usually made from garnacha. They are among he best rosados in Spain. Drink them young, when they are at their most delicious. Most rosados are full in flavor, rounded, spicy, fruity (red currants) and often quite strong in alcohol. In Navarra itself rosado is drunk with mixed hors d'oeuvres such as *pimientos del piquillo* (grilled pickled sweet/spicy red peppers), tomatoes with fresh mayonnaise and *jamón serrano* (raw mountain ham). Also delicious with escargot or tapas. Drinking temperature: 10–12 °C (50–54 °F).

The ordinary tinto vino joven of Navarra can be drunk with anything, even with the hearty Dutch cuisine (kale with sausage and suchlike). These fresh, fruity wines are also ideal for a picnic,

A bit old-fashioned, but still delicious!

At Chivite they are working hard on the future

lunch or barbecue. Drinking temperature: 12–14 °C (54–57 °F).

The tinto crianza require a nice piece of meat. As they have been cask-matured they have more to offer than their younger siblings. In bouquet and flavor you can trace a touch of vanilla, but it is mainly red fruits that dominate. Drink these excellent wines with cold meats (patés and terrines of rabbit, for example), fried chicken or turkey, coarse sausages or lamb cutlets (*chuletas*). Drinking temperature: 14 °C (57 °F).

The tinto reserva and gran reserva are little gems. Independent top bodegas such as Chivite, Magaña and Virgen Blanca make more traditional wines that in their youth contain more tannin than the cheaper wines from the Bodegas Coóperativas. They also have more flavor and strength, more finesse and breadth. These wines are recognizable from the great diversity in bouquet and flavor: vanilla (wood), blackcurrants, redcurrants, cherries, herbs (bay), licorice, etc. Serve these reserva and gran reserva with lamb, such as *cordero asado*, or beef with a garnish of fried mushrooms or *trufas* (truffles). Reserve a little wine for a spicy idiazábal or roncal cheese. Drinking temperature: 15–17 °C (59–63 °F). (17 °C (63 °F) for the gran reserva).

The first-rate sweet moscatel wines of Navarra deserve special

The best rosado in Navarra?

Navarra tinto crianza

Navarra produces some first-rate red wines

mention. These old-fashioned, syrupy, dark brown wines are reserved only for the true enthusiast, but the fresh, fruity and enormously seductive Moscatels, made by modern methods, such as Capricho de Goya from the Camilo Casilla bodega or the Ochoa or Chivite Vino Dulce de Moscatel are among the loveliest

muscat wines in the world. You can drink these divine wines with a fresh dessert, but because of their intrinsic quality they do not really need any accompaniment! Drinking temperature: 8–10 °C (46–50 °F).

Moscatel old style, heavy and sultry

Modern Moscatel, elegant, fruity and sensual

ARAGÓN

The autonomous region of Aragón, between Navarra and Cataluña, covers quite a large area from the foot of the Pyrenees to the Sierra de Javalambre, about 30 miles northwest of the town of Valencia. The most important towns in Aragón are Zaragoza, Huesca and Teruel. Three of Aragón's four wine-growing regions are right next to each other, to the west (Campo de Borja) and south-west (Cariñena and Calatayud) of the town of Zaragoza, in the province of the same name. The fourth wine-growing region (Somontano) is situated higher up and further east, to the east of the town of Huesca, almost on the border of Cataloña. Here too it is almost unbelievable how quickly and how well these four regions (especially Somontano) have adapted to the demands of modern vinification methods. Aragón was once notorious for its heavily alcoholic wines that were supposed to give its weaker siblings more strength. In a not too distant past wine here was sold almost entirely in bulk. Today the DO wines are gaining increasingly more ground, due to modernization in the bodegas themselves, but also to better supervision and control in the vineyards. The important thing is that all four regions have been able to maintain their own identity and authenticity. Unfortunately the quality of these wines is still largely unknown, even in Spain itself.

CAMPO DE BORJA

The wine-growing area of Campo de Borja is concentrated around the three towns of Ainzón, Albeta and Borja. In the Middle Ages Aragón wines already had a good reputation. After the *Phylloxera* plague obtaining a large number of high-alcohol wines was more important than improving quality. The wines were transported in bulk to secret destinations or delivered to the many wine bars in the town of Zaragoza. DO recognition was not obtained until 1980 and since then the winegrowers have been working slowly but surely on improving the quality and the image of these wines.

The soil of Campo de Borja consists mainly of a subsoil of limestone, with a few ancient rocks here and there, which provide good drainage, and an upper stratum of brown (alluvial) sand. The vineyards at the foot of the Moncayo are slightly higher up 1,950 ft than in the rest of the region 980 ft. The climate is the purest continental type. The white wines are made from viura (macabeo), the red and rosé wines from garnacha and cencibel (local name for the tempranillo), sometimes supplemented with a little mazuela or cabernet sauvignon.

The Campo de Borja blanco are fresh, spicy and quite simple. Drink them as an aperitif or with *migas* (oven dishes of breadcrumbs and a bit of this and that: an efficient and very tasty way of finishing up leftovers!) Other possible combinations: *sopa de ajo* (sharp garlic soup with lemon), *bacalao al ajoarriero* (for devotees of garlic and hake) or tronchón cheese. Drinking temperature: 8–10 °C (46–50 °F).

The Campo de Borja rosado are, above all, intended to be drunk young. Rosados harvested from Garnacha in a warm area are often hearty wines with a fair amount of alcohol. Those of Campo de Borja, however, are also surprisingly fruity and fresh. You can serve these excellent rosados all year round with spicy fish dishes or with chicken dishes incorporating garlic, paprika and Spanish pepper. Drinking temperature: 10–12 °C (50–54 °F).

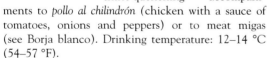

Campo de Borja

The Campo de Borja tinto (vino joven) also need to be drunk young. They are usually fresh and fruity, rounded and high in alcohol. Drink these wines as thirst-quenching accompaniments to *pollo al chilindrón* (chicken with a sauce of tomatoes, onions and peppers) or to meat migas (see Borja blanco). Drinking temperature: 12–14 °C (54–57 °F).

The Campo de Borja tinto crianza (at least six months in barricas and the rest of time in the bottle, minimum of three years old) has a lot of fruit, a hearty body and a fair amount of alcohol (13 to 14%). Serve this wine with *chuletas* (cutlets) or any other barbecued meat, possibly with *chilindrón* sauce. Drinking temperature: 14 °C (57 °F).

The Campo de Borja tinto reserva and gran reserva (at least one and two years respectively in barricas and one and three years respectively in the bottle) give you even more value for money. The long maturing in the wood and the bottle gives them a little more wisdom and roundness and to some extent compensates for the high alcohol percentage (13 to 14%). Drink these wines with fried or roast meat, for example *jabalí asado* (roast

wild boar) or other (furred) kinds of game. Drinking temperature: 16–17 °C (61–63 °F).

CARIÑENA

This is the oldest of Aragón's DOs (recognition in 1960). The vineyards are situated around the town of Cariñena in the province of Zaragoza. This town has been an important center for wine-growing and trade since time immemorial. The well-known cariñena grape (French: *carignan*) took its name from this town and then followed its own path via Cataluña to French Catalonia and the Rhône valley. The soil in the district of Cariñena is very much like that of Campo de Borja: subsoil of limestone and rocks with an upper stratum of brown (alluvial) sand. Close to the river, however, the subsoil is made up of slate and the upper stratum is rather more alluvial. Here too the climate is continental. In the spring night frosts regularly occur. The most important grapes of cariñena are the garnacha and cencibel (tempranillo), supplemented with a certain amount of cariñena, mazuela and cabernet sauvignon (red wines), and viura, possibly supplemented with garnacha blanca or parellada (white wines).

At one time the wines of Cariñena were renowned for their high alcohol percentage. Now they are often avoided for the same reason. The modern consumer prefers light, elegant wines. This is a great problem for an area in the hot sun! Yet the new generation of winegrowers has been quite successful in making very acceptable wines. Owing to the extreme heat of the summer and the type of soil, it is impossible, though, to make light-footed little wines in Cariñena. A blessing for lovers of characteristic spicy wines. Most of the red wines today have an alcohol percentage of 12.5–13%, which is considerably lower than the previous 15–18%.

The Cariñena blanco are fresh and reasonably dry. Because of the high acidity of viura (macabeo) the wines remain reasonably pleasant. Drink them as aperitifs, at meals with fish, poultry, migas or the local specialty *ternasco asado* (roast lamb first marinated in white wine with lemon and herbs). Drinking temperature: 8–10 °C (46–50 °F).

The Cariñena rosados are like those of Campo de Borja, but are slightly stronger in flavor and often heavier on alcohol. Drink them with lamb, migas with fish or chorizo, *pollo al chilindrón* (chicken with tomatoes, onions, paprika peppers and small Spanish peppers) or with a spicy, herbed hake dish such as *bacalao al ajorriero*. Drinking temperature: 10–12 °C (50–54 °F).

The red wines have the same age classification system as the other Aragón wines. The ordinary Cariñena vino joven is not cask-matured and is drunk young. The crianza has matured for at least six months in the wood and the rest of the time in the bottle, the reserva at least one year in barricas and at least one year in the bottle and the gran reserva at least two years in barricas and three years in the bottle. A feature is that the vinos jóvenes are mainly made from garnacha, while the older wines contain more tempranillo. You can drink the vinos jóvenes as fresh, but hearty, thirst-quenchers with all meat dishes. Drinking temperature: 12–14 °C (54–57 °F).

The crianza, reserva and gran reserva call for a hearty chunk of meat or game. They can be well worthwhile due to their strength and relatively high alcohol percentage. Their full and rounded flavor makes them excellent wines for cold winter days. Drinking temperature: 14–16 °C (54–61 °F).

Cariñena also has a long tradition in the area of old, sweet wines which are intentionally and frequently brought into contact with oxygen in the open air and later in large casks. These *rancio* wines do not, however, have the finesse of their French cousins.

Cariñena

CATALAYUD

This DO is definitely the least known of the four Aragón wine-growing areas. Unjustly, for while the wines of Campo de Borja and Cariñena are full and powerful, those of Catalayud show more finesse and elegance. Since the area is protected by the Cordillera Ibérica in the east and the Sierra de la Virgen in the north, the climate is more moderate than in the two previously mentioned regions. The wines therefore have a better balance between acidity and alcohol. The soil of Catalayud is made up of limestone on loam with an upper stratum of sand and loam in the north and of slate and gypsum in the south. The higher situated vineyards at the foot of the Sierra de la Virgen reach almost 900 m (2,950 ft), while the average height of the vineyards in the valley of the river Jalón fluctuates around 450 m (1,470 ft). The entire region has a continental climate. However, the wine-growing area remains far cooler than in Campo de Borja and Cariñena, owing to the high position of the vineyards and the cool mountain winds. A number of young winegrowers have realized the enormous potential of the area and their initial results are very promising. They have learnt to distill the characteristic aromas of Catalayud by improving the hopelessly antiquated equipment and relating terrain, climate and grape variety better to one another.

The white wines are made from viura (macabeo) and malvasía, now and then supplemented with garnacha blanca and the native juan ibáñez grape. Drink these fresh, friendly wines as aperitifs, with fish, chicken or white meat. Also delicious with a portion of tronchón cheese. Drinking temperature: 8–10 °C (46–50 °F).

The rosados are rather better in quality, full and fresh, but also quite fruity. They are mainly made of garnacha tinto. You can serve these wines with a regional buffet or with a selection of meats, fish, poultry or even lamb. Look at the label for the alcohol percentage: some rosados de Catalayud contain 14% alcohol! Drinking temperature: 10–12 °C (50–54 °F).

The tintos are excellent vinos jóvenes. Serve these pleasant, honest red wines with a barbecue, a picnic or simply with a chunk of (Spanish) cheese. Drinking temperature: 12–14 °C (54–57 °F).

The still rare crianzas en (gran) reservas made from garnacha, mazuela, tempranillo and cabernet sauvignon have a warm, full flavor, combined with a certain freshness and elegance. Drink these wines with all kinds of red meat, with game birds and small furred game or roast poultry. Because of their strength these wines are a good compliment to rich, spicy sauces. Drinking temperature: 16–17 °C (61–63 °F).

Calatayud tinto

SOMONTANO

Somontano, in the province of Huesca, is the most surprising region of Aragón for connoisseurs. Thirty years or so ago no one had ever heard of Somontano wines. Today you find them everywhere, in qualities from 'honest and tasty' to outstanding. Somontano is not hampered by an old-fashioned, suffocating tradition of wine-making. Experiments are being made in all areas and this can include the terrain and the climate. The best results emerge from a combination of traditional grape varieties and techniques with modern, better adapted grape varieties and vinification methods. The quality of wines made from daring combinations such as tempranillo and cabernet sauvignon, moristel and cabernet sauvignon, macabeo (viura) and chardonnay, and macabeo and Alcañon, is truly amazing. Imported grapes, such as gewürztraminer and pinot noir also do extremely well in Somontano.

The vineyards are situated on the sides of small mountains, at a height varying from 980 to 1,950 ft. The soil consists of a mixture of heavy clay and sandstone in the higher vineyards, supplemented by a certain amount of alluvial soil in the Ebro valley. Everywhere the soil contains a large quantity of minerals and trace elements – a blessing for wine-making. The climate is continental, but the proximity of the Pyrenees, which act as natural protection from the cold northerly winds, is quite beneficial for wine-growing.

The native grape varieties of Somontano, the white alcañon and the black moristel (not to be confused with monastrell!), go happily together with the rather more Spanish grape varieties of viura (macabeo) and garnacha. However, there is

Calatayud blanco

Somontano Pinot Noir

a huge amount of experimentation with numerous new grape varieties, such as tempranillo, cabernet sauvignon, merlot and pinot noir (black grapes) and chenin blanc, chardonnay, riesling and gewürztraminer (white grapes). The traditional white Somontano wines are made from Viura and Alcañon. They are fresh, light, dry wines that should be drunk young. The modern white wines are well though-out cuvées of viura, alcañon and chardonnay or chenin blanc. They are much fuller and surprisingly delicious. There are also some very interesting wines made from 100% riesling or 100% gewürztraminer. It is impossible to give appropriate advice on what to eat with each of these wines, but in general you can serve the traditional wines as an aperitif or with fairly light starters, while the more modern wines combine very well with fish or poultry dishes. Of course, a portion of tronchón is also always welcome! Drinking temperature: 8–10 °C (46–50 °F) for the traditional wines, 10–12 °C (50–54 °F) for the more modern ones.

The pleasant rosados of Somontano have the finesse and elegance of the best wines and the warmth and strength of the south. Drink these distinctive wines with fried or roast meat, or with grilled or fried sea fish with spicy sauces. Drinking temperature: 10–12 °C (50–54 °F).

The ordinary vinos jóvenes tintos of Somontano are pleasant, light wines made from moristel or garnacha. Great accompaniments at parties, meals *al fresco* and lighter varieties of meat. Drinking temperature: 12–14 °C (54–57 °F).

The crianzas and (gran) reservas contain less moristel and garnacha, but more tempranillo and/or cabernet sauvignon. Maturing in the cask gives these substantial wines more roundness and a good balance between alcohol and body. These magnificent and particularly exciting wines deserve the best meat, furred game or roast game birds you can afford. Keep a drop for a slice of mature Catalan garrotxa. Drinking temperature: 16–17 °C (61–63 °F).

Somontano Gewürztraminer

CATALONIA AND THE BALEARICS

The climate in the whole of Catalonia (Cataluña) is distinctly influenced by the Mediterranean, particularly in the coastal strip, where the air humidity is highest. The further and higher you go inland, the cooler the (micro) climate becomes. From Ampurdán-Costa Brava in the north up to and including Terra Alta in the south, society is closely associated with the sea and the mountains. This is reflected in the eating habits of the Cata-

Outstanding red wine from Somontano

lan people, which include a great deal of fish and seafood and from the mountains a lot of meat.

Catalonia has been famous for its red wines for years. They used to be predominantly heavy, sweet, old, oxidized wines of the *rancio* type (e.g. tarragona) or coarse, powerful and, above all, very alcoholic dry wines of the *priorato* type. Alcohol percentages of 13.5–18 were quite normal. Although you will still find many heavy red wines in these regions, today, owing to improved equipment and vinification techniques, first-rate red wines are produced in Catalonia. Just like in neighboring Somontano, there has been and still is much experimentation in Catalonia, but now growers know which grapes produce the best yield. The whole of Catalonia (and a large part of Spain!) ought to be eternally grateful to the great innovators Miguel Torres Sr and Jr for the magnificent work they have done in the Penedés. Incidentally, Catalonia supplies more than 90% of the Cava production.

AMPURDÁN-COSTA BRAVA

This is the furthest north of Catalonia's DOs, at the foot of the Pyrenees and directly bordering on France. Empordá-Costa Brava today makes outstanding, modern, light and, above all, fresh wines that are avidly bought by the visitors to the beaches of the Costa Brava, but are also increasingly finding their way abroad. This district has been allowed to use the DO designation since 1975.

The soil of Empordá-Costa Brava is formed by the limestone-like foothills of the Pyrenees. Almost everywhere the ground is covered in a thin, fertile stratum. Although the wine-growing region reaches as far as the sea, the best vineyards are situated further inland particularly on the hills in the sheltered valleys and on the sides of the western small mountains, at a height of about 200 m (650 ft). The climate is distinctly Mediterranean; however, the area cools down considerably, due to the Pyrenees. Many cold winds regulate the temperature and air humidity. One of these winds, the notorious Tramontana (Tramontane on the other side of the mountains) is feared most because of its great and often destructive force. To protect the vineyards from this wind the vines are firmly tied to poles. The grape variety cultivated the most is the mazuelo (local name of the cariñena), principally used for the many rosés, followed by the garnatxa (garnacha) and the white xarello, macabeo and garnacha blanca. They have been experimenting here for several years with 'foreign' grape varieties, cabernet sauvignon, ull de llebre (tempranillo) and the white parellada, for example, with varying results.

Catalan label from the maker of famous organic quality wines

Besides the rosados, blancos and tintos, outstanding Cavas are also produced in Empordá-Costa Brava. The largest producer in the area, the Perelada Group (Cavas del Ampurdán en Castillo de Perelada) has for many years given preference to and carried the DO Empordá-Costa Brava. If you happen to be in the area, be sure to pay a visit to Castillo de Perelada, the heart of Perelada, which houses very impressive centuries-old wine cellars and a wonderful glass and wine museum (visits by appointment).

The Castillo Perelada Cavas are excellent and favorably priced. Drink Cava extra brut, brut reserva or Chardonnay as an aperitif or with starters and sophisticated fish dishes, brut rosado as an aperitif or with starters, special fish dishes or even light meat starters and the sublime Gran Claustro at celebratory events, large and small.

Empordà-Costa Brava rosado

The rosados, made from garnatxa or garnatxa and cariñena, possibly with a dash of Ull de llebre (tempranillo) are excellent. They are dry, supple and fruity, with a distinctively elegant cherry red color. Surprisingly pleasant is the slightly sparkling Cresta Rosa from Cavas del Ampurdán, a soft, fruity rosado that has obtained its refreshing bubbles by natural fermentation (cuve close method). All Empordá rosados are the perfect accompaniment to delicacies from the Mediterranean Sea, such as *langostinas* (langoustines), or with sausage, such as the famous *embutidos de Vich* (spiced meat products from the little mountain town of Vich). Drinking temperature: 10–12 °C (50–54 °F).

The rare Cabernet Sauvignon rosados are of a totally different caliber from the other rosados: beautiful in color (light strawberry red), very fruity and fresh and with an elegant, sophisticated structure, combined with the warmth of the Mediterranean Sea. Drink them for example with starters of meat or poultry, terrines or patés. Drinking temperature: 10–12 °C (50–54 °F).

Most of the Empordá-Costa Brava white wines are made from garnatxa blanca and macabeo, possibly supplemented with the juice of garnatxa tinta to give it more backbone and xarello or even chardonnay for more roundness. All these wines are without exception fresh, fruity, modern wines that should be drunk

Cabernet Sauvignon rosado

quickly. A very special wine is the slightly sparkling fish wine Blanc Pescador from Cavas del Ampurdán. This wine is obtained by natural fermentation (cuve close).

Drink all these white wines as aperitifs or with light crustacean, shellfish or fish dishes. Also delicious with the local garrotxa. Drinking temperature: 10–12 °C (50–54 °F).

The rare 100% chardonnay wines, which are still experimental, but all the same particularly delicious, retain their attractive color and characteristic fruity aromas by short cask-maturing in French oak barrels. There is just a hint of vanilla in the background. The texture of these wines is light and elegant and reminiscent of the good Chardonnays from French-Catalan Limoux.

Delicious with *langosta* (lobster), grilled simply *a la plancha* or incorporated into a dish, such as *langosta a la catalana*, which includes onions, carrots, garlic, herbs, brandy and a tiny bit of …. chocolate! You can of course also go for a rich fish dish (e.g. monkfish). Drinking temperature: 12 °C (54 °F).

The red wines are usually made from a cuvée of garnatxa and cariñena. A large proportion of these wines are vinos jóvenes, intended to be drunk quickly, for example with a nutritious Catalan single-pan meal, such as *coneja con caracoles* (doe rabbit with snails and herbs) or *tortillas* (substantial omelettes). Drinking temperature: 12–14 °C (54–57 °F).

For several years better Empordá-Costa Brava wines have been coming on to the market. They are primarily intended for export. If you look carefully you will find excellent crianza and reserva wines (e.g. at Castillo de Perelada). The crianza wines are usually matured in American oak casks, giving them a decidedly sickly and vanilla-like aroma and flavor. The flavor is deep, warm and particularly pleasant.

Drink these wines with grilled lamb cutlets, *costillas*, often served with garlic sauce, *alioli*, or various piquant sauces, such as *sofrito*, *picada* or *Romesco*. But you can, of course, drink them with any other grilled meats, with game birds, rabbit or poultry. Drinking temperature: 14–16 °C (57–61 °F).

Chardonnay blanco seco

The magnificent reserva tintos (twelve months first in American, then French oak casks and two years in the bottle) hold much promise for this area. The grape varieties used are the traditional garnatxa and cariñena, to which preferably about 40% cabernet sauvignon and 20% mazuela (tempranillo) is added. The result is assured: dark red wines with amber-colored hues and a full, elegant warm flavor, in which the wood complements, rather than dominates the fruitiness. Excellent wine at a very reasonable price. Drink this

reserva (Castillo de Perelada) with better kinds of meat, preferably roasted or fried (*asados*), or with game birds and light furred game. Drinking temperature: 16–17 °C (61–63 °F).

Also from Castillo de Perelada comes a rare 100% Cabernet Sauvignon which has been matured first in American and then French oak casks for eighteen months and then several years in the bottle. This wine is full, quite rich in tannin, but well balanced (alcohol, tannins and acids). Drink this aromatic, complex wine with a really special cut of beef. Drinking temperature: 17 °C (63 °F).

If you want to try a very unusual, traditional gran reserva of 80% cariñena and 20% garnatxa, you should go to Cellers Santamaría. Magnificent, full, warm wine that is best drunk in company

Reserva tinto

with *asados*. Drinking temperature: 16 °C (61 °F).

Finally an extra mention for the old-fashioned rancio wine made from garnatxa d'emporadá. These wines are very sweet and syrupy and often have distinct aromas of burnt coffee and cocoa. Although they often do duty as a sweet aperitif or winter-warmer, I recommend to you the more unusual combination of a glass of good Garnatxa with *langosta a la catalana*, a casserole of lobster, incorporating brandy, garlic, saffron, vegetables and chocolate. It is quite easy to get used to a good rancio wine. Drinking temperature: depending on use 8–16 °C (46–61 °F).

ALELLA

The wines of Alella received their DO recognition as early as 1956. The history of this small wine-growing region brings us back to Roman times and maybe even slightly earlier. The original district for producing Alella wines is around the small town of Alella, at a height of about 295 ft.

100% cabernet sauvignon

The soil in these old vineyards consists primarily of a granite subsoil with an upper stratum of sand. Since 1989 the more recent vineyards of the Vallàs officially belong to the Alella district. These vineyards are much higher, at the foot of the Cordillera Catalana (up to 835 ft), on a soil of limestone subsoil with a sandy upper stratum. These higher vineyards remain somewhat cooler than those around Alella, in spite of the warm Mediterranean climate. Most of these lower lying vineyards are well protected, though. Alella makes white, red and rosé wines.

The white Alella wines are primarily made from pansá blanca (the local name for xarello) and Garnacha blanca, sometimes supplemented with macabeo or even partly replaced by the 'foreign' chenin blanc and chardonnay. The traditional Alella wines are characterized by a surprising freshness and fruitiness.

Drink these light, dry white wines as aperitifs, with the famous Mediterranean dishes of fish, crustaceans or shellfish, or with fresh garrotxa goat's cheese from the Vallàs. Drinking temperature: 8–10 °C (46–50 °F).

The rare – still to some extent experimental – 100% Chardonnay wines are very promising. It appears that the Chardonnay does particularly well in the gravel-rich upper stratum of the Alella vineyards. These Chardonnays are elegant, full, fresh, fruity and rounded. They go excellently with crustaceans, such as *langosta* (lobster) eaten in large quantities locally. Drinking temperature: 12 °C (54 °F).

The rosados and tintos of Alella are made from the unique pansá rosada, the ull de llebre (tempranillo) and the garnatxa (Tinta and Peluda). Although in general they are of very acceptable quality, you will not come across these wines very often abroad. Drink these wines during your visit to the area with one of the many local specialties, such as *embutidas* (spiced meats) and *escudellas i carn d'olla* (a famous meat casserole with egg and vegetables). Drinking temperature: rosado 10–12 °C (50–54 °F), tinto 12–14 °C (54–57 °F).

PENEDÉS

Thanks to the innovative and meticulous work of the Torres family, Penedés has become world-famous in a very short time. One tends to forget that not so very long ago very little of any consequence grew under the sun of Penedés. Most of the wines made were rancio wines of moderate to reasonable quality. Hardly anywhere else in the world has there been such a rapid response to the changes on the wine market in such a short time (about thirty years) as in Penedés. The breakthrough in this district is also due to the sudden explosive demand for Cavas. Because the district does not have a grand history of wine, the best companies are able to experiment almost without hindrance with various varieties of grapes and vinification methods. To begin with mostly white wines were produced, using the same grapes as Cava as a basis. The initial results with xarello, macabeo and parellada could not, however, be described as anything more than acceptable. Then they discovered that the chardonnay not only thrived in the local climate, but also lent itself well to the large-scale, almost Californian-style, new vinification policies of the most modern Catalan bodegas. Vinification methods also changed radically: Miguel Torres was the first wine-maker in Spain to start making wine in stainless steel tanks, keeping a constant check on temperature. The cold vinification method helped to change the ponderous white wines into fresh, fruity wines that went equally well with the local fish dishes and with modern cuisine. This daring changeover has turned out to be a great success. Only later did they experiment with red wines, with varying success. Naturally, these red wines also had to be made of French grape varieties, preferably the most aristocratic, such as cabernet sauvignon, cabernet franc, merlot and pinot noir. Here too initial results were disappointing. The best wines came from cuvées of native and foreign grapes, such as garnatxa, cariñena, ull de llebre (tempranillo) and cabernet sauvignon. Grapes such as samsó and monastrell also occur in these cuvées now and then. Only a few companies have been able to make first-rate red wines on a level with the white.

Penedés is situated just below Barcelona, spread across two provinces, Barcelona and Tarragona. While San Sadurní d'Anoia is the center of Cava production and trade, the world of still wines is concentrated around the village of Vilafranca del Penedés. The vineyards lie

Miguel Torres, the man who made Penedés world-famous

between the Mediterranean coastal strip and the central high plain, the Meseta. Along the coast are the vineyards of the Baix Penedés (820 ft high). This is the warmest area and the wines produced here are intended for everyday use. The slightly higher lying vineyards of the Medio Penedés 820–1650 ft produce the bulk of the quality wines. The vineyards of the Alt Penedés are a little higher still (1650–2625 ft) and therefore cooler. Here, at the edge of the Meseta, the very best grapes are produced for the top wines. Although as a rule the lowest regions are the warmest and the highest the coolest, there are so many microclimates in this region of 12,350 acres that there is a suitable combination of grapes, soil and microclimate for every winemaker. The soil varies considerably less than the climate. The coastal strip has a sandy upper stratum, while the uplands contain more clay. However, the subsoil is very calcareous everywhere and contains a high proportion of trace elements, which are very beneficial for the growth and health of the vines.

The Penedés white wines are extremely varied. Most of them are cuvée wines of local and foreign grapes. The base grapes for Cavas (parellada, macabeo and xarello) are often blended with chardonnay or sauvignon blanc, allowing numerous types and varieties of flavor. In general the ordinary white wines of the Penedés are dry, fresh and fruity, primarily intended to be drunk young. These great aperitif wines can also accompany *mariscos* (shellfish), *langostinos* (small lobsters) or *gambas*, especially if they are served with *aioli*. Drinking temperature: 8–10 °C (46–50 °F).

The better white wines are often made from one or a maximum of two grape varieties. The dry versions contain 100% chardonnay, 100% parellada, 100% riesling, 85% sauvignon and 15% parellada or 85%

chardonnay and 15% parellada. Each one of these wines is well worth discovering and they all have very individual character. You can offer them as aperitifs, or with shellfish and crustaceans, fish, white meat and poultry. Drinking temperature: 10–12 °C (50–54 °F).

The top wines of Penedés are undoubtedly the cask–matured wines made from 100% chardonnay (Milmanda from Miguel Torres or Jean Leon Chardonnay, for example). These wines are powerful, rich in bouquet and flavor, fresh and sophisticated, with very nice acids. Bouquet and flavor are reminiscent of vanilla, grilled hazelnuts, butter,

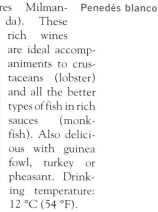

Penedés blanco

toast and cocoa (Jean Leon Chardonnay) or of fresh melon and exotic fruits, butter, toast, vanilla and truffle (Torres Milmanda). These rich wines are ideal accompaniments to crustaceans (lobster) and all the better types of fish in rich sauces (monkfish). Also delicious with guinea fowl, turkey or pheasant. Drinking temperature: 12 °C (54 °F).

Blanco of 100% Garnatxa   **Blanco of 100% Chardonnay**

The slightly sweet wines of the Penedés are also very surprising. In particular the slightly sweet wines made from muscat and gewürztraminer are especially exciting, with rich aromas of spices, flowers and fruit (lavender, aniseed, rose, orange-blossom, peach and sweet apples). You will also come across the strangest aromas in the surprising wines made from parellada, such as quince, ripe bananas, sweet grapes, honey and acacia. Drink the Muscat/Gewürztraminer wines (e.g. Viña Esmeralda from Torres) with light starters such as avocado and prawn cocktail, melon and jamón serrano, asparagus and ham on the bone or with poultry or pork in (oriental) sweet and sour sauces. Drinking temperature: 8–10 °C (46–50 °F).

Jean Leon top Chardonnay

One of the nicest white wines in Spain

The dry rosados of the Penedés are mainly made from garnatxa and cariñena and are fresh and fruity (cherries, plums), with floral nuances (iris, mimosa). You can serve them as aperitifs, with a few slices of chorizo, olives and garrotxa cheese and with paella, *gambas a la plancha* or *gambas al ajillo* (large barbecued prawns, with or without garlic), pasta dishes with saffron and tomato cream sauce or with oriental cuisine (in particular Thai). Drinking temperature: 10–12 °C (50–54 °F).

Among the red wines of Penedés you will find Spanish-style wines, made primarily from tempranillo and garnatxa, but also wines that seem more European, made from cabernet sauvignon, pinot noir, merlot and cabernet franc, possibly blended with tempranillo.

A few tried and tested wine and food combinations are: vino joven Tempranillo with meat paella, light meat dishes; Garnaclia/Cariñena with casseroles, game birds and poultry, Pinot Noir/Tempranillo with Asados (roasts), chicken, lamb and rabbit and Cabernet Sauvignon/Tempranillo with roast meat, fillet of beef and game. Drinking temperature: 12–14 °C (54–57 °F).

The top red wines, made from grapes from one or two of the better vineyards, deserve rather more culinary attention. A few suggestions are: Pinot Noir with grilled meat, game and creamy cheeses and Cabernet Sauvignon (reserva) with roast fillet of beef, rib or game. Drinking temperature: 16–17 °C (61–63 °F).

Penedés also has a few sweet wines. The Moscatel wines are made from Muscat (Grano Menudo and/or Alexandría) and are particularly aromatic (orange-blossom, honey, crystallized orange peel, lemon peel, currants, roses, geraniums, lilies, tobacco, spices). Buy a well-known and, above all, reliable brand, such as the Torres Moscatel d'Oro and the Vallformosa Moscatel. Drink these sweet wines on their own, purely for pleasure. Drinking temperature: 6–8 °C (43–46 °F).

Here and there you will still come across a few old-fashioned rancio wines made from Garnaclia. Better than these are the dessert wines made from Garnaclia and Cariñena, made in stainless steel tanks and then matured in American oak casks. It is difficult to tell what you can taste! Probably a suggestion of dates, plums, red fruit jam, spices and vanilla. Here too we offer you a very exciting culinary combination: *langosta al Sangre Brava*, a casserole of lobster with a Sangre Brava wine sauce. Drink the Torres red liqueur wine Sangre Brava with it… sublime! For the less adventurous they are excellent combined with the fresh Catalan *crema quemada* or *crema catalana*, the famous egg cream with a thin, caramelized crisp topping. Drinking temperature: 8–12 °C (46–54 °F).

TARRAGONA

Tarragona is the largest DO region in Catalonia. The wine-growing area is a continuation of that of Penedés, tucked between the Mediterranean and the foot of the Cordilleras Corstero Catalanas. The region is bordered in the south-west by the vineyards of Terra Alta. In the south-western part of the area is the enclave of Priorato, also renowned for its heavy red wines. The trade in Tarragonese wine is concentrated around the capital of the province of the same name and the small town of Reus. In the western part the small town of Falset is the center for the Tarragona Classica.

Tarragona is sub-divided into two sub-districts. The vineyards of El Camp de Tarragona (about 75% of the DO) lie at a height varying from 40 m (130 ft) near the coast to 195 m (640 ft) at the foot of the Cordilleras. The soil consists principally of an upper stratum of limestone and loam on an alluvial-type subsoil. The south-western part, below the Priorato enclave, from the town of Falset to the vineyards of Terra Alta, is situated higher up: around the town of Falset itself the vineyards are situated up to a height of 450 m (1,475 ft) and in the most westerly part, the valley of the Ebro, at about 105 m (345 ft). The soil of this Comarca de Falset consists of a subsoil of granite with a thin upper stratum of loam and limestone around Falset and an

Tinto Tempranillo

Delicious with grilled meat

Slightly sweet wine made from Muscat and Gewürztraminer

Delicious fruity rosado

Drink great wines with roast beef or game

Cabernet Sauvignon reserva

Moscatel, fresh and sweet

alluvial soil in the valley of the Ebro. The climate is mainly Mediterranean, but the higher vineyards remain slightly cooler in the summer. The requisite rainfall comes mainly in the spring and fall, while the summers are warm, dry and long. In the valley the winters are mild, higher up somewhat more severe (semi-continental). The most important grapes in Tarragona are the white macabeo, xarello, parellada and garnacha blanca, and the black garnacha, mazuelo (cariñena) and ull de llebre (tempranillo). Naturally Tarragona has not escaped the experimental planting of, among others, cabernet sauvignon, merlot and chardonnay. Only cariñena and garnacha may be used for the vineyards of the Comarca de Falset. In total six different types of wine are made in Tarragona:

- El Camp blanco and rosado: dry, fruity wines for everyday use. The El Camp tintos, primarily made from garnaclia, possibly supplemented or even replaced by one of the other permitted black grapes, are great wines for parties or everyday meals. Drinking temperature: blanco 8–10 °C (46–50 °F), rosado 10–12 °C (50–54 °F) and tinto vino joven 12–14 °C (54–57 °F).
- the better El Camp red wines, which contain a larger proportion (sometimes even 100%) of tempranillo and are very suitable for cask-maturing. Tarragona has crianza, reserva and even gran reserva wines, but you rarely come across them outside the area. Delicious with red meat, lamb or grilled poultry. Drinking temperature: 14–16 °C (57–61 °F).
- the Falset tintos, which are spicy and heavy, with at least 13% alcohol. You will not often come across these red wines outside the area, either. Drink them in Spain with game, fried or grilled red meat, fried pork with spicy red sauce or pungent sheep's cheese from the mountains. Drinking temperature: 14–16 °C (57–61 °F).
- the Tarragona Classico (also written as Clásico): the old-fashioned Tarragona liqueur wine, mostly made from 100% Garnacha. The wine must contain at least 13% alcohol and have matured for at least twelve years in oak casks. Every one of these is a genuine museum piece. Drink this sweet red Tarragonese wine on its own after meals. Drinking temperature: according to taste 8 °C (46 °F) or at room temperature (for those with a sweet tooth).

Finally there are the old-fashioned Tarragona rancio wines, which often come out at more than 17% alcohol. These wines have been allowed to mature for a time in the warm sun in glass demi-johns. The flavor is reminiscent of a dry Madeira wine, but with far less finesse. Drinking temperature: 8–10 °C (46–50 °F).

It is a real shame that so much potential for making good wines is denied simply to make a quick profit. On the export market there is still far more bulk Tarragonese wine sold than bottled quality wine. Unfortunately the figures do not show what happens to this bulk wine. Luckily the Spanish themselves are setting a good example by buying increasingly more bottled Tarragonese wine, which should – hopefully – give the winegrowers and foreign buyers something to think about.

PRIORAT/PRIORATO DOC

Priorat – Priorato in Castilian – is one of the oldest wine-growing regions in Catalonia. The landscape is perfectly interpreted by the wines: the strength of the mountains, the heat of the sun, the gentleness and sincerity of the valleys, the heavenly aromas spread by the mountain winds, the tough granite soil, the glittering of the little mica stones in the sun…few wines in the world have such a good story to tell as those of Prioritat. A Carthusian monastery (Priorat) was built on the spot where, about a thousand years ago, a shepherd had a vision of angels entering heaven via a secret staircase. Only ruins remain of that monastery today, but the village built around it, Scala Dei (the staircase to God), still exists and is a prosperous wine center.

Priorat has been renowned for its powerful, warm and very alcoholic red wines for centuries. While most kinds of yeast stop working at around 14.5 or 15% alcohol, fermentation continues in Priorat up to as much as 18% alcohol – unique in the world. Because of their high alcohol percentage and their enormous strength these wines keep very well and they also have no problems in traveling. Although increasingly more blanco and rosado is being produced in the Priorat, there is a hard core of aficionados for the rare red Priorat. These are quite unique wines, which, in spite of their high percentage of alcohol still have enough strength, body, finesse and, above all, elegant acids to be first-rate. You ought at least once in your life to taste a glass of genuine, classic Priorat. These wines are among the most expensive in Spain, so if it's cheap it is not genuine Priorat!

The Priorat district is very hilly: the hills of Montsant reach a height of about 3,940 ft and are intersected by deep river valleys. The vineyards are situated at a height of 330–1,970 ft, on a special soil that looks rather like a striped tiger-skin, the *licorella*.

This kind of soil is as unique as the wines produced here. The underlying soil of volcanic origin has alternating bands of reddish quartzite and black slate. The fertile upper stratum is formed by broken up slate and mica. The steep vineyards on the hills of Montsant are reminiscent of those in the Douro valley in Portugal. Since the sides of the hills are so steep, the vines are often planted on terraces, to stop them being washed away. Needless to say, this type of cultivation allows no room for mechanization. Even the climate of Priorat is different from elsewhere. The continental climate is softened to some extent by the warm southeasterly Mistral, while the cold and often damp north winds blow right into the valleys. In general the winters here are quite cold, but not extreme, while the long summers are warm and dry.

Red Priorat from Scala Dei

The grape variety most frequently used in Priorat is garnacha (tinta and peluda), sometimes supplemented with mazuelo (cariñena). Garnacha blanca, macabeo and a minimal amount of pedro jiménez are used for the rare white wines and the liqueur wines. For several years experiments have also been going on in Priorat with different varieties of grape, including chenin blanc, pinot noir, syrah and cabernet sauvignon. Most of the experiments take place in a flatter, lower area around Gratallops. They are trying to find out how well these foreign grapes adapt here and whether they can be used singly or in combination with other (native) grapes. Initial results are very promising. The region around Scala Dei, situated higher up, still continues to produce only traditional wines, however.

The vinos jóvenes blancos, rosados or tintos, some of them experimental, are in general fresh, pleasant wines for everyday use. They are made to drink young with local or modern European cuisine. Drinking temperature: blanco: 8–10 °C (46–50 °F), rosado 10–12 °C (50–54 °F) and tinto vino joven 12–14 °C (54–57 °F).

There are also the famous red Priorat wines, in the qualities of crianza (at least one year in the cask and a minimum of three years old), reserva (at least one year in the cask and at least two years in the bottle) and gran reserva (at least two years in the wood and at least four years in the bottle). Depending on their age, the wines are of varying shades of black, intensely aromatic (blackberries) and very full-bodied, with an alcohol content of 13.5 to 18%. One of the best and most spectacular Priorat wines is made by the renowned Spanish oenologist José Luis Pérez. This is the Martinet bru, an impressive monument to wine, while the slightly more modern Clos Martinet could be a forerunner of what Priorat might become this century. It is less alcoholic and much fruitier.

Traditionally a full-bodied Priorat is drunk with heavy, nutritious meals such as *escudella i carn d'olla*, a Catalan meat casserole with egg and vegetables. Also great with old-fashioned game stews (wild boar, venison, hare) or grilled rib of beef or T-bone steak with a hearty sauce. Drinking temperature: 14–16 °C (57–61 °F).

Priorat also makes excellent rancio wines that have been matured in the warm sun (condensed in glass bins or casks in the warm sun). This takes place in full contact with the open air, so the wines also oxidize. The Priorat rancio have simultaneously something of Madeira about them, with the strength of a Maury or Banyuls and the terrain flavor of good port. Drink them as a warm winter aperitif or after meals with a chunk of mature cheese and some nuts. Drinking temperature: as aperitif chilled 8–12 °C (46–54 °F), after meals at 16–18 °C (61–64 °F).

Finally there are the liqueur wines, *liquorosos* or *generosos*, made from garnacha and pedro ximénez. The best ones are like a good oloroso sherry. Great as an aperitif or with sheep's cheese, nuts and a few fresh, sweet grapes. Also delicious with *bel y mató*, a specialty of fresh cream cheese and honey, and *menja blanca*, an excellent dessert made of ground almonds, cream, brandy and lemon. Drinking temperature: 8–12 °C (46–54 °F).

TERRA ALTA

The soil of this rather inaccessible mountain region consists of a lower stratum of limestone and clay with a deep, poor upper stratum. The vineyards are situated at an average height of 1,310 ft, on well-aired and porous soil. The climate is continental with slight Mediterranean influences. The traditional wines of Terra Alta are the strongly oxidized rancio wines, which find increasingly fewer buyers. Far more interesting are the new developments concerning the more modern, light and fresh white, red and rosé wines.

You will find the Terra Alta blanco in various qualities, from fresh, light, dry vinos jóvenes to full, rounded reservas (six months in the wood and a minimum of three years old), and also semi-sweet to liqueur-like wines (generosos).

Drink the vinos jóvenes (macabeo, garnacha blanca) as aperitifs or with the traditional *pan con tomate y jamón*, a slice of Catalan rustic bread, lightly rubbed with a clove of fresh garlic and covered with slices of tomato, jamón serrano and sprinkled with plenty of good olive oil (virgin extra). Also delicious with a mixed grill of sea fish, *parillada de pescado*. Drinking temperature: 8–10 °C (46–50 °F). The reserva wines should be served with better types of fish, such as *rape* (monkfish) or *rodoballo* (turbot). Drinking temperature: 10–12 °C (50–54 °F). The semi-sweet to liqueur-like ones are best with fresh desserts such as *mel y mató* (fresh cream cheese and honey). Drinking temperature: 8–9 °C (46–48 °F).

The Terra Alta rosados are principally vinos jóvenes, made from garnacha and intended to be drunk young. They are fresh, light and very pleasant rosados, which combine well with fish, chicken, rabbit or meat paellas, *embutidas* (spiced meats), spiced single-pan dishes with chorizo or morcilla (black pudding), grilled fish and grilled or roast chicken and meat. Drinking temperature: 10–12 °C (50–54 °F).

The Terra Alta tintos can be young, fresh and light, of the vinos jóvenes type, or else adult, full and well-balanced, such as the crianza (six months in the wood, a minimum of three years old), reserva (minimum of one year in the wood and four years old) and gran reserva (minimum two years in the wood and six years old). These substantial wines have an average alcohol percentage of 13–13.5%. Serve them with red meat, game dishes or fried or roast leg of lamb. Drinking temperature: 14 °C (57 °F) crianza or 16 °C (61 °F) (reserva, gran reserva).

CONCA DE BARBERÁ

This wine region is tucked between the wine-growing areas of Tarragona and Costers del Segre. The Conca de Barberá, including the capital Montblanc, is bordered and sheltered by mountain ranges. The soil is particularly suitable for producing the base grapes for Cavas. In recent years, however, more and more time and money have been put into the production of rosados and tintos. The most modern bodegas have extended or even completely renewed their equipment. Cabernet sauvignon and merlot have been introduced, as well as the native trepat (probably a version of Garnacha), garnacha and ull de llebre (tempranillo). Initial results are particularly promising. The vineyards are relatively low-lying, in the valleys, at 655–1,310 ft. The subsoil consists primarily of limestone and the upper stratum of alluvial soil, with a great deal of lime. The climate is distinctly Mediterranean, but is moderated (and cooled) to some extent by the sheltered position of the Conca.

There are five types of Conca de Barberá wines:

- blancos made from parellada and macabeo, which are fresh and fruity and intended for quick consumption. Drink them, for example, as an aperitif, with *mariscos* (seafood), grilled sea fish, young goat's cheese or fish paella. Drinking temperature: 8–10 °C (46–50 °F).
- the experimental blancos made from chardonnay. Drink these hearty, full, rounded, above all, cheerful wines with better kinds of fish, such as *rape* (monkfish) or *rodoballo* (turbot) or with *langosta* (lobster). Drinking temperature: 10–12 °C (50–54 °F).
  - the 100% parellada blancos, which are fresh, light, dry and aromatic wines that are very much in vogue at the moment and make very good aperitifs or accompaniments to *mariscos* (seafood), for example, or *parellada de pescos* (mixed grill of sea fish). Drinking temperature: 8–10 °C (46–50 °F).
  - rosados, which are equally fresh and light, with a lot of fruit. They are principally made from garnacha, sometimes with trepat. Drink these wines with *embutidos* (spiced meats), grilled sea fish, fish, chicken or rabbit paella, or with local single-pan dishes with chorizo or morcilla. Drinking temperature: 10–12 °C (50–54 °F).

Conca de Barberá blanco

- tintos, which are increasingly often cuvées of garnacha and ull de llebre (tempranillo). The vinos jóvenes are very pleasant and, drunk young, can accompany almost anything. Drinking temperature: 12–14 °C (54–57 °F). The first crianza and reserva wines are very promising. There are some with a cuvée of garnacha and ull de llebre and others of cabernet sauvignon and ull de llebre (rare). The latter are of better quality, but the former give the impression of being more Spanish and less European. In any case both are being continued. The crianzas and reservas should be drunk with roast or grilled red meat, lamb and waterfowl and game birds. Drinking temperature: 16–17 °C (61–63 °F).

LÉRIDA (COSTERS DEL SEGRE)

The Segre is a tributary of the Ebro, which flows from the Pyrenees through the province of Lleida. The four sub-districts of the DO Costers del Segre lie on both sides of the river: Artesa (north east of the town of Lleida), Vall de Riu Corb and Les Garrigues (east of Lleida) and the smaller Raìmat (around the small village of the same name, to the west of Lleida). The soil of Costers del Segre consists almost everywhere of a sandy upper stratum on a subsoil of limestone. The climate is continental.

Costers del Segre has a long history as a wine supplier to the town of Lleida. The district's motto used to be: "Quantity first, nice flavor all the better". For the past thirty years or so a small core of innovative bodegas has been busy experimenting with grape varieties and vinification styles.

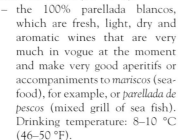

Conca de Barberá tinto

Superior red wine from Conca de Barberá

One name is indissolubly linked with Costers del Segre, that of Raìmat. This huge domain of about 7,400 acres (2,470 acres vineyards) was for many years the property of Raventós family (of the Codorníu Cava) and contained one of the most high-tech bodegas in Spain. This bodega was the driving force behind the great renovations in Costers del Segre. Increasingly more winegrowers have now distanced themselves from the mediocre little wines you will still come across in the wine bars in Lleida. The 'new style' wines, including Raìmat, are of a completely different caliber. While the traditional winegrowers go no further than macabeo, parellada and xarello for the white (base grapes for Cava) and garnacha with ull de llebre (tempranillo) for the red wines, modern winegrowers go for other possibilities. For instance, garnacha blanca and above all chardonnay have been added to the list of white grapes and cabernet sauvignon, merlot, pinot noir, monastrell, trepat and mazuela (cariñena) to the list of red. The best results are obtained in general with a cuvée of cabernet sauvignon, tempranillo and merlot or cabernet sauvignon and merlot.

The modern white wines are principally made from 100% chardonnay or a cuvée of chardonnay, macabeo and xarello. The better Chardonnay wines undergo short cask-maturing, which gives them a little extra weight and roundness. Drink these wines as an aperitif or with meals of the better types of fish, lobster, crab or even veal and poultry

CASTELL DEL REMEI

MERLOT 1996

COSTERS DEL SEGRE
DENOMINACIÓ D'ORIGEN
ELABORAT I EMBOTELLAT A LA PROPIETAT DEL CASTELL DEL REMEI PER CAMERLOT SL. PENELLES. LLEIDA. ESPAÑA RE-3635. L-MOS. PRODUCT OF SPAIN.
75CL 13% VOL

Fantastic Merlot

CASTELL DEL REMEI

BLANC PLANELL
2000

COSTERS DEL SEGRE
DENOMINACIÓN DE ORIGEN
MACABEO, SAUVIGNON BLANC
Y CHARDONNAY. VINO JOVEN
FERMENTADO EN FRÍO A 16°C.
COLOR AMARILLO MARFIL PÁLIDO
CON AROMAS BALSÁMICOS
VEGETALES A BOJ Y FLORALES A VIOLETA
GLICÉRICO Y MELOSO EN BOCA
CON REMINISCENCIAS A MANZANA
ELABORADO EN LA PROPIEDAD CASTELL DEL REMEI

ESTATE BOTTLED

Costers del Segre blanco

Raimat Cabernet Sauvignon

CASTELL DEL REMEI

GOTIM BRU
1998

COSTERS DEL SEGRE
DENOMINACIÓN DE ORIGEN
TEMPRANILLO, MERLOT Y
CABERNET SAUVIGNON. VINO
CRIADO DURANTE 10 MESES EN
BARRICA DE ROBLE AMERICANO.
COLOR CEREZA CUBIERTO. AMPLIO,
ESPECIADO, CON AROMAS A MADERAS,
CUEROS, BAYAS NEGRAS Y CASIS.
POTENTE ESTUCTURADO, SABROSO EN BOCA
ELABORADO EN LA PROPIEDAD CASTELL DEL REMEI

ESTATE BOTTLED

Gotim bru, ten months in the wood

in creamy sauces. Drinking temperature: 10–12 °C (50–54 °F).

The modern rosados range from quite drinkable to very pleasant, but do not reach the standard of the Costers del Segre white or red wines. The most satisfying results so far have been obtained with 100% merlot (Castell del remei)! When you are drinking this wine it is hard to tell whether it comes from the South of France, Italy or Spain. Drink these rosados with meat selections, at parties, lunches and picnics designed for pleasure and not for philosophizing about wine. Drinking temperature: 10–12 °C (50–54 °F).

The red wines, from crianza to reserva, are very worthwhile, particularly if you consider the price. The Raìmat Abadia reserva and the Raìmat Cabernet Sauvignon reserva are typical examples of an intelligent, loving approach to high-tech wines with respect for tradition. These excellent wines are of particularly good quality and reasonably priced. Drink them with a really special piece of meat, beef or lamb, chicken, game birds or waterfowl or small furred game. Drinking temperature: 16 °C (61 °F).

BINISSALEM

Binissalem is a relatively small DO wine-growing region (771 acres) on the island of Majorca (Mallorca), the only one to receive DO recognition in the Balearics and, what is more, the first outside mainland Spain. Winegrowers in the Balearics have made enough wine for local consumption for years. When the Balearics were discovered by Club Med and millions of tourists in the 1960s, the local wine trade went flat out. Most of the bodegas were content with this, but a few progressive wine-makers felt that more could be achieved. Their battle for quality and recognition was crowned in 1991 with the highly sought-after DO status.

The vineyards of Binissalem are situated on Majorca's high plain, above and across from Palma de Mallorca. The soil consists of limestone and a little clay and is very porous. The climate in the Balearics is typically Mediterranean. The choice of grapes is particularly interesting. The native grapes manto negro, callet (red) and moll (white) are used here, if wished blended with 'Spanish' grapes such as ull de llebre (tempranillo) or monastrell (both red) and macabeo and perellada (both white).

The blancos and rosados are fresh, light wines that need to be drunk young. Some bodegas are experimenting with short caskmaturing for white wines, with varying results. Great wines as aperitifs, with fish, paella and meat selections and with local specialties such as *acelgas con pasas y piñones*, an excellent dish of Spanish spinach, pine nuts, raisins, croutons and garlic, or the famous *sobresada mallorquina*, a wonderful sausage, soft in texture but spicily sweet in flavor. Leave a little wine over for the fresh and sour, but rather sharp mahón cheese. Drinking temperature: 10–12 °C (50–54 °F).

The tintos are decidedly fuller and richer in alcohol than the blancos and rosados. Try the typical crianzas and reservas of José L. Ferrer (Bodega Franja Roja) or the crianza of Herederos de Hermanos Ribas. You will definitely have to go to Mallorca to try these wines. So little of them is made that they are not exported. Drink these wines with meat dishes, preferably *asados*, fried or roast, but any good piece of meat with a rich sauce will go with them. Drinking temperature: 14–16 °C (57–61 °F).

THE DUERO VALLEY

We have already dealt with Bierzo, which is a designation of origin of Castilla y Léon. Officially Bierzo forms an entity with the four other wine-growing regions of Castilla y Léon. For geographical, and in particular, climatological reasons we are dealing with Bierzo (Léon) separately from the other regions, all in Castilla. The four remaining regions are located along the banks of the river Duero (Douro in Portugal). The DOs of Toro and Rueda lie to the south of Valladolid in a rectangle formed by the towns of Zamora, Salamanca, Segovia and Valladolid. The DOs of Cigales and Ribera del Duero are located to the north and east of Valladolid respectively.

The climate in the Duero valley is continental, but slightly less severe in the higher-lying regions (some vineyards reach to a height of 2,625 ft. In the neighborhood of the Duero and Pisuerga and in the higher regions there are changeable microclimates that are very favorable for wine-growing.

Surprisingly, partly due to the town of Valladolid and the famous university of Salamanca, the demand for good wine in this area is so great that most of the bodegas do not even need to export. The home market

CASTELL DEL REMEI

ODA 1998

COSTERS DEL SEGRE
DENOMINACIÓN DE ORIGEN
SELECCIÓN DE MERLOT,
CABERNET SAUVIGNON
Y TEMPRANILLO. CRIADO
DURANTE 12 MESES
EN BARRICA NUEVA
DE ROBLE AMERICANO.
COLOR CEREZA INTENSO
RICO Y PROFUNDO EN AROMAS
A VEGETALES, FRUTAS MADURAS, CACAO,
TORREFACTOS, PODEROSO Y RICO EN TANINOS.
VINO NO FILTRADO
ELABORADO EN LA PROPIEDAD CASTELL DEL REMEI

ESTATE BOTTLED

Oda, twelve months in the wood

accounts for the majority of customers. Non-Spanish wine drinkers can count themselves lucky with the export wines, which are of a very high standard, especially those of Ribera del Duero (red) and Rueda (white). Because the Castilians have always been great meat eaters, there is a constant need for full-bodied red wines (Toro, Ribera del Duero). Lovers of river fish can also find salvation in the local waters and the cellars of Rueda, which make marvelous white wines. Rueda and Ribera del Duero (and also Bierzo) have now got a name for themselves among wine connoisseurs. Names like Toro and Cigales still sound strange, though, to most people. Yet the wines from these areas – particularly that of Toro – offer excellent quality at a more than reasonable price.

TORO

Since its DO recognition in 1987 Toro has turned out to be a real asset to the top division of Spanish wines. The region covers only 6,200 acres and has currently only seven bottling bodegas. The area is very dry and has a continental climate with particularly low rainfall. The towns of Toro and Morales de Toro are the two most important trade centers in this designation of origin. Owing to the extremely hot climate and particularly because of the great drought, for many years the wines made here were heavy, almost syrupy, very alcoholic red wines. Thanks to radical modernization of the equipment and a completely different outlook on wine-making, the local bodegas have been able to elevate the Toro wines (particularly the red) to the best in Spain. In the north of the Toro district the soil consists of an upper stratum of sand and a hard subsoil of limestone. In the direct vicinity of the rivers Duero and Guareña the soil is more alluvial in type with a fertile upper stratum. Most of the vineyards are situated at a height of 1,790–2,460 ft. The climate is true continental. Because the vineyards are higher up, they are slightly cooled in the summer when the nights close in and by the gentle west winds. The most important grapes for Toro wines are the tinta de toro (a younger sibling of tempranillo) for the red and the malvasía for the white wines. Black garnacha and white verdejo grapes are used as supplements.

The white Toro wines made from malvasía (sometimes supplemented with verdejo) are fresh, soft, elegant and, above all, very floral in bouquet and flavor, with a touch of fruitiness.

Drink these wines young, as an aperitif or with the local *truchas montañesas* (mountain trout, often boiled in white wine or quickly fried) or salmon trout from the Esla, Aliste or Tera. A glass of Toro blanco also tastes fantastic with the local cheese zamorano. Drinking temperature: 8–10 °C (46–50 °F).

The Toro rosados are fresh, full and round and are slightly reminiscent of Navarra wines. They offer both fruit and warmth (up to 14% alcohol), which makes them just right for both sea fish dishes and grilled chicken, rabbit or even lamb or pork. Recommended combinations are: *arroz con cordero* (rice with lamb

cooked in the oven), *cochomillo asado* (roast sucking pig), *gambas al ajillo* (large prawns with garlic) and fish dishes incorporating garlic, olive oil, Spanish pepper and other piquant additions. Drinking temperature: 10–12 °C (50–54 °F).

The Toro tintos jóvenes are fresh, fruity and very pleasant. All Toro red wines must, by the way, consist of at least 75% Tinta de Toro. The climate and soil help to produce warm wines with a great deal of body. Alcohol percentages of around 14–15% are definitely no exception. It is striking that in spite of the high alcohol percentage these wines are better balanced than other wines from warm regions. This is mainly due to their lovely, fine acids. Even the simplest Toro tintos are a pleasant surprise.

Toro blanco

Drink an ordinary Tinto joven still at its fruity stage with, for example, grilled chicken, lamb, pork or beef roasts. The area around Zamora is not for nothing renowned for its Aliste and Sayago cattle and its sucking lambs. Drinking temperature: 12–14 °C (54–57 °F).

The Toro crianza and (gran) reserva are of exceptional class. They have a great deal of body, roundness, strength and warmth, but still the renowned freshness of the Toro wines. Warmly recommended with meat dishes cooked in the oven or barbecued, such as *cordero/lechazo asado* (roast lamb/sucking lamb) or *cochimillo asado* (roast sucking pig). You can also serve these wines with furred game or waterfowl. Drinking temperature: 16–17 °C (61–63 °F).

Toro tinto

RUEDA

Rueda is the area *par excellence* for white wine. This wine-growing region of almost 14,000 acres has been renowned since 1980 for its magnificent white wines. The climate is quite severe, continental, with deceptive frost attacks that cause a natural drop in yield. The ground consists of very poor calcareous soil and the vineyards are at a height of 2,300–2,625 ft. They have been making excellent wines here for centuries, but Rueda's breakthrough has really come since the arrival of the famous wine merchants from Rioja (Marqués de Riscal).

Rueda produces five types of wine: the simple Rueda (minimum 50% verdejo, supplemented with palomino or viura), the Rueda Superior (minimum 85% verdejo, usually supplemented with viura), the sparkling Rueda (minimum 85% verdejo) and the unusual liqueur wines Pálido Rueda and Dorada Rueda.

Rueda is primarily bottled young, but may have been cask-matured for a while. Particularly with the latter, the use of sauvignon, a new grape to the area, is coming increasingly into vogue. It is an ideal aperitif wine, but is also excellent with *espárragos* (asparagus), *mariscos* (seafood) or even *truchas* (trout). Drinking temperature: 8–10 °C (46–50 °F).

The Rueda Superior has rather more character than the simple Rueda. Although it may also be bottled young, the best wines have been cask-matured for six months or more. These wines smell of grass, hay, herbs and aniseed or wild fennel. They are an excellent accompaniment to the local river fish dishes, *ranas al ajillo* (frog's legs with garlic), sea fish in

Thoroughly cask-matured Rueda reserva

rich sauces (for example *besugo*, sea bream), crustaceans (*cigala* or *langosta*, scampi or lobster), white meat (*ternera*, veal) or a piece of not too old zamorano cheese. Drinking temperature: 12 °C (54 °F).

Rueda espumoso is made according to the *método tradicional* and has been lying in the bottle on its sediment for at least nine months (so, the same as a Cava). Some Rueda espumosos can seem quite full-bodied with their 13% alcohol, but most fluctuate around 12%. Drink these espumosos as aperitifs or as a refreshing contrast with a sweet dessert. Drinking temperature: 6–8 °C (43–46 °F).

The old-fashioned sherry-like liqueur wine Pálido Rueda is a *vino de flor*, just like its distant cousins from Jerez de la Frontera. In other words, during fermentation a film of wine yeast forms on the wine, protecting it against further oxidation. The wine has to mature for at least three years in oak casks before it can be sold. You can drink this wine with a minimum of 15% alcohol as an aperitif or after meals, for example with a hand-

ful of nuts and some zamorano. Drinking temperature: 10–12 °C (50–54 °F) or if you wish at room temperature.

The possibly even more old--fashioned liqueur wine Dorada Rueda is more like rancio: the wine has been in frequent contact with oxygen and aged more quickly, usually in the warm sun. These wines with a minimum of 25% alcohol may be sold only after at least three years maturing in oak casks. You can use them as old-fashioned, heavy aperitifs, if you like sweet wines, or after meals on their own or accompanied by a few *rebozos Zamoranos* (refreshing lemon cakes) or *pantortilla de Reinosa* (flat aniseed biscuits made of flaky pastry). Drinking temperature: 6–8 °C (43–46 °F) or serve at room temperature.

Rueda Viura + Sauvignon

CIGALES

Only fifteen bodegas bottle Cigales wine. This region, on both sides of the river Pisuerga, covers scarcely 6,700 acres. Cigales (DO since 1991) has a long history as a supplier of magnificent rosados. As early as the thirteenth century these wines were welcome guests at the Castilian court. Today first-rate red wines are also made in Cigales.

The climate of Cigales is continental. Owing to the ocean winds there is more rainfall here than in the rest of the Castilian wine-growing area. The vineyards are situated in the valley or on the sides of the slopes at a height of 2,300–2,625 ft. In the summer it is very hot here during the day, but the nights cool the vineyards down to such an extent that all the right circumstances are provided for producing superb wines. For the last ten years every effort has been put into complete renovation of the bodegas. When this is completely finished the whole world will hear about Cigales! The soil in Cigales consists primarily of limestone with a fertile upper stratum, strewn with large lumps of rock here and there, which provide good drainage.

The bulk of Cigales' wines consist of rosados (75%), considered to be among the best in Spain. The rosados should contain at least 50% Tempranillo (here called Tinto del País), if they want to claim the right to DO, possibly additionally supplemented with black grapes such as garnacha or even white grapes (verdejo, albillo or viura). It is quite customary here to make rosados by vinifying a blend of black and white grapes together. This gives the wines the strength of the black grapes and the freshness and aromas of the white grapes. The fairly recent designation of Cigales Nuevo is a vino joven with a minimum of 60% Tinto del País and a minimum of 20% white grapes. Its great freshness and fruitiness, coupled with slightly less alcohol, make the wine suitable for those new to wine-drinking or the student population. Drink this young wine at a party, a picnic or a barbecue and, above all, do not give too

Rueda Sauvignon, Rueda Superior and table wines from Castilla y Léon

much thought to it. Drinking temperature: 10–11 °C (50–52 °F).

The true Cigales rosados (therefore without 'nuevo' on the label) are made with the same percentage of grapes, but usually have more body, meatiness and alcohol. The aromas are very fine and elegant, principally fruity and fresh. These wines have a character all of their own and know how to seduce even the greatest haters of rosé wines. Drink these full-bodied rosados, for example, with sea fish, fried or roast chicken, lambs kidneys or other delicacies accompanied by garlic, olive oil, paprika peppers, Spanish pepper and chorizo. Drinking temperature: 10–12 °C (50–54 °F).

The best rosados have been cask-matured and are sold as crianzas. These wines are usually made principally from red grapes with a minimum of 60% tinto del país and a minimum of 20% garnacha or viura, for example. These rosados, which have been matured in the wood for at least six months, deserve the best oven-cooked fish (for example *dorado*, gilthead sea bream, or *lubina*, wolf fish) or poultry, lamb or game bird roasts. Drinking temperature: 12 °C (54 °F).

Finally, the Cigales tintos, made from a minimum of 85% Tinto del País, supplemented with garnacha and/or cabernet sauvignon, are on the rise. The first tinto crianza and even reserva wines have now arrived and are simply excellent. Surprising in these red wines is the combination of seductive fruitiness and very masculine strength and body. Drink these full-bodied red wines with roast beef or grilled or roast lamb. Drinking temperature: 12 °C (54 °F) for the tinto, 14 °C (57 °F) for the crianza and 16 °C (61 °F) for the reserva.

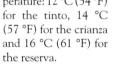

Cigales rosado

RIBERA DEL DUERO

In this 28,400 acre wine-growing region, situated in the heart of the diamond-shape formed by Burgos, Madrid, Valladolid and Soria, the best and certainly the most expensive wines in Spain are produced. Presumably everyone has heard of Vega Sicilia, but there are numerous other wonderful bodegas to be discovered in this region. Fortunately they do not all charge the same astronomic prices for their wines. Even so, the price for a good Ribera del Duero (such as Vega Sicilia, but there are

Cigales tinto

more top wines) is still considerably lower than that of similar quality French wines. It is definitely worth looking further in the area and to go for the second grade wines that offer relatively almost the same quality for a lot less money.

It is difficult to imagine that a wine like the famous Vega Sicilia has only been allowed to be sold as DO since 1982. Before then the wines from the banks of the Duero were just simple vinos de mesa. There was already strict control of the vineyards and wines of the small town of Roa in the twelfth century. While the aristocracy from the Rioja area was busy experimenting with strains of Bordeaux grapes, as well as the native Tempranillo, the aristocracy of Ribera del Duero was doing exactly the same, with – so it would seem – even greater success.

The best vineyards lie at a height of 1,850–2,200 ft, which is quite high in European terms. The rest of the wine-growing area is spread out in the valleys and at the foot of the hills. The ground consists of calcareous soil with an alluvial-type upper stratum near the river, calcareous clay at the foot of the hills and gypsum and limestone with a large number of trace elements in the higher vineyards. The climate is a combination of severe continental and moderate oceanic influences. For wine-growing the most important thing is that there is a great difference between the hot days and the cool nights, providing optimal growth. This is all the more important because, in view of the height of the best vineyards, the summers do not last long. Night frosts can occur even in the fall. A delay in the blossoming or growth of the grapes can have fatal consequences.

The grapes used here are, as well as the classic tinto del país, (tempranillo, also called tinto fino), cabernet sauvignon, malbec, merlot and garnacha. Although the great majority of Ribera del Duero wines consists of tintos, excellent rosados are also produced here.

The Ribera del Duero rosados are principally made from garnacha (also sometimes called tinto aragonés), possibly softened with a little white albillo. The ordinary vinos jóvenes are very pleasant rosados that you can drink young. The crianza rosados have been cask-matured and are slightly fuller and more adult. You can drink both types of wine as aperitifs, in Spanish style with *tapas*. The crianza wines can also accompany the nutritious local specialties of Burgos and the surrounding area, such as *morcillas*, (black pudding), *salchicas de Villarcayo* (sausages) and *jamón de cerdo blanco* (raw ham), together with the delectable *hogaza*

The top wine *par excellence* of both Ribera del Duero and Spain

– rustic bread. Serve the better rosados with *caracoles* (escargots) or *callos* (tripe). Drinking temperature: 10–12 °C (50–54 °F).

The simple vinos jóvenes tintos are intended to be drunk young. They are fresh, fruity wines (blackberries) that can wash down the local specialties without costing a fortune. Drinking temperature: 12–14 °C (54–57 °F).

The crianza wines have been kept for at least twelve months in oak casks and are stronger in flavor. They may not be sold before their third year. These wines are still very fruity, broad and elegant. You can serve these crianza with any type of red meat, or else, for example, with *perdiz* (partridge), *codornices* (quails) or *conejo* (rabbit). Drinking temperature: 14 °C (57 °F).

The full-bodied reservas have been kept for at least one year in wooden barricas and one year in the bottle. These wines call for fried or roast meat, such as *cordero asado* (roast lamb), *asado de buey* (roast beef) or *liebre* (hare). Drinking temperature: 14–16 °C (57–61 °F).

Ribera del Duero crianza

The top wines, the gran reservas, are the lot of only the few. Not only due to the high price, but above all because so little is made and most of the bottles are whisked off to royal or ministerial tables or to the best restaurants. If you have the opportunity of buying a Ribera del Duero gran reserva, do not hesitate. Drink these magnificent wines with the very best meat, for example fillet of beef with *hongos* (mushrooms) and *trufas* (truffles), or with *ciervo* (venison), *corzo* (venison from roe deer) or *jabalí* (wild boar; choose a tender piece). Drinking temperature: 17 °C (63 °F).

Not only the grandiose wines of Vega Sicilia (*Unico gran reserva!*) are worthwhile: some bodegas supply excellent wines often at a considerably lower price. Recommended bodegas for their good ratio of price to quality are:
Hnos. Perez Pascuas (Pedrosa de Duero):
  Viña Pedrosa gran reserva

Ismael Arroyo (Sotillo de la Ribera):
  Valsotillo reserva
  Valsotillo gran reserva

Peñalba López (Aranda de Duero):
  Torremilanos (gran) reserva

Protos (Peñafiel):
  Protos reserva

Rodero (Pedrosa del Duero):
  Ribeño crianza
  Ribeño reserva
  Ribeño gran reserva

Señorío de Nava (Nava de Roa)
  Señorío de Nava reserva

Vega Sicilia (Valbuena del Duero):
  Valbuena 5th año reserva

Ribera del Duero gran reserva

THE MESETA

The region of the Meseta is huge and almost flat. The wine-growing area comprises the DO regions of Vinos de Madrid and Méntrida (below Madrid), La Mancha and Valdepeñas (between Madrid, Ciudad Real and Albacete) and the brand-new DO Ribera del Guadiana in Extremadura, near the border of Portugal. The Meseta has an average height of 1,790 ft. The climate is continental. Anyone wanting to make wine here needs to have nerves of steel, a great deal of enthusiasm and, above all, outstanding basic materials. Not all vines can thrive in such extreme conditions. This area is primarily renowned for its plonk. But some outstanding red wines are also made that go very well with the other gastronomic specialties of the area: mutton and sheep's cheese. The districts of La Mancha, Valdepeñas and Ribera del Guadiana deserve a large pat on the back for their incredible race to catch up and the equally spectacular and radical turn-around in recent decades. They are focusing on producing serious, adult quality wines still at a reasonable price. However, it is disgraceful to see how the European wine trade only seems to be interested in the bottom end of wine production. In this foreign wine-buyers are decades behind the local winegrowers.

Torremilanos reserva

VINOS DE MADRID

Madrid, the capital of Spain, for centuries enjoyed more renown as a great buyer of wine than as a producer. The

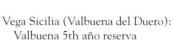

Señorío de Nava reserva

Ribera del Duero reserva

**Vega Sicilia Valbuena
5th año reserva**

Vinos de Madrid have been on the market only since 1990. These wines are produced in the immediate vicinity of Madrid. In view of the great potential for local sales, no attempt is currently being made to promote Vinos de Madrid outside the area. You will therefor rarely find these wines outside the Meseta.

In fact, wine was made in this region before were the Spanish capital existed, in 1561, albeit only for the personal use of the local farmers. The granting of the DO must principally be seen as a kind of 'political' choice, to give the local winegrowers an incentive to go for higher quality. And it seems to be working, even if wine is still made here and there that hardly deserves the name of wine.

There are three sub-districts in Madrid's wine area, which totals almost 12,350 acres: Arganda, Navalcarnero and San Martín de Valdeiglesias. The soil of these three districts gives the wines individual character: in San Martín Valdeiglesias the soil consists of a brown upper stratum on a subsoil of granite, in Navalcarnero of a light, sandy upper stratum on a subsoil of sand and clay and in Arganda of an upper stratum of loam and clay on a subsoil of granite with some limestone here and there. All these kinds of soil are quite poor and therefore very suitable for wine-growing, though it should be mentioned that the soil of Navalcarnero is possibly slightly less porous and remains slightly more swampy than that of Arganda and San Martín. The climate is typically continental, with hot summers and very cold winters. Any rainfall usually falls in spring and fall, brought on southwesterly winds. The red wines are made here from garnacha and tinto fino (tempranillo), the white from malvar, albillo and airén. It is worth noting that the three sub-districts each have a different preference in choice of grapes. Arganda uses tinto fino for red and malvar and airén for white, Navalcarnero uses garnacha for red and malvar for white and San Martín prefers garnacha for red and albillo for white.

The blanco, rosado and tinto vinos jóvenes of Madrid are in general pleasant, light and fresh for the white and rosé wines and slightly stronger and spicier for the red. Drink these wines with everyday meals, at parties, barbecues or just in the evenings with a chunk of manchego or ibérico. Drinking temperature: blanco 8–10 °C (46–50 °F), rosado 10–12 °C (50–54 °F) and tinto 12–14 °C (54–57 °F).

The rare crianzas of 100% tinto fino (tempranillo) or, for example, 85% cent tinto fino and 15% garnacha are definitely worthwhile, especially in view of the very low price. However, do not expect miracles – yet. The rustic strength and character of the vinos jóvenes are to some extent tamed and harmonized by the short caskmaturing. Drink these slightly better wines – which will certainly get even better – with lamb dishes, for example, possibly barbecued or with a piece of mature manchego or ibérico. Drinking temperature: 14–16 °C (57–61 °F).

MÉNTRIDA

This area to the south-west of Madrid (around the towns of Méntrida and Torrijos) was also renowned for its cheap and heavily alcoholic plonk, which could be sold without difficulty to the Madrid catering industry. Even when the authorities embarrassed the unambitious wine region by granting it a DO in 1960, there was little change in the apathy of the local bodegas. Not until the neighboring wine areas of Madrid were given their own DO and the sales market of Méntrida was threatened did they come to in Méntrida: not out of fear, more out of a sense of honor. From 1991 they began rapidly to replace or at least improve their own equipment. The type of wine was to a certain extent adapted to the wishes of the modern consumer: lighter in alcohol and texture but rather more sophisticated in flavor.

The vineyards of Méntrida are situated at a height of 200–500 m (655–1,640 ft), on a subsoil of light clay containing limestone, with an upper stratum of sand. The climate is continental. Most of the rain comes in the fall and the winter. Méntrida has only red and rosé wines. The grapes cultivated most are the tinto aragonés (garnacha), followed by tinto de Madrid or tinto basto and cencibel (tempranillo). The government has ordered that, on replanting, the Tinto de Madrid and part of the Garnacha must be replaced with Cencibel, which is better suited to the soil and the climate of Méntrida.

Vinos de Madrid

The rosados and tinto vinos jóvenes are fresh, light, pleasant and fruity. The crianzas are slightly fuller in flavor and are full of promise for the future of this district. Drink the young wines with lunch, with fried or grilled lamb or with the local sheep's cheeses. The crianzas deserve a nice leg of lamb or a pork or beef roast. Drinking temperature: 10–12 °C (50–54 °F) for the rosados, 12–14 °C (54–57 °F) for the vinos jóvenes tintos and 14–16 °C (57–61 °F) for the crianzas.

LA MANCHA

In area this is by far the largest DO in Spain at 482,000 acres. In the huge wine-growing region of La Mancha, where Don Quixote once battled against the windmills, the winegrowers fought against what they called 'the arbitrary measures of the EU'. Even now not everyone in La Mancha is fully aware of the gigantic surplus of wine in Europe. When they cold-bloodedly started making inventories in Brussels and came to the conclusion that fifty percent of the European area was made up of Extremadura, Aragón, Valencia and La Mancha, it seemed obvious that these would be the areas to be extensively redeveloped. While the message was understood in Aragón and Extremadura, most of the winegrowers in Valencia and particularly those in La Mancha could not see the point of the drastic reduction in the wine-acreage, as witnessed by the wild scenes of angry Spanish winegrowers on the borders with France. Yet it is of great importance to everyone, even to the winegrowers of La Mancha themselves, that better and, above all, less wine is produced. Fortunately there are more and more market-oriented bodegas that have joined battle against the mediocre name of the La Mancha wines. These bodegas have modernized their equipment and are focusing on producing quality wines. Thanks to the efforts of innovative bodegas like these, La Mancha is increasingly gaining a profile synonymous with quality, reliability and a reasonable price. More and more bottled wine from La Mancha is being bought both inside and outside Spain. Bulk buying for export has been drastically reduced. For several years now the steadily growing home demand for La Mancha wines has been greater than the amount of wine exported.

The vineyards of La Mancha are situated at heights of 1,600–2,115 ft. In general the land consists of a subsoil of clay and an upper stratum of brown sand. The better vineyards are situated on a subsoil of clay and limestone, with an upper stratum of red and brown sand containing loam and lime. The climate is typically continental, very cold in the winter and very hot in the summer. Thanks to the mountains surrounding the area the vineyards are protected against the damp winds from the sea and the ocean. White, red and rosé wines are made here. The whites can be seco (dry), semi-seco (medium dry), abocado (slightly sweet) or dulce (sweet). Airén, macabeo and pardilla are used for the white wines and cencibel (a younger sibling of tempranillo), garnacha, moravia, cabernet sauvignon and merlot for the reds. Because La Mancha is the largest wine-growing district in Spain – and one of the largest in the world – and the grape cultivated most is airén, this grape is also the grape cultivated most in the world. However, the government is ordering wine-growers gradually to replace the old airén vines with cencibel (tempranillo).

Thanks to the latest technology (including cold vinification) the white wines made from airén are very fresh and fruity, with surprising aromas of celery and freshly mown grass. As there is a surplus of this grape, the price of the wines is on the low side.

Apart from as an aperitif, you can also drink these wines with river or sea fish and with the local ensalada manchega (salad including hake, tuna and hard-boiled eggs), perdices estufadas (casserole of partridge in white wine) or with the many versions of the tortilla (country omelette). Drinking temperature: 8–10 °C (46–50 °F).

The rosados are made from 100% moravia or a cuvée of several black (almost always including garnacha) and sometimes also white grapes. Drink these fresh, young rosados with salads, tortillas, queso manchego frito (fried manchego cheese), mojete (a kind of vegetable ratatouille) or moreruelo, the almost infamous strong and spicy liver paté. Drinking temperature: 10–12 °C (50–54 °F).

The La Mancha vinos jóvenes tintos are light and fruity and actually go with almost anything, from hearty Dutch hotpots (kale with sausage) to light types of meat. They are also ideal wines for student parties due to their low price. Drinking temperature: 12–14 °C (54–57 °F).

The better La Mancha red wines are matured in oak casks (usually American). In particular, those made of 100% cencibel (tempranillo) are surprisingly good for the comparatively low price. Cuvées of cencibel, cabernet sauvignon and possibly merlot are also first-rate. Some bodegas, finally, make very correct 100% cabernet sauvignon crianzas, but these have a less Spanish feel.

Drink all these wines with grilled or roast lamb, asados of beef or pork or, for example, with the local caldereta de cordero, an excellent casserole of spiced lamb, tomatoes and Spanish peppers. Drinking temperature: 14–16 °C (57–61 °F).

VALDEPEÑAS

A quick glance at the wine map of Spain reveals that Valdepeñas is actually an enclave in the south of La Mancha. The traditional trade center of Valdepeñas is at the heart of the wine-growing region of the same name. Valdepeñas is slightly lower lying than the rest of the Meseta, in a broad valley surrounded by small mountains, on the border between the Meseta and Andalucía. The Valdepeñas wines, as so often on the Meseta, used to be thick, sultry and heavy on alcohol. It seemed as though time had stood still and the same wines were being produced as in the time of the Romans. The wines were stored in enormous pottery jars, the famous tinajas, which were often covered only by a few straw mats.

When the railway reached Valdepeñas in 1861 they decided to focus on quality. Less was produced, but of increasingly better quality, and sold to wealthy consumers, in Madrid, on the coast and even in America and the Philippines. When the Phylloxera louse destroyed the vineyards of Valdepeñas, this policy of quality proved to have paid off. There was enough in store to wait for the next

Airén, the grape cultivated most in the world, produces mainly mediocre and a few reasonable wines

Cencibel (Tempranillo) is increasingly taking the place of Airén

harvest (three years after planting the new vines grafted on American root stock). Already at that time the winegrowers could see the sense in strict

La Mancha's most famous wine

La Mancha reserva

quality control and, above all, the importance of a mutual wine-growing policy. This has made Valdepeñas into a respected and, above all, progressive wine-growing region. With today's technology – in particular fully computer-controlled temperature regulation of the vinification – they are now capable of making fresh and fruity wines in Valdepeñas, as well as the fine, full-bodied red wines. The soil of Valdepeñas ('valley of the rocks') is very rocky. The subsoil consists of limestone, often not more than 10 in beneath the surface of the ground. The yellowy red thin upper stratum is a mixture of crumbled lime and alluvial clay.

Most of the vineyards are situated at a height of 1,970–2300 ft. The climate is pure continental. Because of the protection of the surrounding mountains there is little rainfall and some places could almost be called desert-like. But if there is rain, it comes down in bucketloads! Although in Valdepeñas too a large

number of airén vines are cultivated, the government is ordering them gradually to be replaced with cencibel (tempranillo).

The blancos jóvenes made from airén are very fresh and fruity, with the renowned plant aromas of celery and fresh-mown grass. These wines are intended for everyday use, as an aperitif or with various light starters, from white meat to fish and shellfish. They are also great for refreshing the palette while eating the local famous, very spicy tripe dishes, the *callos*, or, for example, with *pisto manchego*, a dish of mixed vegetables and scrambled eggs. Drinking temperature: 8–10 °C (46–50 °F).

The rosados are usually vinos jóvenes that should be drunk within a year of harvesting. They are fresh, light and cheerful rosados, made of cencibel (tempranillo), often supplemented with white airén.

The tinajas are covered with a straw mat

The distinctive yellowy-red soil of Valdepeñas during the harvest

Quench your thirst with these friendly rosados while eating the nutritious and often quite spicy sinlepan dishes of this area, such as *lágrimas de aldea* (stew of pork, potatoes, black pudding and chorizo). Drinking temperature: 10–12 °C (50–54 °F).

The Valdepeñas tintos vinos jóvenes made from cencibel, like the rosados, are very pleasant thirst-quenchers with spicy stews. Drink them young, at 12–14 °C (54–57 °F).

The crianzas and (gran) reservas of Valdepeñas made from 100% cencibel are definitely worthwhile. Not only are they very nice wines that combine the fruitiness of cencibel with the sweetish, vanilla flavoring of the oak, often American, but the price is also still unbelievably low. The gran reservas are velvet-smooth, round, full and

The tinajas are still used for temporary storage

Cencibel (tempranillo)

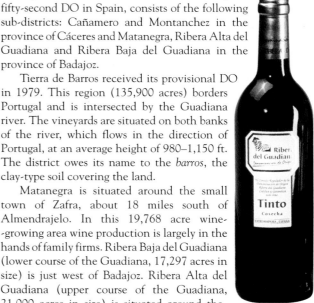

Ribera del
Guadiana

usually contain less tannin than those of Navarra, Rioja and Ribera del Duero.

Drink these wines with a delicious piece of barbecued or roasted lamb (*asado de cordero*) or with *atacaburra* (casserole of rabbit with garlic). Drinking temperature: 16 °C (61 °F) for the crianzas and 7 °C (63 °F) for the (gran) reservas.

RIBERA DEL GUADIANA

This youngest of Spain's DOs (1997) is in Extremadura, the area bordering Portugal, in the extreme west of Central Spain. Previously the wines coming from this district bore the name of one of the sub-districts, Tierra de Barros.

For a long time Extremadura revolved around the cork industry and the olive trees. Since the drastic modernization of wine-growing hopes have grown for an even better economical future. From a gastronomic point of view a visit to Extremadura is a pleasant surprise, with the famous *jamón ibérico* and *chorizo*, lamb and mutton, goat's meat, olive oil and many local cheeses, of which ibores and serena are the best known.

The climate of the Ribera del Guadiana is continental, but softened by the proximity of the Atlantic Ocean. The two rivers Guadiana and Tajo provide a good degree of humidity of air and ground. The summers here are very hot and the winters particularly mild. One thing the winegrower does not have to worry about is night frost. The soil consists mainly

of a mixture of clay and reddish brown sand, with lumps of limestone here and there.

While this book was being written, Ribera del Guadiana was granted a provisional DO, something quite unique in the history of wine-growing. In fact almost everything here revolves around the better red wines of the Tierra de Barros, which account for about 80% of the DO production. Only 8,483 acres of the total of 216,089 acres cultivated area is allowed to bear the DO designation. In 1998 there were still fewer than thirty bodegas that satisfied the strict requirements of the DO. This number will grow considerably in the future, as soon as more bodegas have replaced the old-fashioned *tinajas* with more modern equipment and their own bottling line. It is expected that within fifteen years the old bulk culture of Extremadura will have been completely done away with. Besides Tierra de Barros, the current DO Ribera del Guadiana, the fifty-second DO in Spain, consists of the following sub-districts: Cañamero and Montanchez in the province of Cáceres and Matanegra, Ribera Alta del Guadiana and Ribera Baja del Guadiana in the province of Badajoz.

Tierra de Barros received its provisional DO in 1979. This region (135,900 acres) borders Portugal and is intersected by the Guadiana river. The vineyards are situated on both banks of the river, which flows in the direction of Portugal, at an average height of 980–1,150 ft. The district owes its name to the *barros*, the clay-type soil covering the land.

Matanegra is situated around the small town of Zafra, about 18 miles south of Almendrajelo. In this 19,768 acre wine-growing area wine production is largely in the hands of family firms. Ribera Baja del Guadiana (lower course of the Guadiana, 17,297 acres in size) is just west of Badajoz. Ribera Alta del Guadiana (upper course of the Guadiana, 21,000 acres in size) is situated around the towns of Don Benito and Villanueva de la Serena, about 75 miles upstream form the town of Badajoz. Montanchez is a small region of 9,884 acres, situated around the small town of the same name, about 43 miles northeast of Badajoz. This district is renowned for its old vines and its olive trees. It is a picturesque area with many softly glowing hills and hospitable valleys. Cañamero, finally, is an even smaller region (about 2,965 acres), in the Sierra de Guadalupe, approximately half way between the towns of Badajoz and Toledo. The small town of Cañamero is in all respects the production center of the district of the same name. The vineyards are situated on the sides of hills, at a height of 1,970–2,625 ft. The soil here consists of slate. In the valleys the vineyards are much lower lying and on alluvial-type soil. The production of this small district is principally in the hands of small, old family bodegas.

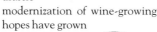

Valdepeñas tinto

Past and present in the cellars of Valdepeñas (Corcovo)

Valdepeñas gran reserva

While Tierra de Barros is allowed to carry the DO designation on the labels, the other districts are officially still *vinos de la tierra*. The DO designation may not appear on the label until the bodega has been approved according to the previously mentioned criteria.

The district is known mainly for its young, fresh and lively wines, which at the moment are still very low in price. The majority of the vineyards are still planted with native white grape varieties such as pardina, cayetana blanca, montúa, eva, alarije and cigüentes. Pardina in particular gives excellent results with today's technology.

You can drink these wines as an aperitif or, for example, with cauliflower florets coated in breadcrumbs and crisply fried in olive oil, *coliflor al estilo de Badajoz* or with the locally much loved anchovy salad *ensalada de boquerones*. Drinking temperature: 8–10 °C (46–50 °F).

The red and rosé wines are made principally from cencibel (tempranillo) and garnacha. Drink the young rosados and tintos with the local *cochifrito*, for example, a wonderful dish of lamb with onions and paprika, or with egg dishes such as *huevos serranos* (tomatoes stuffed with raw ham, covered with egg and cheese) or *huevos a la extremeña* (potatoes, chorizo, ham and tomato sauce, covered with egg). With a good rosado you can also try the excellent *riñones* (gently fried lamb's kidneys). Drinking temperature: 10–12 °C (50–54 °F) (rosados) or 12–14 °C (54–57 °F) (tintos jóvenes).

The red crianzas and (gran) reservas are very promising and have a lot to offer. One local combination is almost obligatory: with *solomillo de cordero*, fillet of lamb marinated in red wine and cooked in the oven. But a *frito típico extremeño*, fried spicy goat's meat, will also appreciate these wines. Drinking temperature: 14–16 °C (57–61 °F).

Tierra de Barros tinto

THE LEVANTE

In the chapter on the Meseta we traveled through the west side of the Castilla-La Mancha. Now it is the turn of the east of the district, Almansa. Almansa is situated on the Levante high plain, near the autonomías of Valencia and Murcia. The climate in this eastern part of Spain varies from distinctly Mediterranean on the coast to semi-continental with Mediterranean influences in Almansa. The weather here is very much like that of Catalonia, though slightly more humid and much hotter. The whole district is open to other countries, partly due to its door to the Mediterranean Sea. Foreign investments and large-scale export of wine have been part of

Tierra de Barros blanco

the Levante for years. They were also well-inclined towards all kinds of wine-growing and scientific experiments from an early stage. Maybe they got this interest and eagerness to learn from the Moors, who were settled here for so long. The Levante, like Catalonia, is very much focused on the sea and its products and is also a very large producer of rice. This explains why the local cuisine has many dishes with fish or seafood and rice. The best known dish is without doubt the famous *paella*. The wines of the Levante in general do not cause much of a stir.

ALMANSA

This wine district is situated in the most easterly part of Castilla-La-Mancha, in the province of Albacete. The climate here is the only thing that resembles neighboring La Mancha, continental and very dry – but when it rains, mainly in the spring and fall, enormous quantities of water fall, often accompanied by devastating hail storms. The soil in this principally red wine region consists of a subsoil of limestone and a fertile upper stratum. Around the two towns of Almansa in the east and Chinchilla de Monte-Aragón in the west the red monastrell, garnacha and cencibel (tempranillo) are harvested, as well as a small amount of white merseguera. The strong point of this district is the red wine made from monastrell, which – as in the surrounding districts of Alicante, Jumilla and Yecla – can give especially good results here. Not all the bodegas are equally well equipped, however, but results obtained so far with this grape are very promising.

The Almansa blancos are light, fresh, modern wines, principally intended for quick consumption. You can serve them as aperitifs or thirst-quenching accompaniments to everything the sea has to offer. Drinking temperature: 8–10 °C (46–50 °F).

The Almansa rosados are fresh, fruity and pleasant rosé wines without too many pretensions. Drink them with fish, seafood or with a (cold) picnic paella. Drinking temperature: 10–12 °C (50–54 °F).

The Almansa tintos occur as vinos jóvenes or crianzas. Serve the often ponderous and alcoholic vinos jóvenes with light meat dishes or seafood casseroles. Drinking temperature: 12–14 °C (54–57 °F).

The better Almansa tinto crianza, reserva and gran reserva of Bodegas Piqueras are very worthwhile and the price is particularly reasonable. Drink these well-balanced and pleasant wines made from Tempranillo and Monastrell with a good cut of meat. Drinking temperature: 14–16 °C (57–61 °F).

VALENCIA

Valencia is one of the largest cities in Spain and the largest wine port. Valencia is also the province around the

Ribera del Guadiana rosado

city of Valencia and the autonomía with Valencia as the capital. Finally, Valencia is also the name of a DO wine-growing region. In the autonomía of Valencia there are two other DO zones: Utiel-Requena in the province of Valencia and Alicante. In the wine-growing region of Valencia enormous pools of *vino común* (plonk) are still produced, to the great annoyance of the European agricultural commission, which would like to reduce the European wine surplus. Unfortunately most of the Valencians still believe that producing gallons of plonk offers greater financial security than making quality wines.

UTIEL-REQUENA

The vineyards of Utiel-Requena are situated around the towns of Utiel and Requena, at a height of 1,970–2,955 ft. In the south the soil consists of loam and clay on a subsoil of sandstone, and in the Magro valley of alluvial soils. The climate is continental and sometimes the temperature differs by as much as 30 °C (86 °F) between day and night. The grape variety cultivated most is the native black bobal, but tempranillo and garnacha are increasingly gaining ground. Among the white grapes, macabeo is the most important, followed by merseguera.

The Utiel-Requena blancos are great wines, but have little 'individual' character. They are light, fresh and fruity and are primarily intended for fast drinkers in the supermarket sector. These cheap little wines can be useful for diluting (over) spicy oriental dishes. Drinking temperature: 8–10 °C (46–50 °F).

The Utiel-Requena rosados are very worthwhile. They are usually made from bobal and garnacha and are full, meaty and powerful. They are definitely rosados for drinking with meals, which are excellent with the local paella, and also with the equally sublime and simple *arroz abanda* (rice cooked in fish stock, served with fish and crustaceans, herbs, saffron and olive oil) or *arroz empedrat* (rice with French beans, tomatoes, garlic and herbs). Buy, according to taste, an ordinary rosado (garnacha + bobal) or a slightly fuller and heavier rosado Superior (100% bobal). Drinking temperature: 10–12 °C (50–54 °F).

The Utiel-Requena tintos come as vinos jóvenes and crianza types. The light, fresh and fruity vinos jóvenes are suitable for student parties, where quantity and a low price are more important than quality of the wine. Drinking temperature: 12–14 °C (54–57 °F). Otherwise you would do better to choose a crianza, usually made from garnacha and tempranillo. Because of the capricious climate and the height of the vineyards, most of the grapes ripen here much faster than elsewhere in Spain. This is why you will find few old crianza wines in Utiel-Requena. It is not customary to make reservas or gran reservas, although some bodegas achieve good results with a cuvée of tempranillo and cabernet sauvignon. Drink the crianzas with red meat (*ternera*), lamb (*cordero*) or with chicken or rabbit paellas. Drinking temperature: 14–16 °C (57–61 °F).

Utiel-Requena rosado and tinto

VALENCIA

The DO of Valencia is largely dependent on export, especially in bulk. Trade is dominated by enormous companies specializing in export. It looks as if things are changing here, partly because more and more bottles of Valencia wine are ending up in Spanish supermarkets, but this will probably never change the export-oriented mentality of the large Valencian wine companies. So there is too much mediocre wine produced in Valencia.

The district is sub-divided into four sub-districts: Alto Turia (north-west of the province of Valencia), Clariano (south of the province of Valencia), Moscatel de Valencia (in the center) and Valentino (also in the center). Alto Turia is the highest and most hilly of the four. Here the vineyards are situated at a height of 1,310–2,300 ft. In Clariano the vineyards are planted on terraces at a height of 525–2,135 ft and in Moscatel and Valentino at a height of 330–1,310 ft. In general the soil consists of a subsoil of limestone and an upper stratum of reddish brown loam, with some alluvial soil in the river valleys. In Alto Turia the upper stratum is slightly more sandy, in Valentino looser and thicker. The climate is distinctly Mediterranean, with continental influences in Alto Turia, where the summers are hotter and the winters colder and where there is less rain than in the other sub-districts, which are closer to the coast. Here and there diverging microclimates occur, which usually bring even more heat. The great differences in temperature between day and night are striking in the whole of Levante.

The DO of Valencia is allowed to use twelve varieties of grapes. Recommended are the white macabeo, malvasía, merseguera, moscatel de alejandría, pedro jiménes and planta fina de pedralba and the black garnacha, monastrell, tempranillo and tintorera; white planta nova and tortosí and black forcayat are permitted. Valencia produces numerous different wines, with regional or sub-regional designations of origin, blanco, rosado, tinto, espumoso, licoroso, rancio, Moscatel dulce and Moscatel licoroso.

Utiel-Requena reserva

Most of the wines are of the vinos jóvenes type, but you will also come across a few crianzas. It is a particular shame that Valencia has possibly the most advanced wine equipment and analysis laboratories, but consumers prefer to buy the cheapest and simplest wines, which puts an enormous check on development in favor of quality.

Alto Turia blancos are fresh, light wines of 100% merseguera. Valencia and Valentino blancos are made from a blend of merseguera, planta fina, pedro ximénes and malvasía and come in seco, semi-seco and dulce. Clariano blanco seco is made from merseguera, tortosí and malvasía.

Drink the dry wines as an aperitif, with fish or shellfish, or with fish paella. They will not be a great asset to your table, more of a silent accompaniment. Serve the semi-sweet wines as an aperitif or with a small fish that has lost it's way to the sea. It is best to avoid the sweet version. Drinking temperature: (semi-)seco 8–10 °C (46–50 °F), dulce 6–8 °C (43–46 °F).

Valencia, Valentino and Clariano rosados are fresh, light and do not have a lot to say for themselves. These rosados also excel at everyday meals with their discreet presence. You can actually use these wines with anything with which you would not dare to serve a real wine … but also with the many versions of paella and other rice dishes, as well as with grilled *dorada* (golden bream) or *lubina* (wolf fish). Drinking temperature: 10–12 °C (50–54 °F).

Valentino and Clariano tintos are just as discreet as their white and rosé counterparts. You can serve these wines with anything, from paella to fish and all kinds of light meat. Drinking temperature: 12–14 °C (54–57 °F).

Tintos crianza made from 100% monastrell or 100% granacha are the most interesting table wines of the area (table wines in contrast to the various sweet or liqueur-like wines of Valencia). There are also secret experiments with cabernet sauvignon, which – especially in combination with tempranillo – brings very good results. Combinations of monastrell and garnacha, possibly with a bit of tempranillo, are very promising. The very best results come from bodegas that have moved away from the old-fashioned vinification methods (concrete or epoxy barrels without temperature control) and have gone over to the most modern techniques, producing more finesse and aromatic strength. Drink all these crianzas with *cordero* (lamb) and *temera* (veal) or any kind of *asados* (roasts). Drinking temperature: 14–16 °C (57–61 °F).

Valencia DO also makes numerous old-fashioned *mistelas* (must distilled with wine alcohol), but prefers to call them *vinos de licor*. Some of them are of

Valencia blanco

outstanding quality, others not noteworthy. Drink these wines on their own or with sweet and sharp fruit salads or lemon or almond cakes. Drinking temperature: 6–8 °C (43–46 °F).

Rancio Valencia or Rancio Valentino are heavy, sweet, alcoholic and fully oxidized wines served as aperitifs or with a starter – for example with fresh, sweet melon. You can also serve them after meals, possibly with chocolates or a fresh nut cake. Drinking temperature: from 6–8 °C (43–46 °F) to 17 °C (63 °F).

Vino de Moscatel dulce and Vino de licor Moscatel are quite simply the best sweet wines in the area, However, do not expect an explosion of fresh aromas, since most bodegas still make old-fashioned, syrupy, unctuous and almost stupefying Moscatel wines.

Valencia tinto

ALICANTE

Alicante is the most southerly Valencian DO. The wine-growing acreage covers quite a large area, from the Mediterranean to the foot of the central Meseta hills. The region is sub-divided into two sub-districts, La Marina, around the Cabo de la Nao above Benidorm, and Alicante, around (and to the northwest of) the town of the same name. Today magnificent red and white wines are made here, and possibly the nicest Moscatel in Spain. A curiosity is the rare Fondillón, a reinforced wine made from 100% Monastrell, matured according to the solera system (see the section on sherry).

In La Marina there is a distinctly Mediterranean climate, with a high level of humidity, hot summers and mild winters. The vineyards are situated at sea level or just above on alluvial soil. Near Alicante the vineyards are slightly higher, up to almost 1,310 ft. The soil consists of limestone and a loose brown upper stratum and the climate – especially inland – has more continental features. It is also somewhat drier here than in La Marina. In the entire region mainly red and rosé wines are made from monastrell, garnacha, tempranillo and bobal. Merseguera, macabeo and planta fina are used for the dry white wines and for the sweet Moscatel Romano.

Alicante blancos are usually made from merseguera, macabeo, planta fina and (increasingly less) moscatel romano. They can be dry (seco), medium dry (semi-seco) or sweet (dulce). These vinos jóvenes are light, fresh and, above all, cheap. The future of Alicante may well lie in the still experimental white wines made from chardonnay and above all from riesling. Initial results – particularly with Riesling – are amazing.

Drink these white Alicante wines as an aperitif, with *mariscos* (seafood) or, for example, with *rodaballo* (turbot) with potato fritters and onion rings. Save a glass for the Valencian cheese tronchón. Drinking temperature: 8–10 °C (46–50 °F).

Alicante rosados are made from monastrell, bobal and tempranillo. Most of them are secos, but you will sometimes come across a semi-seco rosado. Due to their freshness, coupled with fruitiness and roundness, they go splendidly with all fish dishes, particularly with *bacalao a la valenciana* (hake with, among other things, rice, tomatoes and hard-boiled eggs), but any paella would be content in such company. Drinking temperature: 10–12 °C (50–54 °F).

There are Alicante tintos of the vinos jóvenes and crianza types. The former are light, fresh and fruity wines for everyday use. The best Alicante tintos are naturally the crianzas (at least six months in oak and a minimum of two years old), which are fuller and richer than the vinos jóvenes. At the moment experiments are being done with cabernet sauvignon, in some cases mixed with tempranillo. Here too results are very promising! Drink these crianzas and the rare reservas with red meat, lamb and small furred game, for example. Try these wines with a *conejo a la valenciana* (rabbit stuffed with paprika peppers, herbs and garlic). Drinking temperature: 14–16 °C (57–61 °F).

Alicante Moscatel vino de licor is an excellent wine, especially when it has been vinified in a slightly more modern way. The color is then golden yellow and clear, and the bouquet is overwhelming, with strong fruity aromas, like musk. The flavor is soft, sumptuous, succulent and broad, with an aftertaste of moscatel grape that lasts a long time. Drink these very successful liqueur wines just as they are, at the most with a fresh, sharp lemon cake. Drinking temperature: 6–8 °C (43–46 °F).

Alicante Fondillón is also a vino de licor, but is stored according to the solera system as in the sherry district (see that section). The principle is simple: each year a number of the oldest wines are bottled. The empty space in the cask is filled up with wines that are one year younger and they are in turn supplemented with younger wines. In this way the young wines go through various levels of casks (20 or more!) and the ultimate wine remains constant in quality. The result is an amber/gold colored wine with shades of mahogany, a hint of vanilla in the bouquet, luxury bread rolls, cake, tobacco, sometimes cocoa or coffee. The wines are well-balanced, elegant, light, succulent and very delicious.

Drink these very rare wines as an aperitif of after meals on a winter's day, with a good book, an interesting story or a game of chess or draughts. Drinking temperature: according to taste 10–12 °C (50–54 °F) or at room temperature up to 18 °C (64 °F).

MURCIA

There are three DOs in Murcia: Jumilla, Yecla and Bullas.

JUMILLA

Jumilla was a respected wine region well before Rioja gained a profile as a wine district. The wines of Jumilla are not on a level with the better Rioja wines, but they have won a place on Spanish and foreign markets. And rightly so, for the quality of the wines has always been reliable. Jumilla's future lies in the better table wines and not so much in the adulterated wines or the rancios.

The vineyards of Jumilla are situated around and to the west of the town of Jumilla. They are relatively new vineyards, because the wine-growing acreage of Jumilla was re-planted after a late invasion of *Phylloxera* at the end of the 1980s … about a hundred years later than in the rest of Spain! So the winegrowers of Jumilla were able to choose the best and most suitable grapes when they replanted: Monastrell, Cencibel (Tempranillo) and Garnacha (black); Mersequera, Airén and Pedro Jiménes (white). Monastrell accounts for around 80% of the cultivation. In Jumilla the vineyards are fairly high up, sometimes higher than 700 m (2,300 ft), which protects them to some extent from the blistering heat of the sun. The soil consists of a subsoil of limestone and an upper stratum of loose, rather sandy reddish brown earth. The climate is strictly continental with extremely hot summers and unusually cold winters with a great deal of frost.

The Jumillo blancos are primarily made from Merseguera, but Airén is being used more and more, partly because it suits foreign buyers better. These blancos are in the best scenario fresh, fruity (green apple), succulent and pleasant. Drink them on a terrace, as an aperitif or with fish dishes. Drinking temperature: 8–10 °C (46–50 °F).

The Jumilla rosados, like the tintos, must contain at least 50% Monastrell. However, in practice it is often more, even up to 100%. The color of these wines varies from salmon- to raspberry-colored. The bouquet is intense and fruity (raspberries, strawberries) with floral nuances. The flavor is fresh, succulent and fruity. Drink these very pleasant rosados with paella, *mariscos* (seafood), fish, chicken or the local chorizo sausages or other meat products. Drinking temperature: 10–12 °C (50–54 °F).

The Jumilla tintos make up the large majority of Jumilla's wine production. Many of these tintos contain 100% Monastrell, but there are also cuvées of Monastrell and Cencibel (Tempranillo). The vinos jóvenes are fresh, fruity (black cherries, dates, currants), succulent and particularly pleasant. The crianzas and (gran) reservas are noticeably marked by wood, without it dominating. The balance between alcohol, acids, body and flavor is particularly striking. Without doubt the future of Jumilla lies in wines of this sort.

Try these Jumilla tintos de crianza with roast meat (*asados*), grilled lamb (*cordero asado*) or with meat, chicken or rabbit paellas. Drinking temperature: 14–16 °C (57–61 °F).

Finally there is a local specialty made from 100% Monastrell: a sweet rancio wine which has sometimes been cask-matured for up to six years and is very aromatic. Drink it preferably as an aperitif or else in the evenings after meals. Drinking temperature: according to taste 10–12 °C (50–54 °F) to room temperature 17–18 °C (63–64 °F).

YECLA

The large bodegas of Yecla have still not fully realized that consumers want greater quality at an acceptable price. Fortunately, for the last ten years or so the smaller bodegas have been working on a great transformation and radical modernization of equipment and .... policy! The lack of success is certainly not due to the soil, which is a subsoil of limestone and clay with a deep upper stratum, or the climate, which is continental. The black grapes used most are monastrell (80%) and garnacha, but tempranillo, cabernet sauvignon and merlot are also being experimented with. Merseguera, verdil, airén and macabeo are used for the white wines. The vineyards are situated on a high plain around the town of Yecla, at a height of 1,310–2,300 ft, sheltered by rolling hills and small mountains.

Jumilla blanco

The wine-growing region is sub-divided into Yecla and Yecla Campo Arriba, the low lands where only monastrell is planted and where the wines are somewhat fuller than in the rest of the DO.

Today Yecla makes several acceptable, fresh, fruity and light white wines without much character, perhaps through lack of acids. Drink these wines as aperitifs or as thirst-quenchers or dilutants with herbed or spicy dishes with which no other wine is possible. Drinking temperature: 8–10 °C (46–50 °F).

The better Yecla blancas are the crianzas (Viña Las Gruesas crianza or Castaño Barrico from Bodega Castaño, Yecla). These wines have powerful aromas, hints of vanilla (wood), a nice fruity bouquet and flavor and slightly more body. Unfortunately the acidity is still slightly too low, but in Yecla technology is not standing still, nor are investments. Offer these wines with fish, steamed chicken or with white meat. Drinking temperature: 10–12 °C (50–54 °F).

The not unpleasant Yecla rosados, usually made from a blend of monastrell and garnacha, are very fruity and succulent. Drink them with assorted meats (*embutidos*), fish, chicken,

Jumilla tinto   Jumilla tinto crianza

poultry, pink roast lamb or with paella. Drinking temperature: 10–12 °C (50–54 °F).

Many of the ordinary Yecla tintos are brought on to the market as vinos jóvenes. They are mostly obtained by macération carbonique (soaking in carbon dioxide) and are fresh, light and very fruity. Drink these everyday wines with anything you like. These wines quickly make friends, but are also soon forgotten. Drinking temperature: 12–14 °C (54–57 °F).

Here too the better wines are the crianzas and reservas (for example Pozuelo crianza and reserva from Bodega Castaño, Yecla). These wines are made from a cuvée of monastrell, garnacha, cencibel (tempranillo), cabernet sauvignon and merlot for the crianza and monastrell and garnacha for the reserva. Both wines are quite dark in color and have wonderful aromas of fruit with distinct nuances of vanilla. The flavor is full, succulent and meaty with soft tannins and not too much alcohol. Drink these wines with meat (*asados*), preferably lamb, or with light furred game dishes, *liebre* (hare), for example. Drinking temperature: 14–16 °C (57–61 °F).

BULLAS

The definitive recognition as a DO region did not come until 1994. Bullas has been waiting in the wings of the elite corps of Spanish viticulture since 1982. The vineyards of Bullas are spread out over quite a large area, most of them in the river valleys, but also on terraces in the surrounding hills. The height of the vineyards varies from 1,640 to just over 2,300 ft, on sandy or alluvial soil. In spite of the short distance from the Mediterranean the climate of Bullas is rather more continental. The black Monastrell and Tempranillo and the white Airén and Macabeo grow here.

Bullas principally makes white wines and rosados, but it is the red wines that are particularly worthwhile. Most of these tintos are sold as vinos jóvenes. They are definitely not light wines, but very fruity, full wines with a good balance between acids, alcohol and fruit. Drink these pleasant wines with light meat dishes or poultry. Drinking temperature: 12–14 °C (54–57 °F). The better wines are cask-matured and the initial results are particularly promising.

ANDALUSIA AND THE CANARY ISLANDS

We end our journey through Spain in the extreme south of the Iberian Peninsula and the Canary Islands lying off the coast of Morocco. Something of everything grows on the Canary Islands and there is plenty of meat and fish. Partly because of the flourishing tourist industry, demand has arisen for a whole series of wines, white, rosé and red, from dry to saccharine-sweet. Thanks to the slightly gentler climate and the volcanic soil the Canary Islands can easily satisfy this demand.

ANDALUSIA (ANDALUCÍA)

In many books you will read that Iberian wine-growing began in Andalucía. That is not entirely true and does not do justice to the ancient Celts from northern Spain, who were already making wine before the arrival of the first sea voyagers. But Andalucía is the place where intentionally organized wine-growing developed after the arrival of the Phoenicians and the Greeks, who planted vineyards around every port of call. In contrast to the Celts, who to begin with wild graper picked in the woods and only much later planted small vineyards haphazardly around their villages, the Phoenicians (later the Carthaginians) and the Greeks maintained their vineyards very well. The same happened with the founding of the city of Cádiz around 1100 BC. The Phoenicians soon discovered how good the local soil and weather conditions were for wine-growing and they began to plant more and more vineyards inland, in the area of present-day Montilla, Huelva and Málaga. The vineyards around the city of Cádiz produced sherry, probably one of the oldest quality wines in the world. Even during the Moorish occupation the local wine-growers were allowed to carry on almost undisturbed. After the Reconquista the port of Cádiz was one of the most important trade ports in Spain and the wine trade flourished like nowhere else in the world. In the twentieth century the tourist industry reinforced the relative wealth of the area. Wine was made in western Andalucía, but principally drunk on the east coast by the many tourists.

The 22¹/₄ million acre autonomía of Andalucía is the second largest (after Castilla-La-Mancha) in Spain and comprises no less than eight provinces: Almería, Cádiz, Córdoba, Granada, Huelva, Jaén, Málaga and Sevilla. The wine production consists almost exclusively of sherry-type wines, from dry to sweet, but there is increasing experimentation with non-fortified, light, fresh wines made according to the most modern vinification methods. The initial results are very promising, including in the area of Contraviesa-Alpujara (Granada). Andalucía is synonymous with tapas – the tasty snacks that go so well with a glass of sherry (or some other Spanish aperitif).

Andalucía is also renowned, of course, for its refreshing, healthy (read: lots of vitamins and …. garlic) cold soup, *gazpacho*, made of tomatoes, cucumber and green peppers. If you like sea fish and shellfish, you will be in your element in Andalucía. As Andalucía is a great producer of oranges and olive oil, there are also many dishes based on these products. Naturally there are also numerous dishes incorporating a (good) dash of sherry in the sauce: *bistec al Jerez* (steak) and *riñones al Jerez* (kidneys), for example. Finally there are the world famous meat products (chorizo, jamón and morcilla) from the small town of Jabugo and the many dangerously seductive sweet desserts and varieties of cake.

CONDADO DE HUELVA DO

This is the most westerly designation of origin in Andalucía. The wines from this district were sold under the name of 'sherry' for a very long time to unsuspecting supermarket customers. Not until 1996 was it definitely decided that only the wines from the DO Jerez de la Frontera & Manzanilla de Sanlúcar de Barrameda were allowed to use the word sherry in and outside Spain. Since then the bodegas of the DO Condado de Huelva have felt themselves obliged to do more to make the name of their district known. The county (*condado*) of Huelva is in the province of the same name, to the east of Portugal. The wine-growing area covers the region between the Atlantic coast and the town of Huelva. The vineyards are quite low lying, less than 98 ft above sea level, on a soil of limestone and alluvial sediments with an upper stratum of reddish brown sand. The climate is actually more Mediterranean than continental, in spite of its westerly position. The summers are warm and long, the winters mild and damp. The grape most cultivated is still zalema, a difficult grape for traditional wine-growing, but excellent for sherry-type wines,

Sherry en tapas

because it produces light wines that oxidize quickly. Listán (local name for palomino), pedro jiménes, garrido and moscatel also occur.

For a number of years very modern, fresh, fruity, dry wines, the vinos jóvenes afrutados, have been made from zalema. Drink these wines with recognizable plant aromas (grass) as aperitifs or at meals with, for example, fish, shellfish, organic meat (*riñonada*, lamb's kidneys and thymus gland) or egg dishes (*huevos serranos*, tomatoes *au gratin* stuffed with eggs, serrano ham and cheese). Also delicious with a chunk of *rondeño* (goat's cheese) from Andalucía. Drinking temperature: 8–10 °C (46–50 °F).

Besides these modern *afrutados* there are the old-fashioned *corrientes*. The distinction is made before harvesting. The grapes destined for the afrutados are harvested earlier and contain proportionately a lot of acids and fewer sugars. The grapes for the corrientes are harvested much later and contain a lot of sugars and fewer acids. The young wines are fortified with wine alcohol to 15.5–17% or 23% alcohol, depending on the style aimed at. The wines containing less alcohol (15.5–17%) usually have a film of wine yeast, the *flor* (literally the 'bloom' or 'flower' of the wine). The film of yeast prevents contact with the outside air and helps the wines to keep their original pale color. They do take on many of the typical yeast aromas. These wines are dry and in Huelva are also called fino because of their refined and delicate bouquet and flavor. This name is used only locally. For the export market these wines are obliged to bear the official designation of Condado Pálido. These Pálidos are cask-matured according to the solera method (see with DO Jerez de la Frontera & Sanlúcar de Barrameda). Characteristic aromas and flavor are yeast, a slight bitterness, salt and nuts. A typical aperitif drink (although slightly heavier than a nice Fino de Jerez or Manzanilla de Sanlúcar de Barrameda), but also delicious with meals with slices of jamón ibérico or serrano, grilled prawns, seafood, smoked salmon, etc. Drinking temperature: 8–10 °C (46–50 °F).

The wines that are more strongly fortified (17–23% alcohol) do not develop a flor, because the wine yeast cells cannot compete with so much alcohol and die. As no film develops on the wine it soon oxidizes in contact with the warm, humid air, resulting in a dark color and heavy aromas. These wines are still called olorosos, or 'sweet-smelling', referring to the heavy, sultry aromas, though for export only the official name, Condado Viejo, is used. These wines are also cask-matured by the solera method. Characteristic aromas and flavor are fresh cake or luxury bread rolls, toast, wood, vanilla and alcohol. For devotees these wines can serve as a (winter) aperitif, but they are more at home after meals, for example with some cheese, nuts and dried fruits. Drinking temperature: to taste 6–8 °C (43–46 °F) or at room temperature.

JEREZ-XÉRÈS-SHERRY

The English did all in their power to gain control of the sources of sherry. They ultimately succeeded by investing in and buying bodegas. This produced renowned sherry houses such as Duff & Gordon, Osborne, Wisdom & Warter and Sandeman. The French also became involved in this peaceful battle, including a certain Pedro Domecq Lembeye from southwest France. Not until later were genuine Spanish bodegas established, mostly by rich Spaniards and Basques returning from the USA.

The unparalleled success of the sherry wines is largely due to the ideal conditions in the triangle of Sanlúcar de Barrameda, Jerez de la Frontera and El Puerto de Santa María, between the rivers Guadalquivir and Guadalete. The vineyards are therefore bathed in full sunlight for about two thirds of the year, from early in the morning until late in the evening (3,000 hours of sunshine or 290 days of sun a year!). Just a little morning dew and a gentle sea breeze provide some cooling. The climate is distinctly Mediterranean. The soil is also perfect for sherry-type wines: the huge, gently rolling albarizas (white organic loam, rich in lime, clay and silicium oxide) store the water during the short rainy season (winter and spring). In the hot summer and fall they form a hard white crust on the surface of the ground, which reflects the sunlight

even further, while the water remains imprisoned in the deep ground and protects the vines from drying out. These albarizas are found only in the previously mentioned triangle of towns, the Jerez Superior region. Past El Puerto de Santa María, in an easterly direction, the zona begins, an area with poor quality clay (barros) and sandy (arenas) soils, which produce wines of poorer quality. The grape varieties used for sherry are the classic listán or palomino, the pedro jiménes (particularly for the sweet olorosos) and the moscatel de alejandro (muscat d'alexandrie).

Harvesting of the grapes begins every year around 10 September. Harvesting is still done by hand, because the vines are pruned very low and the grapes – in view of the extreme heat – have to be handled very carefully. Pedro jiménes and moscatel are used for the sweet wines. To increase the sugar content of these sweet grapes they are laid on esparto grass mats during the daytime. The grapes are exposed to the sunlight in this way for at least two days (at night they are covered because of the night humidity). In the Jerez district the press-houses are usually in the vineyards themselves or in the immediate vicinity, just outside the towns. The stalks are removed from the bunches and the grapes are pneumatically pressed. Seventy liters (18 gallons) of must is obtained from 100 kg (220 lb) of grapes. Only this 'first must' can be used for making sherry. Straight after pressing, the must is pumped into large (stainless steel) tanks of 10,500 gallons. Fermentation, which is started by wild yeast cells (Saccharomyces apiculatus) and continued with genuine wine yeast cells (Saccharomyces ellipsoideus), takes place at a completely automatically controlled temperature. Fermentation takes in total about seven days. Then follows a long period in the cask, in which the young wines settle down and can develop their specificity. The young wines are tested, classified and marked cask by cask. The cellar-master uses the ancient rayas system for this: one stripe (= raya) for the finest wines with pure aromas (base wines for fino, manzanilla and amontillado), one stripe with one dot after it for the wines with a great deal of character and body (base wines for olorosos), two stripes for wines that have neither the character and body for olorosos nor the pure aromas for finos, and finally three stripes for the wines that are rejected and will go to the distillery. The wines marked with one stripe are fortified with wine alcohol up to 15–15.5% and sent to the maturing chambers (criaderas) for fino, manzanilla and amontillado sherry. In contrast to most wines, where contact with oxygen should be kept to a minimum, the casks in this case are actually left open. These sherries, however, have no opportunity to oxidize. A film of yeast cells forms spontaneously on the surface of the wine, the flor, which seals the wine completely from outside air. During the aging process the yeast cells will be fed by alcohol and give the wines a typical aroma. The yeast cells are living organisms that are more active in the summer and become weaker and even die off in the winter. This means that the flor film is thinner in the winter than in the summer, when old yeast cells are replaced more quickly by new ones.

The wines marked with one stripe followed by one dot are fortified up to a minimum of 17.5% alcohol. This causes the yeast cells to die off and no flor film develops on the wines. These young wines are sent to the criadera for the olorosos, where maturing will take place in direct contact with the outside air. The fine and delicate wines, which do not oxidize due to the development of flor, are therefore called fino sherry. These wines keep their light color. The strong wines, full of character, which do not undergo flor development in connection with the higher alcohol percentage develop typical oxidation aromas. These wines are called *oloroso*, an aromatic, sweet-smelling sherry. They are darker in color.

The wines continue to mature slowly in the *criaderas* (maturing chambers). Maturing takes place in American oak casks each holding 600 liters (158 gallons). The casks are not completely filled (only five sixths of the total capacity), in order to allow the flor to develop (fino, manzanilla, amontillado) or to increase the surface of the wine that comes into contact with oxygen (olorosos).

At one time Jerez wines were always given a year number. Because the demand for sherry was growing so explosively, the need arose for a new system in which the quality of the wines could be guaranteed year in year out. Not until around the year 1830 did they begin using the solera system in the criaderas: three rows of casks are stacked on top of one another (criadera) on the understanding that the wine on the ground (Spanish *suelo*: this is where the name of the system comes from) is the oldest of the three and the top the youngest. When some wine needs to be bottled, it is tapped from the bottom casks. The empty space created is filled by the wines one row above; the empty space created here is in turn filled with wines that are another row higher. This step by step process can continue for ever. Some soleras consist of numerous rows, following one another in age, of three or more casks. In this way finos and manzanillas can easily go through fourteen criaderas in just over three years!

After going through the solera system the wines are tested and marked again. The purest wines continue as finos, while the finos that have ultimately developed more as an oloroso, without having the strength of these, are called palo cortado. When the maturing process is complete the wines are clarified and if necessary gently filtered.

VARIETIES OF SHERRY

At better wine merchants you may well find sherry wines from one specific year. These products, usually expensive but of outstanding quality, represent an extremely small minority and will not be dealt with separately here. We will use the Spanish classification system.

DRY WINES

– fino: a straw-colored wine, always dry and fresh, with the characteristic bouquet and flavor of nuts (almond, walnut), wood and flor. Alcohol: 15.5%. Superb aperitif, but also a good accompaniment to soft cheese (ibores from Extremadura, for example), white fish and appetizers. Combines excellently with smoked salmon or raw serrano ham. Drinking temperature: 10 °C (50 °F).

– amontillado: the name derives from neighboring Montilla. The style of these wines is like those of Mantilla and the name means something like 'in Montillian style'. These wines are darker in color than the other finos. They have matured for longer than most finos (ten to fifteen years instead of a minimum of three years). The flavor and bouquet are fresh and reminiscent of hazelnuts. Alcohol: 17.5%. Winter aperitif, but also an excellent accompaniment to starters with white meat or dark fish. Drinking temperature: 12–14 °C (54–57 °F).

– oloroso: these sweet-smelling wines that have had full oxidation are much darker in color than the finos, from amber-colored to mahogany. The flavor and texture of these wines, which are dry by nature, are full and strong, with distinct nuances of walnuts. To avoid confusion with the *oloroso dulce* (cream) *olorosos seco* often appears on the label. The wines smell sweet, but are dry with an alcoholic finishing touch that gives the tiniest impression of plumpness. Alcohol: 18%. Surprising accompaniments to red meat, game patés and cheese (garrotxa from Catalonia, for example). Drinking temperature: 12–14 °C (54–57 °F) for young olorosos, 14–16 °C (57–61 °F) for the older ones.

– palo cortado: the color of these wines inclines towards mahogany and the flavor is dry, well-balanced and reminiscent of hazelnuts. They are particularly rare dry wines that combine the soft, round flavor of amontillados with the fullness and character of olorosos. Alcohol: 18%. If you have the opportunity of tasting this wine, try it in combination with idiazábal from the Basque country or Navarra. Drinking temperature: 14–16 °C (57–61 °F).

SWEET WINES

– pale cream: these soft, pale wines are very much like a fino in appearance, but are slightly sweet and have a sophisticated and delicate flavor. Alcohol: 17.5%. They go surprisingly well with patés and fresh fruit. Also excellent with the soft, creamy tetilla cheese from Galicia. Drinking temperature: 8–10 °C (46–50 °F).

Fino de Jerez

Oloroso sherry

– rich cream: also called cream or oloroso dulce. These wines are made on the basis of oloroso and therefore have a great deal of body and character. The basic wines come from the pedro ximénes, sometimes supplemented with Moscatel, and are on average five to fifteen years old. The flavor is sweet, full, strong and soft at the same time. Alcohol: 17.5%. This wine is usually served as an old-fashioned dessert wine. Personally I prefer it combined with a good ripe zamorano from Castilla y Léon or ibérico cheese. Drinking temperature: 12–14 °C (54–57 °F).

– Pedro Ximénes, also known as PX. This dark wine (mahogany) is quite rare. It smells and tastes of raisins with hints of burnt coffee or cocoa. The wine is made from PX grapes dried in the sun. Alcohol: 17%. This wine is often served with sweet cake and why not? Choose mocha or chocolate cake. Also delicious are chocolates filled with PX cream. Combining it with a pungent cheese, roncal from Navarra or serena from Extremadura may sound unusual, but is worth a try. To those looking for the height of culinary sophistication I recommend a combination with a not over--ripe cabrales, a pungent blue cheese from the Asturias! Drinking temperature: 16–18 °C (61–64 °F) (if preferred, much colder).

MANZANILLA DE SANLÚCAR DE BARRAMEDA

Manzanillas are wines of the fino type that may only be produced in the harbor town of Sanlúcar de Barrameda. These wines are slightly lighter and often far more elegant than the other finos. The position near the sea and the gentle sea breeze blowing through the storage cellars of the bodegas gives these wines a very individual character. The Manzanilla de Sanlúcar de Barrameda has recently been granted its own DO and is increasingly to be distinguished from the sherry wines from Jerez de la Frontera or El Puerto de Santa María. This is partly an – understandable – reaction to the very unsatisfactory situation for Manzilla producers that almost all the money for promotion of sherry wines is spent on the finos. Although Manzanillas are certainly no poorer in quality than finos, they are presented as such. This has come to an end thanks to the setting up of their own promotion bureau by Manzanilla producers, on the initiative of, among others, the renowned Barbadillo bodega.

The color of Manzanilla is pale to straw-colored, the

Rich cream sherry

bouquet is fresh and slightly plant-like with distinct touches of 'flor'. The flavor is slightly saltier and, above all, drier than that of finos. The finishing touch is often a pleasant bitterness. Alcohol: 15.5%. An aperitif wine *par excellence*, but also wonderful with seafood and manchego. Drinking temperature: 10 °C (50 °F).

Manzanilla is most delicious when it is fresh. Outside Spain the Manzanilla bottles are left for far too long. To make export Manzanilla last longer the wines are filtered before bottling. Unfortunately this means that these Manzanillas lose their sophisticated character. Genuine Manzanilla is a product that tastes different every season. So, if possible, buy Manzanilla en Rama, which is bottled four times a year and sold in half bottles.

MÁLAGA

The DO of Málaga is situated in the province of the same name and consists of two districts: the western sub-district on the coast around Estepona and the northern sub-district around the town of Málaga up to the border with the provinces of Granada and Córdoba. Only the latter sub-district is of interest to us. Almost everywhere the soil consists of a limestone sub-stratum with a calcareous upper stratum. On the coast, however, the soil contains more ferruginous clay with some quartz and mica here and there. The climate is distinctly Mediterranean on the coast and more continental inland. Málaga has only two varieties of grape: moscatel in the coastal strip and pedro ximénes in the interior.

The Málaga dulce wines are made from over-ripe grapes that have been additionally dried in the warm sun. The juices obtained in this way are very concentrated and sweet. During fermentation the wines are fortified with wine alcohol to about 18%. A thick, sweet syrup, *arrope*, is also added. For these wines only *lágrima* (juices obtained without pressing, simply from the grapes' own weight) and *pisa* (first pressing) musts are used. The Málaga dulce lágrima is made only from the first free run (the lágrima). These wines are slightly finer in flavor than ordinary dulces. All Málaga dulce wines of any quality undergo solera maturing (see: sherry). A good Málaga dulce is

Pedro Ximénez (P.X.)

Manzanilla

Manzanilla en rama, spring
bottling

Summer bottling

Fall bottling

Winter bottling

very fruity, sweet and succulent with strong aromas of wood, raisins, caramel and burnt cocoa or coffee.

Drink this wine after meals with some cheese and nuts. Drinking temperature: according to taste, chilled 8–10 °C (46–50 °F), slightly chilled 12–14 °C (54–57 °F) or at room temperature 16–17 °C (61–63 °F).

MONTILLA-MORILES

The wine-growing region of Montila-Moriles is situated around the towns of the same names in the province of Córdoba. The best soils are in the central part of the district, the Superior wine-growing region. As in the Jerez *albarizas* (here also called *alberos*), these are soils rich in lime and good at storing water, so the vine-

yards do not dry out in the hot summers. The rest of the wine-acreage consists of sandy soils, in Jerez called *arenas*, but here *ruedos*. The vineyards are situated at a height of 980–2,300 ft. The climate is Mediterranean, almost subtropical in the south (Moriles) and with continental influences in the height of the interior (Montilla).

The most important grape here is pedro ximénes (75%), followed by moscatel and in the more recent vineyards a certain amount of airén (here called layrén or lairén), Torrontés and baladi for a few modern, still experimental wines. These experimental wines, the vinos jóvenes afrutados, are, at their best, light, fruity and fresh white wines. A relief in themselves in a baking hot area where almost exclusively heavy sweet wines are made. Great as an aperitif or, for example, with fish, shellfish or with local specialties, such as *callos a la andaluza* (steamed tripe) and *caracoles a la andaluza* (snails with, among other things, garlic, almonds, peppers, tomatoes and lemon). Drinking temperature: 8–10 °C (46–50 °F).

Vinos crianzas are wines that are not fortified, contain a minimum of 13% natural alcohol and have been matured in the wood for at least one year. They come in seco (dry), semi-seco (medium-dry) and dulce (cream). For a sweet flavor a little sweet syrup or *vinos de licor* (*mistela*) is added to the by nature dry wines.

Vinos generosos have a natural alcohol content of more than 15%. These wines are subjected to a solera system (see: sherry) to keep the quality homogeneous. They are available in the following types:

- fino seco: dry, lightly colored with a fine, pungent bouquet and flavor. Often reminiscent of Provençal herbs. Alcohol: 14–17.5%
- amontillado: dry, gold or amber colored, strong bouquet and flavor of hazelnuts, soft and full. Alcohol: 16–18%.
- oloroso: oxidized (no 'flor'), mahogany color, very aromatic, velvety soft, dry or slightly sweet. Alcohol: young wines 16–18%, old 22%;
- palo cortado: oxidized, mahogany color, very aromatic, somewhere between an oloroso and amontillado. Alcohol: 16–18%;
- Pedro Ximénes: probably the best wine of Montilla-Moriles, made from 100% over-ripe grapes, further dried in the sun after harvesting. Because of the enormous concentration of sugars the must for these wines cannot completely ferment out naturally. So *spirit* (wine distillate) is added to the saccharine-sweet must. This results in a very dark wine with a sugar content of more than 272 g/liter (4³/₈ oz per pint).

Serving temperatures and advice on accompanying food are the same as for the Jerez wines (see that section).

CANARY ISLANDS

The Canary Islands are of volcanic origin. In Tenerife, La Palma and Lanzarote, among other places, the volcanoes are still active. The climate on the islands is quite varied, with the mountains catching most of the rainfall, brought by the northeasterly winds. As much as eight to fifteen times as much rain falls on Tenerife, El Hierro, La Gomera and La Palma a year than on Fuerteventura and Lanzarote. The eastern islands often have to contend with the warm wind from the Sahara, the Scirocco. The average annual temperature can certainly be called mild. Except in the mountains the islands are never or hardly ever in danger of frost.

The food culture of the islands is rich, varied and healthy. There are plenty of sea fish (including herring and wolf fish), marine animals (squid) and shellfish (mussels, clams, and suchlike). Strangely enough, the islands do not have any freshwater fish – apart from a few tropical fish. Numerous fruits and vegetables grow on the fertile volcanic soils. There is also a vast choice of meat. You will not find large game on the Canary Islands, but there are hares, rabbits, partridges and quails.

The Canary Islands' wine-growing has a rich past due to the Malvasía wine, once renowned in England, a full, sweet wine which is midway between Madeira wines and Spanish olorosos. However, you will no longer find many good Malvasías. Wine-growing has developed enormously since the 1980s and particularly in the direction of table wines (in contrast to rancios, generosos and suchlike). This is partly due to the explosive growth in tourism on the islands. In order to be able to satisfy the demands of the many visitors, old vineyards have been grubbed and replanted with well suited grapes such as the native negramoll or listán negro. The equipment has been completely modernized and there is a thriving trade in local wines. The wine district of Tacorante-Acentejo was the first to be recognized as DO and La Palma, El Hierro, Valle de la Orotava, Ycoden-Daute-Isora, Valle de Güimar, Abona and Lanzarote soon followed. The Canary wines are sold for the most part in local restaurants and wine-shops and the rest goes to the duty-free shops. You hardly ever find Canary wine outside the islands. Because of this exceptional position the winegrowers and cooperative bodegas can ask quite high prices, by Spanish standards, for their wines. The most important wines are:

– La Palma Malvasia seco, semi-dulce and dulce
– La Palma Negramoll tinto
– La Palma Vino de Tea (retsina-type red, white and rosé wines cask-matured for six months in pine casks)
– El Hierro blanco, rosado and tinto
– Valle de la Orotava blanco and tinto crianza
– Ycoden-Daute-Isora rosado and tinto
– Tacoronte-Acentejo tinto
– Valle de Güimar blanco, rosado and tinto
– Abona
– Lanzarote Malvasía seco, semi-dulce and dulce

PORTUGAL

Portugal has much to offer, including a rich culture and history, green landscapes in the north, picturesque towns and harbor villages, magnificent beaches, mountains in the interior and, above all, a very surprising choice of wine and food.

LANZAROTE

EL GRIFO
MALVASÍA SECO
2000

12,5 % Vol.　　　PRODUCE OF SPAIN　　　75 cL

EMBOTELLADO POR EL GRIFO, S.A. - R.E.1776-GC - EL GRIFO - ESPANA

Lanzarote Malvasia seco

The climate in Portugal is in general quite moderate. The south has the warmest and driest climate, moderate Mediterranean. Portugal has a total of 989,000 acres of vineyards, enough to provide about 10 million hectoliters (220 million gallons) of wine a year. Almost 25% of the entire population still makes its living directly or indirectly from wine-growing. Portugal has been exporting wines since the fourteenth century and was the first country officially to guarantee a designation of origin (Porto-Douro). Almost everywhere Portuguese wine-growers have made up for their lost ground in technology in recent decades. The high-tech *adegas* or independent *quintas* have become fully automated. All the same, the best quintas (independent wine companies) combine respect for ancient wine tradition with the guarantee of hygiene and convenience provided by the latest technology.

Under the terms of the European Community Portuguese wines are sub-divided into different categories.

VQPRD (VINHO DE QUALIDADE PRODUZIDO EM REGIÃO DETERMINADA)

Wines of good quality and limited quantity, which must be produced in the area of origin and only from grapes from the demarcated designation of origin. These include the DOC and IPR, and also the high quality liqueur wines VLQPRD (Vinho Licoroso de Qualidade Produzido em Região Determinada) and the better sparkling wines VEQPRD (Vinho Espumante de Qualidade Produzido em Região Determinada).

DOC (DENOMINAÇÃO DE ORIGEM CONTROLADA)

Quality wines made from grapes from a strictly demarcated region and produced in the area of origin. Demarcation is done on the basis of geographical uniformity (position, soil, climate), typical characteristics and style of the wines and the local traditions of wine preparation.

You are welcome anytime in Portugal (Quinta do Convento)

The green north

IPR (INDICAÇÃO DE PROVENIÈCIA REGULAMENTADA)

IPR wines are strictly bound to a geographical area and have a very individual character. They are, in fact, placed in a kind of waiting room where they have to prove themselves worthy candidates for the higher designation of DOC for a minimum of five years.

Ancient slate poles for securing the vines in the Douro

VINHOS REGIONAIS

Better table wines with demarcated designation of origin, comparable to the various other European regional wines.

VINHOS DE MESA

Wines for everyday consumption without specific designation of origin, comparable to European table wines.

THE WINES

The wine-growing regions below are listed according to geographical position, from north to south. Port and Madeira are dealt with separately at the end. Portuguese wines that we shall not discuss further here, but which you really ought to try are:
- Valpaços/Tras-Os-Montes IPR
- Chaves IPR
- Planalto Mirandês IPR
- Távora-Varosa DOC
- Lafoes IPR
- Beira Interior DOC
- Obido DOC
- Lourinha DOC
- Alcobaça IPR
- Arruda DOC
- Alenquer DOC
- Encostas d'Aire IPR
- Portuguese rosé

VINHOS VERDES DOC

This wine-growing region is situated in northwest Portugal. The strength of the Vinho Verde area lies in its combination of a very favorable microclimate, suitable soil (granite with an upper stratum of sand and humus), the gentle relief and the excellent old traditional grapes. The vineyards of the Vinho Verde district make up about 10% of the total area of vineyards on the Portuguese mainland. The largest production regions are Viana de Castelo, Porto and Braga. The vines here, unlike elsewhere, are not trained low, but in fact very high, to prevent the grapes from rotting. The vines are trained on trellises, pergolas or even cross-shaped concrete structures and usually picked from below, often from a platform behind a tractor.

The vinhos verdes (literally: green wines) owe their name to the magnificent green of the surrounding countryside, and not, as some malicious tongues would have it, to the high acidity of the wines! Vinhos verdes come in white and red, from dry to slightly sweet.

Drink a vinho verde young, within one or two years of picking. The wines made from 100% Alvarinho from the subdistrict of Monçao, the vinhos verdes Alvarinho, can be kept slightly longer.

Vinhos verdes brancos are perfect aperitifs, especially as they have a suggestion of carbon dioxide about them. This delicate fizziness is

Denominação de Origem Controlada Dão

One of Portugal's many vinhos regionais, which comes from Alentejo

Tras-Os-Montes also produces many vinhos regionais

As well as DO wines, Beira produces many regional wines

obtained in a completely natural way, by bottling the wines quickly after the second fermentation (malolactic or milk fermentation). Most of the wines contain about 10% alcohol.

Vinho verde branco seco has slightly more alcohol

Apart from as aperitifs, you can also serve these fresh, fruity white vinhos verdes with lunch. At meals they combine excellently with shellfish and crustaceans, fish or cold meat. Try *gambas picantes* (spicy grilled prawns with garlic and chili sauce). Drinking temperature: 8–10 °C (46–50 °F).

The vinhos verdes Alvarinho are of better quality and contain slightly more alcohol. Drink them with better varieties of fish or with chicken, veal or pork. Try *santola no carro* ('spider crab in a carriage': stuffed crab with herbs cooked in the oven). Drinking temperature: 10–12 °C (50–54 °F).

Vinhos verdes tinto are equally as light and refreshing as the white but have just that little bit more body. They taste even more delicious straight from the cask, simply put on the table in a carafe. Bottling does most wines more harm than good.

Drink them with lunch, with meaty kinds of fish (monkfish, lamprey) or with all kinds of poultry or meat dishes. Try *arroz de pato de Braga*, a rice dish with duck and garlic sausage. Drinking temperature: 10–12 °C (50–54 °F).

Vinho verde branco usually has a slight sweetness

DOURO DOC

The Rio D'ouro (golden river) gave its name to this district in north-eastern Portugal, which has been famous for its wines for more than two thousand years, principally for the vinho do porto (port). It seems that increasingly more table wines are being made in the Douro valley. In recent years more of these table wines have been produced than port!

The vineyards of the Upper Douro Valley begin about 62 miles inland from the harbor town of Porto. Most of the vineyards are planted on hills with a soil

of ancient rock and granite. The climate in the valley is relatively dry and semi-continental. Good quality white and red wines are produced here. Malvasia fina, rabigato, viosinho, donzelinho or verdelho, for example, are used for the white wines and bastardo, mourisco tinto, tinta roriz, tinta francisca, touriga nacional or tinto cao, for example, for the red.

Great lunch wine

Douro brancos are fresh, lively and very aromatic wines. The flavor is delicate and sophisticated, definitely not too heavy. These wines with a minimum of 11% alcohol have to have undergone at least nine months maturing in the bottle before they can be sold. Drink these white Douro as an aperitif or with fish or seafood. Try *pescado frito*, crisply fried fish coated in breadcrumbs. Drinking temperature: 10–12 °C (50–54 °F).

Some Douro tintos are young, fruity and almost playful, while others are in fact quite sturdy and powerful. This is partly to do with the choice of grapes, the vinification technique used and the length of cask-maturing. All red Douro must be at least eighteen months old before they can be sold and contain a minimum of 11% alcohol. The modern wines are very

In the Doura valley a great deal of red wine is made too.

rich in color, fruity, velvety soft, succulent and full of flavor. The traditional wines are quite dark in color and very aromatic, often almost rustic (granite terrain). Drink a red Douro with red meat, game or mature cheeses (tomar or rabaçal). Try *cocido de grao*, a spicy stew that includes chickpeas, pork and chorizo. Drinking temperature: modern wines 12–14 °C (54–57 °F), traditional wines 14–17 °C (57–63 °F).

BAIRRADA DOC

The climate of the Bairrada district is distinctly influenced by the Atlantic Ocean. The name 'bairrada' is derived from the Portuguese word for clay or lime *bairro* or *barro*, which refers to the local soil. First-rate wines are made here, with a great deal of extract and a great deal of color. Bairrada wines are seductive charmers. They are available in red, white and rosé. Grapes used for the rare white wines (about 10% of production) include bical and rabo de ovelha (also known as rabigato) and for the rosé (10%) and red (80%) Baga and Rufete. Acceptable sparkling wines are also made in Bairrada according to the méthode traditionelle. The majority of the production is in the hands of the *adegas coöperativas* and a few independent quintas.

Bairrada branco is very rare, but definitely worth discovering. In particular those wines that have had a (short) time maturing in the cask are surprisingly delicious. You can drink these fresh, sophisticated wines young, or they can mature for a few extra years.

Drink a Bairrada blanco with fish, white meat, chicken or even young cheese. Try *frango no churrasco*, grilled chicken. Drinking temperature 8–10 °C (46–50 °F).

Simple but very pleasant Douro tinto

The Bairrado rosado is slightly spicier than the white, but not as full as its red namesake. Ideal with lunch, with mixed dishes (fish + pork) or with the local greatly renowned sucking pig. Try *frango piri-piri*, casseroled chicken with a piquant sauce (piri-piri), vegetables and a pinch of cinnamon. Drinking temperature: 10–12 °C (50–54 °F).

The Bairrada tinto has a strikingly intense bouquet and a broad, full flavor. It is a powerful wine with a great deal of character and a long after-taste that improves with a few years maturing in the bottle.

Drink this wine with red meat, game and mature cheeses. Try *cacarola de cabrito*, stewed goat's meat (or lamb) with red peppers, red wine, onions, carrots, potatoes, garlic and coriander leaves. Drinking temperature: 12–14 °C (54–57 °F) for young wines, 14–17 °C (57–63 °F) for the older wines.

As well as white, red and rosé wines, Bairrada also makes good white sparkling wines and excellent wine spirits.

DÃO DOC

The Dão district is situated just below the wine-growing region of the Douro. The district is in the central part of Portugal, between the Spanish border and the Bairrada wine-growing district, and is surrounded by moun-

tain ranges that protect the vineyards from the damp winds of the Atlantic Ocean and the extreme continental cold. The north and center of the region consist of a soil of hard granite and the south of slate or stone chips. The vineyards are situated on terraces on the steep sides of the mountains, as in the Douro valley. The climate is quite moderate, with in general warm and dry summers and cold falls. Mainly black grapes thrive on the granite soil, while the white grapes do better on the slate or stone chips. The traditional grapes of the Dão include alfro-

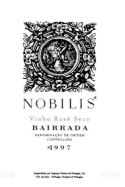

Bairrada branco

Bairrada tinto reserva

Bairrada rosado

chero preto, tinta pinheiro and touriga nacional for the red wines and the ancient barcelo, bical, cercial and uva cao for the white. All Dão wines must contain at least 11% alcohol. Since the vineyards are so spread out and are small in size the role of the large cooperatives (adegas coöperativas) is of huge importance. Yet the number of domains (quintas) maturing and bottling their own wines is steadily increasing. This in itself is a good sign for the future.

The Dão branco must have been matured for a minimum of six months before it is sold. Some wines are stored in the wood for a short time. Modernization of the vinification means that today excellent, dry, fresh, fruity white Dãos can be made that go particularly well with fish, chicken and white meat. Try *pescada/moda de Beira Alta* (hake baked in white Dão wine, with, among other things, potatoes, mushrooms, tomatoes and onion). Drinking temperature 8–10 °C (46–50 °F).

The Dão tinto must have had a minimum maturing time of eighteen months. In its youth this Dão tinto is ruby red in color and quite austere and full. After a few years maturing it develops a velvety smooth flavor full of character and a very complex bouquet. Some old wines bear the designation 'reserva' or 'garrafeira'. By the way, drinking a Dão tinto always has a beneficial effect on the digestion!

Drink this wine with pork, grilled meat, game and cheese. Try *coelho a Beira*, rabbit stewed in red Dão wine, with, among other things, onions, garlic and bacon. Drinking temperature: young 12–14 °C (54–57 °F), old/reserva/garrafeira 14–17 °C (57–63 °F).

TORRES VEDRAS DOC

As in the surrounding vineyards above Lisbon, the climate here is moderate, with subtropical and Mediterranean influences. The soil contains lime, clay, shingle and calcareous loam. The white wines are aromatic and fresh, but it is principally the red wines of Torres Vedras that stand out from the rest. The Torres Vedras tintos VQPRD are ruby red in color, soft and fruity with a hint of wood, full and round. Drink them with (red) meat or cheese. Drinking temperature: 14 °C (57 °F).

The Torres Vedras tintos reservas VQPRD are pomegranate red in color and have a very complex bouquet. They are rich in aromas and nuances of flavor, full, rounded and velvety soft. Drink these wines with (red) meat, possibly in rich sauces, or with grilled or braised poultry. Try *perdiz//Guincho*, braised partridge with cabbage, onion and bacon.

Dão branco

Drinking temperature: 16–17 °C (61–63 °F).

The Adega Coöperativa de Torres Vedras also makes excellent regional and table wines.

BUCELAS DOC

This region lies in the valley of the river Trançao, about 15 miles from the town of Lisbon. The area has a strange microclimate, very cold in the winter and warm in the summer. There are great variations in temperature. The soil here consists of a mixture of clay and lime. The wines of Bucelas have enjoyed a good reputation for more than a century. Unfortunately lack of quantity stands in the way of the world breakthrough that, especially in view of their intrinsic quality, they richly deserve. The wines are white, dry, aromatic and, above all, intended to be drunk young. Older wines lose their fresh acids and become slightly milder, but gain in intensity of aroma.

Dão tinto

Drink these wines with crustaceans and shellfish or with fish. Try *filetes a Portugesa*, fish fillets (whiting, sole) in Portuguese style, with tomato sauce. Drinking temperature: 10–12 °C (50–54 °F).

CARCAVELOS DOC

Carcavelos wines are among the best and most famous in Portugal. Until fairly recently they were in danger of dying out due to sweeping urbanization. This small wine-growing region

Torres Vedras is still greatly underestimated and is therefore cheap!

at the mouth of the river Tagus has a pleasant, moderately Mediterranean climate, directly influenced by the ocean. The soil consists of lime with odd spots of basalt. Special sweet liqueur-type wines are made here, with a magnificent amber-colored appearance and a very aromatic bouquet. The wine is mellow, velvety and very sophisticated. Drink this wine with melon or fresh figs, for example, and a small portion of cheese, or just on its own after meals. Watch out: this wine contains 18 to 20% alcohol! Drinking temperature 6–8 °C (43–46 °F).

COLARES DOC

Wine was being made in this small region near Sintra on the Atlantic coast as early as the thirteenth century. The vineyards are regularly subjected to strong sea winds. The climate is moderately oceanic and the soil consists of sand, a little clay and some patches of basalt.

The white wines made from the Malvasia grape are light and aromatic and go extremely well with all delicacies from the sea. Do not drink these wines too young; they often improve after a few years in the bottle. Try *pargo assada*, baked sea bream with tomatoes, onion, garlic and coriander. Drinking temperature: 10–12 °C (50–54 °F).

The red wines are particularly spicy and harsh when they are young. So let them rest for a few years. They then become mellower, more aromatic and better in flavor. Red Colares are an excellent accompaniment to grilled or roast meat or game. Try *iscas*, marinated and baked (lamb's) liver with bacon and garlic, or *bifes de porco grelhado*, pork kebabs with onion, peppers, garlic, lemon juice, olive oil and fresh mint. Drinking temperature: 14–17 °C (57–63 °F).

RIBATEJO DOC

The history of this wine-growing region northeast of Lisbon begins well before the birth of Portugal. The wine-growing region is situated around the low basin of the Tagus. The climate is subtropical with Atlantic and Mediterranean influences. The ground consists of clay, lime, sand and alluvial soil. Something of everything is produced here, dry and sweet wines, red wines, some cask-matured and others not, and very acceptable sparkling wines. The white wines are mild, fruity, often velvety smooth in texture and can accompany any fish dish, particularly boiled fish. The red wines are usually pomegranate red in color, hearty and rich but with plenty of fruit. The best red wines can be kept for at least ten years. Drink them with grilled or roast red meat. Try *bife de cebolada*', steak with an onion and red wine sauce. Drinking temperature: 8–10 °C (46–50 °F) for the white wines, 14–16 °C (57–6 °F) for the red wines.

PALMELA DOC

On the peninsula around Setúbal the climate is subtropical and the soil consists of lime, sandstone, clay and shingle. The red wines produced here (including from Periquita) are strong and spicy. They become mellower and better as they age. Drink them with roast or braised meat. Try *Borrego estufado*, braised shoulder of lamb with garlic, onion, carrots, white celery, leeks and tomatoes. Drinking temperature: 14–17 °C (57–63 °F).

MOSCATEL DE SETÚBAL DOC

Moscatel del Setúbal is, in my opinion, one of the best fortified wines in the world. It is made on the peninsula of Setúbal, on the banks of the Sado. The climate here is subtropical and the vineyards lie on a soil of clay and lime. The wines are made from Moscatel, with its distinctly recognizable bouquet and flavor. Drink this sweet, rich, honey-like wine after meals or with a not over-sweet dessert. Try *salada de laranjas*, a fresh, sharp salad of oranges and figs with honey. Drinking temperature 6–10 °C (43–50 °F).

ALENTEJO DOC

Alentejo lies to the (south) east of Lisbon and covers a fairly large area where wine and olive oil have been produced since time immemorial. The majority of the wine production is in the hands of enormous *adegas coöperativas*.

Red wines make up the majority of the production, but there is an ever- increasing demand for good, reasonably priced white wines. The enormous region (more than 32,100 acres) of vineyards) is flat and mainly dry and rocky. The climate is Mediterranean with Atlantic influences. The summers here are very warm and dry. In total more than twenty varieties of grapes are used. A number of sub-districts of the Alentejo have been granted provisional recognition in the form

Palmela

of their own IPR (Portalegre, Borba, Redondo, Reguengos and Vidigueira). It is expected that these regions will soon be promoted to DOC. The DOC Alentejo comprises the remaining sub-districts of Granja/Amarleja, Evora and Moura, but also serves a generic purpose: the wines from all the IPR regions of the Alentejo can be blended together into DOC Alentejo. Granja/Amereleja is not yet allowed to bear an independent designation. For the time being the wines of this Alentejo region come under the generic DOC. Evora was once a famous wine-growing region and is now working on its revival. Judging by the quality of the new wines it will probably not be long before Evora too obtains its own IPR and eventually DOC.

PORTIMÃO DOC/TAVIRA DOC/ LAGOS DOC/LAGOA DOC

The climate in the Algarve is subtropical and the soil consists principally of sand. The Algarve's wine-growing traditions date from before the arrival of the Moors. The wines produced here are very characteristic of hot, dry regions.

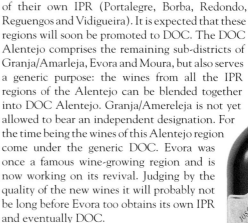

Moscatel de Setúbal

The white wines are quite mild in acids, fine and delicate, but often contain a large amount of alcohol (up to 13%). Drink these wines with fish, white meat or crustaceans and shellfish. Try *salada atum e batata*, a particularly tasty salad of potatoes, tuna, egg and tomato, or *ameïjoas na cataplana*, a typical casserole of cockles (small seafood), chorizo, ham and coriander leaves in a piquant *piri-piri* sauce. Drinking temperature: 8–10 °C (46–50 °F).

The red wines are soft and velvety, with a lot of alcohol and little body and acids. They taste great with all meat dishes. Try *trouxa de vitela*, marinated, grilled veal with red onion, red pepper and garlic. Drinking temperature: 14–16 °C (57–6 °F).

BISCOITOS IPR/GRACIOSA IPR/PICO IPR

Wine is also made in the Azores, but you will very rarely come across it outside the islands. In the Biscoitos wine-growing region, on the island of Terceira, very interesting liqueur wines are produced, mainly from Verdelho. The volcanic soil gives these wines a very individual character. Wine was already being produced on Graciosa and exported in the sixteenth century. On Pico excellent wines are made from Verdelho. This 'Verdelho do Pico', very popular in the nineteenth

Alentejo still has many relatively good regional wines

century, is a 'generoso' (liqueur wine) of especially good quality, comparable with the best Madeira. The wine owes its strength, character, charm and aromas to the volcanic soil (basalt), the high temperatures and the regular rainfall. Each vine is planted in a hole in the dark basalt soil and then protected by a low round wall.

PORT DOC

Port or porto takes its name from the harbor city of Porto, today Portugal's second city. Porto is close to Vila Nova de Gaia, where most of the port wines are stored, bottled and marketed.

In the seventeenth century the French and the British were entangled in a violent battle with Europe as the stake. The then French minister Colbert decided to introduce huge taxes on the export of Bordeaux wines. The British found alternatives in Spain (Navarra) and Portugal (Douro). However, the British were not the only ones interested in Portuguese and Spanish wines.

Vinho regional from Alentejo

The Dutch too, who were looking for wines as the base for their brandies, had found a niche for themselves in Portugal. It was the Dutch who gave the British the idea of adding some wine alcohol to the Douro wines to help them to stand up better to the long, rough voyage home. These new, fortified wines soon found a ready market in British taverns. The British soon discovered that the wines in the Douro valley from the monasteries between Lamego and Pinhão were much fuller, more robust, more complex and more pleasant than the others. It was in 1679 that enterprising English traders first added a little Portuguese *aguardente* (wine alcohol) to the must during vinification. They had learned this from the monks of Lamego, who had already discovered the secret of *beneficio* (fortifying wine). It produced excellent, albeit unexpected, results: since fermentation was stopped at an early stage, the wines were sweeter, fuller, rounder, fruitier and, above all, less harsh! In no time this drink became extremely popular both in Portugal and England. Experiments with letting the wines mature longer were a great success. The first vintage port wines developed due to the arrival of the cylindrical bottle. Large numbers of British wine merchants arrived in Porto to set up new businesses there. Trade was concentrated in the nearby harbor town, named by the Portuguese O Porto (the harbor or port), later shortened to Porto.

At the end of the nineteenth century *Phylloxera* and later mildew almost completely destroyed the wine acreage in the Douro valley. All the vineyards were replanted on immune American root stock.

They then began to leave some wines longer in the cask. This was the first time a distinction was made between the cheap, young, fruity 'drink of the masses' (the ruby) and the more expensive, rarer vintage port

The Douro valley, a breath-taking wine-growing region

matured in the cask, the 'civilized' port for the upper classes. In 1906 the government decided that from now on port wines could be exported only from the port of Porto and that they had to contain a minimum of 16.5% alcohol. Since 1921 it has been compulsory for the wines to be cask-matured for a minimum number of years and since 1926 only the trading houses resident in Villa Nova de Gaia have been allowed to export. Since 1933 the quality and authenticity of port wines has been strictly controlled by the mighty Instituto do Vinho do Porto. In 1985 the law was relaxed and from then on wines were also allowed to be matured in the Douro valley and exported from there (via a trading office in Porto/Villanova de Gaia). In 1997 came the most radical change: the ban on bulk transport and bottling of port wines outside the area.

Port is actually a 'generoso', a fortified wine. The official European designation for these wines is in full: Vin Liquoreux de Qualité Produit dans une Région Délimitée (VLQPRD). As a mark of respect for the

The Nacional vineyard, here in the morning shade, is the only one that still has vines from before the Phylloxera plague!

quality of their wine the Portuguese wine companies are allowed to continue to put the name 'generoso' on the bottle. However, you will rarely come across this designation outside Portugal.

In the Alto-Douro valley the vineyards are protected from extreme influences of the oceanic climate by the 4,590 ft high Marao mountains. The vines are forced to excel themselves in order to reach the scarce water. Because the roots need to go deep (sometimes as much as 65 ft deep), the plant takes in a lot of nutrients from the deep strata, which is good for the strength of the aroma. The soil in the western foothills of the Iberian high plain (meseta) consists primarily of stone chips, with patches of granite and silex (flint). The great variations in temperature are extremely beneficial for the development of aromas and flavorings. The vineyards are situated on the sides of the mountains, which are about 1,640 ft high, on both sides of the Douro and its tributaries and are divided into three very different sub-districts:

– Baixo Corgo, with the low Corgo and Douro valleys. The relief is much gentler and the region more accessible and this is therefore the most productive part of the Douro wine-growing area. It is also the land of polyculture, with olive, almond and orange trees growing next to or between the vines. In general there are a large number of vineyards here with high yields and, relatively speaking, slightly lower quality.

– Cima Corgo, the central part of the Douro valley. Here polyculture has almost disappeared. This is the country of many isolated quintas, disjointed terraces and wooded mountain peaks. This is where the better wines come from, much fuller and more complex than those from Baixo Corgo.

– Alto Douro, a steep, almost desert-like region with little rainfall and a great deal of sun. Thanks to the latest techniques this area is emerging more and more from its isolation. The soil is exceptionally suitable for wine-growing. The problem is transport in and out: it will be a long time before the necessary infrastructure is in place.

and supported by substantial stone walls. The vines are planted close together, which forces the plants to compete with one another and improves the strength of the aroma.

These terraces are expensive to maintain though, and difficult to work on. The so-called 'patamares', narrower terraces without walls, but with a sloping bank are more modern.

Here the vines are often planted in every other row, which lowers the yield and possibly also to some extent the strength of the aroma, but has the great advantage that it enables better maintenance and even mechanization.

Finally there is the Ao Alto system, in which the vines are planted square on the slope. This system, being used more and more frequently, can, however, only be used on gently sloping inclines, usually up to 32 degrees.

Yet the Ao Alto system is sometimes employed on steeper inclines, with regular channels or paths to stop erosion. A plus point of this system is the possibility of achieving higher yields.

Polyculture: vines and orange and olive trees (Quinta das Heredias)

CLASSIFICATION OF VINEYARDS

The complex Portuguese inspection system is based on terrain and climate rather than strains of grape. The vineyards are divided into categories according to geological, topographical and climatological parameters. Of importance, for example, are the height of the vineyards in relation to the river (130–1,480 ft is ideal),

TERRACES, PATAMARES AND AO ALTO

Port, a 'genial' (generoso) drink

Countless terraces have been built to prevent erosion and to make working on the very steep slopes len ardnous.

The original terraces were narrow and protected only by rows of stones piled on top of one another. Now the terraces are wider

New terraces on steep mountain sides

local microclimates (the amount of rainfall is especially significant), incline (well drained steep slopes prevail over heavy, flat terrain low in the valley), position (in relation to the sun and the wind) and of course type of soil (stone chips score better than stone chips + granite and loess, for example; the number of stones in the

Ancient terraces on the banks of the Douro

upper stratum is also significant). Finally, in adding up the points, the way in which the vineyards are managed, the yield, the density of cultivation, and so on are also considered. The more points, the higher the ranking from A to F. Twice as much is paid for grapes from top vineyards (100% A) than for grapes from the

The old terraces produce outstanding quality, but are expensive (and dangerous) to maintain and use

lowest vineyards (E and F). The Instituto do Vinho do Porto still also decides, based on the quality of the vineyards, how much port and table wine they are allowed to make. The better vineyards are allowed to make more port and the worse ones more table wine.

VARIETIES OF GRAPES

The eighty-seven varieties of grape recommended here are not all used at once by any means. There are

Patamares

five very popular varieties: touriga nacional (complexity, strength, fine aromas and aging potential), roriz (elegance, fine, fresh acids), barroca (depth and sultry fruit aromas, velvety smooth texture), touriga francesca (fruit and body) and cao (elegance, lightness, complexity, aging potential). Grapes used for white port and the white Douro wines include mal-

Ao alto system

vasia fina, rabigato, codega, gouveio, viosinho and donzelinho.

THE HARVEST

Nowhere in the world can the harvest have been as difficult as in the Douro valley. Now, of course, the terraces are much wider and the access roads allow trucks in. Today the grapes are picked into small bins, which do less damage to the grapes and therefore help to prevent any spontaneous fermentation. If the vineyards are very close to the press-houses the grapes are still brought to the quintas in large bins. The harvest normally takes place from the beginning of September until the end of October. Once the grapes are in, they are pneumatically pressed and further processed. Only a few top quintas, such as Quinta do Noval, still work with the old-fashioned granite lagares, in which the grapes are still trodden in the famed manner of folklore.

Top A vineyards at Quinta do Noval

Portuguese wine-growers are looking for alternatives to this traditional treading. In most of the quintas they use systems that keep the mixture of skins constantly in motion and tread it down. This method is systematically used for port of average quality. At the Symington group's Quinta do Sol (including Dow's and Graham) automated lagares are used, in which silicone pads imitate treading by foot. This continually introduces oxygen into the fermenting must, activating the fermentation still further. The result is amazingly good.

WINE PREPARATION

Douradal

Once it has been fully trodden or pressed (the second, gentle pressing is also used here), the press-cake goes to processing companies and the divine smelling juices are pumped into storage tanks. On the way to or on arrival at the tanks or casks, wine alcohol of 77% is gradually added to the still fermenting juices. In general about 16–20% alcohol is allowed per volume of fermenting must. As it is added gradually, the alcohol can blend well into the must without destroying the fruity aromas. Ultimately, after this operation, the young fortified wine will have an alcohol percentage of about 18%, which can eventually be increased further. The quality of the *aguardente* is of great importance for the ultimate character of the port. After the harvest the fortified wines are, if necessary, transferred by pumping and blended to make them more homogeneous. It is still too early to decide what type of wine they will become, but a first selection will be made on the basis of quality.

What is planted in the vineyards naturally has an influence on the quality and character of the wines, just as whether they are harvested haphazardly or separately by grape and section of land. Growers who harvest all the grape varieties separately, preferably one section of land at a time, and vinify them separately keep all their options open. Naturally the basic conditions differ from year to year, but most of the houses employ their own style and clear guidelines. Therefore the wines from two

Smoothing out the grapes as they arrive in the traditional lagares

Treading continues day and night

Tiredness sets in, no more nice rows

The better the cuvee, the smaller the lagares
(Quinta do Noval, lagar for the Nacional Single Quinta)

brands from one and the same group can be completely different; one, for example, slightly sweeter and more sensual, the other drier and richer in tannin. The first serious selection is aimed at setting the best wines apart (for vintage and colheita). The rest of the harvest will be assessed again later, with increasingly clearer distinctions being made. According to a kind of pyramid system over time a constant watch is kept to see how a wine is going to develop. The top of the pyramid consists of the very best, a special vintage cuvée. If the quality is not adequate for this, the wine that would normally produce this top cuvée is downgraded, usually for another vintage. The wines that do not have the vintage quality and desired characteristics are set apart for later. The best wines will be used for the colheitas, among other things. The wines that are just below these are reserved for the 'aged

The LBV 95 is resting here for
a well-known Belgian customer

tawnies', then the special tawny and finally what is left is processed into ruby.

THE WINES

Port is one of the most imitated drinks in the world, but the quality of a good port is never equaled anywhere else. Port is sun in a bottle, but is also indissolubly linked with its earthy beginnings, the soil of stone chips and ancient rock. This makes it different from the port-type wines made elsewhere.

'A glass of port' has become a fairly common expression, where 'port', like sherry, cognac, Champagne, Burgundy and Bordeaux, has become synonymous with a brand product. A pity, because there are all types and flavors of port. Sometimes an erroneous distinction is made between wines matured by oxidation and by reduction. This, however, is not wholly correct. The first oxidation takes place in the lagares and the young fermenting must, to which alcohol is added, has already been slightly oxidized. In the two to three years all port wines spend in the cask extra oxidation also takes place through the pores of the casks. Only after this can a distinction be made between wines that mature further in the cask (therefore undergo further oxidation) and wines that continue to mature further in the bottle. It would be better to refer to oxidative (tawny) or oxido-reductive (vintage). Only a wine vinified and stored in stainless steel and then bottled straightway is a reductive wine, which is certainly not the case with port.

PORTO BRANCO/WHITE PORT

For centuries port was always red. Since 1935 white port has also been made, in the same way as red port, except for the fact that white grapes are used (including malvasia). White port can have various levels of sweetness, from saccharine sweet and syrupy, or even "like tears", as the Portuguese call it (*lágrima*), via the softly sweet *meio-seco* and full sweet doce to extra dry (*bone-dry, crispy dry*). A relatively new trend has been set by the fresh, reductive, dry, less alcoholic (16.5%) *leve seco* wines which do good service as aperitifs.

White chilled port (extra-seco, seco or meio-seco) is delicious as an aperitif. The slightly cheaper varieties are also suitable for smart cocktails, but don't tell the port purists – for them drinking white port is a 'crime' in itself. It is very trendy to fill a glass a third full with not too sweet a white port, put in two ice cubes, a slice of lemon and to fill it up with Schweppes Indian Tonic. A sublime summer aperitif with a handful of fresh almonds fried in olive oil!

The soil

TINTO ALOIRADO/RUBY

Ruby port owes its name to the lovely ruby red color of the young port. A ruby port has undergone a minimum of three years maturing in the cask, after which it is bottled immediately. As the wine is matured for less time in the cask, ruby port is a relatively cheap product and therefore very popular. Ordinary ruby is composed of wines from the most recent vintages blended together. At its best it is a ruby red, fresh, very fruity wine, but some cheap rubies taste far too harsh and sour, even caustic, and also flat and thin. Fortunately there are companies, such as Dow's, that prove a ruby is also worthwhile, particularly as an aperitif on a long winter's evening!

Not all glasses of port are alike

ALOIRADO/TAWNY

As the name indicates, a tawny is a wine of a 'tan' color, depending on the year and the length of time matured in the cask, from brownish orange to almost transparently amber-gold. This color comes from the longer cask-maturing time, by contrast with the ruby and vintage wines, which are bottled quickly. The tawny port wines are also cuvées from several vintages. Young tawny is bottled after three to five years, tawny reserve after about five years in the cask. Good tawny wines are elegant and sophisticated in flavor, with a slight nuance of oxidation. The fruitiness of the young wines has become more mellow, with aromas of figs and other dried fruits (nuts). The alcohol seems to become more amalgamated and the flavor is often slightly sweet. A good tawny is not cheap: good tawny is often a blend of cheap ruby and white port.

Sweet white port   **Dry white port**

AGED TAWNY

Where the label states ten, twenty, thirty or even forty years old tawny, this does not refer to the age of the wine, but the average age of the wines that were blended for this aged tawny. Often half to three quarters of the wine consists of one vintage, supplemented with young or old wines. The intention is to give the consumer constant quality and character. The aim is to produce elegance, finesse and increasingly more complexity with a lot of freshness and mellow oxidative tones.

COLHEITA

Colheita (pronounced 'col-yay-ta') means 'harvest' in Portuguese. The colheita are tawny wines from one specific vintage, which must be stated on the bottle. A colheita must mature for at least seven years in the cask before it can be sold. The year of bottling is also stated on the bottle. The color is much lighter than that of a vintage port and the flavor is full, complex and powerful, with undertones of herbs, spices and dried fruits.

Ruby port

The real *aficionado* drinks his red port at the end of the meal, for example with gâteaux and desserts that are not too sweet.

VINTAGE

Vintage port comes from just one harvest year (vintage) and is usually of outstanding quality. Good wines from an exceptional year are set apart at once, or after one year. After two years cask-maturing a decision is made as to whether the wine is to be declared vintage port, whereupon it still has to be approved by the Instituto do Vinho do Porto. The approved wines are then bottled immediately and mature further in the bottle. A good vintage port must be left for at least ten to fifteen years before it can show its true character. In top years the best wines may be kept for several decades. Long maturing in the bottle and the large concentration of dry matter causes a considerable amount of sediment to develop in the bottle. It is therefore necessary to decant a vintage port before use. Leave older port bottles standing upright for at least twenty-four hours before decanting them. You need a fine quality cheese to go with good vintage port. In Portugal go for the delectable local cheeses like mature queijo de la serra, azeitao, queijo de la Ilha or otherwise an English cheese (Cheddar, white and blue Stilton) or even Dutch (extra mature farmhouse Gouda, genuine farmhouse Stolwijker). Of course you can use the older wines simply as a philosophical companion during a brainteaser game or a stimulating discussion.

Tawny port

LATE BOTTLED VINTAGE/ CRUSTED PORT

Crusted port (usually a specialty of Dow's) is a Late Bottled Vintage without a vintage (it is made from two or three different vintages), which is not filtered, causing a crust of sediment to form on the inside of the bottle. They are rich, full, dark wines which definitely need to be decanted before use. A cheap and often surprisingly delicious alternative to the more expensive ports.

10 years old tawny

The Late Bottled Vintage have been matured in the wood for five to six years. They are fuller and more complex than most ruby and tawny ports, but are not up to the quality of vintage port. They have two great trump cards, though: in contrast to a vintage port they can be drunk straight after bottling and they are cheaper.

VINTAGE CHARACTER

These wines have an average age of three to four years and often represent a convenient way of selling excess stocks to the unsuspecting consumer.

Only a few wines, often not even specified as of 'vintage character', but with imaginative names like Nova LB port, are of very acceptable quality. The price argument seems to be the most decisive one here.

SINGLE QUINTA

Quinta is the Portuguese name for a wine estate. Some quintas,

Colheita port

such as Dow's Quinta do Sol, are not even surrounded by their own vineyards. In the quinta grapes are processed into wine and port, but they certainly do not have to come from their own vineyards. Many wine-houses buy in a proportion of the grapes for their products in the low and middle market segments. Some well-known wine-houses do not even own a quinta. Normally the word 'quinta' is not even stated on the label, apart from the odd exception. It does appear on Quinta do Noval bottles, because this is the registered name of the company. It is a completely different matter if 'single quinta' appears on the label, or 'Quinta (do Bomfim) vintage'. These are vintage wines exclusively made from grapes from vineyards owned by the wine estate concerned.

Some quintas are world-famous, thanks to their superb quality throughout the centuries, Quinta da Roeda

Single Quinta Nacional vintage port

Crusted port   **Late Bottled Vintage (LBV)**

A good vintage character

(Croft), Quinta do Bomfim (Dow's), Quinta do Noval (Axa Millésimes) and Quinta de Vargellas (Taylor), for example.

KEEPING PORT

A good port, irrespective of type, goes on developing in the bottle and should be stored with care. Port does not have infinite life and should not be stored upright, as often happens in shops. The better wines, in particular, but also the best rubies, may come to a premature end if they are stored upright (or even worse under hot lamps), because the cork dries out.

VINTAGE/COLHEITA YEARS

Even in top years it may well happen that a particular wine-house has a failed harvest and does not declare any vintage. In reverse it more often occurs that it is not a top year everywhere, but that some wine-houses still declare their best wine vintage. Lists of top years are only a guideline, because in some lesser years some houses may well have made a superb wine, such as Dow's in 1980 or Quinta do Noval Nacional in 1996. According to statistics the years below were the very best of last century: 1908, 1912, 1927, 1931, 1935, 1945 (in many people's opinion the year of the century), 1955, 1963 (best year after WW II). 1966, 1970, 1977, 1985, 1991, 1994 and 1997.

MADEIRA DOC

Madeira lies in the Atlantic Ocean, about 1,000 km (620 miles) south-west of Portugal

Good wines sometimes hide behind imaginative names

and only 370 miles west of the North African coast. The island has a moderate climate and is quite humid. The landscape is dominated by green woods,

The small, but outstanding, Quinta das Heredias

The large, excellent quality Quinta do Noval

numerous flowers and a 6,560 ft high volcanic mountain. The vineyards are situated at the foot and on the low southern slopes of this mountain. Because of the high air and ground humidity the vines have to be trained upwards along slats (*poios*). This, together

Quinta do Bomfim

with the very hilly terrain, makes working conditions especially hard.

Madeira wines are fortified wines, like port. The type of wine and the flavor are totally determined by the varieties of grapes used, stated on the label. The alcohol percentage of Madeira is on average 18–20%. Maturing takes place in large casks in a heated (by the sun) room (*estufas*). This causes the wine to oxidize and develop the typical 'port-like' bouquet and flavor, a process called 'maderization'. For the better wines maturing continues in above-ground cellars, the *canteiros*, which are heated by the sun. Madeira wines are often blends of different vintages, apart from a few exceptions.

SERCIAL

Pale, dry, light wines with fine acids, a very pleasant bouquet and a very individual, spicy flavor, which make excellent aperitifs. Drinking temperature: 10–12 °C (50–54 °F).

VERDELHO

These wines are darker in color than the Sercial, less dry and less sophisticated, but have a seductive bouquet and flavor of fresh grapes, honey and a slight smokiness. Ideal as a winter aperitif or after meals with a chunk of (sheep's) cheese, a few nuts and dried figs. Drinking temperature: 10–13 °C (50–55 °F).

BOAL (BUAL)

Full, rich, velvety smooth, sweet wines, which are better not drunk as aperitifs, but preferably during an informal evening with friends, a game of chess or with a good book. Drinking temperature: 10–14 °C (50–57 °F).

MALVASIA (MALMSEY)

This is the sweetest Madeira, very dark in color, heavy, almost syrupy, with a surprisingly elegant bouquet and a particularly full flavor. Delicious with chocolate gâteau! Drinking temperature: 8–14 °C (46–57 °F), depending on the time of drinking, the season (in the winter it can be drunk a little warmer) and the company (the more 'romantic', the warmer, but not at room temperature).

ITALY

Since the arrival of the Greeks Italy has been known as Oenotria, the wine country. The Hellenes, lovers of wine and feminine beauty, discovered the charms of the Italian peninsula very early on, around 800 BC. They introduced many Greek grape varieties into the south of the country and cultivated their own vineyards. The inhabitants of northern Italy had already started making wine before the Greeks (principally Cretans) founded their settlement in the south of present-day Italy. These Etruscans, who had close ties with the surrounding Celtic races, conquered the southern races (the original Italians) and came under the influence of Greek civilization. From this cultural fusion there developed a very cultivated Etruscan civilization that between 600 and 400 BC

played an important role in the history of present-day Italy. Eventually the power of the Etruscans became too great a threat and they were attacked simultaneously by the northern Celtic tribes and the southern Greek settlers. Latium, with its capital Roma, took control. Roman civilization was deeply influenced by the Etruscan cultural legacy. The Romans' drive to expand was responsible for introducing wine-growing to the Italian peninsula as early as the third century BC. Eventually the Romans would organize and extend wine-growing over the whole of Europe. Since for centuries Italy consisted of numerous states of varying sizes and not until 1861 was there any question of a united Italy, it was impossible to establish a large-scale wine industry. For a very long time Italy remained a huge, chaotic, mosaic of small wine-growing regions and vineyards. It seemed as if every Italian had a vineyard in his back yard. It was not until 1963 that any kind of structure was applied, with a law for protected designations of origin DOC (Denominazione di Origine Controllata). In 1992 the whole thing was further clarified and adapted to European standards of wine-growing.

Madeira Boal (Bual)

ITALIAN WINE-GROWING

Italy is a long, narrow peninsula, shaped like a wader. At the foot of the boot is the island of Sicily, shaped like a bunch of grapes and above it Italy's other large island, Sardinia. Wine-growing in Italy is not clearly demarcated into regions. The wine acreage covers the whole of the peninsula, with the exception of the highest mountains. These mountains are in the north of the country, running from west to east (the Alps), and in the center and south, running from north to south (the Apennines). Yet these mountain

Madeira Malvasia (Malmsey)

regions, which form the backbone of the country, account for 40% of the total wine-growing area! Vineyards thrive in every sheltered valley. Between the two mountain regions is the fertile Po valley. Although Italian wine-growing is determined by numerous microclimates, it is possible to say that the north of Italy has a continental climate and the south a Mediterranean climate. The extreme temperatures are mitigated by the fact that the vineyards are never very far from the sea. In northern Italy the ground consists in general of calcareous soil and in the south and Sicily of volcanic soil.

In terms of total production Italy, regularly alternating with France, is the largest wine producer in the world. In recent decades the government has done everything in its power to lower overall production figures and to steadily improve the quality instead. At the end of the 1970s Italy was still producing a pool of 77.5 million hectoliters (20,500,000 gallons); by the end of the 1980s this had been reduced to 57.4 million (15 million gallons) and by 2000 to 52 million (13,700,000 gallons). As well as this improvement in favor of the quality of the wine, Italian legislation was put under the microscope and where necessary drastically improved. The dirt-cheap alcoholic lemonades that used to be sold as Lambrusco and the kitschy 'fiasco' bottles in baskets in which a whole range of mediocre Chianti used to be sold are no more. Fortunately the majority of wine drinkers now know that Italy is a wonderful wine-growing country where great names like Barolo, Barbaresco, Brunello and Chianti and less familiar names like Taurasi, Salice Salentino, Greco di Tufo, Aglianico del Vulture guarantee an unforgettable voyage of discovery. Although a large number of Italian wines that are not quite so wonderful are still sold in bulk (usually to pep up weaker but more expensive French wines), the proportion of quality wines has

The distant past inspires many Italian label makers

increased enormously within the total production. In 2000 almost half the Italian wine production consisted of DOC/DOCG wines. Add to this the steadily growing group of IGT wines (including many great wines that do not meet local vinification requirements) and you have an idea of the general quality of Italian wines.

ITALIAN WINE LEGISLATION (1963/1992)

The act of 1963 was inspired by the French AOC act. In all DOC regions the grape varieties to be used, the yield per hectare, the minimum alcohol percentage and a number of aspects relating to wine-growing were legally established. This act also allowed for a stricter, more controlled and guaranteed designation of origin: the Denominazione de Origine Controllata e Garantita (DOCG). Because in some cases this act was treated too drastically and in others too leniently, the former minister of agriculture Giovanni Gloria decided to change it. The new Gloria act provided for more extensive classification, easy for everyone to understand and, above all, convenient to carry out.

VINO DA TAVOLA (VDV)

This is the lowest ranking for Italian wines. Origin and varieties of grapes used are not stated on the label, but it is obligatory to give the name of the maker, the alcohol percentage and the color (blanco, rosso, rosato). In general these are simple plonk produced in large quantities.

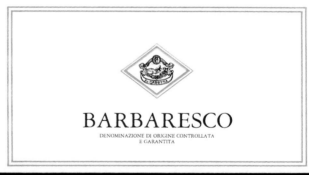

Barbaresco, classic, but still too much in the shadow of Barolo

INDICAZIONI GEOGRAFICHE TIPICHE (IGT)

This is a new ranking, comparable to the French vins de pays. For these wines the following must all be stated on the label: demarcated production zone, variety/ies of grape used and specific vinification techniques, the alcohol percentage, the color and the name of the maker. This intermediate category was an attempt to prevent top wines, from Tuscany, for example, still having to be sold as vino da tavola.

DENOMINAZIONE DI ORIGINE CONTROLLATA (DOC)

For these wines the previously mentioned label requirements apply, plus strict geographical demarcation of the wine-growing zone and strict control of the grape varieties used, yields and the minimum alcohol percentage.

DENOMINAZIONE DI ORIGINE CONTROLLATA E GARANTITA (DOCG)

The same standards apply to these, but compliance with them is far more strictly supervised. The wines must also be repeatedly tested if they want to be accorded the DOCG designation.

GRAPE VARIETIES AND TYPES OF WINE

Italy is a veritable labyrinth of vineyards, where the interested wine enthusiast can come across more than 2,000 different varieties of grapes. The majority have been growing on the peninsula for almost 3,000 years! You will still find ancient native grapes, and also varieties introduced by the Greeks and finally the more modern varieties, mostly from France. In 2000 Italy had 21 DOCGs, 301 DOCs and 121 IGTs. You will come across almost every kind of wine imaginable in Italy, including magnificent dry sparkling wines (spumante), made according to the traditional method used in the Champagne area or according to the charmat/cuve close method, seductive sweet sparkling wines made from Moscato, dry, fresh, light and fruity white wines, full-bodied white wines that have undergone cask-maturing in small French barriques, semi-sweet (abboccato) or sweet (dolce) white wines, light and fruity rosé wines, or else full-bodied, powerful red wines and finally various specific, late vintage wines (passito), such as the sweet Recioto and vin santo and the dry Recioto Amarone. Whatever you desire. Italy has it!

VALLE D'AOSTA

The picturesque valley of Aosta is situated in the north of Piedmont, at the foot of the mighty Mont Blanc and

A simple vino da tavola can be very surprising

the Matterhorn. From a linguistic and cultural point of view the Aosta valley has more in common with the French-speaking Swiss and the French from Savoy than with the rest of Italy. This can be seen in place names and also in the name of the local wines – excellent by the way – which unfortunately you do not come across so frequently outside the area. Production is quite limited and the inhabitants and passing tourists are quite

capable of handling it. As well as the wines mentioned here, the (pomegranate) red wines of Arnad-Montjovet with their characteristic bouquet and flavor of almonds and the red wines of Torette with their surprising bouquet (from pot-pourri roses to almonds) are worth trying.

BLANC DE MORGEX ET DE LA SALLE DOC

Particularly delicious, soft, delicate dry white wine with a remarkable bouquet of mountain herbs and grass and a fresh flavor, partly due to the often present trace of carbon dioxide. Although this wine is drunk here with the local cheese fondue of toma and fontina, I prefer it in combination with a freshly caught stream trout *filetti di trotta alla fontina* (with fontina and raw ham). Fantastic! Drinking temperature: 8–10 °C (46–50 °F).

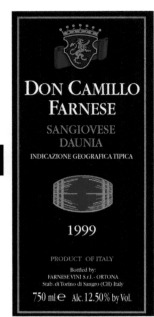

IGT

DOC

DOCG

CHAMBAVE DOC

This DOC comes in red (rouge/rosso) and white (Muscat/Moscato and Muscat flétri/Moscato passito). The red Chambave, made from, among others, petit rouge, dolcetto, gamay and pinot noir, are smooth, aromatic (violets) and harmonious wines that go with any

ITALIAN TERMS ON THE LABEL

abboccato/amabile	slightly sweet wine (10–20 g sugar per liter) ($^1/_6$–$^1/_3$ oz per pint)
annata	vintage
asciutto	dry wine (same as secco)
cantina	wine cellar/wine company
cantina sociale	cooperative wine cellars
chiaretto	another name for rosato
classico	comes from the heart of the wine-growing district
contenuto	contents
consorzio	official umbrella wine-growing organization
cooperativa viticola	cooperative wine cellars
dolce	sweet wine
fattoria	wine domain (where the vines grow)
grado alcolico	alcohol percentage
imbottigliato	bottled
… all'origine	at the domain
… nel'origine	
invecchiato	cask-matured
metodo classico/	
tradizionale	méthode traditionelle (sparkling wines)
passito	wine from late harvested, semi-dried grapes
profumato	very aromatic
riserva	wines with extra (cask/bottle) maturing
secco	dry wine
superiore	more alcohol than its namesakes, sometimes better
tenuta (viticola)	wine domain
uve	grapes for wine
vendemmia	vintage
vino bianco	white wine
vino frizzante	slightly sparkling wine
vino liquoroso	liqueur wine, 16–22% alcohol, very sweet
vino novello	white or red *vin nouveau* (macération carbonique)
vino rosato	rosé
vino rosso	red wine
vino santo,	
vinsanto	wine from semi-dried grapes, pressed months after harvest
vino spumante	sparkling wine with a second fermentation in the bottle

kind of meat. Drinking temperature: 12–14 °C (54–57 °F).

The Chambave Muscat (Moscato) are very aromatic dry white wines which make good aperitifs. Drinking temperature: 10–12 °C (50–54 °F).

The Chambave Muscat flétri (Moscato passito)

contain more alcohol (minimum 16.5%) and are quite sweet. Here too the bouquet and flavor are pure Muscat. Delicious with not over-sweet desserts. Drinking temperature: 8–10 °C (46–50 °F).

DONNAZ DOC

Very elegant dry red wine made from nebbiolo, among others. Lovely red color, delicate and aro-

Recioto Amarone

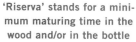

'Riserva' stands for a minimum maturing time in the wood and/or in the bottle

matic (nuts, almonds) in bouquet and flavor, with a discernible bitterness in the aftertaste. Excellent with roast meat. Try *costoletta alla Valdostana*, veal cutlet coated in breadcrumbs with melted fontina and (white) truffles! Drinking temperature: 13–15 °C (57–59 °F).

ENFER D'ARVIER DOC

A lovely pomegranate red color, soft and delicate bouquet and flavor, a velvety smooth texture and a slight bitterness as a finishing touch. Great accompaniment to the whole meal. Drinking temperature: 12–14 °C (54–57 °F).

Italian labels

NUS DOC

The Nus rouge (rosso) is a dry, velvety smooth red wine with unusual plant aromas (freshly mown grass). Can accompany the whole meal. Drinking temperature: 12–14 °C (54–57 °F).

The Nus Malvoisie is made from pinot gris and is a dry, full-bodied, very aromatic white wine that can accompany the whole meal. Drinking temperature: 10–12 °C (50–54 °F).

The Nus Malvoisie flétri (passito) is sweet and very aromatic (resin, wood, nuts, chestnuts). Delicious on a cold winter evening by an open fire or with a not over-sweet dessert containing nuts and/or dried fruit. Drinking temperature: 10–12 °C (50–54 °F) (in the summer it can be a little colder).

VALLE D'AOSTA DOC

Valle d'Aosta produces many generic wines under the DOC of the same name, in blanc (bianco), rouge (rosso) or rosé (rosato), but also müller-thurgau, pinot gris, pinot noir (made as white), chardonnay, petite arvine, or gamay, pinot noir, premetta, fumin and petit rouge as mono-cépages. Most of the white wines are dry, fruity and fresh and the red light, fruity, dry and often quite rich in tannins. Drink the white wines at 10–12 °C (50–54 °F) as an aperitif, with starters or fish and the red at 12–14 °C (54–57 °F) with meat dishes.

PIEDMONT

Numerous rivers, including the Po, descend here from the mountains (Alps) to form beautiful valleys in the lower lying regions. The capital of Piedmont, Turin, is known for its heavy industry, but the rest of the area has remained faithful to the traditional agricultural sector. The valleys of Piedmont make a welcome contrast to the mighty mountain peaks of the Alps. The southern-most part of the area is reminiscent of gently rolling Tuscany. Piedmont is rich in traditions, mostly from the abundant farming life. The local cuisine is renowned for its hearty dishes that make full use of garlic and herbs. So it comes as no surprise that the red wines of the district are full-bodied and strong, especially the wines made from the nebbiolo grape much in evidence here. Wines have been made in Piedmont since time immemorial, as witnessed by the many mentions in Greek and Roman literature. Today Piedmont, toget-her with Tuscany, is the temple to Italian oenology.

ASTI SPUMANTE DOCG AND MOSCATO D'ASTI DOCG

Sparkling Asti spumante is obtained by natural fer-mentation in the bottle (the best) or in closed fermen-tation vats. The color is clear, from light straw-colored to golden-yellow. The bouquet is reminiscent of the seductive muscat grapes that form the basis of this wine. The flavor is soft, delicate, fruity and sweet. Women often prefer this wine as an aperitif, well chilled, but a good

Asti spumante can also accompany a fresh, tangy fruit salad. Also delicious as a festive wine at an informal reception. Drinking temperature: 6–8 °C (43–46 °F).

The slightly bubbly Moscato d'Asti is a clear straw color and has the particularly intense bouquet of muscat. The flavor is aromatic and sweet, but because of the fine acids in it this wine leaves an impression of freshness on the taste-buds.

Drink this very seductive wine with a fresh fruit salad or on its own purely for pleasure, after dinner in the summer. Guarantees shivers down the spine. A true Moscato d'Asti is certainly not cheap, but then a cheap imitation will not give you the shivers down the spine! Drinking temperature: 8–10 °C (46–50 °F).

BARBARESCO DOCG

This red wine, made from nebbiolo, gets its name from the district of Barbaresco in the province of Cuneo. It is a particularly good wine, its color a full, deep red with a suggestion of orange. The bouquet is very aromatic (including bay) and the flavor full, rich and sufficient-ly dry. The young wine can still be quite harsh, but an aged Barbaresco becomes velvety smooth. An ordinary Barbaresco must undergo a minimum of two years matu-ring, a riserva four years.

Drink this wine with roast beef or furred game. Try capret-to arrosto, spicy roast goat's meat. Drinking temperature: young 13–15 °C (57–59 °F), aged 16–17 °C (61–63 °F).

BARBERA DOC

Three types of wine are made from the barbera grape. All three are ruby red in color in their youth and pome-granate red when aged. Do not drink these wines too young because they are too rich in tan-nins. After a few years maturing in the bottle they become fuller and softer. Choose the 'superiore' version with just that little bit more alcohol than the ordinary Barbera, which makes the wine better balanced. The Barbera d'Alba is made exclusively from the barbera grape. Barbera d'Asti and Barbera del Monferrato may also contain a maximum of 15% freisa, grignolino or dolcetto. Barbera del Monferrato – in contrast to its two siblings – sometimes has a slight sweetness about the flavor and sometimes a little carbon dioxide that tickles the tip of the tongue. You can serve these three wines with any red meat dish, preferably roasted. Drinking temperature: 13–15 °C (57–59 °F).

Moscato d'Asti, a famous ambassador from Piedmont

BAROLO DOCG

Probably the best known red wine from Piedmont. This Barolo is also made from nebbiolo and, like Barbaresco, comes from the province of Cuneo. The cradle of the Barolo is in the Langhe, near the small town of Barolo. This Italian top wine is deep pomegranate red in color, very intense and aromatic in bouquet (including bay, rosemary and alcohol) and full, powerful and rich, with a considerable alcohol content (minimum 13%). A young Barolo is almost undrinkable, because it is particularly harsh (a lot of tannins). Leave it at least ten years. Ordinary Barolo has to be at least three years old before it can be sold (that does not necessarily mean it is ready to drink!), while the riserva must be at least five years old. Do not buy cheap Barolos – they are characterless commercial wines. If you do not wish to pay the

Moscato d'Asti

price (average 20 Euro) for a good Barolo, buy a good Barbaresco or Gattinara.

Drink these musclemen from northwest Italy with strong-flavored food, preferably beef or furred game (wild boar) in rich sauces. Try *manzo al Barolo*, an excellent dish of roast beef first marinated in Barolo and then braised in the marinade on a low flame. Drinking temperature: 16–18 °C (61–64 °F).

Moscato d'Asti

BRACHETTO D'ACQUI DOCG

Red wine made in the provinces of Asti and Alessandria from brachetto grapes, possibly supplemented with aleatico and moscato nero. Intense in color, from ruby red to pomegranate red, very subtle muscat aromas, sweet, soft in flavor, slightly sparkling to true spumante. Minimum alcohol content 11.5%. In Italy the Brachetto d'Acqui is often served with desserts. Also great in the winter by an open fire. Drinking temperature: depending on the season and the time of drinking 6–10 °C (43–50 °F).

CAREMA DOC

This rare red wine from the north of the province of Turin is made from nebbiolo. The unusual thing about this wine is that the grapes are soaked for a long time before pressing. This technique, already used in the sixteenth century, gives the wine extra aromas (pot pourri roses!), a beautiful pomegranate red color and a velvety smooth and very broad flavor. This

Barolo and Barbaresco

Barbaresco

Carema is a powerful seducer rather than a muscleman. The wines must be a minimum of four years old before you buy them.

Drink this wine with roast veal or game. Try *camoscio alla Piemontese*, a local casserole made from the meat of the chamois goat (or you can use ibex). Drinking temperature: 14–16 °C (57–61 °F).

DOLCETTO DOC

Of all the wines made from the dolcetto grape the Alba is the most familiar, though not necessarily the best. This Dolcetto d'Alba is a reddish purple color and has a pleasant, fruity bouquet and a full flavor, with a slight bitterness that is slightly reminiscent of bay. In general

Barbera d'Alba

Barbera d'Alba

it is best to choose the 'superiore' version, with slightly more alcohol. Drink these wines with any main dish you like involving red meat, poultry or roast pork. Drinking temperature: 12–16 °C (54–61 °F).

The list of Dolcetto wines: Dolcetto d'Acqui, Dolcetto d'Alba, Dolcetto d'Asti, Dolcetto delle Langhe Monregalesi, Dolcetto di Diano d'Alba, Dolcetto di Dogliani and Dolcetto d'Ovada.

ERBALUCE DI CALUSO/ CALUSO DOC

This white wine is available in a still version and in spumante, passito and passito liquoroso. The still and spark-

Two superb top quality wines

ling wines are dry and fresh, with a great deal of fruit in bouquet and flavor. Drink the spumante as an aperitif (6–8 °C/43–46 °F)) and the still white with fish dishes (8–10 °C/46–50 °F). Serve the excellent, sweet, full-bodied, smooth passito and passito liquoroso (a minimum of five years old and minimum 13.5% and 17.5% alcohol respectively) with or after dessert (6–8 °C/ /43–46 °F).

FREISA DOC

Freisa is an old native grape from Piedmont. The name is very similar to the French word for strawberries, *fraise* (Italian: *fragole*) and surprisingly enough this special red wine often does taste of strawberries, as well as raspberries with a hint of roses. There are two Freisa DOCs: Asti and Chieri. Both wines are available in dry (secco) or sweet (amabile), still, bubbly (frizzante) or even of course sparkling (spumante naturale). You must definitely try these almost forgotten wines during a visit to Piedmont. Choose the better kinds, not the cheapest, as they are often still unstable and start fermenting again in the bottle!

Drink a still dry Freisa with the main course and the other wines with dessert. Drinking temperature: dry Freisa 10–12 °C (50–54 °F), sweet and sparkling 6–8 °C (43–46 °F).

GATTINARA DOCG

Nebbiolo is the base grape for Gattinara. This red wine comes from the area around Gattinara in the province of Vercelli. Gattinara has enjoyed great fame for centuries, in spite of its low production. The color of the wine is deep pomegranate red with a hint of orange. The bouquet is somewhat more sophisticated than that of Barolo or Barbaresco and inclined to floral nuances, such as violets. The flavor is slightly less strong than that of its two sturdy siblings from Piedmont, but it is still definitely a masculine wine: full-bodied, well-balanced and rich. Especially in the aftertaste you can detect a bitterness characteristic of Gattinara, which makes this wine extremely suitable for roast beef or game dishes. An ordinary Gattinara must be at least three years old and contain a minimum of 12.5% alcohol; a riserva is at least four years old and contains 13% alcohol. In top years (with a lot of sun) a Gattinara can rival a Barolo! Try *lepre al sivé*, the local jugged hare. Drinking temperature: 14–16 °C (57–61 °F).

GHEMME DOCG

This is one of the best red wines in northern Italy as regards the ratio of price to quality. Admittedly these wines never reach the standard of nebbiolo top wines like Barolo, Barbaresco or Gattinara, but a good Ghemme costs considerably less and is very enjoyable to drink! The color is pomegranate red, the bouquet intense, very pleasant, floral (violets) and sophisticated. The flavor is full and round, with the typical slight bitterness as a finishing touch. A good Ghemme usually

Dolcetto d'Alba

Brich dij Nòr
DOLCETTO DI DOGLIANI
DENOMINAZIONE DI ORIGINE CONTROLLATA

1999

IMBOTTIGLIATO ALL'ORIGINE DAL VITICOLTORE
ROMANA CARLO
DOGLIANI (CN) - ITALIA
PRODOTTO IN ITALIA

0,75 ℓ. e   NON DISPERDERE IL VETRO NELL'AMBIENTE   13,5% vol

Dolcetto di Dogliani

matures for at least four years before it is sold. This wine also goes perfectly with roast red meat or furred game. Drinking temperature: 14–16 °C (57–61 °F).

GAVI/CORTESE DI GAVI DOC

One of the few white wines from Piedmont. The popularity of this Gavi or Cortese di Gavi is out of proportion to its actual qualities, but it is nevertheless a great wine: fresh, delicate and sufficiently dry. There

are also frizzante and spumante versions with the name Gavi.

These excellent fish wines are delicious, for example, with *trota alle erbette*, flambéd trout with fresh herbs. Drinking temperature: 8–10 °C (46–50 °F).

GRIGNOLINO DOC

Two red wines made from the grignolino grape have the right to the DOC designation: Grignolino d'Asti and Grignolino del Monferrato Casalese. The second wine in particular is rated very highly by wine connoisseurs. They are both lighter red wines with a beautiful reddish orange color, a delicate bouquet and flavor and a dry, slightly bitter finishing touch. You can serve these wines with any meat dish. Drinking temperature: 13–15 °C (57–59 °F).

Four trump cards from Piedmont

MALVASIA DOC

In Piedmont you will find two wines made from the malvasia grape: Malvasia di Casorzo d'Asti and Malvasia di Castelnuovo Don Bosco. Although they are made of different malvasia varieties they are very similar. Both these red sweet wines are very fruity in bouquet and flavor and sometimes have a slight tingle of carbon dioxide. Alcohol percentage: 11–12%. Drink them with less sweet desserts. Drinking temperature: 8–10 °C (46–50 °F).

NEBBIOLO D'ALBA DOC

This wine, made from the nebbiolo grape, from the area around Alba tastes especially good. It is full, round, and velvety smooth, with a long aftertaste. Read the label carefully before opening a bottle; as well as this delicious dry red wine there is also an *amabile* version that can be really sweet! Also available as spumante. The dry red wines deserve a little extra maturing in the bottle. Buy them in top years when they almost reach the standard of a good Barbaresco or Gattinara.

Drink a dry Nebbiolo d'Alba with red meat or roast pork or lamb. The sweet and sparkling versions are delicious with a dessert. Drinking temperature: dry 13–15 °C (57–59 °F), sweet or sparkling 6–9 °C (43–48 °F).

SIZZANO DOC

Another magnificent red wine made from nebbiolo, this time from the area around Sizzano on the hills of Novarra. This wine is less full-bodied and powerful than a Barolo or Barbaresco; it is more like a Gattinara, delicate and soft, with a floral undertone (violets) rather than the Italian culinary herbs that characterize Barolo and Barbaresco. This wine must mature for a minimum of three years before it can be sold. Drink it with fried or roast red meat. Try *stufato di manzo con cipolla*, casseroled beef with onions. Drinking temperature: 14–16 °C (57–61 °F).

Gavi and Langhe Arneis

OTHER DOC WINES FROM PIEDMONT

Less well known, but definitely no less in quality, are the red wines made from Boca (violets, pomegranate), Bramaterra, Colli Tortonesi Barbera, Fara (violets), Gabiano and Lessona. Also interesting are Roero rosso, Rubino di Cantavenna, Ruché di Castagnole Monferrato and Verduno Pelaverga, Under the names of Piedmont, Langhe and Colline Novaresi you also come across various wines made from different varieties of grapes. Some are of first-rate quality.

Of the white wines I can recommend the fresh, dry Cortese dell'Alto Monferrato, which goes well with light starters (best of all with fish). Also very worthwhile are the generic wines from the Langhe: Favorita, Arneis, Monferrato (Casalese Cortese!), Piedmont (including Pinot Bianco, Pinot Grigio and Cortese) and Roero (Arneis) and the sweet Muscat wines from Loazzolo.

LIGURIA

Liguria is one of the smallest, but loveliest regions in Italy. The capital of Liguria, Genoa, is a port. The Mediterranean Sea has a strong influence on local eating habits. A large amount of sea fish is eaten and there is a plethora of white wines. Liguria is protected in the north by foothills of the Apennines, making the area into a miniature Paradise. Most of the vineyards are on the slopes of the first hills, facing the south and the Mediterranean. It is difficult to find a Ligurian wine outside Italy, although a few Cinqueterre sometimes make it abroad.

CINQUETERRE/CINQUETERRE SCIACCHETRÀ DOC

This is without doubt the best wine in Liguria, straw-colored, made from Vermentino, Bosco and Albarola. The wine has a subtle bouquet, a dry, fresh, pleasant flavor and goes very well with all the local fish specialties. Try *cappon magro*, a festive dish with all kinds of varieties of shellfish and crustaceans. Drinking temperature: 10–12 °C (50–54 °F).

Cinqueterre Sciacchetrà is a sweet version of Cinqueterre, made from partially dried grapes. The flavor is fuller than that of the ordinary Cinqueterre, but can vary from almost dry to quite sweet. Minimum alcohol percentage: 17%! Drink the almost dry version as an aperitif and the sweeter one with or after dessert. Try *castagnaccio*, a chestnut cake with pine nuts and raisins, which is not too sweet. Drinking temperature: almost dry wine 10–12 °C (50–54 °F), sweeter wine 8–10 °C (46–50 °F) or less.

Nebbiolo d'Alba

OTHER WINES FROM LIGURIA

Liguria has many generic wines, in other words one DOC but several variations, each from a different variety of grape.

Of the white wines the Vermentino from Riviera Ligure di Ponente and that of Colli di Luni are real musts. If you prefer to eat something other than fish, you will be in your element with a Colli di Luni rosso (choose a riserva), a Colli di Levanto rosso, a Pigato or Rossese from Riviera Ligure di Ponente or a Rossese di Dolceacqua' (also just called Dolceacqua, this wine smells and tastes of fresh strawberries). These red wines are very pleasant, not too heavy, round and soft, with a typical touch of bitterness in the aftertaste.

Try *coniglio al Rossese*, rabbit with tomatoes, garlic and olives, or *tagliatelle verdi con salsa alla Ligure*, green tagliatelle with a sauce of cep, garlic and fresh herbs. Drinking temperature: 12–14 °C (54–57 °F).

There are some very interesting examples of generic wines to be found

LOMBARDY

Lombardy, Lombardia in Italian, is right in

Colli Tortonesi
Barbera

Moscato

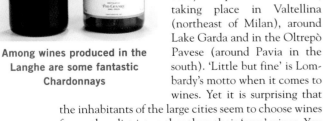

Among wines produced in the
Langhe are some fantastic
Chardonnays

the middle of northern Italy, from the foot of the Alps to the valley of the Po. Various tributaries of the Po flow from the Alps, the best known probably being the Ticino. Water is one of the features of this area, which has no less than four large lakes: Lago Maggiore, Lago di Como (Lake Como), Lago d'Iseo and Lago di Garda (Lake Garda). Lombardy is quite a large area with several famous towns and cities, including Milan, Como, Bergamo, Pavia, Cremona, Brescia and Mantua.

Wine-growing in Lombardy is quite concentrated, taking place in Valtellina (northeast of Milan), around Lake Garda and in the Oltrepò Pavese (around Pavia in the south). 'Little but fine' is Lombardy's motto when it comes to wines. Yet it is surprising that the inhabitants of the large cities seem to choose wines from other districts rather than their 'own' wines. You will often look in vain for bottles of Lombardy wine in the shops of Milan. However, this is not a problem for wine-growers, since consumption of local wines in the countryside almost equals production. There is little left for export.

Lombardy's cuisine is primarily renowned for its numerous creamy versions of risotto and *osso buco*, a wonderful casserole dish of calves' shank in red wine sauce.

FRANCIACORTA DOCG

The wine-growing region of Franciacorta is between Brescia and Bergamo, on the banks of Lago d'Iseo. Very good wines are made in the gentle, windy climate. The sparkling wines are particularly renowned.

The Franciacorta crémant is made from chardonnay and/or pinot bianco, the Franciacorta rosé from pinot nero (minimum 15%) and chardonnay and/or pinot bianco. The better Franciacorta spumante are the white wines made from chardonnay, pinot bianco and/or pinot nero (without skins). The wines are a magnificent deep straw color with a hint of green and occasional golden reflections. The bouquet is fresh and full, the flavor sappy, fresh and sophisticated. You can go on serving these wines throughout the meal, but they are really at their best before or after meals. The Franciacorta spumante is a must with *vitello tonnato*, a surprising dish of veal steak with a delicate sauce of tuna and cream. Drinking temperature: 6–9 °C (43–48 °F).

Franciacorta also makes a few very pleasant still white and red wines. The great red wines are made from cabernet sauvignon, cabernet franc, merlot, barbera and nebbiolo. They are sold under the name of Tierre di Franciacorta DOV bianco or rosso.

VALTELLINA SUPERIORE DOCG

For this wine they are allowed to add a maximum of 5% of other grapes (see Valtellina DOC) to chiavennasca. The color is then ruby to pomegranate red, the bouquet heavy when the wine is young and rather more subtle when it is older, and the flavor quite rich in tannins and bitter-sour in the early years and softer, fuller and rounder after a few years maturing. The ordinary wines are put on sale only after a minimum of two years and the rare riserva after four years. The Valtellina superiore really come into their own with roast red meat or furred game. Drinking temperature: 12–14 °C (54–57 °F) (young) to 14–16 °C (57–61 °F) (aged).

VALTELLINA SUPERIORE SASSELLA/ VALTELLINA SUPERIORE INFERNO/ VALTELLINA SUPERIORE GRUMELLO/ VALTELLINA SUPERIORE VALGELLA

These four wines are crus of Valtellina superiore. This means they come from very strictly demarcated regions (Sassella, Inferno, Grumello and Valgella). The wines are slightly better and fuller than the ordinary Valtellina superiore. Especially those from Sassella are of outstanding quality. Drink these wines with a festive dinner, with roast game (wild boar, hare), for example. Drinking temperature: 14–16 °C (57–61 °F).

OLTREPÒ PAVESE DOC

A relatively small area with one designation of origin but twenty different types/varieties of grapes. As the name suggests, this wine-growing region (about forty municipalities) is near the town of Pavia and the river Po. The vines grow on hills in the south of the province. Oltrepò Pavese come in red, white, rosé, sparkling (spumante) and slightly bubbly (frizzante):

– Oltrepò Pavese rosso (also in riserva)
– Oltrepò Pavese rosato (rosé with a slight fizziness)
– Oltrepò Pavese Buttafuoco (usually with a slight fizziness, also in frizzante)
– Oltrepò Pavese Sangue di Giuda (red; slightly sweet with a fizziness from subsequent fermentation

Franciacorta brut

– Oltrepò Pavese Barbera (red; in dry, medium dry and sweet and in slightly bubbly, bubbly and slightly sparkling)
– Oltrepò Pavese Bonarda (see Barbera)

Franciacorta rosado

– Oltrepò Pavese Riesling Italico (white, dry, sometimes a slight fizziness; there is also an elegant spumante and a fresh frizzante)

Franciacorta bianco

– Oltrepò Pavese Riesling Renano (white, more severe than Riesling Italico; also in spumante)
– Oltrepò Pavese Cortese (white; also in frizzante and spumante)
– Oltrepò Pavese Moscato (sweet white wine with fresh acids, very aromatic; still, sparkling and bubbly versions)
– Oltrepò Pavese Moscato liquoroso (17.5–22% alcohol; the dry vinified version is a rarity)
– Oltrepò Pavese Malvasia (white; dry, medium dry or sweet; still, sparkling or bubbly)
– Oltrepò Pavese Pinot Nero (red, white and rosé; also in frizzante or spumante

Franciacorta rosso

– Oltrepò Pavese Pinot Grigio (also in frizzante)
– Oltrepò Pavese Chardonnay (still, frizzante and spumante)
– Oltrepò Pavese Sauvignon (modern wine)
– Oltrepò Pavese Cabernet Sauvignon
– Oltrepò Pavese spumante (bianco or rosato, made according to the metodo classico)

SAN COLOMBANO DOC

To the northeast of Pavia is a fairly small wine-growing region with a big name. In the seventh century an Irish monk soon succeeded in converting the local population by teaching them how to make wine. The wines of San Colombano have since become a household name in spite of their rarity. The vines, principally croatina and barbera, grow on low hills of lime and sand, which are rich in minerals and trace elements. The soil gives strength and character to the wines. San Colombano rosso (still or vivace, slightly fizzy) has a lot of backbone and roundness. This red wine can accompany any meal. Drinking temperature: 12–14 °C (54–57 °F),

VALTELLINA DOC

The Valtellina valley is a veritable wine paradise. The vines here grow on steep, rocky hills suspended above the river Adda. The local wines have to conform to strictly controlled requirements as to origin, processing and treatment of the grapes. All the wines must be vinified and matured in the district of production. Under these DOCs come:

– Valtellina red wines made from chiavennasca (local name for nebbiolo), possibly supplemented with pinot nero, merlot, rossola, pignola valtellinese or brugnola. The type of Valtellina depends on the cuvée used, but they are nearly all recognizable from their lively red color, a subtle and characteristic bouquet and a dry, sometimes spicy flavor rich in tannins. You can continue drinking these wines throughout the meal, but they prefer red meat and game. Try *petti d'anitra*

Oltrepò Pavese rosso

all'uva, breast of duck with a red grape sauce. Drinking temperature: 14–16 °C (57–61 °F);
– Valtellina Sfursat: a very different wine made from partially dried grapes. Drink these almost orange-colored, heavy (minimum 14.5% alcohol) sweet wines with an appropriate dessert, such as *sciatt*, a deep-fried pastry made of buckwheat and wheat flour, cheese and grappa. Drinking temperature: according to taste 6–8 °C (43–46 °F) or 10–12 °C (50–54 °F).

Oltrepò Pavese Bonarda

VALCALEPIO DOC

This region lies on opposite sides of Lago d'Iseo, close to Bergamo. East of Bergamo the soil consists of a mixture of clay and lime and in the northwest of pebbles, stone chips/slate and clay. The wines are made from old native grapes (moscato di scanzo, merera, incrocio

terzi) and more modern varieties (pinot bianco, pinot grigio, chardonnay, merlot, cabernet sauvignon and cabernet franc). The wines are sold under the designation Valcalepio rosso or Valcalepio bianco. Both types of wine are the fruits of a successful marriage between tradition and modernism.

Valcalepio rosso is made principally from cabernet sauvignon and merlot, with different supplements depending on the wine-maker. The color is usually ruby red with flashes of pomegranate red. The bouquet is pleasant, vinous and aromatic and the flavor is dry and characteristic of both grapes (blackcurrant, pepper, cherries). A riserva must mature for at least

Oltrepò Pavese Cortese is made from
the Cortese grape

three years and contain 12.5% or more alcohol. Serve a Valcalepio rosso with roast meat. Drinking temperature: 14–16 °C (57–61 °F).

Valcalepio bianco is usually made from pinot bianco, chardonnay and pinot grigio, in varying combinations. Each wine is unique, but the best wines are an intense straw color, have a sophisticated bouquet and a dry, well-balanced distinctive flavor. Serve these wines as an aperitif or with fish dishes. Drinking temperature: 10–12 °C (50–54 °F).

Finally, there is also a Moscato passito, made by an old-fashioned method, which is of particularly good quality. It is a sweet red wine, ruby to cherry red in color, with some pomegranate red here and there. The bouquet is very typical of a red Moscato: intense, full of character and sensual. The flavor is sweet, but well-balanced, thanks to the fine acids. A nuance of bitter almonds is sometimes noticeable in the aftertaste. This wine must mature for at least eighteen months and contain a minimum of 17% alcohol. Wonderful after meals or as a winter warmer. Drinking temperature: depending on the season and your preference 8–12 °C (46–54 °F).

BRESCIA

Brescia is not a DOC, but a wine-growing region around the town of the same name and Lake Garda. The district comprises the designations of origin Botticino, Capriano Del Colle, Cellatica, Garda, Garda Bresciano, Garda Classico, Lugana and San Martino Della Battaglia. The area produces many types and flavors of wine. Here I shall give you a few guidelines for each designation of origin to make your choice easier. As most Garda DOC wines are made in Veneto, see that section.

BOTTICINO DOC

Wine-growing region with the village of the same name as epicenter. The vines grow on rocky hills around Brescia. The soil consists of clay, marble and limestone. The wines are made from barbera, marzemino, sangiovese and the many variants of schiava grapes. Botticino wines are in general ruby red in color with pomegranate red nuances, warm and full in bouquet and extremely pleasant. Great accompaniments to the whole meal. Drinking temperature: 13–15 °C (57–59 °F).

CAPRIANO DEL COLLE DOC

White wine made from trebbiano and red wine from sangiovese, marzemino and barbera, possibly supplemented with merlot and incrocio. The red wine is ruby red in color, quite light, sappy and well-balanced. This wine goes with anything. Drinking temperature: 12–14 °C (54–57 °F).

The white wine actually has more to offer than the red. It is a dry, fresh wine with a lot of backbone. It can be somewhat brutal, particularly in its youth. Excellent accompaniment to freshwater fish. Drinking temperature: 8–10 °C (46–50 °F).

CELLATICA DOC

The vineyards are situated on a subsoil of lime and clay. Cellatica rosso is made from marzemino (minimum 30%), barbera (minimum 30%), schiava (minimum 10%) and incrocio or cabernet franc (minimum 10%). The wine is very pleasant, velvety smooth and well-balanced, with a slight touch of bitterness in the aftertaste. Wines with a minimum of 12% alcohol and one year maturing may bear the designation 'superiore'.

Excellent accompaniments to the whole meal. Drinking temperature: 12–14 °C (54–57 °F) (rosso), 14–16 °C (57–61 °F) (superiore).

RIVIERA DEL GARDA BRESCIANO/ GARDA BRESCIANO DOC

These wines are made only on the Bresciano side of Lake Garda. This DOC has been in existence for thirty years. The vineyards get plenty of sun and water, so it is always beautifully green here. The soil is very complex and does not have any clear uniformity. White, red, light red and rosé wines and spumante are produced under this DOC name.

Garda Bresciano bianco is made from riesling italico and/or riesling renano with the addition of a maximum of 20% other grapes. The wine is light straw-colored with a hint of green. The bouquet is aromatic, slightly herby and the flavor soft, almost velvety, with a distinct touch of bitterness and a hint of salt. Due to its texture this wine goes equally well with fish and white meat and poultry. Drinking temperature: 10–12 °C (50–54 °F).

Garda Bresciano rosso is made from gentile, santo stefano, mocasina, sangiovese, marzemino and barbera. Some wines are made from one variety only; in others two or more grape varieties are blended. Therefore thousands of different types of flavor are possible for this wine. Definitely characteristic of this area is the ruby red color and the touch of bitterness in the aftertaste. Great accompaniments to meat dishes. Drinking temperature: 12–16 °C (54–60 °F), depending on the type.

Garda Bresciano Chiaretto (claret, clarete, clairet) is a light red wine made from the same grapes as for Garda Bresciano rosso. The color is usually cherry red and the flavor quite soft and round, with a characteristic touch of bitter almond in the aftertaste. An excellent companion at meals, which actually goes with anything. Drinking temperature: 10–14 °C (50–57 °F).

Garda Bresciano Groppello, ruby red wines made from gentile, groppellone and groppello, are full, soft and round, with a pleasant touch of bitterness in the aftertaste. The better wines bear the designation 'superiore'. Particularly suitable as a wine to go on serving throughout the meal. Drinking temperature: 12–14 °C (54–57 °F).

The spumante rosato/rosé made from groppello are very unusual. Deliciously full and fresh at the same time. Excellent winter aperitifs. Drinking temperature: 6–10 °C (43–50 °F).

LUGANO DOC

Lugano wines come from south of Lake Garda. The wines made here from trebbiano can be still or sparkling. Typical of this wine is the slightly salty character given to it by the mineral soil. The color varies from pale and greenish yellow when it is young to golden-yellow after several years. The bouquet is fine and pleasant, the flavor dry, fresh and smooth, with a good balance between acid, body and alcohol. Drink the sparkling version as an aperitif and the still wine with (river) fish. Drinking temperature: 8–10 °C (46–50 °F).

SAN MARTINO DELLA BATTAGLIA DOC

This small region has the same climate and the same mineral soil as Lugana. San Martino della Battaglia is obtained from tocai friulano (green sauvignon). The color is lemon-yellow, the bouquet very inviting and intensely aromatic and the flavor dry and full, with a slight bitterness in the aftertaste. Excellent wines with fish. Drinking temperature: 10–12 °C (50–54 °F).

There is also a San Martino della Battaglia Liquoroso, which is much darker in color (straw color), very fruity and seductive. The flavor is full, smooth and pleasantly sweet. This well-balanced wine contains at least 16% alcohol. Delicious with less sweet cakes and pastries or after meals. Drinking temperature: 6–10 °C (43–50 °F).

VINI MANTOVANI

Garda DOC wines are also made south of Lake Garda, though administratively they belong to the province of Mantua. They do not differ very much from the other Garda wines, though. Well known varieties include pinot bianco, pinot grigio and merlot. Good frizzante are also made, mostly from pinot bianco, chardonnay and riesling.

The Colli Morenici Mantovani del Garda DOC deserve special mention. These wines come from south of Lake Garda, so in fact from the best hills (Colli) above Mantua. The wines have just a little more to offer than the other Garda wines. Pinot bianco and garganega are used as base grapes for the bianco and rondinella, rossanella, negrara, sangiovese and merlot for the rosato and rosso.

South of the town of Mantua are the vineyards of the Lambrusco Mantovano DOC. This wine still contains a considerable amount of carbon dioxide, obtained from natural fermentation. As many as four different lambrusco grape varieties may be incorporated into them, possibly supplemented with ancellotta, fortana or uva d'oro. This dry or sweet wine is ruby red in color and tastes fresh and sappy. The Italians drink the dry wine (and unfortunately also the sweet) during the entire meal. Try it if you like with fried chicken dishes (dry) or red fruit salads (sweet). Drinking temperature: 10–12 °C (50–54 °F). There is also a lighter rosato.

Lugana superiore

TRENTINO-ALTO ADIGE

Trentino-Alto Adige, also known as South Tyrol, is bordered by Lombardy in the west, Veneto in the south and Switzerland and Austria in the north. The capital of Trentino (Italian-speaking) is Trento and that of Alto Adige (German-speaking) is Bolzano. The area is divided in two by the Adige, the second longest river in Italy. The north has an almost continental climate, while the climate in the south is much warmer and gentler. Trentino-Alto Adige is a kind of transition region between Austria and Italy. The Austrian and also Swiss influence can sometimes be seen in the German spelling of the wines. You will find Santa Maddalena and Magdalener, Caldaro and Kalterersee and Alto Adige and Südtirol side by side. The grapes have two names too. As these wines are often exported to Switzerland, Austria and Germany, you will often find the German names on the labels.

This region is also considerably influenced by Switzerland and Austria culturally and gastro-nomically, with many different kinds of sausage, bacon, Sauerkraut, stream and lake trout, oven-roasts, dumplings, rye bread, potatoes and apple strudel. The Italian-speaking inhabitants on the other hand prefer pasta, polenta, gnocchi and absolutely delicious Venetian cakes. Some of the German names, such as 'Sauerkraut' or 'Knödel' are 'italianized' into 'crauti' and 'canederli'.

Because the vineyards are located high up, at the foot of or even actually in the mountains, white wines are in the majority here. Logically the white wines contain the fresh acidity needed for the often fatty food. The great difference in temperature between day and night during the period before the harvest gives the wines an incredibly strong aromatic bouquet, which makes them highly recommended. The red wines too, mostly from Trentino, situated further south, have a charm all of their own. Also very popular are the fresh, rosé wines, full of character, made in the northern part.

The vineyards of the generic designation of origin Alto Adige DOC are situated on the slopes of the mountains, on terraces, making work on them and harvesting very difficult. Alto Adige wines are therefore never really cheap, but they are particularly delicious. There are countless different wines made from a single grape variety (sometimes supplemented up to a maximum of 15% with a different grape variety).

ALTO ADIGE

Countless generic wines of varying quality and character are included under the name Alto Adige. They are made from a single variety of grape, the white, for example, from chardonnay, moscato giallo or pinot bianco and the red and rosé wines from cabernet, merlot or pinot noir.

A FEW REMARKABLE WINES

MOSCATO ROSA (ROSE MUSCATEL)

Unusual ruby red muscat wine, very typical in bouquet and flavor: velvety smooth, sweet and seductive. Can be kept for several years. It is difficult to match this wine with anything. You could try it with 'Krapfen Tirolese', fried jam fritters. Drinking temperature: 6–8 °C (43–46 °F).

LAGREIN SCURO (LAGREIN DUNKEL)

The big brother of Lagrein rosato. Full ruby red color with a few reflections of pomegranate red, very pleasant in bouquet (fresh grapes) and velvety smooth in flavor. There is also a riserva (minimum two years old). This is a wine you can drink and enjoy throughout the meal. Drinking temperature: 10–14 °C (50–57 °F), depending on its age.

ALTO ADIGE MERLOT

Full, rounded wines with discernible plant undertones in bouquet and flavor. The riserva are extra elegant and full-bodied (minimum two years maturing). Although they go with almost everything, these wines have a slight preference for meat, especially beef. Try 'gröstl', an oven dish of beef, onions and potatoes. Drinking temperature: 12–16 °C (54–61 °F), depending on age.

ALTO ADIGE CABERNET-CABERNET FRANC-CABERNET SAUVIGNON/ ALTO ADIGE CABERNET-LAGREIN/ ALTO ADIGE CABERNET-MERLOT

Usually great wines that are ruby red to orange in color. They are dry and aromatic and have quite a light texture and sometimes a considerable amount of tannins. The flavor is full and distinct (plant undertones). Wines that have undergone two years extra maturing bear the designation riserva. In general these are far better than the ordinary Cabernet. Great wines for poultry, terrines and beef dishes. Drinking temperature: 14–16 °C (57–61 °F).

Alto Adige Cabernet (Sauvignon and franc)

There are also first-rate wines made from cabernet and lagrein or cabernet and merlot. Here too the wines that have had two extra years maturing are allowed to put the word riserva on the label.

Alto Adige Pinot grigio

Alto Adige Chardonnay special cuvée

ALTO ADIGE PINOT NERO (BLAUBURGUNDER)

Ruby red color with hints of orange. Typical pinot noir bouquet and a mild, full, round flavor, dry and slightly bitter in the aftertaste. Delicious with meat, especially beef, and hearty variety meats. A riserva has to undergo a minimum of two years maturing. Drinking temperature: 10–12 °C (50–54 °F), 12–14 °C (54–57 °F) for the riserva.

There is also an excellent, dry, white sparkling wine made from pinot nero: the Alto Adige Pinot Nero spumante. Wonderful as a winter aperitif. Drinking temperature: 6–10 °C (43–50 °F).

ALTO ADIGE MALVASIA (MALVASIER)

Surprisingly, this Malvasia is not white, but red. Drink this full, harmonious, powerful wine with red meat. Drinking temperature: 12–14 °C (54–57 °F).

ALTO ADIGE SCHIAVA (VERNATSCH)

If you are thinking of the white wine, Vernaccia, you are in for a disappointment. This red wine is light in color, bouquet and flavor, quite unremarkable and yet really quite delicious in its own way. There is a discernible slight hint of bitter almonds in the aftertaste. Goes with anything. Drinking temperature: 10–12 °C (50–54 °F).

Alto Adige Merlot

ALTO ADIGE SPUMANTE

White sparkling wine made from pinot bianco and/or chardonnay, possibly supplemented with pinot nero and/or pinot grigio (maximum 30%), in dry (extra brut) and less dry (brut) versions. Ideal aperitif. Drinking temperature: 6–8 °C (43–46 °F).

Alto Adige Chardonnay

Alto Adige Cabernet Sauvignon

THE ALTO ADIGE CRUS

As well as the previously mentioned generic wines Alto Adige produces wines from more narrowly demarcated regions. The quality of the majority of these wines is often greater than that of ordinary Alto Adige. All the wines mentioned come under their own DOC.

COLLI DI BOLZANO (BOZNER LEITEN)

This small wine region in the district of Bolzano produces red wines from a minimum of 90% schiava, possibly supplemented with pinot nero or lagrein. The color is varying shades of ruby red, depending on the vinification and the grape ratio. Bouquet and flavor are soft and fruity. Delicious wine without too many pretensions. Can be served throughout the meal. Drinking temperature: 12–14 °C (54–57 °F).

MERANESE DI COLLINA/MERANESE (MERANER HÜGEL/MERANER)

These red wines made mainly from schiava are produced on the hills above the little town of Merano. They are ruby red in color, soft and fruity in bouquet and sappy and pleasant in flavor. Wines without any great pretensions that go with almost anything. Drinking temperature: 12–14 °C (54–57 °F).

SANTA MADDALENA (SINKT MAGDALENER)

The vineyards for these superb wines are situated on the hills around Bolzano. Schiava grapes, possibly supplemented to a maximum of 10% with pinot nero and/or lagrein, lend their character to this wine. The color is ruby red to an intense pomegranate red, the bouquet subtle and seductive (a hint of forest violets) and the flavor velvety smooth, full, round and sappy with a slight touch of bitter almonds in the aftertaste. Good maturing potential. Heavenly wines that you can quite happily drink throughout the meal, especially with red meat and game. Try 'pollo cacciatore', chicken with onions, tomatoes and olives braised in vermouth. Drinking temperature: 14–16 °C (57–61 °F).

TERLANO (TERLANER)

The vineyards of Terlano lie parallel to the Adige in the province of Bolzano. These white wines are made from pinot bianco (weißburgunder), chardonnay, riesling italico (wälschriesling), riesling renano (rheinriesling), sylvaner (silvaner), riesling x sylvaner (müller-thurgau) or sauvignon, with a minimum of 90% of the grape mentioned or blended together (bianco). The young wines are all greenish yellow and the older ones rather more yellow. They have fresh acids and a very aromatic bouquet and flavor.

Drink a Terlano as an aperitif or throughout the meal. The Chardonnay likes to accompany freshwater fish in creamy sauces, Riesling Italico prefers fried fish, trout with almonds, for example. Drinking temperature: 8–10 °C (46–50 °F) (Chardonnay 10–12 °C (50–54 °F).

The spumante – dry (extra brut) or slightly less dry (brut) – is fresh, fruity, aromatic and elegant. Excellent aperitif. Drinking temperature: 6–8 °C (43–46 °F). Wines made in the central zone of the production region of Terlano are allowed to carry the additional designation of 'classico'.

VALLE ISARCO (SÜDTIROL-EISACKTALER)

The vineyards of this designation of origin are situated fairly high up (sometimes above 1,970 ft) and require a great deal of extra work. The region is in the neighborhood of Bolzano, in the valley of the river Isarco. Mainly white wines are produced here, made from pinot grigio (ruländer), sylvaner (silvaner), veltliner, riesling x sylvaner (müller-thurgau), kerner and traminer aromatico (gewürztraminer) and a red wine made from schiava, the klausner leitacher. The white wines all have a hint of green and are fresh, subtle, fruity and sappy. The pinot Grigio and the Traminer Aromatico are in general slightly fuller in flavor than the other wines.

You can serve any of these wines as an aperitif or throughout the meal. Sylvaner and Veltliner love fried fish, Müller-Thurgau braised fish and poultry. Drinking temperature: Sylvaner, Veltliner and Kerner 8–10 °C (46–50 °F), the others 10–12 °C (50–54 °F).

The Klausner Leitacher is ruby red in color and has quite a soft bouquet and a fresh, acidy, full flavor. Drink it with red meat. Drinking temperature: 12–14 °C (54–57 °F).

VALLE VENOSTA (VINSCHGAU)

Small wine-growing region of traditional attitude that produces primarily white wines from chardonnay, kerner, riesling x sylvaner (müller-thurgau), pinot bianco (weißburgunder), pinot grigio (ruländer), riesling and traminer aromatico (gewürztraminer). A small amount of red wine is also made from schiava (vernatsch) and pinot nero (blauburgunder). The fruity, aromatic white wines all have a hint of green and a fresh bouquet and flavor.

Serve the Pinot Bianco and the Chardonnay as aperitifs, Chardonnay also with fish in creamy sauces, Pinot Grigio with river cray fish or substantial kinds of fish, the Riesling with fried or poached fish and all the other wines throughout the meal. Drinking temperature: Pinot Bianco and Kerner 8–10 °C (46–50 °F); Chardonnay, Pinot Grigio, Traminer Aromatico and Müller-Thurgau 10–12 °C (50–54 °F).

Schiava is ruby red in color, very pleasant and fruity in bouquet and flavor and can accompany the entire meal. Drinking temperature: 12–14 °C (54–57 °F). The Pinot Noir is also ruby red, but with a few hints of orange. The bouquet is quite characteristic, from plant to animal (manure), and the flavor is full, smooth and well-balanced. Discernible slight bitterness in the

aftertaste. Serve this wine with red meat or poultry. Drinking temperature: 12–14 °C (54–57 °F).

CALDARO/ LAGO DI CALDARO (KALTERER/ KALTERERSEE)

This is another famous quality wine from the Alto Adige. The vineyards are in the neighborhood of the well known Lake Caldaro. Excellent red wines are made here from the various schiava variants, sometimes supplemented with pinot nero or lagrein. The color varies from ruby red to dark red and the bouquet and flavor are smooth, fruity and elegant. You can often detect a characteristic hint of bitter almonds in the aftertaste. There is also a 'classico' that comes from the central region and a 'classico superiore' with 1% more alcohol than an ordinary Caldaro. Ideal wines that can accompany the entire meal. Drinking temperature: 12–14 °C (54–57 °F).

TRENTINO

The southern part of the Trentino-Alto Adige area also makes good white wines, of course, but more, and in general, better red wines than the northern part (Alto Adige). Most of the vineyards are on the hills of the Adige, Cembra, Lagarina or Meren valleys above Lake Garda. Only in the Rotaliana valley are the vineyards situated at the bottom of the valley. Characteristic of Trentino are the immense pergolas (called 'trellis' locally), over which the vines grow. This trelliswork ensures that the vines grow high above the ground, which means that less foliage develops and the grapes get maximum benefit from the sun. In this way air circulates among the vines and protects them from the treacherous night frost. This area is in the midst of development, not only in terms of wine preparation and growing and pruning techniques, but also in terms of experimental strains of grapes. Numerous experiments are going on with the rebo grape, a cross between merlot and marzemino. In Trentino most of the wines are made from a single grape variety. Chardonnay is the most popular (50% of the white grapes, 15% of the total production) for white wines. Chardonnay Trentino DOC and the excellent spumante Trento Classico are made from chardonnay. Among all the other white grapes that grow here there is one special native one, the nosiola. This very aromatic grape gives a delicate and fruity character to Nosiola Trentino, and in particular to the delectable vino santo Trentino DOC. Schiava holds the prize for red wines, making up, believe it or not, 30% of the total grape cultivation. For those who like it Trentino makes probably the nicest grappas (eaux de vie, wine spirits) in the whole of Italy!

CASTELLER DOC

Red or rosé wines made from schiava, possibly supplemented with lambrusco, merlot, lagrein or teroldego (maximum 20%). These wines are ruby red or pink in color, quite light in texture and velvety smooth in flavor. They are 'asciutto' (dry) or 'amabile' (slightly sweet to sweet). These wines keep well.

Serve the dry wines throughout the meal, fairly cold (12–14 °C (54–57 °F)). You can serve the sweeter wines after the meal with a red fruit salad or even during the meal with poultry or pork in a sweet fruit sauce. Drinking temperature: 8–10 °C (46–50 °F).

SORNI DOC

There are two kinds of Sorni, a white made from nosiola, possibly supplemented with müller-thurgau, pinot bianco and sylvaner, and a red made from schiava, teroldego and possibly lagrein.

The Sorni bianco is straw-colored with a hint of green and quite unremarkable in bouquet and flavor. Simply tasty and fresh. This wine goes with anything, especially fish and light meat starters. Drinking temperature: 8–10 °C (46–50 °F).

The Sorni rosso is much more expressive in bouquet and flavor. It is an elegant, aromatic wine that goes down well with the entire meal. Choose, for example, a Scelto (Auslese), which has rather more alcohol and roundness. Drinking temperature: 12–14 °C (54–57 °F).

TEROLDEGO ROTALIANO DOC

A unique wine made from teroldego, a native of Trentino, which thrives particularly well in the flat valley of Rotaliana north of Trento. This is the only place where it seems able to develop to its full finesse. Everywhere else in Italy that this grape variety has been planted results have been mediocre to abominable.

The Teroldego Rotaliano rosso is very intense in color (ruby red with glimmers of purple when the wine is young) and has a typical bouquet of violets and raspberries. In the aftertaste you can detect a pleasant bitterness and hints of roasted almonds. Like some of the Loire red wines, it is better to drink this Teroldego rosso either in its youth or not until eight to ten years after it has been harvested. In the intervening period the wine often suffers from reduction (the wine has completely shut down and refuses any form of dialogue). Drink this wine with red meat or grilled poultry. Drinking temperature: young 10–12 °C (50–54 °F), aged 14–16 °C (57–61 °F).

The Teroldego Rotaliano rosso superiore has rather more alcohol and texture. This is certainly true of the riserva wines, which have to mature for at least an extra two years. You must definitely eat roast meat with this. Drinking temperature: 14–16 °C (57–61 °F).

There is also a rosato (Kretzer) made from teroldego, which is a beautiful pink to light pomegranate red color and has an intriguing floral, fruity bouquet and a light, sappy, rounded flavor. Here too you can detect roasted almonds and a slight bitterness in the aftertaste. Excellent wine for a country buffet, all year round. Drinking temperature: 10–12 °C (50–54 °F).

TRENTINO DOC

Generic designation of origin for white and red wines. It is very difficult to give a complete overview of these wines because every wine-grower has his own cuvée and technique.

The Trentino bianco is made from chardonnay and pinot bianco, is straw-colored and pleasant but not exactly remarkable. Great wine as an aperitif or with fish. Drinking temperature: 8–10 °C (46–50 °F).

The better white wines are obtained from a single grape variety. In this case the wines bear the name of this grape as well as that of Trentino DOC. The best wines are usually the Chardonnay Trentino, but excellent wines are also made from pinot bianco, pinot grigio, riesling italico, riesling renano, traminer aromatico and müller-thurgau. Pinot bianco and riesling renano are most suitable as aperitifs, but also go very well with any kind of fish. The other wines can be served throughout the meal. Drinking temperature: Pinot Grigio, Traminer, Müller-Thurgau and Chardonnay 10–12 °C (50–54 °F), the rest 8–10 °C (46–50 °F).

The subtle wines made from the native nosiola are really worth getting to know. Do not expect miracles, however, but rather a pleasant discovery of a special variety of grape, fine and delicate with pleasant fruit in the bouquet and flavor and a slight bitterness in the aftertaste. Delicious as an aperitif, even more delicious at meals with sophisticated fish or white meat starters or main courses. Drinking temperature: 8–10 °C (46–50 °F).

Finally there is also a first-rate sweet white wine made from moscato giallo. There is also a liqueur-like version of this wine, the liquoroso. Excellent on its own after a meal, well chilled at 6–8 °C (43–46 °F).

Super sparkling wines are also made from chardonnay and pinot bianco. These spumante make particularly good aperitifs. Drinking temperature: 8–10 °C (46–50 °F).

The Trentino rosso DOC is made from cabernet and merlot and has almost always been matured in wooden casks. Depending on the maker and the origin, the wines can be light and friendly or else full and strong. The latter mature well. Drink the light and friendly types when they are still at their fruitiest with terrines, patés or meat starters, at about 12 °C (54 °F). The fuller wines deserve to be left for longer and then go particularly well with roast meat or game. Keep a glass for a tasty chunk of mature cheese, such as asiago or grana padano, for example. Drinking temperature: 14–16 °C (57–61 °F).

The other red wines from Trentino are made from one single or two varieties of grape and are very typical of grape and terrain. There are wines made from cabernet sauvignon and/or cabernet franc, merlot, marzemino, pinot nero and lagrein. All of them first-rate wines, but the better ones are definitely the riserva wines, which have had at least two years extra maturing. You can combine these red Trentino wines to your heart's content with various kinds of meat, though a riserva is best with roast red meat or game and Marzemino with fried pork or lamb. Try all these wines

Trentino Pinot grigio

sometime with a chunk of montasio cheese. Drinking temperature: 14–16 °C (57–61 °F).

A pungent spumante is also made from pinot nero and goes well with meat starters or poultry. Drinking temperature: 10–12 °C (50–54 °F).

VALDADIGE DOC (ETSCHTALER)

These wines exist both in generic white, red and rosé versions and in varietal wine made of one or more grape varieties. The grape variety shown on the label must then account for at least 85% of the wine. For ordinary Valdadige bianco there is a large choice of grapes: pinot bianco, pinot grigio, riesling italico, müller-thurgau, chardonnay, bianchetta trevigiana, trebbiano toscano, nosiola, vernaccia and garganega. There is therefore no prime example of a Valdadige bianco. What can be said of them is that in general they are straw-colored, pleasant and fresh, with a good bouquet and not always equally dry. Here and there you will actually come across a wine with a certain amount of residual sugar. Drink these wines as aperitifs or throughout a meal. Drinking temperature: 8–12 °C (46–54 °F), depending on the type of wine.

There are numerous possible versions of the ordinary Valdadige rosso too. For these wines the choice is between the three schiava varieties, lambrusco, merlot, pinot nero, lagrein, teroldego or negrara. Depending on style and type this Valdadige rosso is light red to deep dark red. The bouquet is often reminiscent of fresh grapes and a handful of herbs and is always pleasant. Not all the wines are equally dry and here too you will come across the odd smooth sweet wine.

Drink a Valdadige rosso with meals, preferably with pork or poultry. Drinking temperature: 12–16 °C (54–61 °F), depending on the type.

The rosato wines are made from the same wines as the rosso. The color of these wines varies depending on the grape varieties used. Bouquet and flavor are fresh, fruity (English sweets, peardrops) and sometimes slightly sweetish. Surprisingly delicious wines without too many pretensions. A great accompaniment to poultry and fried/roast white meat. Drinking temperature: 10–12 °C (50–54 °F).

The other wines, made primarily from a single grape variety, are quite characteristic (grape + terrain). In general the white wines are straw-colored, fresh, sappy and sometimes a teeny bit sweet (Pinot Grigio). Drink Pinot Bianco and Chardonnay as aperitifs or with fish and Pinot Grigio with white meat or poultry. Drinking temperature: Pinot Bianco 8–10 °C (46–50 °F), Pinot Grigio and Chardonnay 10–12 °C (50–54 °F).

The red wines are made from the three schiava varieties (gentile, rossa and grigia), possibly supplemented with other, non-aromatic grapes. The wines are ruby to pomegranate red in color, slightly aromatic, fresh and acidy, smooth and sometimes slightly sweet. They can accompany the entire meal, but often go very well with roast pork with plums or sharp sauces. Drinking temperature: 14–16 °C (57–61 °F).

VENETO

The region of Veneto is a veritable paradise for lovers of nature and culture, and also for the most discriminating gastronomes. The area has held on to its agricultural role throughout the centuries. From the Dolomites in the north to the fertile valley of the Po and from Lake Garda to the Venetian coast there is a certain feeling of *joie de vivre*. The landscape is gently rolling, green and inviting. The climate is particularly favorable, from mildly continental in the north to Mediterranean in the south. The hospitable, cheerful inhabitants owe their daily nourishment to the rich countryside. The flavor and aroma of the natural ingredients are retained in the simple dishes. The wines, of which Soave, Bardolino and Valpolicella, in particular, have become world-renowned, echo the same unbounded *joie de vivre*.

RECIOTO DI SOAVE DOCG

As with Recioto della Valpolicella, selected, partially dried grapes are used for this wine. The result is a full, very aromatic white wine, golden in color. The flavor is full and fruity, from slightly sweet to very sweet. However seductive and excellent these wines may taste, do not forget that they contain a minimum of 14% alcohol.

Drink these wines with not over-sweet desserts. Because of the distinct touch of bitter almonds this wine goes well with desserts based on Amaretto biscuits, hazelnuts and mascarpone. Drinking temperature: 10–12 °C (50–54 °F).

BARDOLINO DOC

The vineyards of this famous designation of origin lie on an alluvial soil from the distant Ice Age, between the right shore of Lake Garda and the city of Verona. Wine has been made here for a long time, since before the time of the Romans. Bardolino wines may be made from corvina veronese, rondinella, molinara and negrara (total minimum of 85%), possibly supplemented with rossignola, barbera, sangiovese and garganega (maximum 15% in total).

Bardolino is a ruby red wine with occasional nuances of cherry red. As it ages, the color inclines towards dark pomegranate red. The wine smells fresh, fruity (cherries), sometimes a tiny bit herby, and tastes

ROSSO
LA FABRISERIA

1999

TEDESCHI

Veneto has many great wines

pleasant, smooth and fruity, with a discernible slight touch of bitterness in the aftertaste. Young wines may still have a slight fizziness, but this becomes less as they get older.

Drink these young, sappy wines with weekday meals, with pasta or quick-fried pork (escalopes). Drinking temperature: 10–12 °C (50–54 °F) (young) to 12–14 °C (54–57 °F).

The Bardolino wines that come from the historic heart of the area have 'classico' on the label. Wines with slightly more alcohol (minimum 11.5%) may be called 'superiore'. You may also come across (mainly in Italy) lighter colored Bardolino wines. These wines are made by the short soaking method and are called 'chiaretto'. They are rather lighter in texture than an ordinary Bardolino, and yet fuller than an average rosé.

There is also a red Bardolino spumante, possibly classico and/or superiore. This dark pink to pale red wine has fine foam, a fairly smooth bouquet and a pleasant, full, dry, sappy flavor. Here too you will find the typical touch of bitterness in the aftertaste. These wines are too heavy to drink as aperitifs and are better served at a festive dinner, with grilled poultry or game birds, for example. Also delicious with fresh strawberries after meals. Drinking temperature: 10–12 °C (50–54 °F).

The brand-new wine, Bardolino Novello, which is rather lighter and fruitier, is very trendy.

VALPOLICELLA DOC

Valpolicella wines have enjoyed great renown since the time of the Romans The famous poet Virgil was a great fan. And Valpolicella's fame has not diminished since

– on the contrary. The wines are made from corvina veronese, rondinella and molinara (minimum 85% in total), possibly supplemented with some rossignola, negrara, trentina, barbera or sangiovese (maximum total 15%).

The wines are light ruby red in color, inclining towards intense pomegranate red as they age. The bouquet is fresh, fruity and sometimes slightly herby. The flavor is dry, velvety smooth, fruity and slightly herby, with a hint of roasted bitter almonds in the aftertaste. With these too there are 'classico' and 'superiore' versions (minimum 1% more alcohol and one year extra maturing).

This wine is promoted in many pizzerias and trattorias to accompany simple dishes. There's certainly nothing against it, but the better Valpolicella classico superiore or the Valpolicella from the area of Valpantena are worth rather more than a pizza or a bowl of pasta.

Try involtini di cavolo Borghese, wonderful cabbage roulades, stuffed with herbed minced beef, covered in a cheese sauce and cooked in the oven au gratin. Drinking temperature: 12–14 °C (54–57 °F).

RECIOTO DELLA VALPOLICELLA DOC

The Italian word for ears is orecchi. Corrupted to recie, it refers to the 'little ears' of the bunches of grapes, in other words the highest part of the bunches that catches the most sun. Recioto wines are made from specially selected grapes. The bunches are cut into two pieces: the bottom part is used for making ordinary Valpolicella and the top part – the little ears, therefore – are gathered separately. These extra ripe grapes are then dried in the warm sun. This means that the water partially evaporates from the grapes, greatly increasing the concentration of sugars and aromatic and flavoring substances in the grapes. This produces a deep dark red wine, with a seductive, full and fruity bouquet (fruit jam, prunes, figs, raisins, etc.) – a wine rich in extracts.

The flavor is full, sultry, very warm (minimum 14% alcohol!) and overwhelmingly sweet. So drink this

Bardolino can also be first-rate

Valpolicella classico

wine after meals or with a not over-sweet dessert. Try pear or peach halves stuffed with a mousse of two-thirds gorgonzola piccante and one-third mascarpone. Drinking temperature: 10–16 °C (50–61 °F).

RECIOTO DELLA VALPOLICELLA SPUMANTE DOC

Dark-colored red sparkling wine, intensely aromatic (see above) and very rich in extracts. Minimum 14% alcohol. Definitely a wine for lovers of strong sensations or of lively, sweet bubbles, with a not over-sweet dessert. Drinking temperature: 6–8 °C (43–46 °F).

Recioto della Valpolicella

Valpolicella classico superiore

RECIOTO DELLA VALPOLICELLA AMARONE DOC

This wine is made in the same way as the sweet Recioto della Valpolicella, but this is a dry version with a minimum of 14% alcohol and two years extra maturing. Not everyone appreciates its charms, but if you can cope with an old-fashioned wild boar cooked slowly in the oven or over an open fire, you could spend an unforgettable evening with this monumental wine. Also conceivable is combining it with old, pungent cheeses, such as grana padano. Drinking temperature: 16–18 °C (61–64 °F).

BIANCO DI CUSTOZA DOC

This is a fairly well known white wine from south of Lake Garda. Partly because so many tourists have drunk this wine and have obviously found it good, Bianco di Custoza has enjoyed a rather inflated status. Not all Bianco di Custoza achieve the same standard, because they can be made from a very wide range of grapes, with all the associated various differences in type and flavor. Wine-growers may choose from trebbiano toscano, garganega, tocai friulano (sauvignon vert), cortese, malvasia, pinot bianco, chardonnay and Riesling Italico, pure or blended together. At best this provides a full, aromatic wine with a lot of sap, body

and freshness and a pleasant slight bitterness in the aftertaste. At worst it can produce a mediocre and tasteless wine.

If you serve a Bianco di Custoza as an aperitif or with fish you will usually be all right, irrespective of the quality of the wine. Drinking temperature: 8–12 °C (46–54 °F).

There is also a spumante in this Bianco di Custoza, made from the same grapes and therefore with the same variations in quality.

SOAVE DOC

The vineyards of Soave, like those of Bardolino and Valpolicella, lie between the eastern shore of Lake Garda and the city of Verona. Around the medieval town of Soave grow the vines of the gargenega that accounts for the lion's share of the famous white wine (minimum 85%). There is a choice of supplementary grapes, including pinot bianco, chardonnay, trebbiano di Soave or trebbiano di Toscana. Although there are all too often lesser Soave-type wines on the European market, a genuine Soave is definitely good. The color is usually quite light, from green to pale yellow, the bouquet not unduly striking and the flavor dry, smooth

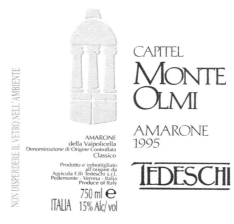

Recioto della Valpolicella Amarone

and pleasant with a slight hint of bitter almonds. This ordinary Soave has a light texture. It is a great aperitif, and also an amiable thirst-quencher at buffets and other informal gatherings.

The Soave classico comes from the historic heart of the area; the superiore has rather more alcohol and must rest for at least five months before it can be sold. The very best Soave is the superb Soave classico superiore, which makes a particularly good aperitif and goes well with freshwater fish.

Serve it at a summer lunch with fresh ciabatta covered in young montasio and thin slices of pear. Drinking temperature: ordinary Soave 8–10 °C (46–50 °F) the better Soave classico superiore 10–12 °C (50–54 °F).

Bianco di Custoza

SOAVE SPUMANTE DOC/RECIOTO DI SOAVE SPUMANTE DOC

These are light colored, aromatic sparkling wines with not too full a texture and are fresh and very pleasant. Characteristic of these wines is the ever- present hint of bitter almonds. In Soave spumante there is a dry

Soave classico

(exra brut) and a less dry (brut) version; in Recioto di Soave spumante only a full, sweet, highly alcoholic version (minimum 14% alcohol).

Drink ordinary spumante as an aperitif or with festive starters and Recioto di Soave spumante with desserts. Try Recioto di Soave spumante with *tortino di Montasio e pere'*, a warm pear cake made of flaky pastry with a hot sauce of melted montasio, cream and amaretto. Drinking temperature: 8–10 °C (46–50 °F).

GAMBELLARA DOC

Gambellara is a pleasant white wine made from garganega, possibly supplemented with other non-aromatic white grapes (maximum 20%). The vineyards of Gambellara are situated on the hills around the small town of the same name southwest of Vicenza. These white wines are in general straw-colored to golden-yellow and have a very pleasant bouquet of fresh grapes. The flavor is usually dry, fresh and acidy, smooth and not too heavy, with a slight hint of bitterness in the aftertaste. In the heart of the area they are allowed to use the term 'classico' on the label. Great aperitif, but also a great wine to serve throughout the meal. Drinking temperature: 10–12 °C (50–54 °F).

Soave classico superiore

GAMBELLARA RECIOTO DOC

The same grapes are used as for ordinary Gambellara, but they are first dried slightly in the sun. This gives them a higher concentration of sugars and aromatic and flavoring substances. The wines are golden-yellow and smell very strongly of over-ripe grapes or raisins. The flavor varies from slightly sweet to very sweet, while some wines can be slightly bubbly. Drink them with less sweet desserts at 6–10 °C (43–50 °F) (the sweeter, the colder). There is also a Gambellara Recioto spumante and a classico.

GAMBELLARA VIN SANTO DOC

This is the top rung Recioto: dark gold-colored with an impressive bouquet of extra-sweet raisins, which is echoed in the sweet, velvety smooth flavor. Minimum 14% alcohol.

Delicious with dessert, especially almond or hazelnut cakes and pastries. Drinking temperature: 6–8 °C (43–46 °F), 8–10 °C (46–50 °F) for enthusiasts.

COLLI EUGANEI DOC

These wines also have a long history, and yet they have never really made the breakthrough. The vineyards for these white and red wines are situated on hills south of Padua. The ordinary Colli Euganei bianco are made from garganega, prosecco (also called serprina), tocai friulano (sauvignon vert) and sauvignon, with the possible addition of pinella, pinot bianco, riesling italico and chardonnay. You've guessed it: no two wines taste alike. The flavor varies from dry to slightly sweet. Drink the dry wines as an aperitif or with light starters (white meat, poultry) and the sweeter ones after a meal or with a fresh, tangy fruit dessert. Drinking temperature: 8–12 °C (46–54 °F) (the sweeter, the colder).

The better wines of Colli Euganei are sold under the name of the dominant grape variety. First-rate Chardonnay (also in spumante), Pinot Bianco and Tocai Italico. Far more original, though, are the mostly dry Pinello wines (also in frizzante), the dry to slightly sweet Serprino (also in frizzante) and the sweet to very sweet Moscato wines. Ordinary Moscato has slight bubbles, giving it a better balance. The better Moscato are made from moscato giallo and sold under the name of Fior d'Arancio (orange blossom). They are very sensual wines, also available as spumante. Fior d'Arancio passito is darker in color, even sweeter, fuller and stronger in alcohol (minimum 15.5%). All of them very sensual wines for anyone contemplating a romantic evening by an open fire. Drinking temperature: Pinello/Serprino 8–12 °C (46–54 °F) (the sweeter, the colder), Moscato 6–8 °C (43–46 °F), Fior d'Arancio/spumante 6–10 °C (43–50 °F), Passito 10–12 °C (50–54 °F).

The ordinary red wines Colli Euganei rosso are produced from a cuvée of merlot, cabernet franc, cabernet sauvignon, barbera and raboso veronese. This gives the wines a great variation in color, bouquet and flavor, making them extra exciting to discover. Most of the wines are dry (watch out for the exceptions), robust, rounded, smooth and full of character. The riserva wines must be at least two years old and contain a minimum of 12.5% alcohol. Very good wines with meals, for example roast pork or even lamb. Drinking temperature: 14–16 °C (57–61 °F).

The best red wines are undoubtedly merlot, cabernet franc and cabernet sauvignon. Go for the older riservas, which offer you comparatively more for your money. All these wines are very well made but are not exactly typical of this area. They could in fact have been made almost anywhere. Nevertheless first-rate wines with meals, particularly with red meat or lamb. Drinking temperature: 14–16 °C (57–61 °F).

MONTELLO/ COLLI ASOLANI DOC

Small designation of origin above Padua. Great Rosso/Rosso superiore, Merlot/merlot superiore and cabernet/cabernet superiore. But it is primarily the white wines that cause a stir.

Still and sparkling wines of first-rate standard are produced from pinot bianco and chardonnay. You can serve the still wines with fish dishes and the spumante as an aperitif.

Only still wines are made from pinot grigio and prosecco. Pinot grigio is always dry, Prosecco dry to slightly sweet. Both wines are very fruity and velvety smooth in flavor. Prosecco is also recognizable from an undertone of bitter almonds. Drink the dry Prosecco as an aperitif or with light starters (white meat, poultry), Pinot Grigio at mealtimes with fried white meat, poultry or fish in rich sauces and the less dry Prosecco with poultry in creamy, sweetish sauces. There is also a Prosecco frizzante naturale. Drinking temperature: 8–10 °C (46–50 °F) for the slightly sweet and/or Prosecco frizzante 10–12 °C (50–54 °F) for the others.

BREGANZE DOC

The Breganze wines are little known outside their own area. However, the wines made here are of outstanding quality.

The ordinary bianco (primarily tocai friulano) loves any sort of fish and the red (primarily merlot) goes with any weekday meal. But it is above all the wines from a single dominant grape that are really worth trying.

The white wines (Pinot Bianco, Pinot Grigio, Vespaiolo, Chardonnay and Sauvignon) are sufficiently dry, aromatic, fresh and elegant. Most of these white wines have undergone a short period of cask-maturing, which makes them more rounded. The Sauvignon and Pinot Bianco are excellent summer aperitifs, Chardonnay a winter aperitif. Although all these wines will go well with fish dishes, I prefer Chardonnay and Vespaiolo with crustaceans and Sauvignon with shellfish.

Torcolato is a very special wine, a sweet to very sweet version of Vespaiolo, reminiscent of the aroma and flavor of fresh, extremely sweet grapes, honey and raisins. With its 14% alcohol (or more) it is an excellent wine for long winter evenings. Drinking temperature: 9–12 °C (48–54 °F).

The better Breganze red wines are Cabernet Franc and/or Sauvignon, Pinot Nero and Marzemino. All three types are very aromatic (brushwood, plant aromas, fruity) and particularly delicious. Admittedly they are not high-fliers, but they can make any weekday meal into an occasion. Drinking temperature: 12–14 °C (54–57 °F).

PROSECCO DI CONEGLIANO-VALDOBBIADENE ROSECCO DI CONEGLIANO PROSECCO DI VALDOBBIADENE DOC

Three wines of equal quality from the region above the triangle of towns of Padua, Vincenza and Treviso. These wines are obtained from the prosecco grape, possibly supplemented with some verdiso, pinot bianco, pinot grigio or chardonnay (maximum 15%).

There are two main types of Prosecco. Prosecco frizzante is slightly bubbly, straw-colored, very fruity, sappy and particularly pleasant. Prosecco spumante is definitely more passionate, fresh, fruity and full in flavor. Both wines are available in 'secco', (dry, light, elegant, hint of bitter almonds), 'amabile' (slightly sweet, very fruity) and 'dolce' (very sweet and fruity). You may well also come across a Prosecco superiore di Cartizze, a wine made in a strictly demarcated region called Cartizze (around San Pietro di Barbozza in Valdobbiadene). As far as flavor goes there is scarcely any difference from the other Prosecco wines. Drink these dry elegant wines as aperitifs or at meals with light starters (white meat, poultry, fish) or sweet desserts (has a refreshing effect). It is better to drink the sweeter versions after meals or with less sweet desserts (Panettone, for example). Drinking temperature: 6–8 °C (43–46 °F) for sweet, (8–10 °C (46–50 °F) for dry Prosecco.

N.B. A number of interesting trendy wines are also produced in the area, including some made from moscato.

VINI DEL PIAVE DOC

You must know them, those large two liter bottles served by the glass in most Italian restaurants. What's the betting they come from the Piave district? Tocai del Piave for the white and Merlot del Piave for the red? In general these wines are very drinkable but most definitely not representative of the whole area. Good wine is also produced in Piave, the district on both banks of the river of the same name.

You will find great Cabernet Franc and/or Sauvignon wines, with just enough plant undertones and tannins to be able to compete with a good French vin de pays (but they are far cheaper) and the Merlot and Pinot Nero are just that little bit smoother than everywhere else... sometimes verging on the sweetish (hence their success with inexperienced frequenters of pizzerias). The better wines have spent longer in the cask and are allowed to carry the designation 'riserva'.

But try something different for a change, a typical Italian

Prosecco di Conegliano Valdobbiadene

wine, the Raboso del Piave, ruby red to pomegranate red, with a seductive bouquet of forest violets and other pleasant woodland smells and a flavor which is dry, robust, strong and masculine, fresh and acidy, sometimes with a considerable amount of tannins, but always full of character and sappy. Excellent with roast meat (fried too). Drinking temperature: 12–14 °C (54–57 °F) to 16 °C (61 °F) for the riserva wines.

Good quality trendy spumante

The choice is simpler with the white wines. Almost everyone knows the golden-yellow, unremarkable Tocai Italiano. Great with a fish pizza or for a school reunion... As long as it is well chilled and drunk in moderation it has its own charms. The same is more or less true of the Pinot Bianco and Chardonnay that are certainly not a very good advertisement for these world-famous grape vari-

Moscato spumante

eties. Far more interesting are the sultry, aromatic Pinot Grigio del Piave or the elegant, characteristic and particularly pleasant Verduzzo del Piave. You can serve any white Piave wines as aperitifs or throughout the meal. Verduzzo also has a secret liaison with substantial sea fish. Drinking temperature: 8–10 °C (46–50 °F) except for Verduzzo and Pinot Grigio 10–12 °C (50–54 °F).

BAGNOLI DI SOPRA/ BAGNOLI DOC

These wines come from the province of Padua, in the neighborhood of the little town of Bagnoli di Sopra. Here the vines grow on a fairly loose subsoil of sediments, containing a great deal of lime. They produce great white (Chardonnay, Tocai Friulano, Sauvignon, Raboso), rosé (Raboso and Merlot) and red wines (Merlot, Cabernet Franc, Cabernet Sauvignon, Carmenāre and Raboso).

Merlot del Piave

The white wines can be dry to slightly sweet, depending on the maker, the style and the grape varieties used. They are all smooth, friendly, tasty wines that can do good service from aperitif to dessert. Drinking temperature: 10–12 °C (50–54 °F), slightly more chilled for the sweeter versions.

The rosé wines are quite light in color, and also in bouquet and flavor. Nothing special, but quite palatable. You will find them from smoothly dry to slightly sweet. Rosé for drinking throughout the meal. Drinking temperature: 10–12 °C (50–54 °F).

The red wines are the best of the three types. They are intense in color, quite aromatic and full in flavor, smooth and rounded. The riserva wines have been cask-matured for slightly longer. You can drink Bagnoli rosso with red meat or poultry, but a leg of lamb or fillet of pork cooked in the oven also goes extremely well with them. Drinking temperature: 12–14 °C (54–57 °F).

LISON-PRAMAGGIORE DOC

Two areas northeast of Venice produce a wide range of wines, all sold under the name of a single grape, as in Alsace.

You will find outstanding wines here made from tocai italico (especially that from the Lison Classico area), pinot bianco, pinot grigio, riesling italico, verduzzo and – it comes as no surprise – the ubiquitous shelf-fillers chardonnay and sauvignon. All these wines are dry, with, very uniquely, a slight residue of sugar in the Verduzzo, Chardonnay and Pinot Bianco. Riesling Italico makes a very appropriate aperitif and all the other wines have a distinct preference for fish. Try Tocai di Lison with *risi e bisi*, the renowned risotto with garden peas from Venice. Drinking temperature: 8–10 °C (46–50 °F), 10–12 °C (50–54 °F) for Chardonnay, Pinot Grigio, Tocai and Verduzzo.

The red wines are obtained from the renowned merlot and cabernet. They do not strictly speaking originate from this area, but are extremely well made. Like all wines of their kind they go mainly with roast or fried red meat. Try to choose a riserva, which has far more to offer. Drinking temperature: 12–14 °C (54–57 °F), 14–16 °C (57–61 °F) for the riserva.

A lovely, and above all original, wine is made from refosco dal pedonculo rosso. This foreign grape is also used in French Savoy under the name of mondeuse and here provides a wine with an intense red color, slightly rich in tannins and bitter in the aftertaste, but rounded and full in flavor. Great accompaniment to red meat, but in particular to fried or roast pork. Drinking temperature: 12–14 °C (54–57 °F).

OTHER WINES FROM VENETO

Some unusual and exciting wines, the Lesini Durello DOC, are made in the hilly area between Verona and Vicenza. They are fresh, fruity and full-bodied still,

slightly bubbly (frizzante) or sparkling (spumante) wines. Great aperitifs. Drinking temperature: 10–12 °C (50–54 °F) for the still wines, 6–8 °C (43–46 °F) for the sparkling.

To complete the picture, I should state here that wines are also produced in Veneto under the designations of origin of Lugana DOC, San Martino della Battaglia DOC and Valdadige DOC, which have already been discussed in the section on Lombardy. The wines of the Colli Berici are also very worthwhile.

One designation of origin, Garda DOC, is also divided between both areas, but the majority of the wines are made in Veneto.

GARDA DOC

The wines of Veneto officially bear the designation Garda Orientale DOC and those of Lombardy simply Garda DOC. The wines are made from at least 85% of the grape variety stated on the label.

Here too you will come across the familiar pinot bianco, pinot grigio, chardonnay, riesling italico, riesling renano and sauvignon. All are first-rate wines. Riesling Italico and Chardonnay are delicious as aperitifs and all the wines are good as accompaniments to fish. Drink Sauvignon with shellfish, Chardonnay or Riesling Italico with crustaceans and Pinot Grigio with poultry or white meat. Drinking temperature: Sauvignon, Pinot Bianco and Riesling 8–10 °C (46–50 °F), Chardonnay and Pinot Grigio 10–12 °C (50–54 °F).

Far more interesting to discover are the white garganega, trebbianello and cortese. All three can be dry or sometimes slightly sweet. They are all quite aromatic and full in flavor. The (dry) Cortese is an exciting aperitif, otherwise all three wines go with fish in rich sauces or with crustaceans. Drinking temperature: 10–12 °C (50–54 °F).

Among the red wines you will again encounter the obligatory Cabernet, Merlot and Pinot Negro, no better or worse than anywhere else in the world, and the original Marzemino and Corvina. The latter two wines are fresh, cheerful and aromatic. Wines with a little more flavor. Serve them with red meat. Drinking temperature: 12–14 °C (54–57 °F).

Finally, there is another white frizzante, dry or slightly sweet and always fruity. The dry version is great as an aperitif and the sweeter one for any festive occasion outside meals. Drinking temperature: 6–8 °C (43–46 °F).

FRIULI-VENEZIA GIULIA

Wine-growing had already been instigated in Friuli long before the west European Celts discovered the virtues of wine. This wine-growing district is in the extreme northeast of Italy, below the Austrian border, next to Slovenia. A large part of the country is mountainous, but wine-growing is concentrated in the green river valleys (Tagliamento, Isonzo) and on the sunny hills. The climate is a happy coincidence of mild Mediterranean (Adriatic Sea) and severe continental (Alps) climate. The soil consists mainly of broken up stone from the Ice Age. The capital Trieste still shows traces of the long Austrian occupation. The second most important town in the neighborhood is Udine. Local culture is a mish-mash of ancient Roman, pan-Italian and Slavic and Germanic influences, making the area all the more exciting. The people are very hospitable and make every visit into a celebration. Although the district is also well known for its excellent sausages, it is the fantastic San Daniele ham and the light, fruity and elegant wines that have made Friuli famous in the culinary world. As in Alsace and in some other areas of northern Italy, wines from Friuli are sold under a generic name, followed by the name of the dominant grape variety.

CARSO DOC

Less well known wines from the neighborhood of Gorizia and Trieste. They come in many versions, including the ordinary rosso (70% terrano grape), Terrano (85% Terrano) and Malvasia.

The red wines are light, dry and full-bodied and pleasant in flavor. They can accompany most dishes. Drinking temperature: 10–14 °C (50–57 °F).

The beautiful straw-colored Malvasia is obtained from the malvasia istriana variety and is very aromatic and fruity. It is a dry, delicious white wine that goes well with sea fish, but also, for example, with fresh cheese (young montasia) and fruit. Drinking temperature: 10–12 °C (50–54 °F).

Friuli Osonzo Chardonnay
and Pinot Nero

FRIULI ANNIA DOC

Another less familiar wine district in the province of Udine. The wines that have the right to this designation of origin (white, rosé and red) can be generic wines (rosso, bianco, rosato) or else wines from a single dominant grape variety. The generic wines are in general of very acceptable quality, but my preference 1 is for the more specific wines. As almost everywhere in northern Italy, great Pinot Bianco and Pinot Grigio are made here and a certain amount of Sauvignon and Chardonnay. You can serve all these wines at meals with fish, Pinot Grigio also with white meat and poultry. The Chardonnay and Sauvignon are first-rate aperitifs, as are the excellent frizzante and spumante made from chardonnay and/or pinot bianco. Drinking temperature: Sauvignon and Pinot Bianco 8–10 °C (46–50 °F), Chardonnay and Pinot Grigio 10–12 °C (50–54 °F), frizzante and spumante 6–8 °C (43–46 °F).

Among the red wines you will come across the almost obligatory Merlot, Cabernet Franc and Cabernet Sauvignon (great wines with distinct plant undertones and a great deal of fruit).

The following wines are interesting and characteristic of this area:

Malvasia Istriana: straw-colored with a hint of green, attractive bouquet, dry, fine flavor. Wonderful with light kinds of white meat. Drinking temperature: 10–12 °C (50–54 °F);

Tocai Friulano: straw-colored to lemon yellow, seductive aromas, sultry, sophisticated and elegant in flavor. Likes a nice fish with a soft, creamy sauce. Drinking temperature: 10–12 °C (50–54 °F);

Verduzzo Friulano: golden-yellow, sensual bouquet and flavor of fresh grapes, sometimes a little rich in tannins, dry, slightly sweet or even sweet. Drink the dry version with starters or fish, the sweeter versions at the end of or after the meal. Drinking temperature: dry 10–12 °C (50–54 °F), sweeter 6–10 °C (43–50 °F) (the sweeter, the colder);

Refosco dal Peduncolo rosso is a full, elegant, fruity wine with a discernible, pleasant hint of bitterness. Ideal partner at informal dinners. Drinking temperature: 12–14 °C (54–57 °F), the older riserva slightly warmer 14–16 °C (57–61 °F).

COLLI ORIENTALI DEL FRIULI DOC

These wines in white, red and rosé are produced in the district above Udine. The white wines, made from, among others, sauvignon, chardonnay and pinot grigio, are not unduly exciting. However do try one of the following original white wines:
- Tocai Friulano: dry, warm and full, likes a substantial fish, or else white meat and poultry. Try *vitello tonnato*, veal in a creamy tuna sauce. Drinking temperature: 10–12 °C (50–54 °F).
- Verduzzo Friulano: fruity, sometimes dry, sometimes sweet, sturdy and often fairly rich in tannins. Drink the dry wine as an aperitif or with white meat (veal) or poultry (guinea fowl), the slightly sweet one with fish or white meat in a sharp sauce and the sweet one with fresh desserts or after meals. Drinking temperature: 10–12 °C (50–54 °F).
- Ribolla Gialla: fresh and harmonious, always dry, sophisticated and elegant. Particularly delicious

with fish (fresh salmon) or white meat in a smooth sauce. Drinking temperature: 10–12 °C (50–54 °F).

– Malvasia Istriana: sultry, herby, aromatic and full. Drink it with substantial fish (turbot) with a sunny, herby sauce, with risotto with young vegetables or with young cheese. Drinking temperature: 10–12 °C (50–54 °F).

– Ramandolo: this wine made from the verduzzo grape is magnificent, intensely golden-yellow in color, very fruity and full, with sometimes a touch of tannin and a robust body. They are always slightly sweet to very sweet wines. Minimum 14% alcohol. The wines from the historic center of the area are allowed to be called 'classico'. Serve a Ramandolo at the end of a good meal in a gathering of family or friends, with a fresh dessert, for example, or a nut gâteau or just on its own after the meal. Try *strucolo*, the local version of Austrian Strudel, here usually filled with ricotta and apples. Drinking temperature: 8–10 °C (46–50 °F) (slightly sweet), 6–8 °C (43–46 °F) (very sweet).

– Picolit: Italy's most unusual sweet white wine and probably one of the most unique in the world. The Picolit grape is characterized by very freakish growth. A remarkable kind of natural selection of grapes takes place in the bunches. Most of the grapes do not reach full growth but drop off prematurely or remain small and hard. The grapes that do fully develop have an enormous amount of extract and aromatic and flavoring substances. These grapes are also harvested late, so that the sun causes the grapes to shrink to some extent. This increases the content of extract, sugars and aromatic and flavoring substances in the grapes. Wines made from

A superb sweet wine of outstanding quality

picolit are comparable to a German or Austrian Trockenbeerenauslese. The color is a very full golden-yellow, the bouquet seductive, sultry, overpowering … The flavor is strong, fruity (ripe fruit), ethereal (plenty of alcohol!), velvety smooth (honey) and full and lingers for a long time. Because its growth pattern is so strange, picolit produces a particularly small amount of wine. This quantity is reduced still further by the late harvest. Understandably, the price of this divine nectar cannot be exactly low, but do try it once at a very special moment. It is preferable not to serve it with meals, but with a great deal of respect and love on a winter evening of romance or appreciation of the arts. Drinking temperature: 8–10 °C (46–50 °F).

As far as the red wines are concerned too, as well as the excellent Cabernet Sauvignon, Merlot and suchlike, several exciting and original wines are produced: Schippettino and Refosco dal Peduncolo rosso are very enjoyable wines with a lot of fruit and character, full, warm and velvety smooth. Refosco also has a discernible touch of bitterness. Serve these wines with typical northern Italian dishes such as 'capriolo in salmi (game in rich wine sauce) or *coda alla vaccinara* (braised oxtail). Drinking temperature: 14 °C (54 °F), for the older riserva 16 °C (61 °F).

Ramandolo, fantastic sweet wine

GRAVE DEL FRIULI DOC

Here too there are many different wines made from one specific grape variety and some generic wines. These wines are made on the banks of the Tagliamento in the province of Udine. You will come across similar kinds of wines here to those of Colli Orientali Friulani. The white wines are made from grapes including Pinot Grigio, Tocai Friulano, Traminer Aromatico and Verduzzo Friulano. The spumante is also of outstanding quality. The rosato is fresh, fruity and unconstrained (also available in frizzante). The red wines are obtained from the two cabernet grapes (possibly blended together), merlot, pinot nero and refosco dal peduncolo rosso.

FRIULI LATISANA DOC

Although less well known outside their own district, these wines are of outstanding quality. Fresh, full white wines made from pinot bianco, chardonnay, sauvignon, malvasia istriana, tocai friulano, verduzzo friulano, traminer aromatico and riesling renano. The spumante is also of a high class.

The red wines also offer good value for money. As well as the Cabernets, Merlot and Pinot Nero you will come across an unusual wine, the Franconia. This is a light, very fruity wine that is midway between a cheerful Gamay and a fresh, herby Portuguese. Wonderful with variety meats or light pasta dishes. Drinking temperature: 12–14 °C (54–57 °F).

COLLIO GORIZIANO/COLLIO DOC

This is definitely one of the best wine-growing districts in Italy as regards white wines, but the red wines also reach a very high standard. The vineyards are situated on the hills ('Collio') on the east side of the river Judrio, near Gorizia. The ordinary bianco is made from ribolla gialla, malvasia istriana and tocai friulano, possibly supplemented up to a maximum of 20% with

Grave del Friuli Refosco

other grapes used locally. It is a straw-colored wine, slightly aromatic, dry, sophisticated, delicate and harmonious. Excellent as an aperitif or throughout the meal. Drinking temperature: 8–10 °C (46–50 °F).

The Pinot Bianco is a light straw color, slightly aromatic and smooth in flavor, fresh with a hint of sweet almonds. Great as an aperitif, but also delicious with pasta dishes with seafood. Drinking temperature: 8–10 °C (46–50 °F).

The Pinot Grigio is often golden-yellow in color, with the occasional coppery sheen, very intense in bouquet, very full and sappy in flavor. Very good with poultry or white meat risotto, among other things. Drinking temperature: 10–12 °C (50–54 °F).

The Ribolla Gialla is an intense straw color with a hint of green. Very exciting bouquet, floral and fruity at the same time. Full, dry, round wine, lively and fresh, which makes a good winter aperitif or goes well, for example, with starters of white meat or poultry. Drinking temperature: 10–12 °C (50–54 °F).

The Sauvignon is light in color and quite intense in bouquet and flavor. The experienced taster will detect a plant (grass) undertone, and also a pinch of nutmeg, acacia honey, white blossom and a hint of herbs. By contrast with many mediocre shelf-fillers from northern Italy, the Sauvignon wines from Collio are of outstanding quality, very characteristic of their grape variety and their terrain. Great aperitifs, but also very suitable for mushroom risotto, pasta dishes and egg dishes. Drinking temperature: 8–10 °C (46–50 °F).

The Tocai Friulano is pure straw color to golden-yellow, with some lemon yellow nuances here and there. The bouquet is very characteristic, delicate and pleasant, the flavor slightly herby, with hints of bitter almonds and nuts. Ideal with poultry, or else as a winter aperitif or with a risotto. Delicious with raw San Daniele ham! Drinking temperature: 10–12 °C (50–54 °F).

Grave del Friuli Pinot Bianco

The Traminer Aromatico wines here are golden-yellow, very aromatic and intense in flavor and improve after a few years extra maturing. Serve these full-bodied, sultry, powerful wines with oilier kinds of fish, with a herby risotto or with fried pork. Drinking temperature: 10–12 °C (50–54 °F).

The Riesling Renano is straw-colored, sometimes golden-yellow after extra maturing, very intense in bouquet and flavor, sophisticated and delicate. Great as an aperitif, but also with meals, for example with risotto with assorted forest mushrooms, pasta dishes with fish or even with grilled fish. Drinking temperature: 10–12 °C (50–54 °F).

The Riesling Italico is a light straw color with a hint of green. Subtle dry wine that goes well with fish. Drinking temperature: 10–12 °C (50–54 °F).

The Malvasia Istriana is straw-colored, very fine and subtle in bouquet, smooth and round in flavor, with a slight plant undertone. Excellent wine with salads of fish or white meat combined with young fresh vegetables. Drinking temperature: 10–12 °C (50–54 °F).

Collio's Chardonnay is also often better than most of the others from northern Italy, Straw-colored, delicate, dry, full-bodied, slightly floral, smooth and very pleasant. Serve it as a winter aperitif or with fish dishes. Try *insalata di aragosta*, lobster salad! Drinking temperature: 10–12 °C (50–54 °F).

The Müller-Thurgau is also surprisingly good. The color is quite dark yellow with flickers of green. The bouquet is very characteristic (green apple, flowers) and the flavor dry, smooth and full. Excellent as a winter aperitif and a good accompaniment to white meat or fish. A real must for those that like them is combining it with snails. Try pasties stuffed with a seafood ragout or a ragout of veal and veal sweetbreads. Drinking temperature: 10–12 °C (50–54 °F).

The Picolit wines here are sweet to very sweet. They are sophisticated, warm, full-bodied white wines that go well with fruit desserts and soft, not over–sweet cakes and pastries. Drinking temperature: 6–8 °C (43–46 °F).

The Collio rosso is usually made from cabernet and merlot. It is a ruby red wine with a plant–like bouquet and a smooth, lively flavor. Serve these full-bodied wines with red meat or fried pork. Drinking temperature: 12–14 °C (54–57 °F) 14–16 °C (57–61 °F) for the riserva.

The other red wines are made from cabernet franc, cabernet sauvignon, merlot and pinot nero. The first three wines have a characteristic plant undertone that clearly distinguishes them from a Bordeaux-type wine. The flavor is full and strong, dry and harmonious. The Merlot also sometimes has a little extra bitterness in the aftertaste. The Pinot Nero is very smooth and full in flavor. Serve the first three wines with fried pork, lamb or red meat. You can also drink the older riserva with game. The Merlot is also very fond of poultry. The young Pinot Nero goes very well with risotto, pasta dishes with cheese and fried white meat. Older wines and riservas are good with game. Try *papardelle alla lepre*, a famous Italian dish of fresh ribbon pasta and jugged hare. Drinking temperature 14–16 °C (57–61 °F).

ISONZO/ISONZO DEL FRIULI DOC

Here too we are talking about outstanding white wines and excellent red wines. The wine-growing region is on the banks of the Isonzo in the neighborhood of Gorizia. The vineyards extend as far as the Slovenian border. The difference in flavor between Collio and Isonzo is not actually very much. A generic bianco is made here from tocai friulano, malvasia istriana, pinot bianco and chardonnay. It can be dry to sweet, but is always particularly fresh and often quite rich in tannins. The other white wines are made from pinot bianco, pinot grigio, tocai friulano, verduzzo friulano, traminer aromatico, riesling renano, riesling italico and of course sauvignon and chardonnay.

They make a delicious spumante from pinot bianco, sometimes supplemented with pinot nero and chardonnay. The spumante made from Verduzzo are also wonderful. Drink these spumante on festive occasions or as an aperitif.

Other suitable aperitif wines are Sauvignon, Pinot Bianco, Riesling Renano, Riesling Italico and Chardonnay.

You can also serve the two Riesling wines with fried fish, the Chardonnay, the Tocai and the Pinot Grigio

Isonzo bianco and Isonzo rosato frizzante

with fish in creamy sauces or with white meat, the Traminer with a herby risotto or pasta dishes with cheese and Verduzzo throughout the meal. Drinking temperature: 8–10 °C (46–50 °F) (Chardonnay, Traminer, Tocai, Verduzzo and Pinot Grigio 10–12 °C (50–54 °F).

The ordinary rosso is made from merlot, cabernet franc and cabernet sauvignon, possibly supplemented with some pinot nero or refosco. You will find this Isonzo rosso in countless types and variations of flavor. Simply experiment; they are all worth it.

Sparkling wine made from Pinot Bianco

Verduzzo spumante

Here too the better red wines are made from the ubiquitously familiar French grapes, cabernet, merlot and pinot nero. These wines are first-rate, with a discernible plant undertone in the first two and a considerable hint of bitterness in the Pinot Nero. All three are, according to taste, good accompaniments to classic meat dishes or fanciful combinations of modern cuisine. Try them with roast venison or wild boar! Drinking temperature 14–16 °C (57–61 °F).

Apart from the original and excellent local passito, the most surprising wines are the young, fruity and more aromatic Franconia (excellent with pork) and the full-bodied, powerful Refosco dal Peduncolo rosso (more at home with roast beef or game). Drinking temperature: Franconia 15–16 °C (59–61 °F), Refosco 16–17 °C (61–63 °F).

Isonzo Pinot Grigio and Merlot

FRIULI AQUILEIA DOC

This is the southern-most of the Friuli wines. The vineyards extend from the Adriatic coast to the border of Isonzo. Here too they make very unadulterated white wines from, among others, pinot bianco, tocai friulano and verduzzo friulano, fresh and fruity rosato from merlot, cabernet and refosco and excellent red from merlot, cabernet franc and cabernet sauvignon. However, again it is Refosco dal Peduncolo Rosso that provides the most original and exciting wines (see also Collio and Isonzo).

EMILIA-ROMAGNA

Emilia-Romagna lies below Lombardy and Veneto and extends from Liguria to the Adriatic Sea. In the south Emilia-Romagna is separated from Tuscany and the Marches by the Apennines. By Italian standards the area is exceptionally flat. This gives

Friuli Aquileia rosso

Three classic Izonso wines

the local wines their own identity and a completely different character from other Italian wines. For most people the name Emilia-Romagna gives little clue as to the origin of the wines. However, the vineyards are easy to localize: between Piacenza and Parma, around Reggio and Modena, around Bologna and in the triangle of Ravenna, Forli and Rimini. The capital of Emilia-Romagna is Bologna, of culinary fame for its Bolognese sauce, *aceto balsamico* (high quality vinegar), parma ham and *parmigiano-reggiano* (Parmesan cheese).

ALBANA DI ROMAGNA DOCG

This is the only DOCG in Emilia-Romagna. This wine, made from the Albana grape, can be made in the provinces of Bologna, Forli and even Ravenna (small enclave in the Bosco Eliceo). The DOCG version can be dry (secco), slightly sweet (amabile), sweet (dolce) or liqueur-like (passito).

The secco is straw-colored, light but sublime in bouquet, fresh, warm and harmonious, with a touch of tannin. Drink this wine while it is young with fish, shellfish or snails (*lumache*), for example. Drinking temperature: 8–10 °C (46–50 °F).

The amabile and dolce are slightly darker in color, the older ones golden-yellow. Here too the bouquet is subtle and elegant rather than powerful. The flavor is very fruity and luxurious. Drink these wines at the end of a meal with cakes or pastries, preferably with fresh, tangy fruit. Try *panettone*, a luxury dessert cake the Italians are mad about. Drinking temperature: 6–8 °C (43–46 °F).

The passito is even darker, from golden-yellow to amber. The bouquet is far more intense, intriguing and intoxicating. The flavor is particularly full and velvety smooth and varies in sweetness depending on the maker, year and type. This wine is mad about petits-fours and other divine pastries, but also likes dried fruit. Try *formaggi erborinati* (herbed cheeses), such as the famous castelmagno from Piedmont – a very unusual but fantastic combination! Drinking temperature: 6–8 °C (43–46 °F).

COLLI PIACENTINI DOC

The wines originating from the area south of Piacenza have long enjoyed great fame. The white and red wines produced here are of outstanding quality. All the wines have a distinct authority, which places them among the loveliest wines in Italy. The Sauvignon, Chardonnay and Pinot Grigio are excellent wines, but the following white wines are far more interesting.

TREBBIANO VAL TREBBIA

This wine is made from ortrugo, supplemented with trebbiano and/or sauvignon (the combination with trebbiano is best). This straw-colored wine has a pleasant, though quite modest, bouquet and comes in a great variety of types and flavors, from dry to sweet, from still to bubbly or sparkling. Drink the dry kinds as aperitifs or with light starters or freshwater fish and the sweet ones on their own after a meal. Try *pesce al vino bianco,* fish in white wine sauce. Drinking temperature: 8–12 °C (50–54 °F) (from sweet to dry).

MONTEROSSO VAL D'ARDA

Dry or slightly sweet wine made from malvasia di candia aromatica, moscato bianco, trebbiano romagnolo, ortrugo and bervedino and/or sauvignon. The wine is straw-colored, very aromatic, still, slightly bubbly (frizzante) or sparkling (spumante). Great aperitif or accompaniment to starters and fish. Serve the sweeter wines with fresh fruit or slightly sweet pastries at the end of a meal. Drinking temperature: 8–10 °C (46–50 °F).

VAL NURE

Made from malvasia di candia aromatica, ortrugo and trebbiano romagnolo. Very pale yellow in color, intensely aromatic, dry or sweet, still, bubbly or sparkling. The dry version is a first-rate aperitif. Good accompaniment to pasta dishes with fresh cheese, light starters, fish, white meat and young cheese, provolone, for example. Drinking temperature: 10 °C (50 °F).

MALVASIA

Very characteristic, intensely aromatic wine, dry, slightly sweet or very sweet and fresh in flavor. Comes in still, slightly bubbly and sparkling versions. Drink the dry sparkling wines as aperitifs, the dry still wines with starters, pasta, white meat and fish and the less dry wines with creamy cheeses (e.g. *gorgonzola dolce* or Gormas). Drinking temperature: dry 10 °C (50 °F), sweet 6–8 °C (43–46 °F).

ORTRUGO

Made from a minimum of 85% ortrugo. This surprising wine is straw-colored with a hint of green. The bouquet is subtle and quite characteristic. The flavor is dry and sappy, with a distinct touch of bitter almonds in the aftertaste. The wine is still, slightly bubbly or sparkling. Serve the latter variation as an aperitif, the still wines with starters, white meat, fish and cheeses that are not too mature. Drinking temperature: 10 °C (50 °F).

You will come across some great generic wines among the red wines, and also first-rate Cabernet Sauvignon and Pinot Nero. However, the following wines are more exciting.

GUTTURNIO

This intensely ruby red wine is made from barbera and croatina. This wine too can be dry to sweet and still to slightly bubbly. Pleasant, but not exactly striking as regards bouquet or flavor. Serve it with a meat risotto or fried meat. The sweet version has a surprising under-tone of almonds in the aftertaste and goes extremely well with fruit salads. Drinking temperature: dry 14–16 °C (57–61 °F), the older riserva wines (minimum two years old) 16–17 °C (61–63 °F) and sweet 8–10 °C (46–50 °F).

BARBERA

Ruby red in color, characteristic and quite aromatic in bouquet and flavor. Sappy, dry, fairly rich in tannins and quite passionate in their youth (carbon dioxide). Serve these Barbera with roast meat or mature, characterful, dry cheeses (older provolone!). Drinking temperature: 14–16 °C (57–61 °F).

BONARDA

Ruby red wine made from a minimum of 85% bonarda Piemontese with a very aromatic bouquet and a flavor that is fairly rich in tannins; it can be dry, slightly sweet or very sweet, still or slightly bubbly. Traditionally this wine is drunk with pasta dishes with meat, but it can also accompany many other dishes. The sweeter version belongs with fruit salads or desserts combining fruit and creamy cheese (mascarpone + gorgonzola). Drinking temperature: 14–16 °C (57–61 °F) for the dry version, 10–12 °C (50–54 °F) for the sweet.

COLLI DI PARMA DOC

The vineyards are situated around the town of Parma on hills of up to 1,300 ft. Although none of the wines produced here are exactly outstanding, they do enjoy considerable renown. There are four different wines here.

COLLI DI PARMA ROSSO

Minimum 60% barbera, supplemented with bonarda piemontese and/or croatina. The wine is ruby red, smells pleasantly fresh and fruity and tastes dry, sappy and harmonious, with the occasional slight touch of carbon dioxide. Serve it with pasta dishes, deep-fried vegetables or meat, roast or fried meat and pungent cheeses (parmigiano reggiano). Drinking temperature: in Italy they drink the wine at 18 °C (64 °F), but most tasters prefer 16 °C (61 °F).

COLLI DI PARMA SAUVIGNON

Very acceptable Sauvignon, delicate, sophisticated and aromatic. The flavor is sufficiently dry, fresh, acidy and harmonious, with a slight touch of bitterness and occasional bubbles. A great aperitif that is also excellent in combination with grilled, boiled or fried fish. Drinking temperature: 10 °C (50 °F).

COLLI DI PARMA MALVASIA ASCIUTTO/SECCO

The best Malvasia wines are made from 100% malvasia di candia aromatica. However, there are a few less sophisticated versions in which malvasia is supplemented to a maximum of 15% with moscato. Depending on the style, the wine will be slightly to intensely straw-colored. The bouquet is very aromatic and characteristic of malvasia. The flavor is fresh, full of character and harmonious. Some of the wines have a slight suggestion of carbon dioxide and some are actually sold as frizzante. There is also a spumante in this Malvasia. Drink the dry and sparkling wines as aperitifs, with starters, with fish or white meat. Drinking temperature: 10–12 °C (50–54 °F).

COLLI DI PARMA MALVASIA AMABILE

This wine has the same features as Malvasia asciutto, but it is sweet. Also exists in frizzante and spumante. Drink the sparkling versions at the end of or after a meal, to give it a festive finish. The still sweet wine is incredibly good in combination with creamy cheeses like gorgonzola dolce and mascarpone + gorgonzola (e.g. Gormas). Drinking temperature: sparkling 6–8 °C (43–46 °F), still wines 8–10 °C (46–50 °F).

LAMBRUSCO REGGIANO DOC

This wine is made from the following grapes: lambrusco salamino, lambrusco montericco, lambrusco marani, lambrusco maestri and ancelotta (maximum 15%). The wine is pink to ruby red and has a fine, persistent foam. The bouquet is fruity, reminiscent of plants and full of character. The flavor is dry or sweet, fresh and fairly light. The Italians serve this wine, dry or sweet, with hearty pasta dishes or casseroles and even with roast pork. Far more surprising and even exciting are combinations with cheese (not too old). Lambrusco is at its best young. Drinking temperature: here too the Italians drink this wine quite warm - about 15 °C (59 °F). Personally I find it more enjoyable at 13–14 °C (55–57 °F).

BIANCO DI SCANDIANO DOC

Within the wine-growing region of Lambrusco Reggiano, around the little village of the same name, is the white wine enclave of Scandiano. This white, slightly bubbly to sparkling wine is made from … Sauvignon! Very surprising wine, very aromatic, fresh and full. Comes in dry (secco), medium dry (semi-secco) and sweet (amabile) versions. Drink the secco as an aperitif or with cold dishes of fish, for example. The semi-secco goes wonderfully with fish in creamy sauces or white meat in fruity sauces. Finally, the amabile is better served with fruit desserts. Drinking temperature: (semi-) secco 9–10 °C (48–50 °F), amabile 6–8 °C (43–46 °F).

LAMBRUSCO MODENESI DOC

This region around Modena actually makes three different DOC wines.

Lambrusco Salamino di Santa Croce, made from lambrusco salamino (90% minimum) and the other lambruscos in the northern zone above Modena. The wine is a beautiful ruby red and has a magnificent, lively effervessence. Bouquet and flavor are very characteristic and particularly pleasant. Both the dry and the sweet versions are very fresh and harmonious. Drink the dry (secco/asciutto) Lambrusco with casseroles and the sweet (amabile) at the end of or after a meal. Both wines taste surprisingly good with chunks of pungent parmigiano reggiano! Drinking

![Lambrusco di Sorbara (VCR)]

Lambrusco di Sorbara (VCR)

temperature: dry 12–14 °C (54–57 °F), sweet 10–12 °C (50–54 °F).

Lambrusco di Sorbara is probably the most familiar, but not necessarily always the best! Some of these wines have more in common with old-fashioned fizzy lemonade than true Lambrusco. The better wines are made from lambrusco di sorbara (60%) and lambrusco salamino (40%). They are ruby red and have a lively effervessence. The bouquet is very pleasant and – only with genuine ones – is reminiscent of wild violets. The flavor can be dry or sweet, but is always fresh and full. Try this Lambrusco di Sorbara with pork dishes or with roast/fried meat. A very successful combination worth trying is with crumbly cheese, such as parmigiano

reggiano and gran padano. Drinking temperature: according to the Italians 14–16 °C (57–61 °F), in my opinion 12–14 °C (54–57 °F), particularly the sweet ones.

Lambrusco Grasparossa di Castelvetro comes from south and east of Modena. The wine is made from lambrusco grasparossa (85%) and other supplementary lambrusco varieties. The color is ruby red with glints of purple, the foam fine and passionate. The bouquet is very aromatic and the flavor dry to sweet, always fresh and full. Drink the dry version with pasta dishes, braised or boiled meat and fried white meat. It is better to drink the sweet version at the end of or after a meal. Drinking temperature: dry 14–16 °C (57–61 °F), sweet 10–12 °C (50–54 °F).

MONTUNI DEL RENO DOC

This white wine is produced northeast of Bologna and owes its name to the dominant grape used, the montuni (minimum 85%).

It is straw-colored with a soft, pleasant, characteristic bouquet and a fresh, full flavor, whether dry or sweet. Both the dry and the sweet version can be served with almost anything, except perhaps red meat and game. Drinking temperature: 10–12 °C (50–54 °F).

COLLI BOLOGNESI DOC

The ordinary bianco (albana + trebbiano romagnola) is a good accompaniment to variety meats and white meat, but never really has the power to excite. Drinking temperature: 8–10 °C (46–50 °F).

The Sauvignon, on the other hand, is an excellent aperitif, fresh, dry, slightly aromatic and full of flavor. It also goes very well with fish and all kinds of starters. Drinking temperature: 8–10 °C (46–50 °F).

The very successful Pinot Bianco is delicate and sophisticated, fresh, warm and harmonious. Great accompaniment to light pasta dishes with soft cheese, fish, shellfish or young cheeses. Drinking temperature: 10–12 °C (50–54 °F).

The Chardonnay is very acceptable, but not all that convincing. The fine, fruity flavor of a young Chardonnay is shown to its best advantage with white meat and fish. Drinking temperature: 10–12 °C (50–54 °F).

The Riesling Italico is far more exciting than the Chardonnay, with a much finer bouquet and a fresher, fuller and warmer flavor. Eminently suitable as a smart aperitif, but also as an accompaniment to raw ham, egg

Colli Bolognesi Pignoletto

dishes and fish. Drinking temperature: 8–10 °C (46–50 °F).

The Pignoletto, made from the grape of the same name, is a very unusual wine. It is a light--colored wine with the occasional hint of green, a very characteristic fine, delicate bouquet and a har-monious, fresh, warm flavor, whether dry or sweet. The wine comes in a still or a slightly sparkling version. Drink the dry Pignoletto as an aperitif, the still dry one with starters, fish and white meat and the sweeter one with young cheese or fruit pastries. Drink-ing temperature: sweet 6–8 °C (43–46 °F), still and sparkling dry 9–11 °C (48–52 °F).

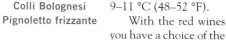

**Colli Bolognesi
Pignoletto frizzante**

With the red wines you have a choice of the light Merlot (dry, sappy and harmonious), the full, sturdy Barbera and the Cabernet Sauvignon. The Merlot goes very well with casseroles of beef or small game, red meat with forest mushrooms and roast game. The Barbera is just right with meats with character, such as furred game, lamb, goat, duck, venison or wild boar. The Cabernet Sauvignon prefers oven-roasted pork, veal or beef. There are also some very high quality riservas made from Barbera and Cabernet Sauvignon. Drinking temperature: Merlot, young Barbera and Cabernet Sauvignon 14–16 °C (57–61 °F), riservas 16–17 °C (61–63 °F).

**Colli Bolognesi
Merlot**

BOSCO ELICEO DOC

This wine-growing area is on the Adriatic coast, above the city of Ravenna. Two white wines and two reds are produced here.

The ordinary bianco is made from Trebbiano Romagnolo (minimum 70%) and sauvignon or malvasia bianca di candia. This straw-colored wine has a light, soft bouquet and a pleasant, smooth flavor. The wine is dry or slightly sweet, still or slightly sparkling. It is definitely not a wine you can keep for long. This great thirst-quencher can accompany light starters, fish or white meat. Drinking temperature: 8–10 °C (46–50 °F).

The Sauvignon (minimum 85%) is supplemented with trebbiano romagnolo. The wine is quite modest in bouquet and flavor, warm, velvety smooth and harmonious. Comes in dry or slightly sweet. Excellent as an aperitif and with fish and white meat. Try *fritto*

misto of fish, a traditional dish of bite-sized deep-fried chunks of fish and vegetables. Drinking temperature: 8–10 °C (46–50 °F).

Merlot produces an acceptable wine here with a typical plant undertones. The wine is dry, sappy, harmonious and fresh and is great with the various local meat dishes, and also with small game. Drinking temperature: 14–16 °C (57–61 °F).

Fortana produces quite strong wines, of the same name, which are also quite high in tannin, but sappy and fresh. Definitely a wine for drinking young, preferably – as the local inhabitants do – with substantial grilled fish with a piquant sauce. It also goes very well with fatter types of meat, such as roast pork, or pasta dishes with Bolognese sauce. Try *spiedini alla Petroniana*, skewers of pork, mortadella and cheese, coated in breadcrumbs and grilled. Drinking tem-perature: 10–12 °C (50–54 °F).

VINI DI ROMAGNA DOC

Another generic designation of origin that produces several very unusual wines. The area is situated in the extreme south of Emilia-Romagna and extends from just below Bologna via Forli to the famous beach resort of Rimini.

ALBANA DI ROMAGNA SPUMANTE

Good quality sparkling version of the DOCG Albana di Romagna. This spumante bears only a DOC desig-nation, though.

TREBBIANO DI ROMAGNA DOC

The dominant grape in this wine, trebbiano, is pro-duced in the neighborhood of Bologna, Ravenna and Forli. The wine is straw-colored, varying in intensi-ty, the bouquet fresh and pleasant and the flavor dry and harmonious. There are still, bubbly and spark-ling versions. Serve these delicious, but not par-ticularly exciting, wines with light starters, fish or white meat. Drinking temperature: 8–10 °C (46–50 °F).

PAGADEBIT DI ROMAGNA DOC

Now this is an exciting wine! It is made from bombino bianco (minimum 85%), harvested in the neighborhood of Forli and Ravenna. The color is an unremarkable straw-color. The bou-quet on the other hand is very characteristic and reminiscent of may blossom: soft, subtle, and very seductive. The wine can be dry or slightly sweet. In both cases it tastes very well balanced because of the wonderful acids. The flavor is sophisticated and particularly pleasant, with a distinct plant undertone. There is also a frizzante version. Serve the dry Pargadebit with fish, crustaceans or shellfish, boiled ham and white meat. The slightly sweet wine tastes

**Sangiovese di
Romagna**

wonderful with lobster or crab, hot or in salads. Drinking temperature: slightly sweet 6–8 °C (43–46 °F), dry 8–10 °C (46–50 °F).

SANGIOVESE DI ROMAGNA DOC

This red wine made from the Sangiovese grape is produced in the neighborhood of Forli, Bologna and Ravenna. The color is ruby red with glints of purple and the bouquet is very subtle and reminiscent of forest violets. The taste is quite dry and well balanced, with a typical slight bitterness in the aftertaste. Drink this wine within four years of harvesting. There is also a superiore (minimum 12% alcohol) and a riserva (minimum two years extra maturing). Serve this wine by preference with grilled lamb or roast pork. Also delicious with pasta dishes with Bolognese sauce or other meat sauces. Drinking temperature: 14–16 °C (57–61 °F), 16–17 °C (61–63 °F) for the riserva.

CAGNINA DI ROMAGNA DOC

Another exciting red wine made from Refosco, here called Terrrano. This wine is made around Forli and Ravenna. The color is purplish red, the bouquet intense and characteristic and the flavor full, sweet and acidy and velvety smooth, sometimes with a considerable amount of tannins. Drink this wine after meals, with rich pastries. Try *castagne arrosti*, a handful of hot, fresh-roasted chestnuts with a glass of Cagnina di Romagna – a little rustic, but excellent all the same. Drinking temperature: 6–8 °C (43–46 °F).

Tuscany produces outstanding red wines

TUSCANY

Glorious Tuscany has excellent wines and a fantastic cuisine. Tuscany's cuisine is totally different from that of Emilia-Romagna, where they are particularly generous with all the good things produced by the land. In Tuscan gastronomy quality is more important than quantity. Tuscan olive oil, for example, is world-famous, but the local beef and poultry are also of high quality. Because there is so much good quality meat available it is not surprising that Tuscany mainly produces red wines that are excellent with succulent beef and poultry.

TUSCAN WINE-GROWING

The Tuscan vineyards are widely spread out over the countryside, from above Pisa to Florence, from Siena to Montalcino and Montepulciano, from below Livorno to the border with Lazio and Umbria and finally on the island of Elba. Apart from the famous wines (Chianti, Brunello and Vino Nobile) there are countless less familiar wines to discover. Particularly now that the prices of some of the top wines from Tuscany have hit the roof, it is worth looking in the still reasonably unknown areas. The wines below are listed from north to south, first the DOCG wines, then the DOC.

CARMIGNANO DOCG

This wine was once one of the top Chianti wines. After years of lobbying and, above all, of making outstanding wines, the inhabitants of the little town of Carmignano first succeeded in having their precious offspring accepted into the DOC family (1975) and then ultimately into the elite corps of the DOCG (1990). The charm of this famous wine is perhaps in the combination of noble French grapes (both cabernets) and distinctive Italian grapes. Carmignano is made from sangiovese (45–70%), canaiolo nero (10–20%), cabernet franc and cabernet sauvignon (both in total 6–15%). As with Chianti, minimal addition of white grapes is allowed: trebbiano toscano, canaiolo bianco and malvasia (maximum 10%). The fairly low yield – by Italian standards – is also important to the quality of this wine. Its color is ruby red, very intense and clear. As it ages it develops nuances of pomegranate red. The bouquet is superb, intense, subtle (forest violets) and seductive. The equally intense flavor is full, rounded, smooth and very elegant. The ordinary Carmignano (annata) must be at least two years old, the riserva a minimum of three. The alcohol percentage must be a minimum of 12.5%. Carmignano ages very well. Owing to its finesse this wine calls for something a bit special: succulent roast beef, wild boar or medallions of red deer, etc. Keep a glass for a chunk of hearty, mellow cheese, such as pecorino Toscano. Try *filetto di manzo alla griglia*, grilled tournedos of beef with herb butter. Drinking temperature: annata 14–16 °C (57–61 °F), riserva 16–17 °C (61–63 °F).

CHIANTI DOCG

This is probably Italy's best-known wine and worldwide one of the most valued. Chianti and Tuscany have been indissolubly linked for centuries. In ancient times countless poets sang the praises of the red wines from the Tuscan hills. In the Middle Ages Chianti had another resurgence, but its great success is mainly due to Baron Bettino Ricasoli, who radically modernized the vinification method at the beginning of the nineteenth century. Since then things have steadily improved for Chianti. Time and again the wine-growers try to translate the legacy of previous generations of wine-growers into wines from this time. The Tuscan wine-houses have not stood still in their attempts to advance and make increasingly better wines. This also had repercussions on legislation. The Chianti area used to be quite large and the variations in quality were enormous. This led to a huge identity crisis. Deceptive dealers wanted to cash in on the success of Chianti and brought some very mediocre and thin wines on to the market. This forced legislators into drastic measures. Chianti has now become a DOCG (since 1996), but not every 'old' Chianti qualifies. All wines have to prove themselves first. Only the better wines are allowed to bear the designation DOCG; the others are only allowed to put the words Colli dell'Etruria Centrale DOC on the label. Chianti DOCG comes exclusively from the following seven zones: the central zone (where the classico wines are made) and the six hills ('colli') surrounding it: Arezzo, Florence, Pisa, Siena, Montalbano and Rufina. There is also a separate zone in the neighborhood of Empoli, but this does not have its name on the label, by contrast with the seven previously mentioned zones. The wines from the heart of the area, as well as the extra addition of 'classico', also have a symbol on the neck of the bottle, the famous black rooster (*gallo nero*). These wines may only be made and harvested on the soil of the following districts: Greve in Chianti, Radda in Chianti, Gaiole in Chianti, Castellina in Chianti and parts of Barberino

Outstanding wines from Tuscany

Val d'Elsa, Castelnuovo Berardenga, Poggibonsi, San Casciano Val di Pesa and Tavarnelle Val di Pesa.

The basic material for this famous wine is sangiovese (75–90%), supplemented with canaiolo (5–10%) and the white trebbiano toscano and malvasia (5–10%). For the classico a maximum of 5% white grapes may be added. White grapes are used to soften the sangiovese, which is sometimes particularly high in tannin, to some extent. The color of a good Chianti is ruby red, very intense and clear. After a few years maturing it inclines more towards pomegranate red. The bouquet is very pleasant, full and delicate. Connoisseurs can also discern here, especially in the classico, a subtle nuance of wild violets. Other characteristics include cherries, blackberries, red fruit, pepper, herbs, licorice and vanilla. The flavor is certainly dry, fresh and sappy, often rather rich in tannins in the initial years. After a few years maturing the flavor becomes much smoother, fuller and more rounded. Chianti wines can be very varied, depending on where they come from and how they are made. The light-footed, cheerful and unconstrained Chiantis are best drunk quickly. The more traditional Chiantis are slightly fuller and deserve to rest for a while. The wonderful riservas are already at least three years old when they come on to

From the Ricasoli range

Chianti Colli Senesi

Chianti classico

the market and can still go on developing for a long time.

Drink a modern young Chianti throughout the meal, without any fuss, at around 14 °C (57 °F). The traditional Chianti wines like roast white meat, pasta dishes, chicken or other poultry (preferably grilled) and tasty, not over-pungent, cheeses; the riservas like grilled or fried red meat, game or pungent cheeses (pecorino Toscano). Try *pollo alla Toscana*, chicken with cep or *pollastralla con prugne*, chicken with prunes. Drinking temperature: 16–17 °C (61–63 °F).

VERNACCIA DI SAN GIMIGNANO DOCG

Wonderful wines have been made in Tuscany for centuries from the grapes of the same name. Since being granted DOCG recognition the makers of this Vernaccia have not stood still. They are constantly working on improvements in quality, not just in the vineyards, but also in the wine-making equipment. San Gimignano is just outside the Chianti classico region. The color of the young wine is quite light and inclines towards gold as it ages. The bouquet is penetrating, elegant, fresh and subtle. The flavor is sufficiently dry, fresh, well-balanced and particularly charming.

Vernaccia di San Gimignano

A slight hint of bitterness is discernible in the aftertaste. There is also a riserva, which has had to mature for at least one extra year. Particularly good as a smart aperitif, but also with all kinds of starters, white meat, fish, shellfish and even fresh, creamy cheeses. Drinking temperature: 10–12 °C (50–54 °F).

VINO NOBILE DI MONTEPULCIANO DOCG

This wine-growing region is southwest of Siena, around the village of Montepulciano, at a height of 820–1,970 ft. The soil of Montepulciano consists principally of layers of sediment. This 'noble' wine from Montepulciano, as the Italians call it, has a long and abundant history. In the seventeenth century it was even called the king of Tuscan wines. However, this designation of origin threatened to fade into the background to some extent when the more popular Chianti wines experienced such a breakthrough. It has only been during the past few decades that every effort has been made to restore the Vino Nobile. A great deal of time and money has been put into new vineyards and equipment, with the result that this DOCG (1980) is now counted among the greatest in Italy. The base for these sublime red wines is sangiovese (here called prugnolo, 60–80%) and canaiolo nero (10–20%). Black or even white grapes can be added to these two grape varieties. The amount of white grapes (including trebbiano) may never exceed 10%, though. The strength of the Vino Nobile is not just in the choice of grapes and the soil, but also in the, by Italian standards, low yield. A Vino Nobile is usually a pretty pomegranate red, with varying degrees of intensity, with occasional glints of orange as it ages. The bouquet is intense, sublime and subtle: whole bunches of forest violets, rather than bowls full of red fruit. The flavor is full and round and sometimes quite rich in tannins when it is young. These are never light wines, with a minimum of 12.5% alcohol (usually far more).

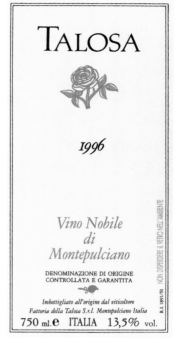

Vino Nobile di Montepulciano

Vino Nobile di Montepulciano riserva

This fantastic classic red wine calls for your best culinary skills. It is ideal in combination with red meat or roast game, grilled game birds or the more mature, pungent cheeses, such as the local pecorino Toscano. In some books it is recommended to open the bottle a few hours beforehand. However, the surface that comes into contact with oxygen in this way is so tiny that there is absolutely no point. It is better to decant the wine into a wide carafe (port carafe or the famous 'duck carafe') no more than half an hour to an hour beforehand. The wine will really be able to breathe in one of these and develop all its aromas. Try *arista*, a wonderful oven roast of pork loin with rosemary and garlic. Drinking temperature: young (preferably not!) 15–16 °C (59–61 °F), aged 16–18 °C (61–64 °F).

BRUNELLO DI MONTALCINO DOCG

Brunello di Montalcino

Probably the best DOCG wine in Italy. The village of Montalcino is south-west of Montepulciano. The soil here consists principally of layers of sediment. It was not until the second half of the nineteenth century that a few fanatical and very competent local wine-growers succeeded in creating a wine that was not only of superb quality, but also aged well. This was preceded by long years of experimenting with various Sangiovese clones. Since then the fame of this Brunello has never diminished – on the contrary. Brunello was the first to be granted the official DOCG recognition in 1980. The soul of Brunello is of course Sangiovese Grosso, which is intentionally pruned low here to keep the yield down. A Brunello may not be sold before its fifth year and a riserva not before its sixth year. All this guarantees impeccable quality. The wine is a beautiful ruby red color, very intense and clear, which inclines towards pomegranate red as it ages. The bouquet is very intense and aromatic and reminiscent of ripe red fruit, with a hint of herbs and wood (vanilla). The riservas also sometimes smell of burnt cocoa or coffee and of licorice. The flavor is full, strong, smooth and warm (minimum 12.5% alcohol, but 13.5% in most wines). The ordinary Brunello is somewhat fruitier and the riserva more herby. Drink an ordinary Brunello with roast or fried red meat and with pungent cheeses. Keep the riserva for the best possible joint of red meat or game. This wine will also feel flattered by pungent, mature cheeses. It is advisable to decant the wine into a wide carafe some time before (at least an hour). Drinking temperature: 17–18 °C (63–64 °F).

COLLINE LUCCHESI DOC

The vineyards in this region are situated on the hills between Lucca and Montecarlo. The area around Lucca is famous for its wonderful olive oil and superb white and red wines. If you take the trouble to discover this area, you will be surprised at the many lovely wines

Colline Lucchesi blanco

made there. Unfortunately, availability of these wines is limited and demand is very high.

The Bianco delle Colline Lucchesi (also called Colline Lucchesi Bianco) is obtained from trebbiano toscano (50–70%), greco or grechetto (5–15%), vermentino bianco (5–15%) and malvasia (maximum 5%). This bianco is light straw-colored, smells smooth and elegant and tastes quite dry, full, elegant and

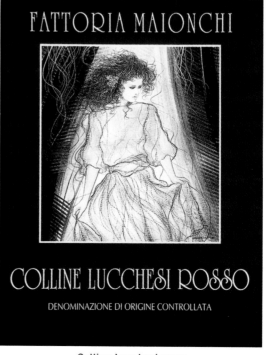

Colline Lucchesi rosso

harmonious. The better wine-houses also produce a few crus under the domain names. These top wines are very rare and of unprecedented quality. Serve the ordinary bianco as an aperitif, with crêpes (bocconcini) or with fresh pasta cushions (tortellini, tortelloni, capelleti or fagotini) filled with ricotta and spinach (*alla Fiorentina*). Keep the better crus for a good fish dish. Try *bronzino al vino bianco*, sea bass poached in white wine.

There are also some very typical wines made from vermentino: not with a DOC label, but with IGT (controlled designation of origin). However they are by no means of lesser quality. Drinking temperature: 10–12 °C (50–54 °F).

The Colline Lucchesi rosso is a full-bodied wine, ruby red to pomegranate red in color. The bouquet is quite soft, but very pleasant. The flavor is delicate, full, well balanced and rounded. Most of the wines contain 12.5–13% alcohol. The red wine goes well with casseroles of white or red meat, oven roasts or substantial pasta dishes. Try *fegato di vitello alla paesana*, calves' liver with bacon and fresh Italian herbs, among other things.

The better wines are produced in small quantities. Among things that distinguish them are the fantastic aromas (such as irises) and the fuller flavor. These top wines feel most at home with substantial dishes like roast or fried red meat or small game. Try *papardelle alla lepre*, wide ribbon pasta with jugged hare, a specialty from Lucca. Drinking temperature: 16–17 °C (61–63 °F) for the best wines.

Needless to say a few 'Super Tuscans' are also made here. These are wines that stand out due to their fantastic quality, but which – because they do not conform to the legal grape percentages – have been downgraded to IGT. For a long time these wines were only allowed to bear the rather unflattering designation of 'vino da tavolo'. Since 1992 they have been allowed to use the new IGT classification. A typical example of these Super Tuscans from Lucca is I Pampini from Fattoria Fubbiano. The same wine-house also produces an extremely rare white Super Tuscan, the Del Boschetto bianco. It hardly needs to be said that the price of these sublime wines is on the high side.

BARCO REALE, ROSATO E VINSANTO DI CARMIGNANO DOC

This is also one of the most recent DOCs (1994). The vineyards lie between the small towns of Carmignano (well known for its DOCG) and Poggio and Caiano at a maximum height of 1,300 ft. The soil here consists of crumbled lime, marble, stone chips and sandstone.

Barco Reale is made from sangiovese (45–70%), canaiolo nero (10–20%), cabernet franc and cabernet sauvignon (6–15%). The color is ruby red and very clear, the bouquet very aromatic and sophisticated and the flavor is full, round, fresh, well-balanced and sufficiently dry. Drink this wine with pasta dishes with meat sauces, poultry or fried white meat. Drinking temperature: 14–16 °C (57–61 °F).

Rosato di Carmignano is made from the same grapes as Barco Reale, possibly supplemented to a maximum of 10% with the white grapes trebbiano toscano, canaiolo bianco or malvasia. The wine is slightly lighter in color, pink with occasional glints of ruby red. The bouquet is pleasant rather than exciting, but the flavor is fresh, full, dry and a little reminiscent of English sweets (pear drops). Drink this cheerful rosé as a winter aperitif or, for example, with the various *fritto misto* of vegetables. Also good with variety meats and white meat. Drinking temperature: 10–12 °C (50–54 °F).

The Vinsanto di Carmignano is obtained from trebbiano toscano and malvasia. The color of this wine varies from straw colored to gold or even amber as it ages. The bouquet is particularly aromatic, fruity, sultry and very characteristic of a vinsanto. The flavor is full, round, velvety smooth, varying in sweetness depending on the type, year and maker. Drink this vinsanto with pastries or fruit desserts. Drinking temperature: dry 10–12 °C (50–54 °F), sweet 6–8 °C (43–46 °F).

Finally there is also the very unusual Vinsanto di Carmignano Occhio di Pernice. This wine is made from sangiovese (50–70%) and malvasia nera. It is a rosé vinsanto (unique!) with a beautiful pink color of varying intensity (the name Occhio di Pernice means partridge's eye and aptly reflects the subtle color of this wine). The bouquet is stunning, warm and sensual, the flavor full, warm (16% alcohol minimum), round, sweet, smooth and sophisticated. This wine certainly does not belong at the table: drink it with your best friend or your partner when you really have something to celebrate, but want to keep things intimate. Simply enjoy it in secret. Drinking temperature: 10–16 °C (50–61 °F), depending on the season and your preference.

BIANCO PISANO DI SAN TORPÈ DOC

This wine-growing region (DOC since 1980) is southeast of the city of Pisa. Outstanding white wines have been made here for centuries from trebbiano (75–100%). The local vinsanto has also enjoyed great renown in Italy.

The fresh Bianco Pisano is quite subtle in flavor and calls for subtle foods, such as braised fish or eel and light starters. Drinking temperature: 8–10 °C (46–50 °F).

The vinsanto is amber-colored, aromatic, full, smooth and sweet. Enjoy it with pastries or fruit desserts. Drinking temperature: 6–8 °C (43–46 °F).

POMINO DOC

Tiny region to the northeast of Tuscany between the villages of Rufina and Pomino. Excellent wines: white, red and white and red vinsanto. The vineyards are situated on high hills, which is beneficial for the concentration of extract and aromatic and flavoring substances.

Pomino bianco is obtained from pinot bianco and chardonnay (60–80%), supplemented with trebbiano toscano. So not an 'original' wine, but certainly very well-made. The color is light yellow with a hint of green, the bouquet fine and pleasant and the flavor fresh, dry and slightly bitter. Without being particularly convincing, this wine can accompany any light starter, fish or white meat. Drinking temperature: 8–10 °C (46–50 °F).

Pomino rosso is made from sangiovese (60–75%), canaiolo, cabernet sauvignon, cabernet franc and merlot. This wine combines the subtlety of a French wine with the passion of an Italian. This substantial wine is full, rounded, sufficiently dry and very well-balanced. The young wines often have a bit of a problem with awkward tannins, but that disappears after a few years maturing. Ideal wines with roast meat or oven dishes and also with poultry on the spit. Also really good with pecorino Toscano. Drinking temperature: young 12–14 °C (54–57 °F), older wines 14–17 °C (57–63 °F).

The Pomino vinsanto white and red (extremely rare) are made from the same grapes as the bianco and rosso. Both come in a dry and a sweet version and they go best with biscuits, petits-fours, pastries or dried fruits. Drinking temperature: 6–8 °C (43–46 °F) to 10–12 °C (50–54 °F), the sweeter, the colder.

Most of the vinsanto is sold as vino da tavola

VINSANTO DEL CHIANTI CLASSICO DOC

A rarity in Italy, a designation of origin for just one sweet wine. This vinsanto, like its companions, has a long and exciting history. Vinsanto is synonymous with friendship and hospitality, with respect for tradition and pure enjoyment. The very best grapes are selected for vinsanto and laid out to dry for a year on straw mats or in small crates, in the open air or in well-ventilated attics. Then they are pressed and the young wines mature patiently in small casks (caratelli). Trebbiano toscano and malvasia are used as the base for the white vinsanto. Sangiovese is primarily used for the rosato, the Vinsanto del Chianti Classico Occhio di Pernice (partridge's eye). Both wines can be dry in varying degrees or else sweet. They are superb wines, smooth, full, aromatic and very distinctive, which are good at the end of a meal with biscuits, almond pastries, fruit gâteaux etc. You can serve the dry vinsanto as an aperitif or on its own with a good book or a stimulating discussion. Drinking temperature: dry 10–12 °C (50–54 °F), sweet 6–8 °C (43–46 °F).

COLLI DELL'ETRURIA CENTRALE DOC

Many wines that do not achieve the required standard for DOCG Chianti can be downgraded to Colli dell'Etruria Centrale DOC. Yet this recent designation of origin is more than a kind of safety net for bad Chianti. Some very great wines are made here, even though they differ as regards grape percentage. As in Colli Lucchesi, some wine-growers refuse to choose from the obligatory four varieties of grape. They believe that the combination of sangiovese and cabernet sauvignon/franc brings far better results. Until recently this was not allowed and so these wines, the Super Tuscans, had to be downgraded to vino da tavola. And that is embarrassing for a wine that is way above average in quality. Now wine-growers who choose this path may use the designation of origin Colli dell'Etruria Centrale

Only wines made within the Chianti district may call themselves DOC

DOC, which makes a higher price easier to accept. Not all the wines of this designation of origin are Super Tuscans, though, and that is no bad thing.

The bianco Colli dell'Etruria Centrale is obtained from trebbiano toscano (minimum 50%), supplemented with chardonnay, pinot bianco, pinot grigio, vernaccia di san gimignano, malvasia or sauvignon (maximum in total 50%). So many flavors, so many wines. In general these white wines are fresh, fruity, sappy and quite light. Great as aperitifs or with light starters. Drinking temperature: 8–10 °C (46–50 °F).

Montescudaio bianco

The rosato and rosso can consist of sangiovese (minimum 50%), cabernet sauvignon, cabernet franc, merlot, pinot nero, ciliegiolo and canaiolo (in total maximum 50%). Here too wine-makers produce everything from light wines to musclemen. All the wines have plenty of fruit and freshness. The red go excellently with grilled or roast beef, the rosé with variety meats (Tuscan sausages!). Drinking temperature: rosato 10–12 °C (50–54 °F), rosso 12–14 °C (54–57 °F), for the Super Tuscans 16–17 °C (61–63 °F).

In the same area very aromatic, fantastic vinsanto is made that is equally as good as its companions with pastries and petits-fours. Drinking temperature: according to taste 6–12 °C (43–54 °F).

MONTESCUDAIO DOC

Great white and red wines from the area around the village of Montescudaio, below Livorno. The white wines in particular benefit from the calcareous soil of tufa. They are made from trebbiano toscano, malvasia bianco, vermentino and chardonnay, the red wines from sangiovese, trebbiano toscano and malvasia. There is also a vinsanto, made from the same grapes as for the bianco.

Drink the fresh, dry and elegant bianco with starters, pasta with cheese, escargots, eel or fish. Drinking temperature: 8–10 °C (46–50 °F).

The red wine is slightly fruity, dry and reasonably high in tannin. It is great with red meat and small game, especially after a few years maturing. Drinking temperature: 14–16 °C (57–61 °F).

Drink the vinsanto, like its siblings from Tuscany, with petits-fours, pastries or fruit gâteaux. Drinking temperature: depending on your preference and the season 6–12 °C (43–54 °F).

ROSSO DI MONTEPULCIANO DOC

The Rosso di Montepulciano comes from the same vineyard acreage as the Vino Nobile. The grape varieties used are also the same: sangiovese (prugnolo, 60–80%) and other black and white grapes. The difference is often in the age of the vines and the yield per hectare: younger and/or very productive vines are responsible for the Rosso di Montepulciano, while the older and/or less productive vines are reserved for the Vino Nobile. The Rosso di Montepulciano therefore does not have the same concentration and strength as its big brother. You can see this already in the varying intensity of the ruby red color. The bouquet is almost as seductive as that of Vino Nobile; here too you can smell the subtle scent of woodland violets. The flavor is dry, well-balanced and often slightly rich in tannins. Because these wines are less concentrated they will often contain less alcohol. This makes them suitable for

Montescudaio rosso

Rosso di Montalcino

many dishes, especially for pasta with meat sauces and cheese, as well as for roast white or red meat. Drinking temperature: 16–17 °C (61–63 °F).

ROSSO DI MONTALCINO DOC

This young sibling of Brunello obtained its DOC recognition in 1983. Since then this rosso has continued to climb. The wines come from the same vineyards as Brunello and here too 100% Sangiovese is used. The yield per hectare is, however, a little higher with this wine and there is no question of four or five years' obligatory maturing. So you will come across young wines already on the market. The best wines (those from the famous house of Banfi, for example) do, though, undergo cask-maturing for at least one year in French oak casks.

Rosso di Montalcino is certainly not a light wine. This ruby red wine with a subtle bouquet of red fruits (and vanilla in the better ones) tastes strong, full, rounded and warm (often more than 13% alcohol). The better wines also often have an undertone of herbs and spices and are very rich in tannins in their youth. Where Brunello calls for your best table manners, this wine conjures up festive, above all friendly, country scenes: dried sausages from Siena, chicken and other poultry, pasta with meat sauces (the famous *pinci* from Siena), roast pork or beef, casseroles, jugged hare, game birds and well matured sheep's cheese (pecorino Toscano). Drinking temperature: 16–17 °C (61–63 °F).

MOSCADELLO DI MONTALCINO

Another scion from the famous Montalcino family. This is a sweet wine made from moscato bianco. This designation of origin has been part of the great DOC family since 1984. As so often in Italy, there are various types of this wine:
- drink the fresh, still, sweet Moscadello at 6–10 °C (43–50 °F) at the end of a meal with your favorite fruit pastry or fruit salad;
- drink the fresh, sparkling, sweet Moscadello with its fine, passionate foam at 6–8 °C (43–46 °F), preferably on a terrace in summer after sundown.
- the full, gold-colored *vendemmia tardiva* (late vintage), which smells of flowers and muscat grapes, is incredibly intense in flavor: sun, honey, a mouthful of muscat grapes, exotic fruits – a veritable work of art! One of the loveliest Muscat wines in the world. You can of course serve it at the end of a meal with a really super cake or dessert or simply with carefully selected, fresh, ripe fruit. The best way to enjoy this wine, however, is towards midnight, with the one you love, on a warm summer evening under the full moon. Drinking temperature: 6–8 °C (43–46 °F).

SANT'ANTIMO DOC

Less familiar designation of origin south-west of the village of Montalcino. Countless different wines are made here.

For a bianco they are allowed to blend several grapes together or use one dominant grape variety, such as pinot grigio, sauvignon or chardonnay. Trebbiano toscano and malvasia are also permitted. Most of the wines are of very acceptable quality and can easily be used as aperitifs or to accompany fish, white meat and poultry. Drinking temperature: 8–10 °C (46–50 °F) (Chardonnay and Pinot Grigio 10–12 °C (50–54 °F).

As well as the ordinary rosso, they make Cabernet Sauvignon, Merlot and Pinot Nero. No great surprises, although some of the large houses (Banfi, for example) make particularly delicious wines from a cuvée of Sangiovese (60%), Cabernet sauvignon and merlot (20% each). Drink these wines with oven-cooked pasta dishes or fried or grilled meat. Drinking temperature: 14–16 °C (57–61 °F).

BOLGHERI DOC

This region is situated on the Mediterranean coast in western Tuscany, between Montescudaio and Massa Marittima. This area was for a long time principally renowned for its sublime rosato. But now another wine has completely outstripped this rosato. This is the Super Tuscan Sassicaia, one of the best and most expensive wines in Italy. At one time this wine was downgraded to 'vino da tavola' due to the suffocating Italian laws on wine-growing. It may now be sold as Bolgheri Sassicaio DOC, because Sassicaio has been adopted as a sub-zone of Bolgheri in the law on designations of origin.

Trebbiano toscano (10–70%), vermentino (10–70%) or sauvignon are used for Bolgheri bianco. So here too countless different variations are possible. Wines containing more than 85% of one of these three grape varieties are allowed to state the name of the grape variety concerned on the label as well as that of Bolgheri. All these wines are fresh and dry, sappy and elegant. They are ideal aperitifs, but they can also accompany all kinds of (sea) fish or vegetable dishes. The Sauvignon has a slight preference for fish dishes with slightly more complex sauces or, for example, skewers of the more substantial sea fish (sword fish, tuna) with lemon and tomato. Drinking temperature: 8–10 °C (46–50 °F).

The Bolgheri rosato is still one of the most delicious rosé wines in the whole Mediterranean region. Today it is made from cabernet sauvignon, merlot and sangiovese, allowing some very exciting cuvées. These dry, sappy, elegant wines call for some delicious grilled fish, *triglie* (red mullet) or scampi, for example. Drinking temperature: 10–12 °C (50–54 °F).

There is also a vinsanto Occhio di Pernice (partridge's eye rosé vinsanto), made from sangiovese and malvasia nera. It is very intense in flavor and quite aromatic. Drink this full, sensual wine with a special cake.

The Bolgheri rosso, like the rosato, is made from cabernet sauvignon (10–80%), merlot (maximum 70%) and sangiovese (maximum 70%). Here too this choice of grapes permits countless possibilities for cuvées, making them particularly exciting wines. Irrespective of the ratio, you can easily combine these dry, full wines with roast white or red meat. Drinking temperature: 16 °C (61 °F).

BOLGHERI SASSICAIA

This top wine must contain at least 80% cabernet sauvignon and may be supplemented with merlot and/or sangiovese. The yield per hectare is considerably lower for Sassicaia than for the ordinary Bolgheri rosso. This produces a powerful, full-bodied wine with a great deal of extract and maturing potential. Sassicaia is matured for two years in oak casks and must further mature for at least five years in the bottle before it can be drunk. Naturally enough, this wine – probably the best Italian red wine – comes with a stiff price ticket, but it is well worth the money. The wine combines the warm-blooded Italian temperament with the civilized elegance of a grand cru from the Médoc. The color is an intense ruby red, the bouquet very aromatic and a tiny bit herby and the flavor intense, full, rounded, velvety smooth, warm and enormously sensual. All lovers of wine ought to try this wine at least once in their lives. And as far as the price goes, by comparison it is much lower than a wine of comparable quality from California, not to mention the absurdly high prices of some grands crus from the Médoc.

Keep this superb wine for special occasions and serve it, for example, with a classic game dish or fillet of beef with truffles and softly fried cep. If you want to make it a little cheaper, but still want a pleasurable meal, try *filetti di agnello al formaggio*, a divine dish of fried lambs' fillet with oyster mushrooms and a sauce made of pecorino Toscano. Decant the wine well beforehand into a wide (duck) carafe. Drinking temperature: 18 °C (64 °F).

MORELLINO DI SCANSANO DOC

This region is below Grosseto and has its epicenter in the village of Scansano. Unfortunately this wine is not very well known outside Italy and yet in Italy it is one of the best known Tuscan wines. In the seventeenth century a few wine-growers introduced the famous Spanish grape variety alicante. Today this grape, together with sangiovese (here called morellino, minimum 85%), caniolo, ciliegiolo and malvasia nera (maximum 15%, including alicante) is responsible for the charm and originality of Morellino di Scansano. You will find various levels of quality in this region, from good to very good. The standard is often partly determined by the yield per hectare: the lower the yield, the better, but then again not too low, because that makes the wines far too heavy. The better Morellino are ruby to pomegranate red when they are older, full, warm, with slight tannins and very dry. The riserva wines must contain slightly more alcohol and have matured for at least two years in oak casks. Drink the young or lighter wines with simple pasta dishes with meat sauce and cheese, the older riserva with better red meat and game

dishes. Drinking temperature: 14–16 °C (57–61 °F), riserva 16–17 °C (61–63 °F).

PARRINA DOC

Tiny wine-growing region in the extreme south of Tuscany, not far from the coast. Local wine-growing goes back to the time of the Etruscans, but the Spanish laid the foundations for today's vineyards. The local wines are not of any particular quality, but because Parrina attracts a large number of tourists, the area enjoys reasonable renown as a wine-growing region. Obtaining DOC recognition encouraged many wine-growers to make more effort to improve quality.

Parrina bianco is made from trebbiano toscano (here called procanico, 30–50%), supplemented with Ansonica and/or Chardonnay. This produces fresh, elegant, smooth wines with a slight touch of bitterness, which are good with light starters, fish and vegetables. Drinking temperature: 8–10 °C (46–50 °F).

Parrina rosato is made on a base of sangiovese (70–100%). It is a light rosé, fresh and elegant, which goes well with variety meats, pasta or egg dishes and casseroles of white meat. Drinking temperature: 10–12 °C (50–54 °F).

Parrina rosso is also made from sangiovese (70–100%) and is somewhat fuller and darker than the rosato. Nevertheless it is a simple, elegant, smooth wine, rather than a muscleman. Ideal with red meat and also with the typical Tuscan dishes with white haricot beans in tomato sauce. Drinking temperature: 14 °C (57 °F).

Finally there is also the Parrina rosso riserva that has a lot more to offer than an ordinary rosso. The two years extra cask-maturing and often a year maturing in the bottle gives this wine more depth and strength. Serve this riserva with better red meat dishes, roast meat, small game or mature cheeses (pecorino Toscano). Drinking temperature: 16–17 °C (61–63 °F).

ANSONICA COSTA DELL'ARGENTARIO DOC

The region of this designation of origin is also in the extreme south of Tuscany. It extends from the border between Tuscany and Lazio to the coast, including the enclave of Parrina. The island Isola del Giglio also forms part of this region. There are good reasons why this is one of the most touristy areas in Italy: beautiful beaches, old villages, many Etruscan, Roman and medieval ruins, etc. The wines are also worth a diversion. The Costa dell'Argentario is the domain of a single grape, the ansonica bianca (at least 85%), which produces very original white wines that are light straw-colored with an occasional hint of green. The bouquet is soft and fruity and intriguing, the flavor dry, smooth and particularly pleasant. Drink this wine, which is full of *joie de vivre*, as an aperitif or with light fish dishes. Try *tagliatelle alle conchiglie*, wide ribbon pasta with a creamy fricassée of, among other things, scallops, peppers and white wine. Drinking temperature: 8–10 °C (46–50 °F).

ELBA DOC

Excellent white, red and rosé wines are made on Elba, the island off the Tuscan coast. Surprising here is the originality of some of the wines that are still made from old native grapes. The French introduced some of their vines to the island and so did the Tuscans. In all, this gives exciting variation to the types and flavors.

The fresh, light, elegant Elba bianco is made from trebbiano toscano (here called procanico, 80–100%). Great wine, as long as it is drunk young, for light starters, fish and seafood. Drinking temperature: 8–10 °C (46–50 °F).

Much nicer, more original, fuller and more intense is the white Ansonica (minimum 85% ansonica). This wine can be dry to slightly sweet. Serve the dry wine as an aperitif, with seafood or with baked or deep-fried fish. The less dry wines go extremely well with creamy pasta dishes and even with crustaceans. Try *calamari fritti con crema di pomodoro*, deep-fried squid fritters with a creamy tomato sauce. Drinking temperature: 10–12 °C (50–54 °F).

A wonderful passito is also made here from Ansonica, which goes extremely well with *tiramisu con cioccolata*, a divine variation on the famous dessert, in which the coffee is replaced by chocolate. Drinking temperature: 6–10 °C (43–50 °F).

They also make an excellent, full, rounded and velvety smooth vinsanto from trebbiano (procanico) and malvasia bianca, which goes with any sort of cake or pastry. Drinking temperature: 6–12 °C (43–54 °F) (the sweeter, the colder).

The fresh Elba rosato consists mainly of sangiovese (here called sangioveto). Drink this light, delicious but simple rosé with grilled fish or crustaceans. Try *triglie al carbone*, marinated red mullet from the grill or barbecue. Drinking temperature: 10–12 °C (50–54 °F).

An original and exciting vinsanto Occhio di Pernice is also produced from grapes including sangiovese (50–70%) and malvasia nera (10–50%). This rosé vinsanto is very warm, full-bodied, intense in flavor and velvety smooth. Drink this wine preferably after meals, during an informal tête-à-tête with a best friend or partner. Drinking temperature: 8–12 °C (46–54 °F) (the sweeter, the colder).

The Elba rosso also contains sangiovese (sangioveto, 75–100%) and is very fruity, full and rounded. Drink this dry red wine with red meat or roast pork or lamb, for example. Drinking temperature: 16 °C (61 °F).

The nicest red wines from Elba are without doubt the Aleatico made from the grape of the same name (100%). This old, native grape variety produces a superb wine, intensely ruby red in color, very aromatic and full of character. The flavor is strong, rounded, warm and slightly sweet. This wine ages very well. Because of its slightly sweet, but definitely not cloying, flavor and its high alcohol percentage (minimum 16%), it is difficult to find foods to go with it. Therefore drink it at the end of a meal, for example with gorgonzola piccante or chunks of mature pecorino Toscano. Drinking temperature: 16–18 °C (61–64 °F).

OTHER INTERESTING DOC WINES FROM TUSCANY
Bianco della Valdinievole, Bianco dell'Empolese, Bianco Vergine della Valdichiana, Bianco di Pitigliano, Colli di Luni, Candia dei Colli Apuani, Montecarlo, Val d'Arbia, Val di Cornia and Monteregio di Massa Marittima.

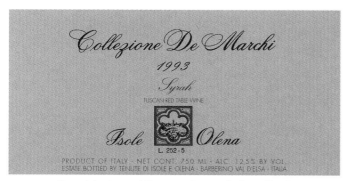

You will find very interesting table wines at any good tenuta

Surprisingly good Tuscan wine made from Syrah

UMBRIA

Umbria is bordered in the east by the Apennines and the Marches (Marche), in the north-west by Tuscany and in the south-west by Lazio. Umbria is one of the five districts of Italy that do not border on the sea. The main focus of this relatively small inland district of Italy is on forestry, agriculture and wine-growing. Umbria is not only the domain of wine-growers and olive farmers, but is also renowned for its saints, including Saint Francis of Assisi,

This is just the place for enthusiasts of country cooking. You will not find haute cuisine here, but primarily dishes from Etruscan and Roman times that have just been adapted to modern demands. In Umbria you can enjoy succulent roast pork with simple sauces

Torgiano rosso DOC and Torgiano DOCG from Lungarotti

made of tomatoes, mushrooms, olive oil and the occasional truffle. After all, Umbria is the world's greatest producer of truffles and Nurcia's truffle market attracts thousands of visitors each year. Umbria's small game dishes are also worth a diversion, as is the famous beef of Perugia, the local lamb, the sheep's cheeses and the lentils. Umbria has an ancient history of wine, but the standard of wine has not always remained constant. The climate is quite difficult to cope with (very cold winters and very warm summers). A great deal of patience and know-how is required to make good wines here. It is only within the last few decades that Umbria has again produced anything worth drinking. The best known wine is, of course, the white Orvieto. But since Giorgio Lungarotti started to take an interest in the old family business it is mainly the red wines of Umbria that take the prizes now. Partly thanks to Lungarotti, two of these red wines have been admitted to the elite corps of DOCG wines.

TORGIANO ROSSO RISERVA DOCG

This wine is among the greatest in Italy. Its history is quite recent, but its quality is timeless. The vineyards for the Torgiano rosso riserva are situated on hills above the mediaeval town of Torgiano, near Perugia. The wine is made from sangiovese and canaiolo, possibly supplemented with trebbiano toscano, ciliegiolo and montepulciano. To meet the DOCG requirements this wine must be at least three years old (cask + bottle) before it can be sold. The Torgiano rosso riserva is a sparkling wine of a beautiful ruby red color, with an elegant, smooth bouquet of red and black fruits, herbs, spices and a hint of tobacco, and a full, rounded flavor. Drink this wine with roast meat or small game birds. Try *palombacci all'umbria*, wood pigeons in red wine sauce with fresh mushrooms. Keep a glass for some hard cheese (pecorino). Drinking temperature: 16–17 °C (61–63 °F).

MONTEFALCO SAGRANTINO DOCG

This wine comes from the sunny hills around the village of Montefalco, slightly below Perugia. Its history begins with the Romans or probably even with the Etruscans. Only relatively recently has this noble Montefalco Sagrantino been allowed to bear the designation DOCG. There are two versions:
– the secco made from 100% sagrantino, which may not be sold until it has had been matured for a compulsory twelve months in wooden casks and

eighteen in the bottle. It is a dark ruby red wine with shades of purple in its youth. Once it has been matured it inclines towards purplish red. The bouquet is intense and fruity, reminiscent of ripe blackberries. The flavor is full, warm (at least 13% alcohol), dry and rich in tannins. A typical wine for those still brave enough to enjoy something old-fashioned: game in red wine sauce, oven roasts with a rich sauce or even pungent (blue-veined) cheeses. Drinking temperature: 16–18 °C (61–64 °F);
the passito made from 100% sagrantino grapes which have to be partially dried in the open air first. Fermentation takes place very slowly according to a centuries-old tradition. The result is a ruby red wine, with a typical aroma of blackberries and a full, rather tannin-rich, sweet, warm flavor (minimum 14.5% alcohol). In line with tradition this wine is served with dry cakes and pastries, but connoisseurs prefer to combine it with roast red meat with a sharp sauce or even spicy Asiatic sweet and sour meat dishes. Drinking temperature: 16–18 °C (61–64 °F) with meat dishes, 14–16 °C (57–61 °F) with cakes and pastries. But if you prefer this wine a little cooler, that is also fine.

Torgiano bianco Grechetto from Lungarotti

TORGIANO DOC

Several outstanding wines are made (white, rosé, red and even sparkling) in the area around Perugia. The white wines are sold under the name of bianco (usually trebbiano + grechetto and others) or under the name of a specific grape variety, such as Chardonnay, Pinot Grigio or Riesling Italico (at least 85% of the grape variety mentioned on the label). All these wines are elegant, fresh, fruity and full of flavor. The Riesling and Chardonnay have a slight preference for fish, the others go with almost anything. Drinking temperature: 10–12 °C (50–54 °F).

Rosato di Torgiano is principally made from sangiovese and canaiolo, vinified with white trebbiano toscano. This produces an intensely colored wine that is very fruity in bouquet and flavor, dry and particularly pleasant. Delicious with variety meats, soft cheeses and egg dishes. Drinking temperature: 10–12 °C (50–54 °F).

Rosso di Torgiano is made from sangiovese and canaiolo, possibly with a little trebbiano toscano. Drink this ruby red, elegant and flavorsome wine with roast meat. Try *perugina porchetta*, roast pork. Drinking temperature: 15–16 °C (59–61 °F).

The other red wines from Torgiano are made from pinot nero or cabernet sauvignon. Both are excellent and very typical of their grape varieties. You can go on serving them throughout the meal. Some tips are: Pinot Nero with roast wood pigeon or braised rabbit, Cabernet Sauvignon with risotto in meat sauce or with semi-hard cheeses. Drinking temperature: Pinot Nero 14–16 °C (57–61 °F), Cabernet Sauvignon 16 °C (61 °F).

The Torgiano spumante – made of chardonnay and pinot nero – has a fine effervessence, a beautiful straw color, a very fruity bouquet (green apples and may blossom) and an elegant, fine, dry and well-balanced flavor. Excellent aperitif. Drinking temperature: 8–10 °C (46–50 °F).

MONTEFALCO DOC

Outstanding white and red wines are produced around the village of the same name. The bianco is made from a minimum of 50% grechetto and 20–35% trebbiano. The wine is light in color, fruity in bouquet and flavor, dry and quite smooth. A typical wine for a soft risotto with fish or light starters. Drinking temperature: 8–10 °C (46–50 °F).

The rosso is made from 60–70% sangiovese, 10–15% sagrantino and another 15–30% recommended red grapes. This wine has a minimum of eighteen months maturing. There is also a riserva, which has been matured for at least twelve months in oak and then eighteen months in the bottle and contains a minimum of 12.5% alcohol. This wine is ruby red in color, subtle in bouquet, full, rounded and harmonious in flavor. Excellent combined with pasta dishes (with truffles!), roast meat or pecorino. Try *capretto*, roast young goat. Drinking temperature: 16 °C (61 °F).

ORVIETO DOC

The renown of this wine goes back to Etruscan times. The Romans discovered it and took it back to Gaul with them. The popes were mad about it. The bodily remains of pope Gregor XVI were even washed in Orvieto

before they were buried. Poets, painters, aristocrats from all over the world were all besotted with the heavenly, sweet wine from Orvieto. Yes, that's right: Orvieto was first a famous sweet wine. The dry version is quite recent. If you look carefully you will still find the old-fashioned wonderful sweet (abbocato/amabile/ dolce) Orvieto. The dry wines predominate, however, especially for export. Trebbiano (here called procanico), verdello, canaiolo bianco (drupeggio) and malvasia are used for Orvieto. The secret of Orvieto is in the soil, the tufa, and in the special microclimate that allows access to the beloved *Botrytis cinerea*. The grapes blessed with this noble rot are used for the sweet wines. The yellow color of the wines varies in intensity depending on the degree of sweetness, but they all have a subtle, elegant, fruity bouquet and a velvety smooth flavor. The secco is dry but smooth and has a discernible slight bitterness in the aftertaste. It makes an excellent aperitif, but also a good accompaniment to green vegetables, fish dishes and light pasta dishes with cream and cheese, for example. It also goes extremely well with white meat, tame rabbit and steamed fish or fish braised in white wine, possibly enhanced with grated white truffle! Try *asparagi*, asparagus with a delicate butter sauce! Drinking temperature: 10–12 °C (50–54 °F).

The abboccato and amabile go surprisingly well with delicate dishes of calves' liver and with soft sheep's cheeses (pecorino di fossa, cenerino). Also good with a slightly sharp fruit salad. Drinking temperature: 8–10 °C (46–50 °F).

The full, rich dolce is made only from late-harvested grapes that have been slightly afflicted by *Botrytis*. You can drink this sultry, particularly sensual wine just as it is after a meal, with your partner or best friends. If you do want to serve it at the table go for classic combinations with foie gras (*fegato di anitra*, duck liver) or gorgonzola dolce. The very best wines are called Muffa Nobile (100% with *Botrytis*) and are particularly rare. These very full-bodied wines – pure liquid gold – are oily, smooth, almost like liqueurs and have a never-ending aftertaste. Drinking temperature: 6–8 °C (43–46 °F).

OTHER INTERESTING DOC WINES FROM UMBRIA
Colli Altoriberini, Colli del Trasimeno, Colli Perugini, Colli Martani and Colli Amerini.

THE MARCHES

The Marches (Marche) are bordered in the west by the Apennines, Umbria and a small dot of Tuscany, in the north by Emilia, in the south by Abruzzo and in the east by the Adriatic Sea. Well known places on the coast are Pesaro and Ancona; inland Macerata and Ascoli Piceno. The whole area is inter-

Verdicchio dei Castelli di Jesi

CASTAGNOLO
SECCO
1998
ORVIETO CLASSICO
DENOMINAZIONE DI ORIGINE CONTROLLATA
SUPERIORE
BARBERANI
VITICOLTORI IN BASCHI
750 ml ℮ IMBOTTIGLIATO DAL VITICOLTORE BARBERANI-ORVIETO   ALIA AZ. AGRICOLA VALLESANTA BASCHI-ITALIA   ITALIA 13% vol.

Orvieto classico superiore

sected by a large number of rivers that flow from the Apennines to the Adriatic. Wine-growing thrives particularly well in the valleys of these rivers (Conca, Foglia, Metauro, Cesano and Tronto). There are three further wine-growing centers: around (Castelli di) Jesi, Ascoli Piceno and Ancona. The people of the Marches live primarily on agriculture and wine-growing, tourism and fishing. You will not find a rich culinary tradition here, but instead a tradition of delicious, nutritious meals.

VERDICCHIO DEI CASTELLI DI JESI DOC

For centuries this was the only known wine from the Marches. It is made between Pesaro and Ancona, around the small village of Jesi. This classic white wine contains a minimum of 85% verdicchio. The color is fairly light, inclining towards straw-colored. The bouquet is soft and subtle (apple, (hazel) nuts, peach) and the flavor fresh, dry and well balanced, with a slightly bitter undertone. Verdicchio dei Castelli di Jesi, like the French Muscadet de Sèvre et Maine, is always a good choice for fish and seafood. If you are looking for extra quality without spending too much more, go for a Verdicchio dei Castelli di Jesi riserva. This wine has had at least two years extra maturing and contains a minimum of 12.5% alcohol. Try *aguglia alla marchigiana*, a divine dish of garfish braised in white wine. Drinking temperature: 10–12 °C (50–54 °F).

VERDICCHIO DI MATELICA DOC

This younger sibling of Verdicchio dei Castelli di Jesi comes from the neighborhood of the village of Matelica at the foot of the Apennines. The ordinary Verdicchio di Matelica is light straw-colored, quite delicate and soft and fruity in bouquet and tastes fresh and elegant, with a slightly bitter undertone. Here too it is better to buy the older riserva that offers more quality and costs only slightly more. This Verdicchio is an excellent accompaniment to fish (not seafood). Drinking temperature: 10–12 °C (50–54 °F).

A great spumante and a divine passito are also produced here from verdicchio.

Rosso Conero and rosso Piceno

VERNACCIO DI SERRAPETRONA DOC

Excellent wine made from partially dried vernaccia nera (here called vernaccia di serrapetrona), possibly supplemented with some sangiovese, montepulciano and ciliegiolo. This Vernaccia is an unusual, naturally sparkling wine, ruby red in color, with an elegant foam, an intensely aromatic bouquet (fresh grapes) and a slightly (amabile) to very sweet (dolce) flavor with a pleasant bitter undertone. It is traditionally drunk at the end of the meal, with some pungent cheese (amabile) or cake. Drinking temperature: dolce 6–8 °C (43–46 °F), amabile 8–10 °C (46–50 °F).

LACRIMA DI MORRO D'ALBA DOC

Rosso Piceno

Unusual red wine made from lacrima, possibly supplemented with verdicchio or montepulciano. This Lacrima is made in the neighborhood of Ancona, near the coast. This is also where most of it is drunk, mainly by the tourists who stay here every year. The color is dark ruby red, the bouquet soft and friendly, the flavor pleasant, dry and smooth. An all-rounder that is bought in large quantities in the local trattorias. Drinking temperature: 14–16 °C (57–61 °F).

Excellent vino da tavola from the Marches

ROSSO CONERO DOC

In my opinion, as regards price to quality ratio this is one of the best red wines in Italy. Not one of the big boys, but particularly delicious all the same. The wine is produced near the coast, between Ancona and Macerata. Montepulciano, possibly supplemented with sangiovese, here produces a clear ruby red wine with a pleasant fruity aroma (blackberries, blackcurrants) and a dry, full, smooth, meaty, rounded flavor. Serve this wine with your favorite casserole, oven roast or chicken dish. The rare riservas are of outstanding quality. Try *faraona*, guinea fowl braised in red wine with onions, tomatoes and fresh Italian herbs. Drinking temperature: 14–16 °C (57–61 °F), riserva 16–17 °C (61–63 °F).

ROSSO PICENO DOC

The vineyards of the Rosso Piceno are below those of the Rosso Conero, between Macerata and Ascoli Piceno. Here too the wine-region follows the coast. This red wine is also made of sangiovese and montepulciano, possibly supplemented with trebbiano or passerina. The color is ruby red, the bouquet soft and fruity (black fruit) and the flavor dry, smooth and quite full. The superiore wines, mostly from the southern part of the wine-growing region, contain just a little more alcohol and seem more full-bodied. Drink the young wines with casseroles or oven-baked pasta dishes, the older ones with roast or fried meat. Drinking temperature: young 14–16 °C (57–61 °F) older wines 16–17 °C (61–63 °F).

As well as the wines mentioned above, they produce excellent vini da tavola in the Marches. One of the best wine producers is Colonnara, in Cupramontana, which makes every wine into a gem.

OTHER INTERESTING DOC WINES FROM THE MARCHES
Bianchello del Metauro, Colli Pesaresi, Esino, Colli Maceratesi and Falerio dei Colli Ascolani.

LAZIO

The district of Lazio extends from the Apennines (Umbria, Abruzzo and Molise) to the Mediterranean (Tyrrhenian) Sea. In the north Lazio borders on Tuscany and in the south on Campania. The river Tiber plays an important role in local wine-growing, as does the capital Rome, which constitutes the largest sales market for the local wine-growers. Most of Lazio's vineyards are situated around Rome. The other wine-growing regions are near Montefiascone in northern Lazio, between Rieti and the border with Abruzzo and above Frosinone in the south of the area. Lazio is best known for its white wines, but some of the red wines are also worth trying.

The entire area has volcanic soil. All the existing lakes (Bolsena, Vico, Bracciano, Albano and Nemi) are in fact former volcano craters. The climate is quite mild, warm and humid, which encourages *Botrytis cinerea* (noble rot). Mountains, volcanoes, the Tiber, the many lakes, the climate, the gentle hills around Rome – all in all this area has the ideal environment for wine-growing. So it is no wonder that the ancient Romans were so enthusiastic about wine: they had the best vineyards in their back yard, on the hills surrounding the city.

Est! Est!! Est!!!:
the story behind the
wine is better than
the wine itself

EST! EST!! EST!!! DI MONTEFIASCONE DOC

This wine has a richer history than its present quality would suggest. It used to be an excellent wine, as witnessed by the famous story from the fourteenth century about bishop Giovanni Defuk. During his many journeys this bishop sent his servant Martino on ahead to look for the best wines. This servant had to write the word 'Est!' (here it is!) on the doors of the inns that served the best wines. In Montefiascone the servant was so impressed with the local wine that he wrote 'Est! Est!! Est!!! on the door of the inn. The name Est! Est!! Est!!! has remained unchanged ever since. The quality, however, is not what it was.

The wine is made from trebbiano toscano, trebbiano giallo (rossetto) and malvasia bianca. It is a light straw color, the bouquet is quite fruity and vinous, the flavor full, round, smooth, harmonious and dry or slightly sweet. It is an excellent accompaniment to the many lake and river fish in this area and also to white meat. The slightly sweet version also goes well with soft, creamy fresh cheeses. Drinking temperature: secco 10–12 °C (50–54 °F), amabile 6–10 °C (43–50 °F) (the sweeter, the colder).

VIGNANELLO DOC

Wine-growing region in the province of Viterbo, below Lago di Bolseno. The bianco is made from various scions of the trebbiano and malvasia families. It is a straw-colored wine with a hint of green, usually quite fruity, dry or slightly sweet and smooth in flavor with a bitter undertone. The superiore versions contain just a little more alcohol and are possibly slightly better balanced. Great wine for a simple fish dish. Drinking temperature: 8–10 °C (46–50 °F).

The Greco di Vignanello is far better in quality and has more character and body. Excellent with fish dishes and also with poultry or white meat. There is also a slightly sweet version which goes well with creamy, fruity sauces. Drinking temperature: 10–12 °C (50–54 °F), slightly sweet 8–10 °C (46–50 °F).

The Greco spumante is definitely worth trying. The foam is fine and elegant, the bouquet seductively fruity and the flavor smooth and a touch mischievous. Wonderful as an aperitif or for drinking in company on long winter evenings. Drinking temperature: 7–9 °C (45–48 °F).

The rosato is a wonderful wine that goes with almost anything and never disappoints. Delicious without any fuss. Drinking temperature: 10–12 °C (50–54 °F).

The rosso is made principally from sangiovese and ciliegiolo. It is a first-rate red wine: warm, full-bodied and round. The riserva has even more to offer at a slightly higher price. Excellent price to quality ratio. Try *abacchio alla Romana*, succulent lamb cooked in the oven with potatoes, herbs and garlic. Drinking temperature: older wines 14–16 °C (57–61 °F), riserva 16–17 °C (61–63 °F).

CERVETERI DOC

Two wines have been made here from time immemorial:
- the exceptionally pleasant bianco made from trebbiano and malvasia, possibly supplemented with verdicchio and other white grapes. Dry or slightly sweet, always with a pleasant touch of bitterness, this is the ideal companion to fish. Drinking temperature: 8–10 °C (46–50 °F), amabile 6–8 °C (43–46 °F);
- the rosso is made from sangiovese, montepulciano and cesanese, possibly supplemented with canaiolo nero, carignano or barbera. This ruby red wine smells of fresh grapes, blackberries and other black fruits and tastes full, dry, sappy and rounded, with a slightly bitter undertone. Great accompaniment to pasta dishes with meat and tomato. Drinking temperature: 14–16 °C (57–61 °F).

CESANESE DEL PIGLIO DOC/
CESANESE DI AFFILE DOC/
CESANESE DI OLEVANO ROMANO DOC

These three white wines are also just called Piglio DOC, Affile DOC or Olevano Romano DOC. They are made from cesanese, possibly supplemented with a maximum of 10% sangiovese, montepulciano, barbera, trebbiano bianco or bombino bianco. The vineyards are situated in the area between the town of Rieti and the border with Abruzzi, at the foot of the Apennines.

These three red wines are in my opinion completely underestimated. They are excellently made wines, ruby red to pomegranate red in color, that smell and taste of freshly picked grapes. They are smooth, full-bodied and round, with a slight bitterness in the background. These wines can be dry (secco or asciutto), slightly sweet (amabile) or even sweet (dolce). The dry version is great with red meat, small game and lamb. Keep the sweet for a salad of red and black fruits, for example, or soft, creamy (blue-veined) cheeses. Drinking temperature: dry 12–14 °C (54–57 °F), sweet 8–10 °C (46–50 °F).

There is also a naturally bubbly (frizzante naturale) and a sparkling (spumante) version, mainly intended for the local market.

Frascati

COLLI ALBANI DOC

White wines (secco, abboccato, amabile or dolce) made from malvasia and trebbiano, possibly supplemented with other white grapes. It is light to dark straw-colored, the bouquet is sophisticated and pleasant and the flavor quite fruity. Drink the dry version as an aperitif, with light starters or with fish and the sweeter versions after meals or, for example, with soft, creamy cheeses or fresh, tangy fruit salads. Drinking temperature: secco, abboccato 8–10 °C (46–50 °F), amabile, dolce 6–8 °C (43–46 °F).

There is also a very acceptable spumante dei Colli Albani.

FRASCATI DOC

Like the previous wines, Frascati comes from the area south of Rome. This white wine from the Roman castles (Castelli Romani) is probably the best known in Lazio. It is made from malvasia and trebbiano, sometimes supplemented with Greco. It is light to dark straw-colored, the bouquet is fruity and delicate and the flavor velvety smooth, sappy, playful, seductive and friendly. Not a difficult wine, nor a wine to philosophize over for hours, but just really delicious. Frascati is produced in average quality secco (asciutto) and amabile and also in an excellent and unusual Canellino version (sweet, made from grapes afflicted by noble rot). Excellent wines, few of which, unfortunately, are exported. Drink the secco (asciutto) as an aperitif and with fish or white meat, the amabile with soft cheeses or fresh, tangy desserts and the Canellino when relaxing after meals. Drinking temperature: secco and amabile 8–10 °C (46–50 °F), Canellino 6–8 °C (43–46 °F) (warmer if wished).

A first-rate Frascati spumante is also produced from the same grapes.

MARINO DOC

Soft, fruity white wine made from malvasia and trebbiano scions. There are dry (secco/asciutto), medium dry (abboccato), slightly sweet (amabile) and sweet (dolce) versions of this Marino. The dry Marino goes excellently with seafood and sea fish, but the other wines are better served at the end of the meal with a fresh, tangy dessert, for example. Try *cozze alla Marinara*, mussels stewed in white Marino wine with a dry Marino. Drinking temperature: 8–10 °C (46–50 °F), sweet 6–8 °C (43–46 °F).

A great Marino spumante is also produced from the same grapes.

VELLETRI DOC

Pleasant white wine made from the Trebbiano and Malvasia families, fruity and soft, dry or slightly sweet. Also comes as spumante, secco or amabile. Serve these wines as aperitifs or to accompany light starters. Serve the sweeter Velletri bianco amabile at the end of a meal with fresh, tangy desserts. Drinking temperature: 8–10 °C (46–50 °F), sweet 6–8 °C (43–46 °F).

The more unusual Velletri rosso is made from sangiovese, montepulciano and cesanese, possibly supplemented with bombino, merlot and ciliegiolo. It is a first-rate wine, ruby red to pomegranate red in color, fruity and rich in bouquet, fairly rich in tannins and full in flavor. The best wines (riserva) are cask-matured for somewhat longer and contain a little more alcohol.

Great accompaniment to meat dishes with tomato sauce. Drinking temperature: 15–16 °C (59–61 °F).

APRILIA DOC

Fairly recent small wine region between Rome and Latina. The local cooperatives spare neither money nor effort to make modern, yet outstanding wines that are held in increasingly high esteem.

The Trebbiano is very fine and delicate in bouquet and flavor and is great with light fish dishes and seafood. Drinking temperature: 8–10 °C (46–50 °F).

The Sangiovese is fruity, fresh, full-bodied and elegant. Goes extremely well with light meat dishes and pasta with tomato sauce. Drinking temperature: 14–16 °C (57–61 °F).

The Merlot is fresh, fruity, seductive and soft, not too heavy – in short, just right. Good example of a very successful modern wine that actually goes with anything. So the perfect wine for the catering industry. Drinking temperature: 13–15 °C (55–59 °F).

CORI DOC

This small wine region is situated between Cisterna and Cori, above Latina. The bianco is made from malvasia and trebbiano and is soft, fruity and particularly pleasant. Drink the dry version as an aperitif or with simple starters, the (semi) sweet versions with fresh fruit desserts or creamy cheeses. By the way, the Cori secco bianco has a weakness for tender vegetable dishes. Drinking temperature: 8–10 °C (46–50 °F).

The rosso is made from montepulciano, nero buono di cori (native) and cesanese. This ruby red wine has a character all of its own and is full, round and smooth in flavor, with a fresh undertone. An all-rounder of this kind cannot really go wrong and you can serve it throughout the meal. A good tip is *pasta alla matriciana*, pasta with a sauce of peppers and tomatoes, bacon and a lot of grated Parmesan or pecorino. Drinking temperature: 14–16 °C (57–61 °F).

MONTECOMPATRI COLONNA/ MONTECOMPATRI COLONNA DOC

These great white wines are produced from malvasia and trebbiano in a small region above Frosinone, in southeast Lazio. Here too you can choose from dry, medium dry, slightly sweet and sweet versions. In general these wines are slightly fruity and pleasant. Drink these Montecompatri Colonna with simple pasta dishes or, for example, with *gnocchi alla Romana*, little balls of semolina with butter and grated cheese. Drinking temperature: 8–10 °C (46–50 °F), sweet 6–8 °C (43–46 °F).

ZAGAROLO DOC

This wine with a history of more than four hundred years is much like the other white wines of Lazio made from trebbiano and, in particular, malvasia. It comes in dry, medium dry, slightly sweet and sweet versions.

Montepulciano d'Abruzzo

The better, more full-bodied wines carry the designation 'superiore'. Serve the dry wines with pasta with butter and grated pecorino or with *saltimbocca alla Romana*, veal escalopes with *prosciutto crudo* (raw ham) and sage. Drinking temperature: superiore 10–12 °C (50–54 °F), secco 8–10 °C (46–50 °F), dolce 6–8 °C (43–46 °F).

OTHER INTERESTING DOC WINES FROM LAZIO
Aleatico di Gradoli, Bianco Capena and Colli Lanuvini

ABRUZZI

The Abruzzi district borders on the Marches in the north, Lazio in the west via the Apennines and Molise in the south. The Adriatic Sea forms the eastern border. Apart from a small coastal strip, this district consists entirely of hills, mountains and valleys. The climate varies from Mediterranean on the coast to continental in the mountains. Places suitable for winegrowing are carefully selected, above and below Pescara, the only real town in the Abruzzi, and in the valley of the river of the same name, the Pescara. The vineyards are situated at the foot of the imposing Gran Sasso and Montagna della Maiella. Only two DOC wines are produced here.

MONTEPULCIANO D'ABRUZZO DOC

The Montepulciano grape was introduced to the Abruzzi almost two hundred years ago and produces here a dry, mellow red wine, fairly high in tannin, sappy and friendly. Depending on the maker, the wine is an excellent all-rounder or a slightly more serious wine. The riserva, at a minimum of two years old, is always to be recommended. Great accompaniment to pasta dishes with meat and tomato sauce, to pecorino and to grilled lamb. Try *maccheroni alla chitarra*, rectangular-shaped pasta with a *ragu* of beef, the Abruzzi's great specialty. The riserva is excellent combined with *rosticini*, grilled pork and lamb on skewers. Drinking temperature: young 12–14 °C (54–57 °F), older wines and riserva 14–16 °C (57–61 °F).

Montepulciano d'Abruzzo Cerasuolo is a beautiful cherry red rosé made from Montepulciano and a pleasant fruity wine that soon gains fans. Try *agnello alla diavola*, lamb with a spicy (deviled) sauce of shallots, reduced white wine and red peppers. Drinking temperature: 10–12 °C (50–54 °F).

The better Abruzzi red wines come from the hills of Teramane, Colli Teramane. As well as the obligatory montepulciano, they are allowed to add a maximum of 10% sangiovese. These wines are fuller and more robust than an ordinary Montepulciano d'Abruzzo, especially the wonderful riserva, which must be at least three years old and contain 12.5% alcohol. Excellent wines for roast meat or oven dishes. Drinking temperature: 14–16 °C (57–61 °F), riserva 16–17 °C (61–63 °F).

TREBBIANO D'ABRUZZO DOC

Great white wine made from trebbiano, smooth and delicate in bouquet, dry, sappy and friendly in flavor. The bulk of this wine is reasonable, but there are also a few outstanding examples. Serve them with fish and poultry. Drinking temperature: 8–10 °C (46–50 °F).

MOLISE

For years Molise was linked with its northern neighbors from Abruzzi. In many books on wine you still come across the name 'Abruzzo e Molise'. This is partly because for a long time the quality of local wine-growing was not good enough to be considered for DOC recognition. Recently, however, the quality of two wines has improved to such an extent that they have been allowed to join the DOC corps. Molise is an agricultural area with a relatively small coastline. Beach tourists do not bother to visit the beautiful interior, which is fortunate for the 'green tourists' who are still able to enjoy the rustic environment in peace.

PENTRO DI ISERNIA/ PENTRO DOC

Less well known wine from Molise, made from trebbiano and bombino (bianco) or montepulciano and san-

giovese (rosato/rosso). The vineyards are situated on sunny hills near the little town of Isernia.

The bianco is fresh, elegant, dry, intense in flavor and quite aromatic. Excellent wine for sea fish, preferably grilled. Drinking temperature: 10–12 °C (50–54 °F).

The rosato is fresh, fruity, dry and particularly pleasant in flavor. Goes very well with grilled scampi or fish with a tomato and garlic sauce. Drinking temperature: 10–12 °C (50–54 °F).

The rosso is quite light, smooth, dry, rounded and not too rich in tannins. This all-rounder is delicious with *melanzane* (eggplant) with a gratin of mozzarella and provolone or zucchini served with a mild tomato sauce. Drinking temperature: 14–16 °C (57–61 °F).

BIFERNO DOC

Only the Biferno rosso enjoys any sort of renown. It is made from montepulciano, trebbiano and aglianico and comes from the area around Campobasso. The wine is a ruby red color that inclines towards pomegranate red as it ages. The bouquet is smooth and pleasant (blackberries, blackcurrants) and the flavor fairly rich in tannins, smooth and dry. The riserva is more full-bodied, more mature (at least three years old) and contains considerably more alcohol (minimum 13%). Drink the ordinary Biferno with fried red meat or pork, the riserva with roast or grilled meat. Try *abbaccio alla cacciatora*, lamb grilled on a log fire with a piquant *sauce chasseur*. Drinking temperature: 14–16 °C (57–61 °F), riserva 16–17 °C (61–63 °F).

As well as the previously mentioned rosso, there is also a fresh, sappy, dry, fruity rosato and a fresh, elegant, aromatic bianco.

CAMPANIA

Campania is an elongated district on the Tyrrhenian (Mediterranean) Sea, in southwest Italy. The countryside, Campania Felix, was popular with the Romans. Not only is the landscape, particularly on the coast, breathtakingly beautiful, but the inhabitants always seem happy and carefree. Naples the capital of Campania, is one of the most sociable towns in Italy. Nowhere can you eat such delicious pizzas and pasta as in Naples. The simple salads of sun-dried tomatoes with mozzarella, fresh basil, salt, pepper and a dressing of wonderful olive oil and vinegar are fit for the gods. So much *joie de vivre* and love is due not only to the unprecedented beauty of the area and the glorious climate conditions, but undoubtedly also to the brutality of those same natural features. Everyone knows the tragic history of Pompeii and Herculaneum, two gems of Roman civilization, wiped from the map by a dramatic eruption of Mount Vesuvius. No one here seems to be losing any sleep over it any more, but life has been drastically affected by this volcano, even only in that the terms life and death are more closely associated with one another in Campania than anywhere else in Italy. While cruel Vesuvius took

Biferno rosso

the lives of thousands, at the same time the volcano gave the area a particularly fertile soil that was to have a positive effect on the entire region. Wine-growing in Campania once again confirms how skilled the Greek and Roman wine-growers were. In spite of today's modern techniques, the better wines of Campania are still produced in the same places as two to four thousand years ago! Descendants of the grape varieties introduced by the Greeks still grow here too, including aglianico and greco.

Taurasi, a fabulous red wine

TAURASI DOCG

This is Campania's only top wine. It is produced near Avellino, below Benevento, in the same way as the white Greco di Tufo. The epicenter of this designation of origin is close to the village of the same name, Taurasi. This beautiful red wine is made from aglianico. The color is ruby red to pomegranate red, the bouquet very aromatic and sensual and the flavor full, well balanced, rounded and harmonious. The surprising thing is the aftertaste that remains for ages. There is also a sublime riserva version with a minimum 12.5% alcohol and at least four years maturing. Serve this fabulous red wine with a really good beef roast, herbed leg of lamb cooked in the oven or fillet of wild boar in red wine sauce. Drinking temperature: 14–16 °C (57–61 °F), older wines and riserva 16–18 °C (61–64 °F).

AGLIANICO DEL TABURNO/ TABURNO DOC

These white, red and rosé wines are produced between Benevento and Taburno in northern Campania. The Aglianico del Taburno rosato, primarily made from Aglianico, is fresh, fruity, elegant and quite smooth. An all-rounder. Drinking temperature: 10–12 °C (50–54 °F).

The Aglianico del Taburno rosso also contains Aglianico, possibly supplemented to a maximum of 15% with other local black grapes. The ruby red young wines have a pleasant and inviting bouquet and a dry, power-ful, often tannin-rich flavor. Only after several years extra maturing do the wines become somewhat smoother. The color then inclines towards pomegranate red. The best wines (riserva) undergo a longer period of maturing: three years instead of two. These pungent wines with a character all of their own are at their best with roast meat. Try *capretto*, roast young goat. Drinking temperature: 14–16 °C (57–61 °F) (older wines and riserva 16–17 °C (61–63 °F).

Taburno is produced in seven versions, one spumante, three white and three red wines (including a mediocre vino novello). Taburno rosso is an attractive ruby red wine, made principally from sangiovese and Aglianico. Drink this pleasant, reasonably full-bodied wine with your favorite pasta dish. Drinking temperature: 14–16 °C (57–61 °F). Taburno Piedirosso is more original, more exciting and of slightly better quality than the ordinary rosso. It is made principally from the native Piedirosso (minimum 85%) and is ruby red in color, distinctive and friendly in bouquet, dry, fruity and full in flavor. Ideal with lighter pasta dishes with meat and tomato sauce. Drinking temperature: 14–16 °C (57–61 °F).

Of the white wines, the ordinary Taburno bianco is particularly pleasant. It is made from trebbiano and falanghina, sometimes supplemented to a maximum of 30% with other white grapes. This white wine is fresh, fruity and elegant. Excellent accompaniment to lightish fish dishes or white meat. Drinking temperature: 8–10 °C (46–50 °F). The Taburno Falanghina, Taburno Greco and Taburno Coda di Volpe are made from a minimum 85% of falanghina, greco and coda di volpe respectively. These three wines are definitely more original and exciting than the ordinary bianco: they are dry, fresh and very distinctive. Serve them with the local fish or white meat specialties or with pasta dishes with cream sauce and (lots of) grated cheese. Also delicious with fish or seafood pizza. Drinking temperature: 10–12 °C (50–54 °F).

SANT'AGATA DE' GOTI/ SANT'AGATA DEI GOTI DOC

A few acceptable wines are produced in the small town of Sant'Agata de'Goti near Benevento. Surprisingly, the white, red and rosé wines are all made from the same grapes. For the bianco the skins of the black grapes used are not included in the fermentation, but they are for the rosato and rosso. The wines made from aglianico and piedirosso are all fresh, aromatic, full-bodied and sophisticated. The bianco is a sturdy aperitif and tastes great with white meat or fish starters. The rosato is a typical lunch wine, while the rosso feels comfortable with almost anything. Drinking temperature: bianco and rosato 10–12 °C (50–54 °F), rosso 12–14 °C (54–57 °F).

Greco di Tufo, one of Italy's loveliest white wines

The other wines from this region are also interesting. A fresh, fruity white wine with an occasional slight fizziness is made from greco. Great accompaniment to (baked) sea fish. Two white wines are made from falanghina: the ordinary one is dry, fresh and fruity and goes well with fish and the passito (minimum 15% alcohol) is sweet, intensely aromatic and velvety smooth. Drink the passito with less sweet desserts. Drinking temperature: 8–10 °C (46–50 °F), passito 6–12 °C (43–54 °F).

The red wines made from aglianico or piedirosso both have individual character and are full-bodied and powerful with a considerable amount of tannins. Of these I thoroughly recommend the riserva. Serve these wines with roast or fried meat. Drinking temperature: 14–16 °C (57–61 °F), riserva 17 °C (63 °F).

GRECO DI TUFO DOC

Famous dry, fresh, elegant and full-bodied white wine made from greco. This wine is produced near Avellino, where the red Taurasi also comes from. The ordinary Greci di Tufo is a genial white wine, but the top wines are veritable gems of finesse. Ideal accompaniment to your best fish dishes. Drinking temperature: 10–12 °C (50–54 °F).

An outstanding spumante is also produced from this greco.

FALERNO DEL MASSICO DOC

Fairly unknown wine-growing region near Caserta, where, however, outstanding red wines are made from aglianico and piedirosso, possibly supplemented with primitivo and barbera. These red wines are powerful, full-bodied, round and quite warm (minimum 12.5% alcohol). The flavor is velvety smooth, making this wine especially popular with all wine drinkers. Excellent wine for grilled or roast lamb. Drinking temperature: 14–16 °C (57–61 °F), riserva 16–17 °C (61–63 °F).

The distinctive and original Primitivo is obtained from the grape of the same name, supplemented with aglianico, piedirosso or barbera. The color is a very intense ruby red, while the bouquet and flavor are reminiscent of over-ripe, freshly picked grapes. The wine tastes full, strong and warm (minimum 13% alcohol) and can be dry or slightly sweet. The better wines are left a little longer to mature and are designated as 'riserva' or 'vecchio'. Although it takes some getting used to for some people, traditionally these wines are served with old-fashioned fried or roast meat. A particularly clever combination is with wild boar. Drinking temperature: 16–18 °C (61–64 °F).

ASPRINIO DI AVERSA DOC

The vineyards of this region lie between Caserta and Naples. The whole enterprise, including the wines, is more of a museum-piece than a representative example of current wine-growing in Campania. In line with tradition the vines are still trained over trees. You can recognize the wines obtained from these vines by the words 'alberata' or 'vigneti ad alberata' on the label. These white wines are quite dark in color, the bouquet is particularly fruity and playful and the flavor dry, fresh and fruity. Serve them with sophisticated fish dishes. Drinking temperature: 10–12 °C (50–54 °F).

Wonderful spumante is also made from 100% asprinio. They are fresh, fruity, elegant dry sparkling wines that are equally good as country aperitifs at outdoor parties or as a warm-up to a formal dinner. Drinking temperature: 8–10 °C (46–50 °F).

CAMPI FLEGREI DOC

Attractive white and red wines from the area of Pozzuoli, just above Naples. The following wines are of much better quality:
- Pér'e Palummo: ruby red to pomegranate red wine made from piedirosso with a very aromatic bouquet. The flavor is quite smooth and dry. Serve it with oven- cooked pasta dishes. The slightly older riserva tastes great with roast meat. Drinking temperature: 14–16 °C (57–61 °F);
- Pér'e Palummo passito: an outstanding passito (minimum 17% alcohol), made from piedirosso, with a very intense bouquet and velvety smooth flavor, from secco to dolce. Drinking temperature: according to taste and depending on type 6–12 °C (43–54 °F) (the sweeter, the colder).

The falanghina grape produces two outstanding white wines here, a still and a spumante. Both wines are fresh, fruity and smooth. Serve them as aperitifs or with fish. Drinking temperature: 8–10 °C (46–50 °F).

ISCHIA DOC

The small wine-growing region of Ischia is on the island of the same name off the coast of Naples. Ischia wines enjoyed great fame at one time. Today they are more tourist wines. They are all of good quality, but only a few reach a really high standard.

The ordinary bianco (forastera and biancolella), the Biancolella and Forestera are fresh, fine, dry white wines that – as you would expect on an island – go very well with the local fish specialties. Try any version of *cozze* (mussels), which are very much in vogue on the island. Drinking temperature: 8–10 °C (46–50 °F). A very successful spumante is also produced from forastera and biancolella.

The rosso and the Pér'e Palummo (piedirosso) are dry, semi-full-bodied red wines, often quite rich in tannins, which are sold in large numbers in the local trattorias. Great accompaniment to red meat and lamb. Drinking temperature: 14–16 °C (57–61 °F). An excellent passito is also made from Pér'e Palummo (Piedirosso).

VESUVIO DOC

This designation of origin is perhaps better known by the name given to it in the area by tourists, Lacryma

Christi. Apparently Christ is once said to have shed a few tears when he saw the large scale of the sins being committed by the people of Naples and its neighborhood. These tears fell on the slopes of the famous volcano, after which the vines grew as never before and produced the very best wines. Masses of tourists are only too eager to take these 'tears of Christ' back home with them. Most of the Vesuvio wines are of particularly mediocre quality and are only used to attract the tourists. If you look carefully, however, you will be able to find a few top wines. The best wines are sold under the name 'Lacryma Christi del Vesuvio' (minimum 12% alcohol), in white, rosé and red.

The bianco is very fresh, dry and particularly pleasant. The best wines are recognizable from the bouquet. Only a few wines have the extremely sophisticated bouquet of the top Lacryma Christi. Serve these austere white wines with fish. Drinking temperature: 8–10 °C (46–50 °F).

The rosato and rosso are all-rounders that can be drunk with anything, even with baked fish. Drinking temperature: 10–12 °C (50–54 °F) for the rosato and rosso with grilled fish, 12–14 °C (54–57 °F) for the rosso with meat dishes. To tempt the tourists still further there is also a reasonable spumante and a liqueur wine (liquoroso) with the same designation of origin.

CASTEL SAN LORENZO DOC

Excellent white wines made from trebbiano and malvasia, fresh, fruity, slightly bitter, smooth and full. Not exactly typical of this area around Salerno. Great accompaniment to fish. Drinking temperature: 8–10 °C (46–50 °F).

There are also a first-rate, sensual Moscato and a Moscato spumante, both very aromatic, velvety smooth and sweet. Serve these wines with fresh desserts. Drinking temperature: spumante 6–8 °C (43–46 °F), Moscato 8–10 °C (46–50 °F).

CAPRI DOC

The unprecedented charm of Capri is certainly not due to its wines. The local bianco and rosso are nice, but definitely not exciting. Drink the white with fish and *vongole* (shellfish) and the red with fried or grilled meat and with pasta or vegetable dishes *au gratin*. Drinking temperature: bianco 8–10 °C (46–50 °F), rosso 12–14 °C (54–57 °F).

PENISOLA SORRENTINA DOC

The vineyards of this region are situated on the slopes of hills, up to a height of 1,970 ft. The bianco Falanghina, Biancolella and Greco is a pleasant aperitif, fresh, dry, sappy and well balanced. Drinking temperature: 8–10 °C (46–50 °F).

The rosso (piedirosso, sciasinoso and aglianico) is a semi-full-bodied, easy-going red wine for everyday meals. Drinking temperature: 12–14 °C (54–57 °F).

The local Lambrusco-type variation, the rosso frizzante naturale, obtained from the same grapes as the rosso, is surprising and sometimes even pleasant. This lightly sparkling red wine can be dry or sweet, but is always velvety soft, sappy, intensely aromatic and fruity, with an occasional slight bitterness in the aftertaste. It is quite difficult to match this wine with anything. The dry wine can be served as a winter aperitif, but it is better in combination with provolone. This wine is also great with the many versions of pizza with meat. The sweet version goes surprisingly well with red fruit salads or cakes and pastries. Drinking temperature: dry 10–12 °C (50–54 °F) (though some Italians drink it at room temperature, which takes some getting used to), sweet 6–8 °C (43–46 °F).

OTHER INTERESTING DOC WINES FROM CAMPANIA
Solopaca (especially Falanghina and Aglianico), Guardia Sanframondi/Guardiolo, Costa d'Amalfi and Cilento.

APULIA

Apulia is one of the largest wine-producing districts in Italy. The region is in the extreme southeast of the country and forms the heel of the Italian boot. Apulia has a long coastline on the Adriatic and Ionian seas. In the west the region borders with Campania and Basilicata, and in the north with Molise. As regards landscape, Apulia is very different from the surrounding districts. There are no longer any mountains, only a few high plains. The climate is distinctly Mediterranean. Local gastronomy is characterized by the large range of sea fish, shellfish and crustaceans, olive oil and fresh vegetables. In Apulia they eat less meat than in the north and center of Italy and if they do eat meat it is mainly lamb. The Greeks began growing wine here eight hundred years or so before Christ. The Phoenicians and later the Romans continued their success. During the occupation of Italy by the French royal troops (sixteenth century) and later by the troops of Napoleon and Napoleon III a great deal of wine constantly disappeared to France. In the twentieth century bulk trade flourished in Apulia, especially owing to the great French demand for full-bodied pungent wines. These wines were blended with sick French wines to be palmed off on the European supermarket clientele as reasonable, cheap 'French' wines. It is incredible how much bulk wine is sent annually from (southern) Italy to France, and yet you will scarcely ever see a bottle of Italian wine in a French supermarket! It is an open secret that these deceptive practices go on. Do not blame the Italians, but think a little more carefully before you buy another anonymous cheap French wine. Fortunately wine-growing has improved enormously in recent years in Apulia too. Growers are increasingly trying to maintain their own identity and to improve the quality. Apart from the wines mentioned here, Gravina (also in spumante) is an interesting DOC wine from Apulia.

SAN SEVERO DOC

Increasingly more wine connoisseurs are discovering these wines from the Foggia area in northern Apulia. These white, red and rosé wines offer very affordable quality. The bianco is possibly the best of the three. It is made from bombino and trebbiano, sometimes supplemented with malvasia and verdeca. This wine is fresh, fruity, dry and well balanced, making it an excellent accompaniment to sea fish dishes. The local spumante made from the same grapes is also of surprisingly good quality. Drinking temperature: 8–10 °C (46–50 °F).

The semi-full-bodied rosato and rosso (both made from montepulciano and sangiovese) are very pleasant, dry, rounded and fruity. Drink the rosato with grilled sea fish or seafood and the rosso with grilled lamb. Drinking temperature: rosato 10–12 °C (50–54 °F), rosso 14–16 °C (57–61 °F).

CACC'É MITTE DI LUCERA DOC

A wonderful, rounded, full-bodied, warm, red wine made from montepulciano, uva di troia, sangiovese, malvasia nera, trebbiano, bombino and malvasia. It is made in northern Apulia, in a wide area around Foggia. Splendid with the local ways of cooking *agnello* (lamb). Drinking temperature: 15–16 °C (59–61 °F).

ORTA NOVA DOC

Also from the north, near Foggia. The rosato and rosso made from sangiovese, sometimes supplemented with uva di troia, montepulciano, lambrusco and trebbiano, are fresh, fruity and full-bodied. Drink the rosato with grilled fish or shellfish and the often tannin-rich rosso with grilled or fried meat. Drinking temperature: rosato 10–12 °C (50–54 °F), rosso 14–16 °C (57–61 °F).

Moscato di Trani

ROSSO BARLETTA DOC

This full-bodied, warm, sturdy red wine is produced near the coast between Foggia and Bari, especially around the village of Barletta. Uva di troia is the base for this wine, possibly supplemented with montepulciano, sangiovese and malbec. The better wines are matured for two years and have the term 'invecchiato' on the label. Excellent wine with all kinds of grilled meat and also with pungent sheep's cheese (pecorino). Drinking temperature: 16–17 °C (61–63 °F).

ROSSO DI CERIGNOLA DOC

This dry, full-bodied, warm, sappy red wine from the same area as the rosso Barletta, but further inland, is made from uva di troia and negroamaro, possibly supplemented with sangiovese, montepulciano and malbec. A very original wine, exciting and absolutely delicious. Drink it with pungent cheeses and grilled lamb with herbs and garlic. Drinking temperature: 16 °C (61 °F), riserva 16–17 °C (61–63 °F).

MOSCATO DI TRANI DOC

This sultry, velvety smooth, sweet Moscato is probably a legacy from the ancient Greeks. Very aromatic Moscato (minimum 14.5% alcohol) and Moscato liquoroso (minimum 18% alcohol). Wonderful on its own after meals or with a fresh, tangy fruit salad. Drinking temperature: 6–8 °C (43–46 °F).

CASTEL DEL MONTE DOC

In this region near the coast in the neighborhood of Bari is the proof that a little bit of high-tech can do no harm. Fresh wines are made here thanks to modern equipment and a slightly higher location of the vineyards:
– the bianco and the Pinot Bianco are light, dry and elegant. Great wines for fish. Drinking temperature: 6–8 °C (43–46 °F);
– the Sauvignon is quite aromatic and is certainly well made, but does not exactly have the power to excite. The name sells better than the wine itself. Nevertheless it is a nice wine as an aperitif or as a thirst-quencher with shellfish and baked fish. Drinking temperature: 8–10 °C (46–50 °F);
– the Chardonnay is also extremely well made and certainly makes a good aperitif, but it is not a wine for purists. Drinking temperature: 10–12 °C (50–54 °F);
– perhaps the most unusual, but also the most delicious wine, is the Bianco da pinot nero. This full-bodied, dry wine is produced from at least 85% pinot nero, a black grape, which here though is vinified without the skins as a white wine. The result speaks for itself. You can, of course, serve this wine with shellfish, but also with crustaceans or even with white meat. Drinking temperature: 10–12 °C (50–54 °F);
– the rosato is made from bombino nero, aglianico and uva di troia. This wine is also a living legacy of the ancient Greeks. Drink this very fruity rosé with grilled fish or shellfish, and also with the wonderful vegetable dishes of Apulia. Drinking temperature: 10–12 °C (50–54 °F);
– the Aglianico rosato is slightly fuller in bouquet and flavor and goes very well with rustic oven dishes. This rosato certainly does not shrink from olive oil, herbs and garlic. Drinking temperature: 10–12 °C (50–54 °F);
– the ordinary rosso (including uva di troia, aglianico and montepulciano) is a genial, dry, full-bodied red wine with occasional strong tannins in its youth. The better wines are the riservas, which are at least two years old. Drink this rosso with roast meat or oven dishes *au gratin*. Drinking temperature: 16–17 °C (61–63 °F);
– the Pinot Nero is a pleasant, dry, full-bodied red wine that goes with anything, especially with tender vegetable dishes. Drinking temperature: 14–16 °C (57–61 °F);

the Aglianico is rather more original and distinctive. Here too go for the better riserva. Outstanding wines with roast or fried meat. Drinking temperature: 16–17 °C (61–63 °F).

ALEATICO DI PUGLIA DOC

Rather old-fashioned sweet red wine made from aleatico, often supplemented with negroamaro, malvasia nera and primitivo. This dark red 'dolce naturale' is obtained by leaving part of the harvest to dry out. The bouquet is full and very aromatic, the flavor warm (minimum 15% alcohol), distinctive and velvety smooth. The degree of sweetness is just right. The 'liquoroso' is much fuller, sweeter and warmer (minimum 18.5% alcohol). The better wines undergo an extra three years maturing (riserva). Drinking temperature: 8–14 °C (46–57 °F), liquoroso according to taste 6–16 °C (43–61 °F).

ROSSO CANOSA (CANUSIUM) DOC

This red wine from the area near Bari is made from uva di trocaia, sometimes supplemented with montepulciano and sangiovese. It is a dry, sappy, full-bodied, pungent wine, often quite warm, which can sometimes be fairly rich in tannins and slightly bitter. The best wines mature for another two years and are slightly more full-bodied, rounder and warmer (minimum 13% alcohol). The rosso Canosa calls for some good roast or fried meat. Drinking temperature: 16 °C (61 °F), riserva 16–17 °C (61–63 °F).

Locorotondo

GIOIA DEL COLLE DOC

Six types of wine are made here between Bari and the border with Basilicata:
– the bianco, made from trebbiano, is fresh, elegant and pleasant. It goes reasonably well with shellfish and extremely well with sea fish. Drinking temperature: 8–10 °C (46–50 °F);
– the rosato (primitivo, montepulciano, sangiovese, negroamaro and malvasia) is dry, fruity and seductive. Goes well with most delicacies from the sea. Drinking temperature: 10–12 °C (50–54 °F);
– the rosso (the same grapes as rosato) is pleasant and uncomplicated. A great red wine for pasta dishes and oven dishes. Drinking temperature: 14–16 °C (57–61 °F);
– Primitivo, made from the grape of the same name, is a full-bodied, heavy, warm red wine (minimum

13% alcohol) with distinct residual sugar. The riserva is even more full-bodied and warm (minimum 14% alcohol). This wine definitely belongs at the end of the meal, with pungent cheeses. Drinking temperature: according to taste 8–14 °C (46–57 °F);
– two sweet red wines are made from aleatico, the Aleatico dolce and the Aleatico liquoroso dolce. Both wines are full-bodied, pungent, sultry and velvety smooth. The dolce is considerably less sweet than the liquoroso dolce and has less alcohol (minimum 15% and minimum 18.5% alcohol respectively). Serve these at the end of the meal with pungent cheeses, or after the meal purely for pleasure. Drinking temperature: dolce 8–12 °C (46–54 °F), liquoroso dolce 6–14 °C (43–57 °F).

LOCOROTONDO DOC

This small wine-growing region is situated between Bari and Brindisi, in southern Apulia. Here very acceptable white wines are made from verdeca and bianco d'alessano, usually supplemented with fiano, bombino and malvasia. Locorotondo is a very pleasant, fresh, elegant dry white wine that is excellent in combination with better (substantial) kinds of fish. This wine is also an excellent aperitif and an unorthodox but surprisingly delicious accompaniment to lukewarm oysters, *ostriche, au gratin*. There is also a reasonable spumante made from this Locorotondo. Drinking temperature: 8–10 °C (46–50 °F).

MARTINA FRANCA DOC

North of Taranto white wines are made similar to those in Locorotondo. This Martina Franca is also light straw-colored with a hint of green, dry, fresh and elegant. As in Locorotondo, a reasonable spumante is also produced from this wine. Great aperitif and good accompaniment to fish, crustaceans and shellfish. Drinking temperature: 8–10 °C (46–50 °F).

OSTUNI DOC

These wines from the area around Brindisi once enjoyed greater fame. The explosive growth of tourism has put wine-growing around Brindisi in a bit of a tight spot.

The bianco, made principally from impigno and francavilla, is a pure, fresh, elegant dry white wine that makes a good aperitif or accompaniment to fish or seafood. Drinking temperature: 8–10 °C (46–50 F°).

Ottavianello, made from the grape of the same name, possibly supplemented with negroamaro, malvasia nera, notar domenico and sussumaniello, is a light, aromatic, dry, elegant red wine. Serve it with fairly light dishes, for example vegetables *au gratin*. Drinking temperature: 14–16 °C (57–61 °F).

BRINDISI DOC

Very reasonable rosato and rosso made principally from negroamaro. The rosato is fresh and fruity with

a pleasant touch of bitterness, the rosso robust, sometimes very high in tannin, slightly bitter and very pungent. The riserva (two years old, minimum 12.5% alcohol) is very much to be recommended. Serve it with gratin dishes, grilled, fried or roast meat and with pungent sheep's cheeses. Drinking temperature: 14–16 °C (57–61 °F), riserva 16–17 °C (61–63 °F).

LIZZANO DOC

A whole range of wines is made just above Taranto:
– the bianco spumante, like the still bianco and the bianco frizzante, is made from trebbiano, chardonnay and possibly malvasia. All three are dry, fresh, elegant and quite fruity. Drink them as aperitifs or with a local fish dish. Drinking temperature: 8–10 °C (46–50 °F);
– the rosato, rosato frizzante and rosato spumante are obtained principally from negroamaro, montepulciano, sangiovese, bombino nero and pinot nero. They are dry, fresh, very fruity wines. Drink the (slightly) sparkling wine as a winter aperitif or smart accompaniment to fish or white meat starters and the still one with fish, crustaceans or poultry. Drinking temperature: 10–12 °C (50–54 °F);
– the Negroamaro rosato is a full-bodied, dry, fresh, elegant rosé that actually goes with anything. Drinking temperature: 10–12 °C (50–54 °F);
– the rosso, rosso novello and rosso frizzante are made from 60–80% negroamaro, supplemented with the

Primitivo di Manduria

Primitivo di Manduria dolce

Rosso Salento

same grapes as in the rosato. They are genial red wines, dry and pleasantly smooth. You can actually serve them with anything. Drinking temperature: 12–16 °C (54–61 °F);
– of much better quality are the Negroamaro Rosso and Malvasia Nera. Both wines offer a great deal of character and body for a relatively low price. Choose the superiore (minimum 13% alcohol). These warm, full-bodied, rounded, dry red wines call for a special joint of meat or a delicious oven dish *au gratin*. Drinking temperature: 14–16 °C (57–61 °F).

PRIMITIVO DI MANDURIA DOC

Four types of heavy, sultry red wines are made from the primitivo grape, which seem to have come straight from ancient Greece. The ordinary Primitivo contains a very little residual sugar and 14% alcohol. In Apulia it is served at the table with heavy meat dishes or with pungent pecorino.

The dolce naturale is considerably sweeter and contains a minimum of 16% alcohol. Like the liquoroso dolce naturale (even sweeter, minimum 17.5% alcohol) and the liquoroso secco (a little residual sugar, minimum 18% alcohol), the dolce naturale goes with cakes and pastries and less sweet desserts. The liquoroso secco, on the other hand, can be served with sweeter desserts and with pungent sheep's cheeses. Drinking temperature: 10–16 °C (50–61 °F) for the secco and ordinary Primitivo, 6–12 °C (43–54 °F) for the dolce and liquoroso dolce.

SQUINZANO DOC

This rosato and rosso are made between Brindisi and Lecce. Malvasia Nera and Sangiovese are used as base grapes.

The rosato is a delicious, full, warm wine (minimum 12.5% alcohol) with a sappy and very civilized flavor. Excellent with grilled sea fish or crustaceans, but also with a succulent leg of lamb cooked in the oven. Drinking temperature: 10–12 °C (50–54 °F).

The rosso is also a full-bodied, robust wine with a minimum of 12.5% alcohol. The better wines (riserva) have undergone two years maturing and contain a minimum of 13% alcohol. Drink these wonderful musclemen with roast or grilled meat or with a pungent sheep's cheese. Drinking temperature: 14–17 °C (57–63 °F).

SALICE SALENTINO DOC

Although only the rosso and rosato Salice Salentino are well known outside Italy, they also make several very pleasant white wines and excellent sweet red wines here.

Salice Salentino rosso riserva

Copertino

The bianco (chardonnay) and pinot bianco (possibly supplemented with chardonnay and sauvignon) are fruity, fresh and lively. Some of the young wines have a passionate touch of fizziness in their youth. The flavor is smooth and friendly. Serve them as aperitifs or with sea fish and crustaceans. Drinking temperature: 10–12 °C (50–54 °F). A reasonable spumante is also produced from pinot bianco.

The rosato is fruity and fresh, dry and smooth, with an occasional slight fizziness in its youth. There is also a rosato spumante version. Drink this cheerful rosato with crustaceans, vegetable dishes and leg of lamb cooked in the oven. Drinking temperature: 10–12 °C (50–54 °F).

The rosso is very distinctive, robust, smooth, warm, full and rounded. The better wines are extra matured for at least two years and contain just that little bit more alcohol. Drink these sturdy dry red wines with oven dishes, vegetables *au gratin* or grilled, fried or roast lamb. Drinking temperature: 15–17 °C (59–63 °F).

ALEZIO DOC

Wonderful dry, full-bodied, warm rosso made from negroamaro, malvasia nera, sangiovese and montepulciano. Drink these succulent, slightly bitter, tannin-rich red wines with grilled red meat. Drinking temperature: 14–16 °C (57–61 °F), 16–17 °C (61–63 °F) for the excellent riserva.

Smooth, coral red rosato made from the same grapes as the rosso. A great rosé with a pleasant freshness and a semi-full body. This wine has a characteristic bitterish undertone. Drink it with grilled sea fish, squid or vegetable dishes *au gratin*. Drinking temperature: 10–12 °C (50–54 °F).

COPERTINO DOC

Excellent rosato made from primitivo, montepulciano, sangiovese, negroamaro and malvasia. The wine is smooth, full-bodied and dry, but definitely not too dry. The bouquet and the flavor are very characteristic, fruity and slightly plant-like at the same time, with a pleasant bitterness in the background. Ideal wine for grilled fish or crustaceans. Drinking temperature: 10–12 °C (50–54 °F).

The rosso is ruby red in color, dry, full-bodied, rounded, sappy and velvety smooth. The riserva is at least two years old and contains a minimum of 12.5% alcohol. Excellent wine with braised red meat, lamb or mature sheep's cheeses. Drinking temperature: 15–16 °C (59–61 °F), riserva 16–17 °C (61–63 °F).

MATINO DOC

First-rate rosato and rosso made from negroamaro, produced in the furthest southeasterly point of the Italian boot (the heel). Drink the rosato with crustaceans, fish, poultry, tender vegetable dishes or succulent lamb. The rosso calls for a casserole or roast meat. Drinking temperature: rosato 10–12 °C (50–54 °F), rosso 14–16 °C (57–61 °F).

Aglianico del Vulture riserva

Aglianico del Vulture

NARDO DOC

This region is near the village of Nardo, in the heel of the boot. Here outstanding wines are made from negroamaro, supplemented with malvasia nera and montepulciano.

The rosato is magnificent in color – somewhere between cherry red and coral – slightly fruity, dry, velvety smooth and seductive, with a slightly bitter undertone. Great wines with crustaceans, fish, poultry or vegetable dishes. Drinking temperature: 10–12 °C (50–54 °F).

The rosso is ruby red in color, intensely aromatic (soft fruit), rounded and full in texture, slightly bitter and rich in tannins. The better wines (riserva) have had two years maturing and contain a minimum of 12.5% alcohol. First-rate wines for pasta dishes with olives and tomato sauce, lamb or not over-pungent sheep's cheeses. Drinking temperature: 15–16 °C (59–61 °F), riserva 16–17 °C (61–63 °F).

BASILICATA

When you leave the heel of the boot you enter Basilicata before you arrive at the toe (Calabria). This area, previously known as Lucania, has only recently come to be called Basilicata again. Basilicata has a uniquely exciting landscape, wild and original, partly determined by the mountainous interior and the short, but magnificent coastline. Basilicata is on the Tyrrhenian (Mediterranean) and Ionian seas and in the west borders on Campania and in the east on Apulia, The entire area is completely dependent on agriculture, wine-growing and green tourism. If you look carefully you will find traces of earlier civilizations in the capital Potenza and the second town Montera. The ancient Greeks and

Romans have left behind a monumental legacy here. They were omnipresent in wine-growing too. The only DOC in the area bears the name of an ancient Greek grape variety, the hellenico, 'Italianized' to aglianico. Local gastronomy is quite rustic. Nutritious combinations of pasta and beans (instead of meat), for example, are often on the menu. Sunday and festive dishes often consist of lamb, and every single part of the lamb is used. By comparison the inhabitants of Basilicata also eat a large number of potatoes as well as the perennial favorite pasta. Vegetables, especially peppers, tomatoes and eggplant, also play an important role here.

AGLIANICO DEL VULTURE DOC

Vulture is the name of a volcanic mountain near Potenza. The soil on the slopes of this ancient volcano is particularly fertile for wine-growing. The location of these vineyards means that the grapes enjoy full sun. If this wine were made anywhere else but in impoverished Basilicata it would without doubt be among the elite of Italian wines: it is a superb wine.

The color varies from ruby to pomegranate red, with orange nuances as it ages. The bouquet is quite subtle and characteristic. The wine tastes full, fresh and powerful when it is young and later somewhat smoother; it is sappy and dry to very slightly sweet. The better wines are kept in the cask for a little longer and contain more alcohol and body. The vecchio has to be at least three years old, the riserva a minimum of five years. Serve this wine with a very special dish of lamb

cooked in the oven. Drinking temperature: 15–16 °C (59–61 °F), riserva 16–17 °C (61–63 °F).

CALABRIA

Calabria is the point or toe of the Italian boot. It is a very

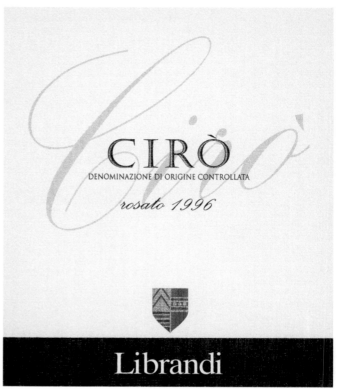

Cirò rosato

wild, but beautiful area of land, surrounded on three sides by sea: the Tyrrhenian (Mediterranean) Sea, the Straits of Messina and the Gulf of Squilace (Ionian Sea). Calabria was at one time the Garden of Eden for the Greeks who were attracted by the beautiful coastal stretch and imposing mountains (Sila). Again it was the ancient Greeks who started wine-growing in Calabria. Though all the famous old wines have disappeared and been forgotten now, in an old, matured Cirò there is still a discernible hint of ancient Greek civilization. As in Greece, sea fish, peppers, eggplants,

Cirò bianco

Cirò rosso riserva

tomatoes, olive oil, olives and garlic predominate. No wonder you come across such wonderful white and rosé wines here. However, it is mainly the red wines that are renowned. As well as the wines described here, Sant'Anna di Isola Capo Rizzuto and San Vito di Luzzi are interesting DOC wines from Calabria.

POLLINO DOC

This small wine-growing region is in northern Calabria. Here a genial ruby red wine is produced that is dry, distinctive and rounded. The superiore version contains slightly more alcohol and has been extra matured for longer (minimum two years). Great wine for lighter meat dishes, oven and vegetable dishes. Drinking temperature: 16 °C (61 °F).

CIRÒ DOC

In the immediate vicinity of the present town of Cirò was the famous ancient Greek temple of Cremista. The fact that this temple was dedicated to Dionysius, the Greek god of wine, indicates how important this place was for the ancient Greeks. The wines of Cremista, the direct ancestors of the Cirò wines, were world famous at that time.

Cirò bianco is made from greco bianco and trebbiano. This wine has always been the lesser sibling of the rosato and the rosso. Yet, in recent years they have been successful in producing very acceptable, fresh, lively white Cirò, ideal with sea fish. Try *pesce spada*, swordfish, preferably grilled, with peppers, tomatoes and garlic, for example. Drinking temperature: 8–10 °C (46–50 °F).

Cirò rosato is made from gaglioppo grapes, possibly supplemented with trebbiano and greco (maximum 5%). This rosato is intense in color, quite smooth in bouquet and dry, full, warm and inviting in flavor. Definitely a rosato for mealtimes (minimum 12.5% alcohol), preferably with fish or seafood pizza, grilled scampi or squid. Drinking temperature: 10–12 °C (50–54 °F).

Cirò rosso is undoubtedly the best wine of the three, maybe the best in Calabria. It is made from the same grapes as the rosato. The basic Cirò (minimum 12.5% alcohol) is dry, sappy, sophisticated, full and warm in flavor. The wines from the heart of the area around the little villages of Cirò and Cirò Marina bear the designation 'classico'. Whether classico or not, a Cirò rosso containing at least 13.5% alcohol is called superiore and the wines that have matured for a minimum of two years are called 'riserva'.

The very best wines are in principle the Cirò rosso classico superiore riserva. Serve these full-bodied, velvety smooth, but sturdy red wines with oven-roasted or grilled meat. Try *abbaccio Calabrese*, a divine casserole of lamb, potatoes, onions, olives and herbs. Drinking temperature: basic wine 16 °C (61 °F), the better and older classico superiore and riserva 16–18 °C (61–64 °F).

LAMEZIA DOC

Reasonable bianco made from greco, trebbiano and malvasia and an outstanding greco bianco that is dry, fresh, smooth and full-bodied. Great wine with sea fish or with the many kinds of fish pizza you can try here. I recommend *pizza Calabrese con tonno*, a wonderful pizza with tuna and anchovies. Drinking temperature: 8–10 °C (46–50 °F), (Greco 10–12 °C (50–54 °F)). There is also a smooth, dry, easy-going rosato that gets on well with anything that comes from the sea. Drinking temperature: 10–12 °C

The rosso is dry, full-bodied, warm, round and fruity. The varieties of grapes used include nerello mascalese, nerello cappucio and marigliana – in other words not your average grapes – that make a very acceptable wine. Look out for the excellent riserva quality, with a minimum of three years maturing, including at least six months in wooden casks. Wonderful with the local casseroles of potatoes, pork, peppers and tomatoes. Drinking temperature: 16 °C (61 °F), riserva 17 °C (63 °F).

MELISSA DOC

Reasonable bianco made from greco, trebbiano and malvasia. Great as an aperitif or with light fish dishes. Drinking temperature: 8–10 °C (46–50 °F).

Excellent rosso made from gaglioppo, greco nero, greco bianco, trebbiano and malvasia. Full-bodied, rounded, warm dry red wine that calls for a tasty joint of roast meat. The 'superiore' has to be at least two years old and contain a minimum of 13% alcohol. Try *abbaccio al forno*, leg of lamb cooked in the oven. Drinking temperature: 16–17 °C (61–63 °F).

DONNICI DOC

Another excellent rosso from mid Calabria. This is produced from gaglioppo, montonico nero and greco nero, sometimes 'softened' by adding the white grapes malvasia, montonico bianco and pecorello. A full-bodied rosato is also made from the same grapes. Both wines are fresh, full, round, and smooth. Serve this rosato with grilled delicacies from the sea and the rosso with casseroles. Drinking temperature: rosato 10–12 °C (50–54 °F), rosso 16 °C (61 °F).

SAVUTO DOC

Dry, full–bodied, characteristic rosato and rosso with an abundant history. Gaglioppo, greco nero, nerello, capuccio, magliocco, canino and sangiovese are used for today's wines. Very interesting and original wines which go well with the local cuisine. Preferably go for a superiore (minimum two years old and at least 12.5% alcohol). Ideal wines for the many oven dishes, including pasta (lasagne), meat, tomatoes and onions. Drinking temperature: rosato 10–12 °C (50–54 °F), rosso 16 °C (61 °F).

SANTA ANASTASIA
Sicilia
INDICAZIONE GEOGRAFICA TIPICA
Bianco

ABBAZIA SANTA ANASTASIA
PRODOTTO E IMBOTTIGLIATO
DALLA AZIENDA AGRICOLA L.E.N.A. S.R.L.
CASTELBUONO · ITALIA

750 ml ℮   ITALIA

**Sicily also produces excellent
white wines**

SCAVIGNA DOC

A fresh, fruity, seductive bianco made from trebbiano, greco and malvasia. The flavor is dry, full and smooth. Excellent aperitif! Drinking temperature: 8–10 °C (46–50 °F).

The rosato is dry, fresh, lively and elegant. This wine not only likes fish and other sea delicacies, but also chicken and even young lamb. Drinking temperature: 10–12 °C (50–54 °F).

They also produce a rather cheeky, full-bodied, dry rosso from galioppo and nerello cappucio. Drink this wine with heavier oven-baked pasta dishes. Drinking temperature: 16–17 °C (61–63 °F).

VERBICARO DOC

The bianco is made from greco, malvasia and guarnaccia bianca. It is an easy-going, fresh, dry white wine without any pretensions. Good as an aperitif or as a simple thirst-quencher during a summer meal. Drinking temperature: 8–10 °C (46–50 °F).

The rosato is dry, elegant, fresh and harmonious. This wine also prefers to remain in the background from genuine modesty. Great with most pizzas. Drinking temperature: 10–12 °C (50–54 °F).

The rosso is made from galioppo (guarnaccia nera) and greco nero, possibly supplemented with some white

1998

ZURRICA
Sicilia
INDICAZIONE GEOGRAFICA TIPICA
Bianco

ABBAZIA SANTA ANASTASIA
PRODOTTO E IMBOTTIGLIATO
DALLA AZIENDA AGRICOLA L.E.N.A S.R.L.
CASTELBUONO · ITALIA

750 ml ℮   12,5% vol. ITALIA

White wine in which you can still taste the soil

grapes. This ruby red wine is slightly aromatic, dry, smooth and round. The better wines (riserva) are matured for at least three years and contain a minimum of 12.5% alcohol. Ideal wines for most oven dishes of pasta and vegetables. Drinking temperature: 15–16 °C (59–61 °F), riserva 16–17 °C (61–63 °F).

IGT wine made from the native Insolia grape

IGT wine made from the native Nero d'Avola grape

GRECO DI BIANCO DOC

This is the southernmost wine-growing region on the Italian mainland. It is situated near Reggio Calabria, in the toe of the boot. A superb straw-colored to golden yellow white wine with an aromatic and distinctive bouquet and a smooth, warm (minimum 17% alcohol) and slightly bitter flavor is made here from greco bianco. Traditionally this wine is served with sweet desserts. Drinking temperature: 10–12 °C (50–54 °F), slightly colder is all right, but preferably not warmer.

SICILY

The triangular-shaped island of Sicily is the largest province in Italy and also the largest island in the Mediterranean. Almost all the peoples who ever had anything to do with the Mediterranean have left traces on Sicily: from Phoenicians to Cretans, from Arabs to Vikings. Sicily's relief is influenced totally by the sea and the volcanoes. More than 80% of the surface area consists of mountains, usually of volcanic origin. Some of the volcanoes are still active. Sicily is also a land of contrasts: cosseted tourists can ski on the highest mountains in the morning and in the afternoon happily lie on one of the many beaches enjoying the sun and the warm sea. Life on the island reminds you instantly of southern Italy, the weather and the landscape, though, more of the north African coast.

Sicily is the largest wine-producing province in Italy, but the inhabitants themselves drink less wine than in many other parts of Italy. So Sicilian wine-growing is largely dependent on the export market. Neither money nor effort have been spared in recent years to expand this export market. Wine-growing on the island has undergone huge changes in recent decades. The full-bodied, sultry, sweet Muscat and Marsala – which were once the pride of the island – have, if possible, been further improved, while more and more new, modern wines have come on to the market. As well as the famous DOC wines they also produce a large quantity of excellent Indicazione Geografiche Tipiche and vini da tavola.

The Sicilians have inherited the cultural and gastronomic baggage of all the people who have ever visited the island. Some, like the Greeks and the Arabs, stayed longer, and they have left more obvious traces than other civilizations. From a culinary point of view Sicily is a veritable paradise for those who like original, natural, fresh, rustic cooking: pasta, pizza, fish, lamb, olive oil, olives, citrus fruits, Mediterranean vegetables and, not to be forgotten, cakes, sorbets and cassatas!

Etna rosso

FARO DOC

Small wine-growing region near Messina, in the north east of the island that produces good red wines from nerello, nocera and sometimes calabrese, gaglioppo and sangiovese. Serve these dry, semi-full-bodied red wines with vegetable or pasta dishes. Drinking temperature: 14–16 °C (57–61 °F).

MALVASIA DELLE LIPARI DOC

This is one of the many Malvasia wines made on the main island or on the smaller Aeolian Islands. This golden-yellow Malvasia from the island of Le Lipari (off the coast of Messina) is very aromatic. It can be made in several ways: entirely from fresh grapes (malvasia), partly from dried grapes (passito), entirely from dried grapes (liquroso) or even pressed with a small amount of currants. The ordinary Malvasia contains a minimum of 1.5% (sic- translator) alcohol, the passito a minimum of 18% and the liquoroso a minimum of 20%. All the wines should be served after meals with less sweet desserts. Drinking temperature: according to taste 10–12 °C (50–54 °F) for the least sweet, 16–18 °C (61–64 °F) or 6–8 °C (43–46 °F) according to taste for the sweeter and heavier versions.

ETNA DOC

Reasonable white, red and rosé wines are produced on the fertile slopes of Etna above the town of Catania.

The bianco and bianco superiore are made from carricante and cataratto bianco, possibly supplemented with trebbiano and minella bianca. Serve these dry, fresh, light, smooth wines as aperitifs or with fish. Drinking temperature: 8–10 °C (46–50 °F).

The rosato and rosso are made from nerello (mascalese and mantellato/capuccio). Both wines are dry, full-bodied, warm (minimum 12.5% alcohol), substantial in texture and quite pungent in flavor. Serve the rosato with *peperoni imbottiti* (stuffed peppers), for example, and the rosso with *palpettone*, the famous Sicilian herbed meatballs. Drinking temperature: rosato 12 °C (54 °F), rosso 16 °C (61 °F).

CERASUOLO DI VITTORIA DOC

Fairly small wine-growing region in the hinterland of Catania. This ruby red wine is made from frappato, calabrese and possibly grosso nero and nerello. The bouquet is full, elegant and a touch herby. The flavor is full, round, warm (minimum 13% alcohol) and dry. Excellent wine with grilled lamb *abbaccio al forno*. Drinking temperature: 16–17 °C (61–63 °F).

ELORO DOC

This wine-growing region is in the southeast of the island, near Syracuse. Six types of wine are produced here:
– a rosato, the color of which inclines towards 'partridge's eye' (gray/orange/pink) and the bouquet is very fruity. The flavor is fruity, fresh and smooth. Great wine with fish and/or seafood pizza. Drinking temperature: 10–12 °C (50–54 °F);
– the rosso is quite rustic, dry and pungent and often contains a fairly large amount of tannins. Serve this

distinctive wine with a bitter undertone with fried or grilled fish. Drinking temperature: 16 °C (61 °F);

– Nero d'Avola is a genial red wine without too many pretensions. Great with pasta dishes with meat sauce. Drinking temperature: 14–16 °C (57–61 °F);

– Frappato has a little more to offer, certainly as regards bouquet. Nice wine for everyday pasta. Drinking temperature: 14–16 °C (57–61 °F);

– Pignatello is a fast seducer, but brings little culinary pleasure. Drink this easy-going red wine with vegetable dishes or with lunch in the country. Drinking temperature: 14 °C (57 °F);

– the Pachino is without doubt the best of all the Eloro wines. The color varies from intense pomegranate red to ruby red with glints of orange-brown. The bouquet is full and very exciting, fruity with a slight touch of animal at the same time. The flavor is full, intense, robust, warm and slightly mischievous. Do go for the outstanding riserva (minimum two years old, including six months in the wood, minimum 12 % alcohol). Definitely a wine for better joints of beef or lamb. Drinking temperature: 16 °C (61 °F), riserva 17 °C (63 °F).

MOSCATO DI NOTO DOC

This wine was already very famous in Roman times, under the name of Pollio. It is produced in the area around Syracuse, in the south east of the island.

The Moscato naturale (minimum 11.5% alcohol) smells intensely of freshly picked muscat grapes and this is also reflected in the flavor. Great wine for not oversweet or complicated desserts. Drinking temperature: 8–10 °C (46–50 °F). (Some people prefer it at room temperature to be able to enjoy the full muscat aroma and flavor, but you then lose some of the elegance and freshness of the wine. It's up to you).

The Moscato spumante (minimum 13% alcohol) is a full-bodied, sultry sparkling wine with a stunning aromatic strength. A wine like this leaves no one unmoved! Drink it after meals, purely for pleasure. Drinking temperature: 8–10 °C (46–50 °F).

The Moscato liquoroso (minimum 22% alcohol) is a fortified wine. It combines the sweet, fruity strength of the Muscat grapes with the warmth and roundness of alcohol. Drink this velvety wine on its own after meals. Drinking temperature: 6–8 °C (43–46 °F).

MOSCATO DI SIRACUSA DOC

Another scion of the Moscato family: seductive, very aromatic, full and elegant – particularly pleasant, but deceptive, as it contains a minimum of 16.5% alcohol! This Moscato is often drunk in combination with sweet desserts, sometimes even with ice-cream. This is actually a crime, as this wine tastes much better drunk in small sips and without accompaniment. Drinking temperature: 6–8 °C (43–46 °F).

MENFI DOC

The wine-growing region of Menfi is near Agrigento. Excellent wines are produced here.

The bianco (insolia, ansonica, grecanico, chardonnay, cataratto bianco, lucido) is light straw-colored with a hint of green. The bouquet and flavor of this southern wine are of a surprising freshness that goes well with fish dishes. Drinking temperature: 8–10 °C (46–50 °F).

The Chardonnay is round, full and pleasant, fruity and smooth. Tasty rather than exciting. Great with sea fish. Drinking temperature: 10–12 °C (50–54 °F).

The Grecanico, though, is an exciting, original wine. It is light yellow in color with a hint of green, fresh, fruity, elegant and inviting. A typical wine for substantial kinds of fish, such as swordfish, *pesce spada*. Drinking temperature: 10–12 °C (50–54 °F).

The Insolia and Ansonica are also fresh, elegant wines that go well with sea fish. Drinking temperature: 10–12 °C (50–54 °F).

The Feudo dei Fiori (insolia, ansonica and chardonnay) is an excellent, fresh, subtle white wine

Moscato di Pantelleria

that is good in combination with fish dishes that are not too heavy. Drinking temperature: 10–12 °C (50–54 °F).

The Bonera and Bonera riserva are both made from nero d'avola, sangiovese, frappato di vittoria and cabernet sauvignon. They are full-bodied, dry wines, fairly rich in tannins, with a lot of character. The Bonera is still quite fruity, while the riserva is rather fuller and warmer (minimum 13% alcohol and at least two years old, including a minimum of one year in the wood). Drink these robust wines with *farsu magru*, beef or veal roulades, stuffed with minced meat, cheese, vegetables and hard-boiled eggs, for example. Drinking temperature: 16–17 °C (61–63 °F).

SAMBUCA DI SICILIA DOC

This is not the famous star aniseed drink Sambuca, but the wine region around the village of Sambuca di Sicilia, near Agrigento.

The bianco (ansonica/insolia, catarratto bianco lucido and chardonnay) is a delicate, fresh wine that soon becomes acquainted with any kind of fish. Drinking temperature: 8–10 °C (46–50 °F).

The Chardonnay is well made, but has little individuality to offer. Good as an aperitif and a great accompaniment to fish and white meat. Drinking temperature: 10–12 °C (50–54 °F).

The rosato, made from nero d'avola/calabrese, nerello, sangiovese and cabernet sauvignon, is fresh, fruity and smooth. Delicious with dishes based on vegetables, such as *caponata* (includes eggplant) and *peperonata* (includes peppers, tomatoes, onions and olives). Drinking temperature: 10–12 °C (50–54 °F).

The rosso and rosso riserva are very intense in bouquet, distinctive, round, full-bodied and smooth. The ordinary rosso has to mature for at least an extra six months, the riserva for at least a year, including six months in the wood. First-rate accompaniments to pasta dishes with meat sauce. Drinking temperature: 15–17 °C (59–63 °F).

Bianco Alcamo

The Cabernet Sauvignon is excellent and slightly less subdued than its big brothers from Bordeaux. Serve this dry, full-bodied, rounded wine with grilled beef or lamb. Drinking temperature: 16 °C (61 °F).

MOSCATO DI PANTELLERIA DOC

Pantelleria is one of the many islands off the coast of Sicily and is near Trapani. Two very surprising wines are produced here that seem to come straight from the time of the ancient Greeks. Both wines have the native Zibibbo Muscat grape as their base.

The Moscato naturale (minimum 12.5% alcohol) is typically Moscato in bouquet and flavor. Partially dried grapes are used for the Moscato vino naturalmente dolce, which increases the alcohol content to a minimum of 17.5%. There is also a divine spumante and a liquoroso. Serve all these Moscato wines with not over-sweet desserts, or on their own after

a meal. Drinking temperature: 6–12 °C (43–54 °F) (the sweeter, the colder).

The passito is made entirely from partially dried grapes. This is a very sensual Moscato with a great deal of strength, sultry fruitiness and warmth (minimum 14% alcohol). There is also an even sweeter liquoroso version with a minimum of 21.5% alcohol. The very best wines are given the designation 'extra'. Then, as well as possessing outstanding quality and finesse, they must contain at least 23.9% alcohol! Drink the passito and passito liquoroso – whether or not 'extra' – after meals, without accompaniment. Drinking temperature: passito 8–10 °C (46–50 °F), liquoroso 6–8 °C (43–46 °F). (Some people prefer them at room temperature. This gives them an even fuller bouquet and flavor, but the wines lose any kind of freshness and become quite ponderous.)

CONTESSA ENTELLINA DOC

Wine-growing region near Palermo, in the northwest of the island. Dry, fresh, elegant and distinctive white wines are made here from ansonica, catarratto bianco lucido, grecanico, chardonnay, sauvignon blanc and müller-thurgau. The better wines, though, are those made from one dominant grape variety, especially those made from sauvignon blanc, chardonnay and grecanico. These three wines are good in combination both with traditional and modern dishes. Drinking temperature: 8–12 °C (46–54 °F).

Marsala

ALCAMO/BIANCO ALCAMO DOC

Definitely the best known white wine on the island. Alcamo comes from the area between Trapani and Palermo in the northwestern part of Sicily. The wine is made from catarratto bianco (Commune/Lucido), possibly supplemented with damaschino, grecanico and trebbiano. The color is light yellow with a hint of green and the bouquet quite neutral. The flavor, on the other hand, is fresh, sappy, extremely fruity and smooth. This is a very good wine for the better kinds of fish, but is also good in combination with simpler pasta dishes. Try *lumaconi con le sarde*, large variety of pasta with a sauce of fresh sardines, fennel, pine nuts, raisins and anchovies. Drinking temperature: 10–12 °C (50–54 °F).

MARSALA DOC

Without doubt the oldest and best known fortified wine in Sicily and probably the most English. The Englishman John Woodhouse, who was the first to ship

TURRIGA®

ISOLA DEI NURAGHI

Indicazione Geografica Tipica

IMBOTTIGLIATO DA ARGIOLAS & C s.p.a. - SERDIANA - ITALIA

750 ML ℮ - ITALIA - 12,5% VOL

La Grande Madre—museo archeologico di Cagliari

The distant past is still alive and well in Sicily

this liqueur wine to England, was the man behind the success story of this famous wine. Another Englishman, Benjamin Ingham, was the first to apply the solera system (known from sherry wines) to Marsala wines. For Marsala you need must from grillo, catarratto, pignatello, calabrese, nerello, damaschino, insolia and nero d'avola, which is distilled with pure wine alcohol to stop the fermentation prematurely and retain the fruit of the must in the wine. The following types exist:

– Marsala fine: minimum one year old, minimum 17% alcohol
– Marsala superiore: minimum two years old, minimum 18% alcohol
– Marsala superiore riserva: minimum four years old, minimum 18% alcohol
– Marsala vergine/Solera: minimum five years old, minimum 18% alcohol
– Marsala vergine/Solera stravecchio/Solera riserva: minimum ten years old, minimum 18% alcohol.

The color of the product is also put on the label:
Oro: golden-yellow
Ambra: amber-yellow to amber-gold
Rubino: ruby red, obtained from black grapes.

The degree of sweetness is also meticulously indicated by the familiar terms secco, semi-secco and dolce.

Every type of Marsala has its own character, color, bouquet and flavor, depending on the original grapes, the sugar content of the must, the amount of wine alcohol added and the length of maturing. You can serve a dry Marsala as a civilized aperitif or with mature cheeses, the slightly sweet with less sweet cakes and

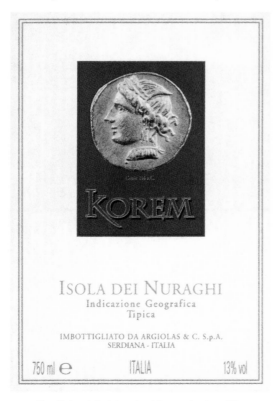

KOREM

ISOLA DEI NURAGHI
Indicazione Geografica
Tipica

IMBOTTIGLIATO DA ARGIOLAS & C. S.p.A.
SERDIANA - ITALIA

750 ml ℮   ITALIA   13% vol

Sardinian label inspired by ancient motifs

Canonau (VCR)

pastries and desserts (for example based on ricotta), the very sweet with fritters and other deep-fried tidbits and the riserva on its own after meals. Drinking temperature: depending on the type and accompaniment 8–18 °C (46–64 °F), according to taste.

You can also buy 'Marsala speciale', which are certainly not among the best wines and have been flavored with eggs, cream, coffee, vanilla and so on. Buy them by all means if you like them, but these are a far cry from Woodhouse's noble drinks!

SARDINIA

Sardinia too is an island of contrasts: a gentle coastline and rugged, steep mountains, very touristy spots and wild, untamed nature. Sardinia, the next largest island

Monica di Sardegna

in the Mediterranean after Sicily, has also been visited by countless civilizations during its long history: Phoenicians, Carthaginians, Greeks, Romans and Spaniards have left their traces in Sardinia. These visitors brought the vine with them. After many centuries, at last a certain balance has been found in Sardinia between the sweet wines praised by the Greeks and Romans and the lighter wines which better suit the tastes of today's wine drinkers. Wine-growing is concentrated at the foot of the mountains, in the valleys and on the flat areas by the coast, where most of the people live. Sardinian cuisine is united in its simplicity: fish, crustaceans, shellfish, grilled pork, goat and lamb, pasta and, of course,

Vermentino di Sardegna

sheep's cheese, such as pecorino. Simple, fresh and exceptionally delicious!

VERMENTINO DI GALLURA DOCG

This Vermentino is produced in the north of the island. It is more subtle and finer than the ordinary Vermentino di Sardegna and is always dry and fresh. Generally this Vermentino also contains more alcohol, especially the 'superiore', which has to contain a minimum of 14%! Ideal with grilled fish dishes. Try *tonno/pesce spada alla griglia*, barbecued tuna or swordfish. Drinking temperature: 10–12 °C (50–54 °F).

CANONAU DI SARDEGNA DOC

The canonau (alicante) grape was brought to the island by the Spanish. Canonau di Sardegna is produced in the southeastern quarter of the island. You may well find the following local additions on the label: 'Oliena', 'Nepente di Oliena' (area around Nuoro), 'Capo Ferrato' (area around Cagliari) and 'Jerzu' (between Nuoro and Cagliari). This ruby red wine is a dry or slightly sweet rosato or rosso with a pleasant, sappy, warm flavor (minimum 12.5% alcohol) all of its own. The riserva in fact contains a minimum of 13% alcohol and has had at least two years maturing. There are also a liquoroso secco with 18% alcohol and a liquoroso dolce naturale with 16% alcohol. Drink the liquoroso secco as an aperitif or with cakes, the rosato with sea fish and seafood, the rosso with grilled lamb and the liquoroso dolce naturale with desserts or after meals. Drinking temperature: liquoroso secco 10–12 °C

(50–54 °F), liquoroso dolce naturale 6–8 °C (43–46 °F) or 14–18 °C (57–64 °F), rosato 10–12 °C (50–54 °F), rosso 16 °C (61 °F) and rosso riserva 17 °C (63 °F).

MONICA DI SARDEGNA DOC

This is a series of wines made from the monica grape, sometimes supplemented with white grapes. Monica di Sardegna is made all over the island. It is an exciting, sappy, seductive ruby red wine, dry or slightly sweet, which is also produced as frizzante naturale and as secco superiore (minimum 12.5% alcohol). Serve the dry version with nutritious vegetables and bean dishes, such as *favata* (a dish of garden beans and pork), and the slightly sweet one with desserts. Drinking temperature: secco superiore 14–17 °C (57–63 °F), slightly sweet 10–14 °C (50–57 °F).

MOSCATO DI SARDEGNA DOC

This beautiful straw-colored Moscato is very aromatic, sophisticated and sensual. The flavor is sweet, elegant and very fruity. Great accompaniment to fresh fruit desserts. In the north of the country you may also come across local additions on the label: 'Tempio Pausania', 'Tempio' or 'Gallura'. Drinking temperature: 8–10 °C (46–50 °F).

VERMENTINO DI SARDEGNA DOC

Straw-colored white wine with a hint of green. The bouquet is soft and subtle, elegant rather than full-bodied, and the flavor is fresh, sappy, dry to slightly sweet, with a touch of bitterness in the aftertaste. There is also

Nuragus di Cagliari

an elegant spumante, which makes a good aperitif. Serve the ordinary Vermentino with sea fish. Try *cassola*, a main course soup of various kinds of sea fish. Drinking temperature: 8–10 °C (46–50 °F).

MALVASIA DI CAGLIARI DOC

These Malvasia wines come from the area around Cagliari. The Malvasia secco (dry) and the Malvasia dolce naturale are full-bodied, warm wines (minimum 14% alcohol), aromatic and sophisticated, with a bitter undertone and a hint of burnt almonds. Traditionally these wines are served at the end of the meal. Drinking temperature: secco 10–12 °C (50–54 °F), dolce 8–10 °C (46–50 °F).

The Malvasia liquoroso secco (dry) and the Malvasia liquoroso dolce naturale are high quality fortified wines, especially the riserva wines which have been matured for more than two years. These aromatic wines contain a minimum of 17.5% alcohol and should be served with dessert. Drinking temperature: 10–12 °C (50–54 °F), dolce 8–10 °C (46–50 °F).

MONICA DI CAGLIARI DOC

This wine made from monica comes in the following types:
– Monica secco (dry) and Monica dolce naturale are ruby red, aromatic and sultry with a full, smooth, seductive flavor. The secco contains at least 14% alcohol, the dolce 14.5%. Serve them at the end of the meal, with pungent sheep's cheese, for example. Drinking temperature: secco 14–18 °C (57–64 °F), dolce 10–12 °C (50–54 °F);
– Monica liquoroso secco (dry) and Monica liquoroso dolce naturale are even more powerful and fuller in flavor and contain at least 17.5% alcohol. If possible buy the excellent riserva (matured for at least two years). Serve them at the end of the meal. Drinking temperature: secco 14–18 °C (57–64 °F), dolce 6–12 °C (43–54 °F).

MOSCATO DI CAGLIARI DOC

Outstanding Moscato, very aromatic and powerful. Available as dolce naturale and the heavier liquoroso dolce naturale. Serve them with sophisticated fruit desserts. Drinking temperature: 6–12 °C (43–54 °F), according to taste.

NASCO DI CAGLIARI DOC

Dry (secco), sweet (dolce naturale), sometimes fortified (liquoroso secco/dry or liquoroso dolce naturale) white wines made from the nasco grape. Outstanding quality, especially the riservas. Drink the dry versions as aperitifs, the sweet with dessert. Drinking temperature: secco 10–12 °C (50–54 °F), dolce 6–10 °C (43–50 °F).

NURAGUS DI CAGLIARI DOC

The nuragus is a very old Sardinian grape variety, probably brought to the island by the Phoenicians. At one time this grape was to be found all over the island. Today wines are made from nuragus only in the south of the island, between Cagliari and Nuoro. These wines are straw-colored with glints of green. The bouquet of these easy to drink, dry to slightly sweet wines is subtle and inviting and the flavor fresh and pleasant. Serve the dry wines as aperitifs or with fish dishes, the slightly sweet ones with fresh desserts or creamy fresh cheeses. There is also a frizzante naturale made from this grape. Drinking temperature: dry 10–12 °C (50–54 °F), slightly sweet 8–10 °C (46–50 °F).

GIRO DI CAGLIARI DOC

These sturdy red wines made from giro come in secco/dry (minimum 14% alcohol) and dolce naturale (minimum 14.5%). Both wines are sultry, extremely aromatic (freshly picked sweet grapes), full-bodied, velvety smooth and warm. Drink the secco with heavier meat dishes and pungent cheeses, the dolce naturale with desserts. Drinking temperature: secco 16 °C (61 °F), dolce naturale 10–12 °C (50–54 °F).

There is also a far more full-bodied liquoroso version of both the secco/dry and the dolce naturale. Serve these wines (minimum 17.5% alcohol) with better desserts. Drinking temperature: secco 16–18 °C (61–64 °F), dolce 10–12 °C (50–54 °F).

CARIGNANO DEL SULCIS DOC

Carignano was also introduced to the island by the Spanish. Today it is used almost exclusively in the area of Cagliari. The rosato is dry, fresh and smooth and can be served with anything. There is also a frizzante. Drinking temperature: 10–12 °C (50–54 °F).

The ruby red rosso is not so pronounced in bouquet, but still delicious, dry, sappy and smooth in flavor. Choose a riserva (minimum 12.5% alcohol and three years maturing). Excellent wines for herby vegetable dishes and grilled pork. The riserva is delicious with *manzo alla Sarda*, spicy beef fillet. Drinking temperature: 16–18 °C (61–64 °F).

MALVASIA DI BOSA DOC

Very pleasant dry (secco), sweet (dolce naturale) or fortified (liquoroso secco/liquoroso dolce naturale) white wines made from the malvasia grape. Drink these wines with better desserts or with pungent cheeses. Drinking temperature: secco 10–12 °C (50–54 °F), dolce 8–10 °C (46–50 °F).

MANDROLISAI DOC

This exciting wine is produced between Nuoro and Oristano. Bovale Sardo, Cannonau and Monica are used as base grapes. The rosato is dry and sappy, full-bodied and harmonious, fresh and smooth, with a slight

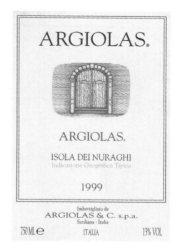

Insola dei Nuraghi IGT   Insola dei Nuraghi IGT

bitterness in the aftertaste. Good with grilled fish (tuna or swordfish) or with squid. Drinking temperature: 10–12 °C (50–54 °F).

The rosso is fairly unobtrusive, fresh, smooth, dry and sappy, also with a slight bitterness in the aftertaste. The better wines (superiore) are matured for two years and contain a minimum of 12.5% alcohol.

VERNACCIA DI ORISTANO DOC

This Vernaccia is a golden-yellow wine with an intensely aromatic bouquet (almond, white flowers) and a warm (minimum 15% alcohol), full, sultry and seductive flavor with nuances of bitter almonds. The superiore and riserva (15.5% alcohol) are fuller and have been matured for longer (three and four years respectively). There are also a liquoroso dolce (16.5% alcohol) and a liquoroso secco/dry (18%), both made from must distilled with wine alcohol. Drink the secco possibly as an aperitif or, like all the dolce versions, with a good dessert or a piece of (dry) cake. Drinking temperature: secco 10–12 °C (50–54 °F), dolce 8–12 °C (46–54 °F).

Fantastic vendemmia tardiva

SARDEGNA SEMIDANO DOC

This white wine is made almost everywhere in the western half of the island. The base grape Semidano produces a straw color with glints of gold, a fruity, elegant bouquet and a smooth, sappy, fresh flavor. If it has a minimum of 13% alcohol this wine can be called superiore. Excellent wines with sea fish. Drinking temperature: 10–12 °C (50–54 °F). A delicious spumante and an excellent passito are made from the same grape.

ARBOREA DOC

Around Oristano three types of wine are produced:
- Trebbiano, a greenish yellow wine with a fairly modest bouquet but an excellent, full, fresh flavor.

This wine vinified into a secco goes very well with sea fish and crustaceans. Try *aragosta arrosta*, grilled lobster. The slightly sweet abboccato goes better with fresh fruit salads or creamy desserts based on soft cheese (mascarpone). Drinking temperature: secco 10–12 °C (50–54 °F), abboccato 8–10 °C (46–50 °F). There is also a delicious Trebbiano frizzante naturale, available in secco and abboccato;
— the Sangiovese rosato is a beautiful cherry red color, inviting but fairly modest in bouquet and dry, sappy and fresh in flavor. Great wine with grilled squid or sea fish and with pasta or vegetable dishes. Drinking temperature: 10–12 °C (50–54 °F);
— the Sangiovese rosso is friendly, dry but soft, rounded and fresh. You can serve this all-rounder with pasta dishes or with zucchini, *melanzane* (eggplant) or *peperoni* (peppers) stuffed with herbed minced meat. Drinking temperature: 16–17 °C (61–63 °F).

ALGHERO DOC

Countless different wines are made in the northwest of the island. The frizzante bianco secco, spumante bianco secco, Torbato spumante secco, Chardonnay spumante secco and Vermentino frizzante are first-rate aperitifs, but also make frivolous companions to seafood. Serve the abboccato or dolce with all kinds of different desserts. Drinking temperature: 8–10 °C (46–50 °F), abboccato/dolce 6–8 °C (43–46 °F).

The still bianco, Chardonnay, Sauvignon and Torbato are great accompaniments to seafood, fish and even white meat. Drinking temperature: 10–12 °C (50–54 °F).

The rosato with its light texture is an ideal wine for lunch or for a quick, uncomplicated meal. Drinking temperature: 10–12 °C (50–54 °F).

The rosso novello, rosso and Sangiovese are friendly red wines that like less heavy dishes: pasta, vegetables or fried young goat's meat or lamb. Drinking temperature: 12–14 °C (54–57 °F).

If you want to give a chic touch to your meal you can serve a rosso spumante secco with the dishes listed above. Drinking temperature: 10–14 °C (50–57 °F).

Save the Cagnulari or the Cabernet (cabernet franc + cabernet sauvignon) for more substantial types of meat. Both wines are very dry and have plenty of tannins. Drinking temperature: 16–17 °C (61–63 °F).

With pungent cheeses or special desserts serve the wonderful honey-like passito or the full-bodied liquoroso. There is also an excellent riserva from the latter wine, which is at least five years old.

OTHER INTERESTING WINES FROM SARDINIA

In the DOCs of Campidano di Terralba and Terralba, and on the island of Nuraghi some very interesting wines are produced, at the moment still under the IGT label, including a fantastic 'vendemmia tardiva' (vendages tardives, Spätlese).

GREECE

If we are to believe the Greeks, they invented both wine and wine-growing and have the vineyards, Dionysos – god of wine – and the sun ... In short the Greeks regard their country as the cradle of all wine-making. Those who study history or have read Chapter One of this book will know that the Greeks most definitely did not invent wine, but in the footsteps of the Phoenicians they did spread it more widely around the Mediterranean. The Greeks also played an important role in the establishment, maintenance, and improvement of countless vineyards from Thrace to Spain by way of Italy, Sicily, and southern France. Every place of civilization around Mediterranean once survived on olive groves and vineyards. That the ancient Greeks were masters in both fields will surprise no-one. The Greeks and before them the people of Crete always were great travelers. Wherever they went they constructed well-defended harbors so they could supply themselves. In order to feed these colonists and the garrison that defended them both olive trees and vines were planted around each of these havens. After the Cretans, the torch of Greek civilization was kept burning by the Spartans and Mycenaeans. At the time of the Trojan War (about 1200 BC) the wines of Thrace and Limnos were already highly respected. You will recall of course the famous story of how Odysseus and his shipmates were held captive by the fearsome Cyclops. Once Odysseus had encouraged the Cyclops to drink large volumes of the strong sweet wine from Thrace the Cyclops fell into a stupor and he and his companions were able to escape. The Greek wines of those times were syrupy, extremely strong, sweet as honey, and exceedingly alcoholic.

The Hellenes gave their name to modern Greece (Ellas). They were excellent traders and feared conquerors. Hellenic towns sprang up all around the Mediterranean, in Sicily, on the present Greek islands, in Italy, and in Turkey. A new wave of trading voyages went out from one of these new towns on the coast of present-day Turkey, called Phocaea. Once more the Greeks created small trading havens, this time on the coast of southern France. In this way they brought their civilization, their olives trees and vines to Massilia – present-day Marseilles –, Nikeia – now Nice – and other towns such as Antibes. In 600 BC the Greeks penetrated inland Gaul along the Rhône, Seine, and Loire. The existing cultivation by the Celtic Gauls of vines was greatly improved. The same happened too in eastern and southern Spain where Greeks established and improved the growing of vines. The best Greek wines of those times came from the islands and from Thrace in the extreme east of present-day Greece. Famous names of those times were Ariousio from Chios and the wines of Lesbos, Thasos, Chalkidiki, Schiathos, Thyra, and Thessalia. Greek power in the Mediterranean region waned following the fall of the immense empire of Alexander the Great and the honor fell to the Romans of carrying forward the development of wine. Greek history after this time was pretty tumultuous.

GREEK WINES

- EOK: wines for the EC, often destined for blending;
- *epitrapezios* table wine – includes all the branded wines, some of which are of exceptional quality;
- *cava*: the best quality table wine, selected with care and matured for at least two years (red three) of which at least one year is in a wooden cask. Wines that fulfill this (usually branded wines) are permitted to ad *cava* to their label. In Greek the word means a special *cuvée* of the cellar master;
- *topikos oinos*: country wines, similar to a French *vins de pays*. Each bottle is coded with the last three numbers representing the year the grapes were harvested;
- *onomasia proelefsios anoteras poiotitos* (OPAP): guarantee of origin status, also known as AOC from the French *appellation contrôlée*;
- *epilegmenos* (*réserve*): used solely for OPAP wines of exceptional quality that have been matured for a minimum of two years (white) or three years (red), of which at least one year must be in a wooden cask;
- *eidaka epilegmenos* (*grande réserve*): even more strictly controlled for quality with minimum maturing of at least three years (white) and four years (red), with a minimum of two years in wooden casks.

After the fall of the Byzantine empire Greece became fairly isolated and was left behind by cultural development occurring in most of Europe. Greece enjoyed no Renaissance but instead was heavily oppressed by the Ottoman occupation. The once renowned wines of Greece fell into decay, with a few exceptions. Only those wines with strong local roots survived the Turkish occupation.

In the late nineteenth century a number of winemakers became established in Naoussa, Attica, and Patras. These producers followed a market-oriented approach and soon dominated the entire Greek wine trade. The Greeks enjoyed a period of boom when the vines of European growers were devastated by *Phylloxera*. Demand quickly arose for healthy red wines such as those of Macedonia, Nemea, and Crete. Once the European crisis began to come under control with the French having grafted their vines onto the root stock of American-type vines, the export market for the Greeks entirely collapsed with enormous economic consequences for the Greek growers who had extensively increased the areas under cultivation. Enormous lakes of excess wine had to be distilled under supervision of the Greek government. The poor economic circumstances rather pushed wine cultivation into a backwater. While almost all the other European wine-producing countries were improving techniques in both the vineyards and wineries the Greeks somewhat vegetated. Only the big producers with their massive brands found a way to survive. The small producers came under enormous pressure. The political instability of the later twentieth century – especially the period of military dictatorship – did not improved the name of the Greek wines. When Greece joined the European Community it was also a difficult time for growers and wine makers. Wages soared and fixed costs went up enormously, forcing the Greeks to significantly raise prices. Since at this same time a great diversity of "new" wines from well-established winegrowing countries (Bulgaria and Romania) and also the wines of the "New World" (South Africa, Chile, Argentina, Australia, and California) won a place for themselves in the market, things became even tougher for Greek wine. The near monopoly position of the major wine houses of Achaia Clauss, Boutaris, Kourtakis, and Tsantalis was increasingly eroded by young independent wine-producers and cooperatives. Only Tsantalis was able to survive with innovation in its marketing strategy and continuing to listen to the customers without allowing quality to slip. The quality of the wines of the smaller independent producers also increased noticeably in the 1990s. The cooperatives got considerable financial help from the Greek government and the European Community. Unfortunately Greek wines are still not well known and their prices are relatively high, making it difficult for the Greeks to break into the market in the rest of Europe. It is anticipated that Greek wine prices will fall, in part because the domestic market has responded well to the improved quality. Efforts are also being made to adapt the image of Greek wine (including the sometimes ponderous labeling) to western norms. Finally efforts are being made on two fronts: increasing numbers of French types of vines are being introduced for Greek export wines while pride is being restored in the better native grapes for the specialty market. The small individual peasant grower with a few vines is disappearing for good from the scene. They are being replaced by a generation of young wine makers who have an eye on quality with a respect for the age-old traditions of Greek wine-making. In short the retsina age appears to now be in the past and a revolution is taking place.

Retsina

GREEK WINE GROWING

Greek wines fall into two market segments: the branded wines and those with the name of their place of origin. Large numbers of just about drinkable wines fall within the branded sector but also some very top quality wines. This is extremely confusing for the European consumer, particularly as some wines with place of origin also appear to be of poor quality. Many Greek wines are already past it by the time they reach European consumers due to either wrong storage or poor transport. The consumer therefore needs considerable knowledge and experience and a great amount of good will. It is therefore best to only buy Greek wines from respected importers who guarantee you good quality.

Greek wine-growing is blessed with an ideal climate for cultivating vines and making wine, especially close to the sea. Many different microclimates, combined with varying local soil conditions such as chalk and rock, and the different varieties of grapes used ensure different characters for the various wines. At present some three hundred different types of grape are grown in Greece. Many of these are of French origin such as sauvignon blanc, chardonnay, cabernet sauvignon, pinot noir, and merlot, but the majority are native and sometimes ancient varieties. The best known of them are assyrtiko (Santorini, Sithonia, Athos), vilana (Heraklion, Crete), robola (Cephalonia), savatiano (Attiki, Beotia, Euboea), Aghiorgitiko (Nemea), xinomavro (Naoussa, amynteon, Goumenissa, Rapsani), mavrodaphne (Achaia, Cephalonia), mandelaria (Paros, Rhodes, Heraklion Crete), moschofilero (Mantinia), muscat (Patras, Samos), and rhoditis (Achaia, Anchialos, Macedonia, Thrace).

RETSINA

Retsina is not a guaranteed origin name but an *apellation traditionelle* or wine with an ancient history and unique character. Retsina in produced in many different wine-growing areas of Greece on the mainland and in the islands. Its origins lie in ancient times when wine was shipped in amphoras sealed with jute cloths soaked in resin. The still fluid pine resin dripped into the wine before becoming hard. This gave the wine its characteristic resinous taste that some liken to turpentine or gasoline...In addition to forming a good seal, the resin proved to have antiseptic properties. No-one became ill from drinking this Retsina – which in those days could not be said of every wine! Modern technology makes the use of resin entirely unnecessary but the Greeks in their tavernas were so wedded to the taste that the resin from local pine trees is still added to the must before fermentation. The resin is removed during clarification but the taste and aroma remain. Most retsina is made in Central Greece with saviatiano and roditis grapes.

The resinous taste of Retsina can vary from slight to strong. Serve the more subtle variety as an aperitif, the stronger ones with *mezedes* starters with plenty of olive oil. Retsina can taste great beneath the Greek sun, with richly stuffed *mezedes*, and the sound of a *bouzouki*

playing...but it is an acquired taste. Drink it at 8–10 °C (46.4–50 °F).

THRACE, MACEDONIA

Thrace (*Thraki*) is in the extreme north-east of Greece, bordering on Bulgaria and Turkey. Thrace, which was once a land of gorgeous, stunningly sweet wines such as those of Thasos, is now something of a backwater. The present vineyards that are mainly planted with vines such as the blue grape mavroudi and pamidi and white zoumiatiko, are principally used for making bulk wine and indifferent table wines. Greek Macedonia is situated to the west of Thrace and borders Bulgaria and the newly independent state of Macedonia. This area also has a long tradition of wine-growing and making. Currently there are four wines with guaranteed origin made here and at least six *oinos topikos* (*vins de pays* or country wines) of excellent quality. Macedonia's vineyards are situated on sunny slopes on the hills inland, along the coast, and on the Chalkidiki peninsula.

AMINDEO OPAP

This is the most northerly wine area of Greece. The climate here is wholly continental and the vineyards are sited at heights of around 2,132 feet. The blue grape varieties of xinomavro and negoska thrive here. Drinking temperature is 14–16 °C (57.2–60.8 °F).

There are both still and sparkling rosé Amindeo wines.

Naoussa

GOUMENISSA OPAP

The growers in Goumenissa, about 50 miles northwest of Thessaloniki, also use the xinomavro and negoska grapes for their local red wines. The vineyards of Goumenissa are sited at about 820 ft high on chalky soil. Goumenissa is a dark red wine with glints of purple. Its nose is reminiscent of ripe fruit such as fig, cherry, and gooseberry, and the well-balanced taste is elegant and smooth, almost caressing in the aftertaste. Serve these red wines with red meat with light sauces of with soft cheeses. Drinking temperature is 16 °C (60.8 °F).

NAOUSSA OPAP

Naoussa is Macedonia's best-known wine. The vineyards are sited on the slopes of the Vermio hills at a height of 492 to 2,132 ft. Naoussa is wholly made from xinomavro grapes. The young wine is aged for at least twelve months in small casks of French oak. The color of the wine is dark red and the nose suggests small fruit like blackcurrant with a hint of spice such as cinnamon and vanilla from the oak. The taste is fulsome, rounded, warm, and rich. This wine is better left for at least two to three years before drinking. The harsh tannin of the young wine is then changed into velvet smooth luxuriance.

Serve these wines with red meat in sauce or well-matured cheese. It is ideal with *stifado* a beef stew. Drinking temperature is 16 °C (60.8 °F).

There are also Reserve and Grand Reserve quality Naoussa wines. These wines are generally cask-aged in French oak for two years. These are deeply-colored red wines with a hint of brown and the nose often exhibits associations with sweet and overripe fruits or even dried fruit such as fig and prune. Oak only plays a modest role in the bouquet and taste, subtle and in the background without dominating. These robust wines contain considerable tannin and need to be laid down for several years. You will then eventually be rewarded with an excellent wine that reaches the level of top

Côtes de Meliton blanc and a superb white Malagousia table wine

French wines. The Naoussa from the house of Tsantali is excellent.

Serve a Naoussa with red meat, game, and strong cheese. Drinking temperature is 17–18 °C (62.6–64.4 °F).

PLAYIES MELITONA/CÔTES DE MELITON OPAP

This nominated origin wine comes from the Chalkidiki peninsula, that lies in the sea like Poseidon's trident. Only two of the 'forks' of the peninsula grow wine. These are Sithonia in the center and Athos to the east.

Excellent red wine from Epanomi

The finest Greek wines came from here from Carras, started in the 1960s by a rich Greek ship owner. Under the watchful eyes of French wine experts, including Prof. Emile Peynaud of Bordeaux, various French and Greek grape varieties were planted on slate and shale soils, such as assyrtiko, athiri, rhoditis, and sauvignon blanc for white wines, and limnio, cabernet sauvignon, cabernet franc, syrah, and cinsault for red wines. Now excellent white, rosé, and red wines are successfully made using a balanced assembly of Greek and French grapes. The greatest wines are made here from vineyards with exceptionally low yields of forty hectoliters per hectare for white wines and as low as thirty hectoliters per hectare for reds. Unfortunately the original business is no longer but the very talented Greek wine expert Gerovassiliou – a student of Prof. Peynad – has in the meantime started his own business. It remains to be seen what happens with the vineyards of Carras. The future of the reds seems to be assured but that of the whites hangs in the balance.

The Côtes de Meliton blanc de blancs (athiri, assyrtiko, and rhoditis) were smooth, light, and dry with a subtle floral bouquet. The Côtes de Meliton Melisanthi (athiri, assyrtiko, and sauvignon blanc) were more fruity (melon and apricot) than the blanc de blancs. The Côtes de Meliton Limnio (limnio, cabernet sauvignon, and cabernet franc) enjoyed maturing for twelve months in wooden casks. These were fine ruby-red in color, elegant, lithe, and a touch spicy. The Côtes de Meliton Chôteau Carras (cabernet franc, cabernet sauvignon, and limnio) were matured for longer.

Constantine Lazaridi Drama wines

These were elegant full-bodied red wines with a fine bouquet and prolonged finish. The Côtes de Meliton Domaines Carras grande réserve (cabernet franc,

cabernet sauvignon, and limnio) remained for at least three years in the cellars of the winery. These were full, exceptionally pleasing wines of elegance and velvety smooth taste with many notes of ripe fruit in both bouquet and taste and with a very long finish. The latter two wines really were wines to lay down for more than ten years without the slightest problem. Carras also produced a superb rosé and two magnificent modern wines: a white Malagousia and red Porphyrogenito. Quite what will happen to these wines and the nominated domain of Côtes de Meliton was entirely unclear as this book went to press.

TOPIKOI OENOI (VINS DE PAYS)

Thrace and Macedonia also have a number of surprisingly good country wines, including Makedonikos, Epanomitikos, the excellent wines of Gerovassiliou, Mesimvriotikos, Agioritikos, and Dramas.

Excellent country wines are made on the border of Thrace and Macedonia by the Lazaridi company. Their equipment is among the most modern in Greece and the vineyards are a text book example of responsible modern viticulture. Lazaridi produce five dry wines under the Amethystos name (white, rosé, red, and fumé) and an outstanding white Chôteau Julia. The white wines are produced from sauvignon, semillon, and assyrtiko, the rosé from cabernet sauvignon and the red from cabernet franc, cabernet sauvignon, merlot, and limnio. Considering the very high quality of these wines, the grapes used, the superb presentation, and the for Greek's pretty high prices, you are far more likely to encounter them in the UK, USA, or Japan than in Greece. Lazaridi proves with these exceptional wines that it is possible to use French grapes without imitating French wines. All Lazaridi's wines have an individual identity and are very aromatic.

IPIROS

Ipiros is not really a wine region but an area of forests and meadows. It does have two exceptional wine enclaves though of which only the first enjoys the recognition of a designated origin.

ZITSA OPAP

Zitsa's vineyards are found to the north of Ipiros, against the Albanian border at a height of about 1,968 feet. Delicious still and sparkling wines are made here from debina grapes. These wines are characterized by their elegance, freshness, and exuberant fruitiness. The sparkling Zitsa is available as semi-

Dry still and medium dry sparkling Zitsa

Dry sparkling Zitsa

Rapsani

sparkling or *imiafrodis krasi* and fully-sparkling or *afrodis krasi* versions.

Drink the semi-sparkling and sparkling wines as an aperitif and the still Zitsa with fish. Drinking temperature is 8–10 °C (46.4–50 °F).

METSOVO

A Greek politician named Averoff dreamed of making the best wine of Greece. Although he never achieved this himself, his company has scaled unprecedented heights and may well make its founder's dreams come true. The vineyards are on south-easterly facing slopes of the Pindos mountains. Fine red wines have been produced here for centuries but unfortunately the ancient vines were entirely destroyed by *phylloxera*. The original vines were replaced by cabernet sauvignon. Excellent Katogi Averoff red wine is made from these grapes. This great wine can certainly be kept for ten years because of the tannin it contains. This ruby red wine is characterized by its intense aromatic power and fulsome taste that is velvet smooth (after maturing). Katogi Averoff is now regarded as one of Greece's best wines and it is very expensive.

Drink this wine with the finest grilled fillet steak or with lamb. A local delicacy is *anaki furnu*, meltingly tender oven-roasted leg of lamb. Drinking temperature is 17–18 °C (62.6–64.4 °F).

THESSALIA

Thessalia is situated to the south of Macedonia and it borders Ipiros to the west, the Aegean to the east, and Central Greece to the south. The area is dominated by the imposing Mount Olympus (9,570 ft) and it is bisected by the Pinios river. Thessalia is clearly an agricultural region. The best vineyards are sited on slopes or close to the sea. The vines planted on flat countryside are for grapes sold to be eaten or for poor wines.

RAPSANI

Rapsani's vineyards are planted on the slopes of Mount Olympus at heights of 984–1640 ft. The climate here is fairly moist and above all cold in the winter. Yet the siting of the vineyards guarantees full sunshine and excellent red wines. The basic grapes used for Rapsani are xinomavro, krassato, and stavroto, which combine to produce a fresh, rich, and elegant red wine.

An ideal wine for all manner of roast or grilled meat. Drinking temperature is 14–16 °C (57.2–60.8 °F).

NEA ANKIALOS OPAP

The vineyards of Nea Ankialos are sited close to the sea near Volos. The rhoditis vines grow at a height of 328–656 ft and their grapes make a fresh and elegant white wine. Serve with seafood or shellfish. Drinking temperature is 8–10 °C (46.4–50 °F).

MESENIKOLA OPAP

Dry wed wines from mesenikola, carignan, and syrah come from the area immediately around the town of Mesinikola.

TOPIKOI OENOI (VINS DE PAYS)
Reasonable to good country wines from this region are Thessalikos, Kraniotikos, and Tirnavou.

CENTRAL GREECE

This area is the center of the Greek mainland, bounded in the north by Ipiros and Thessalia, in the west by the Ionian Sea (Mediterranean), and in the east by the Aegean. Vast quantities of wine are produced here (about one third of all Greek wine) but the region only has one guaranteed source of origin wine other than the *appellation traditionelle* retsina. The other wines are all table wines or country wines. Enormous investment has been made in this region in recent years in French grapevines and the better native varieties. The first results are extremely encouraging, especially the wines of Domaine Skouras and Hatzi Michaelis.

Fine *topikos oinos* (vins de pays) are Thevaikos, Ritsonas Avlidos, Peanitikos, Attikis, Vilitsas and Attikos, Pallinitikos, Playies Kitherona, and Vorion Playion Pentelikou.

IONIAN ISLANDS

The Ionian Islands (*Eptanesos*, the seven islands) lie to the west of the Greek mainland on a latitude with Ipiros, Central Greece, and parts of the Peloponnese. Vines are cultivated on virtually all of these islands. The conquest by the Turks in this part of Greece – also known as Eptanessos or the seven islands – was of sufficiently short duration that the inhabitants were able to continue to cultivate vines and make wine.

The wine industry in the most northerly island of Corfu (Kerkyra) has been somewhat depressed by the rise of tourism and the growing of olives. Here too though excellent white wines are made such as that from the house of Ktima Roppa. This is an old-fashioned and traditional wine with the culture of 'flor' (a film created by the fermentation) in the same way as sherry. The wine is a lot like dry sherry. The grapes used are robola and kakotrychi. New businesses are developing modern-style dry white wines of elegance using the native kakotrychi grapes. Production of this new wine is very limited.

Very little wine worth mentioning is produced at present on the islands of Paxi, Lefkas, and Ithaki (with the exception perhaps of Lefkas's Santa Mavra).

KEFALLINIA ROBOLA OPAP

Robola, also known as rombola, is one of the finest white grape varieties of Greece. This grapevine thrives extremely well on Cephalonia, the largest of the seven Ionian islands, thanks to both the weather and soil structure. The summers are hot but there are light sea breezes to provide the necessary moisture and cooling. The vineyards are sited at 1,968 ft and sometimes as high as 2,952 ft. Robola's color is fairly pale yellow with a tinge of green. The bouquet, with hints of hazelnut and citrus fruit, is seductive and the taste is mellow, elegant, and extremely pleasant.

This wine combines well with all delicacies from the sea but also cheese and soft vegetables. Try a Robola with a combination of white and green asparagus with a mellow lemon cream sauce – delicious! Drinking temperature is 10–12 °C (50–53.6 °F).

KEFALLINIA MAVRODAPHNE OPE

This is a first class sweet red wine made from mavrodaphne grapes. At first glance it resembles a ruby port in looks. Drinking temperature is 8–12 °C (46.6–53.6 °F) or 14–16 °C (57.2–60.8 °F) according to preference.

KEFALLINIA MUSCAT

This is a first class sweet muscat wine that is very aromatic. Drinking temperature is 6–10 °C (42.8–50 °F).

Other fresh and fruity white wines are made on the island of Cephalonia e.g. Sideritis, Tsaoussi, and Zakinthos and several reasonable reds from aghiorgitiko, mavrodaphne, or tymiathiko that are fresh, fruit, and very aromatic but not always particularly dry.

VERDEA

On Zakinthos just as on Corfu, a fresh green white wine in the style of a Madeira is made that is known as Verdea. This is an excellent aperitif but it also combines very well with Greek *mezedes* or with freshly-grilled sardines. Drinking temperature is 8–10 °C (46.4–50 °F).

EASTERN AEGEAN ISLANDS

The Aegean is spread out to the east of mainland of Greece and the coast of Turkey and is filled with countless islands. Vines have been cultivated on these islands and wine made for at least 6,000 years and the sweet, luxuriant wines of Limnos, Lesbos, Chios, and Samos are legendary. Each island has its own microclimate and soil structure which ensure wines of an individual character.

Samos vin doux

LIMNOS OPAP

The designated origin wine of Limnos is a dry white wine made from muscat of Alexandria grapes. The island of Limnos is volcanic in origin and fairly arid. There are not many trees but there are gently undulating hills rising to 1,476 ft and valleys in which the wine-growing and agriculture is concentrated. This white Limnos wine is yellow-green in color with a very fruity nose of fresh muscat grapes. The taste is fulsome and rounded.

Samos vin de liqueur

An excellent aperitif, ideal with asparagus and other soft vegetables, good accompaniment for soft fish. Drinking temperature is 10–12 °C (50–53.6 °F).

Several acceptable red wines are also made on the island of limnio grapes.

LIMNOS MUSCAT OPE

This is a superb sweet and luxuriant muscat wine that is very aromatic with suggestions of roses and honey. The taste is fulsome, rounded, and velvet smooth. Serve with fresh deserts or after a meal. Drinking temperature is 6–12 °C (42.8–53.6 °F).

SAMOS

The island of Samos is much more hilly than Limnos but it is ideal for growing vines. These are cultivated on terraces carved out of the sides of the two mountains on the island to a height of 2,624 ft. Muscat grapes thrive extraordinarily well here but the superb taste of the Samos wines is largely due to the great care taken with the grapes on the vines and in the winery. The cooperatively organized growers have completely renewed their wine-making equipment in recent times with modern horizontally-operated pneumatic presses, computer-temperature control, stainless steel tanks, and new oak casks. The quality of Samos wines was already excellent but not always uniform. Consumer tastes have also changed so that heavy and sticky wine without freshness is no longer popular. By controlling the temperature during fermentation, a much fresher and more balanced wine is now made.

Dry white Samena wine from muscat grapes

Samos Vin Doux Naturel and Samos Vin Doux Naturel Grand Cru are natural sweet wines with alcohol content of around 15%. These are golden yellow wines with a floral nose (roses in particular), and suggestion of ripe fruit and honey. The rich taste is rounded and fatty, and although sweet, remains reasonably fresh.

Ensure you serve a Samos vin doux naturel after food. Drinking temperature is 6–12 °C (42.8–53.6 °F) according to taste.

A Samos vin de liqueur is modified with wine alcohol, making it both sweeter and more alcoholic than the ordinary Samos vin doux naturel. It is a wine for the most precious moments in life. Drinking temperature is 6–8 °C (42.8–46.4 °F).

Samos nectar is another natural sweet wine with alcohol of 14%. This wine is made with partially dried grapes and it is aged in wooden casks. This is a fuller and richer wine than the previous three Samos wines but is exceptional both in taste and class. Definitely a wine to drink for the more intimate moments. Drinking temperature is 6–8 °C (42.8–46.4 °F).

Samos also produces a small amount of dry white wine from muscat (Samena) grapes. This is a very interesting and exciting wine to combine with fish or soft vegetables (asparagus) and shellfish. Drinking temperature is 10–12 °C (50–53.6 °F).

PELOPONNESE

From the mainland of Attika the Peloponnese are reached across the Straight of Corinth. The Peloponnese form a predominantly agricultural region of Greece, famous for its sultanas and Corinthian grapes that are better known as currants. It is a fairly hilly region, dominated by Mount Taygete (7,896 ft). Most of the vineyards are in the north, including the guaranteed origin wines of Patras, Mantineia, and Nemea. In addition to these three wines, the Peloponnese also produce a large quantity of reasonable to good table wine and topikos oinos.

Patraiki Mavro-daphne   Patras Muscat

The increasingly common modern wines made with the well-known French grapes of chardonnay, sauvignon blanc, ugni blanc, cabernet sauvignon, cabernet franc, merlot, grenache rouge, and carignan etc. are surprising but not exactly exciting. These grapes do produce outstanding results though when combined with Greek varieties such as mavrodaphne or agiorgitiko.

PATRAS OPAP

Patras is in Achaia, in the north west of the Peloponnese. The local vineyards are mainly sited on chalk-bearing soils on slopes around the town of Patrai or Patras, at heights of between 200 and 450 metres (656 and 1,476 feet). The basic grape used here is the rhoditis, which produces superb white wines that are fresh, fruity, very elegant, and dry.

An ideal wine for fish, shellfish and vegetable dishes, but also delicious as an aperitif. Drinking temperature: 8–10 °C (46.4–50 °F).

MAVRODAPHNE ATRON/PATRAS MAVRODAPHNE OPE

The famous Patraiki Mavrodaphne (or Mavrodaphne Patron) red liqueur wine originates from the area around

Nemea   Special Nemea from organic vineyards

Trifyllias red

MANTINIA OPAP

Mantinia is the most southerly of the three major designated wines of the Peloponnese. Fresh, light, dry white wines are produced here from the native moschofilero grape. The vineyards are situated on a plateau at about 2,132 ft in the vicinity of the ruins of the ancient town of Mantinia.

This is an elegant white wine that makes a good accompaniment for fish, poultry, and vegetables but it also very suitable to drink as an aperitif of with fresh fruit or even soft cheese. Drinking temperature is 10–12 °C (50–53.6 °F).

TOPIKOI OENOI (VINS DE PAYS)
Vins de pays from this region worth considering are: Peleponnesiakos, Trifyllias, Playies Petrotou, Pyllias, Playies Orynis Korinthias, and Letrinon.

THE CYCLADES

The Cyclades Islands are stretched out in the Aegean Sea to the southeast of the Peloponnese. The best known of the islands is the astonishingly beautiful Santorini (Thira).

SANTORINI OPAP

Santorini (Thira) was once known as Kallistè, or 'the most beautiful', and this is certainly true of this island that is one of the most picturesque throughout the Mediterranean region. Many photographers dream of taking photographs of the island's steep cliffs that plunge over three hundred metres (984 feet) to the sea on top of which the fairy tale town of Thira is perched. The island is of volcanic origins and this can be readily seen in the geology. There are varying layers of pumice stone, chalk, and shale. The array of colors in the ground here is quite extraordinary with black, gray, red, and brown through to purple. The charm and individual style of Santorini's wines are the result of a combination of the volcanic geology and a moist and hot climate. Santorini makes a range of different wines from dry to very sweet.

The dry white Santorini is wholly made from assyrtiko grapes and it is elegant, fruity (citrus fruit), lively, with a fulsome taste that includes a slightly fiery tingle. It is ideal with fish, seafood, poultry, or veal. Drinking temperature is 10–12 °C (50–53.6 °F).

The dry white Santorini Fumé wines are partially fermented in small oak casks and aged for about six months in their own sediment. This wine has definite traces of vanilla (from the wood) and hints of hazelnuts, toast, smoke, and white flowers in its nose and taste. Drink this very aromatic wine with grilled fish or shellfish. Drinking temperature is 10–12 °C (50–53.6 °F).

The most exciting wine from the island is probably that made from assyrtiko, mixed with aidani and athiri. The wine known as Nycteri is either dry or sweet but always extremely fruity and aromatic with

Patras. This wine, made with the eponymous grapes, is a full-bodied and sturdy wine that is spicy and very aromatic. It is aged in wooden casks for a number of years. It makes a good and inexpensive replacement for red port although it has its own character which resembles that of a port or oloroso sherry.

An ideal accompaniment for melon and other fresh fruit and can be used as a port-type aperitif. It is far better though drunk as an accompaniment to after dinner chatter. Drinking temperature is 6–14 °C (42.8–57.2 °F).

PATRAS MUSCAT/PATRAS RIOU MUSCAT OPE

Exceptional fresh sweet but fresh muscat wines. They are golden in color, luxuriant and rather like honey. Serve after dining and at intimate moments. Drinking temperature is 6–10 °C (42.8–50 °F).

NEMEA OPAP

Nemea, or the blood of Hercules, is made from agiorgitiko grapes picked from vineyards at heights of 656–2,624 ft that are close to Mount Kilini. After Naoussa, Nemea is the most popular of the Greek wines. Nemea wines are aged for at least twelve months in casks of French oak. The color is intense purple to mauve and the very aromatic bouquet suggests prune, peach, cinnamon and other spices. The fulsome taste is complex, rounded, robust, warm, and well-balanced. This wine suits meat dishes that are not heavily spice or mature cheese. Drinking temperature is 16–17 °C (60.8–62.6 °F).

Ilios and Chevalier de Rhodes

a fulsome rich taste. The Vin Santo made from overripe assyrtiko and aidani grapes is also very exciting. The color is yellow with orange glints. The bouquet is reminiscent of citrus fruit while the taste is simultaneously fresh and luxuriant. Locally this wine is drunk as an aperitif but you might find it better after a meal or with a fresh desert. Drinking temperature is 6–8 °C (42.8–46.4 °F).

PAROS OPAP

The vineyards on the island of Paros grow two types of grapes, white monemvassia and red mandilaria. Paros wine is made from combining these two varieties. The vines are grown on terraces and their manner of pruning is relatively uncommon. The vines are pruned to keep them low in habit but their side shoots may be up to 16 ft long making a very strange sight. Paros wine is cherry-like in color, which is characteristic of the mandilaria grape. Its bouquet is full of fruit and floral notes while the mellow taste is fulsome and rich with fairly substantial tannin. This is definitely a wine for roast meat, preferably lamb. Drinking temperature is 16–17 °C (60.8–62.6 °F).

THE DODECANESE

These islands are in the eastern Aegean to the south east of the Cyclades. The Greek 'Dodekanisos' means 'twelve islands' but only the islands of Rhodes and Kos are dealt with here. In the case of Kos it almost exclusively produces poor to reasonable quality table wine.

RHODES OPAP

Wines from the island of Rhodes are fairly well known in Europe due both to its good quality and the island's history. The Knights Templar used Rhodes as a staging post during the times of the Crusades. The ruins of their famous fortifications (Krach) are still there to be seen. The vineyards of Rhodes in the north have underlying chalk or slate/shale while those of the south are sited on sandy soil. The climate is ideal for wine-growing with hot summers that are low in rainfall but with cooling from the northerly Etesian wind and yet again warming for the south of the island by southerly breezes.

Rhodes brut of CAIR

Rhodes makes two good still wines and a fine sparkling one:
– the Ilios (Greek for 'sun') made from athiri grapes is an elegant, slightly aromatic, lithe and pleasing white wine that serves well as an aperitif or can accompany all manner of fish and white meat dishes. Drinking temperature is 8–10 °C (46.4–50 °F).
– Chevalier de Rhodes, made from mandilaria, is an excellent red wine with a purple to mauve color, a soft aromatic nose but a sturdy yet elegant taste with the necessary tannin. Ideal for roast meat from the oven. Drinking temperature is 16 °C (60.8 °F).
– Rhodes brut like the other two is made from athiri grapes by the Compagnie Agricole Industrielle de Rhodes (CAIR). Despite its designation as brut, this sensual and naturally sparkling wine, made by the traditional method, is not absolutely dry. Its power lies in abundant fruitiness and mellow, almost caressing taste. For those who do not find this wine convivial enough, there is also a demi-sec version. Serve Rhodes brut on any festive occasion as a chic aperitif or just as itself. The demi-sec is more of an evening wine for after dinner. Drinking temperature is 6–8 °C (42.8–46.4 °F).

RHODES MUSCAT OPE

This is a sultry and seductive wine from muscat trani grapes. The color is golden yellow and the very aromatic bouquet has floral notes and hints of honey. The taste is sweet but remains elegant and fresh. The wine contains 15% alcohol. Serve after dinner or at moments of intimate pleasure. Drinking temperature is 6–8 °C (42.8–46.4 °F) but can be served less chilled depending on the occasion and the season.

CRETE (KRITI)

In terms of size, Crete is the fifth largest island in the Mediterranean region. Many may recall the stories from their school days of Knossos and the palace of King Minos, where the Greek hero Theseus slew the Minotaur and fled with the beautiful Ariadne.

Crete is a small and elongated island to the south of the Greek mainland. The 162 miles long island is dominated by the mountains of Lefka Ori (8,047 ft) and Idi (8,353 ft). The vineyards are spread out in the central and eastern parts of the island. The mountains protect the vines from the hot and dry winds from Africa. There are four guaranteed origin wines that have been nominated on Crete and just

White and red Peza

one country wine, Kritikos. This is made as a dry white (sylvaner, sauvignon blanc, and ugni blanc and other grapes), rosé (kotsifali, mandilaria, romeiko, and others), and red (kotsifali, mandilaria, and liaitiko).

Very old-fashioned types of rancio wines are still made in the west of the island near Chania, using grapes from ancient native romeiko and liatiko vines, which may be mixed with some grenache. Crete is responsible for twenty percent of all Greek wine production. Another unusual aspect of Crete is that *phylloxera* never set foot on the island and hence the vines originate from very old varieties.

ARCHANES OPAP

Archanes wines were once the rage of Europe. These full-bodied and spicy red wines that are easily drunk were the first Greek wines to reach supermarket shelves. They originate from the south of the island around Heraklion (Iraklio). Wines have been made here for at least 4,000 years as proven by the ancient wine press at Vathipetro, which originates from Minoan times. The wines are made from kotsifali and mandilaria grapes. These are normally ruby red wines that are lithe, rounded, and elegant with a very pleasing taste but quality in recent times has been extremely variable. An ideal accompaniment for fairly simple dishes such as stews. Drinking temperature is 14–16 °C (57.2–60.8 °F).

DAPHNES OPAP

A red liqueur wine of good quality, made from liatiko grapes that is full-bodied, pleasing, and very aromatic. This wine is a relic from ancient Cretan civilizations and almost as old as the liatikos grape vines, which were cultivated during Minoan times.

Drink this fairly old-fashioned wine with strong cheeses or fresh fruit. Drinking temperature is according to taste either 6–8 °C (42.8–46.4 °F) or slightly below room temperature (12–14 °C/53.6–57.2 °F).

There is also a dry version of the red Daphne.

PEZA OPAP

This ancient Cretan red wine is made from kotsifali and mandilari grapes. It is a dark mauve wine with a slightly unusual vegetal and fruity taste but it is pleasing and supple. Both alcohol, of not less than 12.5%, and body are normally in good balance with each other but in recent years the quality of this wine has not been consistent from every producer. It is always an experience though to taste a good Peza, for instance with pork or lamb. Drinking temperature is 16 °C (60.8 °F).

Peza also produces a white wine made from ancient and native vilana grapes. This wine is greenish yellow and is fairly aromatic and fruity with reasonable freshness and suppleness of taste. An excellent aperitif but also for all manner of seafood. Drinking temperature is 10–12 °C (50–53.6 °F).

SITIA OPAP

The vineyards of Sitia are situated at the eastern tip of the island at a height of about 1,968 ft. The ancient grape varieties that thrive here are liatiko used for red wines and vilana for white wines.

Sitia white is fairly green in color with a fresh taste that is supple and pleasing rather than exciting. Drink it with not to strongly-tasting fish. Drinking temperature is 8–10 °C (46.4–50 °F).

Dry red Sitia is fairly dark in color with a mild nose and fulsome, supple, and comforting taste. Perfect for simple meat dishes, preferably grilled. Drinking temperature is 14–16 °C (57.2–60.8 °F).

There is also an ancient type of sweet version of the red wine, comparable with a Daphne.

BALKAN COUNTRIES

FORMER YUGOSLAVIA

The former Yugoslavia was known as a supplier of excellent wines and the wine industry had just started a rejuvenation when all hell burst upon this paradise for lovers of life. After the fragmentation of the former country in tragic circumstances the wine industry has to re-establish quality and its image. People also have to learn to cope with their new freedom and to relinquish practices dating from the pre-Communist era. Not all have succeeded in doing so. The contrast between the old-fashioned state-controlled wine industry that was managed from on high and the individual, professional, and eager to work smaller private concerns is enormous. The old state concerns have no money for renovation and improvement. Smaller companies are much more interesting for potential investors. It is hoped the local wine industry will restore itself in this millennium.

SLOVENIA

Slovenia was the first country to leave the federation of the mighty Yugoslavia. Slovenia was always the most European member of the former Yugoslavia because it borders on Austria and Italy on one side and Hungary and Croatia on the other, making it a transitional place between east and west. The landscape of Slovenia is extremely varied. The north of the country is mountainous, inland is flat or gently undulating and the southeast has a beautiful stretch of coastline. The climate is generally central European and continental with mountain influences in the north and Mediterranean one in the south.

SLOVENIAN WINES

Slovenia has the Celts to thank for its vineyards. The Romans quickly discovered the fresh and lively wines of the ancient Slovenians that were quite different from the unctuous heavy wines of Italy, Spain, and Greece. A crusading army paused in the hilly countryside around Ormoz in the Middle Ages and after sampling the local wine they renamed it Jeruzalem. The wines of Jeruzalem Ormoz now play a prominent part among the wines of Slovenia. The church also stimulated wine-making and in the days of the Austro-Hungarian empire, Austria and Hungary ensured a golden era for Slovenian wine. An end of this euphoria occurred with the *phylloxera* plague. In the twentieth century Slovenian wine did not achieve what might be expected of its potential capacity but it did survive, even in international markets. One of the most important international wine events took place in Ljubljana for forty-five years as world homage to the persistence of the Slovenians.

The Slovenian wine laws are very complex and strict, extending much further than most European laws controlling production and sale of wine. Hence sugar is not permitted to be added to the quality wines (Vrhunsko vino) except in disastrous seasons and only with low quality wines. Acidity may not be reduced by chemical means or enhanced (in order to make the wine fresher), although acid may be added to table wines as a preservative (e.g. citric acid). Slovenian wine may not be bottled outside Slovenia and bulk export is strictly forbidden. Matters such as transport, storage, and turnover speed outside the country unfortunately still fall outside the law.

In addition to the classification of wines by place of origin (see below), Slovenia also classifies them by quality in a similar way to other European countries.

NAMIZNO VINO (TABLE WINE)
Ordinary table wine may originate from any part of Slovenia.

NAMIZNO VINO PGP
The better table wines only come from the three main wine-growing areas of Podravje, Posavje, or Primorje. These are called *dezelno vino* (regional wine) and bear the broadest form of origin name: "Prizano Geografsko Pooelko" (guaranteed origin), abbreviated as PGP.

KAKOVOSTNO VINO ZKGP
Wines that come from defined sub areas (e.g. Brda or Koper) are known as "Zasciteno in Kontrolirano Geografsko Porelko", shortened to ZKGP. All these wines fall within the middle to top quality range and must be tested annually for color, bouquet, and taste.

VRHUNSKO VINO/VRHUNSKO VINO PTP
These are the "crème de la crème" of Slovenian wines. To achieve this designation (high quality) a wine must first be admitted to Kakovostno Vino ZKGP. Only the wines that score highest in official tastings may bear this title.

Top wines that not only originate from a defined sub-area but are also produced according to strict vinification method are allowed to bear the category "Priznana Tradicionalno Poimenovanje", abbreviated as PTP. This literally means "traditionally accepted name" and applies only to such illustrious wines as Kraski Teran and Dolensjkai Cvicek.

WINE AREAS

The small country of Slovenia has no fewer than fourteen different wine areas. These are grouped together in this book into three main areas: Primorje, Podravje, and Posavje.

PRIMORJE (PRIMORSKI VINORODNI REGION)

Although most of the Primorje (by the sea) region is some way from the coast, the sea's proximity does influence the local climate. The continental and Mediterranean climates meet one another in Primorje. This results in countless strongly alcoholic and dry red wines, especially from the area around Koper. Primorje is the only Slovenian region that makes more red wines than others. The white and rosé wines here are also full-bodied, powerful, warm, and with little acidity. The local cuisine is heavily influenced by the Italians, especially neighboring Fruili. In turn Slovenian food has found its way into northern Italian cooking. Slovenian gastronomy is characterized by the use of olives, olive oil, raw ham, fresh sea fish, game, hearty vegetable flans, and meat and or vegetable dishes.

BRISKO (BRDA)

The red wines are reasonable but sometimes rustic and uneven. They also produce excellent sparkling wines from here, made from chardonnay, beli pinot, rebula, and prosecco. There are also fresh white wines made from rebula, beli pinot,

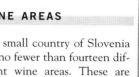

Vrhunsko, quality wine

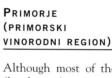

Chardonnay from Brda

Cabernet Sauvignon from Primorje

Vipava Sauvignon

Vipava Chardon-
nay Barrique

Vipava Merlot
Barrique

sauvignon blanc, sivi pinot, chardonnay, furlanski tokay, and malvasia (malvasija) but with the exception of some of the rebulas, these are not really very convincing. Ideal thirst quenchers or as accompaniment for fatty pork dishes. Drinking temperature is 8–12 °C (46.4–53.6 °F).

VIPAVA

This is an excellent dry white wine and most of them are usually quite modern in style and taste. Grapes used are rebula, sauvignon blanc, beli pinot, chardonnay, furlanski tokay, laski riesling (welsch riesling), malvasia (malvazija), zelen, and pinela, with the last two frequently totally underestimated. These grapes far better represent the authenticity and strength of this region than the other imported varieties. The Sauvignon and Chardonnay are outstanding and refined aperitifs. The more native wines combine very well with fish, poultry, other white meat dishes, and also with fresh cheese. Drinking temperature is 8–12 °C (46.4–53.6 °F).

There is a surprisingly delicious, fresh, and mellow rosé made from barbera and merlot that are exceptionally delicious with a summer cheeseboard or the whole year with fish and poultry. Drinking temperature is 10–12 °C (50–53.6 °F).

The ordinary red wines (modri pinot, prosecco, refosc) are very acceptable. Some wines, such as the Merlot Biljenski Grici, Barbera, and Cabernet, are of excellent quality, particularly in view of their prices. Serve with roasted meat or small game. Drinking temperature is 12–14 °C (53.6–57.2 °F).

The best white and red wines are aged in small oak casks, although these are often made from inferior Slovenian timber which imparts a strong, almost resinous taste that entirely stifles any finesse in most white wines. This is a great shame for behind the strong taste of the wood there is a fresh, pleasing wine of great potential. This applies to the Chardonnay Barrique and Merlot Barrique of Vipava.

KRASKI/KARST

The truly ancient and famous Kraski Teran wine originates from Karst. This is made from refosc grapes which are related to the Italian variety of refosco and the wine is said according

Chardonnay
from Koper

to popular belief to work as a tonic for health. This ruby red wine with glints of purple is very fruity (redcurrants) in both bouquet and taste with a velvet smooth texture but not excessively alcoholic. Teran is traditionally drunk with red meat and game. Drinking temperature is 16 °C (60.8 °F).

Other wines made here include fairly uninteresting sparkling wines, charming white wines and excellent reds from refosc, cabernet sauvignon, merlot, modri pinot, and prosecco.

KOPER

More than 70% of the production here consists of red wines that are chiefly made from refosc. This is a wine area with a future, although the winery installations are far from ideal owing to shortage of money. Most wines lack too much freshness to compete well in foreign markets, yet there is considerable potential here in the combination of soil and ideal weather conditions. It is all waiting for foreign investment.

The dry white wines such as Sauvignon Blanc, Chardonnay, and Beli Pinot are not recommended due to their lack of freshness. Much wine is fairly coarse and devoid of either character or style.

If however you should choose an old-fashioned syrupy white wine such as Malvazija, Sivi Pinot, Sladki Muskat, or Rumeni Muskat, then you will get value for money. These wines deserve suitable table companions in the form of grilled pork, goose, or duck. Drinking temperature is 10–12 °C (50–53.6 °F).

The wine made from overripe grapes selected by hand and picked late is excellent, whether or not the grapes have been visited by *botrytis* (the noble rot). Extremely interesting wines include the Chardonnay Izbor (Auslese), Malvazija Pozna Trgatev (Spätlese), sweet Sladki Refosc, and an extremely rare passito made from cabernet sauvignon (suseno grozdje).

The red wines like most of the local rosés are of reasonable quality but these red wines could also benefit from more modern vinification methodology. Many of the wines give a somewhat overblown appearance (too much wood, too much tannin, lots of alcohol, but otherwise little individual character). Choose from the better crus where possible from the cabernet sauvignon, cabernet franc, refosc, malocrn, merlot, modri pinot, and prosecco. Drink these stronger reds with roast meat or sturdy stews. Drinking temperature is 16 °C (60.8 °F).

PODRAVJE (PODRAVSKI VINORODNI REGION)

The climate here in the extreme northeast of Slovenia is continental of a Central European nature. This helps the area to produce fine, fresh, elegant, and aromatic white wines. Podravje is also renowned for its delightful sweet wines (pozna trgatev and izbor). Podravje borders Hungary and Austria in the north, and Croatia to the east. The cooking specialties of the neighboring countries have left their mark on the kitchens of Podravje. Its local fare includes numerous sorts of decorated bread, substantial flans, and goose and duck dishes. The fresh sharp acidity of the local wine combines extremely well with the fatty nature of the local cuisine. In addition to wines listed below, the Rieslings and Chardonnays from Premurske Gorice and wines of centrally-sited Slovenske Gorice are worth considering.

RADGONA-KAPELSKE GORICE

A very promising wine area best known for its individual style Traminer and superb Zlata Radgonska Penina. This is the first Slovenian sparkling wine made by the traditional method.

Other excellent wines include Pozne trgatve (Spätlese), Arhivska vina (riserva), and Jagodnii izbor (Beerenauslese). Choose the most sultry wines such as those from rumeni muskat or sivi pinot and the best crus such as Perko or Rozicki, which produce the very best Traminer.

There are first class fresh and dry white wines made from laski riesling and zeleni silvanec.

LJUTOMER ORMOSKE GORICE

The white wines from this area are certainly among the best in Europe. Unfortunately the means are not to hand to make their wines better known. The wines from the local cooperative Jeruzalem Ormoz should have a great potential market in Europe. For excellent pinot

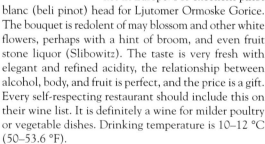

Sauvignon
from Ormoz

blanc (beli pinot) head for Ljutomer Ormoske Gorice. The bouquet is redolent of may blossom and other white flowers, perhaps with a hint of broom, and even fruit stone liquor (Slibowitz). The taste is very fresh with elegant and refined acidity, the relationship between alcohol, body, and fruit is perfect, and the price is a gift. Every self-respecting restaurant should include this on their wine list. It is definitely a wine for milder poultry or vegetable dishes. Drinking temperature is 10–12 °C (50–53.6 °F).

Wines are made from sauvignon blanc throughout Slovenia and these sell well and quickly but only the Sauvignon from Ljutomersko-Ormoske – and in particular from the cooperative referred to above – are really worthwhile. Gooseberry, hay and grass, asparagus, citrus fruit, and a hint of smoke in the background can all be discerned in this wine that resembles a very good Sancerre. This wine is so smooth, almost like salve and yet extremely fresh and aromatic. This is an outstanding wine for a fantastic price. Serve this sublime Sauvignon as an aperitif or with the best fish dishes. Drinking temperature is 8–10 °C (46.4–50 °F).

Further excellent dry white wines are also made from varieties such as renski riesling, laski riesling, and

sipon. You may find fine medium dry to semi-sweet whites like those of sivi pinot, rulandec, and chardonnay. Tasting a medium dry Chardonnay takes some getting used to but the sunny, very aromatic, fulsome, and warm taste even convinces died-in-the-wool Chardonnay enthusiasts.

Wines made from late harvested grapes (Spätlese) of excellent quality include Pozna Trgatev made from chardonnay, laski riesling, renski riesling, and sauvignon blanc, the Jagodni izbor (Beerenauslese) made from sipon, and Ledeno vino (Eiswein) using laski riesling. Despite their very sweet nature, these wines are unbelievably fresh due to the fine acidity which is characteristic of this area.

MARIBOR

The oldest vines in the world according to the Slovenians are those of Maribor. Some $9^{1}/_{4}$ gallons of wine are still made each year from 450 years old Kölner blauer or zametna crnina (black velvet) grapes. This very special wine is bottled in miniatures that are sold with a certificate of authenticity. This is a highly desirable item for collectors of wine curios. In addition to this rarity there are also excellent fresh and elegant white wines made here from grapes such as laski riesling and rumeni muskat. The local sauvignon blanc is perhaps less pronounced than that of Ljutomersko-Ormoske, but it is certainly of high quality.

Maribor also produces excellent sweet wines: Izbor (Auslese), Jagodni izbor (Beerenauslese), Suhi jagodni izbor (Trocken Beerenauslese), and Ledeno vino (Eiswein).

Finally a number of fresh and light red wines are also made here from varieties like portugalka and zametovka that combine well with more fatty dishes. Drinking temperature is 12–14 °C (53.6–57.2 °F).

HALOZE

Almost exclusively white wines are made from the hills of Haloze, on the border with Croatia. The chalk soil imparts great beauty and elegance to these wines. These are further examples of wines that are totally underestimated by the European wine buyers. The prices for the quality are extraordinarily low for wines so completely western European in character.

The best of the whites are made from laski riesling, sipon and traminer. The sweet Pozne trgatve, Izbori, Jagodni izbori, Suhi jagodni izbori, and Ledeno vino wines are very good too.

POSAVJE (POSAVSKI VINORODNI REGION)

Several rivers ensure the necessary moisture in this region. Posavje is situated south of Podravje, next to the Croatian border. The area has a mainly central European continental climate moderated by the influence of the Mediterranean to the south, especially in Bela Krajina. Every type of wine is produced here from fresh to sweet, from light to moderately full-bodied, and

355

white, rosé, and red, still or sparkling. Posavje is also renowned for its excellent late harvest sweet wines from Spätlese (Pozna trgatev) to Eiswein (Ledeno vino), and others produced from grapes carefully selected such as ilzbor, jagodni ilzbor and suhi jagodni izbor.

In Smarje-Virstanj they produce excellent Laski Riesling and Sivi Pinot; in Bizeljsko-Sremic all manner of reasonable to good wines including rare port-type wines; in Dolensjka the wines include the well-known Cvicek ; and finally from Bela Krajina come the Metliska Crnina – probably the best red wines of Slovenia – and excellent Pozne trgatve, Jagodni izbori, and Ledeno vino.

CROATIA

Croatia, that was once an idyllic country for vacations, renowned for its rich culture, gastronomy, and superb wines is still recovering from the wounds of the war with the former Yugoslavia. There is hope though for the very near future. Most of the vineyards and wineries were totally destroyed by the war. The Croatian government and the European Community have ensured that new vineyards are planted in the best places and that new wineries are built with latest equipment – an improvement on the hopelessly outdated installations of before the war. Greater freedom has also arisen from the removal of the pro-Communist pressure from Belgrade. The economy has improved and countless talented wine makers were able to privatize their businesses following independence. Those working for themselves are more highly motivated than for an "Agrokombinat" or state agricultural company. Time will tell but the first signs suggest a speedy recovery. Croatian wine-making is on the right path and will be better than before.

Croatia is not a huge country and yet has wine-growing of 650 square kilometers, consisting mainly of a fairly large number of small areas. One of the attractive aspects of Croatian wine-growers is their preference for improving native varieties of grapes to the rapid imitation of "European" wines. This makes it more difficult for them to sell their very specific wines of local character but will eventually be rewarded as increasing numbers of consumers are discovering that the native grapes guarantee greater authenticity of the *terroir*.

Croatia can be loosely divided into two large wine areas: the interior and the coastal area (including islands).

THE INTERIOR

Most wine growing areas are close to Zagreb. There are seven areas

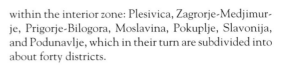

Grasevina

within the interior zone: Plesivica, Zagrorje-Medjimurje, Prigorje-Bilogora, Moslavina, Pokuplje, Slavonija, and Podunavlje, which in their turn are subdivided into about forty districts.

The best wine areas are:
Sveta Jana-Slavetic (Plesivaca)
Moslavina (Moslavina)
Virocitica-Podravina-Slatina (Slavonija)
Kutjevo (Slavonija)
Erdut-Daljoaljmas (Podunavlje)

THE BEST WINES
Many of the vineyards in this part of Croatia were destroyed so the judgment is temporary.

GRASEVINA

Grasevina is the local name for welsch riesling, known in Slovenia as laski rizling or riesling. Some very special white wines are made here from grasevina, especially in the district of Kutjevo in Slavonija. This fine, elegant, and fresh dry white wine deserves to be served with tender white meat or poultry. Drinking temperature is 10–12 °C (50–53.6 °F).

Other good white wines include those made from Rhine riesling, gewürztraminer, chardonnay, and sauvignon blanc. None of these wines though has the same finesse as the Grasevina from Kutjevo.

Small amounts of red wine are now also being made in the interior of Croatia, principally from frankovka grapes.

THE COAST

This is the most important area for Croatian wine. Most of the vineyards here are sited along the coast and on countless islands close to the coast. The position is ideal with steep rocks above the Adriatic and a Mediterranean climate that is hot and dry. Unfortunately the Balkan wars have had a tremendously bad effect on the wine industry, directly through destruction and indirectly through loss of manpower. Although the coastal area was more directly affected than the islands, the economic consequences are clearly apparent on the islands of Krk (Vrbnicka Zlahtina), Hvar (Ivan Dolac), Korcula (Posip), and above all on Peljesac (Dingac, Postup).

The coastal region officially consists of four areas (Istria and the coast, Northern Dalmatia, the interior of Dalmatia, and Central/Southern Dalmatia. These are in turn subdivided into some 50 districts.

The best wine-growing areas are:
Porec (Istria/ coastal strip)
Rovinj (Istria/ coastal strip)
Primosten (Northern Dalmatia)
Neretva-Opuzen (Central/Southern Dalmatia)
Ston (Central/Southern Dalmatia)

Cara-Smokvica (Central/Southern Dalmatia)
Dingac-Postup (Central/Southern Dalmatia)

THE BEST WINES

Excellent wine is made in Porec and Rovinj in the region of Istria (Istra) from malvasia (malvazija) grapes. These fresh and fruity dry white wines are delicious with fish, and shellfish and a superb choice for the locally popular lobsters. Drinking temperature is 10–12 °C (50–53.6 °F).

Istra also has several interesting red wines of which the first choice should those made from teran grapes. The merlot from Istria is well made but lacks identity.

VRBNICKA ZLAHTINA

Red Kastelet

The island of Krk (to the southeast of Rijeka) is the home of Vrbnicka Zlahtina, a delightful white wine made from white zlahtina grapes (zlahtina bijela), a native specialty of Krk. Like most Croatian whites, Vrbnicka Zlahtina is fulsome and rounded but also outstandingly fruity in both the bouquet and taste. It therefore combines well not only with the local seafood but also with most vegetarian dishes, grilled pork or even veal, grilled poultry, and all casseroles of white meat or poultry in a white wine sauce. Drinking temperature is 10–12 °C (50–53.6 °F).

KASTELET

Two very acceptable wines originate from the chalky surrounds of Kastel, slightly north of Split. These are the white and red Kastelet wines. The white is an approachable and fresh dry wine that is excellent with fish (drinking temperature 8–10 °C/46.4–50 °F). The red is made from plavac mali and vranac grapes and is a very pleasing full-bodied and amenable wine that will grace any outdoor meal. Drinking temperature is 10–12 °C (50–53.6 °F).

PLAVAC

The island of Brac lies off the coast from Split. Plavac made here is a very nice red wine. The best Plavec comes from the small town of Bol to the south of the island. Bolski Plavac is a very special red wine that is full-bodied, powerful, and fleshy and ideal for grilled and oven-cooked dishes. Drinking temperature is 14–16 °C (57.2–60.8 °F).

Ivan Dolac

IVAN DOLAC

The island of Hvar to the south of Split is renowned for its red Ivan Dolac. This wine is solely made from grapes in a small enclave of just 19 acres from which the plavac mali grapes are hand picked. Ivan Dolac is one of the better Croatian reds and it is full-bodied, powerful, warm, and rounded. Serve it with the many grill specialties of this area. Drinking temperature is 16 °C (60.8 °F).

FAROS

Another good red from the island of Hvar is made from plavac mali. It is delicious with meat and oven dishes. Drinking temperature is 14–16 °C (57.2–60.8 °F).

POSIP

The island of Korcula is just south of Hvar and at a similar latitude to Peljesac. The superb Posip white wine is made here, probably the best known Croatian white. The wine is made from the native variety of grape from which it gets its name and has been made from these grapes for centuries. The grapes are entirely hand picked. Posip is a delightful full-bodied, rounded, and powerful white wine which elevates itself from the others by its superb fruitiness in both its nose and taste. An ideal accompaniment for grilled fish and seafood, white meat, or poultry. Drinking temperature is 10–12 °C (50–53.6 °F).

DINGAC AND POSTUP

The very elongated island of Peljesac is about 31 miles north of Dubrovnik. The vineyards are very difficult to reach and the growers once transported their grapes on donkeys along dangerous narrow tracks but since a 1,312 feet long tunnel was built through the mountains about twenty-five years ago they have been able to bring the grape harvest in quickly to the wineries in Potomje. Cultivating vines in this terrain

Postup

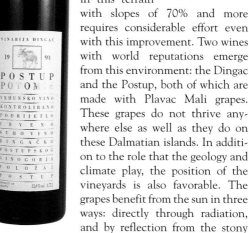

Dingac

with slopes of 70% and more requires considerable effort even with this improvement. Two wines with world reputations emerge from this environment: the Dingac and the Postup, both of which are made with Plavac Mali grapes. These grapes do not thrive anywhere else as well as they do on these Dalmatian islands. In addition to the role that the geology and climate play, the position of the vineyards is also favorable. The grapes benefit from the sun in three ways: directly through radiation, and by reflection from the stony ground and from the sea. These are ideal circumstances for this native variety of grape.

Dingac is made from vines on the steepest hills in the center of the island where the position is most favorable in respect of sea and the sun. These wines are full-bodied and warm (alcohol 13–15%), powerful, fleshy, and exceptionally delicious. The better vintages of Dingac can readily be kept for five years and sometimes ten, with the very best years keeping for fifteen years or more.

Postup is made more towards the north of the island where the slopes are less steep. Postup is clearly related to Dingac, with similar quality but with less bite, body, and flesh than Dingac. Despite this, Postup is still an excellent warm, full-bodied and powerful wine that generally possesses greater finesse and elegance than a Dingac.

Both wines demand roast or grilled meat, preferably beef, goat, or lamb. Postup also combines well with the local meat stews that are popular in the Balkans. Drinking temperature is 14–16 °C (57.2–60.8 °F) for a Postup and 16–17 °C (60.8–62.6 °F) for a Dingac.

PROSEK

This liqueur wine smells and tastes deliciously of over-ripe grapes and slips down very readily, especially if served chilled on a sunny terrace. Yet with its alcohol of 15% this wine is more treacherous than people think. Drink it in moderation therefore. Drinking temperature is 10–12 °C (50–53.6 °F).

BULGARIA

Statistics show that Bulgaria has achieved great success through the modernization and adaptation of its wine industry. New "French" grape varieties that are successful have been planted with great haste, such as cabernet sauvignon, merlot, sauvignon blanc, and chardonnay and inexpensive wines that are easily drunk when young are made in great volume which have conquered the European market through intelligent marketing. The problem is that Bulgarian wine is boring, lacking any character of its own. And this in spite of Bulgria's rich history of wine-making, producing good wines from native grapes such as pamid, mavrud, melnik, gamza (red), and rkatziteli, misket, and dimiat (white). These sell less readily though than the cheaper Chardonnay and Sauvignon. This is a great shame, not least because the Bulgarians would gladly sell better quality réserve wines but since the public has accepted the cheap image of Bulgarian wine it is difficult to sell them more expensive wines. There is also far more competition and the Bulgarians hardly took advantage of the opportunities presented following the collapse of Communism to start up independent wine producers. People remained loyal to the old factory-scale giant wine cooperatives but it is just these great fossils that lack money for investment.

The climate in Bulgaria is a combination of a maritime one from the Black Sea, a Mediterranean climate in the south, and Central European climate in the center and north of the country. The geology permits the production of high quality wines on a large scale. Nothing seems to stand in the way of Bulgaria making top quality wines. The ultra modern wineries are extremely efficient and the vinification methods are well managed…now hopefully the first steps might be taken in the right direction!

Bulgaria has had a European-style wine law since 1978 concerning the quality and origins of wines from defined areas. The standard wines are comparable with French vins de table and have the lowest demands attached but

Controliran Region: wine from a defined area

Réserve wines are cask aged

these Bulgarian "country wines" are often of very reasonable quality which is not always true of French table wines. The "Origine Géographique Déclarée" corresponds with French "Vins Délimité de Qualité Supérieure" (VDQS). Greater quality demand is made of these wines plus a defined area of production. The "Controliran Region" corresponds with the French AOC and is a guarantee of place of origin but not necessarily of better quality.

The addition of "réserve" on the label is a guarantee of better quality. This indicates the wine has been selected for quality and matured in small wooden casks (barriques).

WINE AREAS

Bulgaria is divided into a number of large regions which in turn are divided into smaller wine areas.

DOLINATA NA STRUMA RAION (SOUTHWEST REGION)

This area is distinguished by its Mediterranean type climate and underlying chalk and sand which are ideal for producing red wine. First class Cabernet Sauvignon is produced in Melnik, which is slightly spicy and mellow. Cabernet Sauvignon/Melnik of Petrich somewhat more powerful and has a fuller taste. The best wines are undoubtedly the réserves made from the native

Fine wine from Melnik

Domaine Sakar
Merlot from
Liubimetz

Domaine Boyer
Merlot Réserve
from Liubimetz

melnik grape. These are powerful, full-bodied and rounded wines with some bite to them.

TRAKIISKA NIZINA RAION (SOUTHERN REGION)

This is the land of the ancient Thracians who were active wine-makers as long ago as 700 BC. It is also the largest wine area of Bulgaria. Because of the favorable climate the majority of the wines here are reds. The superb full-bodied and rounded wine that was characteristic of the area, made from native mavrud grapes, is still produced in Assenovgrad. Mavrud wines are relatively speaking rare by comparison with other Bulgarian wines but they are of excellent quality.

Delicious mellow Merlots originate from Haskovo that are well-rounded and cask aged for a number of years. These are very acceptable but have little Bulgarian character. The Merlot from neighboring Stambolovo is better. This wine receives a long period (in Bulgarian terms) ageing in wooden casks and it tastes wonderful. The best Cabernet Sauvignons and Merlots originate around Mount Sakar in the Strandja region, such as Lyubimets.

ROZOVA DOLINA RAION (THE SOUTHERN BALKANS)

This is the domain of cabernet sauvignon. High quality Cabernet Sauvignon and Merlots of European style come from Oriachovitza (Controliran region). Cabernet Sauvignon from Plovdiv is fairly powerful and at first acquaintance resembles a French wine. Perhaps the finest Chardonnay from Bulgaria originates from Sliven but here too the juicy Merlots and Pinot Noirs country wines dominate.

DUNAVSKA RAVINA RAION (NORTHERN REGION)

Suhindol (Controliran region) make fine Gamza, on its own and also in combination with French grapes such as merlot. True

Cabernet Sauvignon
from Plovdiv

Genuine Gamza

Modern Gamza
with Merlot

Gamza wines are superb, spicy, aromatic, full-bodied, rounded, and powerful. Young Gamza wine is often very high in tannin, and this is equally true of melnik and other native Bulgarian blue grapes. Merlot grapes make the wines more mellow and enable it to be drunk sooner. In addition to this Gamza/Merlot there are also reasonable Cabernet Sauvignon wines made in this area which are light, fresh, and elegant. These wines also have a creamy texture and discernible blackcurrant bouquet.

Rousse is situated right alongside the Romanian border. Many of the white wines produced from this area are slightly sweet to sweet. The combination for example of welsch riesling and native misket produces surprising results. These sultry sweet white wines manage to stay quite fresh with light spicy undertones thanks to the addition of welsch riesling. Excellent welsch riesling wines are also made which are generally high in residual sugars. This wine is fresh, fruity, and floral with a mellow and pleasing taste.

Rousse makes
very acceptable
red table wine

There are also acceptable French-style wines made from cabernet sauvignon, merlot, and cinsault.

Svischtov (Controliran Region) is part of the Rousse (or Russe) area. Powerful full-bodied and aromatic red wines are made around Svischtov from grapes such as cabernet sauvignon. The northern position here makes these Cabernet wines less heavy than similar wines from Melnik or Plovdiv. They are even more elegant and fresh and offer much more than copies of French wines with no identity. Here they have succeeded in making the most chauvinistic of French grapes to speak with a Bulgarian tongue.

They are excellent wines with characteristic aromas in the bouquet of mint, spices, vanilla, redcurrant, and blackcurrant. Despite its powerful nose and taste this wine remains smooth in texture so that it quickly wins friends.

Simple white wine from Targovishte

Simple but good drinkable rosé

CHERNOMORSKI RAION (EASTERN REGION)

This region on the Black Sea has a moderate maritime climate that is suitable for white wines.

Burgas lies close to the Black Sea coast and produces reasonable white wines. Ugni blanc grapes provide the bulk for these wines and muscat the sweetness and aromatic properties. Many of these wines are not particularly dry and plenty of them are quite sweet.

Preslav is sited a little further inland but is still clearly influenced by the presence of the Black Sea. First class dry and fruity Chardonnays are produced here on chalky soil and also simple, but tasty rosé wines.

Novi Pazar (Controliran region) also forms part of this area and produces a first class Chardonnay that is full, fruity, powerful, and elegant.

Fine Chardonnay from Khan Krum

ROMANIA

Romania produces about 211,360,000 gallons per annum (approx. 10% of French production) from 679,250 acres in of vineyards, placing it in the European top ten wine--producing countries.

The climate and the geology in Romania is very beneficial for wine growing. The Romanians continue with the local wine traditions and native grapes and although grape varieties of French origin are grown it is the native varieties that get special support. This is entirely right since consumers are increasingly choosing quality and originality at an acceptable price. Romania fits this demand perfectly. The only obstacle in the way of well deserved success is perhaps lack of infrastructure and good means of distribution. Much still needs to be done too to improve the image of Romanian wine. Romanian wines are often lumped together with Bulgarian in people's thoughts and this is a shame for Romania has much greater potential than its southern neighbor.

This 30-year old Riesling was still very drinkable!

SOUTHERN CARPATHIANS

This wine area lies in the foothills of the Southern Carpathian mountains, between the mountains and the southern plateau. Dealu Mare in particular is quite well known and gains grudging respect from connoisseurs. Excellent wines are made here from cabernet sauvignon, merlot, and pinot noir from vines grown in ferruginous soil. Well-known districts of Dealu Mare are Valea Calu-

Romania is still very poor

gareasca, Tohani, Urlati, Ceptura, and Pietroasele. The superlative Tamaioasa Romaneasca and Grasa dessert wines are made from native grapes bearing these names that are grown in the gently undulating hills of Pietrosele. Excellent but light dry whites are made from native feteasca regal and tamaioasa romaneasca grown on terraces on the Arges hills, perhaps with addition of some 'borrowed' sauvignon blanc, welsch riesling, and muscat ottonel. The vineyards of Segarcea are situated to the south of the town of Craiova, from where mainly cabernet sauvignon reds emerge.

EASTERN-CARPATHIANS (ROMANIAN MOLDOVA)

This area bordering the Ukraine (Russian Federation) has soil chiefly consisting of a mixture of humus and chalk. Here too wines are made from the native feteasca alba, feteasca regala, feteasca negra, and galbena grapes, possibly supplemented with or even supplanted by imported grapes such as Rhine riesling, welsch riesling, pinot gris, traminer, or sauvignon blanc. Cotnary, which is one of the best known vineyards of Romania, is in this area where two great dessert wines are produced. One uses grasa and the other from tamaioasa romaneasca, with unusual nose of roasted coffee. Babeasca neagra red wines from Nicoresti area are also of interest and also the fine dry whites made of Husi in the Dealurile Moldovei region. Considerable amounts of cheap whites and reds are made around the area of Tecuci Galati close to the Ukrainian border.

TRANSYLVANIA/BANAT

Transylvania, associated with bloodthirsty horror stories of the local Count Dracula is an area with a magnificent natural landscape with great tracts of woodland, castles, and a few renowned wine areas. Fine sweet white wines are made here and a few excellent dry whites, in particular those from Tirnave. The basic grapes used are feteasca regala, feteasca alba, welsch riesling, muscat ottonel, and sauvignon blanc. Recently they have also begun to make very acceptable sparkling dry

wines by the traditional method. In Alba Iulia they produce full-bodied dry or sweet whites that are filled with extract from fully ripened feteasca alba, feteasca regala, welsch riesling, and pinot gris. Several interesting dry whites are made from the same native grapes in Bistrita. A great deal of everyday local Romanian wine originates from Banat that is made from kadarka grapes. There are also a few reasonable wines made from the ferruginous soils around Minis (kadarka and cabernet sauvignon) and from the area around Recas by the river Bega (cabernet sauvignon).

DOBRUDJA

This area is mainly known for the vineyards of Murfatlar. The climate is very hot and the soil is much the same as in Champagne in France: light, brittle, and chalky. Medium dry and sweet whites of great class originate from the Murfatlar vineyards made from feteasca regala, chardonnay, welsch riesling, and pinot gris. There are also excellent dry to medium dry reds and whites made from babeasca neagra, cabernet sauvignon, merlot, pinot noir, muscat ottonel, and tamaioasa romaneasca. The Chardonnays that have been visited by *botrytis* (the noble rot) are of world class.

Drinking temperature for sweet wines is 6–10 °C (42.8–50 °F), medium dry 8–10 °C (46.4–50 °F), dry white wines 10–12 °C (50–53.6 °F), and red wines 14–16 °C (57.2–60.8 °F).

FORMER SOVIET UNION

It is some time since the policies regarding the wine industry in the former Soviet Union and Comecon countries was determined in Moscow. Countries that were once Soviet dominated have become independent. Hungary, the Czech Republic, and the Slovak Republic have chosen their own destinies. Moldova is now also independent and on the right road but needs time. The huge wine plants that were required to produce quantity before quality have generally been dismantled throughout the former Soviet Union. Increasing numbers of smaller companies have been established, each of which has to fight against ingrained attitudes to achieve any renewal and modernization. In wine-growing areas in these countries much is either happening or has gone to total rack and ruin.

MOLDOVA

Despite the severe oppression in the Soviet era, the Slavic culture never really took hold in Moldova. In the times of the Czars, Moldova's wine industry flourished greatly. When *phylloxera* decimated the vineyards of Western Europe, certain French growers set up in Moldova in order to survive the crisis who brought French varieties of grapevine with them.

Moldova's climate is ideal for growing grapes and making wine from them: it is cold in winter and hot in summer, which is particularly beneficial for white wine. Despite this it is difficult to find any good wines in Moldova. The taste of Moldovan wine is not really very western. These are very acidic wines with little bouquet that are heavily oxidized which is not the image to promote. Efforts to change this are underway with support from the UK, the Netherlands, and France but things are not straightforward and the underlying competition between the various investors does not ease the situation.

The basic grapes used are the native feteasca alba, rkatsiteli, and saperavi. Feteasca provides very fruity white wines with a nose of peach and apricot though without the required freshness. Rkatsiteli stands out because of its spicy and floral bouquet combined with a pleasing freshness. Saperavi are blue grapes that provide red wine with backbone and a greater potential for aging. In addition to the native grapes mentioned, Moldova also makes wide use of French grapes such as the white sauvignon, riesling, and aligoté. Aligoté is a grape from Burgundy that is only occasionally used in quality wines such as Aligoté de Bouzeron. In Moldova though aligoté plays a major role because of the high acidity. Moldovans are crazy about ten year-old fully oxidized Aligoté wine. There are also excellent sherry-type wines made from blends of aligoté, sauvignon blanc, riesling, and rkatsiteli. An unusual wine that is certainly not inferior to sherry is sold in Moldova under the old name for Jerez of Xérés (which is strictly forbidden outside of Moldova). The best whites are made by the Englishman Hugh Ryman, working with the cooperative of Hincesti. These are an excellent full and powerful Chardonnay that is rich and fruity, and a Rkatsiteli which is very fruity and exceptionally pleasant.

Hincesti-Ryman also make a very acceptable Merlot and Cabernet. The best reds are made either wholly of cabernet sauvignon or with the addition of saperavi, such as the wines of Rochu & Negru which are very similar in style to an excellent Bordeaux red. Finally, several sparkling wines are also produced here though most are so highly oxidized that little pleasure is to be derived from them. The rare undamaged and still fresh examples though are of very good quality. Moldovan wine production has not yet completed its evolution from the Communist era but most observers consider it obvious that Moldova has a great future.

UKRAINE

Recently much effort has been invested in the area around Odessa and Nikolajev, close to the Black Sea, and around Dnjeprpetrovsk on the Dnjepr, to replace the old but highly productive varieties of grapes with better quality new ones such as riesling and cabernet sauvignon. Economic uncertainly has meant a decline in the Ukrainian wine industry. At present little positive can be said about the Ukraine. Once the sparkling wines of the Crimea – much of which originated in Moldova – were a by-word. These wines also do not appear to have a rosy future.

Czar Nikolai II had huge wine cellars constructed in the village of Massandra and the entire wine collection from the royal palace was transferred there. There is still an enormous collection here of the oldest bottled wines, each more famous than the next, dating from 1775. These wines are sold at auction for staggering sums of money.

Sweet red Crimean sparkling wine

RUSSIA

During the time of Perestroika the Russian government carried out a policy of dissuading people from their wide-scale problem of vodka drinking. The wine industry was subsidized and consumption of wine (instead of vodka) was encouraged. Enormous wine plants or Kombinats produced a never-ending flow of syrupy, full-bodied, and often heavily oxidized white and red wines, ranging from somewhat on the dry side to extremely sweet. These wines were produced in the Black Sea region, around the Sea of Azov (Krasnodar), the Don basin, Stavropol, and the Crimea, and also utilized imported bulk wine from Bulgaria, Moldova, Hungary, and Algeria. These foreign bulk wines were blended with wines from native grapes which lost their own identity behind a Russian label. Given the current uncertain economic situation in Russia and the significant lack of funds, the Russian wine industry has gone to total rack and ruin. The quality of wine has fallen sharply and it is impossible to give a clear picture of the current state of Russian wine. The Russians themselves have no idea what the future holds and the consumption of vodka has soared.

White rkatsiteli wine from Georgia

Red saperavi wine from Georgia

GEORGIA

Georgia, which is sandwiched between Russia and Turkey, produces a tremendous volume of good white, rosé, red, and sparkling wines but these are rarely seen outside of the country.

Some Georgian wines are unlikely to charm Western consumers because of their earthy tones and somewhat tart acidity. This results from the old--fashioned wine-making methods that are still in regular use in which entire bunches of grapes being left to ferment and more or less 'forgotten' for a time in earthenware pitchers. Georgian wines can easily be recognized by the decorative labels with at least six or seven gold medals on them on somewhat ungainly bottles. White wines are dominated by the two native grapes varieties of rkatsiteli and mtsvane. Several strange but high quality dry wines are made from these two types of grape. These are Tsinandali, Gurdzhaani, and Vazisubani. The equally excellent Napareuli wine is made solely from rkatsiteli, and Manavi uses just mtsvane. Tsitska, Tsolikauri, and Bakhtrioni are all made from native grape varieties of the same name. These wines and the Manavi and Vazisubani previously mentioned are all firm, fruity, and harmonious wines. Tsinandali, Gurdzhaani, Napareuli, and Manavi are all aged in wooden casks for at least

Georgian wines

three years. These wines are not truly fresh but they have marvelous fruitiness and a very elegant nose with a light and mellow fruity taste (by Georgian standards).

Those who truly wish to try the authentic and very localized taste of old-fashioned Georgian wines (from earthenware pitchers) should try the Rkatsiteli, Sameba, or Tibaani. The color of these dry white wines – made from pure rkatsiteli in the case of the first and from rkatsiteli and mtsvani in the case of the others – is between dark yellow and amber. The bouquet is somewhat fruity, suggesting perhaps currants with clear sherry-like undertones. All these three wines are more alcoholic at 12–13% than the other white wines mentioned.

Full-bodied red wines are made here from saperavi (Kvareli, Napareuli and Mukuzani) and cabernet sauvignon (Teliani). All these wines are cask aged for at least three years. These are not only full-bodied wines, they are also strong in tannin and have moderate levels of alcohol (12–12.5%) and are fairly fruity with suggestions of overripe fruit and currants.

Serving temperatures for Georgian wine are 10–12 °C (50–53.6 °F) for dry whites, 16–17 °C (60.8–62.6 °F) dry reds, 10–12 °C (50–53.6 °F) sweet reds, and between 6 and 8 °C (46.4 °F) for sweet whites and sparkling wines.

ARMENIA

Armenia might be the birthplace of the grapevine, with the stories of Noah's Ark that is thought to have been set in the region of Turkey, Iran, Azerbaijan, and Georgia, between the Black and Caspian Seas. Armenia is best known for its excellent brandies produced close to Mount Arafat but the country also makes a number of very acceptable quality red wines, such as those in the south-west of the country in the area around Yeghegnadzor. These are sturdy wines that are high in tannin and with high levels of acidity. They should be decanted some time before serving, preferably with lamb or goat. Drinking temperature is 14–16 °C (57.2–60.8 °F).

HUNGARY

Hungary is a relatively small Central European state. The climate is determined by changing fronts from three different climate systems: the severe Russian continental climate, the pleasant Mediterranean climate, and remnants of a moderate maritime climate. Winters are moderately cold and the summers are hot.

The Hungarian economy has two facets. On one hand there are enormous former state enterprises and on the other young and vigorous independent companies with a certain flair but this latter category is riddled with craft anachronisms and inertia.

Seventeenth century wine press

Hungary has a rich wine-making tradition

The gap between the rich and poor seems to be getting bigger but in contrast with the immediate past there is also a new middle class arising and improved living standards.

HUNGARIAN WINE-GROWING

Hungarian wine-growing dates back to the time of the Roman emperor Probus who had vineyards planted on slopes along the Danube in about 276 AD. These vineyards were significantly extended during the period that the Austro-Hungarian Empire flourished. During the period of Soviet domination Hungary was required to produce large amounts of steel so that the wine industry was to a large extent neglected. Hungarian wines of that era disappeared almost entirely to the USSR. The loss of Russia as export market was not immediately replaced by new markets in Western Europe. The quality levels required in Europe were far higher and the Hungarian wine industry was in dire need of renovation.

While the large former state concerns found it extremely difficult to attract capital (too big, to static, too old-fashioned) some dynamic wine makers found their salvation in the form of foreign investment. The terroir was good, the prospects very promising, and the investments were not big by western standards. New vineyards were planted, older ones replaced, complete

new wineries constructed and adapted to modern demands. Only the companies that produced products of superior quality had any chance in the markets of Western Europe. Power, money, and who-you-know still have a role to play in the Hungarian wind industry but that is changing and the younger companies are being taken more seriously even in the domestic market. This has much to do with several dynamic wine-growers and business such as István Szepsy, Tibor Kovács, János Arvay, Attila Gere, and Tibor Gál.

Hungary's great diversity in wine has its origins in the curiosity of three different climate types (maritime, continental, and Mediterranean). Furthermore Hungary also possesses some unique varieties of grapes. The Hungarians generally have great respect for both tradition and character although the question is which tradition? For the former state industries tradition seemed to stretch back no further than the past forty years but many of the newer companies are seeking the soul of the more traditional Hungarian wines of before World War II and before the Russians.

Tibor Kovács (Hétszölö, Tokaj)

István Szepsy (Királyudvar, Tokaj)

most important widely planted are the white varieties of olasrizling (Italian riesling, welsch riesling), furmint, rizlingsilváni (Müller-Thurgau or rivaner), hárslevelü, chardonnay, and cserszegi füszeres (of which wines by Hilltop Neszmély were introduced in the UK under the name of "The unpronounceable grape"), red and rosé wine varieties kékfrankos, zweigelt, kékoporto, kadarka, merlot, cabernet sauvignon, and cabernet franc.

HUNGARIAN LABEL TERMS

bor	wine
száraz bor	dry wine
felszáraz bor	medium dry wine
félédes bor	medium sweet wine
edes bor	sweet wine
asztali bor	table wine
tájbor	country wine (vin de table)
minöségi bor	defined origin wine
eredetvédelem bor	defined origin named wine

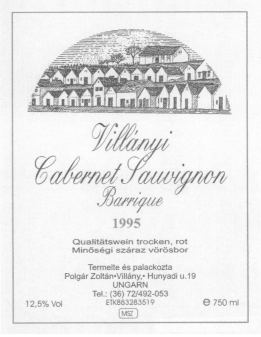

Minösegi száraz vörös bor: dry red quality wine from Villány

HUNGARIAN WINE TERMINOLOGY

Hungarian wine law is extremely strict in respect of nominated areas of origin and the choice of grapes and soil. In common with the French law, on which it is based, the rules provide no guarantee of quality of the wines.

HUNGARIAN GRAPES

The country grows many native varieties in addition to the well-known European (French and Austrian) types. The

János Avay, former wine-maker of Disnókő, the face of Tokay for outsiders for a long time

Below you will find the more important ones and some of their characteristics in Hungarian wine.

CABERNET SAUVIGNON AND CABERNET FRANC
Very popular in Villány. Very acidic and tannic when young but more mellow later. Characteristic bouquet of freshly cut green peppers (paprika), blueberries, bilberries, and cherries.

CHARDONNAY

Hungarian Chardonnays are often very acidic, especially from areas in the north. Apart from the Chardonnay of for instance Villány or Siklós, the majority of Hungarian Chardonnays lack the rounded, full, and creamy character with typical bouquets of butter and hazelnuts. In Etyek and surrounding area in particular they often possess a bouquet of apple, melon, or citrus fruit.

CIRFANDLI

In contrast to what is often claimed this has nothing to do with the Californian Zinfandel grape. It is originally a northern Italian variety introduced through Austria. The taste of this idiosyncratic grape is spicy and mild.

EZERJÓ

Literally meaning (thousand good) you are wished a thousand good things and need them in drinking Ezerjó wine. Most are very acidic and have a characteristic bouquet of citrus fruit, especially of grapefruit.

Cabernet sauvignon yields several great Hungarian wines

FURMINT

The basic grape for Tokay (Tokaji) wines. In the past furmint was vinified by the oxidative method that produced freshly acidic sherry-type wine with a hint of Granny Smith apples in bouquet and taste. Today made by reductive methods furmint wines are much fresher in bouquet and taste with great aromatic properties containing much fruit.

HARSLEVELÜ

Literally translated the name is lime or linden leaf. It is a late-ripening variety that is prone to *Botrytis cinerea*.

Very exciting wines are produced in Mór from ezerjó grapes

This is the second most important grape for Tokaji Aszú (Tokay) wines. Depending on where it is picked and the method of wine making it can have a bouquet of pears (reductive) or sherry-like aromas and honey (oxidative). Debröi hárslevelü even develops aromas of peach, milk, and substantial honey.

IRSAI OLIVÉR

This relative of the muscat grape is very aromatic and is mainly used in blended wines.

JUHFARK

Literally "sheep's tail": a very old-fashioned grape with a high level of acidity. Thanks to modern techniques this grape now produces very acceptable wines with relatively more mellow acidity and unusual bouquets of banana, cooked beans, butter, nuts, chestnuts...

KADARKA

This was once the most important blue grape of Hungary but because it is far too sensitive for the Hungarian climate it has largely been replaced. It no longer for instance forms part of the quality wines from Eger because most kadarka wines were too irregular in quality. Some growers though – and not the poorest – believe in the quality of kadarka. In Szeksard and Villány for instance several good Kadarka wines are made that can be distinguished by the vegetal and spicy bouquets which are slightly reminiscent of blue grape skins.

KÉKFRANKOS

This widely used grape is also known as blaufränkisch. With a few exceptions (Sopron, Villány) most kékfrankos wines are simple, freshly acidic, fruity, and light-bodied.

KÉKNYELÜ

This "blue voice" is a specialty of Badacsony on Lake Balaton. Extremely exciting aromas of grass and flowers combine with mineral undertones from the volcanic soil in which it grows.

KÉKOPORTO

Also known as portugueser. Delivers rich, full, velvet smooth, and seductive wines when well made as in Villány.

LEÁNYKA

These grapes produce dry and sweet wines, especially in Matraalja and Eger. Both the dry and sweet wines are characteristically mildly acidic.

Irsai olivér is often used in blends

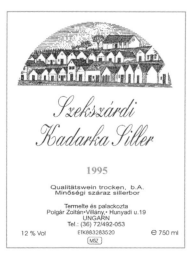

Juicy rosés are made from kadarka grapes

MERLOT

Hungarian merlot has aromas of freshly-sliced green peppers (paprika) and a hint of what is best described as cooked beans. Most of them are light and mellow. Those from Villány on the other hand are full, tannic, and robust.

OLASRIZLING

Also known as welsch riesling (wälschriesling) or riesling italico. Very widespread in Hungary. This type of grape produces firm wines with considerable body and aromas of roasted almonds.

ZÉTA

A cross between a furmint and a bouvier that is widely used in the Tokay (Tokaj) region. Ripens early with good acidity and fruitiness. Previously known as oremus.

OTTONEL MUSKOTÁLY

Muscat ottonel is world-renowned for its mellow acidity and floral bouquet.

PINOT BLANC

Not widespread by produces good results in Hungary. Soft and mellow wines that are delicate and fruity.

PINOT NOIR

In Villány they call pinot noir 'nagyburgundi'. There it produces, with or without cabernet sauvignon, rich, full, and very aromatic wines. In Etyek pinot noir is being more widely planted for sparkling wines.

RAJNAIRRIZLING

Also known as Rhine riesling. These grapes produce rare but exceptional wines in Hungary. Characteristic aro-

Merlot from Villány

Hajósi Kékfrankos is often stronger than other versions

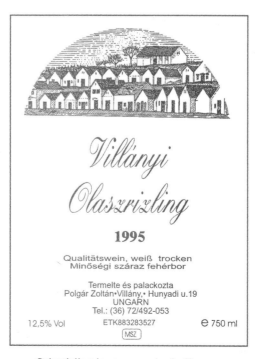

Oslasrizling is very popular in Hungary

367

mas include a slightly smoky scent and taste with vegetal freshness.

RIZLING SZILVÁNY

This fine local name is a synonym for the German/Swiss Müller-Thurgau or Luxembourg rivaner. During the Russian era it was widely planted but it now less used.

SAUVIGNON BLANC

World-famous grape that is achieving increased success in Hungary. Hungarian Sauvignon Blanc is mainly very vegetal (grass) with hints of citrus or exotic fruit (kiwi or lychee).

SÁRGA MUSKOTÁLY

The yellow muscat or muscat de lunel is fresher than its sibling ottonel muskotály. Very aromatic (fresh muscat grapes).

SZÜRKEBARÁT

The local name, literally "the gray monk", for pinot gris which in Hungary results in crude, ponderous, honey sweet

Some Olásrizling is cask-aged

and uninteresting wines but also fortunately a few (dry and sweet) fresher examples that are more modern and light. It certainly earns its place in the area around Badacsony.

TRAMINI

This is not the ordinary traminer as the name suggests but gewürztraminer. Some Hungarian wine makers use the correct name on the label: piros tramini. Has characteristic aromas of muscat and spice with floral notes (roses).

ZÖLD SZILVÁNI

Better known as (green) sylvaner or silvaner. Produces fairly neutral wines with vegetal nuances.

ZÖLD VELTELINI

Better known as grüner veltliner, originating from Austria. Is widely used around Sopron where it often results in uninspiring fresh wines with vegetal aromas.

ZWEIGELT

Another grape of Austrian origin. Zweigelt mainly produces light tannin-rich reds with bouquets of freshly-ground black pepper.

HUNGARIAN WINE AREAS

It is impossible in short to describe all the wine areas of Hungary so the emphasis is placed on the best of them.

In 2001 there were at least 22 different wine areas in Hungary of which the best are Sopron, Ászár-Nesmzmély, and Etyek (northwest), Mátraalja, Eger, and Tokajhegyalja (north east), Hajós-Baja (south east) Villány, Szekszárd, and Tolna (south west), and Badacsony (north east), Balatonfüred-Csopak, Balatonfelvidéki, and Balatonboglári (northeast and Lake Balaton). Wine areas that produce poor to reasonable wines such as Kunság and Csongrád are left out of the picture.

SOPRON

The Sopron wine area borders Austria and is greatly influenced by that country. Sopron's main tour de force is its Kékfrankos red wine. This is masculine and powerful wine that is high in tannin, full-bodied, and acidic with discernible bouquet of morello cherry, bilberry, and peppers (paprika).

Perfect wine for roast meat and stews (*pörkölt* of game) and oven dishes. Drinking temperature is 14–16 °C (57.2–60.8 °F).

Leave the area's cheaper wines for thirsty tourists and immediately choose instead the better wines such as Hilltop Soproni Sauvignon Blanc 'Kamocsay Borok' – one of the finest Hungarian Sauvignon Blancs – or Weninger Soproni Kékfrankos from the famous Austrian wine company that manages its own vineyards in Sopron.

For export the labels often bear Pinot Gris instead of Szürkebarát

Good robust wine from zweigelt

SOMLÓ

This tiny area between Sopron and Lake Balaton surrounds the town of this name. Very alcoholic and oxidized white wines are made here on underlying clay, basalt, and sandstone that are very acidic and high in minerals. The principal grapes are juhfark, furmint, olaszrizling, and hárslevelü. Somloi Jurfark is certainly not a western-style wine but many Hungarians, including professional tasters, continue to find this wine superb. This is inexplicable for many because even the best wines act like a rasp on the tongue. The bouquet has notes of hot butter, nuts including chestnuts, or even of beans that succeed in slightly diminishing this effect.

PANNONHALMA-SOKORÓAJA

This is one of the smaller wine areas of Hungary to the south of Györ. The soil consists mainly of loess and ancient forest humus. Several very acceptable full-bodied and sturdy white wines with a rich taste are made here from grapes such as tramini and olaszrizling. They combine well with pan-cooked pork, veal, or poultry. Drinking temperature is 10–12 °C (50–53.6 °F).

ASZÁR-NESZMÉLY

These are two small wine areas to the north-west of Budapest where the first-class Hilltop Neszmély produces mainly white wines from olaszrizling (riesling aromatico, Italian riesling, welsch riesling), rajnai riesling (Rhine riesling), rizlilngszilváni (Müller-Thurgau), and leányka (mädschentraube). Very fresh,

Famous Soproni Kékfrankos of Weninger

intensely fruity, and exceptionally pleasing. Delicious with goose, duck, or fish. Drinking temperature is 10–12 °C (50–53.6 °F).

MÓR

This is an elongated area to the north of the town of this name where ezerjó grapes produce white wine that is fairly acidic. The wines from this area have strong grapefruit bouquets and are at their best with substantial fare, preferably pork, goose, or rabbit. Drinking temperature is 14–16 °C (57.2–60.8 °F).

Pannonhalma

ETYEK

Etyek to the west of Budapest is the closest wine area to the capital. Those who like their wine harsh will certainly find it here. Chardonnays here are greener than anywhere else and rarely convincing. Some wines even smell strongly of sulfur but these are best ignored. The Sauvignon Blancs of Etyek Vinum and Hungarovin (György Villa Selection) are more reasonable. The best wines are perhaps the less commercial ones such as Etyeki Királyléanyka of Etyekvinum and Olaszrizling

György Villa of Hungarovin. Their acidic nature makes them best for fatty dishes such as pork. Drinking temperature is 8–12 °C (46.4–53.6 °F).

Etyek produces an outstanding sparkling wine (pezgö) by the traditional method. These are wines than can readily compete with most Champagnes except the top cuvées. Two that are recommended are François Président and Törley Brut, both from Hungarovin, a joint venture with the German sparkling wine house of Henkell.

MÁTRAALJA (MÁTRA MOUNTAINS)

En route between Budapest and Eger you pass through

Neszmély vineyards seen from Hilltop

Hilltop in Neszmély, pause and learn amidst the vineyards

Chardonnay of Szölöskert or the Mátraaljai Chardonnay of Mátyás Szöke) but they cost much less than the average Hungarian Sauvignon or Chardonnay. In short if you are wise you will buy from the Mátra region. All the wines are of very acceptable quality and fine for accompanying poultry or even lamb. Drinking temperature is 8–12 °C (46.4–53.6 °F).

EGER

The town of Eger is situated in a hilly area about 81 miles east of Budapest. The volcanic soil here also seems highly beneficial for wine-growing. The Eger Bull's Blood or Egri Bikavér is world famous but of variable quality. Some do not even deserve to be called wine while others are stupendous.

Fine quality Törley brut

The finest wines come from Vilmos Thummerer and Tibor Gál. Although excellent white wines are made here from grapes such as leányka, királyleányka, pinot blanc, olasrizling, and chardonnay the top honors go to the superb Egri Cabernet Sauvignon and Egri Bikáver. These possess great strength yet remain elegant and well-balanced. They can also be laid down for a considerable time. Other highly recommended top wines are Cabernet Franc and Cabernet Sauvignon of Bela Vincze and Egri Bikavér of PPP-Tamás Pók.

Drink the better Egri Bikavér with game, poultry in slightly spicy sauce, game stews, or oven dishes. Drinking temperature is 16–18 °C (60.8–64.4 °F) depending on the quality. Warmer is better with the best quality wines.

TOKAJ-HEGYALJA

Gently undulating hills, cool valleys, winding rivers teeming with fish, rustic villages in pastel colors and storks all conspire to make the area around Tokaj extremely picturesque.

The Tokaj area is best known for its Tokay (Tokaji), which is like liquid gold. It is not surprising that the bidding in Latin 'Oremus!' (Let us pray!) is above the entrance to the town's cellars. Tokay is no ordinary wine but a gift from Bacchus!

Eger produced a special 2000 cuvée for the Millennium

István Bozoki, king of the Móri Ezerjó

Gyóngós and the beautiful 31 miles long Mátra range of mountains. The entire area is covered in dense woodland and is an ideal wine-growing and walking area. The soil is of volcanic origin and hence ideal for growing grapes for wine. The wines are mainly dry to sweet whites. The hárslevelü and szürkebarat here are good.

Some recommended white wines are Abasári Olaszrizling of Sándor Kiss and Gyöngyöstarjáni Chardonnay and the Királyleányka of Mátyás Szöke. The much rarer red wines are surprisingly good, such as the Zweigelt and Gyöngyöstarjáni Cabernet Sauvignon of Mátyás Szöke and the Nagyrédei Vinitor Kékfrankos of the Szölökert Cooperative. Some of the rosés are also worth while considering. The most surprising wines are probably the superb Sauvignon Blancs and Chardonnays. Not only are these wines of great style and quality (like the Mátra Hill Sauvignon Blanc and

Visit István Bozoki's small wine museum

WINE STRUGGLES

Probably no other wine region in Hungary has seen such major changes as Tokajhegyalja since the ending of Soviet domination. The arrival of foreign investors after the green light for privatization quickened the pace of the renewal process but this also caused an enormous identity crisis in the region.

There had already been a bitter struggle between the old guard and the dynamic renovators over the rusty remnants from the old regime. This was not just about the style of what had once been the world's most famous wine but a complex issue concerning economic, sociological, and above all political issues. The antagonists are the Tokay renaissance movement on the one hand who defend the interests of the best independent wine makers of Tokaji and on the other the giant Tokaji Kerekedöház that is an inheritance of the old state-run days and still in the hands of the Hungarian government. Most of the members of the renaissance movement work with modern techniques while the former Borkombinat adheres to the old oxidative methods. The struggle turns mainly on the future of the state concern that is in possession of enormous cellars of unsold and possibly unsaleable supplies of Tokay. The cost of maintaining these become

Exciting dry white from Eger

Egri Bikavér of Tamás Pók: one of Hungary's best reds

TOKAJ, TOKAJI OF TOKAY?

There are various names similar to Tokaj that can cause confusion for the consumer.
- Tokaj is a town in the north east of Hungary, historic center of Tokay or Tokaji wines.
- Tokaji is the Hungarian name for wines from Tokaj. The genitive form is used and hence a Cabernet France from Sopron becomes a Soproni Cabernet Franc, Hajósi wine comes from Hajós, Villanyi from Villány etc. So wine from Tokaj becomes Tokaji Aszú or Tokaji Furmint.
- Tokay is still more widely used for wines from Tokaj in English and to confuse matters further, the French use Tokay for their Pinot Gris wines (see Pinot Gris/Alsace).
- Tocai is the Italian name for two different grapes: welsch riesling in most of Italy and sauvignon vert or sauvignonasse in Friuli. It is unclear how the name tocai came into use here. The Italians will no longer permitted to use tocai on their labels from March 2007.

increasingly onerous and the number of staff has had to be significantly cut. The first clashes followed privatization in 1989. The foreign companies (especially the French of Disnókö, Hétszölö, and Magyar Pajos) made a radical start and irritated the cash-strapped ex Borkombinat concern. The foreigners broke with the tradition of oxidization and pasteurization. In common with France and almost everywhere else in the world sulfur was added to the wine to prevent further fermentation in order to retain

The top of Disnókö (wild-boar hill)

the delicate primary aromas. The quality of the casks was also significantly improved and indeed the wines from these foreigners was much fresher, fruitier, and purer than those of the old kombinat. István Szepsy has already experimented with reductive methods before the arrival of the foreigners. The battle reached a climax in 1995 when the Hungarian wine authorities (OBB) threatened to reject the Aszú of Disnókö. The

In Eger they prefer their red wine with grilled meat

The Burgundian-style vineyards of Hétszölö:
revolutionary for Tokaj

Disnókö was once disputed but now widely praised for
the high quality of its wines

French almost made an international political incident of it but after much negotiation things were calmed.

That this time bomb between the Hungarian authorities and foreign investors could exploded at any time was shown in 1999 when the OBB did reject the wine of Hétszölö for "not being sufficiently oxidized." Some members of the renaissance movement threatened a boycott of the OBB or otherwise to leave the description Aszú off the labels. After difficult negotiations however a revision of the wine law permitted modern Tokay and significantly reduced the period of cask maturing. Peace seems to have returned to Tokaji. After a historical and tragic low point, Tokay wine is once again flourishing at home and abroad thanks to reforming people like István Szepsy, János Arvay, András Bacsó, Tibor Kovács, and the late Gábor Tepliczki.

CLIMATE

The secret of Tokay wine lies in its microclimate that in the fall ensures morning mists that are then burnt off later in the day by the hot sun. These are ideal conditions for *Botrytis cinera* which more or less removes all the moisture from the grapes, leaving a high concentration of sugars and aromatic substance in the grapes.

The withered grapes (known locally as *aszú*) are picked by hand.

Wine is naturally created under the pressure of the grape's own weight (*eszencia*) that has intense flavor. This *eszencia* is added to the 'base' white wine. The higher the number of containers or *puttonyos* that are added, the greater is the quality of the wine with a maximum of six *puttonyos*. The required quantity of *aszú* grapes is weighed these days with one *puttonyos* equal to 20 kg (44 lb) before being added to the must (in good years) or to other white wines used as a basis. The wine is then aged in wooden casks. The length of ageing is dependent on the method of vinification (traditional or modern). Tokaji Aszú is then usually bottled in half liter 'belly' bottles and left for some years

in the impressive cellars of Tokaj. Rare Tokaji Aszú Eszencia wine is made in exceptional years equivalent to seven or eight *puttonyos*, and then left for decades before being sold. Take care not to become confused with the ordinary Eszencia, which is also sold separately and is virtually pure nectar.

In addition to the superior Tokay wines, Tokay also produces white wines from furmint grapes. In those years when too few *aszú* grapes can be harvested or people cannot be bothered to sort the grapes they make Tokaji Edes Szamorodni. The name Szamorodni is Polish for 'as it comes' which recalls the times when Poland forged new links with Hungary. There are also a sweet (Edes) and dry (Száraz) version.

Considerable foreign investment and time has recently gone into improving the soil, new planting, new equipment, and better hygiene control of the

István Szepsy can laugh again after troubled times

grapes and wines. This has resulted in an enormous improvement in the quality. The vinification method varies totally from that of the former state company. These modern business try to retain the freshness of the fruit and wine and to avoid contact with oxygen (the reductive method) in contrast with the slow oxidative approach used by the Tokaj Kereskedöház. Wines made by the reductive method not only smell and taste better, they are drinkable much sooner! This means the consumer does not have so long to wait and that the price is relatively cheaper.

Start of the *Botrytis* infection

The desired result: "aszú grapes"

The absolutely top quality wine among the foreign companies is Disnókö (Axa of France). Their Tokaji Aszú 5 and 6 *puttonyos* are superb with a deep amber color and very elegant bouquet of sun-dried apricots, quince, tobacco, leather, almonds, coffee, toast, and acacia honey (5 put.) sun-dried apricots, white truffles, *Botrytis*, tobacco, cedar wood (cigar boxes) honey, dates, prunes, and toast (6 put.) They also possess strength, finesses, and fine acidity which keeps the unctuousness in balance. Secretive tastings of the 5 and

The aszú grapes are individually picked by hand

The result of intensive labor

6 put. wines of '95, '96, '97, and the eszencia of '99 left a very deep impression on me. For those who do not wish to wait so long and seek a not too expensive wine the Tokaji Szamo-rodni Edes 1993 is an absolute must with superb aromas of overripe fruit including peach and apricot but also raisins, almonds, vanilla, and various flora aromas (lilies-of-the-valley, may blossom) that are present in the overtone.

The entire range of Aszú wines from Hétszölö (GMP-Suntory, France/Japan) are very impressive but the most intriguing wine was the Hárslevelü Késöi Szüretélésü

Tasting from the cask: István Szepsy and Zoltán Demeter of Királyudvar

Liquid gold

of Tokay and the only survivor who can say how the old Tokay wines were made. His family has worked in the production of Tokay for generations and István himself can recall how his grandfather made the wine. He can still recall the smell and flavor of them. None of the old generation of wine-makers survives and of the present-day makers only István can recall these times. Until 1996 István made rare jewels of wines in the garage of his home and conditioned them in the family's underground cellars. In 1996 he established the new company of Királyudvar with the American patronage of Anthony E. Hwang. They chose the former royal court buil-

(vendages tardives/late harvest). Also recommended are the top wines of Pajzos (superb Muscat vendages tardives), Oremus (of Vega Sicilia of Spain), and Royal Tokaj Wine Company (with Hugh Johnson as a shareholder and promoter). The smaller Hungarian family companies also produce good wines despite limited means. Good to excellent wines are those of János Arvay (former wine maker of Disnókö), Zoltán Demeter (also second wine-maker of Királyudvar), Vince Gergely (Uri Borok), and Himesudvar.

ISTVÁN SZEPSY AND KIRÁLYUDVAR

The star of István Szepsy has been in the ascendant in the past decade. He is regarded as the best wine-maker

A jewel from the Szepsy family's own production

dings of Királyudvar as their base. These neglected buildings were fully restored and reopened with festivities in 2000. The first Királyudvar was harvested in late 1999 from their own vineyards. The results are extremely promising as well as the superb harvest of 2000 with sugar in the Eszencia of more than 800 grams per liter!

The criticism of the traditionalists is cut short by István with: "It is pure nonsense to say the modern wines are 'reductive' and the traditional ones 'oxidative'. Oxidization always occurs in the Aszú grapes themselves and hence also in the eszencia. The elegant tones of oxidization are derived from there, not languishing in musty casks that are only three-quarters full. The modern wines are much better and have a longer life through their higher concentration of acidity, alcohol, and sugar. The wines made by the kombinat are pasteurized leaving no room for improvement in the bottle. The liquid is dead. With

Making a top wine starts in the vineyard

Wine-tasting area at Disnókö

Attention to detail at Disnókö

modern methods this opportunity is there by earlier bottling." His opinion is gaining greater acceptance in Tokaj and much farther afield. Anyone who has tasted István's wines can immediately endorse his words. Something fine is blossoming again in Tokaj that will bring this region to unparalleled heights.

TOKAY WINE/WINES OF TOKAJ

- Furmint: old-fashioned wine with traditional oxidized taste like the wines of the Jura and Jerez. Drinking temperature is 8–12 °C (46.4–53.6 °F).
- Szamorodni Edes: often served in Hungary as an aperitif or with goose liver. This is certainly not inappropriate provided the rest of the meal is accompanied by Aszú wines. Alternatively you can drink this sweet wine with fresh desserts or after dinner. Drinking temperature is 8–10 °C/ 46.4–50 °F (but cooler is also possible).
- Szamorodni Száraz: this dry wine has much in common with a Fino Jerez (sherry) and is a first-class aperitif or with smoked fish, light hors d'oeuvres, and more fatty meat (pork, mutton, goose etc.). Drinking temperature is 10–12 °C (50–53.6 °F).

A superb late-harvest Késöi Szüretélésü from hárslevelü

- Aszú: serve this sublime wine with fresh desserts or pastry, with fruit (juicy pears, peaches, apricots), with mature cheese, or simply on its own after dinner. I do not recommend combing it with goose liver for neither the wine or the liver benefit. Drinking temperature is 6–10 °C (42.8–50 °F) according to taste.

HAJÓS-BAJA

The south of Hungary is blessed with a Mediterranean-type climate moderated by maritime influences. This makes the area a paradise for birds. Only the wines of Brilliant Holding of Hajós are worth considering, which produces fresh rosés and superb reds under very hygienic conditions using the latest technology (no chaptalization, aging in wooden casks, use of nitrogen during bottling, and longer Portuguese corks).

Szepsy's private réserve

Drink the rosé wines with pan-cooked poultry, robust fish dishes, or with meat. The reds demand a fine piece of meat or poultry. Drinking temperature is 10–12 °C (50–53.6 °F) for the rosés and 14–17 °C (57.2–62.6 °F) for the reds.

SZEKSÁRD

This area is one of the oldest wine regions of Hungary and has an ideal microclimate plus a fertile sedimentary soil of loess. Szeksárdi Bikavér (Bull's Blood) has an excellent reputation and an older history than that from Eger. This wine is dark red and its bouquet is reminiscent of redcurrants with suggestions of toast. The taste

Harvest home, the future is bright

is dry, fresh, very tannic, fulsome, and rounded. Perfect with pan-fried or roasted meat. Drinking temperature is 15–17 °C (59–62.6 °F).

In addition to outstanding red wines (merlot, cabernet sauvignon, cabernet franc, kadarka, and kékfrankos), Szekszárd also produces excellent kadarka rosé and whites (chardonnay, sauvignon blanc, and olaszrizling). Heartily recommended are Takler Ferenc, Vesztergombi Ferenc, and Vida Péter.

One wine that deserves a special mention is the sublime Bátaszéki Sauvignon Blanc of Akos Kamocsay of Hilltop Neszmély.

Their Sauvignon Blanc is undoubtedly one of the finest Hungarian whites. It possesses a bouquet in which newly mown grass, wild chervil, stinging nettles, and suggestions of elderflower can be discerned.

Superb as an aperitif but also with a starter (asparagus) or refined fish dishes. Drinking temperature is 9–10 °C (48.2–50 °F).

TOLNA

Tolna is a new wine area that was part of Szekszárd until recently. Although the name of Tolna is little known outside of Hungary, wines of exceptional quality are made here by Eurobor (Zwack & Antinori). Although the official name is Möcsényi Kastélyborok the wines is better known under the name of the village of Bátaapáti.

TOLNAI MÖCSÉNYI ZÖLD VELTELINI

This wine is fresh and fruity that even the most spoilt fish

Szamorodny is often omitted from the label

will happily swim in it. Drinking temperature is 8–10 °C (46.4–50 °F).

TOLNAI MÖCSÉNYI TRAMINI

A subtle, elegant, and very fine wine to combine with rich fish dishes and white meat. Drinking temperature is 10–12 °C (50–53.6 °F).

TOLNAI MÖCSÉNYI SAUVIGNON

The Sauvignon Blanc newest member of the family is delightful with vegetal notes of green peppers (paprika), asparagus, and mangetout (Pisum sativum). An excellent aperitif of good companion for white meat, poultry, or fish in a fine sauce. Drinking temperature is 9–10 °C (48.2–50 °F).

Excellent wine from Hajós

TOLNAI MÖCSÉNYI CHARDONNAY

This cask-aged wine is generally very characteristic of the grape with an immediate and rich bouquet and excellent balance between fresh acidity and rounded body. A chic aperitif and excellent accompaniment for poultry, white meat, and fish in a rich sauce. Drinking temperature is 10–12 °C (50–53.6 °F).

TOLNAI MÖCSÉNYI KÉKFRANKOS

A fresh and elegant crystal-clear rosé and a classic deep red wine with a mellow but full-bodied texture.

TOLNAI MÖCSÉNYI SPECIAL RESERVE

The top cuvée is a blend of cabernet sauvignon and cabernet franc. This Special Reserve is very rich and complex, filling the mouth with flavor, with a good balance between spice and body. The finish is prolonged and superb. This wine needs to be kept for at least two to three years before drinking. It is ideal for better steak. Drinking temperature is 17–18 ° (62.6–64.4 °F).

N.B. Although only the grapes originate from the Tolna region and the wine is made elsewhere, Csersegi füszeres of the very successful Hilltop (Neszmély) deserves a special mention if only for the self-deprecating humor of its label.

Elegant and refined modern Furmint

Commercial but very acceptable Szeksárdi Bikavér

VILLÁNY-SIKLÓS

This is the most southerly of Hungary's wine areas and it consists of two parts, both situated at the foot of the Villányi mountain. Siklós is predominantly known for white wines and Villány for fine reds. There are six top wine producers in Villány that give us the feeling that something really fine is developing here. It is surely no coincidence that the six best wine-makers of Hungary originated from Villány. They are Attila and Támas Gere, Zoltan Polgár, Ede Tiffan, Joszef Bock and Vylyan's Tibor Kovacs. It is anticipated that the red wines of Villány will be among the finest in Europe in a few years.

Each wine-maker has an individual style but the power and depth of the red wines is apparent, which is the result of the great care with which the grapes are selected, the volcanic soil, and the very beneficial climate.

VILLÁNYI ROSÉ

Some wine-makers produce a light rosé that is fairly unconvincing. The best rosés from here though are those made from kékfrankos and kékoportó, possibly with a little pinot noir, zweigelt, or kadarka. These are very fresh and elegant wines that are fruity and full-bodied. The rose's from Ede Tiffan and Gere Weninger is particularly recommended.

Totally suited for lighter meals, soft vegetable dishes, but also for freshly and lightly poached salmon or other robust seafish.

In Hungary they often serve rosé with creamy dishes spiced with paprika. Drinking temperature is 10–12 °C (50–53.6 °F).

A fish should swim three times: in water, in fat (or oil), and in Zöldveltelini

VILLÁNYI KÉKOPORTÓ

The better Kékoportó wines (Vylya, Tamás Gere) are intensely colored, fresh, concentrated, fruity, velvet smooth, fruity, mellow, and slightly tannic. There are also excellent cask-aged Kékoportó Barriques (Vylyan). Drink this authentic and festive wine with lighter meat dishes or roast poultry (barrique). Drinking temperature is 14–16 °C (57.2–60.8 °F) or 16–17 °C (60.8–62.6 °F) for the Barrique.

VILLÁNYI KÉKFRANKOS

An authentic full-bodied and rounded fresh red wine that is full of tannin that combines well with roast meat but also most *pörkölt* stews. (Tamás and Attila Gere, Jószef Bock, or Zoltán Polgar). Drinking temperature is 14–16 °C (57.2–60.8 °F).

VILLÁNYI PINOT NOIR

The pinot noir grape thrives here too on volcanic soil. Vylyan is the pinot noir specialist. Serve this It is a full-bodied, fiery, and powerful wine with delicate acidity and distinctive taste of *terroir* with poultry or small game. Drinking temperature is 14–16 °C (57.2–60.8 °F).

VILLÁNYI MERLOT

These are good wines with definite bouquet of cedar wood, blackcurrant, and hint of roses, possessing a fulsome and rounded taste and velvet smooth texture. These wines are superbly made but never either excit-

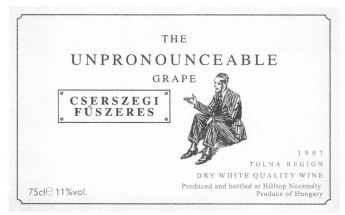

Unpronounceable maybe but very delicious

ing or typically Hungarian. Suits most types of meat. Drinking temperature is 14–16 °C (57.2–60.8 °F).

An exception of world class is the Merlot Of Vylyan which truly is sublime and gets better as the vines get more mature. By aiming for low yields they are aiming

Talentum, the top cuvée from Bátaapáti

at world class here. Vylyan's wines are not light-footed affairs but robust with appropriate aging in wood. Following several more years aging in the bottle they are supremely exciting and very complex. The Merlot from Vylyan deserves the very best piece of steak or roast sirloin. Drinking temperature is 17 °C (62.6 °F).

VILLÁNYI CABERNET FRANC
Cabernet franc is certainly not a native grape variety and in the rest of Hungary this wine would be inconsequential but here in Villány on volcanic soil it does extremely well and develops a character of its own. It is dark in color while the nose is reminiscent of ripe plum or even prune, and blueberry, while the taste is

Attila Gere during the annual gastronomic festival in Budapest

Dynamic Vylyan winery in Villány

fulsome, firm, and rich, with the required tannin. A superb accompaniment for roast meat. Drinking temperature is 16 °C (60.8 °F).

The Cabernet Sauvignon from Villány is filled with color, very aromatic with suggestions of berries and peppers, with a fulsome and powerfully fiery taste with considerable tannin. These wines of superb class have great potential for aging well, especially those that are cask aged – and good potential for laying down. Drinking temperature is 16–17 °C (60.8–62.6 °F).

Highly recommended are Bock cuvée (1995), Attila Gere Kopár, and Attila Gere & Weninger Cabernet Sauvignon Barrique.

SPECIAL CUVÉES
The best wines from Villány are generally found in the "special cuvées." In addition to various classic combinations (cabernet sauvignon, cabernet franc, and merlot) there are also Franco-Hungarian blends (cabernet sauvignon and cabernet franc with e.g. kékfrankós or kékoportó) and pure Hungarian cuvées (kékfrankos and kékoportó). One of these blends produces results not known elsewhere that is guaranteed its own identity: the impossible combination in French terms of cabernet sauvignon and pinot noir. From these very special cuvées I particularly recommend those of Vylyan (Montenuovo) and Joszef Bock (Duennium cuvées).

VILLÁNY WHITE WINES
Although Villány is best known for its reds and Siklós for its whites, there are some Villány whites. Try the 100% olaszrizling, tramini, and Chardonnay Barrique that are excellent or the superb Hárslevelü and Muskotály.

SIKLÓSI WHITE WINES
The white wines of Siklósi are generally of reasonable to good quality. They are made from grapes such as olasrizling, hárslevelü, and chardonnay. The first two yield aromatic dry wines of character that are excellent as an aperitif with lighter fish dishes. The chardonnay

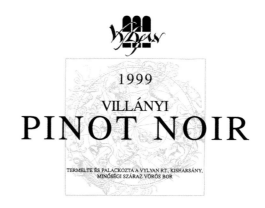

1999
VILLÁNYI
PINOT NOIR

TERMELTE ÉS PALACKOZTA A VYLYAN RT. KISHÁRSÁNY, MINŐSÉGI SZÁRAZ VÖRÖS BOR

750 ml   PRODUCE OF HUNGARY   alc.13,5 % vol.

Villányi Pinot Noir

general yields full and rounded warm wines that go well with fish, white meat, or poultry. Drinking temperature is 10–12 °C (50–53.6 °F).

THE BALATON
The area surrounding Lake Balaton is ideal for sun worshippers and watersports enthusiasts. The climate is mild in winter and hot in summer (above 25 °C/77 °F). The water temperature varies in the summer between 20 and

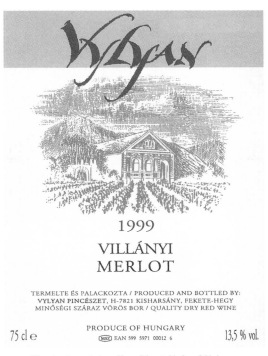

1999
VILLÁNYI
MERLOT

TERMELTE ÉS PALACKOZTA / PRODUCED AND BOTTLED BY:
VYLYAN PINCÉSZET, H-7821 KISHARSÁNY, FEKETE-HEGY
MINŐSÉGI SZÁRAZ VÖRÖS BOR / QUALITY DRY RED WINE

75 cl e   PRODUCE OF HUNGARY   13,5 % vol.
MSZ EAN 599 5971 00012 6

The truly outstanding Pinot Noir of Vylyan

Sublime Bock cuvée 1995

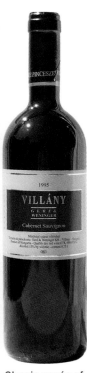

Classic cuvée of
Gere & Weninger

26 °C (68–78.8 °F), during which time the water temperature varies between 20 and 26 °C (68 and 78.8 °F).

In addition to still wines, area around Lake Balaton produces several very acceptable sparkling wines.

BALATONBOGLÁR

The soil of the most southerly of the three wine areas around Lake Balaton is a mixture of sand and clay. It was formerly known as Del-Balaton. Most of the winemakers no longer produce ponderous, heavy, and oxidized wines as was once the case. The young wines are fresh, mild, light, and fruity and are chiefly made from irsai olivér, tramini, olaszrizling, chardonnay, and muskotály (Muscat). There are also a few reds made from merlot, cabernet sauvignon, cabernet franc, and kékfrankos. The local reds and whites here are generally very simple affairs but the exception is the superb, taut wines of Chapel Hill in Balatonboglár which are full of character. These wines originate from small areas of land on volcanic soil. The Chapel Hill Sauvignon Blanc and those of Ottó Légli are very surprising.

BALATONFELVIDÉK

This is most westerly of the three areas on the northern shore of Lake Balaton. Until recently it

was known as Balatonmellék but this name is now reserved for a new wine area between the western end of Lake Balaton and the Austrian border, formerly known as Zalai that has yet to produce any worthwhile wine. The soil of Balatonfelvidék consists of chalk, marl, and some tufa, interspersed with volcanic outcrops. This makes the area ideal for white wines and hence it is planted with olaszrizling, rajnai rizling, rizling szilváni, szürkebarát, sauvignon blanc, chardonnay, and some other white grape varieties. The outstanding winemaker Sander Tóth makes excellent aromatic, full-bodied, and classic-style Chardonnay, but also exceptionally sensual wines such as the Aldozói Zöldveltelini and Zenit.

BADACSONY

This fairly small wine area is sited around the town of this name on the northern shores of Lake Balaton. The soil chiefly consists of basalt and other volcanic types. This imparts high acidity,

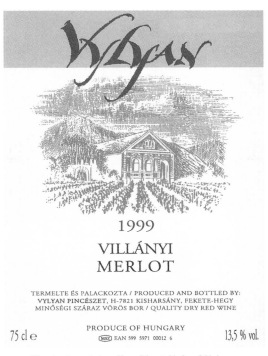

1999
VILLÁNYI
CABERNET SAUVIGNON
SELECTION

TERMELTE ÉS PALACKOZTA / PRODUCED AND BOTTLED BY:
VYLYAN PINCÉSZET, H-7821 KISHARSÁNY, FEKETE-HEGY
MINŐSÉGI SZÁRAZ VÖRÖS BOR / QUALITY DRY RED WINE

75 cl e   PRODUCE OF HUNGARY   13,0% vol.
MSZ EAN 599 5971 00092 8

Villányi Cabernet Sauvignon

Exceptional
Vylyan cuvée

1997
VILLÁNYI CUVÉE
CABERNET SAUVIGNON - MERLOT - ZWEIGELT

AZ EZREDFORDULÓ
ALKALMÁBÓL ÖSSZEÁLLÍTOTT
VILLÁNYI CUVÉE /
CUVÉE FOR THE NEW MILLENNIUM.

MINŐSÉGI SZÁRAZ VÖRÖS BOR /
QUALITY DRY RED WINE

TERMELTE ÉS PALACKOZTA /
PRODUCED AND BOTTLED BY :
VYLYAN Rt., H-7821 KISHARSÁNY,
FEKETE-HEGY

PRODUCE OF HUNGARY
MSZ

5 995971 999475

alc.13 % by vol.   750 ml

Duennium rear label

Lake Balaton

a rich bouquet, and fulsome but fiery taste to the local wines. The area's specialty is an exceptionally sultry, slightly sweet to sweet wine that is made from late harvested kéknyelü, szürkebarát, tramini, rajnai rizling, and muskotály (muscat) grapes. But there are also many fresh and scented dry white wines that are made from olaszrizling, zöld veltelini, and sauvignon blanc, plus full-bodied, rich chardonnays. All the wines of Szent Orban Pince, the wine business of globetrotter Huba Szeremley, are recommended.

BALATONFÜRED-CSOPAK

This is the most north-westerly of the areas around Lake Balaton, situated around the town of Csopak. The soil is mainly underlying strata of volcanic origin with shale, ferruginous sandstone, rock, and chalk. White wines are produced here from grapes that include olaszrizling, rajnai rizling, and rizling szilvány, and reds from cabernet franc, merlot, pinot noir, and zweigelt, plus rosés from merlot, zweigelt, and kékfrankos. Balatonfüred wines are full-bodied, powerful, and rounded, while those of Csopak possess greater finesse, acidity, and elegance. The special cuvées of Figila Mihály are outstanding.

THE CZECH
AND SLOVAK REPUBLICS

The Czech and Slovak Republics have been separated now for a few years. Both countries have a turbulent history, and hopefully they are now in a period of peace and tranquillity. The economic situation in these countries is still far from ideal. With regard to wine, attention is mainly focused on The Slovak Republic, while the Czech Republic is more of a place of pilgrimage for beer lovers – everyone knows the Pilsner

Urquell and the true Budweiser. In fact, the Czech Republic was so important for the development of beer that a beer from Plzen (Pilsen) became the prototype for all Pilsener beers. Nevertheless, grapes are cultivated in both countries. Viticulture suffered a great deal from the many wars and years of occupation. The Romans planted the first vineyards in the third century AD. Viticulture thrived during the Austro-Hungarian Empire, particularly in The Slovak Republic. Unfortunately, the vineyards were also destroyed there by the *Phylloxera* louse at the end of the nineteenth century. Following the final collapse of the Austro-Hungarian Empire (1918), the history of Czechoslovakia experienced a very black period with disastrous consequences for viticulture. For fifty years the enormous state-run businesses experimented with an emphasis on quantity rather than quality, even though The Slovak Republic in particular had been famous for centuries for the quality of its wines. During the 1950s the area of vineyards was further expanded in The Slovak Republic, but it was at the end of the 1960s in particular that the

Three top wines by Huba Szeremley (Badacsony): Kéknyelü, Szürkebarát (Pinot Gris), and priceless Zeus spätlese

country was able finally to start a period of slow recovery.

Underground cellars of Figula Mihály

CZECH REPUBLIC

The Czech Republic covers the western part of the
former Czechoslovakia and consists of the two regions,
Bohemia and Moravia. From the reign of Charles IV
through the late eighteenth century, grapevine cultivation constituted an important branch of agriculture.
It subsequently began to decline, and farmers started to
grow sugar beet and other cash crops as the area covered by vineyards decreased. Only in the second half of
the twentieth century was the wine industry revived.
Czechs now drink around 3 3/4 gallons of wine per
inhabitant per year. About 17,960,000 gallons of wine
is made locally annually, and another 13,210,000 gallons is imported.

The drawback of Czech and Moravian viticulture
is that the emphasis was placed on the grape variety
and the importance of the location of the vineyard was
underestimated. The wine industry also lacked regu-
latory legislation of the type introduced into other
European countries. That is the reason why even quality wines exported to elsewhere in Europe were classified as table wines. A law governing viticulture was
finally passed in 1995. The classification is based on
the sugar content of the grapes, which are therefore
divided into 3 categories – table wine, quality wine,
and choice quality. The whole territory is divided into
2 regions, containing 16 vine-growing areas. The law
also lists the grape varieties that may be cultivated in
each area.

The grapes selected for cultivation consist of a mixture of foreign and domestic varieties. The white
varieties include Vetlínské zelené, Ryzlink vlašský,
Müller-Thurgau, Ryzlink rýnský, Sauvignon, Tramín
červený and Muškát moravský and the "blue" varieties
include Svatovavřinecké, Frankovka, Modrý Portugal,
Rulandské modré, Zweigeltrebe and André.

The Bohemian viticulture region is the smallest in
area (1,606 acres) and is also the furthest north. The
prevailing conditions are not particularly propitious,

however, the average yearly temperature being only
46.4 °F, and on rising to 57.2–59 °F in the growing season. There are 1600–1800 hours of sunshine a year and
the annual rainfall varies from 19–22 inches. Most of
the vineyards are situated on the southern slopes and
the soils are largely calcareous, although there is also
some eroded basalt. In climatically favorable years,
lighter, more acidic but distinctly full-bodied wines are
obtained.

There are 6 vine-growing areas in the region. The
largest is the Mělník region. The soil here is lighter,
and so quickly warmed by the sun, and it provides good
conditions for growing Rulandské
modré, Svatovavřinec, Red Traminer and Ryzlink rýnský. As early as
1896, the production of sparkling
wine was begun in the cellars of
Mělník castle, using the *méthode
champenoise* (fermentation in bottles). The Mělník wine Ludmila also
has a long tradition; it is sold in
distinctive bottles shaped like an
inkpot.

The vineyards of the Roudnice region are located on the
shores of the river Labe, around
the town of Roudnice. The best
red Roudnice wines are Svatovavřinec and Modrý Portugal,
and the best white wine is made
from Green Sylvaner grapes.

The Žernosec region is located on southern slopes of
the Bohemian mid-mountain
range (Středohoří). White varieties are mainly grown here
–Ryzlink rýnský, Red Traminer,
and Müller-Thurgau.

The Mostec region is the
furthest north in the Czech
Republic and the grapes here are
of the typically northern type,
being rather acidic. A specialty

Müller-Thurgau

Frankovka grapes
produce simple,
but fresh, pleasant
red wines.

Grapevine trained over steel wool

is the production of kosher wines under the supervision of the Chief Rabbi of Prague.

The Moravian wine-growing region is situated in southern Moravia. There is a thousand-year-old tradition of grape-growing for wine-making in Moravia, but grapes were only grown extensively for the benefit of the Roman legions stationed here in the third century AD. Currently, about 29,650 acres of vineyards are cultivated in Moravia. The area is divided in 10 grape-growing regions. The Znojmo region is located near the town of Znojmo near the Austrian border, in the lea of the Czech-Moravian hills. The local soil is mainly gravel or loess. Most of the wines made here are white, from varities of Ryzlink rýnský, Vetlínské zelené, Ryzlink vlašský and Müller-Thurgau. Drinking temperature: 50–53.6 °F.

The Velké Pavlovice region is known as the red wine region. The blue varieties Frankovka, Svatovavřinec, Rulandské modré and Modrý Portugal are predominately grown. Drinking temperature: 53.6–57.2 °F.

The Mikulov region has 2 centers: Mikulov and Valtice. The Mikulov vine-growing area boasts one of the warmest microclimates in Moravia. On the southern, calcareous slopes of Pálava, the Ryzlink vlašský, Rulandské bílé and, more recently, the Chardonnay varieties ripen to excellent quality. Near the city of Valtice grapevines have always been widely grown. This has required large cellars for storing the wine. One such cellar exists that has a capacity of 171,700 gallons and dates from 1430. It is still in use. Besides of the basic white varieties, blue varieties—Frankovka, Rulandské modré and Cabernet Sauvignon—are also grown.

The Brno region lies south of Brno and its main centers are Židlochovice and Dolní Kounice. The varieties predominantly grown in Židlochovice are Moravian Muskat, Red Traminer and Irsay Olivér. The resulting white wine is aromatic. In Dolní Kounice, blue varieties–Frankovka, Svatovavřinec, and Modrý Portugal are predominately grown on the gravely soil, resulting in full-bodied, robust wines.

The vineyards of the Kyjov region are located on the southern flank of the Žďárnický forest, which shelters the vineyards from the

The Slovakian side of the Tokay hills

The familiar Czech 'inkpot' bottle used for Ludmila wines

The Excellent Rhone Riesling

Rhone Riesling grapes produce simple, but very acceptable, wines

northern winds. Since this region is fairly far north, early-maturing white grapes are cultivated here, in particular Müller-Thurgau.

The Bzenek region has an ancient wine-making tradition, the first written document about Bzenek vine cultivation dating from the year 1078. The center of viticulture was Bzenek castle, where sparkling wine was first produced in the cellars in 1875. A French nobleman who found a retreat here disclosed the secret of the méthode champenoise. The Bzenek region is proud of having the oldest Moravian quality domain name, Bzenek Lipka.

The Uherskohradišťsko region lies at the northern end of the Moravian region. The most common varieties here are Müller-Thurgau, Moravian Muscat, and Ryzlink rýnský.

The Strašnice region´s vineyards lie on the slopes of the White Carpathian mountains. White wines are made from White Rulander, Gray Rulander, Green Sylvaner, Ryzlink rýnský, and Müller-Thurgau. The best-known wine is Blatnický Roháč, made from a blend of White Rulander and Green Sylvaner grapes.

THE SLOVAK REPUBLIC

Slovakia is smaller than the Czech Republic, but a much larger area is under vine cultivation (75,610 acres). The whole grape-growing area is divided into 8 regions, 6 in the west and 2 in the east.

The most important region is Malokarpaty (Small Carpathians). Here, the vineyards are located on slopes of the foothills of the Carpathian mountain range, near the Ukrainian border, where the climate is warm with mild winters. White varieties such as the Green Veltliner, Müller-Thurgau, Ryzlink vlašský, Dívčí hrozen, Sauvignon, and in the Rači are grown along with the blue Frankovka and Blue Portugal are grown predominately.

Climatically the best growing region in Slovakia is the Nitra region. The main varieties grown here are Ryzlink vlašský, Ryzlink rýnský, White Ruland, Red

Traditional wine made from the Moravian Muskat grape, as indicated by the label.

Traminer, Green Veltliner, and Müller-Thurgau. Dry wines are produced here whose flavor is distinctive and full-bodied.

The Modrokamensko region has vineyards on the slopes of the Slovakian Red Mountains. White varieties such as Müller-Thurgau, Ryzlink vlašský and the Dívčí hrozen are planted here predominately, but there are also

Slovakian Tokay

Slovakian vineyards extend over the Hungarian border

red varieties, such as Frankovka and Svatovavřinecké.

The Tokay region is the most famous of the Slovakian viticulture regions.

The technique for producing Tokay wines is the same as that practiced in the Hungarian Tokay region. Traditional steps are taken to produce Tokay selections (azsu) and Tokay au naturel dry and dessert wines. For many years, the Hungarians have tried to obtain the exclusive right to use the Tokay appellation. The problem was solved to some extent during the Communist era, when Slovakian Tokay was imported into Hungary and sold as Hungarian Tokay. After the fall of Communism, the vineyards on both sides of the border were privatized and the Slovakian wine producers started to sell the wine themselves. This upset their Hungarian neighbors considerably and the argument is still far from settled. Slovakian Tokay wine is of a quality equal to the Hungarian product and is usually bottled in clear glass 1 pint bottles.

AUSTRIA

After the great fiasco of 1985 (the anti-freeze scandal), Austrian wines have once again been able to resoundingly convince the world of their great class, diversity and fascinating character. Despite their noble past, Austrian wines are not wines which you drink wearing white gloves with your little finger raised in the air: they are cheerful, informal, inviting wines, reflecting the culture and picturesque landscape.

The very good
Ruland white

HISTORY

Austria has a fairly long tradition of wine growing. There were already vines growing in Burgenland almost 5,000 years ago. Vienna, the capital of Austria, was famous for its wine in Roman times, as evidenced by the many wine accoutrements discovered in archeological digs. Once again it was Emperor Probus who encouraged the planting of vineyards here. The village of Zagersdorf (Burgenland) was already known as a wine-growing village in 700 BC. Following a period of stagnation, Charlemagne revitalized Austrian viticulture. In the fifteenth century monks continued its development, especially along the banks of the Donau (Danube). The very first Trockenbeerenauslese made its appearance in 1526. The drinking water in the towns in those days was of such

An idyllic landscape does not guarantee that the wine will have a flowery bouquet, of course.

poor quality, and the majority of beers were equally undrinkable and unsanitary, that the Austrian people started drinking wine on a grand scale. When the quality of beer improved slightly and could be drunk without ill effects, wine consumption declined to more normal levels. Because of the extremely heavy taxes on growing and making wine, its production was no longer very profitable. However, Empress Maria

"Austrian wines are full of music." (Langelois)

Theresa and her son, Emperor Joseph II reduced the taxes and gave wine growers the freedom to sell wines directly from their own estates, which led to the development of the many 'Heuriger' inns, where new wines can be sampled and drunk, together with delicious snacks. The vineyards and wine taverns of Austria were probably the most cheerful places in the whole of Europe. However, this euphoria came to an abrupt end after the severe frosts of the late nineteenth century. The vines had no time to recover, because shortly thereafter the first fungal disease appeared (*oidium*) and *Phylloxera* lice spread from Western Europe. Vineyards in Austria were also completely destroyed by this *reblaus*, or grape louse, as *Phylloxera* was locally known. The indigenous Austrian grapes were grafted onto immune stock, and eventually wine growing flourished once more after an interval of many years.

Austrian viticulture became independent after World War I and could no longer count on the possible assistance of the other states of the former Austro-Hungarian Empire. This led to the start of a great regeneration of vineyards and wine-making, with particular improvements in matters of quality. After World War II, new methods were developed for training the vines (using high trellises), older and inferior varieties of grapes were replaced by better ones, and all the wine-growing systems were completely renewed and expanded. In 1985, Austrian wine once again faced a serious setback: 'anti-freeze' (diethyleneglycol) was discovered in the wine of a number of producers. This had been added to the wines as chaptalization. This fraud, which only took place on a very modest scale, resulted in an enormous scandal, which irrevocably damaged the image of Austrian wine. Austrian wines have regained the high ground again through new wine laws, increased controls and the passion of growers for both their product and their country. True wine connoisseurs throughout the world are familiar with the superb and fascinating wines of Austria. It is to be hope for the benefit of today's generation of growers that the general public will also rediscover Austrian wine.

WINE GROWING

The composition of the soil in Austria is extremely varied, which explains the great diversity of wines. In the Weinviertel and the valley of the Danube, the loess soil produces elegant and fruity wines. Along the Danube valley, particularly around Wachau) there are also occasional deposits of iron ore. In the Thermal springs region (near Gumpoldskirchen) there is also some limestone. The soil in Burgenland consists mainly of slate, marl and sand, which produces full-bodied, meaty wines. Finally, the wines from Steiermark derive their strength and fiery character from the volcanic soil. The climate is particularly favorable for wine growing, since Austria has a continental climate. Another very important factor for Austrian viticulture is that of water. The Danube and its tributaries, together with the Neusiedler See, not only provide sufficient water for the vines, but the water also reflects the warmth and light of the sun. The evaporation resulting from the heat in turn tempers the sun's heat. Around the Neusiedler See this creates a moist warm microclimate for *Botrytis cinerea*, which is responsible for the excellent Trockenbeerenauslese. Finally, the height of planting of the vineyards also plays an important role: in most wine-growing regions they are situated at a height of 656–1,312 ft, except in Steiermark, where they can be at a height of 1,968 ft.

GRAPE VARIETIES

Austria is clearly a country which produces white wine. Slightly more than three quarters of the wines are white. These white wines have fresh, elegant acidity and a great deal of fruit. The alcohol content varies between 10.5–14% alcohol.

GRÜNER VELTLINER
This indigenous variety of grape still accounts for the lion's share of Austrian wines (more than one third of the vines that are planted). Its characteristics are pepper, grapefruit, fresh acidity, lively wines which can be drunk when young, but also kept for some time.

WÄLSCHRIESLING (WELSCH RIESLING)
This is an extremely popular quality grape. It is characterized by green apple, hay, flowers, fresh acids and a slender elegance.

MÜLLER-THURGAU (RIESLING+SYLVANER)
Although a long way behind the grüner veltliner, this grape comes in third place after the wälschriesling. Its characteristics are a light muscat aroma and meadow flowers, and it should be drunk when young.

Most vineyards are at a height of 650–1,300 ft

WEISSBURGUNDER (PINOT BLANC)

This wine is characterized by almonds, nuts, a powerful structure, a compact character and balance.

NEUBURGER

This indigenous variety produces wines that age well. It is characterized by mild acidity, an aroma of nuts and is full-bodied.

The hot, humid area of the Neusiedler See at Rust

RIESLING

This Rhine riesling produces excellent wines for laying down: characteristics: roses, peaches, apricots, fruity aromas, elegance, fresh acids.

MUSKAT OTTONEL

Characterized by light muskat aromas, a light and slender structure.

TRAMINER (GEWÜRZTRAMINER, ROTER TRAMINER)

In Austria, the traminer usually produces sensual, supple and feminine wines that are very tempting. Characterized by aromas of flowers (roses), spices.

RULÄNDER (PINOT GRIS)

Full-bodied sturdy wines are made with the ruländer with a great potential for aging. Characterized by honey, sweet.

ZIERFANDLER

Indigenous variety that produces mild fruity wines, rich in extracts. It is often used together with the slightly less elegant rotgipfler.

Grüner Veltliner

Weissburgunder Federspiel (Wachau)

ROTGIPFLER

Another indigenous variety of grapes for fruity mild wines rich in extracts, though they are slightly less elegant and sophisticated than those of the zierfandler.

Riesling Federspiel (Wachau)

MORILLON (CHARDONNAY)

This grape has also recently been discovered in Austria. Austrian Chardonnay wines are fresh, with the characteristic aromas of green apples and a lot of fruit.

MUSKAT - SYLVANER (SAUVIGNON)

Characteristics: a strong vegetal character with grassy nuances and frequently a hint of elderflower.

OTHER WHITE GRAPES

Roter veltliner, bouvier, gelber muskateller, goldburger and sylvaner.

ZWEIGELT

Zweigelt is an indigenous black grape obtained by crossing the Saint Laurent and blaufränkisch. Characteristics: cherries, morellos, with a lot of backbone, rich in tannins and fresh.

BLAUER PORTUGIESER

This is the Austrian counterpart of the Hungarian kékoportó. Characteristics: pansies, hay, fruity aromas, mild, little alcohol or acidity.

BLAU FRÄNKISCH

The Austrian counterpart of the Hungarian kékfrankos. Characteristics: red fruit, spices, cinnamon, powerful, high in tannin.

SAINT LAURENT

Old-fashioned variety, probably from Alsace. Characteristics: cherries, morellos, dry and balanced, velvety when the youthful tannins have broken down.

BLAUER BURGUNDER (PINOT NOIR)

An old favorite, which produces full, round and soft wines with little acidity in Austria.

BLAUER WILDBACHER

Older indigenous variety, specially used in rosé wines. Characteristics: raspberries, blackcurrant, grass, often quite a lot of acids, dry, should be drunk young.

OTHER BLACK GRAPES

More and more top wine growers are producing excellent wines using cabernet sauvignon, cabernet franc, and merlot. In terms of percentages, these three varieties of grapes are not really representative of Austrian wine. Nevertheless, the cabernet sauvignon particularly produces good results: wines rich in tannin with cha-

Blaufränkisch

racteristic aromas of blackcurrants, and strong grassy and herbal undertones.

WINE CLASSIFICATION

Reading an Austrian label is a fairly complicated matter. Wines are classified according to the geographical origin of the grapes or wines and according to the variety of grape, methods of wine making, quality requirements, sugar

A rare, excellent Saint Laurent

content of the must and final taste of the wine. For quality wines, the origin of the grapes is the same as the origin of the wines. However, this is not the case for simple table wines.

QUALITY AND MUST WEIGHT CLASSIFICATIONS

According to the new wine law of 1985, quality wines must be made with a single variety of grapes. There are three categories, each determined by the amount of sugar in the must, expressed in KMW degrees (1 °KMW – Klosterneuburger Most Waage –corresponds to 1% sugar in the must).

TABLE WINE/TISCHWEIN

These wines may be made of grapes from all over Austria. The only indication that must be shown on the label is 'Wein aus Osterreich'. A table wine must contain at least 8% alcohol and 10.6 ° KMW.

VINS DE PAYS

These wines may only originate from a single geographically determined wine-growing region and must be made from the legally permitted varieties of grapes. The yield is limited to 6,750 l/ha. Furthermore, the wines must contain min. 8.5% and max. 11.5% alcohol, as well as min. 14 ° KMW and max. 6 g/l residual sugar.

QUALITÄTSWEIN

These wines may only come from a single geographically determined wine-growing region and may only be made with the legally permitted varieties of grapes. The must may be enriched (added sugar, chaptalized) with max. 4.25 kg per 100 l of must, up to max. 19 °KMW for white wines and 20 °KMW for red wines. However, both white and red wines must contain at least 15 °KMW and respectively 9% and 8.5% alcohol. All wines must have a label with a control number.

KABINETT

These wines are really Qualitätsweinen. They can be seen as a sort of special reserve. The biggest difference from the ordinary Qualitätsweinen is the prohibition on enriching the must either with sugar or with extremely sweet or reduced must (Germany: Süssreserve). This prohibition also applies for poor years. Furthermore, the wines must contain max. 13% alcohol, max. 9g/l residual sugar and min. 17 °KMW.

PRÄDIKATSWEIN

The Prädikatswein (Spätlese to Trockenbeerenauslese and Eiswein) must show a year and contain at least 5% alcohol. The must may not be enriched. There are seven different types of Prädikatswein which are distinguished on the basis of the weight of the must and the method by which the wine is made:
– Spätlese, min. 19 ° KMW, made exclusively with completely ripe grapes. (N.B. More and more frequently the label states Qualitätswein instead of Spätlese. In fact, Austrian Spätlese wines are virtually always made very dry and contain min. 13% alcohol. As the grapes are harvested in the best

Kabinett

vineyards when they are very ripe, there is no need for any extra sugar to maintain a balance with high acidity);
– Auslese, min. 21 ° KMW, made exclusively with carefully selected and completely ripe grapes;
– Eiswein, min. 25 ° KMW, made with frozen grapes with an enormous concentration of aromas and taste. When the frozen grapes are pressed, the water is left behind with the skins;
– Beerenauslese, often abbreviated to BA, min. 25 °KMW, made with overripe grapes, affected by *Botrytis*;
– Strohwein, min. 27 °KMW, made with grapes which have been dried on a bed of straw in the open air for at least three months, comparable to vino santo or vin de paille);
– Ausbruch, min. 27 °KMW, made with overripe grapes partly dried by *Botrytis*;
– Trockenbeerenauslese, often abbreviated to TBA, min. 30 °KMW, made exclusively with grapes dried by *Botrytis*.

In the Wachau region, where enriching the must is strictly prohibited, a different classification is used for white wines;
– Steinfeder, light and elegant wines with min. 10.7% alcohol.
– Federspiel, elegant and slightly more powerful

Spätlese trocken with the simple indication 'Qualitätswein'

wines, min. 17° KMW, max. 11.9% alcohol;

– Smaragd, full-bodied wines, rich in extracts, and with a great deal of character, min. 18° KMW.

DESCRIPTION OF TASTE

The label on Austrian wines tells you how dry or sweet the wines tastes. You should certainly make a distinction between the residual sugar content and the original sugar content in the must (KMW, must weight). It is often the case that a wine of which the must contained a great deal of sugar actually tastes dry: i.e., it does not contain any residual sugar. However, this wine, which is made rather dry (e.g., Spätlese or Auslese), contains relatively more alcohol than the sweet versions of the same wine. In this case the sugars are converted into alcohol during the fermentation process.

– extra trocken: brut, very dry, max. 4g/l.
– trocken: dry, max. 9 g/l and max. 2 g less acidity than sugars (i.e., 7 g sugars, min. 5 g acidity).
– halbtrocken; medium dry, max. 12g/l
– lieblich, halbsüss: medium sweet, max. 45 g/l.
– süss: sweet, like a liqueur, min. 45 g/l.

Beerenauslese

Eiswein

Steinfeder (Wachau)

Federspiel (Wachau)

Smaragd (Wachau)

Trockenbeeren-auslese

The famous Ruster Ausbruch

WINE-GROWING REGIONS

Austrian wine growing is mainly concentrated in the east and southeast of the country. Because of the Alps in the west, cultivation of vines is hardly possible there. In the west, Austria borders on Germany and in the south it borders on Italy, but the vineyards lie near the Czech, Hungarian and Slovenian borders. The area of Austria cultivated with vines (125,712 acres) was subdivided in July 1999 into four main areas: the *Weinbauregionen* of Weinland, Wien (Vienna), Steiermark, and Bergland.

WEINLAND

The wine-growing area of *Weinbauregion* Weinland covers a fairly large area of the Czech/Hungarian border close to Vienna (115,007 acres). It is subdivided into two subsidiary regions, known as *Weinbaugebiete*: Niederösterreich and Burgenland.

NIEDERÖSTERREICH (LOWER AUSTRIA)

WEINVIERTEL (WINE QUARTER)

This is the largest of the sixteen Austrian sub-regions (39,489 acres). Approximately one third of Austrian wines are produced here. This region is universally known for its very characteristic 'Kellergassen'; long, narrow streets in the local villages with rows of friendly wine cellars where it is possible to taste

(Spätlese) trocken from Langelois (note the high alcohol content!)

You can taste wines everywhere in Austria.

and buy the wines. Wines of grüner veltliner varieties, which account for no less than 50% of the production, are very well known. The region also produces the white wines, Wälschriesling, Rheinriesling, Weissburgunder and Chardonnay, as well as Blauer Portugieser and Zweigelt (red). The soil of the Weinviertel consists mainly of heavy loam and limestone.

KAMPTAL

Kamptal is mainly known for its very good Grüner Veltliner with a characteristic peppery aroma and very

fresh acidity. Other good and excellent wines, usually from the village of Langenlois, include the Riesling and Chardonnay (white) and the excellent red Zweigelt, Pinot Noir and Cabernet Sauvignon. Kamptal leads the way in the whole of Europe with its organic approach to viticulture. The soil of this region, which has an area of 9,582 acres, consists of clay and a little limestone. The white wines are still in the majority, but red wines are gaining ground all the time.

KREMSTAL

This wine-growing region, with an area of approximately 5,495 acres near the town of Krems, produces excellent Grüner Veltliner, Riesling and Chardonnay. The soil consists of granite, (in the west) or clay and loess (in the east and south), producing elegant white wines, which are fruity and extremely aromatic.

WACHAU

This extremely high quality wine-growing area (3,595 acres) in the picturesque valley of the Danube

Austria is in the lead with regard
to environmentally-friendly viticulture.

produces excellent Grüner Veltliner, Neuburger, Chardonnay and Weissburgunder. The vineyards are on terraces on the steep hillsides above the Danube. The soil consists mainly of igneous rock. This produces the best white wines in Austria, although the competition from Südsteiermark is increasing all the time.

Niederösterreich is quite a green area.

A view of the steep hills of Wachau
from the southern banks of the Danube

TRAISENTAL

This small region (1,766 acres) lies around and above the town of Sinkt Polten, and only stretches as far as the Danube in a few places. The soil consists of loam and sand, producing extremely fruity Grüner Veltliner, Wälschriesling, Rheinriesling and Chardonnay.

DONAULAND

Donauland (6,832 acres) is a region on either side of the Danube between Krems and Vienna. The loamy soil with clay and some limestone produces excellent grapes: grüner veltliner, riesling and weissburgunder.

CARNUNTUM

The 'gemischter Satz', mixed viticulture, is still applied in Carnuntum (2,525 acres). Several different varieties of

Langeloiser Grauund
Weissburgunder
(Kamptal)

grapes are planted in the same vineyard. The vines benefit from the twofold influence of the Danube and the Neusiedler See. The soil consists mainly of clay, sand, gravel and chalk. Characteristic wines are the Grüner Veltliner, Wälschriesling, Weissburgunder, Chardonnay (all white) and Zweigelt and Saint Laurent (red).

THERMENREGION (THERMAL SPRINGS REGION)

This is the southernmost region of Lower Austria (Niederösterreich), south of Vienna and west of the Neusiedler See. The name of this region (6,310 acres) is based on the large number of hot springs of volcanic origin which are found here. The soil consists of a heavy, rocky subsoil with an upper layer of clay and limestone. The historical and commercial epicenter of the region is Gumpoldkirschen. The white wines produced here are full and very aromatic, while the red wines are strong and full-bodied.

BURGENLAND

The large region of Burgenland actually consists of two separate areas, both next to the Hungarian border. The northern region (Neusiedler See and Neusiedler See-Hüggelland) is directly influenced by the Neusiedler See, while the southern parts (Mittelburgenland, and Südburgenland) are less affected by this. The total area of this wine-growing region is 39,409 acres.

NEUSIEDLER SEE

The hot and dry Central European climate, in combination with the presence of evaporation from the Neusiedler See, forms the basis for the success of this region. It

The border between Wachau and Krems

is an ideal climate for *Botrytis,* and this fungus results in extremely good Prädikat wines. The strength of this region lies in the Edelfäule wines (noble rot), the Stroh wines, Eis wines and other sweet wines made, for example, with the wälschriesling, weissburgunder, bouvier and muskat ottonel grapes. However, the red wines are also excellent: Saint Laurent, Blaufränkisch, Cabernet Sauvignon and Pinot Noir (21,072 acres).

NEUSIEDLER SEE-HÜGELLAND

This region lies to the west of the Neusiedler See. The relatively large region (12,641 acres) is mainly known for its tempting sweet wines, such as the famous Ruster Ausbruch. The white wines are made with the wälschriesling, weissburgunder, neuburger, sauvignon and chardonnay grapes. Excellent red wines are also produced with the blaufränkisch, zweigelt and cabernet sauvignon grapes in the area of the picturesque town of Rust. Most vineyards have soil consisting of clay, sand, limestone and heavy loam.

MITTELBURGENLAND

Here the soil is slightly heavier (clay). The majority of wines are red wines: they are excellent dry red wines, full, powerful and rich in tannin, made with, the blaufränkisch and zweigelt grapes. Attempts to mature the wines in wood in small barrels (barriques) have been very successful. In addition to the red wines, some reasonable Wälschriesling and Weissburgunder wines are also produced (4,568 acres).

SÜDBURGENLAND

Until recently, Südburgenland was the smallest wine-growing area in Austria (1,126 acres). The wines produced here reflect the unparalleled beauty of the idyllic landscape. Extremely powerful red wines are made with the blaufränkisch and zweigelt grapes on the hills, where the soil consists of loam, clay and sand, as well as a few good white wines made with wälschriesling and muskat-ottonel grapes.

WIEN (VIENNA)

Vienna is not only a great cultural and historical city with a rich history of wine-making, but also one of the very few major European cities where wine is actually made. Wine is produced in the immediate vicinity of Vienna, as far away as possible from the industrial areas. These wines are of

The town of Rust with the Neusiedler See in the background

Excellent red wine from the Neusiedler See region

Magnificent cuvée from Burgenland

Neusiedler See: an oasis in Rust

Excellent sweet Wälschriesling

The Neusiedler See region is well known for its luxurious, sweet white wines.

With these grapes, affected by *Botrytis*...

...the amiable Willi Opitz from Rust makes some of the best sweet wines in Europe.

reasonable quality and are mainly intended for local catering establishments and the inhabitants of Vienna. They come from vineyards with a soil of soft slate mixed with clay and limestone. They are mainly white wines made with the grüner veltliner, neuburger, chardonnay, traminer and riesling grapes.

STEIERMARK

Total wine-growing area: 8,856 acres.

SÜD-OSTSTEIERMARK
This is a fairly large region (2,970 acres), east of the city of Graz. The soil consists of a mixture of clay and volcanic rock and the climate conditions are extremely favorable (hot and humid). Very acceptable wines are produced here with the wälschriesling, weissburgunder, traminer, ruländer, Rheinriesling and chardonnay grapes.

WESTSTEIERMARK
This region is much smaller than Süd-oststeiermark (1,188 acres) and lies west of Graz. The exclusive specialty of the region is an extremely fresh, fruity rosé (aromas and taste of blackcurrants): the Schilcher, made

To know more about the whole of Burgenland, you could visit the wine museum in Rust.

with blauer wildbacher. The best wines come from vineyards with a soil consisting of gneiss and slate.

SUDSTEIERMARK
The beautiful, softly undulating green landscape in the south of Steiermark (4,697 acres) is reminiscent of the Tuscan hills in Italy. The wines (Wälschriesling, Sauvignon blanc, Chardonnay – known here as Morillon – and Muskateller) are of an excellent quality and increasingly compete with the top wines from Wachau. Because of the small scale of local viticulture, the wine growers focus exclusively on quality and originality. Many of these young wine growers have great plans for the future, and it will not be long before they break through on the international market.

BERGLAND

This new wine-growing region is very modest with regard to the total wine-growing area which is only 42 acres! The Weinbauregion Bergland comprises the tiny regions of Voralberg, Tirol, Kärnten, Oberösterreich and Salzburg.

SWITZERLAND

Switzerland is an unbelievably beautiful country with breathtaking mountains and deep valleys, many lakes, picturesque towns and villages and a great deal more. The Swiss (culinary) culture is also universally admired and praised. Swiss chocolate, cheeses, air-dried Graubünder (Grisons) meat and other delicacies are famous all over the world. However, talking about Swiss wines leads to lively discussions. According to opponents, Swiss wines are absurdly expensive and of very moderate quality. After all, you cannot make a good wine with an inferior grape such as the chasselas. On the other hand, fans of Swiss wines actually mention the original Swiss terroir as an argument, as well as the extremely successful combination of the soil, location and grape. They will quickly add that Switzerland not only produces white wines, and that the prices are the logical consequence of the difficult working conditions. For an objective taster, Swiss wines are extremely

COMBINATIONS OF FOOD WITH AUSTRIAN WINE

- Cold starters (salmon, raw ham): dry white wine, e.g., Grüner Veltliner, Riesling or Wälschriesling.
- Cold meats: dry rosé, e.g., Zweigelt rosé, Blauer Portugieser rosé or Schilcher.
- Game paté: rosé or soft red wine made with the blauer portugieser.
- Paté of veal or poultry: exciting white wines, e.g., Grüner Veltliner trocken or Weissburgunder.
- Smoked fish: dry white wines with a great deal of extract, e.g., Weissburgunder, Chardonnay or Grüner Veltliner.
- Lobster (cold, e.g., in salads): dry white wines which are very powerful, e.g., Riesling Spätlese trocken, Chardonnay or Ruländer trocken.
- Other shellfish and crustaceans: vibrant white wines with fresh acids, e.g., Grüner Veltliner, Riesling or Weissburgunder trocken.
- Eggs: mild or slightly herbal white wines, e.g., Neuburger, Sylvaner, Müller-Thurgau, Rotgipfler.
- Hot starters (e.g., vol-au-vents, etc.): powerful, aromatic white wines or rosé, e.g., Sauvignon blanc, Muskateller trocken, Goldburger or Blauer Portugieser rosé.
- Hot lobster or coquilles St. Jacques: round white wines rich in extracts, e.g., Chardonnay.
- Hot seafood: fresh, aromatic white wines, e.g., Sauvignon blanc, Muskateller or Müller-Thurgau trocken.
- Mushrooms: red wines which are not too heavy, e.g., Zweigelt or Blauburger.
- Pies, rice: light, dry white wines, e.g., Grüner Veltliner, Riesling or Sauvignon blanc.
- Pastry with cheese: powerful white or rosé wines, rosé. e.g., Zweigelt rosé, Schilcher or Chardonnay.
- Pastry from the oven: medium heavy red wines, e.g., Blaufränkisch, Saint Laurent or Merlot.
- Fish (fried): dry white wines, e.g., Riesling, Sylvaner or Sauvignon blanc.
- Fish (in light sauce): dry or medium dry white wines, e.g., Wälschriesling or Grüner Veltliner.
- Fish (in rich, creamy sauce): white wines rich in extracts, e.g., Weissburgunder or Ruländer.
- Fish (in red wine sauce): use the same red wine as for the sauce, but make sure they are not wines which are high in tannin.
- Fresh salmon, hot: your very best rosé.
- Eel (stewed in chervil sauce): aromatic white wines, powerful rosé wines or light red wines which are not matured in wood, e.g., Blauer Portugieser.
- Tender vegetables (asparagus): soft white wines, e.g., Sauvignon blanc, Müller-Thurgau or Weissburgunder.
- Vegetables with a strong taste (cabbage, beans): light or medium-heavy red wines, e.g., Zweigelt, Blauer Portugieser or Blaufränkisch.
- Mushrooms (as a main course): powerful red wines, e.g., top Zweigelt, Blaufränkisch, or Saint Laurent.
- Poultry (braised, steamed): dry, full white wines, e.g., Riesling.
- Poultry (roast, grilled): mild or full white wines, e.g., Sylvaner or Neuburger.
- Goose, duck: red wines, e.g., Saint Laurent or Merlot.
- Veal, pork and lamb (cooked): medium heavy white wines, e.g., Riesling or Grüner Veltliner with some residual sugar, Neuburger or Sylvaner Spätlese.
- Veal, pork and lamb (roast): dry white wines rich in extracts or light red wines, e.g., Grüner Veltliner, Blauer Portugieser or Zweigelt (not matured in wood).
- Beef: light or powerful red wines, which may or may not be matured in wood (barrique), e.g., Zweigelt, Blaufränkisch or Blauburger.
- Game: powerful, heavy red wines which have been matured in wood, e.g., Cabernet Sauvignon, Blauer burgunder or Merlot.
- Raclette, fondue: fresh, fruity, dry white wines, e.g., Grüner Veltliner or Wälschriesling.
- Semi-mature cheeses (Tilsiter): full-bodied, dry, white wines, e.g., Weissburgunder, Chardonnay or Riesling.
- White cheeses: full-bodied, ripe and fruity red wines, e.g., Blaufränkisch or Merlot.
- Red bacteria cheeses (Limburger): strong, red or white wines, such as mature Grüner Veltliner, Blauburger or Zweigelt.
- Blue cheeses: good sweet Auslese, Ausbruch, or Trockenbeerenauslese (TBA), white wines.
- Apple strudel: Spätlese.
- Pancakes: Kabinett or Spätlese.
- Pastry/pancakes with whipped cream: Auslese made with the Müller-Thurgau, traminer, weissburgunder, ruländer or neuburger grapes.
- Desserts made with fruit or nuts: Spätlese or Auslese made with the muskat-otonel, traminer, rotgipfler or zierfandler grapes.
- After dinner with (good) friends: Eiswein, Strohwein, or Ausbruch.
- In very tranquil surroundings: Beerenauslese (BA), or Trockenbeerenauslese (TBA).

FREIE WEINGÄRTNER WACHAU

Spitzer

Tausend Eimer Berg

RIESLING
SMARAGD 1995

Delicious with better types of fish

Austrian viticulture is experiencing an upward trend.

HISTORY

The Romans introduced Roman vines in Switzerland about 60 BC. Old indigenous varieties of grapes such as the amigne, arvine and rāze probably date back to Roman times. The Romans planted vineyards in the south of Switzerland (Ticino, Valais), around all the lakes and rivers (e.g., in the valleys of the Rhône and the Rhine) and in the north of Switzerland. After the collapse of the Roman Empire and following the Barbarian invasions, it was again the monks who restored and developed viticulture here at a later date. The wine was needed for the Mass (the blood of Christ), and therefore had to flow abundantly. After the Middle Ages, more and more laymen started to own vineyards. The wines of those days had a lot in common with the extremely poor wines which are sold nowadays in some roadside restaurants and ski resorts: acidic and green. In order to make these wines more drinkable the Swiss added just about anything with a strong taste, from honey to fruit juices and herbs. In the seventeenth century, so many Italian and French wines were imported into Switzerland that the wine-growing area was significantly reduced. Viticulture particularly lost ground in

Wallis in September, breathtakingly beautiful

fascinating and have great class. Admittedly, the wine which is served for much too much money in most ski resorts to tourists is no better than a sharp, almost undrinkable liquid. However, these expensive aprés-ski wines are certainly not representative of the quality of Swiss wines. There are many excellent white wines in Switzerland, particularly the wines made in the immediate surroundings of the great lakes. Some Merlot wines from Ticino can compete without any problem with even the very best French wines. But it also true that the prices of some of the wines, particularly at the lower end of the market, are kept artificially high by the protectionist approach of the Swiss government and because the Swiss consumption of white wine is almost as large as its production. However, a visit to the terraces of Dézaley, Epesses or Sion shows that cultivating a terrace costs almost as much as the whole vineyard itself! Fortunately, the Swiss government appears to be prepared to help with this by providing subsidies to maintain the famous Swiss terraces, possibly with the help of UNESCO. In 2002, the borders will open for good for wines other than Swiss white wines. The prices will then have to be revised if Swiss viticulture is to survive, but the future of the wine growers who focus on quality and authenticity will eventually be assured.

mountain areas and concentrated on the hills, in the valleys and around the lakes. As a result of the *Phylloxera* plague at the end of the nineteenth century and the subsequent expansion of the large towns on the shores of the lakes, the Swiss wine-growing area was reduced by half in a short time. Throughout almost the whole of the twentieth century, the emphasis in Switzerland was more on quantity than on quality, which did not do the image of Swiss wines much good. Because of large quantities of artificial growth stimulants the vines were forced to 'piss' wine, the term used for ensuring excessive yields. In the 1960s and particularly the 1970s, it became clear that this could not go on. The soil was turning to rock, there was increasing erosion and the terraces suffered enormously. Under pressure of the government and because of the honesty and alertness of the best wine growers, these poor practices came to an end. Wine growers who had deridingly been described until then as "living fossils", were suddenly regarded as saviors in a time of need. Their respect for nature and the consumer was adopted almost everywhere. Lower yields, fewer artificial fertilizers (preferably none), no more insecticides and pesticides, a compromise between the interests of nature and of man in which nature should never pull the short straw: this was to be the new policy. Fortunately, the message was received. In 2002, the borders of Switzerland will open completely to all foreign wines. Up to now, only red wines could be freely imported, because the Swiss production did not cover consumption. From 2002, Swiss wine growers with high quality wines will once again give Switzerland a chance on the international wine market.

WINE GROWING

Despite the many mountains, the situation for Swiss viticulture is extremely positive. Most vineyards are concentrated in valleys or around lakes. In the valleys, vineyards are warmed up by the föhn, warm air in the mountain areas (particularly in Valais and in Grisons (Graubünden) and the northeast). The surface of the water in the lakes reflects the light and heat of the sun

(Neuchâtel, Geneva and Vaud). Because the soil of many vineyards around the lakes consists of igneous rock and boulders, the vines are heated in three different ways. Many Swiss vineyards have 'three suns', as the local wine growers poetically call this phenomenon: the direct sun, the sun of the rocks and the sun of the water. The sunniest regions of Switzerland are Ticino (which also has the tail end of a Mediterranean climate), Valais and Vaud; it is not surprising that the best Swiss (red) wines come from these areas. As the soil of the Swiss wine-growing regions is quite diverse, I will describe it for each region.

Switzerland has at least twenty varieties of white grapes and more than ten black varieties. Most belong to the so-called 'specialties' of a wine-growing area. The Swiss wine-growing regions are subdivided into three large regions: Suisse Romande, Ticino, and Ostschweiz. In the French-speaking region (Suisse Romande) the chasselas is the king of the white grapes (90%); the pinot noir and gamay of the black grapes (together 99%). In Ostschweiz, the riesling x sylvaner (alias Müller-Thurgau) is the dominant white grape (90%), while the pinot noir dominates the black grapes (100%). Finally, the Merlot is particularly important in Ticino (88%).

CHASSELAS (GUTEDEL)

Chasselas grapes accounts for 40% of Swiss vines and the variety is therefore the most characteristic Swiss grape. It plays a dominant role in Valais, Vaud, Neuchâtel, Geneva, Fribourg, and Berne, but is also well represented in Ticino, Schwyz, Solothurn and Basel. Chasselas vines thrive in the Swiss climate and geological conditions. Outside Switzerland, some chasselas is also found in Alsace, in Germany (where it is known as gutedel) and in the Loire region. Like pinot blanc, it is a fairly neutral grape which derives all its strength from the soil. Chasselas is often regarded as a weak variety because it produces moderate wines in Alsace. However, this is a very shortsighted view because the special conditions in Switzerland produce surprisingly good results. As chasselas grapes derive all their strength and

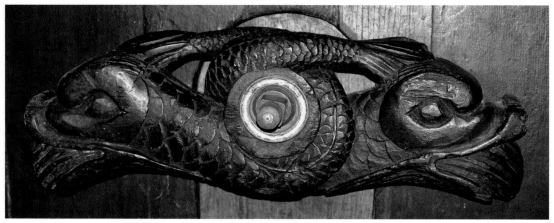

Old decoration on a barrel in Neuchâtel (Montmollin)

diversity from the soil, Swiss Chasselas wines are quite fascinating! If you taste wines from Dézaley, Epesses or a Fendant from Valais one after the other, you will discover three completely different wines.

SYLVANER (JOHANNISBERG)
Although it originally comes from the banks of the Danube, this grape is often referred to as the 'Rhin' (Rhine) in Valais. In general the sylvaner produces fresher, fuller and more aromatic wines that the chasselas.

RIESLING
A specialty from Valais (Sion), Vaud and Neuchâtel.

RIESLING X SYLVANER (MÜLLER-THURGAU)
This is the most important grape of Ostschweiz. It dominates in sixteen of the twenty-four wine-growing areas, and is present as a specialty in seven others. It is only in Ticino that wine growers see nothing in this Swiss creation of Müller, a researcher from Thurgau. The muscat aroma and fine, fruity character are characteristic of the riesling x sylvaner.

PINOT GRIS (MALVOISIE, GRAUER BURGUNDER, RULÄNDER, TOKAYER)
This famous variety produces excellent results particularly in Valais (as the malvoisie): full, ripe, elegant wines.

PINOT BLANC (WEISSBURGUNDER)
A specialty in Vaud and in Ostschweiz. The pinot blanc can produce extremely diverse wines, from light, elegant, fairly neutral wines to heavy, full-bodied rich wines.

CHARDONNAY
A specialty in Suisse Romande. Excellent results in Valais, Vaud, Geneva and Neuchâtel.

GUWÜRZTRAMINER
Not widely cultivated, but present in twelve wine-growing regions as a specialty. In general, very good results.

RAUSCHLING
This was once one of the most important varieties of grapes in the area around Zurich. It was slowly but steadily replaced by the more productive riesling x sylvaner. However, in recent decades increasing numbers of young wine growers seem to want to save this variety from oblivion. This is a good development, because this grape results in splendid original wines.

AMIGNE
Indigenous variety of grape from Valais in the neighborhood of Vétroz.

ARVINE (PETITE ARVINE)
Indigenous variety from Valais which produces extre-

Riesling x sylvaner or müller-thurgau (Coire/Chur)

Pinot gris/malvoisie (Coire/Chur)

mely surprising and very fascinating aromatic wines with a great deal of strength and complexity and a very characteristic taste of the terroir: slightly salty. This is a completely undervalued variety of grape which has also recently been introduced in the Rhône valley by way of an experiment, thanks to the inspired wine grower Michel Chapoutier from Tain l'Hermitage.

ERMITAGE (MARSANNE BLANCHE)
On the subject of Hermitage, this ermitage comes from the French Rhône valley. It is a specialty in Valais, where it often produces sweet, rich wines full of character which age very well.

HUMAGNE BLANC
Old-fashioned indigenous grape, which is a specialty in Valais. The highly aromatic wines are full and powerful and were said to have a fortifying effect. They were often prescribed as a tonic.

MUSCAT (MUSCAT BLANC A PETITS GRAINS/MUSCAT OTTONEL)
Both types of muscat are found in Valais. They are used to make mainly fruity, aromatic, light wines which should be drunk when they are young.

PAIEN (HEIDA, SAUVIGNON BLANC)
This extremely specific variety of grape is also found in the French Jura (vin jaune!) and in Savoie. It is a specialty from the Viãge valley in Valais.

RÈZE
This was once used for the famous glacier wine in the area around Anniviers. Unfortunately this variety of grape has now almost entirely disappeared.

OTHER AND NEW VARIETIES OF GRAPES
Swiss wine growing has not stood still. On the contrary, new varieties have been produced from crossing existing varieties. Obviously the aim of this cross-fertilization is to improve the quality of these wines even further. For example, the freisamer was the result of crossing the sylvaner and the pinot gris, and the highly promising charmont is the result of crossing the chardonnay and the chasselas. Finally, some sauvignon and sémillon are also used occasionally.

PINOT NOIR (BLAUBURGUNDER, SPÄTBURGUNDER, CLEVNER)
The pinot noir is widely represented in Switzerland (approximately 27% of the total vines planted). It the only variety of grape used in Ostschweiz and Neuchâtel and is also dominant in many smaller regions of Suisse Romande. It is only in Ticino, Vaud, Geneva and Fribourg that it is not in the majority, and it is not found in some areas of Appenzell.

GAMAY
Gamay comes third in Switzerland behind chasselas and pinot noir, accounting for approximately 14% of the vines that are planted. This fairly productive variety of grape thrives mainly in Vaud, Valais and Geneva.

MERLOT
Merlot is used mainly in Ticino (approximately 75% of the total Merlot production), but also in the Italian-speaking part of Graubünden (Mesoccodal valley), in Valais, Vaud and the area around Lake Geneva. The merlot ripens late, and therefore requires a great deal of sun; for this reason it is mainly found in the vineyards that are furthest south.

BONDOLA
A unique indigenous grape from Ticino.

HUMAGNE ROUGE
A late-flowering specialty from Valais. With sufficient sun it can produce a very special wine with fascinating wild aromas.

CORNALIN
Another indigenous specialty from Valais. This variety of grape has a few passionate fans, and as there is a very small supply available, the wines made with cornalin are a highly prized rarity.

OTHER AND NEW VARIETIES OF BLACK GRAPES
A few wine growers, mainly from Ticino, use the malbec. The syrah is also sometimes found in Valais and Ticino, while the cabernet sauvignon and cabernet franc are found in Ticino and Geneva. New varieties of grapes based on experimental crossing include the gamaret and the B 28, both resulting from crossing the gamay x reichensteiner and the diolinoir, resulting from the black diolly x pinot noir. The gamay x reichensteiner B 28 is found only in the Jura, the diolinoir only in Valais.

Pinot noir (Coire/Chur)

TICINO
DENOMINAZIONE DI ORIGINE CONTROLLATA
MERLOT
L'ARIETE ®

Valsangiacomo

75 cl e   12,5% vol.

F.LLI VALSANGIACOMO FU VITTORE SA - CHIASSO
VINO SVIZZERO

Merlot is the most popular variety of grape in Ticino.

IL FORNO

TICINO
DENOMINAZIONE
DI ORIGINE
CONTROLLATA
CABERNET
FRANC
DI PEDRINATE

12,5% Vol.   S.A. F.LLI VALSANGIACOMO
CHIASSO   75 cl e

**The first Cabernet wines can also be
found in Ticino.**

WINE CLASSIFICATIONS

Swiss wines are made in a comparable way to those in France, Germany, Austria and Italy. However, there is one exception to this, the Schiller. For this rosé, a specialty from Ostschweiz, black and white grapes which have often been planted in the same vineyards are harvested together. The grapes are pressed together, producing the light rosé color, and are then processed as for white wine. In Valais there is also another specialty, a 'blanc de noirs', i.e., a white wine made with black pinot noir grapes, which is made without the skins. This unusual wine is known as the Dôle blanche. A similar wine made with the pinot noir is produced in Ostschweiz as the Federweisser or Weissherbst.

Switzerland also produces excellent sparkling wines, although these are not so well known. The best use the méthode traditionnelle, and they are much better for only slightly more money.

The Swiss are very thirsty, and the production of white wines can only just quench their enormous thirst. As most of the white wines are not wines for laying down, they are often sealed with a screw top which is fine for wines intended to be drunk while young. Do not be surprised therefore if you are given an excellent bottle of Fendant with a screw top in a top restaurant. The Swiss do not have no hang-ups about this, and the wine does not suffer. Swiss white wines are rarely spoilt by the taste of the cork. Some table wines are also sealed with ordinary bottle tops, and these should be drunk fairly quickly.

There are two indications which are compulsory on Swiss labels: the name or code of the maker/bottler or dealer and the quality indication of the wine.

Like most other European countries, there are three quality categories in Switzerland:
– wines without a geographical indication and/or indication of the variety of grape, (e.g., vin rouge, vin blanc, vin de table). These are always wines which are intended for rapid consumption and are usually sold in liter bottles, with or without an ordinary bottle top;
– wines with a geographical indication and/or indication of the variety of grape. These wines come

VALSANGIACOMO
Merlot del Ticino
SPUMANTE
METODO CLASSICO
FERMENTAZIONE IN BOTTIGLIA
F.LLI VALSANGIACOMO FU VITTORE SA CHIASSO

**Switzerland also makes excellent sparkling wines,
such as this 'blanc de noirs' made with the
merlot from Ticino.**

RISERVA DI BACCO®

TICINO

DENOMINAZIONE DI ORIGINE CONTROLLATA

MERLOT

DEI COLLI DEL MENDRISIOTTO

F.LLI VALSANGIACOMO FU VITTORE SA

CHIASSO

75 cl ℮ vino svizzero 12,5% vol.

Classical label from Ticino

Example of a label of wine with a controlled geographical indication

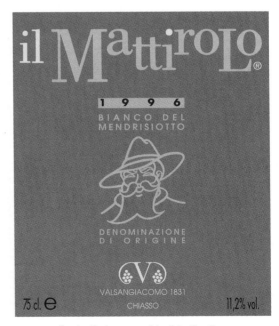

Controlled geographical indication

from a large wine-growing area, e.g., from Suisse Romande (vin rouge Romand). The name of the variety of grape can precede the geographical indication, e.g., Gamay de Romandie;

– wines with a controlled geographical indication (appellation d'origine contrôlée). These wines may indicate the place of origin in the normal way, e.g., Neuchâtel appellation d'origine contrôlée, the geographical indication with an indication of the variety of grape, such as Gamay Vaudois AOC, Merlot Ticino AOC or even a recognized traditional name for a specific wine from a specific wine-growing area: Fendant AOC, Dôle AOC.

TICINO

Like Ticino, part of Graubünden (Mesolcina, Poschiavo) is Italian-speaking. For the sake of convenience these regions will be discussed together. Mesolcina and Poschiavo only produce red wines made with the merlot grape and several black hybrid varieties. Almost the entire harvest is sold to firms in Ticino.

Ticino is the fourth wine-producing canton in Switzerland. Before the *Phylloxera* plague, the wine-growing area covered approximately 17,297 acres; nowadays it is only 1,200 hectares (2,965 acres)! Ticino is subdivided into two regions: the southern Sottoceneri

and the northern Sopraceneri. The border between the two regions is formed by the Monte Ceneri. The soil of Sottoceneri consists mainly of a mixture of limestone, minerals, clay and sand. The vineyards lie on either side of the picturesque lake of Lugano. Sopraceneri has a soil with less limestone but more granite and sand. In both areas the lakes, Lago Lugano, Lago Maggiore, and to a lesser extent, Lago di Como, play an important role, amongst other things, because they temper the hot Mediterranean climate to some extent.

MERLOT DEL TICINO

Obviously the ultimate wine from Ticino is the Merlot del Ticino denominazione di origine. The merlot grape was introduced in Ticino after the destruction of the vineyards by *Phylloxera*. In blind tastings, some Merlot wines obtain astonishingly high marks. Two top wines can even compete with the famous Pétrus, as shown by the results of many tastings. Fortunately, the sympathetic wine growers are more concerned at the moment with making wine than with marketing!

Obviously not all Merlot del Ticino wines are of the same caliber as the top wines. Most are tempting, light and supple with few acids and tannins. The color is usually garnet and the aroma is reminiscent of wild black cherries with hints of red fruit. Only the better wines are matured in wood and have a lot of tannin; they become velvety as they age. These better wines are also stronger and more powerful. The best wines have the sought-after VITI quality seal which states: Controlo Ufficiale di Qualita, the official quality control.

You could drink a simple Merlot with pasta, casseroles, roast chicken, fowl and cheeses which are not too ripe or strong. Tip: 'gnocchi al gorgonzola', homemade gnocchi made with potatoes in a strong gorgonzola sauce. Drinking temperature is 12–14 °C (53.6–57.2 °F).

Serve better, stronger Merlot matured in wood with roast meat, e.g., roast lamb or beef or with hare or other small game. Tip: 'coniglio val bredetto con polenta', an excellent rabbit casserole served with traditional polenta. Drinking temperature is 14–17 °C (57.2–62.6 °F).

There is also a white Merlot (delicious with pasta with a nut sauce or fish) and an excellent light Merlot rosé (ideal with pasta with a mild tomato sauce or with crawfish or trout). Drinking temperature is 8–10 °C (46.4–50 °F) for the Merlot bianco and the Merlot rosato.

NOSTRANO

Nostrano is certainly the oldest and most traditional wine from Ticino. It is made with the indigenous bondola, with the possible addition of freisa, bonarda or malbec. This wine is sometimes slightly coarse, but it is utterly fascinating.

It goes perfectly with the cuisine from local taverns ('grotto'), especially with the Luganiga and Ticinese sausages! Drinking temperature is 14 °C (57.2 °F).

There is also a bianco version of this Nostrano. This is delicious with cooked pork and other meat. Drinking temperature is 8–10 °C (46.4–50 °F).

BONDOLA

Serve this rustic red wine made with 100% bondola with casseroles. Tip: 'osso bucco del Ticino', the local

The now famous Valsangiacomo Rubro Merlot which has been thoroughly matured in wood

La dolce vita in Ticino

Delicious with pasta and gnocchi

Excellent Merlot to have with small game and polenta

version of the famous Italian dish. Drinking temperature is 14 °C (57.2 °F).

OTHER WINES FROM TICINO

Occasionally you will find Ticino spumante (aperitif, fish dishes, 5–6 °C/41.0–42.8 °F). Ticino Pinot Nero (duck, rabbit, 14 °C/57.2 °F) and various white wines made with the chasselas (fish, rabbit, soft cheese, 8–10 °C/46.4–50 °F), Chardonnay (risotto of fish or shellfish, 10–12 °C/50–53.6 °F). Sauvignon (aperitif, starters of pasta in a white creamy sauce, 8–10 °C/46.4–50 °F), Sémillon (vegetables, rabbit, 10–11 °C/50–51.8 °F) and Riesling x Sylvaner (tender vegetables, shellfish, fish, 10–11 °C/50–51.8 °F). There are also several white blended wines made with the chasselas, sauvignon and sémillon grapes which are delicious with fish, 8–10 °C (46.4–50 °F).

SUISSE ROMANDE

Situated in the (south) east of the country, the French-speaking wine-growing areas account for the lion's share of Swiss wine growing. Although Bern, Fribourg, Neuchâtel and Vaud are certainly not unimport-

ant, it is Valais which is responsible for the best quality and the largest volume. Anyone who thinks of Suisse Romande is immediately reminded of the white wines made with the chasselas which do not achieve the same quality or diversity of taste and types anywhere else in the world. These wines indicate the name of the variety of grape and the place of origin, a geographical indication without an indication of the variety of grape (Neuchâtel) or even a traditional name (Fendant, Perlan). The chasselas also has a number of famous crus, sometimes no larger than the wine-growing area of a single village or even hamlet: for example, Dézaley, Epesses, Yvorne and Aigle.

This diversity is possible because the chasselas is naturally fairly neutral and takes over the qualities of the terroir. The better the terroir, the better the wine! In addition to the chasselas, the red wines of the pinot noir and gamay play an increasingly important role. While the wine-growing area for white wines is growing very slowly, it has mushroomed in recent years for red wines. Perhaps this is related to the growing demand for red wine grown in Switzerland and the liberated trade in foreign wines. A great deal of red wine is imported from the French Côtes du Rhône, as well as a lot of Burgundy and Beaujolais.

Rare sparkling wine from Ticino

The vineyards of Dézaley and Epesses

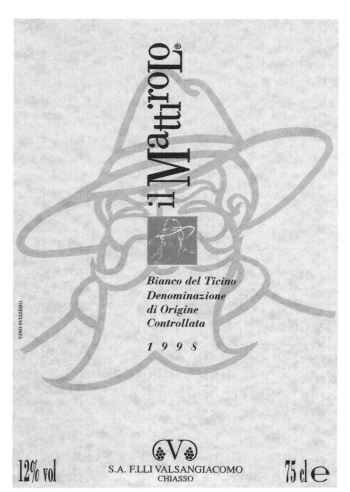

Delicious white wine

VALAIS (WALLIS)

The vineyards of Valais produce about 40% of the total wine production in Switzerland. Although Valais is known all over the world for its Fendant and Dôle, it is above all the indigenous specialties which have attrac-

ted the attention of wine connoisseurs. Anyone who takes the time to discover the unique wines of Valais will be in love with this rugged but beautiful region for the rest of his life. Valais lies at the foot of the Alps along the valley of the upper Rhône on either side of the town of Sion. In the north and south, the region is protected from excessive rainfall by the high Alps. Most of the vineyards are on the terraces on the steep hillsides hanging above the Rhône valley. The ingenious systems of irrigation from the past have been replaced by spraying systems in many instances. The valley and above all, the steep hillsides, get a lot of sun, which encourages the growth of the grapes. The hot mountain wind (föhn) keeps temperatures extremely pleasant long into the fall, so that the grapes have a good chance to ripen. The soil consists mainly of loose poor soil, which retains the heat as well as water very well. As in other places in Switzerland, the soil in Valais is rather diverse: from grit to chalk, gravel and slate.

The chasselas accounts for approximately 45% of the total production, followed by the sylvaner (often referred to here as 'gros Rhin'), and the countless specialties, such as the indigenous amigne, arvine or petite arvine, humagne blanche and rāze and the imported grapes, muscat, paìen (savagnin blanc), marsanne blanche, etc. Many of these varieties are used to make wines with grapes harvested late, which may or may not have partly dried in the sun (flétri). Three old indigenous varieties of grapes have been revived (gwäss or gouais, lafnetscha and himbertschna), but they still only account for a very small share. Of the black grapes, the pinot noir particularly thrives in the limestone soil of Valais, while the gamay prefers slightly less limestone. Other black grapes which thrive here include the humagne rouge, cornalin, syrah, diolinoir and durize.

AMIGNE

Amigne wines are rare, elegant, rich and temptingly sweet wines with the tough character of the slate and limestone soil of Vétroz. If you ever have a chance to

Vineyards at Sion (Wallis)

Specialties such as amigne and petit arvine are grown in these small steep vineyards, which produce only a small yield.

buy an Amigne wine, don't ask about the price: just buy it. Then use your best foie gras recipe and keep a glass to drink with a gratinée of fresh fruit and sabayon which has been popped under the grill. The gates of heaven will open for you! Drinking temperature is 8–10 °C (46.4–50 °F).

ARVINE (PETITE ARVINE)

While the last two white wines should be drunk within three to four years after the harvest, the wines of the (petite) arvine should really be laid down. These wines have a very strong personality, with tempting fruity aromas and usually quite a lot of alcohol (13% or more) and sometimes some residual sugar. This specialty thrives on very steep, rocky soil. The yield is fairly low, but the price of this jewel is still reasonable.

Serve the (Petite) Arvine sêche (dry) with the characteristic salty taste and aromas of citrus fruits with fish and shellfish, poultry or sweetbreads, or with cheeses. The (petite) Arvine flétrie (partly dried grapes) is an excellent sweet wine. Serve it with foie gras (duck liver), soft blue cheeses or fresh desserts. Drinking temperature is 8–10 °C (46.4–50 °F) for dry wines, 6–9 °C (42.8–48.2 °F) for sweet wines.

DÔLE BLANCHE

This is a very interesting wine made with the same black grapes as those used for the Dôle: pinot noir, min. 80%, and gamay. It is excellent accompanying poultry, white meat, or soft cheeses. Drinking temperature is 8–12 °C (46.4–53.6 °F).

ERMITAGE

Ermitage or marsanne blanche is a grape from the French Rhône valley which produces excellent dry white wine here: the Ermitage sec, but above all, a wonderful sweet Ermitage flétri. The later comes from the vineyards on the steep hills of Sion, Fully and Sierre.

Few wines develop such an impressive series of aromas as a top Ermitage flétri.

Serve a dry Ermitage with better types of fish, white meat or poultry and the sweet Ermitage flétri with foie gras (duck liver), delicate fish and fresh desserts made with fruit and acacia or lime blossom honey. Drinking temperature is 8–12 °C (46.4–53.6 °F) for dry wine, 6–9 °C (42.8–48.2 °F) for sweet wine.

FENDANT

Fendant is undoubtedly the visiting card of Valais and provides living proof that wonderful wines can be made even from a soft grape like the chasselas which grows in the most rugged type of soil. Anyone who tastes a good Fendant is caught up in a joyful dance, without any fuss or reservations. The Fendant is certainly not a philosophical wine, but is pure undiluted pleasure. Every Fendant is an ambassador for Valais, but also and above all, of its own terroir. For example, a Fendant from Sion tastes very different from one which comes from Sierre. However, in general, it can be said that the best Fendant is a dry, lively, fresh white wine with a great deal of juice and a clearly identifiable undertone of flint.

The Fendant is an ideal aperitif, but is also excellent accompanying cheese fondue, raclette and most cheese dishes. It is also delicious with cold meats, fish, (smoked) salmon, shellfish, poultry and soft (mountain) cheeses. A light fruity Fendant should be drunk at a temperature of 8–10 °C (46.4–50 °F), a Fendant with lots of character at 10–12 °C (50–53.6 °F).

HUMAGNE BLANCHE

This 'magical' white wine from Valais has a fortifying (tonic) strength. Whether or not this is true, they are excellent wines, though they are difficult to find. They are also very good with dishes containing truffles! They are also delicious with soft cheeses. Drinking temperature is 8–12 °C (46.4–53.6 °F).

Fendant de Sion
(Valais)

JOHANNISBERG

This is the second well-known white wine from Valais. It is made with the sylvaner grape, which also flourishes here. These wines are mild, soft, round, sometimes full and always with the characteristic light aroma and taste of muscat. It is precisely because of these surprising muscat aromas that this wine makes an excellent aperitif, but like the best Muscat wines it is also very good with asparagus! In addition, the Johannisburg combines perfectly with fish (including raw fish such as sushi and sashimi!), hot starters with mushrooms, poultry or white meat in a cream sauce (pastries) and soft creamy cheeses. Drinking temperature is 8–12 °C (46.4–53.6 °F) (the better the wine, the less cold it should be).

MALVOISIE

A dry, sweet wine is also made with partly dried grapes of the malvoisie (pinot gris) variety. A dry Malvoisie combines perfectly with mushrooms, fish and oriental dishes (curry!). The Malvoisie flétrie is the perfect partner for duck liver, soft blue cheese and fresh, acidic, fruity desserts. Dry malvoisie should be drunk at a temperature of 8–12 °C (46.4–53.6 °F), sweet malvoisie at 6–9 °C (42.8–48.2 °F).

PAIEN

The wines made with paien ('heida': heathen) are also exceptional. This old indigenous variety grows at heights of over 3,280 ft and is still found in the French Jura and in Savoie (savagnin), in some vineyards in Alsace and Germany (traminer) and occasionally in Italy (tramini). The wines are fresh and very dry, with identifiable fresh aromas of green apples. They are delicious with soft vegetable and potato dishes. Drinking temperature is 8–10 °C (46.4–50 °F).

RÂZE

The rare wines made with the râze grape are still made in very small quantities in Anniviers. This vin des glaciers (glacier wine) is extremely acidic and green when you drink it too young. However, if you allow it to age, it develops very unusual and fascinating aromas. Try it with cheese dishes. Drinking temperature is 6–9 °C (42.8–48.2 °F).

OTHER WHITE WINES FROM VALAIS
Valais also makes a number of other excellent white wines though only in very small quantities: Chardonnay (increasingly popular and delicious with fish with a slightly sour sauce), Gewürztraminer (foie gras, curry, oriental dishes), Gouais (fish), Himbertscha (fish, cheese), Lafnetscha (savory pies, cheese), Muscat (foie gras, warm starters, fresh fruit desserts), Pinot Blanc (shellfish, salmon, vegetables), Riesling (fish, oriental dishes), Riesling x Sylvaner (starters, fish) and Sauvignon (aperitif, vegetables, fish).

GAMAY ROSÉ

Gamay grapes impart an amiable playfulness to this light rosé which suits any informal occasion, preferably outdoors in bright sunlight. Drinking temperature is 8–10 °C (46.4–50 °F).

OEIL-DE-PERDRIX

This light, cheerful rosé, made with 100% pinot noir, will accompany any lunch or summer buffet without any problems. It is delicious with soft meat such as rabbit, chicken or guinea fowl. Drinking temperature is 8–10 °C (46.4–50 °F).

CORNALIN

A fruity, generous red wine made with the eponymous grape. It is fairly rich in tannin in its youth, generous and friendly after maturing for some time. It is excellent accompanying cold meats, fowl and cheese. Drinking temperature is 12–14 °C (53.6–57.2 °F).

DÔLE

This famous red wine from Valais should contain at least 80% pinot noir, possibly supplemented with gamay or other black grapes from Valais, such as humagne, syrah or cornalin. The Dôle is a typical Pinot Noir: generous, fruity, velvety soft, round and harmonious.

Drink this wine with beef, particularly with casseroles. Tip: 'viande des Grisons et asperges', an excellent combination of air-dried beef from Grisons and asparagus, e.g., with a hollandaise sauce. Drinking temperature is 14 °C (57.2 °F).

GORON

Goron is the little brother of the Dôle, with slightly less alcohol and a lighter structure. This pleasant, light, generous and fruity wine is often served with cold meats or light meals. Drinking temperature is 12–14 °C (53.6–57.2 °F).

HUMAGNE ROUGE

Despite its name, this red Humagne has nothing in common with the white

Oeil-de-perdrix   Dôle (Valais)
(rosé) from Sion

Humagne. A Humagne rouge is very aromatic and slightly coarse; it is best left to mature for a few years. It is excellent accompanying game and mature cheeses. Drinking temperature is 14–16 °C (57.2–60.8 °F).

PINOT NOIR

A 100% Pinot Noir is fuller than a Dôle, with richer aromas and taste nuances, more body and more character. It is an excellent wine with red meat, game and mature cheeses. Drinking temperature is 14–16 °C (57.2–60.8 °F).

SYRAH

Here too, the macho syrah grape produces strong powerful wines with a great deal of extract and rich aromas. It is an excellent wine with roast beef or game and mature cheeses. Drinking temperature is 14–16 °C (57.2–60.8 °F).

VAUD (WAADTLAND)

Vaud is one of the most beautiful wine landscapes in Switzerland. The region actually consists of two parts, the northern shores of Lac Léman (Lake Geneva) and the southern part of the Lac de Neuchâtel. These two regions are subdivided into six smaller districts: Chablais (Aigle), Lavaux (between Montreux and Lausanne) and La Côte (between Lausanne and Nyon) near Lac Léman, and Côtes de l'Orbe, Bonvillars and Vully, near the Lac de Neuchâtel. The two lakes provide extra cooling and moisture when it is very hot and extra light and heat in the fall, when the sun is shining. There is slightly less rainfall in the western area (La Côte) than in the east (Lavaux and Chablais), while the latter profits more from warm mountain winds (föhn). Although some vineyards are higher than 1,968 or even 2,296 ft, they are at an average height of 1,312–1,640 ft. The soil in Vaud consists of limestone, grit, sandstone, clay and rock. The wines of Vaud are characterized by their geographical indication, and not by the varieties of grapes used.

CHABLAIS

This wine-growing region comprises five geographical indications: Bex, Ollon, Aigle, Yvorne and Villeneuve. The white wines made with the chasselas are fresh, lively, elegant and rich. They can be identified by their relatively high mineral content (magnesium in Aigle and Villeneuve, minerals in Ollon, a great deal of flint in Bex, chalk in Ollon and Bex). The Chablais also reflect their terroir in their aromas: flowers and aniseed (Bex), wet stone, resin and roses (Ollon), flowers, fruit, flint and burnt or smoky soil, with a hint of caramel at a later age (Aigle), hazelnuts, peaches and apricots (Yvorne) and slate, flint and fruit (Villeneuve). These perfect aperitifs are also excellent accompanying fish, shellfish and crustaceans, poultry, white meat and soft cheeses. Drinking temperature is 10–12 °C (50–53.6 °F).

The tower of Dézaley-Marsens

LAVAUX

Lavaux has six geographical indications (Montreux-Vevey, Chardonne, Saint-Saphorin, Epesses, Villette and Lutry) and two grands crus: Dézaley and Calamin. Nowhere else in Switzerland has the landscape been so beautifully transformed by human hands as here, particularly in the areas around Dézaley and Calamin. There are thousands of rows of terraces hanging above Lac Léman, forming a magnificent scene, particularly in the fall.

The chasselas produces structured wines here, fuller and more robust than in the west of the region, with more of the taste of the terroir. Discover all of them: lemon balm and mint (Montreux-Vevey), pear and

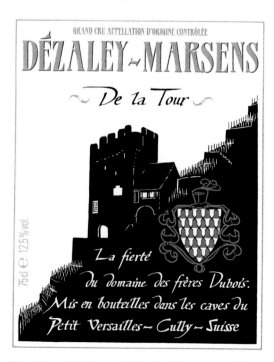

The 'wine of the tower', Dézaley-Marsens grand cru, made by the Dubois family

Devilishly delicious and heartwarming, the 'Braise d'enfer' ('hot coals from hell') from Epesses

Tasting by candlelight in an old wine barrel, by way of aperitif (Dubois family, Cully)

blackcurrant (Chardonne), pineapple, truffles and white pepper (Epesses), and grapefruit and roses (Lutry). Some top wines, such as those from Dézaley, have surprising aromas of almonds, toast, tea and honey which tend towards hazelnuts, beeswax and candied fruit as they mature (Dézaley-Marsens, Dubois).

Serve a Lavaux as an aperitif with starters. Top wines from Dézaley are crazy about grilled lobster and coquilles St. Jacques! Drinking temperature is 8–10 °C (46.4–50 °F) for Lavaux, 10–12 °C (50–53.6 °F) for Dézaley and Calamin.

The red wines from Lavaux are also very worthwhile, such as those from Saint-Saphorin (cherries, kirsch; slightly bitter, full and round) and Villette (red fruit, wild strawberries, blueberries, raspberries, blackberries; mild and generous). Serve these wines with tender meat in sauces which are not too rich or heavy. Drinking temperature is 12–14 °C (53.6–57.2 °F).

LA CÔTE

Approximately half of the wines from Vaud come from this area between Geneva and Lausanne. It is a gently undulating region with picturesque villages, large country houses and castles. The most striking characteristic of the local wines is their often slightly effervescent character and their elegance. They are much lighter than the wines from Lavaux and Chablais, but also have a great deal to offer: particularly their floral and fruity aromas. La Côte does not have a grand cru, only twelve geographical indications: Morges, Aubonne, Perroy, Féchy, Mont-sur-Rolle, Tartegnin, Côteau de Vincy, Bursinel, Vinzel, Luins, Begnins and Nyon.

The white wines from La Côte are very good aperitifs and excellent with starters, fish, poultry, white meat and cheeses. Tip: try this wine in the asparagus season – it is magnificent! Drinking temperature is 8–10 °C (46.4–50 °F).

The red wines from Lavaux are also very worthwhile.

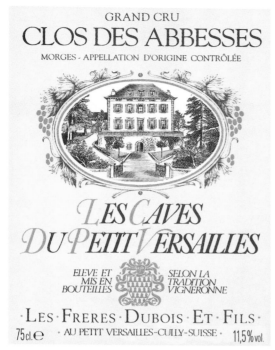

Clos des Abbesses, Morges

BONVILLARS, CÔTES DE L'ORBE, VULLY

Although these three wine-growing areas are on the shores of the Lac de Neuchâtel, they are certainly part of Vaud. On the other hand, the wines are very similar to those of Neuchâtel: fresh, light, elegant, and often slightly sparkling. These wines made with the chasselas go well with cold meats, fish, shellfish and even oysters. However, they are most convincing as an aperitif. Drinking temperature is 8–10 °C (46.4–50 °F).

SALVAGNIN

This red wine made with the gamay and/or pinot noir, from the Vaud, is fresh fruity and supple. When it is drunk young and cool it is excellent in combination with the various fish specialties from Lac Léman. Slightly less cool and not so mature, it is a good accompaniment for cold meats, starters, poultry and small game. Drinking temperature is 12 °C (53.6 °F) with fish, 12–14 °C (53.6–57.2 °F) with meat.

OEIL-DE-PERDRIX

These light, cheerful, generous rosé wines mainly come from Vully and Bonvillars. The color is described by the 'eye of a partridge' slightly between a pale pink and orange. This rosé, made with the pinot noir and/or gamay, goes well with cold meats, but can also be served very well with a summer meal or a winter lunch. Drinking temperature is 10–12 °C (50–53.6 °F).

GENEVA

After Valais and Vaud, Geneva is in third place of the wine producing cantons of Switzerland. The landscape immediately around Geneva varies much less in height than in the other two wine-growing areas. This means that the vineyards are slightly larger and that mechanization is possible, which does not detract from the quality of the wines in any way, although it does affect the price. In Geneva, attempts have also been made to rationalize viticulture in recent decades, and to look for the best varieties of grapes for quality wines. The region is surrounded by mountains which protect the vineyards from the rain. Lake Geneva (Lac Léman) protects the vineyards from night frosts during the periods of growth and flowering. In this region the types of soil are also rather diverse. Almost everywhere the soil consists of a maximum of one-third clay, except in the region of the Jura where there may be slightly more clay. There is more limestone in Lully and Peney, the higher vineyards in Dardagny and the surrounding area have more limestone and sandstone and loess, and there is more gravel in the vineyards close to the lake. The ubiquitous chasselas has been replaced to some extent by aromatic varieties of grapes such as the chardonnay, gewürztraminer and aligoté (a specialty from Lully). The gamay is the dominant black grape, followed by the pinot noir and the merlot. Recently some new varieties have been introduced: gamaret and gamay x reichensteiner B 28, cabernet franc and cabernet sauvignon. Geneva is still developing at a great rate, and there may be many surprises in store in the next few decades.

The wine-growing area of Geneva is subdivided into three smaller regions: Entre Arve et Lac, Entre Arve et Rhône and Mandement. Mandement is the largest of the three (approximately two thirds of the production). However, the most fascinating wines unquestionably come from the area between Arve and Rhône (mainly from the hills of Bernex, Confignon, Lully and Sévenoze), where the soil consists of gravel and limestone and leaves a big impression on the wines (including aromas of flint).

CHASSELAS DE GENÈVE/PERLAN

You often find this wine with the geographical indication (canton or municipality): Jussy, Choulex, Lully, Dardagny, Russin, Peissy, Satigny and Chouilly. Because of the strict rules aimed at restricting the yield, the quality of this Chasselas de Genâve has improved enormously in recent decades. It has a fresh and floral aroma and a lively, fresh, dry taste, which is often slightly sparkling.

It is excellent as an aperitif or for accompanying smoked salmon, fish, oriental dishes or cheese specialties. Drinking temperature is 8–10 °C (46.4–50 °F).

OTHER WHITE WINES FROM GENEVA

The Chardonnay (aperitif, crustaceans, crawfish, delicate fish, fresh cheese), Pinot Blanc (delicate fish) and Pinot Gris (paté, foie gras) are excellent. The Muscat (soft blue cheeses, slightly caramelized fruit) and the Gewürztraminer (oriental dishes, aperitif) are very aromatic and of a good quality. The Sauvignon (aperitif) is pleasant, but not particularly exciting. Finally, the Aligoté from Lully is an extremely good aperitif, but also excellent with fish starters.

GAMAY DE GENÈVE

Again this wine can be found under the generic name (Gamay de Genève), or under the name of the municipality where it is produced. It is fresh, fruity, full, generous, friendly and juicy as a Gamay should be. It is an excellent wine with cold meats, small game, grated vegetables and desserts of red fruit (strawberries!). Tip: 'gratin de cardons', a creamy gratin of cardoon, an old-fashioned vegetable which belongs to the thistle family. Drinking temperature is 10–12 °C (50–53.6 °F).

PINOT NOIR DE GENÈVE

This is a very fine red wine, fruity and generous. It is excellent accompanying poultry, patés and terrines, small game, duck and cheeses. Drinking temperature is 14 °C (57.2 °F).

OTHER RED WINES FROM GENEVA
The first results obtained with the cabernet franc and cabernet sauvignon are very promising. The merlot

(which is still fairly rare) has been thriving for some time in the higher vineyards. The wine is very good with fish in red wine sauce, hare and other small game and even with a juicy joint of lamb. Drinking temperature is 14 °C (57.2 °F).

OEIL-DE-PERDRIX/GAMAY ROSÉ

These two different rosé wines are uncomplicated, fresh, fruity and friendly wines to accompany any summer meal. Drinking temperature is 8–10 °C (46.4–50 °F).

NEUCHÂTEL

The wine-growing area of Neuchâtel lies on the left shores of the eponymous lake and is divided from France by the Jura mountains. The climate is fairly mild, sunny and dry. Because of the water in the lake, the winter is mild, but the fall is often misty which can jeopardize the harvest. The soil in this region at the foot of the Jura consists mainly of mountain limestone with the occasional rocks, loam or loess. The soil contains many minerals which can often be clearly identified in the taste of the wines. The most striking feature in the area around Neuchâtel is the patchwork of small vineyards. Only a few houses have larger vineyards.

White wines are in the majority here; this almost goes without saying in a chalky soil. The chasselas accounts for about 75% of the grapes; in addition, you will find the pinot gris, the riesling x sylvaner and the chardonnay, as well as occasionally sylvaner, riesling and gewürztraminer. The pinot noir for red wines is also used for an extremely attractive Oeil-de-Perdrix (rosé).

The Pinot Noir is at home everywhere in Switzerland

Fairly large uninterrupted vineyard
(Montmollin, Neuchâtel)

Rustic scene in the vineyard

Early morning mist in Neuchâtel

NEUCHÂTEL

This refers to Chasselas wines. The best wines come from the villages of Cressier, Auvernier, Cortaillod, Boudry and La Béroche. The surprising characteristic of this Chasselas (not quite as full as their cousins from Valais and Vaud) lies in the elegant bubbles and salty undertone. In the local wine bars, this wine is served fairly high in the glass so that it is slightly sparkling and there is occasionally a star of carbon-dioxide bubbles. You can see adults change into happy children when the wine forms this star ('Le vin fait l'étoile').

It is best to serve these exciting and fresh wines as an aperitif, with raw fish (sushi, sashimi!), shellfish, cheese dishes and cheeses. The unusual combination of Chasselas with sweet apple tart or even shortbread is very surprising. Drinking temperature is 8–12 °C (46.4–53.6 °F) (the better and fuller the wine, the less cold it should be).

NEUCHÂTEL PINOT NOIR

The Pinot Noir from Neuchâtel is often rather rough and high in tannin when it is young, but becomes softer and more friendly as it ages. The taste is fresh, elegant, complex and fairly traditional. Serve this wine with starters, cold meats, sausages, casseroles and mature cheeses. Drinking temperature is 14 °C (57.2 °F).

Attractive assortment of white, red and rosé wines from Neuchâtel (Montmollin)

NEUCHÂTEL OEIL-DE-PERDRIX

The color of this rosé will remind any huntsman immediately of the color of the eyes of a dying partridge. The brown color disappears slowly to turn into a pinky-orange hue, which is characteristic of this sort of rosé. These are elegant, fresh wines made with the pinot noir, excellent with fish, cold meats and fresh cheeses. However, you do not need any excuse to enjoy a glass of Oeil-de-Perdrix. Drinking temperature is 8–10 °C (46.4–50 °F).

OTHER WINES FROM NEUCHÂTEL

The Chardonnay from Neuchâtel is extremely good and is quite similar to a good Burgundy. It is excellent as an aperitif, but also good with fish, poultry, white meat or vegetables. The other specialties are quite rare: the Gewürztraminer is aromatic, but not really powerful (aperitif, starter with fruit, fish in creamy fruit sauce), the Pinot Blanc is light and elegant (cold meats, fish, and the Pinot Gris is superb (fish, white meat, poultry). The Riesling x Sylvaner and the Sylvaner are not always convincing. The latter should be drunk as an aperitif, and a better Riesling x Sylvaner can be served with sweetbreads, fish or poultry in a mild creamy sauce. There are also small qualities of sparking wines of reasonable quality.

FRIBOURG

The wines from Fribourg are produced to the east of the lake of Neuchâtel. The vineyards of Vully lie between the lake of Neuchâtel and the lake of Morat. The soil consists of clay, sand and a chalky sandstone and the climate is noticeably milder because of the lakes. Again the chasselas is king, but there are also some interesting specialties such as the freisammer, a cross between the sylvaner and pinot gris. In addition, there is an excellent Oeil-de-Pedrix and a wonderful Pinot Noir.

CHASSELAS FRIBOURGEOIS

Wines from Vully, Faverges and Cheyres are fresh, elegant, fruity and fairly light. They clearly reflect their terroir. They are excellent as an aperitif but also delicious with fish, vegetable dishes and the local cheeses, including (gruyère and vacherin). Drinking temperature is 8–12 °C (46.4–53.6 °F) (the better the wine, the less cold it should be).

PINOT NOIR FRIBOURGEOIS

Extremely fruity wines (raspberries) with a great deal of body and juice. Excellent with small game, poultry, mature cheeses. Drinking temperature is 14 °C (57.2 °F).

OTHER WINES FROM FRIBOURG

Of all the other – rare – wines from Fribourg, the fresh and elegant Oeil-de-Perdrix (fish, cold buffet), the full Chardonnay (fish, rabbit, white meat), the sultry Pinot Gris (fish, poultry, mature cheeses) and the Gewürztraminer (oriental chicken dishes, foie gras, sharp cheeses) are the best.

JURA

This is a very recent wine-growing area. The first vineyards were only planted in 1986 and the first harvest was in 1990. This is curious because the location and the mild microclimate are extremely favorable as is the rocky soil. Up to now, the red wines made with the pinot noir (cherries, red fruit) have been more convincing than the white wines made with the riesling x sylvaner. In a few years' time, the vines of the pinot noir will reach their peak and the expectations are very high. Excellent results have also been obtained with the pinot gris (honey, candied fruit, exotic fruit).

BERNE (BERN)

The canton of Bern forms the actual border between Suisse Romande and Ostschweiz. Most of the vineyards lie around the Lac de Bienne (Bielersee), north of lake of Neuchâtel. The rest of the vineyards lie close to the lakes of Thoune and Brienz in the vicinity of Interlaken. The vineyards of the lake of Bienne have a soil consisting of limestone (left shore), or chalky sandstone (right shore). The soil of the lake of Thoune consists of a subsoil of rock covered with a thin layer of earth. In addition, these vineyards benefit from the positive effects of the föhn.

CHASSELAS

Again the chasselas is dominant and produces fresh elegant, slightly effervescent wines on the chalky soil. On the right shore, the wines are slightly fuller and heavier, but less elegant. Serve the Chasselas from Berne as an aperitif, with fish or with cheese dishes. Drinking temperature is 8–10 °C (46.4–50 °F).

PINOT NOIR

Full, fruity, round, generous wines which are never too heavy. Serve the wines from the lake of Bienne with any meat dishes, from pork to lamb, with poultry or – as long as it is cooled – with firm fish. Tip: 'gigot d'agneau en gibier', roast leg of lamb marinated like game. Drinking temperature is 12 °C (53.6 °F) with fish, 14 °C (57.2 °F) with meat.

OSTSCHWEIZ

German-speaking Swiss people call this region East Switzerland, but 'Northeast' would be more accurate for this enormous area, which covers more than one third of Switzerland from the east of the line connecting Thun, Bern, Solothurn and Basel and to the north of the line connecting Thun and Chur. This German-speaking region comprises no fewer than sixteen cantons. Despite the enormous size of Ostschweiz, the wine-growing area is fairly small (only 5,683 acres) and the tiny vineyards are very scattered. The largest winegrowing cantons in the northeast are those of Zurich, Schaffhausen, Aargau, Graubünden (without Misox/Mesolcina, see Ticino), Thurgau, St. Gallen and Basel. The cantons of Schwyz, Bern (Thunersee), Luzern, Appenzell, Solothurn, Glarus, Zug and Unterwalden together account for only 2.5% of the total production of Ostschweiz. The wine-growing area of Ostschweiz was dramatically decimated by the *Phylloxera* plague and the stricter quality requirements. The greatest decline was in the area around Basel (also as a result of the growth of the city), in Thurgau and in Solothurn.

The climate of Ostschweiz is not really very favorable for wine growing. It is too cold and too wet. Nevertheless, the conditions are excellent in the immediate vicinity of the many lakes (Thunersee, Brienzersee, Zurichsee, Zuger See, Vierwaldstätter See, Walensee, Bodensee), the rivers (Rhine, Aar, Reuss, Thur) and in the valleys where the föhn blows (St. Gallen, Graubünden). The lowest vineyards are found at a height of 984 ft near Basel, the highest (1,968 ft) in the Duchy of Graubünden. The main threats to viticulture in Ostschweiz are the lengthy winter frosts or the fatal spring frosts during the flowering period. Over the centuries the creative Swiss wine growers have developed countless methods to protect the vines from the cold. In addition to the well-known spraying technique and stoves, local wine growers employ a very original method: the vines are given a skirt of straw or even wrapped up in a warm robe.

The soil of Ostschweiz varies from west to east. In the west, near the Jura, the soil contains more limestone, in the middle there is more chalky sandstone and in the east, there is more slate and grit. As the fall is fairly damp and cold in Ostschweiz, only varieties which mature early thrive here. For white grapes this is the riesling x sylvaner (Müller-Thurgau), for black grapes the pinot noir. The black varieties of grapes represent no less than 70% of the total vines planted. Occasionally you will find other varieties of grapes in small quantities: the räuschling is a white specialty from Zurich, and the Limmatdal is increasingly attracting attention. In

Pinot Noir vineyards at Chur/Coire (Ostschweiz)

Picturesque scene in the Herrschaft at Maienfeld

addition, you will occasionally come across the gewürztraminer, the pinot blanc, the pinot gris (often called the tokayer here), the freisamer, the ebling, the chardonnay, the chasselas and the more complete (Graubünden). The choice is more restricted as regards black grapes. Occasionally you will come across the new grapes, gamaret and B 28 (both gamay x reichensteiner).

For the sake of convenience, Ostschweiz is subdivided into three main subsidiary regions: the west (Bern or Thunersee, Unterwalden, Uri, Luzern, Zug, Aargau, Solothurn and Basel), the central region (Schwyz, Glarus, Zurich, Thurgau and Schaffhausen) and the east (Graubünden, St. Gallen and Appenzell).

RIESLING X SYLVANER

The name of the canton or municipality of origin is indicated on the label. In general, these are fresh, fruity, elegant wines with a hint of muscat. Serve them as an aperitif with tender vegetables (asparagus), warm, creamy starters (vol-au-vents), fish, white meat, pork, poultry and soft cheeses. Tip: ham and cheese fritters from St. Gallen with a mild tomato and basil coulis. Drinking temperature is 8–12 °C (46.4–53.6 °F) (the lighter the wine, the colder it should be).

BLAUBURGUNDER/CLEVNER

This wine is made with the pinot noir throughout Ostschweiz. The wines vary a great deal from very light fruity wines to rough wines rich in tannin. In general, the best Pinot Noir comes from the Rhine valley in Graubünden and St. Gallen where it is often matured in wooden barrel (barriques). Serve an 'ordinary' Blauburgunder/Clevner with dried meat from Graubünden, cold meats, poultry, kid or lamb and all sorts of cheeses. Drinking temperature is 12–14 °C (53.6–57.2 °F).

Serve the Blauburgunder/Clevner barrique from St. Gallen and Graubünden with heavier peasant fare, casseroles, small game, duck and any sort of mature cheese. Tip: Mutton casserole with white cabbage and potatoes. Drinking temperature is 14–16 °C (57.2–60.8 °F).

FEDERWEISSER/SCHILLER/SÜSSDRUCK

In Ostschweiz these poetic names refer to the various rosé wines made with the pinot noir (blauburgunder, clevner). These lively wines are often extremely fruity, soft, elegant, friendly and generous. Serve these wines with fish or dishes made with tender small game, poultry, oriental dishes, sausages etc. Tip: 'Churer fleischtorte', savory meat pie from Chur, or 'Churer fleischkröpfli', meat fritters from Chur. Drinking temperature is 8–12 °C (46.4–53.6 °F) (the fuller the wine, the less cold it should be).

GERMANY

Germany is one of the top ten wine-producing countries. A large proportion of the production is intended for export, while Germany also imports a great deal of wine itself. This illustrates the complexity of the German situation. It seems that both the best, and unfortunately also the worst German wines disappear abroad, and that the Germans themselves are more inclined to drink a beer or a foreign wine than a German wine. In comparison with countries such as France, Italy and Spain, German wine consumption is quite low.

Although the government has always maintained that the German system of controls is watertight and unquestionably the best in Europe, experience has shown that there is a great deal that can go wrong with cheap German wines. Again a number of dealers (not necessarily of German origin) were more interested in making money quickly than in serving as ambassadors for German wine. This is an unfortunate situation and the image of German wines is still suffering as a result in some countries. Producers of "lemonade" selling their creations in bad faith, with imaginative names such as 'Alte Wein Tradition' or 'Kellergeister' are also responsible for damaging the image of German wines. Until recently, the sublime top wines from Germany appear to have gone to only a small group of true connoisseurs. However, because of the absurd prices of Bordeaux wines (especially Sauternes), more and more people are looking for good alternatives for great and still affordable sweet wines. For these people, and actually for any true wine lover, Germany has a great deal to offer.

For a long time there did not seem to be anything between the heavenly top wines and the disgusting drinks which do not even deserve to be called wine. However, in the last few decades, the demand for good, affordable German wines has increased. There has also been an explosive growth in the demand for dry German wines. This has meant enormous efforts on the part of German wine growers, as they were not really known for their ability to adapt quickly. Nevertheless, most wine growers have managed to adapt to the changes in the market very well in a relatively short time. Better ways of guaranteeing the quality of the wines were found for a price acceptable to everyone. This was a great challenge and the Germans have certainly risen to the occasion.

Bernkasteler Doctor (Mosel-Saar-Ruwer), one of the best German wines

hard work of centuries and endless research into the most suitable varieties of grapes have turned Germany into a splendid wine-growing area against all expectations. German viticulture is extremely complex, and subdivided into thousands of small vineyards (Einzellage), each with its own microclimate. This is precisely what makes German wines so fascinating!

Once again it was the Romans who introduced vines to the banks of the Rhine and to the Rheinpfalz. Much later it was Charlemagne in particular who gave fresh encouragement to wine growing. Small wineries sprang up everywhere, in which wines could be tasted and sold, both with or without a nutritious meal. Later on, it was the turn of the monks to tend the vineyards and where possible, expand them. These monks played a key role in selection of the most suitable varieties for specific types of soil. Monastic vineyards ceased when Napoleon conquered Germany. These vineyards were divided up and sold to private owners and local authorities. The nineteenth and twentieth centuries were the golden age of German viticulture. Names such as Schoss Johannisberg (Rheingau) were music to the ears of most European sovereigns and heads of state. After losing two world wars, the Germans were probably in need of appreciation, warmth and consolation, and this was clearly reflected in the sudden enormous popularity of sweet wines. However, tastes change quickly, and nowadays, dry German wines are gaining ground all the time, though without any negative effect on the best sweet wines which will always continue to be popular.

HISTORY

Since the unification of Germany it has been one of the biggest countries in Europe. However, only a very small part of the country is suitable for cultivating vines. The majority of German wine-growing areas are in the south and southwest, with two small exceptions in former East Germany, along the banks of the Elbe and Saale. In the other regions, the Rhine and its tributaries (Neckar, Kocher, Jagst, Tauber, Main, Nahe, Saar, and Mosel) play a major role. In fact, Germany is certainly not an obvious wine country, because the location of the wine-growing areas is well north of the magical fiftieth degree of latitude. However, the perfect location of the vineyards in relation to the sun, the often undulating landscape and, above all, the reflection of the heat and light of the sun by the many rivers are factors that are decisive for the success of German wine. These rivers also protect the vineyards against the disastrous night frosts in spring. The

Modern, dry quality wine

WINE GROWING

Although some wine growers are successful in producing a number of excellent red wines, Germany is predominantly a white wine country, chiefly because of its climate. Admittedly, the quality of red wines has improved enormously, but the price of these very acceptable wines is still often too high for the quality on offer. Slightly more than 85% of the wine-growing area of Germany is planted with white grapes. Before German reunification, there had been a considerable increase in the proportion of black grapes being planted, from 13% in 1984 to almost 19% in 1994. As the wine-growing areas of the former East Germany cultivated mainly white grapes, this proportion fell once more. There have also been changes in the choice of grapes, towards quality at the expense of quantity. For example, the extremely productive Müller-Thurgau is increasingly losing ground to the higher quality riesling grape. In addition to these two important varieties of grape, you will also find the kerner, silvaner, scheurebe, bacchus and many other varieties. The spätburgunder (pinot noir) is king of the black grapes, followed by the blauer portugieser, the blauer trollinger, etc. The sophisticated fruitiness and relatively low alcohol content is characteristic of all German wines, including dry wines.

VARIETIES OF GERMAN GRAPES

MÜLLER-THURGAU
This grape still accounts for a quarter of the total vines planted. It is a cross between the riesling and the silvaner, first introduced by the Swiss professor H. Müller from Thurgau, who created it. These grapes ripen early and are therefore very suitable for Germany, where it is sometimes cold and damp in the fall. Characteristics: floral aromas, low level of acidity, and a slight undertone of muscat. Drink this wine young.

RIESLING
This is undoubtedly the very best variety of grape in Germany. In terms of percentages it is still just behind the Müller-Thurgau, but it is steadily gaining ground. This grape ripens late and under the best conditions it can produce extremely good wines, very aromatic and harmonious. Characteristics: fine, elegant, fruity aromas, delicate acids which give the wine backbone and a taste full of character. Because of the high level of acidity, the best wines age very well.

SILVANER (SYLVANER)
In Franconia (Franken) particularly, this is a traditional variety of grape which is somewhere between the early Müller-Thurgau and the late riesling, in terms of ripening. Characteristics: soft aromas, fresh and mild, pleasant and often uncomplicated taste, full and generous. Drink the wine young.

KERNER
The kerner is a cross between the black trollinger and the white riesling. It seems to be becoming increasingly popular, partly because this grape ripens early. Characteristics: lively wines with a light undertone of muscat, and a fresh level of acidity (usually drunk young). It is more like the riesling than the trollinger.

SCHEUREBE
Like the Müller-Thurgau, this scheurebe is a cross between the silvaner and the riesling. Characteristics: lively, very fruity, with separate aromas and nuances of overripe grapes, or even currants. Drink the wine young.

RULÄNDER/GRAUBURGUNDER (PINOT GRIS)
The ubiquitous pinot gris is extremely popular in Germany. However, it is a difficult variety of grape in these climate conditions. When you find a bottle made with the grauburgunder, it is usually a dry wine, while the indication ruländer is actually used for sweeter wines. The grapes ripen at more or less the same time as the silvaner and produce full, robust wines which are very round and have a soft sultry taste. Characteristics: aromas of soft fruits, nuts and almonds. Should be kept for a few years.

OTHER VARIETIES OF WHITE GRAPES OF GERMANY
There are a large number of white grapes from Germany, each with their own character:

- bacchus: floral, fruity wines with surprising undertones of caraway seed and spices;
- elbling: mild, elegant and lively with hints of (green) apples;
- faberrebe: light undertone of freshly picked muscat grapes, a very tempting taste;
- roter traminer (gewürztraminer): surprisingly floral wine with an almost feminine undertone of roses. On the other hand, the taste is full and intense;
- gutedel or chasselas: light wines with identifiable aromas of nuts and a friendly taste. Easy and quick to drink;
- huxelrebe: often with a fairly high level of acidity and a herbal taste with an undertone of muscat;
- morio-muskat: fairly spicy with curious hints of fresh lavender and muscat;
- weissburgunder: soft, fresh and elegant with fruity aromas reminiscent of (green) apples.

SPÄTBURGUNDER
In Germany the pinot noir produces velvety, full, elegant red wines with aromas of forest fruit and an undertone of almonds. Only top wines can be laid down for some time.

PORTUGIESER
This blauer portugieser produces light, friendly, aromatic and generous wines which are supple and easy to drink.

TROLLINGER
The blauer trollinger ripens late and is a specialty from Württemberg. The wines are fresh, with a high level of acidity, fruity and lively. Drink these wines young.

OTHER VARIETIES OF BLACK GRAPES OF GERMANY
- the dornfelder: an extremely fascinating variety of grape, very intense color and highly aromatic (red forest fruit, elderberries);
- lemberger: thoroughly fruity, from black cherries to blackcurrants;
- müllerebe (schwarzriesling): the German counterpart to the pinot meunier, well known in the Champagne. Delicate, extremely fruity wines with characteristic aromas of morels and bitter almonds.

GERMAN WINE CLASSIFICATION

The German wine classification closely follows the European directives for table wines and vins de pays, as well as quality wines. In addition to the compulsory indications shown below, all wine bottles must have an AP number (official tasting number), a code number with which the consumer can trace the wine back to its source. In addition, the name of the variety of grape that it used may only be shown on the label if it accounts for at least 85% of the basis of the wine.

GERMAN TABLE WINES
These are simple, easy-to-drink wines. If the indication 'Deutscher' is missing, the wine does not originate (wholly) from Germany.

GERMAN VINS DE PAYS

These wines are comparable to the French vins de pays. They are fresh, lively and simple, but often manage to reflect the character of their own region astonishingly accurately. They are made 'trocken' or 'halbtrocken'.

QUALITÄTSWEIN BESTIMMTER ANBAUGEBIETE (QBA)

These are quality wines from a defined area of production. The geographical indication of the general place of origin must be shown on the label though the variety of grape or precise place of origin is not compulsory (vineyard or municipality)

QUALITÄTSWEIN MIT PRÄDIKAT (QMP)

This group consists of six categories, based on the weight of the sugar in the must and the harvesting technique. This indication only concerns the percentage of sugar in the must, not in the wine. It is possible to make a dry wine (with slightly more alcohol than average) from originally very sweet must of grapes harvested late (Spätlese). These QmP wines may not have sugar added in any way.

KABINETT

The grapes are harvested when they are just ripe for these wines.

Spätlese
(Rheinpfalz)

SPÄTLESE

Overripe grapes are harvested for these wines. The difference between Kabinett and Spätlese is at least one extra week's ripening.

AUSLESE

The very best bunches of overripe grapes are picked for these wines.

BEERENAUSLESE

For Beerenauslese, only the very best grapes, which have been affected by *Botrytis*, are picked by hand.

TROCKENBEERENAUSLESE

The grapes for these wines must be partly dried by the sun and affected by *Botrytis*. Obviously they are also very carefully selected.

EISWEIN

This is a separate category which is not necessarily affected by botrytis, though it does require overripe grapes, probably dried, which may only be harvested after a night frost of at least -7 °C (-44.6 °F). This leads to an enormous concentration. The frozen water is left behind when the grapes are pressed; the extremely sweet and aromatic content is collected drop by drop.

Beerenauslese

QUALITÄTSWEIN GARANTIERTEN URSPRUNGS (QGU)

This is the most recent category of the German wine classification (1994), which gives the wine-growing areas the freedom to subject deviating local wines to a compulsory quality control. For example, in this way a wine-growing area can determine that all the Sylvaner produced in that area must be dry.

QUALITY SEALS

If you do not want to immerse yourself in German quality classifications, there is another foolproof way of buying a good German wine. Every year a voluntary competition is held under the auspices of the German Ministry of Agriculture (DLG). The wines that are submitted must already have obtained a mark in the AP test which is higher than the minimum number of points required to obtain an AP number. The wines are then again tested by professional tasters and granted a Gütezeichen. This seal guarantees the quality of the wine, and at the same time indicates the level of sweetness: a yellow seal means trocken (dry wine), a green seal means halbtrocken (medium-dry), and a red seal indicates a sweeter wine which has a good balance between sweetness, fruitiness and acidity. You can buy these wines without any qualms, but that does not mean that wines without a seal are no good. However, if you do not wish to take a risk, the wines with a seal are a good choice. A seal with a band around the neck of the bottle gives an even better guarantee. Only the very best wines to be submitted from every region are provided with this sort of band. The winners of the regional competition receive a gold, silver or bronze award while those of the national competition win a grosser, silberner or bronzener Preis. These wines generally provide excellent quality for their price.

GEOGRAPHICAL INDICATIONS

Apart from the quality requirements and various descriptions, there are a number of geographical restrictions in Germany which must be shown on the label with the quality control system. For example, there are various names which should be arranged, progressing from general to

TYPES OF WINE

- German white wine ('weiss') is made with white grapes, red wine ('rot') with black grapes and rosé wine ('Weissherbst') from a single variety of black grape and must be a QbA or QmP.
- Rotling is also a rosé wine, but is made by pressing black and white grapes together.
- Schiller, a specialty from Württemberg is also a rosé and is made like an ordinary Rotling, but must be a QbA or QmP.
- Badisch Rotgold is a rosé from Baden made only with ruländer (pinot gris) and spätburgunder (pinot noir), which are pressed together. The wine must be a QbA or QmP.
- Perlwein is a red or white wine with natural or added carbon dioxide. These wines are slightly sparkling.
- Deutscher Sekt is a sparkling wine of good or excellent quality made according to the méthode traditionnelle, with a second fermentation in the bottle. Some wines are also given a geographical indication (Sekt b.A.). The very best wines can be identified by the indication Qualitätsschaumweine b.A., sparkling quality wines with a controlled geographical indication.

specific indications. You could assume that the 'more specific the name, the better the quality, but in practice there are some exceptions to this'.

ANBAUGEBIETE
This is the most general indication (generic) and comprises a whole region. For example: Mosel-Saar-Ruwer.

BEREICH
The Bereich is a defined subsidiary region of the Anbaugebiete. To continue the example given above: Mosel-Saar-Ruwer, Bereich Zell/Mosel.

GROSSLAGE
This is a small area with an identifiable specific wine-growing area such as a municipality. For example: Mosel-Saar-Ruwer, Bereich Zell/Mosel, Grosslage Schwarze Katz.

EINZELLAGE
This is the last indication: it usually concerns just a single hamlet. An Einzellage, must cover at least 5.43 acres. For example: Mosel-Saar-Ruwer, Bereich Zell/Mosel, Grosslage Schwarze Katz, Einzellage Zeller Domherrenberg.

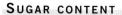

German Sekt

SUGAR CONTENT

As in the rest of Europe, the sweetness of the wines is shown on the label. However, the Germans do not mean exactly the same as the French by 'trocken' (dry). A French dry wine (sec) can have a maximum of 2 g (in exceptional cases 4 g) of sugar per liter. However, a German trocken can contain up to 9 g of sugar per liter (halbtrocken less than 19 g/liter). This means that most German dry wines are easier to drink.

NEW NAMES FOR DRY GERMAN WINES

Since 2001, the two magic words Classic and Selection have simplified the choice of wines for fans of German wines. Starting with the harvest of the year 2000, the label could use these two new terms. The term 'Classic' shows the consumer that a wine is characteristic of a specific wine-growing region. This wine is of a high quality and tastes dry, rich, powerful and aromatic, which makes it extremely suitable for accompanying a meal. The term 'Selection' indicates a wine of the new dry top class of German wines. In order to use these terms, the wines must come from strictly defined wine-growing areas with extra attention devoted to low yields and hand-picked grapes. These wines may not be bottled before 1st September of the year after the harvest. In other words, the wines made with grapes harvested in 2001 may not be bottled and put on the market before 1st September 2002.

WINE-GROWING REGIONS

Viticulture in Germany extends, on the one hand, from the north of the Bodensee up to the river Ahr above Koblenz, and on the other hand, the two areas around Dresden and below Halle. Altogether there are thirteen wine-growing areas, eleven in the (south)west and two in the east of the country. Each wine-growing area has a number of different wines: the taste and type are determined by the soil, the weather conditions (microclimates), the skills and demands of the wine growers and, of course, the demand of the consumers. The northern wines are usually white, softly fruity, subtle in taste and aroma and with sharp acids; those from the south are usually fuller and more powerful in taste and aroma but more mildly acidic. The most important characteristics of each of the wine-growing areas are described below, moving from the south to the north.

BADEN

Baden lies in the southeast of Germany and forms a fairly long strip from the northern shores of the Bodensee, via the famous Schwarzwald (Black Forest) (Freiburg, Baden-Baden) up to Karlsruhe and Heidelberg, slightly below the confluence of the Neckar and the Rhine. Baden is the second largest wine-growing area in Germany and produces a great variety of wines. The soil of Baden consists mainly of loess, loam, gravel, some limestone and volcanic rock. The varieties of grapes include the Müller-Thurgau, ruländer, gutedel, gewürztraminer and riesling for the

Modern white wine from Badisch with an Italian accent

full, round white wines, often with herbal or spicy aromas; spätburgunder for the velvety soft, round and lively red wines and the delicious, refreshing Weissherbst. Local specialties include 'Felchen' (excellent lake trout from the Bodensee) and 'Kalbsbries' (sweetbreads of veal).

WÜRTTEMBERG

The vineyards of Württemberg lie on the hills above the Neckar and its tributaries. This region starts at Tübingen and extends through the capital Stuttgart to Heilbronn and Bad Mergentheim. Württemberg is the largest wine-growing area in Germany for red wines. Approximately half of the vineyards are planted with black grapes. The soil in this region consists of sediment, limestone with many fossilized shells, marl and loess. Unfortunately the splendid wines from this region are hardly ever found outside the area of production. The local population cannot think of any better way to show their appreciation of their own wine growers than to drink all the wines themselves. Varieties of grapes: trollinger, müllerebe, spätburgunder, portugieser and lemberger for the very fruity red wines and riesling, Müller-Thurgau, kerner and silvaner, for the robust, powerful, often slightly coarse white wines. Local specialties: 'Spätzle' and 'Maultaschen' (pastries).

HESSISCHE BERGSTRASSE

This area is a tiny strip of land between Heidelberg and Bensheim. It is bordered by the Rhine in the west and the beautiful Odenwald in the east. The soil consists almost entirely of loess, which is excellent for white wines. Again you will rarely find these wines outside the area where they are produced. Varieties of grapes: the riesling is king here, followed by the aromatic Müller-Thurgau and the subtle silvaner. Most wines are elegant and fruity with fine acids. Extremely refreshing. Local specialty: 'Bratkartoffeln mit Sülze' (fried potatoes with sour headcheese and herb sauce).

FRANKEN (FRANCONIA)

The vineyards of Franconia are on the hills on the banks of the Main by Würzburg and Aschaffenburg. The soil consists mainly of loess, sandstone and limestone. Franconia has been famous for centuries for the Steinwein from Würzburg. It became so popular that it gave its name to all the wines from this region (Stein), and the amusing but utterly impractical green Bocksbeutel bottles which are very difficult to stack in racks meant for round bottles. Varieties of grapes: mainly Müller-Thurgau and silvaner. Fairly dry, robust wines with a high level of acidity and full structure. Local

specialties: 'Spargel' (asparagus), 'blaue Zipfel' (sausages).

RHEINPFALZ

The Rheinpfalz is the most 'French' German wine-growing area. It is only a very small distance from the French border and the older wine growers from Rheinpfalz remember the time when many French people came to buy wines from Rheinpfalz. In some places a few people still speak fluent French, mainly south of the town of Landau, once a French garrison town. The most southerly vineyard in Rheinpfalz, the Schweigener Sonnenberg, is actually in France, but by way of historical exception, the German

The traditional Frankische Bocksbeutel

wine growers are permitted to take the harvest to produce German wine. The soil of the Rheinpfalz consists mainly of loam, clay and eroded limestone. In terms of area, this is the second wine-growing region of Germany and also the most productive. The best vineyards are in the north of the region, mainly around Wachenheim, Forst, Deidesheim and Ruppertsberg. They are very well known for their excellent Riesling wines.

Varieties of grapes: in addition to the powerful, full, aromatic and elegant Riesling, there are a number of good white wines in this region, made with, for example, the Müller-Thurgau, kerner, silvaner, and morio-muskat. The rarer red wines, made, for example, with the portugieser, are soft, mild and fruity. The dornfelder also produces excellent results. Local specialties are: 'Saumagen' (ex-Chancellor Kohl's favorite dish: the stomach of a pig filled with meat, potatoes and herbs), 'Leberknödel' (soft liver balls), and 'Zwiebelkuchen' (onion tart).

RHEINHESSEN

This wine-growing region, between Worms in the south and Mainz in the north, is situated in a loop of the Rhine and its tributary, the Nahe. This is by far the largest wine-growing region of Germany in terms of area, but comes second (after Rheinpfalz) in terms of production. The wines of Rheinhessen were once very famous, particularly during the time of Charlemagne. The region became famous overnight because of the excellent quality of the wines from

Excellent Riesling from the Rheinpfalz

the vineyards around the cathedral of Worms, the Liebfraukirche. This Liebfraumilch, which was once of an extremely high quality, can now be produced in four regions: Rheinhessen, Rheinpfalz, Rheingau and Nahe. The current wines, which are of a quality ranging from reasonable to disgustingly sweet and flat, unfortunately have nothing left in common with the legendary old wines.

The soil of Rheinhessen consists of loess, limestone and sandstone and provides inventive wine growers with countless possibilities. The very best wines from Rheinhessen undoubtedly come from the area of Nierstein, where the riesling particularly produces excellent results on the sunny terraces above the Rhine.

Varieties of grapes: riesling (mild, fruity wines with a round full taste), Müller-Thurgau and silvaner for white wines; portugieser and spätburgunder for red wines. One of the best red wines from Germany is the full, fruity, classical spätburgunder from the village of Ingelheim, in the Grosslage Kaiserpfalz. Local specialties: 'Spargel' (asparagus), and 'Süsswasserfisch' (freshwater fish).

A true Niersteiner which does not deny its origin.

NAHE

Nahe lies to the west of Rheinhessen on either side of the eponymous river. The soil in the north of this region (around Bad Kreuznach) contains a lot of loam and sand; further south there is more quartz and porphyry. In terms of its wines, Nahe is a link between the aromatic wines of the Mosel, the elegant wines from the Rheingau and the mild wines from Rheinhessen. Varieties of grapes: Müller-Thurgau, riesling and silvaner, which produce elegant, subtle and aromatic wines here. Local specialties: 'Soonwälder Frischlingsrücken' (boar's back with mushrooms and a typical German garnish of pears stuffed with mountain cranberries, stewed in red wine with cinnamon) and a series of excellent desserts and pastries, including 'Trauben Torte' (grape tart).

Delicious, modern, dry riesling (Rheinhessen)

Trocken Graubungunder (Nahe)

RHEINGAU

Rheingau is the geographical center of German wine growing. This relatively small region lies on the northern bank of the Rhine between Hochheim and Lorch. Apart from the small Grosslagen of Daubhaus (above Hocheim), Steil (by Assmannshausen) and Burgweg (by Lorch), the Rheingau consists of a single uninterrupted region on the slopes of the Taunus. The forested peaks of this mountain, high above the vineyards, which gradually descend down to the Rhine, form an unforgettable spectacle. Rheingau is famous for its marvelous wines and the major role which it played in the history of wine in Germany. The basic principles of the current German wine laws were drawn up here, and the first wines from late harvests were produced here, as well as the first Trockenbeerenauslese. The riesling thrives here better than anywhere else, in a soil of loess, loam and eroded slate.

Varieties of grapes: the celebrated Riesling wines from Rheingau are elegant, fruity, fresh and have great class. The better wines often have a sharp, almost herbal character and enough acids to be laid down for a few years. The excellent Spätburgunder from Assmannshausen is also famous. Local specialties include 'Blutwurst', 'Hausmacherwurst' and 'Lauchkuchen' (leek tart).

MITTELRHEIN

At the confluence of the Nahe and the Rhine, four wine-growing areas come together: Nahe, Rheinhessen, Rheingau and Mittelrhein. Mittelrhein is an extensive wine-growing region from Bingen through Bacharach and Koblenz to just past the mouth of the Ahr. The vineyards are situated on terraces on steep hillsides on either side of the Rhine. The landscape is truly magnificent, as are the many castles and picturesque villages. Mittelrhein is also worth a trip for its wines, which can hardly be found outside this region. They are characterized by their terroir: slate on the slopes and slightly more clay by the river. Varieties of grapes: the riesling also produces the best

Excellent wine from the Rheingau

wines here: elegant, fruity and with a good structure and sometimes a high level of acidity. The wines made with the Müller-Thurgau and kerner are slightly softer but still have fairly sharp acids. Local specialty: 'Sauerbraten' (sweet and sour beef casserole with red cabbage).

MOSEL-SAAR-RUWER

This well-known wine-growing area stretches from the valley of the Saar, the Ruwer and Mosel, from Saarburg through Trier to Koblenz. Again the landscape is breathtaking. The vineyards lie on steep hillsides on the banks of the meandering Mosel. The slopes consist mainly of slate, and contain many minerals give the wines an extra finesse. True Mosel wines are delicious, but not all wines from this region deserve these superlatives. To put it mildly, there are still too many fair to almost undrinkable sugary wines parading as Mosel. Wine merchants acting in bad faith and foolish buyers who are only out to make a profit have given the name of these wines from Mosel-Saar-Ruwer a very bad name. Varieties of grapes: the true wines from the Mosel owe their reputation to their rich aromas, their elegant character and great class. There are many types of Mosel wines, from soft, fruity and friendly wines to spicy, rich and extremely aromatic wines. The better wines are definitely those made with the riesling, especially around the famous villages of Bernkastel, Piesport, Wehlen, Brauneberg, Graach, Zeltingen and Erden. Apart from the riesling, the Müller-Thurgau and the old fashioned elbling also flourish here. Local specialties: 'Süsswasserfisch' (freshwater fish) and all sorts of game.

AHR

The Ahr is one of the smallest German wine producing areas. It lies to the south of Bonn, near Bad Neuenahr-Ahrweiler. The rugged impressive valley of the Ahr is a true paradise for lovers of nature and hikers. Once you arrive on the plain of the Eifel, there is nothing that tastes better than a cool glass of red Portugieser wine. The Ahr produces red wines, although the volcanic soil with a lot of slate is also extremely suitable for good white wines. However, there were already so many good white wines in Germany and the area of the Ahr was so limited that it was considered more profitable to plant black grapes here. Varieties of grapes: two black grapes, the

Excellent Riesling from the Mosel-Saar-Ruwer

spätburgunder and the portugieser produce velvety-soft, elegant and fruity red wines. The riesling and the Müller-Thurgau produce elegant, fresh, lively and very aromatic wines. Local specialties include trout from the Ahr, 'Pilzen' (mushrooms) and 'Schinken' (hams from the Eifel are utterly delicious).

SACHSEN (SAXONY)

This is one of the two new wine-growing areas of Germany (former east Germany). Together with the second new area, Saale/Unstrut, it is the most northerly wine-growing area in Germany. The small area of Sachsen lies furthest east on the banks of the Elbe on either side of the city of Dresden. The soil of the vineyards is very varied, including sand, porphyry, and loam). Varieties of grapes: the Müller-Thurgau, the weissburgunder and the traminer produce dry, fruity wines with a refreshing level of acidity. The rare local wines are light and mild and the Elbtal Sekt is very acceptable. Local specialties: goose, carp and roast mutton.

SAALE/UNSTRUT

This small area below Halle is the most northerly wine-growing area in Germany and, together with those in England, in the whole of Europe. The severe continental climate forces the wine growers to harvest the grapes very quickly. Therefore you will find few sweet wines and certainly no late harvests! Most of the wines are dry and often quite acidic. White grapes thrive particularly on a soil of sandstone with many fossilized shells, but the rare red wines prove that these are possible as well. Varieties of grapes: the Müller-Thurgau is productive and undemanding (fresh wines with a pleasant aroma of grapefruit). However, the wines made with the silvaner are better (soft and fresh with milder acids and an aroma of citrus fruit). The best locations are reserved for the riesling, which produces excellent results, especially on limestone (fresh, powerful and full with a characteristic aroma of pears). In addition, there is the weissburgunder (green apples) and the traminer (mild and round), as well as the portugieser (tempting aroma of raspberries, although the wine is often slightly rough). Local specialties include: 'Klösse' (potato dumplings), goose, game and 'Thüringer wursten' (herb and garlic sausages).

GERMAN WINE AND GASTRONOMY

German wines are fascinating with meals not only because they are absolutely delicious but also because they often contain little alcohol (and therefore do not make you so tired), and they have fresh acidity which cut through fatty foods. However, German wines are also excellent as an aperitif or for drinking after a meal, precisely because of their fresh and light elegance. You do not even have to think about food to open a bottle of German wine: most can be enjoyed very well without being accompanied by a meal! Although most of us would probably opt for a bottle of Châteauneuf du Pape or a Barolo to drink with a dish of game, a powerful Spätburgunder Spätlese trocken is certainly worth a try. In fact, German wines can accompany almost anything. In Germany they will even tell you that there is a German wine for the spiciest and sweetest dishes, though I prefer to leave extremes to others. I prefer not to drink wine with extremely spicy oriental meals, and I would not drink an expensive wine with very sweet chocolate desserts, except perhaps for a Banyuls, Maury or Pedro Ximénes. The best combinations of wine are the combinations in which the meal and the wine complement each other directly, (e.g., soft, creamy and slightly earthy asparagus with a similar wine, such as a Müller-Thurgau from Rheinhessen or Franconia), or actually supplement each other with their differences in character (e.g., a fresh acidic wine which can slightly neutralize a rather fatty pork dish without detracting from the taste, such as a young Riesling or Kerner from the wine-growing area in the north). However, be careful about some seemingly 'logical' combinations, such as sweet desserts and sweet wines often incorrectly referred to as 'dessert wines'. Too much sweetness is counterproductive and despite the fresh character of German sweet wines, it is not a good idea to serve a Trockenbeerenauslese with an extremely sweet cream cake! Some tried and tested combinations are suggested below: it is up to you to make a choice.

- Aperitif: Deutsche Sekt, Qualitätsschaumwein, QbA, Kabinett.
- Shellfish and crustaceans: (halb)trocken Riesling, Ruländer, Müller-Thurgau, Silvaner or Kerner QbA and Kabinett.
- Fish, fried, without a sauce or in a light sauce: Riesling, Kerner, Silvaner, Grauburgunder, Weissburgunder or Müller-Thurgau QbA, Kabinett, Auslese trocken, Spätlese trocken.
- Fish in a rich sauce: Riesling, Grauburgunder, Weissburgunder, Silvaner, Müller-Thurgau, Kerner, Auslese trocken, Spätlese trocken.
- Pastries, risotto with a light sauce: Kerner, Silvaner, Riesling, Müller-Thurgau trocken/halbtrocken QbA or Kabinett.
- Pastries, risotto with a rich sauce: Scheurebe, Ruländer halbtrocken, Spätlese, Auslese or Grauburgunder, Riesling, Weissburgunder, Auslese trocken and Spätlese trocken.
- Offal: Riesling, Weissburgunder, Kerner, Müller-Thurgau, Silvaner Auslese trocken, Spätlese trocken or Scheurebe, Gewürztraminer, Ruländer Auslese and Spätlese.
- Poultry, Fowl: Riesling Auslese trocken, Riesling Spätlese trocken, Grauburgunder, Kerner, Weissburgunder Spätlese trocken, Auslese trocken, Spätburgunder Weissherbst Spätlese/Auslese trocken, Lemberger Spätlese trocken, Trollinger Spätlese trocken, Spätburgunder Auslese trocken.

- White meat: Weissburgunder, Silvaner, Müller-Thurgau, Riesling Auslese trocken, Spätlese trocken.
- Pork: Riesling Auslese trocken, Riesling Spätlese trocken, Trollinger Spätlese trocken, Lemberger Spätlese trocken.
- Sausages, ham etc. (hot): Silvaner Auslese trocken, Silvaner Spätlese trocken, Spätburgunder Weissherbst Auslese/ Spätlese trocken, Trollinger Spätlese trocken, Lemberger Spätlese trocken.
- Beef: Spätburgunder Auslese/Spätlese trocken.
- Lamb/game: Spätburgunder Auslese trocken.
- Soft cheeses: QbA and Kabinett, (halb)trocken Kerner, Silvaner, Müller--Thurgau.
- Medium cheeses: inter alia, Riesling (halb)trocken, QbA or Kabinett, Kerner, Silvaner, Müller-Thurgau Kabinett
- Blue cheeses: Beerenauslese, Trockenbeerenauslese, Eiswein.
- Strong cheeses: Spätburgunder Auslese trocken, Lemberger, Trollinger Auslese trocken, Gewürztraminer Spätlese/Auslese trocken.
- Fresh desserts: Auslese, Beerenauslese, Trockenbeerenauslese, Eiswein.
- Extremely sweet desserts: Deutscher Sekt or a refreshing dry white wine, or no wine.

Magnificent Riesling Spätlese trocken for better dishes of white meat and poultry

TEMPERATURE FOR DRINKING WINE	
Type of wine	
Extremely sweet wines (Trockenbeerenauslese, Eiswein)	6–8 °C (42.8–46.4 °F)
Light young white wines (up to max. Kabinett)	8–10 °C (46.4–50 °F)
Full, rich white wines (halbtrocken Spätlese, Auslese, etc.)	10–12 °C (50–53.6 °F)
Rosé, Weissherbst, Schiller	8–10 °C (46.4–50 °F)
Rotling, Badisch Rotgold	
Light young red wines (e.g., Portugieser, Trollinger)	11–13 °C (51.8–55.4 °F)
Rich red wines (e.g., Spätburgunder Spätlese)	13–14 °C (55.4–57.2 °F)
Rich red wines matured in wood (barrique cuvées)	14–16 °C (57.2–60.8 °F)

BENELUX

LUXEMBOURG

WINE GROWING

Traces of cultivation of vines have been found in Luxembourg dating from pre-Roman times. Very probably the local inhabitants were already growing wines on the banks of the Moselle, six centuries before Christ. However, it was the Romans who introduced good practices and planted and maintained the first orderly vineyards. The monks took over their work and expanded the vineyards wherever possible. In 1709, the wine-growing area was almost entirely destroyed by severe frosts and had to be planted again. Under Austrian rule, wine growing was prohibited as a form of polyculture. Farmers had to choose between agriculture and viticulture. After the French Revolution, the churches and aristocracy had to surrender their vineyards to the real wine growers. After the fall of Napoleon, the Grand Duchy of Luxembourg lost its land on the right bank of the Moselle, that became part of the Kingdom of the Netherlands. The Dutch lived up to their reputation and imposed enormous taxes on the wines of these Luxembourg wine growers who were not particularly rich in the first place (no less than half of the sale price!). As a result, the disappointed wine growers did not even take the trouble to harvest the grapes in years when the quality and/or quantity of the grapes was disappointing. Many vineyards were not maintained very well, and the quality declined. At the end of the nineteenth century viticulture revived in Luxembourg for a while, when Germans started to buy the local wines on a large scale. At that time, the majority of vines planted in Luxembourg were elbling grapes, and the Germans were interested in this to cover their own shortages. Therefore this revival was more of an economic nature than of a qualitative nature, and was not really very good for the image of Luxembourg viticulture. However, the grape louse *Phylloxera* was responsible for a radical replanting of the vineyards at the beginning of the twentieth century. After the World War I, increasing numbers of Luxembourg wine growers opted to improve the quality, despite the extremely poor post-war economic situation. Partly as the result of government intervention, the wine growers were able to continue their policy focusing on quality, culminating with the creation of the 'marque nationale' recognition for the better wines in 1935. The next step was in 1959, when the better wines were further subdivided into 'vin classé', 'premier cru', and 'grand cru'. In 1985, the best Luxembourg wines were permitted the recognized European geographical indication 'Moselle Luxembourgeoise – appellation contrôlée'. In 1988, the term 'marque nationale' was also used for the best sparkling wines, and in 1991, the by now extremely successful geographical indication, 'crémant de Luxembourg' was introduced.

The vineyards of Luxembourg were all on the left banks of the Moselle. The wine-growing area starts at the French border in Schengen and ends on the German border in Wasserbillig. The Moselle valley is approximately 984–1312 ft wide and is flanked by gently undulating hills. The vineyards lie at an average height of 150 to 250 meters (492–820 ft) above sea level. The soil varies between marl in the Reumich canton (south) to rocky chalk in the Grevenmacher canton (north). The landscape also varies from a gently undulating landscape near Reumich (well known for its mild, almost rounded wines) and a rugged landscape at Grevenmacher (known for its elegant, sharp wines with a characteristic terroir). Because it is never really too hot or too cold (the river tempers extreme temperatures) the grapes are able to grow and ripen in peace.

GRAPE VARIETIES

Luxembourg produces mainly white wines and a small amount of red. Quality wines are made with quality grapes. You can recognize Luxembourg wines immediately by the name of the variety of grape on the label.

RIESLING
The noblest grapes from Luxembourg, which ripen late and produce excellent wines in good years: fruity, elegant, delicate and with a good class.

PINOT GRIS
This little brother of the pinot noir produces full, robust, aromatic wines rich in extracts with a very individual character.

PINOT BLANC
Another member of the pinot family which produces mainly fresh, elegant, supple and very pleasant wines.

AUXERROIS
This is a cousin of the pinot blanc which produces full, aromatic, fruity and elegant wines. The best ones have a strong backbone and age well.

GEWÜRZTRAMINER
Well known in Alsace, but also in Austria and

Riesling from Wormeldange

Germany. This variety ripens late and produces excellent wines, tempting and sultry, with surprising aromas of roses and spices.

RIVANER

The rivaner is none other than the riesling x sylvaner from Switzerland, i.e. the Müller–Thurgau. The grape ripens early and produces mild, often rounded wines with a friendly taste

ELBLING

Once this was the Luxembourg grape (end of the nineteenth century) but it is now used exclusively for light wines which are pleasantly fresh and thirst–quenching.

PINOT NOIR

The only black grape in this list. In years which are not very sunny, the pinot noir produces fresh, light, elegant and fruity red and rosé wines. In very sunny years they are more rounded and strong.

WINE CLASSIFICATION

Only good wines from Luxembourg have the easily identifiable label on the neck of the bottle indicating 'Moselle Luxembourgeoise, appellation contrôlée marque nationale'. Some wines indicate this for aesthetic reasons (they often have their own label around the neck) on a label on the back. 'Marque nationale' means that the wine has been controlled by the government, consists of 100% Luxembourg grapes and corresponds with the quality standards imposed by the EU. Obviously these wines must also by bottled in the area of production. In order to obtain the recognition the wines must be approved by a professional panel and provided with an inspection number. To guard against any possibility of fraud, there is yet another control, this time in the cellars of the producer concerned.

MARQUE NATIONALE

During this inspection, the wines are given points from 0–20. All the wines which are given at least 12 points are given the indication 'marque nationale, appellation contrôlée'. For the Elbling this is the highest which can be awarded. All other wines may compete for a higher classification.

VIN CLASSÉ

All wines which gain at least 14 points may call themselves 'vin classé', which means that these wines scored slightly higher than average. For the Rivaner this is also the highest score that is possible. Other wines can gain a higher score.

PREMIER CRU

All wines which gain at least 16 points, are given the description:' 'premier cru' (literally 'first class crop'). Only the Riesling, Pinot Gris, Pinot Blanc, Auxerrois, Gewürztraminer and Pinot Noir can obtain this high score.

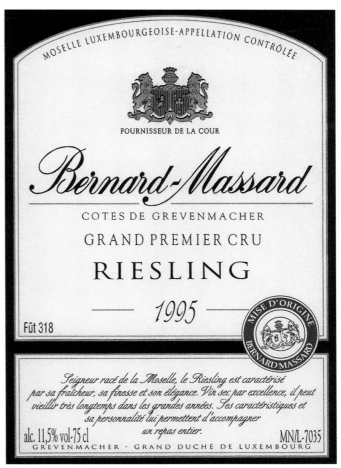

Grand premier cru

GRAND PREMIER CRU

All premier cru wines may participate in the next extremely strict quality test. Any wine that scores more than 18 points is permitted to use the extremely prestigious term, 'grand premier cru'. This rarely happens and only the very best Luxembourg wines are able to achieve this.

CRÉMANT DE LUXEMBOURG
APPELLATION CONTRÔLÉE

Only wines produced using the méthode traditionnelle or the méthode cuve may compete for the marque nationale and only the best sparkling méthode traditionelle wines may use the classification 'crémant de Luxembourg'. For this, they must comply with the strict requirements of the 'marque nationale', as well as the following requirements: every wine is given its own document clearly revealing the whole progress from still wines to the final product; the yield when it is pressed may not be higher than 100 liters of juice from 150 kilos of grapes (211 pints per 330 lb); all wines must mature for at least nine months in local cellars after the second fermentation in the bottle (compulsory); the pressure in the bottles must be at least 4 bar (atmosphere); the total amount of SO2 (sulfur dioxide) may not be more than 150 mg/liter; the corks and the labels must

Excellent Riesling from Grevenmacher

Crémant de Luxembourg

indicate 'crémant de Luxembourg'. It is not surprising that the crémant de Luxembourg is seen by connoisseurs as the best crémant in Europe! In tastings, the crémant de Luxembourg beats the famous French crémants every time.

WINES

Elbling wines and some Rivaner wines may be drunk young, but the best Luxembourg wines certainly deserve to be laid down for some time. Because of the northerly location of the vineyards, these wine often contain high levels of acids. Resting for some time will make them improve even further and give them a better balance. This certainly applies to the great wines made with the riesling, gewürztraminer and pinot gris.

MOUSSEUX DU LUXEMBOURG

The ordinary sparkling wines from Luxembourg are pleasant and fresh. They are typical summer or terrace wines, which can be drunk at any informal occasion. Drinking temperature is 6–8 °C (42.8–46.4 °F).

CRÉMANT DE LUXEMBOURG

Because of its elegant sparkling character, and subtle aromas, a crémant de Luxembourg can add a certain cachet to any time of the day. It is a fantastic aperitif, particularly with subtle snacks, with salmon, poultry, shrimps or creamy cheeses. You can continue to serve the crémant with light starters, fish (preferably poached or in a light sauce), shellfish, white meat and poultry. Finally a crémant de Luxembourg finishes off any meal perfectly, better than most other (sparkling) wines. Drinking temperature is 6–8 °C (42.8–46.4 °F).

ELBLING

This dry wine often has fairly sharp acidity. This means that it is extremely suitable for an informal summer lunch or a picnic. Make sure that you have enough (fatty) cold meats, some fresh bread and creamy butter. It is also delicious with fresh fried fish from the river. Drinking temperature is 8–10 °C (46.4–50 °F).

RIVANER

Very fruity, mild, and sometimes rounded wine which goes with almost anything. It is a friendly, generous wine as an aperitif and quenches the thirst and loosens tongues during the meal. Drinking temperature is 8–10 °C (46.4–50 °F).

PINOT BLANC

This fresh, delicate wine is suitable with any meal. The best combinations of all are with milder and more subtle dishes, e.g., poached fish (salmon, trout) or with veal in a creamy white wine sauce. Tip: 'medallion de veau aux asperges' (veal with asparagus in a mild sauce). Drinking temperature is 8–10 °C (46.4–50 °F).

AUXERROIS

This white wine is often fuller and rounder than the Pinot Blanc. Make use of this to serve it with mild dishes which have slightly more 'bite' such as frog's legs, sweetbreads in a creamy mushroom sauce, ham from a suckling pork, chicken liver paté or a delicious fresh goat's cheese. Tip: 'noix de Saint Jacques au colis d'écrevisses' (coquilles Saint Jacques (without the shell) in a mild sauce of crawfish). Drinking temperature is 10–12 °C (50–53.6 °F).

PINOT GRIS

Most Pinot Gris wines are rounded and full, with a light, rounded undertone and herbal nuances. These are very tempting wines which combine well with poultry and fowl, but also with firm-fleshed fish in a cream sauce. Tip: 'pintadeau aux truffes et pommes fondantes' (a delicious dish made with young guinea fowl stuffed with chicken livers, apple, raisins, herbs and truffles, served with sweet and sour apple purée and a light truffle sauce. Drinking temperature is 10–12 °C (50–53.6 °F).

RIESLING

This is the king of Luxembourg wines, fruity, elegant, robust and complex. Some of the dishes you should try this with include the local truite au Riesling (trout poached in Riesling), and 'poularde au riesling' (young chicken poached in Riesling). Any fish will be honored to partner this King Riesling in a meal. The locally popular pike perch (sandre) will certainly not reject such an invitation. Serve it with fresh tagliatelle and leeks julienne. Riesling is also excellent accompanying less formal dishes such as the local sauerkraut dish, 'choucroute / la Luxembourgeoise', with excellent warm ham. Tip: 'écrevisses' (crawfish). Drinking temperature is 10–12 °C (50–53.6 °F).

GEWÜRZTRAMINER

Gewurztraminer wines are characterized by strength and sultriness, while retaining a civilized elegance. Locally it is often served with foie gras,

One of the best Luxembourg Riesling wines

but my own preference is for the heavenly combination with the cheese which is made both in Alsace, and in Germany and Luxembourg: Munster. This red bacteria cheese will bring out the beast in you when it is served hot on toast or after the main course (at room temperature). Drinking temperature is 10–12 °C (50–53.6 °F).

PINOT NOIR

The Luxembourg Pinot Noir is not quite as full as the wines of Burgundy and Alsace. Its strong aspects are its pleasant fruitiness, playful freshness and tempting character. Of course, this Pinot Noir combines reasonably well with all sorts of red meat (certainly in this locality because you will not find anything more full-bodied to drink). However, if you are looking for the very best combination you will soon come across some soft, crisply-fried offal, such as 'ris de veau' (sweetbreads of veal). Tip: 'gigot d'agneau aux flageolets' (juicy suckling lamb roasted with beans). Drinking temperature is 12–14 °C (53.6–57.2 °F) for lighter varieties, and 14–16 °C (57.2–60.8 °F) for fuller wines made in sunny years.

BELGIUM

Cultivation of vines dates back to the twelfth century in Belgium. A hundred years ago the Belgium vineyards declined, partly as a result of the *Phylloxera* plague. Things picked up at the end of the twentieth century. Wine growing is still a hobby in most places, but a small number of vineyards have managed to put Belgium back on the map of wine producing countries. Most wine growers use the grapes which are suitable for northerly regions such as the Müller-Thurgau, kerner and riesling (white) and the pinot noir, gamay and dornfelder (red). The Belgians are known throughout Europe for their knowledge of wine and appreciation of the good things in life. Therefore producing their own superior wine is part of this. The fact that it is taken seriously is clear from the official European

A real wine castle in Belgium: Genoels-Elderen

Chardonnay vineyards at the castle of Genoels-Elderen

recognition of Belgian viticulture in the form of two geographical indications.

HAGELAND APPELLATION CONTRÔLÉE

The appellation d'origine contrôlée Hageland lies in the triangle Leuven-Diest-Tienen in Belgian Brabant. Vines were cultivated there as long ago as the twelfth century and possibly even earlier. The region experienced its heyday in the fourteenth and fifteenth centuries, and even in the sixteenth century there was a flourishing trade with neighboring Flanders and Holland. The success of the wine growers in Hageland, which is a rather northerly region, is due to the higher location of the vineyards, on the hillsides where the soil consists mainly of sand and a strong ferruginous subsoil, and to the will and perseverance of a handful of wine enthusiasts who have managed to revive wine growing in this region. However, the AOC Hageland will probably never be more than an exaggerated hobby. Most vineyards are so small that they cannot even meet the rapidly rising demand of local catering establishments and private buyers. All the vineyards are fairly recent, at most twenty years old and some are not even ten years old.

HASPENGOUW APPELLATION CONTRÔLÉE

One Belgian wine-growing area sticks out far above the rest, both in terms of quality, and as regards area and professionalism: the wine Château Genoels-Elderen, the only one in Belgium, just outside Riemst. This estate is owned by a Dutch family which has revived the wine-growing culture of Haspengouw and Belgium over the centuries. The Rennes family has planted high quality vines in separate vineyards around this romantic castle since 1990. Altogether they have now planted 18 hectares (800 acres), mainly with chardonnay, but also with pinot noir, and a few experimental vines of pinot blanc, auxerrois and pinot gris.

The two Chardonnay wines from Genoels-Elderen which often win international prizes are full, elegant, complex and highly aromatic. They derive their strength from the chalky marl soil in Haspengouw, which has a slight covering layer of loam. In contrast

Chardonnay blue   Chardonnay gold   Pinot Noir

with the many other vineyards in Belgium, the wine Château Genoels-Elderen has highly professional pressing, fermentation and storage systems, as well as excellent cellars. The yield obtained here per hectare is very low, less than 320 gallons per acre. The cellar master, Joyce Kékkö-van Rennes, deliberately opts for quality over quantity. The wine Château Genoels--Elderen produces approximately 60,000 bottles annually (95% Chardonnay, Pinot Noir and little bit of Pinot Blanc). Four wines are produced: the white Pinot, the black Chardonnay (from the newest vineyards) the golden Chardonnay (from the best and oldest vineyards) and the Pinot Noir. The golden Chardonnay is of exceptional quality.

In addition to the top vineyards at Genoels--Elderen, a few other smaller wine growers are also entitled to use the geographical indication of Haspengouw. For example, the quality of the wines produced in Borgloon is reasonable, though it is significantly lower than Genoels-Elderen.

THE NETHERLANDS

As in Belgium, many small Dutch farmers make their own 'wine'. However, many of these wines are made with grape extracts or greenhouse grapes and therefore fall outside the scope of this book. The wines which are interesting to us are obtained from grapes harvested in the region of production from real open-air vineyards.

There are more than a hundred small vineyards in the Netherlands, as well as ten larger professional vineyards of more than two acres. The Dutch vineyard guild supervises Dutch viticulture, though in an advisory rather than controlling capacity. The vineyards of the beautiful Limburg hills around Maastricht are famous (Apostelhoeve, Hoeve Nekum, Château Neercanne), as well as those of Brabant (De Linie). However, wine is made almost everywhere in the Netherlands, except in the northernmost provinces of Friesland and Groningen. The most 'serious' vineyards are currently in the provinces of Limburg, North Brabant and Gelderland. As it is too cold in the Netherlands for most classical grape varieties, it is often necessary to opt for varieties which ripen quickly and which are resistant to cold winters, early night frosts and fungal infections caused by damp weather in spring. Only on the south-facing or southwesterly hills in Limburg is it possible to ripen the classical grapes without any problems (pinot blanc, auxerrois, riesling, pinot noir). Elsewhere, the wine growers have to select varieties which are more suitable for the uncertain Dutch weather conditions. Resistant strains developed in testing stations, for example in Germany, are becoming increasingly popular. Some very suitable varieties include triomphe d'Alsace, regent, Léon Millot, seyval blanc and phoenix. These varieties are well known for their productivity under the most difficult circumstances. The regent in particular produces wine of an acceptable quality. However, the best wines are still made with the sensitive classical grapes mentioned above, as well as from the qualitatively inferior, though undemanding Müller-Thurgau, and kerner. The results of varieties of black grapes which are less well known than the pinot noir/spätburgunder, but are more suitable for Dutch viticulture, are also very promising: these include the dornfelder, zweigelt, trollinger and portugieser.

One of the oldest Dutch wineries is the Apostelhoeve in the Jeker valley near Maastricht. The former owner Hugo Hulst was the first person in the Netherlands to become professionally involved in viticulture. His wines, which are based on the wines of Alsace, are highly praised internationally. He planted riesling and Müller-Thurgau grapes on the steep slopes of the Louwerberg. Because of the chalk subsoil of marl covered with a thin layer of loess, the good location in relation to the sun and the protection against the cold westerly winds, the grapes have every opportunity to ripen fully. Recently the wine cellar was thoroughly renovated and the quality of the wines is better

Apostelhoeve Riesling and Müller-Thurgau from Maastricht

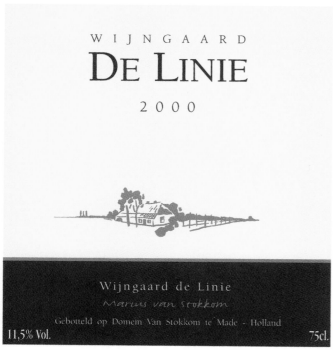

De Linie, Brabant wine from Made

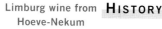

than ever before. Mathieu Hulst has taken over the winery after a few years of work experience in Alsace. The Apostelhoeve is still in the forefront of Dutch viticulture.

Two up-and-coming talents are the Bollen family, also from the Jeker valley near Maastricht (Hoeve Nekum), and Marius van Stokkum from Made in Brabant (De Linie). Other interesting wines include the Pinot Noir made by Peter Harkema (Château Neercanne, Maastricht), the red wines made by Dassen and Dullart (Domaine des Blaireaux, Maastricht) and the organic red wines made by Jan Oude Voshaar (Wageningse Berg, Wageningen).

UNITED KINGDOM

Until recently, wine-making was seen as a bit of a joke in the UK, but it is now taken 'bloody seriously' by fanatical English and Welsh wine growers!

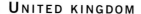
Limburg wine from Hoeve-Nekum

HISTORY

Vitis labrusca or Vitis vinifera vines were already being cultivated in the British Isles before the arrival of the Roman legions. The Celts also knew how to make beer and wine, and above all how to drink them. During the Roman occupation, vines were already growing on the undulating hills of southern England. Vineyards were usually situated around the impressive villas of important Roman officers and representatives.

Curiously the many invasions (including the Saxon and Norman invasions) had virtually no effect on English viticulture. At the end of the first millennium, growing wines was usually the task of the (mostly French) monks who cultivated them for wine for the Mass, but also to make medicinal tonics with the wines. When Eleanor of Aquitaine became Queen of England in 1152 she married Henry II, and the whole area south of Bordeaux, as far as the Spanish border, fell under English rule. The wines from Bordeaux which were already famous (e.g., from Saint-Émilion, Pomerol and Graves), were shipped to England in great volume. In those days, drinking wine was a status symbol. Many English landowners tried to plant French vines in the British Isles, with varying degrees of success. As the French wines were more popular than the indigenous wines and the price was quite reasonable (certainly much cheaper than maintaining a vineyard), English viticulture lost a large proportion of its own loyal customers. Many of the English wine growers switched over to cereals and sheep (for wool). The next blow to English wine growing came two centuries later in 1348 when the Black Death left its deadly traces amongst the poorest people of the land. As a result of the decimation of the labor force, many vineyards were no longer adequately maintained and started to decay. The controversial divorce of Henry VIII led to a definitive break between the Anglican Church and Rome, with the irrevocable result that many of the regular priests and monks left. All the abbeys and monasteries were, which was disastrous for the maintance of the last few English vineyards, though it was not fatal, because despite everything, a number of tiny wine-growing areas survived this disaster. However, it was the end of commercial wine growing in England.

From the early eighteenth to the end of the nineteenth century, cultivation of vines and wine making survived in England through the enthusiasm of a number of fanatics, including Charles Hamilton (Painshill, Cobham, Surrey) and the Marquis of Bute (Castle Coch, Cardiff, Wales). Attempts by individual landowners to establish an estate with kitchen gardens and a vineyard were definitively dashed with the arrival of the Phylloxera louse at the end of the nineteenth century. As in the rest of Europe, wine growing simply did not exist until after the World War II. It was only then that the idea resurfaced of making England and Wales wine-producing countries once again. Both in England and abroad the first pioneers met only ridicule and obstacles. No one believed that the glorious days of the past could be revived in England. One of these pioneers was the Major General Sir Guy Salisbury-Jones, a popular hero who, like many other former soldiers wished to live a quieter life after the war and considered that viticulture was a splendid occupation for a gentleman. Other important pioneers included Lieutenant Colonel Robert & Margaret Gore-Browne (Beaulieu Estate) and Malcolm MacKinnon (Hendred). At the end of the 1960s there were twenty-five serious vineyards in England, and in the 1970s this number grew enormously and the English Vineyards Association, now the UK Vineyards Association, was established. While many enthusiasts were still making a drink like wine at home with grape concentrates (the notorious 'British wines'), the number of commercial open-air vineyards increased enormously. Perhaps the steady improvement in quality was even more important than the increase in the area covered by vines. Some wineries invested enormous amounts in research and in improving the varieties and the wine-growing conditions. The first wineries developed with professional and well-stocked wine cellars with a reception area, tasting room and shop. Guided tours are given in many of these, explaining all there is to know about viticulture and wine.

WINE-GROWING CONDITIONS

At the moment, there are approximately 450 true vineyards in the British Isles, in England, Cornwall, on the Isle of Wight and in Wales. It is always very difficult for a potential wine grower to find the right location because the position of the vineyards (height, soil, sun wind, soil, etc.) is vitally important in such a cold, damp climate. It is only when all these circumstances are ideal that it is possible to produce wine. The location on a hillside, on slopes facing south with a maximum of sunlight and warmth is important for the success of an English/Welsh vineyard. In the second place, the soil must be well drained, as the vines do not like to have their roots in water. It should certainly not be too cold on the hillside. The wind should be able to blow freely but must not blow too hard through the vineyard. The hill should not be too damp, because damp and a lack of sun attract the dreaded fungi. A slightly drier environment will not do any harm, but a damp environment certainly will. Finally, the vineyard should not be too close to the sea, as the winds could blow too much sea

English vineyards at Lamberhurst

salt onto the vines. The more the vineyards comply with these requirements, the greater the chance that it will be possible to produce good wines.

The soil is also extremely important. In the British Isles there is an enormous diversity of different soil. In East Anglia, clay soils are dominant, almost always flecked with flint or coarse gravel. You will find loam and sand on the banks of the Thames, occasionally with some gravel as well. Chalk, sandstone and clay are common in Kent, but you will also find chalky rock (in Canterbury: Elham Valley, Nicholas at Ash), loam and sand (in Tenterden and Biddenden) loam and sand, clay and sandstone (in Lamberhurst). The famous vineyards of Carr Taylor (Sussex) have a soil of sand, and a subsoil of soft slate containing iron and other metals. Other parts of Sussex are dominated by clay and/or sand. In Hampshire you will find more limestone (Winchester), but also loam with gravel (Wellow). A little further southwest, sand and rock are dominant. On the Isle of Wight, some of the northern vineyards have a heavy clay soil (Barton Manor), while the southern vineyards of Adgestone have a hard, chalky soil. The soil in Wiltshire consists mainly of greensand and limestone, while Dorset is mainly limestone. You will find soft loam in the southwesterly vineyards of Cornwall with occasional granite. Devon is well known for its wonderful sandstone and slate, which provides excellent drainage. Wales and the Welsh Borders mainly have soils consisting of sand and clay with occasional red sandstone (Three Choirs).

WINE-GROWING AREAS

In England and Wales there is not yet an official government imposed geographical indication recognized by Europe. Of the approximately 450 British vineyards (2,557 acres) about 95% are located in England, the remainder in Wales. The vineyards are managed by 115 wineries, mainly situated in the southeast, southwest, Wessex and Anglia. More than 90% of English/Welsh wines are white. The northern border for open-air vineyards is at Whitworth Hall, actually not very far from the Scottish border. The most northerly wineries are provided with grapes from colleagues further south. The triangle Whitworth, Wroxeter and Windmill are in the North and the Midlands (Mercia). Most vineyards do not have any commercial aims. It is only in the most sheltered and warmest spots that it is possible to produce serious wines. Wales does not have as many wineries and vineyards, but the quality of some of the wines is truly excellent! The Welsh Borders (between Wroxeter and Tintern) supply the best Welsh wineries with splendid grapes, in particular, Three Choirs in Newent. The local wines made with bacchus, reichensteiner and schönburger are extremely good. East of Wales you will find the wine-growing area of the Thames and the Chiltern Region. Most of the vineyards are between Oxford and Wantage near Reading and Slough, and between Aylesbury and Hemel-Hempstead. Even further east, in East Anglia, there are vineyards between Norwich, Cambridge, Chelmsford and Ipswich. Further

Biddenden Schönburger (Kent)

Hidden Spring (East Sussex)

south, there are the now famous vineyards of Kent and The Weald (East Sussex). This is an extremely productive region and new vineyards are appearing every day. Excellent wines are produced for example in Biddenden, Elham, Tenterden and Lamberhurst.

The vineyards of Surrey and West Sussex are west of Kent and East Sussex. Even further west, there are the vineyards of Hampshire, the Isle of Wight, Wiltshire and Dorset. Finally, the vineyards of Devon and Cornwall are the southernmost British wine-growing area.

The main wine-producing regions are in the southeast (including East Sussex, Hampshire, the Isle of Wight, Kent, Oxfordshire and West Sussex), Anglia (including Essex and Suffolk), Wessex (including Somerset), the southwest (including Devon) and South Mercia (including Gloucestershire).

VARIETIES OF GRAPES

For a good wine, particularly in northern wine-growing areas, the choice of a suitable variety of grape is very important. The varieties which are used in the British Isles are subdivided into three categories:

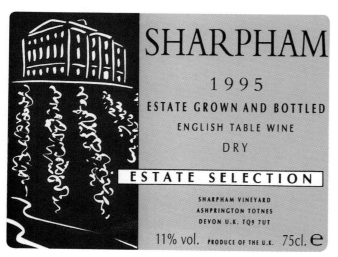

Devon white wine

Good Huxelrebe (Kent)

Müller-Thurgau, popular and recommended in England

Some acceptable wines are also made with the ortega

RECOMMENDED VARIETIES OF GRAPES

These are the varieties of grapes which have been shown to guarantee the best results for the local conditions. These are huxelrebe, madeleine angevine, Müller-Thurgau, reichensteiner, schönburger and seyval blanc.

Of all these varieties, it is above all Müller-Thurgau, seyval blanc and reichensteiner that are particularly popular, although Müller-Thurgau does not seem to thrive so well in England. It is only in good years that the grapes ripen fully. The seyval blanc, a well known hybrid variety from France, which is also popular in Canada and produces reasonable wines even in poor years, is often blended with Müller-Thurgau. Reichensteiner, a cross with Müller-Thurgau, produces many good wines, even in poor years. The wines are fruitier than those of Müller-Thurgau. Schönburger, from Germany, is also a relatively recent product of the laboratory. This grape produces excellent results, particularly in Kent and Somerset. Above all, this variety appears to thrive in England and is resistant to attacks of gray rot and other fungi. The madeleine angevine produces fairly mild wines with tempting aromas of muscat, and is usually blended with harder varieties of green grapes to give the wine a better balance. The huxelrebe does very well in the best spots, but is useless in most places, especially on a chalky soil. However, as long as it is planted in the right location and the yield is deliberately kept low, it can produce excellent wines with sultry aromas of muscat.

PERMITTED VARIETIES OF GRAPES

These are excellent varieties of grapes which could play a major role in English viticulture. The list of more than 35 names includes the following, which are the most popular: bacchus, chardonnay, dornfelder, kerner, kernling, ortega, pinot noir, regner, siegerrebe, triomphe d'Alsace, wrotham pinot and wurzer.

Of this group, bacchus is the most widespread. It is a cross of sylvaner x riesling x Müller-Thurgau and produces better wines than ordinary Müller-Thurgau. The best of the bacchus wines excel because of their aroma of muscat.

The pinot noir hardly ever ripens fully. This grape is used mainly to produce lighter rosé wines.

EXPERIMENTAL VARIETIES OF GRAPES

These are varieties of grapes which can only be 'tested' under the supervision of the local viticulture authorities. Phoenix is a typical example.

ENGLISH AND WELSH QUALITY WINES

Once again, I would like to emphasize the distinction between 'British wines' which are hardly drinkable, made with imported grape juice and the regulated 'English' and 'Welsh wines' from England and Wales. The grapes which are harvested are often too low in sugars and too acid for balanced wines. In the British Isles, as in other vineyards in the north, 'chaptalization' is

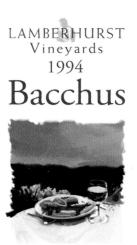

The bacchus produces excellent results

permitted. No less than 3.5-4.5% alcohol can be obtained by adding sugar under the government regulations (EU norms). This is referred to as 'amelioration'. It is also permitssible to add a little bit of concentrated grape juice (known in Germany as 'Sussreserve') to the fermented wine to give it slightly more rondeur and a fuller taste. This practice is sometimes adopted with wines that are naturally too acidic. English and Welsh wines are usually fresh, aromatic white wines between dry, to 'off-dry' (very slightly sweet) or medium-dry. The aroma often contains subtle, floral components. The greatest strength of these wines is their fresh, thirst-quenching character. In addition to still white wines, a few 'pink wines' (rosé), red wines and sparkling wines are also produced. The latter are particularly becoming increasingly popular. This is not surprising in view of the fact that a good champagne, for example, is made with fresh, almost acidic white wines with subtle aromas.

Bordeaux (Vinexpo Wine Fair), but is not recognized as a quality wine in Brussels. In fact, only a tiny percentage of all the English/Welsh production is recognized as 'quality wine'.

A NUMBER OF RECOMMENDED WINERIES

Biddenden Vineyards, Biddenden (Kent)
Lamberhurst Vineyards, Lamberhurst (Kent)
Carr Taylor Vineyards, Westfield, Hastings (Sussex)
Three Choirs Vineyards, Newent (Welsh Borders)
Sharpham Vineyards, Totnes (Devon)
Chiltern Valley, Old Luxters, Hambleden, Henley on Thames (Oxfordshire)

QUALITY CONTROL

The British would not be Brits if they did not rail against the European wine laws to some extent. The English and the Welsh had their own classification and were quite satisfied with this. They even considered their requirements to be stricter than those of the EU. Why should they have to adapt to the European quality classification accepted by all the other states? The fact that this would make it easier for the rest of Europe did not sway the opinionated Brits at all, as most British wines would never reach the mainland of Europe anyway. Since 1991, English and Welsh wines have been admitted to the European category of 'quality wines'. These wines are subdivided into two quality classes: 'English/Welsh table wine' for the simpler wines, and 'English/Welsh vineyards quality wine'. A third category is in the offing: 'English/Welsh country wine'. The main problem for the recognition of English/Welsh wine is that many wines are made with hybrids and despite the sometimes surprisingly good results, these may not apply for a high quality classification. For example, it can happen that an English wine made with seyval blanc wins a whole range of gold medals in

Sharpham, also good red wine

Excellent wines and beautiful labels from Hidden Spring

English table wine

1994
Beenleigh
CABERNET SAUVIGNON/MERLOT
English Table Wine

Estate Grown and Bottled by
BEENLEIGH MANOR VINEYARDS, DEVON, UK.

12.5%vol   PRODUCE OF THE UK   75cl

Beenleigh: excellent vineyards in Sharpham

The middle east

The Mediterranean Sea was enormously important for European (and therefore later intercontinental) viticulture. In the past, all the civilized – and sometimes less civilized – nations used to travel by sea, but the vineyards of most new settlements were also originally in the immediate vicinity of the sea. For example, the Greeks and the Romans were very important for the development of viticulture in those countries, but even long before the Greeks and Romans, the Phoenicians (present-day Lebanon), Egyptians, Persians (Iran) and the people around Mount Ararat practiced organized forms of viticulture. Unfortunately, most Islamic countries have suppressed viticulture to an enormous extent with a fundamentalist interpretation of the holy book of Islam, the Koran.

TURKEY

Like the Greeks, the Turks also like to claim that their country is the cradle of viticulture. All the stylized maps of Turkish viticulture will show you the rickety wooden boat on the much too small peak of a mountain on the border between Turkey, Azerbaijan and Iran. They claim to have found the remnants of Noah's ark on the peak of Mount Ararat, more than 16,404 ft high. He not only had all his animals, but also a handful of vines! Once upon a time, a boat certainly landed on this mountain, but whether it was Noah's has yet to be proved. However, all historians confirm that vines have been cultivated in the area immediately surrounding this mountain (and in the surrounding countries) for a very long time. From 4000–1500 BC the Hittites and their predecessors cultivated grapes in central Anatolia. Alexander the Great later added this country to the great Greek Empire. Up to the time of the invasions of the Arabs and Turks, Anatolia was well ahead of all the European wine producing countries. This came to a definitive end with the fall of Constantinople in 1453. After a long period when grapes were used only for consumption or for industrial purposes (grape sugar, vinegar), Turkish viticulture revived briefly at the end of the nineteenth century. Up to 1914, Turkish wines were regularly found throughout Europe. The outbreak of World War I and the disastrous consequences for the Ottoman Empire, as well as the constant conflicts between Greece and Turkey put and end to the success of the Turkish wine industry. Fundamentalism forced most wine growers to change over to the production of grapes for consumption. However, in 1928 the Turkish government announced that Islam was no longer the official religion, and Turkish viticulture was revitalized. Up to today, this Turkish viticulture consists, on the one hand, of the official growers under a state monopoly (Tekel), and on the other hand, of private wineries.

Kavaklidere is the most dynamic winery in Turkey.

WINE-GROWING REGIONS

Turkish viticulture is mainly concentrated in the middle of the country and on the western and southern coasts. Wine is also produced in the continental part of Turkey, bordering Greece. The huge area of vineyards is still not entirely used for viticulture. Despite the often perfect appearance of some of these vineyards, many grapes are still grown for the daily consumption of grapes (these are actually extremely sweet and delicious). Many vineyards also produce sultanas.

The most productive region lies along the Aegean sea (approximately 41% of the volume), followed by the coastal strip of the Mediterranean Sea (approximately 20%), the southern part of Central Turkey (approximately 11%), the south east (approximately 8.6%), Marmara (approximately 8.5%), the eastern part of Central Turkey (5.3%), and finally the northern part of Central Turkey (4.8%). The better wines certainly come from Central Turkey (Kavaklidere wines, Ankara), but if you look long enough, you will also find some very acceptable and good wines along the coast, including Doluca, Istanbul.

The oldest wine-growing area in Europe could well be in Cappadocia, near Nevsehir in Central Turkey. It is certainly one of the most astonishing and fascinating spectacles in the world. Imagine vineyards with small shrubs just above the ground growing in a lunar landscape. It is the perfect set for a wonderful science fiction film.

There are no fewer than 1,253 different varieties of grapes in Turkey, some of which are only used for consumption or raisins. The most popular varieties of grapes for wine are the oküzgögü, bogazkere, papazkarasi, kalecik karasi, cal karasi, gamay, cinsault and carignan (for red wine and rosé), and emir, sultanine, narince, sémillon and misket (for white wine).

THE BEST-KNOWN WINES

Not all Turkish wines are available in liquer stores, though the best are. The following wines of the state-run Tekel company are worthwhile:

BUZBAG

This red wine made with the oküzgögü and bogazkere comes from Eastern Anatolia (Elazig). It has a dark red color with a light blue reflection when it is young. It is certainly not a very nice wine when it is drunk too young, as it is too rich in tannin. Therefore it is recommended to lay this wine down for at least two or three years, and it will become full and soft, with a pleasant, though by no means tempting aroma.

A Buzbag goes well with most Turkish meat dishes and 'pizze' or 'pitza' (Turkish pizza). Drinking temperature is 14–16 °C (57.2–60.8 °F).

Buzbag

HOSBAG

The Hosbag is made with gamay and is mainly available in Germany. It is a light, thirst-quenching wine, slightly coarse and good with Turkish meals which are not very sophisticated. Drinking temperature is 12–14 °C (53.6–57.2 °F).

TRAKYA

Trakya, the Turkish name for Thrace, the European part of Turkey, produces the grapes for these red and white wines. The white Trakya is made with the sémillon which produces extremely acceptable, light, fruity wines in and around Tekirdag. Serve these wines to quench your thirst with a Turkish meal. Drinking temperature is 8–10 °C (46.4–50 °F).

The red Trakya is made with papazkarasi grapes and comes from the small island of Avsa in Marmara. It is a dark red wine with a good balance and fairly full. Drink it with meat dishes at a temperature of 14–16 °C (57.2–60.8 °F).

The following wines from the Villa Doluca in Istanbul can be recommended:

VILLA DOLUCA

This wine is available as a white, red or rosé wine. The white wine made with the sémillon is fruity and rounded, the fruity and slightly fresh rosé is made with the cinsault and cal karasi, and the pleasant, elegant and rich red wine is also made with cinsault and cal karasi. These three wines are excellent accompanying fish dishes, salads, pizzas and meat dishes. Drinking temperature is 8–10 °C (46.4–50 °F) for white, 10–12 °C (50–53.6 °F) for rosé and 14–16 °C (57.2–60.8 °F) for red.

Villa Doluca, excellent and reasonably priced

ANTIK

These Antik wines are of a slightly better quality than the previous three Villa Doluca wines. The white wine (sémil-

Villa Doluca, red

lon) is full and round with a very individual character. The red wine (cinsault, cal karasi, etc.) is velvety soft, round and warm. Both deserve better fish dishes (Antik white), and meat dishes (Antik red). Drinking temperature is 10–12 °C (50–53.6 °F) for white, 14–16 °C (57.2–60.8 °F) for red.

The best winery in Turkey, Caves Kavaklidere in Akyurt near Ankara, produces a whole series of pleasant to extremely good wines. A selection of the most interesting wines include:

ALTIN KÖPÜK

This is the only sparkling wine from Turkey made in accordance with the méthode traditionnelle. The grapes (emir) come from the region of Cappadocia (Central Turkey). The color is a pale yellow with hints of gold, the aroma is reminiscent of quince, apple, banana and pomegranate. The taste is fresh, fruity and well balanced. It is excellent as an aperitif or to finish off a meal, and very refreshing with sweet desserts. Drinking temperature is 6 °C (42.8 °F).

Excellent festive aperitif

CANKAYA

Emir, narince, sémillon and sultanine grapes form the basis for this wine. These grapes from Thrace, Anatolia and the Aegean coastal strip. The color is light with a hint of green. The wine has a fresh aroma of citrus fruit and a green vegetable undertone. The aftertaste also suddenly includes some floral and herbal nuances. It is a fresh, full and fruity wine with a good backbone.

It is excellent with poultry dishes, but also with white meat and fish. Drinking temperature is 8–10 °C (46.4–50 °F).

Fresh, full and fruity wine

EFSANE

Monocépage (one variety of grape) of the sultanine from the Aegean coastal strip. A very aromatic wine (melon, pear, pineapple, citrus fruit). This fresh, fruity

wine is good as an aperitif, but also with fish, seafood and light starters. Drinking temperature is 8–10 °C (46.4–50 °F).

MUSCAT

This surprising white wine made with misket grapes from the Aegean coastal strip is very aromatic: white fruit, citrus fruit, fresh mint. It has a very fresh and fruity taste, with clear hints of freshly picked muscat grapes.

It is a very pleasant aperitif and excellent accompanying fresh fruit and desserts. Drinking temperature is 8–10 °C (46.4–50 °F).

OZEL BEYAZ SPECIAL

The grapes used for this wine: emir, narince, sémillon and sultanine come from Thrace, Anatolia and the Aegean coastal strip. It has an intense yellow color with aromas of white fruit, pineapple, melon and candied fruit, and an extremely complex taste and aroma. The wine is fresh, fruity and well-balanced. It should certainly be allowed to rest for three or four years after the harvest. An Ozel Beyaz Special is excellent with sea fish. However, it can also accompany spicy meals. Drinking temperature is 8–10 °C (46.4–50 °F).

SELECTION BEYAZ

This top white wine from Kavaklidere is also made with the emir, narince, sémillon and sultanine grapes from Anatolia, Thrace and the Aegean coastal strip. The color is a golden yellow and the aroma is extremely tempting: from green apples to bay leaves, herbs and dried fruit. The taste is fresh, complex and balanced, full and round, and stays for a long time. Dried fruit dominates at the end. This wine can certainly age for seven to ten years.

Very acceptable white wine, good for laying down

Serve a Selection Beyaz with your best sea fish, preferably grilled, but also, for example, with grilled white meat or poultry. Drinking temperature is 10–12 °C (50–53.6 °F).

LAL

This is a surprisingly delicious rosé made with the cal karasi from the Aegean coastal strip. It has a light garnet color with

Lal, an excellent rosé

aromas of freshly picked grapes and red fruit (including strawberries). This rosé has a fresh, round, fruity taste.

Serve this extremely pleasant rosé with your lunch, with exotic starters, salads, pitzas (Turkish pizzas) and grilled fish or fish kebab. Tip: 'köfte' (grilled meat kebab) or soft offal (the 'white kidneys' or testicles, e.g., of sheep) with a light herbal tomato sauce. Drinking temperature is 10–12 °C (50–53.6 °F).

Yakut rubis, a ruby red color and delicious taste

YAKUT RUBIS

Made with the bogazkere, oküzgögü and carignan from Southeast Anatolia and the Aegean coastal strip. It has a ruby red color with purplish tinges, a warm and fruity aroma which is immediately reminiscent of red fruit and a full and round taste with the necessary tannins when it is young.

It is an excellent wine with grilled lamb, kebabs and sheep's cheese. Drinking temperature is 14–16 °C (57.2–60.8 °F).

KALECIK KARASI

This is an excellent red wine made with the eponymous grape from Anatolia. It has a beautiful ruby red color, a wonderful aroma with animal undertones and hints of cocoa, prunes, and green paprika. It is a full, complex, robust wine with a lot of backbone. It can certainly age for six to eight years. This wine needs a good piece of beef. Drinking temperature is 16–17 °C (60.8–62.6 °F).

Complex wine with a lot of backbone

OZEL KIRMIZI SPECIAL

Made with the alicante bouchet and carignan from the Aegean coastal strip. This is a very pleasant wine with tempting aromas of prunes, cherries and figs and a full, fruity, supple and warm taste with a light herbal finale. It combines well with red meat or veal with a sauce and with various sheep's cheeses. Drinking temperature is 16–17 °C (60.8–62.6 °F).

SELECTION KIRMIZI

The best bogazkere and oküzgögü grapes from Southeast Anatolia produce this excellent wine with a beautiful bright red color. It has a surprisingly fruity (strawberries, almonds) and exotic aroma (prunes, figs, nuts, hazelnuts), with an animal undertone. The taste extends these aromas and is full, warm and rounded with the necessary tannins. It is a good wine to lay down for at least seven to ten years.

Serve this wine with game or beef casseroles with herbs. Drinking temperature is 17–18 °C (62.6–64.4 °F).

Kavaklidere also makes extremely acceptable (medium) sweet white wines and portlike wines. Anyone who goes to Turkey and is interested in the best wines can try to buy a few bottles of old Kirmizi wines from Kavaklidere. These top white and red wines are sold with a wax seal instead of the normal capsule.

CYPRUS

Cyprus is a fairly large island off Turkey, near the coast of Syria and The Lebanon. The island has a turbulent historical and cultural past and has been subdivided for the last thirty years into a Greek part (80% of the population) and a Turkish part. With regard to viticulture, Cyprus also has an important and impressive past. For centuries, the sweet Cypriot wines (like sherry and port) were highly valued by London wineries. Cyprus is inextricably linked to one wine: the Commandaria. This full, warm, soft, sweet dessert wine which is like a Madeira is made in twenty villages at the foot of Mount Troodos, north of Limassol. The quality and taste of the wine depend on the ratio between the mavron and xynisteri grapes. Every village and every winery has its own recipe for producing this wine.

Cyprus also makes excellent red wine with the mavron grape (80% of the vines planted). These are dry, full wines, strong and rich in tannin. They are sold under the names Othello and Afamés and like the Kokkinelli rosé, they seem extra heavy because of the lack of fresh acids. Dry wines are produced with the white xynisteri grape (such as Aphrodite and Arsinoë), which also lack the necessary acids, so that they soon become boring. In addition, these wines oxidize fairly quickly. Finally, a light sparkling wine, the Bellapais, is made with the sultana grape.

THE LEBANON

The Lebanon and Syria are descendants of the famous Phoenician civilization. Wine was made in both these countries in classical times. These wines were famous throughout the inhabited world. Lebanese viticulture – which has been long forgotten because of the conflicts between Christians, Jews and Muslims – has made an enormous comeback since the 1980s. Although Gaston Hochar laid the basis for what was later to become the famous Chôteau Musar as far back as 1930, it is thanks to his son Serge that Lebanese viticulture was revitalized.

Surprisingly fruity wine

The Lebanon is a long, fairly narrow strip of land with high mountains (Qurnat es-Swada, 10,114 ft) and poor roads. Because of the unstable political situation, the business of viticulture is rather precarious. Only the Christian population is permitted to produce wines. The vineyards are in the Beka valley, a plateau at a height of 1,640–3,280 ft, situated between two mountain ranges. There is no lack of sunlight and warmth, but there is a lack of water. The climate of this valley is comparable to that of the Rhône valley. The soil is very suitable for viticulture: the white wines come from the chalky soil, the red wines from gravel soil. French grapes are used (cabernet sauvignon, cinsault, mourvèdre, carignan and grenache) for red wines, and indigenous grapes for white wines. There is some confusion about these grapes because Lebanese wine growers are utterly convinced that the obaideh and merwah grapes which they use are simply (the ancestors of) the present-day chardonnay and sémillon.

The Château Musar made by Serge (the wine maker) and Roland Hochard is by far the best wine in Lebanon, but the wines of Kefraya and Chôteau Ksara are also worthwhile.

The white wines of Château Musar have a greater finesse than those of Kefraya and Ksara. However, all three wines have a full taste and structure. Nevertheless,

Good wine from Château Ksara

they are all well balanced because of their surprisingly fine and elegant acids. These wines are often slightly too heavy to serve as an aperitif, except perhaps for the fairly commercial, though delicious blanc de blancs from Ksara. Drink the other wines with shellfish or sea fish at a temperature of 10–12 °C (50–53.6 °F).

The better rosé wines from the Lebanon are full, fruity, well balanced and very juicy. They are pleasant wines which are delicious all the year round, for example with a good sea fish or poultry dishes with herbs. Drinking temperature is 10–12 °C (50–53.6 °F).

Château Musar blanc

The simple red wines such as Clos St. Alphonse or the Réserve du Couvent from Ksara are surprisingly fruity (raspberries, blackcurrants) and fresh, with a characteristic peppery taste. These wines combine very well with red meat, preferably grilled, Mediterranean casseroles and even small game. Drinking temperature is 14–16 °C (57.2–60.8 °F).

The top Lebanese wines are extremely complex, full, round and with a strong structure and powerful tannins. Characteristic aromas: cedar wood, ripe fruit (raspberries, strawberries, blackcurrants), herbs and spices, (pepper). Despite their strength, these wines remain very fresh, and contain quite a lot of alcohol (13–14%!), which means they

Excellent wines from the top vineyard, Musar

Ksara vin gris

Delicious white, red and rosé wines from the
Lebanon

are still well balanced. Wines such as the Château
Musar and to a lesser extent Château Ksara are suitable
for laying down for quite a long time.

Serve these strong wines, which are similar to
the better Rhône wines with firm, complex red
meat or game. Because of their strength, these top
Lebanese wines are good with spicy food, but it
would be a pity to drink them with dishes that are
too hot or spicy. Drinking temperature is 16–17 °C
(60.8–62.6 °F).

ISRAEL

According to orthodox Jews, the world has
only existed for about 5,000 years. The earth
did not exist before the Bible, the Book of the
Dead, and therefore there were no vineyards
either. They will tell you that it is obvious
that all the words which relate to 'wine'
(from 'vin' and 'vinho' to the Latin 'vinum'
and the Greek 'oinos') are related to the
Hebrew word 'yayin', which means wine.
Whether or not this is true, it is a fact that
viticulture was already practiced in Anatolia
(Turkey, Armenia, Kazakhstan, Uzbekistan,
Tajikistan, Persia, Mesopotamia, Egypt and
… Palestine 4,000 to 5,000 years ago. Between 2000 and 1500 BC viticulture was well-
advanced in Palestine. The Egyptian and
Roman rulers almost succeeded in eradica-
ting viticulture there but it was the Saracens
who finally managed to do this. Under Mus-
lim rule vineyards were no longer officially

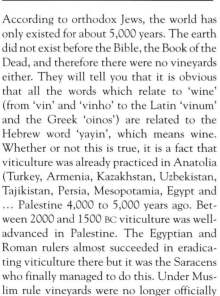

Lebanese
red wines can
mature well.

allowed. Nevertheless, the crusaders later found beautifully maintained vineyards near Bethlehem, Naza-
reth and Mount Carmel. However, up to the end of the
nineteenth century, viticulture in Israel was a thing of
the distant past. In 1870, the first agricultural college
was founded in Palestine. The vineyard of the local
monasteries (including those of the German Templars)
were given a lot of attention once again. With the arrival of the first Zionists in Israel in 1882, the new vineyards were planted with vines that had been taken from
Bordeaux and the southwest of France. Baron Edmond
de Rothschild financed this. With his help, quality
vineyards were established in Rishon Le Zion, south of
Tel Aviv and Zichron Ya'acov, south of Haifa. Modern
viticulture was born in Israel.

For many years viticulture in Israel was based on the
French example. The Société Coopérative Vigneronne
des Grandes Caves (Carmel), which was still linked to
the Rothschild family, represented more than three
quarters of Israeli viticulture. However, since the
1980s more and more new wine makers have adopted
'new world' techniques, (especially from California and
South Africa) to make their wine fresher, fuller and
more delicious. Computer technology has also been
introduced in Israel. Many Israeli wines are still kosher.
This does not have any influence on the technology
that is used, but does imply that from the moment that
the grapes enter the wine cellars, everything – from the
grape to the fermentation tanks and bottling lines –
may only be touched by practicing Jews. Therefore Israeli kosher wines are no better or worse than any other
wines, they are only more 'Jewish'. However, not all
Israeli wines are kosher.

75 cl.   13,5%   vol.   PRODUCE OF LEBANON

1990

MARQUE   DÉPOSÉE

Château Musar

★

GASTON HOCHAR
PROPRIÉTAIRE VITICULTEUR
IMPORTED BY: CHATEAU MUSAR (UK) LTD - HAMPTON, UK

MIS EN BOUTEILLES AU CHATEAU   L. 3. 230   GHAZIR - LIBAN

Châteaux Musar, the best Lebanese red wine
and one of the best red wines from
Mediterranean regions

WINE-GROWING REGIONS

Israel has five large wine-growing regions:
– Galilee: a mountainous region, in which the Golan Heights (volcanic soil, very suitable for viticulture) tempers the heat of the sun. The wine-growing regions of High and Lower Galilee and the area around Mount Taborg all lie in Galilee;
– Samson: a low-lying, hilly region with the southern coastal strip and the low-lying area of Judea;
– Shomron: the area around Mount Carmel and the northern coastal strip. The wine-growing region, which used to be called Zikhron-Ya'acov, is the largest and still the most important region in the country (white, red and rosé wines);
– The hills of Judea: around Jerusalem and Hebron (red and white wines for local consumption);
– The Negev mountains: a fairly recent wine-growing area near Ramat Arad, in the south of the country (white and red wines for local consumption)

Israeli wine growers still use many French varieties of grapes. The most important are: cabernet sauvignon, merlot, pinot noir, carignan, grenache, alicante bouchet for red wines; sauvignon, sémillon, chardonnay, clairette and muscat d'Alexandrie for white wines.

THE WINES

Carmel Mizrachi of the Société Coopérative Vigneronne des Grandes Caves is still the absolute market leader in the domestic and export market. Outside Israel, the name Rothschild is rarely seen on the bottles. In Israel itself, the best wines are found under the name Rothschild and Rothschild Private Collection. When they are exported, the wines are often called Carmel Selected. All Carmel wines are kosher. In the past, the bottles often had extremely old-fashioned labels. Nowadays, the labels reflect the fresh new wind of change which is blowing in Galilee and Samson, etc. Carmel makes excellent white, red and rosé wines. They are characterized by a certain modernity, fresh acidity, a lot of fruit and a pure, supple and amenable taste. For example, the sauvignon blanc is extremely suitable as an aperitif, but for non-Jews, it is also excellent with shellfish. Drinking temperature is 8–10 °C (46.4–50 °F).

Sémillon, Chardonnay, and Chenin blanc require more complex dishes, such as river fish (carp) or sea fish (preferably grilled or in a rich sauce). Drinking temperature is 10–12 °C (50–53.6 °F).

The Cabernet Sauvignon is by far the best of all the red wines. Admittedly it is fairly commercial, but it is extremely fruity and intensely aromatic. For example, it is excellent with grilled lamb chops. Drinking temperature is 16 °C (60.8 °F).

Israeli kosher Sauvignon blanc

Dry Sauvignon from Galilee

Carmel is also known all over the world for its traditional ceremonial wines, Muscat (white), and Sacramental (red). They are both very sweet and are rarely used outside Jewish circles.

OTHER RECOMMENDED WINES
The Golan Heights Winery in Ramat Ha'Golan has vineyards at a height of 1,312–3,937 ft. The soil of the vineyards consists of volcanic basalt forming an excellent layer of drainage and producing beautiful wines. Very good wines are produced with the names Yarden, Golan and Gamla. The Chardonnay and Sauvignon blanc are particularly good. They go perfectly with grilled fish and poultry. Drinking temperature is 8–12 °C (46.4–53.6 °F). The Cabernet Sauvignon is one of the really good red wines, fairly classical and yet modern, with exuberant aromas of plums and blackcurrants, quite a lot of wood (vanilla), and a hint of pepper in the aftertaste. They are ideal accompanying roast beef, steaks and medium hard cheeses. Drinking temperature is 16 °C (60.8 °F).

Domaine de Latroun, which has been in the hands of the Trappists since 1890, makes some interesting wines with a French character between Jerusalem and Tel Aviv. The best is undoubtedly the rustic, aromatic Pinot Noir with animal undertones, which is excellent with roast poultry or duck. Drinking temperature is 14–16 °C (57.2–60.8 °F).

The Margalit Winery produces excellent Cabernet Sauvignon from Galilee: soft with aromas of oak (vanilla) and butter, a lot of fruit and a full round taste. It is delicious with roast lamb or beef, but also surprisingly good with hard goat's cheese. Drinking temperature is 16–17 °C (60.8–62.6 °F).

Since 1994, the Soreq Winery has made very interesting wines in Tal Sachar Mochav (Samson). The wines of Soreq are not kosher.

Cabernet Sauvignon from Galilee

Traditionele Muscat

Sweet red Sacramental for ritual feasts

There are excellent, full, ripe, but also fresh Chardonnays with tempting aromas of peaches and nuts excellent accompaniment for any grilled sea fish. Since this wine is not kosher, you can drink it with a succulent lobster. Drinking temperature is 10–12 °C (50–53.6 °F).

Soreq also makes a fairly robust, rustic Cabernet Sauvignon with a lot of fruit and hints of wood. It is delicious with grilled beef and medium hard (goat's) cheese. Drinking temperature is 16 °C (60.8 °F).

The Baron Winery makes very elegant, correct and creamy wines using the méthode traditionnelle wines with soft, fruity aromas and a pure, elegant taste. They are excellent as an aperitif or on festive occasions. Drinking temperature is 8 °C (46.4 °F).

MALTA

Malta is a medium-sized island in the Mediterranean Sea, below Sicily. A few very moderate green wines are produced here and an attempt has been made to produce reasonable muscat wines.

Sun-ripened grapes

Africa

When you think of Africa, you'll probably think first of South Africa, and this is quite understandable because most quality wines are produced there. However, wine is also made in other African countries including Zimbabwe and Egypt, and above all in the North African countries of Tunisia, Algeria and Morocco. Viticulture in North Africa is only possible in regions just behind the coast or, as in Egypt, along the large rivers. The Mediterranean Sea is able to temper the heat and, above all, the dry conditions, to some extent. However, you cannot expect any wonderful wines from Egypt, Tunisia, Algeria or Morocco: in recent years North African viticulture has declined significantly. In these three large wine-producing countries splendid, full round wines with a rustic but very pleasantly warm character were produced for years. However, for economic reasons and because of a lack of interest in the product (partly resulting from the influence of Islamic fundamentalism), the wines produced nowadays in large quantities are flat and lacking in character. The collapse of the Russian market has also taken its toll in Algeria. The governments of all three countries are trying to restore the finesse of the wines, but it simply isn't possible to produce a 'cool Bordeaux' type of wine under heavy, hot Côtes du Rhône conditions! With a better understanding of viticulture and a love of the product, good wines could be produced in all three countries as long as the terroir is respected.

EGYPT

The Egyptians were already producing wine from vineyards on the banks of the Nile about 5,000 years ago. Owning a vineyard was a matter of great prestige, but it was above all the slaves who drank the enormous quantities of wine. In those days it was not possible to keep wine long and it had to be drunk quickly. The rare better nectar was reserved for the Pharaohs and high priests. Wine was also very popular as a ritual offering made to the gods, and the Pharaohs would take full jugs of wine and luxurious goblets with them into the afterlife. In daily life, the elite preferred to drink beer, which was much more refreshing and thirst-quenching in those days than the heavy and extremely sweet wines. A great deal of the wine was made in line with the thought than anyone who looked after their slaves well, and gave them good wine, would have slaves who worked willingly. The Greeks and Romans also discovered these wines. As a result there was a great revival in Egyptian viticulture. Unfortunately, strict Islamic laws abruptly put an end to this. For a long time Egyptian viticulture only existed on the ancient drawings and in

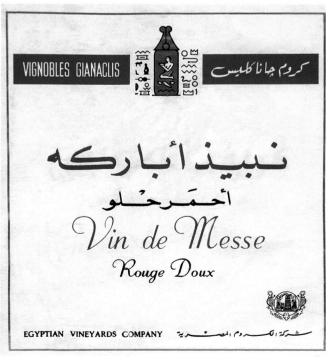

There are also sweet wines for the Mass in Egypt.

the texts of Greek and Roman writers. At the beginning of the twentieth century an attempt was made by, amongst others, Nestor Gianaclis to revive Egyptian viticulture on the chalky banks of the Nile. Modern Egyptian wines are a cross between the wines of the Old and New World: the techniques used are similar to those used in California, but the quality of the wines still leaves a great deal to be desired.

TUNISIA

About 3,000 years ago, the Phoenicians introduced wine growing to Tunisia. For the local population this was the start of 3000 years of foreign occupation. The Phoenicians (Utica, Carthage) were followed by the Romans. They also engaged in local viticulture. With the introduction of Islam, North African viticulture came under heavy pressure. It was only in 1881 that the French profited from the weakness of the Turkish Empire and occupied Tunisia in their turn. In 1920, legions of French farmers went to Tunisia where they helped to revive viticulture together with the local population. The French used the wines, particularly the robust, full, red wines, to help their own weak wines. When Tunisia gained independence in March 1956, this was a sign to improve the quality of Tunisian wines. Unfortunately, things seem to have gone wrong in the last few years. The once famous, dry Muscat wines and sultry red wines have lost a great deal of their character. The storage and transport of the wines also leave a great deal to be desired. Some wines are best drunk in situ, because once they travel outside their own area of production, they are not always treated very well. This means that they sometimes arrive in Europe very tired.

TUNISIAN WINES

The wine-growing areas in Tunisia are Cap Bon (24,710 acres), subdivided into the regions of Khanguet, south of Tunis, Grombalia-Takelsa on the north coast, and Kelibia, also on the coast; Tunis (4,942 acres) with Sidi Thabet-Mornag, and Tébourba; Bizerte (4,942 acres) and Beja-Jendouba (2,471 acres). Some acceptable red and rosé wines under the name Sidi Salem, which combine well with the local cuisine, are produced in Khanguet in the Cap Bon region (alluvial sediments and gravel). The red Vieille Cave is a soft, rich and supple wine, which deserves attention. Drinking temperature is 16 °C (60.8 °F). The Grombalia-Takelsa region, also in Cap Bon, produces some rather pleasant white, rosé and red wines. Most of the good red and rosé wines come from the region around Tunis.

MUSCAT SEC DE KELIBIA

The famous Muscat wines made with the muscat d'Alexandrie come from Kelibia. The old-fashioned Muscat sec de Kelibia was sultry and extremely aromatic and

Muscat sec de Kelibia

this explosion of fruit was followed by an excellent, tempting taste and a long, pure aftertaste. The modern Muscat sec de Kelibia is less convincing. Drinking temperature is 10–12 °C (50–53.6 °F).

MUSCAT

Full, powerful, and aromatic sweet Muscat wines with a fairly high alcohol percentage also come from Kelibia, as well as from Rads and Thibar. Drinking temperature is 6–8 °C (42.8–46.4 °F).

TEBOURBA

The red and rosé wines from Tebourba are extremely interesting. The rosé is made with noble grapes such as the grenache, the syrah and the mouvèrdre. They are fresh, but powerful and reasonably complex, an excellent wine to accompany the local couscous, fish tagines or grilled fish or meat. Drinking temperature is 10–12 °C (50–53.6 °F).

The red wine is full, generous and round and can also accompany couscous, or the traditional 'méchoui' (a whole lamb roasted on the spit). Drinking temperature is 16 °C (60.8 °F).

COTEAUX DE TEBOURBA

Excellent rosé wines (saignée method) made with the grenache and cinsault, etc. These are supple, elegant and juicy wines which are quite fresh. They are delicious with grilled fish, or fish tagines. Drinking temperature is 10–12 °C (50–53.6 °F).

KSAR DJERBA

These are excellent rosé wines made with the syrah, cabernet sauvignon and mourvèdre grapes. They are fresh, powerful, full and well balanced. Excellent with couscous, fish tagines, grilled fish, and even grilled lamb. Drinking temperature is 10–12 °C (50–53.6 °F).

KOUDIAT

One of the few constant factors in Tunisian viticulture. An excellent red wine with a profound taste. This wine asks for elegant meat dishes (beef). Drinking temperature is 16 °C (60.8 °F).

Koudiat, always reliable

The rosé is also excellent and reliable. It is reasonably full, fresh, fruity and round and goes well with grilled fish or fish baked in the oven, as well as fish tagines, or vegetable dishes. Drinking temperature is 10–12 °C (50–53.6 °F).

Magon,
former glory

MAGON

This red wine, made with the cinsault and alicante grapes, named after a writer from ancient Carthage, was once a delicious round wine, full of warmth and with a sultry character. Nowadays this wine has also become more supple. It is still an elegant, velvety soft wine, which goes well with meat dishes that are not too heavy. Drinking temperature is 16 °C (60.8 °F).

COTEAUX DE MORNAG

Fruity, fresh and balanced red wine with a rich, supple taste. Excellent with meat dishes or with fowl. Drinking temperature is 14–16 °C (57.2–60.8 °F).

MORNAG

Châteaux Mornag grand cru rosé is a fresh, sunny, full wine made with the cinsault, mourvèdre and carignan grapes, amongst others. It is ideal with grilled fish or with fish tagines. Drinking temperature is 10–12 °C (50–53.6 °F).

Châteaux Mornag grand cru rouge was once a full, round wine with a warm character. However, the passion and fire have disappeared from this grand cru, which has become more supple as a result of the addition of merlot grapes. Nevertheless, the mourvãdre and grenache still give this wine enough backbone to be combined with grilled or roast beef. Drinking temperature is 16 °C (60.8 °F).

Sidi Saad, an excellent red wine in a rather kitsch amphora deserves a special mention. These are specially selected cuvées of the grand cru Mornag. This wine ages well and should be at least three years old if you really want to enjoy it. Drinking temperature is 17 °C (62.6 °F).

Château Mornag
grand cru rouge

COTEAUX DE CARTHAGE

This is a fresh, supple, elegant, slightly oily rosé made with the cinsault and mourvèdre grapes, amongst others. It is good with fish dishes or juicy lamb. Drinking temperature is 10–12 °C (50–53.6 °F).

The red Coteaux de Carthage are supple, but full and round, with an oily structure. They are excellent with grilled or roast lamb. Drinking temperature is 16 °C (60.8 °F).

Rode Coteaux
de Carthage

ALGERIA

Every country has its own way of expressing its own chauvinism. In Algeria, the umbrella wine-growing organizations are pleased to tell you how the Arabs propagated vines in Spain and spread viticulture throughout Europe. We now know better. Wine growing was probably introduced in Algeria by the Medes and Persians approximately 4,000 years ago. One of the best-known Algerian wine-growing areas is still know by the name of the Medeans, viz., Medea. The Persians and Medians were followed consecutively by the Phoenicians, Greeks and Romans, who expanded viticulture in Algeria. In 1200, North Africa was overrun by Arab invasions. Up to 1830 and the arrival of the first French colonists the vineyards were used mainly for grapes for consumption. In 1938, the total wine-growing area of Algeria was no less than 988,400 acres, enough to produce 581,240,000 gallons of wine! The French used the robust, warm wines to strengthen their own southern everyday wines. Following the independence of Algeria in 1962, viticulture soon declined. The Algerians had to make money quickly and they produced even more in enormous quantities, exporting to the Soviet Union amongst other places, where the wines were given a striking Russian label. Since the collapse of the Russian market, Algeria has been forced to adapt the quality of its products to the strict requirements of western countries. If Algeria is to break through definitively onto the world market, it will have to opt clearly for quality and a lack of ambiguity. The current authorities in the country appear to be promoting some flexibility in the policy on viticulture. For example, up to 2005, no less than 9.9 million acres of arable land (cereals) will be used for olive trees, fruit and vineyards. It is expected that an extra 1,853,250 acres of vineyards will be added in the space of four years, which would be a disaster for the producers of table wine in southern France, Spain and Italy who are already beset by many difficulties.

Just as the traditional European wine-growing areas have decided to reduce their area to concentrate on quality, rather than on volume, the Algerian authorities have opted for large-scale expansion.

ALGERIAN WINES

The seven large wine-growing areas of Algeria lie behind the broad coastal strip in the north of the country. Three of these areas are in the district of Algiers, the other four in that of Oran. The better wines have the status 'Vin d'Appellation d'Origine Garantie' (AOG). The district of Algiers comprises, from east to west, the AOG Aïn Bessem-Bouira, the Coteaux du Zaccar and Médéa; the district of Oran comprises Dahra, Coteaux de Mascara, Monts du Tessala, and Coteaux de Tlemcen.

It is easy to be brief about white Algerian wines: most are undrinkable. Because the heat and the lack of temperature controls during the transport of the grapes, the wines have already oxidized before they are bottled. The rosé wines are much better, but the best wines are unquestionably the reds.

AïN BESSEM-BOUIRA

These wines are not very well known, but are very acceptable red and rosé wines made with the carignan, cinsault and grenache noir (min. 60% in total), possibly supplemented with e.g., cabernet sauvignon and pinot noir. Minimum alcohol content: 11.5%.

COTEAUX DU ZACCAR

Slightly better wines than the previous wines, meaty and full, made with the cinsault, carignan, grenache, pinot noir and syrah. Minimum alcohol content: 12%.

MÉDÉA

Splendid wines from vineyards at higher altitudes (up to more than 3937 ft) on the plateau of Nador. These full-bodied, warm, robust wines are made with a blend of carignan, cinsault and morastel, etc. Minimum alcohol content: 12%.

Medea

DAHRA

In general, an excellent, full-bodied, warm wine made with the carignan, cinsault, pinot noir, syrah, grenache, and morastel. Mini-

mum alcohol content: 12.5%. This is a good wine to lay down.

COTEAUX DE MASCARA

According to connoisseurs, this is the best wine from Algeria. It is full, warm, robust, and reflects its terroir of sand and sandstone, and the sunny climate. It is made with cinsault, carignan, grenache, mourvèdre, syrah, cabernet sauvignon, and morastel. Minimum alcohol content 12.5%. This is a good wine to lay down.

MONTS DU TESSALA

These wines are made with the same varieties of grapes as the Coteaux de Mascara, but they have a slightly less full structure and lack the rondeur of the Coteaux de Mascara. Minimum alcohol content: 12%. This is a good wine to lay down.

COTEAUX DE TLEMCEN

These wines, also produced southwest of Oran, are made with the same varieties of grapes as the Coteaux de Mascara and the Monts du Tessala. However, they are fuller than the Tessala, though not as round and broad in taste as the Mascara. Minimum alcohol content: 12.5%.

Cuvée du Président

SERVING TIPS

All Algerian red and rosé wines are more or less rounded, full and warm, but always with fresh fruity acidity. They do possess the necessary tannin, though often not the more sophisticated kinds. All rosé wines combine very well with fried or grilled fish, and those from Oran are also good with fish couscous, fish tagines and shellfish, though they are also very good with merguez (spicy sausages), chicken tagines, lamb kebabs (brochettes) or even roast lamb or grilled lamb chops. Drinking temperature is 10–12 °C (50–53.6 °F). The red wines combine with almost every sort of meat, particularly casseroles, or with chicken, beef or lamb couscous or with any sort of meat or poultry tagine. Drinking temperature is 14–16 °C (57.2–60.8 °F).

CUVÉE DU PRÉSIDENT

Although this is not an AOG, this wine is probably one of the best of Algeria. It is well-balanced, usually approximately 13% alcohol, full but elegant, and with a slightly more classical character than the other wines which tend to be more rustic.

Coteaux de Mascara

MOROCCO

Morocco is a blessed country with two coasts: one on the Mediterranean Sea and one on the Atlantic Ocean. Here too, the Phoenicians discovered that it was particularly suitable for wine growing at a very early stage. The Phoenicians were followed by the Romans after Carthage was defeated. Beautiful wines were produced in Morocco for centuries. This came to an abrupt end when the Arabs conquered the country. For more than a thousand years the vineyards served only to supply dessert grapes. When Morocco was occupied by the French at the beginning of the twentieth century, the situation changed and wine making was revived.

MOROCCAN WINE GROWING

Morocco has three different climates: a Mediterranean climate in the east, an oceanic climate in the west and a semi-continental climate in the interior of the country. Together with the different types of soil (loess in the east, limestone in Meknes, and sand on the west coast), these differences explain the variation in the methods in production and types of wine. The most important wine-growing area is that of Meknes-Fes, in the hinterland of Rabat and Casablanca, at the foot of the Middle Atlas. This area produces almost half of Moroccan wines. In addition, wines are produced on the Atlantic coast, on the Mediterranean coast, and in Gharb, Doukkala and Moulouya. Moroccan wines have a fairly rustic character, a reasonable alcohol content (12–12.8%) and moderate level of acidity. The wines are pleasant in an uncomplicated way, rather than sophisticated. The rare, dry white wines are mainly made with the clairette, ugni blanc and maccabeo; the most modern wine (Beni M'tir) with the chardonnay, chenin blanc, sauvignon and vermentino. The muscat is used for sweet white wines, the grenache and cinsault for rosé wines, and the grenache, cinsault, carignan, syrah, mourvãdre for red wines. The inferior alicante bouchet is used less and less, while on the other hand, the tempranillo, cabernet sauvignon, cabernet franc and merlot are used more and more. The Moroccan wineries, particularly the progressive Celliers de Meknes, are a guarantee of good wines. Of the three North African wine producing countries, Morocco has been the most consistent in recent decades.

Morocco produces many moderate to reasonable everyday wines for local consumption. There are still many French, Spanish and Portuguese people living in Morocco. The rest of the market consists of the many tourists who visit the country every year. Only the better wines are described below.

CAP BLANC, BLANC DE BLANCS

This is a very dry white wine made with the clairette and the ugni blanc. It is slightly aromatic and has a very fresh taste with fruity undertones. It is delicious as an aperitif, outside in the sun, but also to accompany shellfish or grilled sea fish. Drinking temperature is 8–10 °C (46.4–50 °F).

KSAR VIN BLANC

A very aromatic dry white wine with aromas of dried flowers, citrus fruit, dried fruit (figs) and herbs and spices (fresh mint, cinnamon, nutmeg). The taste is velvety soft. It is an excellent wine from a warm country which combines well, for example with sweetbreads of veal in olive sauce, tongue, salmon, bass or gray mullet. Tip: 'pastilla' (a thin, crisply fried puff pastry package, stuffed with pigeon breast, with almonds and walnuts). Drinking temperature is 10–12 °C (50–53.6 °F).

GUERROUANE GRIS

This is the lighter of the two Guerrouane rosé wines, with a tendency towards a salmon color. Fruity aro-

Guerrouane Gris

mas (mainly strawberries with a hint of fresh almonds), subtle vegetable nuances (fennel, star anise) and a light peppery undertone. It is a wine with two faces, tempting and elegant at first, with a robust and powerful aftertaste. It is excellent with chicken dishes, for example with capon with almonds or with tomatoes and onions. It is also fantastic with dishes of sea fish (sea bass or swordfish). Drinking temperature is 10–12 °C (50–53.6 °F).

GUERROUANE ROSÉ

This wine is significantly darker in color than the last rosé: the color tends towards a light cherry red but remains quite clear. The aroma is reminiscent of fresh fruit (strawberries, melon, citrus fruit) with hints of the riper aromas of coffee and roasted almonds. The wine is juicy, round, civilized, friendly and has a slightly soft aftertaste. It is delicious with grilled sea fish. Tip: 'hellema', fish with olives, garlic and tomato. Drinking temperature is 10–12 °C (50–53.6 °F).

Guerrouane rouge, Domaine Menara

Guerrouane rouge Toulal

GUERROUANE ROUGE

This wine has a ruby red color and is fresh, aromatic and fruity (strawberries, raspberries, a hint of fresh figs and some riper fruit), with a full and soft taste, a sultry structure, generous and juicy. It is a great charmer which goes very well with good meat such as ostrich (a specialty of the Tuareg), camel meat (fillet steaks) or beef. Drinking temperature is 16 °C (60.8 °F).

BENI M'TIR

These red wines, of good to very good quality, can be identified by the aromas of ripe varieties of fruit (figs, blackberries, peaches, candied citrus fruit) and the spicy undertones of peppermint, pepper and cinnamon. Almonds can also be recognized in the aftertaste. Some of the wines, particularly younger wines, also have an aroma of freshly sliced paprika. In general, these Beni M'tir wines are tempting wines with a great deal of class, generous, intense and complex. Clearly a wine for complicated dishes, for example, fillet of beef with prunes. Drinking temperature is 16–17 °C (60.8–62.6 °F).

Beni M'Tir

GRIS DE BOULAOUANE

This Gris de Boulaouane appears in many guises. Some of the wines are bottled in France and are not always equally reliable. Because the wine is well known in France, unfortunately a great deal of inferior Boulaouane is sold. This is coarse and slightly oxidized. Gris de Boulaouane wines are difficult to find, but it is best to opt for the original bottling. This fresh, light and aromatic wine is excellent with couscous and tagines made with poultry and grilled sea fish. Drinking

Boulaouane gris & rouge

temperature is 10–12 °C (50–53.6 °F). In fact, there is also a red Boulaouane, which is full--bodied, warm and round, and is excellent with chicken and meat couscous. Drinking temperature is 16 °C (60.8 °F).

RABBI JACOB

There is nowhere in the world where Jews and Muslims live together as peacefully as in Morocco. The Rabbi Jacob does not have a geographical indication, but is it a full-bodied, delicious and reliable red wine which is made so that it is kosher. Drinking temperature is 16 °C (60.8 °F).

SOUTH AFRICA

Throughout the last decade, South Africa has experienced extreme political, social and ethnic changes. In South Africa of now, where the economy is trying wearily to recover, wine making should be able to give this country an especially strong economic boost. It seems that South African wines are set to conquer Europe and the rest of the world, particularly the UK and The Netherlands. The wine growers in South Africa proudly maintain that their country is the oldest of the "new world wine countries". This is not true though since vines were not introduced into South Africa until 1655, while the first vineyards were planted in Mexico and Japan around 1530, followed by Argentina and Peru in 1560. It certainly is true though that South Africa planted vineyards before California (1697) and New Zealand (1813). When Jan van Riebeek was sent to South Africa by the Dutch United East Indian Company, he could have had no idea how wonderful the local wines would later become. His brief was to arrange rations and drink for the voyaging ships of the UEIC. Much has changed since the establishment of Cape Town in 1655 and the first official harvest of Cape wines in 1659. The first person to take an important step towards the expansion and improvement of the Cape wine industry, was the successor to Jan van Riebeek: Simon van der Stel. Unlike his predecessor, he had an understanding of wine production, and knew how to find the best locations for the plantations. The next step was the arrival of the French who compensated for the Dutch lack of wine knowledge. The Huguenots were penniless being religious refugees and so they made the wine and the Dutch dealt with the sales. However, in the 18th century a breakthrough into the European market was yet to be made. A new market was created for South African wines, when the country came under British rule. After the ending of hostilities between the French republics and the rest of Europe, French wines were no longer taboo, and the door was once again

Rabbi Jacob, kosher wine from Morocco

firmly shut to South African wines. These were very difficult times for the South African wine production. An effort was made in 1918 to introduce some order and stimulus into the wine industry with the founding of the South African "Cooperative Winegrowers Association" (CWA). It was the start of a second childhood for the South African wine industry. After the end of apartheid, together with the associated economic isolation, the South African wine growers started an intensive program of planting, soil cultivation, irrigation and the developing of pruning methods. The emphasis has now moved onto the vineyard, while previously many wines were "made" in the cellars, a very positive development. There is also a lot of effort put into the improvement and use of grape strains and clones. Other plus points aiding the South African wine industry include new environmentally conscious and humanitarian policies, together with subsidies from the government and from the Wine Industry Trust Funds which enables prospective wine growers to purchase wine growing land. The recruitment of a new army of wine growers is essential for the future of the South African wine industry, and without financial assistance many small ethnic companies would never have had a chance. The authorities have also raised the standards for healthcare, education and housing for the workers on the existing (large) wine estates. Finally, under an initiative from the CWA, a new environmentally friendly system has been introduced, the IPW (Integrated Product of Wine), where a variety of wine growing aspects are addressed such as recycling of packaging material and water purification. This is a part of Vision 2020, an ambitious plan intending to turn South Africa into one of the world's foremost wine producing countries.

Old South African wine from the period of apartheid

WINE GROWING CONDITIONS

South Africa is located in the Southern Hemisphere, exactly in the narrow zone most favorable for growing wine. It may sound strange, but the South African climate can best be described as similar to that of the Mediterranean. The best wine growing areas are found at the foot of the mountains in the valleys, where the grapes get plenty of sun. In the winter, the temperature drops to a maximum of 32–50 ° F, while cool sea breezes supply the vineyards with the required moisture. The heaviest rainfall is between May and August. The soil varies from granite at the foot of the mountains, to sand stone at Table Mountain, and soft slate at Mal-

TWO OCEANS

1
9
9
7

W E S T E R N   C A P E

CAPE
SAUVIGNON BLANC

PRODUCT OF SOUTH AFRICA

12%vol   DROSTDY WINES LTD   DE OUDE DROSTDY, TULBAGH   0,75l

Exceptional position between two oceans

mesbury, with slate and loam at the rivers. However, considerable differences can be seen from vineyard to vineyard, making the "estate wines" (wine from small domains) particularly interesting. The wine production is largely in the hands of cooperative wineries (85% of production) with the CWA being the most important. As of 2001, there were eighty-two estate wineries, seventy cooperatives and seventy-three independents, together with a number of wholesalers. The estate wineries produce wines from their own grapes, all of the cooperatives make wine using grapes from their own members. The wholesalers also produce wine using their own grapes, however they also buy in grapes and wines to sell under their own label.

WINE GROWING AREAS

Since 1973, South Africa has been using a clear identification system for the origin of their wines, based in part on geographical and climatic zones. South Africa has five large wine regions, sub-divided into fourteen districts, accounting for a total of approx. 250,000 acres of vineyards. The districts may be divided further into wards consisting of a number of different domains, usually within the confines of one district. Franschoek is actually a ward of the Paarl district in the Coastal Region. Some wards do not make up part of a specific district, but fall directly under a wine region such as the Durbanville ward and Coastal

The seal on this bottle guarantees that this wine is made from cabernet sauvignon in the Paarl district

Region. Finally there are the independent wards such as Oranjerivier (Orange River) and districts like Piketberg, Overberg (which include the celebrated wards of Walker Bay and Elgin) and Douglas.

The quality wines from the recognized wine regions carry a special seal on the bottle which guarantees the authenticity, the origin and the harvesting year of the grapes used.

Almost all of the wine regions in South Africa are located in the south west, between Capetown and the coast, however wine is also produced in the north and eastern parts of South Africa: Olifants River, Orange River and Klein Karoo. The following are the most well known wine producing regions.

ORANGE RIVER

A fairly unknown, independent ward on the Namibian border. Acceptable wines for a reasonable price. Little export.

OLIFANTS RIVER

The Olifants River wine region is just to the south of Orange River and almost parallel to the coast. The climate between Koekenaap and Citrusdal is somewhat dryer (less rainfall and higher temperatures) than in the vicinity of Capetown. The wines are extremely pleasant with very acceptable prices, but sadly more for the local drinkers.

PIKETBERG

The summers in the Piketberg region are particularly hot. Irrigation is essential here, as rainfall is minimal throughout the year. First rate wines for acceptable prices.

SWARTLAND

The Swartland District (Coastal Region) lies between Piketberg, Darling. Malmesbury and Tulbagh. This is where the wines start to improve, and where once outstanding sweet port like wines were produced. Two types of wine are now produced here: light, tasty, and cheerful wines that are certainly not expensive.

Tinta Barocca from Switzerland

(e.g. Swartland) but also top quality classical wines made from noble grapes (e.g. Alles Verloren).

TULBAGH

Tulbagh is a tiny district of the Coastal Region, south east of Swartland. Depending on the micro-climate and the soil type, reasonable to good cooperative wines are produced here together with excellent classical wines (in Europe, the Drostdy Hof and the Twee Jonge Gezellen are especially well known).

WELLINGTON (PAARL)

Wellington is a ward in the district of Paarl in the Coastal Region, about from Capetown. This is the home port of the CWA and without doubt the most well known wine region (also because of the annual wine auctions and tasting sessions at Nederburg). There are of course simple and cheap wines produced, but Wellington has some exceptional top wines (including the houses known in Europe, KWV, Laborie, Landskroon, Nederburg and Simonsvlei). The climate here is just like the Mediterranean with long summers, and just enough rainfall to avoid dependence on irrigation. The best known of this region's wines are the white Sauvignon Blanc, Chenin Blanc (Steen) and Chardonnay, along with the red Pinotage and Cabernet Sauvignon.

FRANSCHOEK (PAARL)

Franschoek is the other ward in the Paarl district of the Coastal Region. The descendants of the Huguenots have made their region a real place of pilgrimage: Franschoek, also producing splendid wines. Apart from the usual varieties of grapes, these French Huguenots prefer semillon. A few of the top South African wine houses are located in Franschoek: Bellingham, Chamonix, Agusta, L'Ormarins, La Motte and Plasir de Merle. The present day (white) wines of Franschoek are often more "French" than today's French wines.

Delicious Cuvée from Franschhoek

DURBANVILLE

This wine area is somewhat troubled by the encroaching suburbs of Cape Town but manages to survive. Durbanville is best known for its good quality red wines but also makes outstanding whites. Neighboring Paarl enjoys much greater fame which is not entirely just but Durbanville is busily working hard to overtake its rival. Names that are known in Europe include Altijdgedacht, Diemersdal, Meerendal, and Theuniskraal.

CONSTANTIA

This wine area is south of Cape Town and by far the wettest of all the South African wine areas. This is also where the first Dutch settlers planted their first vineyards. Constantia was famous for many years for its superb sweet Muscat wines but now produces wines of every type of good to

Two excellent red wines from Franschhoek

outstanding quality. The best-known wine houses of Constantia are Buitenverwachting, Groot Constantia, and Klein Constantia.

STELLENBOSCH

Stellenbosch, A district in the Coastal Region is not only the area that makes the highest quality wines, it is also the research and study center for the wine industry. Renowned wines such as Alto, Bergkelder, Jacobsdal, Kanonkop, Le Bonheur, Meerlust, Middelvlei, Neil Ellis, Rust en Vrede, Simonsig, Thelema, and Uitkijk originate from this area close to Cape Town.

Stellenbosch is also famous for the quality of its blended red wines and also for superlative white and varietal wines. Kanonkop probably produces the finest Pinotage of South Africa.

The most famous
red wine in
Stellenbosch

WORCESTER

Worcester is a district in the Breede River Valley region. This is a fairly large wine area that is responsible for about a quarter of the South African production. The many different soil types and varied microclimates between the Breede River Valley and its tributaries means that there are widely differing wines ranging from reasonable to good. A great deal of wine is also distilled here to make a very acceptable local brandy by KWV among others.

OVERBERG (WALKER BAY, HERMANUS, ELGIN)

This tiny and virtually unknown area lies on the south coast about halfway between Cape Town and Bredasdorp. It is a relative newcomer that promises much for the future. The soil is broken slate and the cool, moist climate guarantees the finest Chardonnay of the country but also excellent Pinot Noir. Two absolutely outstanding wines are Hamilton-Russel and Wildekrans.

ROBERTSON

This is a fairly large wine area between Worcester and Klein Karoo. It was once famed for its fortified sweet wine. Today it produces superb whites and reds of which the Chardonnay and Shiraz are truly outstanding. You

Fine Chardonnay
from Robertson

Top quality from
Stellenbosch

can also find several sublime pure Shiraz wines in contrast with other areas where shiraz is almost systematically blended with other grapes such as cabernet sauvignon. There are plenty of good wine houses such as Rietvallei, Robertson, Rooiberg, Van Loveren, Weltevrede, and Zandvliet.

KLEIN KAROO

The largest wine region of South Africa is Klein Karoo, which is also the most easterly area. It is very hot in summer here and irrigation is essential. Klein Karoo is famous for its sweet fortified wine but also for the surprisingly fresh and fruity Chenin Blanc (Steen).

WINES AND TIPS FOR SERVING

Cheap commercial wines from all regions (white, rosé, red, sometimes in a small bag-in-box of 5 liters or more) are fine for every occasion from student parties to street parties, from barbecue (the South Africans prefer to say "braai") to a national buffet. White wine should be poured around 8–10 °C (46–50 °F), rosé 10–12 °C (50–53.6 °F) and red 14 °C (57.2 °F)

CAPE RIESLING/KAAPSE RIESLING

In spite of the name this is not riesling as we know it in Europe but a different grape, the crouchen blanc, of which the origins are unclear. It is often used to make very acceptable table wines but also produces some good firm wines with interesting vegetal aromas such as straw and grass. A fine aperitif wine and delicious with a light starter. Try it with homemade chicken liver paté. Drinking temperature is 8–10 °C (46.4–50 °F).

COLOMBARD

This grape variety (sometimes called "colombar") hails originally from the French south-west, origin of most of the Huguenots. Its yields fresh and fruity wines that are excellent as an aperitif or to served with grilled fish. Combine with fish au gratin. Drinking temperature is 8–10 °C (46.4–50 °F).

STEEN (CHENIN BLANC)

These grapes originate from the Loire. The grape is particularly used for its fine acidity. In South Africa though it delivers surprisingly mellow wines that are almost sweet as well as dry as chalk examples that are fresh and fruity. The Steen is suitable as an aperitif or with a light starter. A local South African dish to combine with this wine is small pasties stuffed with pike, eggs, cheddar and herbs. Drinking temperature is 8–10 °C (46.4–50 °F).

STEIN

Stein wine is always semi-sweet or sweet and is made from the steen or chenin blanc grape.

Sauvignon Blanc

Beautiful Chardonnay from Franschhoek

Believed by many to be the best South African Chardonnay

Pinotage from Stellenbosch

wines have the familiar aromas and taste characteristics as the noble red wines. Sugar contents: Laatoes/ Late Harvest 20–30 g sugar/liter (0.7–1 oz/34 fl oz); Spesiale Laatoes/Special Late Harvest 20–50 g sugar/liter (0.7–1.7 oz/34 fl oz); Edeltoes/Noble Late Harvest more than 50 g sugar/liter (1.7 oz/34 fl oz).

PINOTAGE

This grape is the true South African specialty. It was formed from a cross based on old root stock with pinot noir, and cinsault (known locally as Hermitage) about which little is known. Prof. Abraham Perold created this variety in 1925 and it combines the reliability of cinsault in terms of volume and quality, even in poor years, with the finesse of pinot noir. Most of the wines are drunk still too young but there are certain top quality Pinotage wines such as Kanonskop, which aged well (five to ten years). Pinotage smells and tastes of dark ripe fruit with hints of spices. (however, some poor cheap varieties have the unpleasant smell of acetone and old rubber tires) Some of the best Pinotage wines contain quite substantial tannin when they are young, but soften after being allowed to mature for a few years. A "must" with a good Pinotage is 'Beesvleis Pinotage', which is a beef stew cooked in Pinotage. Drinking temperature is 16 °C (60.8 °F).

SAUVIGNON BLANC

Sometimes also known as fumé blanc as in the USA. South African Sauvignon Blanc wines are very herbal with definite notes of grass, with peppery undertones. The taste is fresh, dry, aromatic, and beautifully rounded. Drink with fruit, fish or even chicken dishes. Combines well with pan-fried mussels with garlic and white wine. Drinking temperature is 8–10 °C (46.4–50 °F).

CHARDONNAY

The special *cuvées* in particular that, are aged in oak barrels, are extremely exciting. Chardonnay is fruity, rich, and rounded with a robust taste. They are more suited to better dishes like salt water fish or shellfish, can also be drunk quite well with a risotto. Serve with grilled or roasted lobster. Drinking temperature is 10–12 °C (50–53.6 °F).

GRAND CRU/PREMIER GRAND CRU

This honorable mention will have been noticed on the label of many a South African white wine. However, do not expect an exceptional wine of superior quality: this is purely an advice from the South Africans that the wines are perfectly dry.

LAATOESWYN/LATE HARVEST

These wines of the late harvest, although not completely "ennobled" by *botrytis* are always sweet and particularly pleasant. The Edellaatoes-/ Noble Late Harvest

CABERNET SAUVIGNON

In South Africa, cabernet sauvignon produces sturdy, highly tannic wines with herbal aromas and hints of red fruit and blackcurrant. There is a good balance between fruit and ripe woody tones. It is superb with red meat and mature hard cheeses. Combines well with roast beef. Drinking temperature is 16–17 °C (60.8–62.6 °F).

MERLOT

This Bordeaux grape appears to be gaining ground in South Africa, especially in the Stellenbosch and Paarl regions. Merlot is a full-bodied and velvet smooth wine with rich and warm nuances that include cherry. Serve this wine with no all too heavy meat dishes. Ideal with saddle of lamb glazed with a mixture of sherry, honey, and thyme. Drinking temperature is 16 °C (60.8 °F).

Cabernet Sauvignon from the Coastal Region

447

Pinot Noir from the famous Meerlust Estate

Tinta Barocca, underestimated, unknown, but certainly not unloved

PINOT NOIR

Pinot noir is a fairly temperamental grape variety that only produces excellent results in good hands and in good years. A good Pinot Noir is characteristically light in color and quite aromatic with herbal notes and those of red fruit in its nose. Serve with roast chicken with a mushroom stuffing. Drinking temperature is 14–16 °C (57.2–60.8 °F).

SHIRAZ (SYRAH)

The Shiraz here is often an amenable if not slightly exotic wine with sensual nose and taste. This wine is often excellent with plenty of warmth and spicy undertones and is ideal with grilled lamb or game. Combined locally with pot-roast of game. Drinking temperature is 16 °C (60.8 °F).

TINTA BAROCCA

Tinta Barocca (spelt differently to Portugal, where this grape originates) is a surprising wine that is full-bodied, warm, exciting, but also fruity, elegant, and refined. Highly delicious by the better barbecues and with all braised meat dishes. South Afri-

cans combine it with braised ostrich. Drinking temperature is 16 °C (60.8 °F).

RUBY CABERNET

This grape was developed fairly recently in California, and is a hybrid of cabernet sauvignon and carignan.

Delicious but rustic Swartland Shiraz

Elegant full-bodied Stellenbosch Shiraz

The most famous South African blend

Although the quality of these wines is not particularly high it deserves a mention, as it is a very popular, light, easily drinkable red wine.

BLENDS

The Bordeaux type blends of cabernet sauvignon/cabernet franc/merlot (Meerlust Rubicon) are often excellent, especially where the process of cask aging in oak is done well. These are superb, full-bodied, rich, and complex wines with blackcurrant and bilberry in their bouquet, mixed with spices and vanilla.

Cabernet-Shiraz are very exciting wines which often age extremely well. Serve this full-bodied, warm, powerful, and complex wine with roast or grilled meat or mature hard cheese. The fairly new Pinotage-Merlots are quite promising. This is a wine filled with taste that combines spice and fruit. All of the blended wines can be served with red meat, lamb, goat or ostrich. Drinking temperature is 16–17 °C (60.8–62.6 °F).

The Rust and Vrede Estate wine is one of the best South African blends

SPARKLING WINES

South Africa makes a number of very good sparkling wines. The best are made by the *méthode traditionnelle* that is known here as *méthode cap classique*. Only a few of these wines, such as the Pongrácz, could compete with the top quality wines from Champagne.

The other sparkling wines that are not made by the traditional *méthode cap classique* but by transfer method have the frivolous name of bottle-conditioned sparkling wine but they can also be very palatable. Drinking temperature is 6–8 °C (42.8–46.4 °F). South Africa also has a number of sparkling wines that are produced in large tanks using the charmat method. These can also be very deserving wines Finally, a number of "sparkling

*Pongrácz:
Top Quality*

*The Krone Borealis is
a méthode cap classic*

wines" are made by adding carbon dioxide. An even lighter variety is known as "perlé". Generally speaking, these wines are not of a high quality.

FORTIFIED WINES

The sweet South African wines such as Muscadel (Muscat of Frontignan) and Hanenpoot (Muscat of Alexandria) can be recommended. The formerly heavy and sultry wines have become fresher. The port and sherry type wines of South Africa can stand alongside the top European originals. They lack some of the finer freshness of the true ports and sherries but compensate for this with their sunny character. The South African "sjerrie" or sherry is available in the types Fino, Amontillado. Oldoroso and Old Brown, from dry to sweet. This port like wine is available in ruby, tawny, vintage, late bottled vintage and white.

*Muscatel from
Robertson*

*An extremely
meritorious port like
wine from Swartland*

*The best-sparkling South African wines are
made by the cap classique method*

The Americas

The American continent contains a relatively small number of wine-producing countries. The Spanish introduced vines into Peru (no longer a true wine-producing country), Argentina, Chile, Mexico, and California, the Portuguese to Brazil, the British to the USA and Canada, the French to Quebec, Uruguay (Basques), and some parts of the USA.

CANADA

The first mention of Canadian wine was in the first half of the seventeenth century, when French Jesuits attempted to make wine from the native, wild vineyards of the *Vitis labrusca*. The wine was of terrible quality and even appeared to be a health hazard. Attempts were made in all corners of Canada to make wine from this extremely rural *Vitis labrusca*, resulting in everything but elegant wines. It was not until 1860 that wine making was started in earnest. About the same time, the first European vineyards were planted in Ontario (the island of Pelee) and British Colombia (Kelowna, Okanagan Valley) using the far superior grape family member of *Vitis vinifera*. Although the first winery was opened in Ontario in 1873, British Columbia had to wait until 1930. Ontario also led the way with their wine legislation. Since it was founded in 1989, the Vintners Quality Alliance (VQA) has been advising the wine growers of Ontario. This body also monitors the strict origin identification policy employed by Canada. British Columbia has also been working hard since the start of the end of the twentieth century on improving the vines, the equipment, and ultimately the quality of the wine. The biggest problem for the Canadian wine industry appeared to be – apart from the almost impossible weather conditions – the inborn inferiority complex or extreme modesty of their Wine growers. Nowadays, Canadian wines are winning awards and followers throughout the world, but it is only just recently that the Canadian Wine growers have started to believe in their success. A real breakthrough is expected in the coming years following the European Union's decision to allow the import of Canadian Ice wine.

WINE GROWING AREAS

QUEBEC
Quebec is the French-speaking province of Canada. The climate is anything but ideal for cultivating vines and making wine. Temperatures can drop to minus 40 °C/minus 40 °F or even lower in winter, which is fatal for vines. A handful of enthusiasts tried a surprising way to protect the vines against the cold of winter. The vines are kept pruned low and before the first frosts they are covered with a layer of earth that is then removed in spring. Apart from this interesting cultivation technique and the hard working nature of the local growers, there is little else positive to say about this wine region. The wines that we tasted were extremely dubious and their prices far too high.

ONTARIO
Ontario is the wine region in Canada with the longest continuous activity. The vineyards are in three districts: the Niagara Peninsula, Lake Erie North Shore, and Pelee Island. These three districts are all close to Lake Niagara. The epicenter of the wine industry is the town of Niagara-on-Lake, where the present-day generation of Wine growers and makers have their origins in Germany, France, Italy, and even The Netherlands. Although Ontario shares the same latitude as the Côtes du Rhône, its climate is much harsher. The summers are hot and winters extremely cold. Wine growing is only possible close to the most southerly of the five Great Lakes, Lake Erie. The soil here consists of a mixture of clay, gravel, and loam which is rich in minerals and

trace elements. The underlying geology consists of hard rock, which gives additional complexity to the wines.

Various hybrid grape varieties are grown here such as seyval blanc and vidal for white wines and Maréchal Foch and baco noir for reds. Although seyval, vidal, and baco noir deliver good to excellent results the Ontario growers are choosing to plant more *vinifera* varieties such as pinot auxerrois, chardonnay, gewürztraminer, pinot blanc, and riesling on the one hand and pinot noir, gamay, cabernet sauvignon, cabernet franc, and merlot on the other.

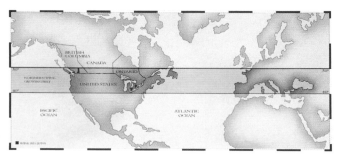

The vineyards of Ontario are on the same meridian as the Rhône, but the climates differ greatly

BRITISH COLUMBIA

Although wine has been made here for some considerable time that left a lot to be desired, the past decade has seen this region striving for the best quality. The old hybrid or even worse native America *Vitis labrusca* vines have increasingly been replaced with *Vitis vinifera* varieties. Wine is made in two districts: the western Fraser Valley and Vancouver Island, and the eastern Okanagan and Similkameen valleys.

The Pinot Noir is gaining more ground

The first two areas and the Similkameen Valley are recent additions that are busily in the process of development. The historical heart of British Columbia lies in the Okanagan Valley where the weather conditions are more suited to growing grapes and making wines. The summers are hot and dry, with little rainfall. The soil consists of rock, fine sand, clay, and alluvial deposits in the south. The more northerly vineyards that are cooler and more humid are mainly planted with French and German grape varieties of auxerrois, bacchus, chardonnay, erenfelser, gewürztraminer, pinot blanc, pinot gris, and riesling, while the more southerly ones have the traditional red varieties of pinot noir and merlot. British Columbia has three types of winery: The Majors are the large wine industries which get their grapes from far and wide, the Estates use only those grown in British Columbia, of which at least 50% is from their own vineyards. They are required to conduct all viticulture and wine making activities within their own winery. The Farms are mainly smaller in scale and must meet the same requirements as the Estates except that 75% of the grapes must come from their own vineyards.

THE WINES

It is best advised to only buy wines that have a VQA neck seal (Vintner's Quality Alliance). These wines are not only strictly controlled in respect of their guaranteed origin but are also quality tested for taste, color, bouquet etc. This gives assurance that you have bought one of the better Canadian wines. Canada also has two levels of guarantee of origin: the broad Provincial Designation Wines category i.e. British Columbia or Ontario, and the more precise wine growing Areas Wines which originate from one of the recognized wine districts such as Okanagan Valley, Similkameen Valley, Fraser Valley, or Vancouver Island for British Columbia, and Niagara Peninsula, Lake Erie North Shore, or Pelee Island for Ontario.

The strength of Canadian wines is their firm and fresh white wines and the sultry, overripe sweet wines. Some wine-makers and growers though, mainly in Ontario, can also make excellent rounded and full-bodied reds. Most of the Canadian red wines though are very light in structure and a bit shallow. The same goes for Canadian wines as elsewhere: do not

Only purchase wine with the VQA neck label

choose the very cheapest wines since a little more money will yield far better quality. The following types of white wine are generally recommended.

VIDAL DRY

This is a fresh and firm dry wine with a bouquet of green

Vidal Dry

apple and sometimes, with the better ones, hints of citrus fruit. Delicious with fish and poultry.

SEYVAL DRY

This wine is less severely dry than the Vidal and it has a nose containing grapefruit and the occasional hint of flowers and spices. Good with fish, shellfish, poultry and creamy pasta dishes.

Seyval Dry

RIESLING DRY

This is a very elegant wine, dry to 'off-dry' (with some sugar residue) with a complex aroma (pear, peach, apple, and spring blossom). Goes well with creamy pasty dishes, fish, white meat and fresh salads.

CHARDONNAY DRY

Most Canadian Chardonnays are fresh and a touch green (apples), partially full-bodied, with a subtle bouquet of butter, wood, and citrus fruit.

The best Chardonnays (bottled sur lie, reserve, and barrel fermented) are more complex, full-bodied, and creamier, with the typical aromas of butterscotch or toffee, toast and croissants. Delicious with shell fish, scallops, strong tasting salt water fish or even veal.

Chardonnay

Drinking temperature is 10–12 °C (50–53.6 °F) for the simpler wines and 12–14 °C (53.6–57.2 °F) for the better examples.

Gewürztraminer Off Dry (with a touch of sweetness)

GEWÜRZTRAMINER

This wine, that is generally vinified as 'off-dry' with sugar residues, is full-bodied and slightly spicy. It has a seductive bouquet in which lychee, melon, peach, and spices can be detected. This should give an immediate hint as to the best accompaniment: Asian dishes, provided they are not too spicy.

GEWÜRZTRAMINER MEDIUM DRY/LATE HARVEST

This one is fuller and more seductive than the 'off-dry' version. It has a good balance between sweetness, alco-

Gewürztraminer Late Harvest

hol, fruit, and acidity. Ideal with semi-soft and blue vane, but also with Asian dishes, poultry terrines or patés, or just as an after dinner drink.

VIDAL MEDIUM DRY/LATE HARVEST

A sweet wine with a bouquet of citrus and tropical fruits and a relatively high acidity, Can be enjoyed on its own, or with a not all too sweet dessert.

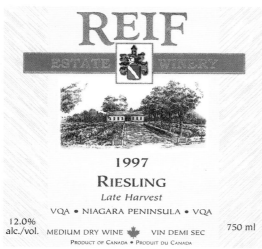

Riesling Late Harvest

RIESLING MEDIUM DRY/LATE HARVEST

Fine medium dry to sweet wines. This wine remains well-balanced thanks to the refined acidity of the Riesling grape. There are very attractive floral aromas and also apple, peach, and honey with the sweeter Late Harvest. To be recommended with creamy fruit sauces, pork, poultry or even fish, fresh fruit desserts, fresh baked goods, fresh goats cheese or just as a drink with friends.

ICE WINE

Ice wine can in principle be made from any type of grape including red varieties like cabernet sauvignon or franc, but with a few exceptions the most interesting of them are produced from vidal and riesling. The method of making ice wines is the same as that for making German or Austrian Eiswein and French Vins de Glace from the southwest of France. The grapes are allowed to hang until frozen by the frost. They are then quickly pressed and the tasteless frozen liquid remains behind with the seeds and skins, with only the honey sweet juices emerging from the press. These juices are so concentrated that the yeast cells, which can normally live up to a level of alcohol of 15%, are finished by 8 or 9%. Ice-wines are very complex, powerful, extremely aromatic wines with notes such as apricot, peach, sweet melon, and honey with vidal grapes and tropical flowers, apricot, citrus fruit, toffee, and vegetal nuances with riesling. After a good meal, enjoy the rest of the evening drinking this wine on its own, together with old friends or your partner. Drinking temperature: Ice wine should be served cold, 8–10 °C (46.4–50 °F) but then allowed to warm up slowly.

ROSÉ

Most Canadian rosés are very lightly structured and not very interesting. However their fruity character and a good level of acidity ensures they go well with cold buffets and rural lunches.

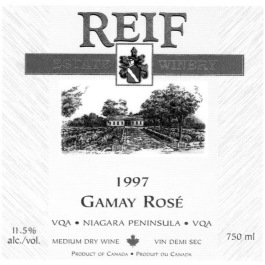

Gamay Rosé

BACO NOIR

This is an extremely surprising French Canadian hybrid which produces quite exciting results in Canada with full-bodied wines with lots of juice and taste that are very scented with suggestions of blackcurrant, blueberries, tobacco, and animal undertones. Some top Baco Noirs slightly resemble better Rhône Syrah wines. Serve with roast lamb. Drinking temperature is 16–17 °C (60.8–62.6 °F).

PINOT NOIR

Canadian Pinot Noir vaguely resembles its Burgundy cousins, only it is somewhat fresher and fruitier. A lovely wine with small wild game, poultry or mature

Baco Noir

OTHER WINES
The best wine houses also make excellent Sauvignon, Aligotés, Viognier, Gamay Blanc and Gamay Rouge. These wines are not very abundant though.

THE BEST CANADIAN WINES
The following wines from the best Canadian wineries are well worth trying.
– Ontario: Château des Charmes, Hildebrand Estates Winery, Inniskillin, Marijnissen Estates, Reif Estate Winery (all Niagara-on-the-Lake); D'Angelo (Amherstburg); Henry of Pelham (St. Catharines); Stoney Ridge Cellars (Winona); Lakeview Cellars (Vineland); Cave Spring Cellars (Jordan); Colio Estate (Harrow); and Pelee Island Winery (Kingsville).
– British Columbia: Calona Vineyards, Quails' Gate,

Sauvignon Blanc

cheeses. Drinking temperature is 14–16 °C (57.2–60.8 °F).

CABERNET

Many Canadian Cabernet wines are a blend of cabernet sauvignon and cabernet franc and sometimes they may even contain merlot! Choose the better wines that are really superb: surprisingly powerful, with an alluring fruitiness and soft tannin. The wines for fine meat dishes, preferably beef. Drinking temperature is 16–17 °C (60–62.6 °F).

Cabernet Sauvignon

Viognier

Henry of Pelham, very reliable

Outstanding ice wine from Château des Charmes

Summerhill, Mission Hill, Cedar Creek, St. Humbertus (all Kelowna); Hawthorne Mountains, Inniskillin Okanoga, Jackson Triggs, Peller Estate (Okanoga); Domaine Combret, Tinhorn Creek (Oliver); and Langley's Estate Winery (Langley).

USA

California is the biggest producer of North American wines. However there are four large wine producing regions in the USA. They are the North East (New York: Finger Lakes, Lake Erie, Hudson River, and Long Island), the South and Mid-West (Texas, Carolina, New Mexico, Georgia, Missouri, Arkansas, and Iowa); California (Napa, Sonoma, and Carneros); and the North West (Washington State, Oregon, and Idaho) but other states are increasingly also producing wines. The wine industry has grown up in the past decades

Californian vineyards, Bernardus, Carmel Valley

and more and more Americans have come to envy the success of the Californian wine growers. Many European wine companies that have felt restricted in the European market have also decided to take an active part in the US industry. The wine industry is still 'big business' in the USA but a new generation of wine

Californian red / white, the largest Californian origin identification

growers has emerged that apart from having a healthy love of the dollar also has a tremendous passion for making good wine. There are increasing numbers of small-scale growers who dare to take on the gigantic Californian wine producers. The American wine industry is now more exciting than ever before.

IDENTIFICATION OF ORIGIN

The wine classification system in America is quite simple. The main identification of origin is by region, e.g. California. To qualify for this classification, all wines must be made with grapes solely (100%) from that specific region.

This is followed by the County e.g. Sonoma County. All wines bearing this identification should originate from California, with at least 75% from the declared County.

Next comes the AVA, American Viticultural Area, which includes the very specific qualities such as climate, soil and/or location. Here it is a requirement that at least 85% of the wine contained in the

Chardonnay from Mendocino County

455

Pinot Noir from A.V.A Oregon

bottle originates from the declared region. The size of these AVA's can vary from being very small to fairly large. It should be remembered that the recognized origin identification only relates to the origin of the wine and not its quality. It is more important that you the consumer is more attentive as to the good name of the wine house, and not to the wine's origin. Especially when you consider that what is on the label is not always what it appears to be… If, for example, chardonnay is mentioned on the label, this means that the wine must contain at least 75% chardonnay. The same applies to the year, a wine producer may add wine from another year up to a maximum of 5%.

In accordance with American legislation, this wine contains a minimum of 75% Chardonnay and a minimum of 95% of the wine from the appropriate year of harvesting.

NORTHEAST

The Northeast has the following officially recognized origin identifications: (AVA's): New York (including Finger Lakes, Lake Erie, Hudson River, The Hamptons (Long Island), New England (Western Connecticut Highlands, South Eastern New England), Ohio, Michigan and Virginia (including Shenandoah Valley).

Vineyards of Lake Michigan

The local wine-growing dates from the illustrious pioneering era in the sixteenth century. Local native species and hybrid grapes were used for a long time (alexander, catawba, delaware, and concord). Results with these grapes were not entirely satisfactory; the wines possessed a distinctive "foxy" aroma and taste that is characteristic of grape varieties of *Vitis labrusca* species. This foxy aroma can best be likened to that of a dirty old pelt on which a layer of old-fashioned fruit preserve has been smeared. In the 1940s improved varieties of French grapes were introduced such as baco noir and seyval. Large scale planting of *Vitis vinifera* vines took place in the 1950s and especially in the 1970s with the great breakthrough occurring thirty years later.

New York's climate is marginal for cultivating vines and making wines. The summers are generally very warm and dry but the winters are often exceptionally raw. Wine growing is only possible where the climate is moderated by the big rivers, lakes, or the Atlantic Ocean. It is extremely important to plant the vines in subsoil that is free draining. Despite government campaigns promoting the planting of *Vitis vinifera* varieties, some still persist with the old-fashioned and inferior

Winter in Ohio

The vineyards are sprayed with water to protect against night-time frost

concord, catawba, delaware, and niagara. The very best wines though are made with chardonnay, riesling, cabernet sauvignon, cabernet franc (Hudson River), merlot, and pinot noir. The wines from such varieties like concord are nothing special. Considerable amounts of sugar are often added to the must to mask the high acidity and strong taste, which certainly do nothing to aid to the wine's finesse. The *Vitis vinifera* wines are very

Healthy crop in Ohio'

taut which is understandable give the climate but they are also extremely aromatic and particularly fruity. These are not high flight wines but the quality is steadily improving.

OHIO

Ohio derives its name from the local native American language for "beautiful river" of the people who lived along the river. Back in the pioneering days the area became known as "the West." Ohio's wine history dates back to the start of the nineteenth century when a lawyer from the Cincinnati area, Nicholas Longworth, had the remarkable idea of planting grape vines along the banks of the Ohio river. The first wines were made from catawba grapes. These were not the ponderous and cloying wines of elsewhere but elegant and light sweet wines. The success quickly led to vineyards being planted around Cincinnati. Ohio was the biggest producer of wine in the USA in 1860 but severe disease problems and the Civil War caused a decline in prominent wine growing position of Ohio, in part due to the lack of manpower.

Wine growing moved northwards because German immigrants discovered how favorable the climate is on the banks of Lake Erie. The grapes benefited from more sunshine and were able to develop over a longer period. The proximity of the lake also gave protection from frost and disease. At the start of the nineteenth century the entire coastline of the lake became a patchwork of vineyards and became known as the 'Lake Erie grape belt'. Countless wineries established themselves on the banks of Lake Erie and trade flourished. The introduction of Prohibition brought an end to this euphoria and a total collapse in Ohio's wine industry. Courageous efforts were made to get wine-making going again after the lifting of Prohibition in 1933 but these were hampered by State officials and politicians and it seemed as if Ohio would disappear completely from the list of wine producing states.

German influences deep in Ohio

A turning point came with the development of Ohio's wine industry in the 1960s. With support from the local agricultural college French-American hybrid varieties of vines were planted in the south of the state. This initiative was quickly followed in the north along the banks of Lake Erie. Since the mid 1960s there has been a steady growth in the number of wineries. In addition to the original French-American hybrids the noble *Vitis vinifera* grapes have also made their entrance. The acreage of vineyards was extended significantly in the 1980s and 1990s. Riesling wines from this area are regularly awarded prizes in the major national tastings.

Measuring the sugar content in the grapes

Harvest time in Ohio

Amish Country Wine, Ohio

Ohio is divided into five wine-growing regions: Lake Erie West, Lake Erie East (both on the banks of Lake Erie), Ohio Heartland, Central Ohio, and the Ohio River Valley Region. Within these zones there are five recognized AVA (American Viticulture Area) areas. These are: Lake Erie, Isle St. George, Grand River Valley, Ohio River Valley en Loramie Creek. The last of these exists only on paper and has no winery in its territory.

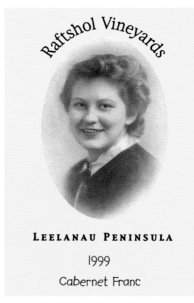

Cabernet Franc from the Leelanau Peninsula

MICHIGAN

Michigan's wine-growing dates back about two centuries. Immediately before the Civil War a number of different diseases virtually wiped out all the vineyards of the large-scale wine-growing area on the banks of the Ohio River, close to Cincinnati. Those brave enough to continue wagered their efforts on once more establishing themselves along the shores of Lake Erie. This was the heyday of Michigan wine-growing and by the late nineteenth century the area of vineyards was extended towards the southeast.

In 1919 there were eight wineries to the southeast of Michigan but unfortunately none of these survived Prohibition. The growers in the southwest fared better thanks to the enterprising nature of Dr. Thomas Welch who produced a non-fermented drink (grape juice) that was originally intended for church services. This grape juice quickly became popular with local people and led to a grape juice industry being established. The Welch's

Grape Juice Company extended the planting of varieties such as concord. Thanks to this activity the "wineries" that produced grape juice were able to survive the period of Prohibition that was harsh for others. After the abolition of Prohibition the blue concord and white niagara grapes – two native *Vitis labrusca* hybrids – were the most popular varieties of grapes. The wines produced with these were sharp and sweet and often rather alcoholic (and fortified) that today's more sophisticated tastes would not relish but these wines were extremely popular throughout the USA. We should not forget that these rather sultry wines were still popular in California in the 1960s! During that decade though there were great changes in American wine-growing and in consumer tastes. Through widespread travel to Europe, Americans increasingly began to appreciate drier wines. This had enormous consequences for wine-growing in Michigan where they specialized in sweet and fortified wines. This led to the demise of all the Michigan wineries then existing, with the exception of St. Julian Wine Company, that still operates.

St. Julian Winery Riesling

The reconstruction began in the 1970s when growers started to plant European varieties of grape vines. This resulted in new studies of the most suitable sites for vineyards and led to the creation of the entirely new wine area of Traverse City. Vineyards were successfully established on the Leelanau and on Old Mission peninsulas. Today one can find many of the classic European varieties being turned into very acceptable wines by the rapidly growing local wineries.

Château Grand Traverse, Old Mission Peninsula

In 2002 Michigan had 13,200 acres of vineyards, making it the fourth largest in the USA. This is misleading though for the majority of these grapes are intended for production of grape juice using native American hybrid grapes (concord and niagara). Only 1,440 acres in Michigan are given over to wine-growing, placing it in eighth place. Despite this the total wine-growing area has expanded by at least twenty-four percent in the past five years and Michigan is now the thirteenth largest wine producer in the USA.

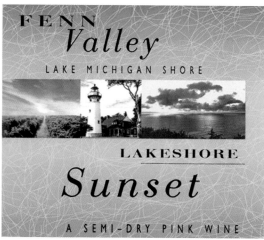

Impression of the lake shore

THE WINES

Michigan produces wine from more than fifty varieties of grapes, including many European types. The most popular are: Johannesburg riesling, chardonnay, pinot gris/pinot grigio, gewürztraminer, pinot blanc/ Auxerrois, cabernet franc, merlot, gamay noir, and pinot noir of the European varieties; vignoles, seyval blanc, vidal blanc, chardonnel, traminette, chancellor, chambourcin, and Marshal Foch of the French-American hybrids; and concord, niagara, and catawba among the American hybrids. Other hybrids used include two that stand out for their relatively high quality. These are chambourcin and vignoles. These French-American hybrids are not sufficiently appreciated and deserve greater recognition. They are very suitable for chilly and damp locations like Michigan and produce very acceptable wines.

The better Michigan wines emanate from within a twenty-five mile radius of Lake Michigan. The lake has a beneficial influence for wine-growing. In the winter the lake protects the vineyards which are further protected under a blanket of snow. The milder temperatures around the lake reduce the risk of early frost and the lake also ensures milder summers and a long period of ripening for the grapes. An additional benefit of the moist warm late summer climate is that it makes it possible to produce late harvest and even ice wines.

SHADY LANE

1999

VIGNOLES

LEELANAU PENINSULA

Vignoles, a much underestimated type of grape

There are four official AVA areas in Michigan: Leelanau Peninsula (northwest, near Traverse City), Old Mission Peninsula (northwest), Lake Michigan Shore (southwest), and Fennville (southwest). Michigan wines are characteristic of the cool climate and have initial freshness followed by finesse and elegance, with a good balance between acidity and sweetness.

CHARDONNAY

Most Michigan Chardonnay is aged in wood. This imparts a full, rich body that is perfectly balanced by aromatic properties in which exotic fruit, citrus fruit, melon, pear, butter, and vanilla can be detected. It is a classic accompaniment for lobster, poultry, or fish in a creamy sauce. Drink it at 10–12 °C (50–53.6 °F).

Superb Riesling Ice Wine from Château Grand Traverse

RIESLING

A lot of Michigan riesling is vinified with the aid of fresh aromas such as oranges and honeysuckle with varying levels of sugar remnants to make "off dry" through to late harvest wines. Off dry and semi-sweet Rieslings go well with pork dishes and young fresh cheeses. The rich full late harvest wines demand a fruit dessert that is not too sweet and they are also delicious with a strong and crumbly hard sheep's milk cheese. Drinking temperature is 8–11 °C (46.4–51.8 °F) (coolest with the sweetest wines).

PINOT GRIS/PINOT GRIGIO

A wide variety of wines are made in Michigan with pinot gris, ranging from light-bodied to fairly full wines that are off-dry to quite sweet. All these wines share the mellow sensuality and stickiness with characteristic aromas of ripe fruit. Those that are less sweet can be served with fish, poultry, pork, or veal in rich creamy sauces. Also delicious with creamy to semi-hard cheese. The sweeter examples are better enjoyed unaccompanied after dinner for their full sensuality. Drinking temperature is 8–11 °C (46.4–51.8 °F) with the cooler temperatures for sweeter examples.

Semi dry Riesling

GEWÜRZTRAMINER

Michigan's Gewürztraminer is a classic example of a good Gewürztraminer, rich and full-bodied with heady aromas of flowers and spices. Ideal as accompaniment for Oriental sweet and sour dishes and Indian curries. Drinking temperature is 8–12 °C (46.4–53.6 °F) with the cooler temperatures for sweeter examples.

PINOT NOIR

The famous Burgundian grape produces light elegant wines here that are full of fruit (redcurrant, blackcurrant) and also a hint of spices and animal undertones. Combines supremely well with roast or grilled lamb or beef but also particularly well with small game. Provided it is well chilled it is a good companion for fresh salmon. Drinking temperature is 14–17 °C (57.2–62.6 °F).

SHADY LANE

1999

DRY RIESLING

LEELANAU PENINSULA

ALC. 11.5% BY VOL.

Dry Riesling

INDIANA

Indiana was the literal center of American wine-growing in the early nineteenth century. Immigrants from Switzerland and Germany lay behind the local wine industry and they concentrated in Switzerland County in the southeast of Indiana. It was here that the first commercial vineyards were planted and the wine from Indiana was reasonably successful in selling to the surrounding states. In common with many other states though Indiana went through a very dark period for wine-growing and the first hint of a resurgence came in 1970. Years later, in 1989, there were only nine wineries in Indiana and they banded together to market themselves and to develop the re-emerging wine industry. There were also serious studies undertaken concerning agricultural improvements for the vineyards and improved methods of vinification for the local wineries themselves. By 2001 Indiana had twenty-five wineries, three of them in Northern Indiana, five in Central Indiana, seven in South Central, and ten in Southern Indiana. The number of wineries continues to grow with a further two to five new ones planned for 2002. In 2001 the twenty-five wineries controlled a mere 216 acres with a further ten due to be added in 2002. The size of the industry remains modest but the quality is improving rapidly. Much more is likely to be heard in the coming decades if Indiana wines.

NEW YORK STATE

The vineyards of New York State extend from Long Island to the shores of Lake Erie. The history of New York wine-growing dates back to the Dutch settlers who planted the first vines 350 years ago on Manhattan Island. The English later extended wine-growing inland but in the east while the French planted along the northern river valleys. By the start of the nineteenth century wine-growing had reached the shores of Lake Erie. After a period of relative success wine-growing fell into neglect until action was taken in the 1970s to get it going once more, when there were nineteen wineries. The come back was spectacular with 150 wineries in New York State in 2002.

New York State recognizes the following wine-growing areas:

LAKE ERIE/CHAUTAUQUA

Lake Erie AVA is also known as Chautauqua and it is second only in size in the USA to California. The majority of its 19,200 acres though are planted with concord grapes that are used for the local grape juice industry.

Leelanau Cellars

Sleeping Bear Red

Premium Dry Red Table Wine

Leelanau Cellars premium dry red table wine

In addition to concord one can also come across some French-American hybrids and even varieties based on the noble *Vitis vinifera* vines in some seven wineries. The local specialties are Seyval blanc and for quality, Riesling.

FINGER LAKES

The larger geographic AVA territory of Finger Lakes surrounds four large lakes: Canandaigua, Keuka, Seneca en Cayuga. Of these Cayuga in particular has a well organized wine industry and the Lake Erie AVA incorporates the sub-AVA of Cayuga Lake. There were fifty-eight wineries active in 2002 in the Lake Erie AVA region. Their specialty is the production of still and sparkling wines from grapes characteristic of cool regions such as riesling, chardonnay, and pinot noir, and also some ice wines.

CENTRAL NEW YORK/LAKE ONTARIO

This is the fastest growing wine area of New York State that is developing rapidly. The local wineries suffer from a shortage of their own grapes and have to buy grapes in from elsewhere.

HUDSON RIVER VALLEY/THE CATSKILLS

The Hudson River is the soul of this wine-growing area to the north of New York City, providing its beneficial softening effect on the otherwise harsh winter climate. Some thirty wineries mainly grow the French-American hybrids of seyval blanc and baco noir but other grapes from cooler climates such as chardonnay are also grown. Recent experiments with cabernet franc look promising.

NEW YORK CITY

The city of New York is not a wine-growing area of course but there are seven wineries that acquire at least eight-five percent of their grapes from the state of New York and may therefore indicate New York State AVA on their labels. There were vineyards on Manhattan in the early seventeenth century but these have long since disappeared.

LONG ISLAND/NORTH FORK/HAMPTONS

Long Island lies off the coast close to New York City and enjoys a mild maritime climate from which its nickname of "the Bordeaux of New York." This is a relatively new wine-growing area that is developing rapidly. The favorable climate enables *Vitis vinifera* varieties to thrive here and the quality of the wine holds much promise for the future. Twenty-nine wineries concentrate on class wines from such grapes as chardonnay, riesling, gewürztraminer, merlot, cabernet sauvignon, and cabernet franc. The vineyards are mainly concentrated around Northeast Northfork and Southwest Northfork.

NEW JERSEY

New Jersey, with its quaintly-named towns, lives up to its title as "The Garden State." New Jersey is renowned for its vegetable and fruit growing but it is also of great interest to wine lovers for its two hundred year old wine-growing. At present there are seventeen commercial wineries spread across both the north and south of the state and the oldest of them is the Renault Winery that dates from 1864 and is still in business. The historical wine-making center of the state is in the south but the north has been developing rapidly in the past two decades. It is likely that we will hear more of New Jersey wines in the positive sense in the coming years. Since 1999 New Jersey has had a strict quality control system known as the Quality Wine Alliance. Based on the European quality control programs, this system guarantees consumers that QWA approved wines meet high standards. The QWA wines can be recognized by their special labels on the bottle. Of the seventeen commercial wineries, the Tommasello Winery has become renowned both within New Jersey and elsewhere.

MARYLAND

Maryland's wine-growing history dates back to the middle of the seventeenth century. Wines were being made in Maryland from native grapes as early as 1648 and in 1662 the first European vines were planted on the right bank of the St. Mary River. Results with these were not particularly good due to lack of experience, the hot summers, and too cold winters. The first officially acceptable wines were produced in 1756 using American hybrid grapevines. Due to the persistence and initiative of some of the wine growers reasonably acceptable wines were produced for many years with both American and European hybrid grapes. The truly serious development of Maryland's wine industry got under way following World War II. The editor of a local newspaper, Philip Wagner, planted his land with numerous different types of hybrid grapevine on what was a fairly large scale for the time. Wagner established his own winery, the Boordy Vineyards and sold his wines along the East Coast of the USA. Maryland wines first became known outside the USA in 1966 thanks to the wines of Dr. G. Hamilton Mowbray of the former Montbray Wine Cellars. Mowbray used European (predominantly French) varieties of grapevines and hybrids and produced quite serviceable wines: seyval blanc, chardonnay, riesling, and cabernet sauvignon. Mowbray and Wagner were awarded the highest French agrarian distinction of the Médaille du Mérite Agricole for their efforts. The driving force behind the recognition of Linganore as the first officially recognized wine area of Maryland in 1976 was Jack Aellen of Berrywine Plantations and Linganore Winecellars. Two areas have now gained recognition: Catoctin and Cumberland Valley in western Maryland. The number of wineries grew to twelve in the 1980s and 1990s.

Maryland wines are produced from ripe grapes of both classic and hybrid vines. The quality is reasonably good but will surely improve further in the coming decades. The Maryland Grape Growers Association suggests the following wines from the entire northeastern states area as accompaniment for the dishes indicated:

Lobster: Dry Riesling, Sauvignon Blanc, sparkling wine
Oysters: Sauvignon Blanc, Riesling
Seafood in a light sauce: Chardonnay, Dry Riesling, Sauvignon Blanc
Seafood in a cream sauce: Chardonnay, Seyval, Vidal Blanc
Shrimps/prawns: Pinot Grigio, Dry Riesling, Sauvignon Blanc, Seyval, Vidal Blanc
Pasta with white sauce (wine or cream): Chardonnay, Pinot Grigio, Vidal Blanc, Seyval
Pasta with red sauce (tomato/wine): Cabernet, Merlot, Chambourcin, Pinot Noir
Chicken: Chardonnay, Pinot Grigio, Dry Riesling, Sauvignon Blanc, Seyval, Vidal Blanc
Turkey: Chambourcin, Cabernet, Merlot, Pinot Noir
Veal: Chardonnay, Pinot Grigio, Seyval, Vidal Blanc, Chambourcin
Ham: Gewürztraminer, Pinot Noir, blush wines
Beef: Cabernet, Merlot, Chambourcin, Pinot Noir
Lam: Cabernet, Chambourcin, Merlot, Pinot Noir
Spicy dishes (Cajun, Oriental): Seyval, Vidal Blanc, Cabernet, Chambourcin, Merlot, Pinot Noir
Chocolate desserts: Cabernet, Merlot, Port, Riesling

PENNSYLVANIA

There are many vineyards in Pennsylvania but the grapes from much of the 13,440 acres are destined for grape juice production. In spite of this the state takes eighth place among the wine producing regions of the USA. With more than seventy wineries, Pennsylvania's wine industry is centered in the following areas: Lake Erie, Pittsburg Countryside, Groundhog Region, Upper Susquehanna, Lower Susquehanna, Lehigh Valley/ Berks County, and Philadelphia Countryside. A substantial proportion of the wines are made with native American grapes or French/French-American hybrids such as catawba, cayuga, seyval blanc, vidal blanc, vignoles etc. In addition to this there are also various wines produced from *Vitis vinifera* varieties such as chardonnay, gewürztraminer, pinot gris, riesling, cabernet sauvignon, and pinot noir.

VIRGINIA

Wine-growing has existed in Virginia for hundreds of years. The first English colonists from Jamestown determined back in 1607 that Virginia was ideal for planting of vineyards. They hoped they would soon be able to start trading wine back to the home country. Initially native vines were planted and the first harvest was pic-

ked in 1609. Wine-making began in earnest in 1611 after experts in the field of wine-making from England settled there. The resulting wines were wholly disappointing though and even the introduction of French winemakers did not improve them. Every effort to cultivate European types of grapevines ended in failure. These proved to be unable to withstand the hot, moist summers and cold winters. A solution was found by crossing American and European vines. These hybrids proved popular at their introduction in the early nineteenth century. The best of them are still grown: alexander, norton, catawba, isabella, niagara, concord, and delaware.

Blue Ridge Mountains, Virginia

The development of Virginia's wine-growing was directly affected by the many battles of the Civil War and the interest in wine-growing was already lessened by the late nineteenth century before the introduction of Prohibition in 1914. By 1950 there were a mere 14° acres of vineyards left in the entire state and these grew dessert grapes rather than those for wine-making. The resurgence began in the 1960s with the planting of American hybrids and then in the 1970s there was a switch to French hybrids for improved flavor and quality. The real breakthrough came in 1982 when it was decided to plant *Vitis vinifera* varieties. The wines made from chardonnay, riesling, and cabernet sauvignon

Oasis winery vineyards in Virginia

were an instant success. In the last decade interest in merlot has grown considerably and the French hybrids of seyval blanc and vidal are also still widely used. By 2002 there were 1,920 acres of vineyards for wine-growing, placing Virginia in eleventh place among US wine-producing states. This is a considerable achievement in under twenty-five years. Virginia now has seventy commercial wineries spread across five areas: Northern Virginia, Eastern Virginia, Central Virginia (the largest producer with the most wineries), Shenandoah Valley, and Southwest Virginia.

THE WINES

CHARDONNAY

Chardonnay is very popular in Virginia. The wines are dry and medium to full-bodied. Depending on whether cask-aged or not and the time in wood they are fruity (apple and citrus fruit) and fresh to opulent and sultry with hints of butter, nuts, and vanilla. The great variety in their taste and body means that these wines have a broad range of accompaniments such as shellfish dishes in a sauce, grilled crustaceans, or fish, poultry, or even veal in a cream sauce. Drinking temperature is 10–12 °C (50–53.6 °F).

Superb chardonnay from Virginia

RIESLING

Virginia Riesling is striking for its fruity and rather spicy aromas. The wines usually contain residual sugars and are rarely off-dry but rather semi-sweet. The body varies from light to rather full. There is generally a strong and fresh bouquet. With sweeter wines one detects a hint of honey, apricot, and peach. Off-dry Riesling is superb to drink as an aperitif or for informal drinking at any time but they also combine well with Oriental and Cajun cooking. A good off-dry Riesling also tastes great with fish in a rich cream sauce, with baked ham with pineapple, and roast pork. Semi-sweet Riesling is fine for after dinner but can also be drunk with fresh desserts that are not too sweet, such as those based on peaches, apricots, citrus fruit, and a little honey. Drinking temperature for off-dry is 8–10 °C (46.4–50 °F) and semi-sweet 8–9 °C (46.4–48.2 °F).

SAUVIGNON BLANC

Sauvignon blanc here yields fresh wines with a bouquet of fresh-mown hay, fresh garden herbs, and green peppers (capsicum). Depending on the style of the wine these Sauvignons can be quite sharply acidic but there are also milder ones with suggestions of freshly-sliced pineapple. The freshness of these wines makes them ideal as an aperitif and they also combine well with all seafood, pasta starters, and poultry. Drinking temperature is 10–11 °C (50–51.8 °F).

SEYVAL BLANC

Virginian Seyval Blanc is generally never full bodied, tending more to fresh and light with considerable acidity and hints of green apples or in the case of the more mature wines of nectarine. This is an ideal aperitif for those who enjoy a sharp white wine but most will enjoy it with a meal of none too lean chicken or with seafood. Drinking temperature is 9–10 °C (48.2–50 °F).

VIDAL BLANC

Vidal Blanc resembles Seyval Blanc in terms of its bouquet and taste. The difference is in the acidity, which with Vidal Blanc is less pronounced in wines that are generally made as off dry or semi sweet with a medium body. Drink it as an aperitif for those who prefer a wine that is less sharp or as an accompaniment for shellfish and crustaceans in a sauce, or with poultry, pork, or fish. Drinking temperature is 8–10 °C (46.4–50 °F).

GEWÜRZTRAMINER

Virginian Gewürztraminer contains residual sugars. They are off-dry to semi-sweet wines. The considerable aromatic bouquet of these wines is striking with sultry hints of spices, roses, and other floral notes. This is ideal wine for Oriental or Cajun food, for grilled or roasted sweet and sour pork, poultry, or fish (off-dry) and also (the semi-sweet) with desserts that are not overly sweet. Drinking temperature is 8–10 °C (46.4–50 °F).

For the sake of completeness two other white wines are mentioned here: the sultry and sensual Pinot Grigio with its bouquet of ripe fruit such as grapefruit and other citrus fruit and a sensually smooth finish and Viognier, with hints of fruit (apricot), floral notes (white flowers), and a hint of spice.

CABERNET SAUVIGNON

Virginian Cabernet Sauvignons are fairly classic examples of "New World" Cabernet Sauvignon wines. They possess plenty of suggestions of vegetal aromas ranging from freshly-sliced green pepper and green olives to the fore together with hints of blackcurrant, peppermint, and leather. These red wines are quite dry and fairly high in tannin when young. Serve with robust meat dishes, especially grilled and roasted beef, lamb, and pork. Drinking temperature is 16–18 °C (60.8–64.4 °F).

High quality wine from Oasis Winery, Virginia

MERLOT

In Virginia the classic merlot grape produces velvet smooth dry wines that are typically characterized by hints of cherry in the nose and underlying vegetal tones similar to cabernet sauvignon, but mellower. Merlot combines well with lamb and beef, wild duck, and pasta dishes with a tomato-based sauce. Keep some back to drink with the cheese, preferably a medium hard one such as Everona Sheep's Milk Cheese from Rapidan, Virginia. Drinking temperature is 16–17 °C (60.8–62.6 °F).

PINOT NOIR

Pinot Noir wines are recognizable by their mellow bouquet of cherry without the vegetal tones of either a cabernet sauvignon or merlot. The color, body, and taste are all lighter than those of classic Bordeaux grapes. Serve these sumptuous and silky wines with beef or lamb, duck breast, pasta dishes with a red sauce and with baked or grilled fish. The combination with subtle Oriental dishes of beef, lamb, or duck using soy or oyster sauce is particularly good. Drinking temperature is 14–17 °C (57.2–62.6 °F).

A few good red wines are also produced in Virginia using cabernet franc and chambourcin grapes. There are also the popular (somewhat sweet) Blush wines, here made from blending a little red wine with white.

Better quality though are the Cabernet Blanc wines that are similar to a French *vins gris*. These are very pale white wines produced from the blue cabernet grapes where the must has been allowed briefly to absorb color from the grape skins. Last but not least, Virginia also produces some excellent sparkling wines by the traditional Champagne method. The best of these are made from chardonnay and pinot noir grapes. These "Brut" wines are mainly dry. Drink them well chilled as an aperitif, for receptions and special occasions, or for more intimate moments.

In addition to the states of the northeast of the USA described above there is also wine production in Connecticut, Delaware, Illinois, Kentucky, Maine, Massachusetts, Minnesota, New-Hampshire, Rhode Island, Vermont, and Wisconsin.

Virginia also produces excellent sparkling wine

SOUTH AND MID EAST

Southwestern parts of the USA are generally not ideal for wine-growing with the exception of certain parts of Texas. But American determination overcomes much and after intense searching a few places have been found in which to plant vineyards.

The South and Mid East region is enormous and the vineyards are spread widely. They lie between Denver in the center, Columbia on the eastern seaboard, south to a line formed by Austin, New Orleans, and Orlando, and finally Florida. The first pioneers, but more particularly monks, planted the first vineyards in New Mexico. The territory now known as New Mexico and Texas was then part of the Spanish Empire. German immigrants introduced wine growing to Missouri, Georgia, and Carolina in the nineteenth century. Other immigrants did the same in Arkansas. These vineyards, which combined European *Vitis vinifera* with many native and hybrid varieties, have never become well known and their wines were all intended for local consumption. When wine growing and making started to catch on in America in the 1960s and 1970s, the growers of Texas, New Mexico, Georgia, and both North and South Carolina saw their opportunity. The area of vines in cultivation in Missouri, Arkansas, Iowa, Arizona, Colorado, Tennessee, Mississippi, Louisiana, and Florida has also been substantially extended and the cultivation and varieties improved during the last decade. The climate is not really favorable, for the summers are extremely hot and the winters severe. It is too dry in the north of the region but irrigation can work wonders. In the south on the other hand it is too wet but here growers seek out

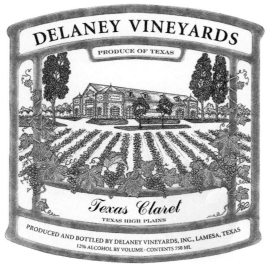

Texas also has its wine châteaux

places that are sighted at higher levels, where it is more windy and drier. The extensive area has a number of official places of origin or AVAs. These include Texas Hill Country, Bell Mountain, Fredericksburg, Escondido; New Mexico, Missouri, and Virginia.

Although there are still many native and hybrid varieties grown in these areas the houses that are really serious about wine are increasingly switching to *Vitis vinifera* varieties. There is one native grape though that springs a surprise: scuppernong, which makes a pleasing and very aromatic muscat-type sweet wine in some of the southern states. All the other native and hybrid varieties are really only intended for local consumption. The most widely used varieties of grape now are chardonnay, sauvignon blanc, riesling, trebbiano, chenin blanc, and colombard for white wines and cabernet sauvignon, cabernet franc, merlot, and zinfandel for reds.

NORTH CAROLINA

The Florentine explorer Giovanni da Verrazano reported the existence of native grapevines in North Carolina back in 1524 that could provide excellent wine. Since that time North Carolina has been inextricably linked with the local scuppernong grapes of the muscadine family (see panel). These native grapes grew extensively along the northern coastal strip of the North Carolina. Scuppernong has been *the* grape of Northern Carolina for centuries. Superb sweet wine similar to a muscatel is made from these grapes. In addi-

SCUPPERNONG IS THE FOUNDATION OF AMERICAN WINE-GROWING

Scuppernong is recorded in books as the earliest type of grapevine to be cultivated in the USA. It was first discovered in 1524 by the Florentine explorer Giovanni da Verrazano, who was in French service. Scuppernong grapevines are a variety of muscadine grapes with the botanical name of *Vitis rotundifolia*. Scuppernong vines are very productive, bearing large bronze-green grapes with a very firm skin. These yield a lot of juice with a powerful muscat aroma. Because of the size of the grapes scuppernong was originally known as the "big white grape". The name was only changed after pioneer settlers planted cuttings from parent plants close to the small town of Cuppernong. The name of scuppernong is derived from *ascopo* in the language of the Algonquin native Americans. meaning "sweet berry tree". The original name "Ascupernung" also makes reference to the river along which the *ascopo* grapevines grew. The name became scuppernong around 1800.

tion to the white scuppernong, that is a variety of muscadine, blue muscadine grapes are also used for red wine. In addition to still sweet white wine there are also sparkling wines made with scuppernong grapes. North Carolina's first officially established commercial winery was the Medoc Vineyard of Sidney Weller of 1835. This soon became twenty-five active wineries in the state. The Civil War was a major drain for the entire country and many of the winemakers did not survive it. With the peace new life was given to wine-making and there was spectacular rapid growth in the number of vineyards and wineries. At the start of the twentieth century North Carolina was the undoubted leader of American wine-growing and making. Prohibition caused a closure of activity with severe long term consequences. In 1947 North Carolina still had thirteen wineries but these had all disappeared by 1950. There was some small scale redevelopment in the 1950s and 1960s. The muscadine grapes still form the cornerstone of the local wine-growing.

The real breakthrough came in 1972 when Jack Kroustalis established what was to become North Carolina's first modern winery. At his Westbend Vineyards, Kroustalis was the first to grow *Vitis vinifera* varieties as in California, such as chardonnay, riesling, sauvignon blanc, cabernet sauvignon, merlot, and gamay.

Westbend Viognier

Jack Kroustalis harvesting Riesling, August 2002

A number of brave persons gambled on establishing vineyards in the 1970s and 1980s with varying success. The harsh winter of 1985 brought an abrupt end to the dreams of many, especially as it was followed by two very hot, dry summers. The area of vineyards in North Carolina was halved to a mere 720 acres. Westbend Vineyards of Jack Kroustalis proved to be a very successful enterprise and in 1988 Kroustalis became the first to set up a modern winery in North Carolina.

The first wine bearing the Westbend label was produced by Steve Shepard, general manager and winemaker at Westbend, in 1990. Westbend wines are made in the classic European style and are well worth getting to know because of their high quality that wins many awards, combined with continuing attractive prices.

Following the settlement of several legal disputes and administrative problems that had held back development a fresh start was made in expanding wine-growing in North Carolina in 1986. By 1999 there were fifteen commercial wineries in North Carolina and the following year this had become twenty, and twenty-two by 2001. The present vineyards consist of 864 acres in production and a further 96 acres of new vines. This total is spread across two hundred separate vineyards.

As elsewhere in the USA North, Carolina wine must contain a minimum of 75% (or 85% for export to Europe) of the grape varieties listed on the label. Winemakers are permitted to use *Vitis vinifera* varieties such as chardonnay, sauvignon blanc, riesling, viognier, sémillon, gewürztraminer, cabernet sauvignon, merlot, cabernet franc, pinot noir, shiraz (syrah), and carminé); French-American hybrids such as seyval blanc, vidal blanc, chambourcin, burdin 8753, and villard noir, *Vitis labrusca* varieties (native American types of grapevine and hybrids) such as catawba, concord, delaware, niagara, norton cynthiana, St. Vincent; and *Vitis rotundifolia* varieties (muscadines or scuppernongs) such as carlos, magnolia, sterling, nesbitt, and noble).

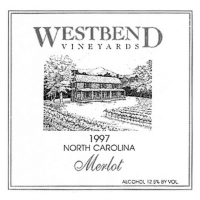

Westbend, the first modern winery of North Carolina

North Carolina vineyards at Biltmore Estate, Asheville

BILTMORE ESTATE WINERY

**Impression of Biltmore Estate –
James Valentine**

The most visited winery of the USA is not in California but in North Carolina! Biltmore Estate lies in the Blue Ridge Mountains and has offered a place to escape to for countless famous and less well-known guests for more than a hundred years. The huge residence was built by the grandson of the railway magnate, "Commodore" Cornelius Vanderbilt, a descendant of a Dutch settler of 1650 known as Jan Aertsen "van der Bilt" (from the Bilt). The majestic house was opened for friends and family on Christmas Eve, 1895 by the grandson, George Washington Vanderbilt. Countless guests enjoyed the hospitality with food from the estate farm and dairy. In 1978 the dairy was converted into the present winery.

**Biltmore Estate Winery is housed
in a converted dairy, that like the
house is 10 years old**

The Biltmore Estate Winery opened its doors to the public in 1985. The first winemaker was a talented Frenchman from Provence, Philippe Jourdain, who established the basis for today's success. He passed the baton of responsibility to the new winemaker, Bernard Delille, in 1995.

At least half a million people visit the imposing winery, the residence, and parkland each year. Nowhere else in the world has as much splendor to be seen as at the Biltmore Estate. The residence itself contains luxurious furnishings, paintings, and other works of art collected over more than a century from throughout the world. Everything has been perfectly maintained for future generations. A visit to the Biltmore Estate takes one back to a different age and another dimension with a spectacle of magnificence for visitors the like of which does not exist.

**President of the Biltmore Estate,
William A. V. Cecil Jr., samples wine
with winemaker Bernard Delille**

The vineyards of the estate are situated in gently undulating hills alongside an artificial lake that was created for the estate. Originally only native varieties of grapes were planted to which French-

The tasting room at the Biltmore Estate winery

American hybrids were later added. Today the vineyards consist of more than sixty-seven acres of European *Vitis vinifera* vines. The Biltmore Estate now produces excellent white wines from chardonnay, riesling, viognier, chenin blanc, and sauvignon blanc grapes. A very acceptable sparkling wine is also made from chardonnay according to the traditional method of Champagne.

Red wines are made from cabernet sauvignon, cabernet franc, merlot, and zinfandel. Although the Biltmore Estate Winery is a relatively new American winery it has managed to win an unbelievable number of awards in the most prestigious competitions in the USA. The inner man (and woman) is not overlooked during a visit to the vineyards, residence, and estate grounds. Seasonal cooking is offered at five different locations ranging from a bistro and café to the luxurious dining room of the

**Turning the sparkling wine as
in Champagne**

house. The estate's own fruit, vegetables, meat, and wine are brought together for an unforgettable combination. For more information about the Biltmore Estate visit http://www.biltmore.com/index.html

TEXAS

T.V. MUNSON (1843-1913)

All the European vineyards were affected by *phylloxera vastatrix* at the end of the nineteenth century. This voracious louse settled in the roots of the vines and prevented the flow of nutrients to the plant. The leaves and grapes wilted and fell off and the harvest was lost. The solution to this problem that was eagerly awaited by the whole of Europe was found by the Texan agriculturist, Thomas Volney Munson, who discovered a type of root stock that appeared to be resistant to the phylloxera lice. European growers were able to graft their own varieties of grapes onto this root stock. The French were so grateful that they awarded Munson the highest decoration in the field of agriculture that could be granted to a civilian making him a *chevalier du mérite agricole*. Munson devoted much of his life to the study and improvement of existing grape varieties. He traveled widely within America and collected hundreds of different varieties from more than forty states. He also studied the local soil conditions and climates of all the states he visited. This made him the most important expert on the subject of wine-growing in the USA. When carrying out a study in Kentucky Munson declared: 'the grape is the most beautiful, most wholesome and nutritious, most certain and most profitable fruit that can be grown. When he died in 1913 Munson was famous throughout the entire world of wine. No-one had previously involved themselves so intensely in wine as him.

Wine has been made since early times in Texas. Franciscan monks produced wine from local grapes in 1662 and at the beginning of the nineteenth century the wine experts of the day were tipping Texas as a potentially good future wine area. Trials were undertaken with numerous native and European varieties of grapevines but the results were not particularly promising. Texan wine-growing concentrated around the ancient

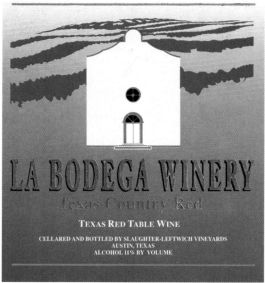

The Mexican past of Texas is still apparent

historic wine area of El Paso and the town of Dallas in 1850. In 1883 the Qualia family established the first officially recognized Texan winery of Val Verde at Del Rio. This winery remains in the hands of the Qualia family. Many vineyards around El Paso were devastated by flooding in 1897. By 1900 the production of and trade in Texan wine was fully developed. The quality of these wines though at that time was so poor and the price of both legal and illicit whiskey so low that the Texan wine business suffered greatly. Prohibition hit the remaining twenty wineries very hard and they remained in considerable financial difficulties even after the lifting of Prohibition. The laws concerning the production of wine had become much tougher and people had lost the art of winemaking.

Around 1960 California first started to establish itself as a serious wine-growing area and the Californians soon started producing wines to rival the famous French wines. Texas was not to be left behind, together with the other major wine areas of the USA: Oregon, Washington State, New York State, and Virginia. Texan wine-growing underwent a promising revival in the 1970s. The local universities researched wine-growing and production thoroughly to seek out suitable locations and varieties of grapes. It was ascertained that certain parts of Texas enjoyed the same ideal wine-growing conditions of some of the French wine regions: open, well-drained sandy soil, warm temperatures by day and cool nights, low humidity, and a constant airflow. The introduction of drip irrigation was sufficient to make Texas a potentially high quality wine area. Methods of vinification were significantly improved. This was the beginning of a new era in which greater emphasis was placed on quality than quantity. Unfortunately not everyone could benefit from these improvements because they lacked capital. Between 1993 and 1996 many large wineries got into financial difficulties. In 1986 Texas had a mere eighteen wineries, that had become twenty-three by 1995 and just a year later had dropped to just eight still operating. These economic problems were worsened by the arrival of bacteria spread by a small insect – the "glassy winged sharpshooter". The *Xylella fastidiosa* bacterium caused the worst problems ever to hit the American wine industry: Pierce's disease (see panel in section on California). In spite of all these set-backs the Texan wine industry managed to fight back. Today, with some forty-two wineries, Texas takes an important place behind California, Washington State, New York State, and Oregon. Quite soon there will be sixty wineries in Texas. This is due in part to an easing of the legal requirements so that promotion and tasting at the wineries is permissible. Regulations concerning the transport of wine within the state of Texas have also been eased. The state government is now supporting the development of Texan wine-growing within its "Go Texan" program by means of the subsidy of new planting of improved quality grapevines. In 2002 there were forty-two wineries and two hundred commercially viable vineyards producing added value to the tune of $105 million for the state of Texas. Apart from the top seven wineries the

Texan wine domains are small, family-run enterprises. In the coming decade the area of vineyards will significantly increase in order on the one hand to reduce overheads and production costs while meeting the increasing demand for the local wines. At present Texas still needs to buy in grapes or even must from other producers and even other states because output from their own vineyards is too low. It is also essential a solution is found for the continuing danger of Pierce's disease. The potential of the (mainly local) market is clearly apparent in order to promise a golden future for Texan wine. It is such a shame for both Americans and Europeans that Texan wine is difficult to buy outside of Texas but keep asking for it for persistence is rewarded!

BECKER VINEYARDS

TEXAS HILL COUNTRY
1996
CHARDONNAY
ESTATE BOTTLED

GROWN, PRODUCED AND BOTTLED BY BECKER VINEYARDS,
FREDERICKSBURG, TX BW-TX-91 ALCOHOL 12.8% BY VOLUME CONTAINS SULFITES.

Texas Hill Country is one of the Texan AVAs

CHARDONNAY

Just as elsewhere, Texan consumers want Chardonnay, the world's most popular grape. Texas is not really the ideal place to cultivate this variety though because chardonnay is susceptible to early frosts in the spring and intense heat in summer, making it liable to Pierce's disease. Despite this, more than eighty percent of Texan wines are produced from chardonnay. In the best cases the Texan chardonnay is a firm and full-bodied wine that combines perfectly with white meat or fish in a cream sauce.

LLANO
ESTACADO

Signature Edition

1997

VINTNER'S SELECT CUVÉE
SIGNATURE WHITE
TEXAS TABLE WINE

PRODUCED AND BOTTLED BY LLANO ESTACADO WINERY
LUBBOCK, TEXAS
ALCOHOL 11.2% BY VOLUME

Texas also produces blends or cuveés
in addition to varietal wines

THE WINES

Texas produces slightly more red wine than white and also some rosé/blush wines. The classic merlot and cabernet sauvignon grapes dominate the red wine production, with much smaller volume of shiraz, pinot noir, and zinfandel being used. Chardonnay is lord and master of white wine, accounting for more than eighty percent of white wine production. The other white wine grapes used are chiefly sauvignon blanc with a little gewürztraminer, riesling, and chenin blanc. In recent years experiments have been carried out with sangiovese, viognier, and muscat grapes. Texas has the following recognized areas (AVAs): Texas High Plains in the northwest, Texas Davis Mountains and Escondido Valley in the southwest, Texas Hill Country with the AVA enclave of Fredericksburg THC in the southeast, and Bell Mountains near Dallas in the northeast.

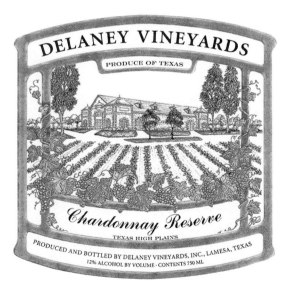

Chardonnay from Texas High Plains

SAUVIGNON BLANC

Texan sauvignon blancs are generally not top wines but most are a perfectly acceptable and tasty wine for informal drinking. Serve as an aperitif or with grilled chicken dishes, pasta, and fish.

Sauvignon Blanc from La Buena Vida

Carefully cask-aged Sauvignon Blanc

CHENIN BLANC

A lot of acceptable commercial wine is produced in Texas from chenin blanc, particularly in West-Texas. There are a few good Chenin Blanc wines to be found and these better ones combine well with roast pork or poultry.

BLUE MOUNTAIN WINES

TEXAS

Sauvignon Blanc

Jeff Davis County

1995
PRODUCED AND BOTTLED BY
BLUE MOUNTAIN VINEYARD, INC. • FORT DAVIS, TEXAS
BWTX85

Alcohol 13.4% By Volume

Robust Sauvignon Blanc for drinking with a meal

1996

TEXAS

CHENIN BLANC

PRODUCED AND BOTTLED BY LLANO ESTACADO WINERY
LUBBOCK, TEXAS
ALCOHOL 11.4% BY VOLUME

Chenin Blanc from Lubbock

RIESLING

Riesling wines from the north of Texas are worth seeking out. Unfortunately these wines are significantly undervalued even by the local consumers. They are a perfect accompaniment for both Oriental and Cajun food.

Spicy and fruity Sauvignon Blanc

MUSCAT CANELLI

These grapes originate from Piedmont in Italy and in Texas they produce simple but pleasing still and sparkling wines of the Asti (spumante) style. These are ideal wines for newcomers to wine drinking and informal celebrations. In Texas this wine is often served with chicken, salads, or cheese.

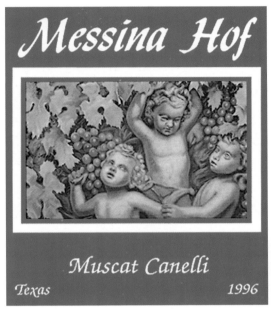

Muscat Canelli from Messina Hof

Modern floral Muscat Canelli is an ideal aperitif

CABERNET SAUVIGNON

The world's most prestigious grape thrives in Texas, particularly in areas where it is protected from severe frosts in spring time. Texan Cabernet Sauvignon from vineyards with a low yield are often of outstanding quality.

Grape Creek Cabernet Sauvignon

They are fruity (blackcurrant), slightly spicy (pepper and chocolate), full of flavor, and medium bodied and mellow on the tongue. They are a perfect accompaniment for roast or grilled beef but also combine well with a large piece of roast pork.

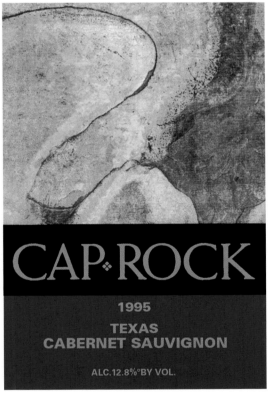

Modern Label for a classic cabernet

MERLOT

Provided the yield is kept low merlot produces excellent wines that are fruity (black cherry), of a fine body, and with good potential for laying down. Serve it with game, particularly with wild boar, duck, or a well-matured American cheddar cheese.

TEXAS
MERLOT
1994

CELLARED AND BOTTLED BY
SLAUGHTER LEFTWICH VINEYARDS
AUSTIN, TEXAS
ALCOHOL 12.5% BY VOLUME

Spiritual nectar from Austin

SANGIOVESE

First results from this variety that is still undergoing trials are remarkably good. Provided the grapes are well ripened when harvested and the new wine is aged for a time in wood the Texan Sangiovese wines are of excellent quality.

ZINFANDEL

In Texas, zinfandel produces a full-bodied red wine and some blush wine. Those from West Texas are particularly recommended. Drink them with duck, quail, or game, and with meat dishes prepared in a sturdy tomato-based sauce.

foot in America – and three centuries before California started to make wine – Florida was already producing wine. Spanish monks cultivate grapevines in order to make wine for the mass (and to consume) in their missions. Today's wine-growing in Florida though is not based on the better *Vitis vinifera* varieties of grapes. Florida's seven wineries produce a few wines from original or improved native muscadine grapes.

TEXAS HILL COUNTRY
1996
VIOGNIER
ESTATE BOTTLED

GROWN, PRODUCED AND BOTTLED BY BECKER VINEYARDS,
FREDERICKSBURG, TX BW-TX-91 ALCOHOL 13.7% BY VOLUME CONTAINS SULFITES.

The viognier grape promises much in Texas

1996

TEXAS
ZINFANDEL

PRODUCED AND BOTTLED BY LLANO ESTACADO WINERY
LUBBOCK, TEXAS
ALCOHOL 11.4% BY VOLUME

Texan zinfandel

Other wines of interest: Gewürztraminer, Viognier, Pinot Gris, Sémillon, Syrah (Shiraz), Cabernet Franc, Petit Verdot, and Pinot Noir.

FLORIDA

The Spanish were the first Europeans to appreciate the delights of Florida. They gave the area the name *florida*, meaning "blooming" in Spanish. This is a very appropriate name for a state with the finest flowers of all America and the most delicious fruit. Florida played an important role in the development of wine-making in America. A century before the "pilgrim fathers" set

NEW MEXICO

The first Spanish to visit the land that is now New Mexico in 1598 brought their own wine with them. The first vines were planted by two monks at the San Antonio de Padua mission in Senecu in 1629. This was a small native American village to the south of Socorro. In common with their other missions in Mexico and South America, the Spanish planted their standard

Pinot Noir from Texas can be very tasty

"mission" vine, an old variety of low value that is better known in South America as Pais. Senecu became the first wine-growing center of New Mexico over the course of forty years, then in 1675 it came to an abrupt halt through attacks by the local native Americans. Wine-growing ran into fresh problems once more in 1680 as a result of the Pueblo revolution. The vineyards were not replanted until 1692. At the start of the nineteenth century New Mexico was well-known and respected for its wine. The area of vineyards was significantly extended but unfortunately this happy situation did not last with severe attacks by nomadic tribes of native Americans that led to insecurity for the local wine-growing. By the late nineteenth century peace had been restored and New Mexico enjoyed a heyday. There was fresh disaster around the turn of that century when the Rio Grande broke its banks and flooded the vineyards. The polluted alkaline silt deposited rotted the roots of the vines and yields dropped dramatically until in 1920 there was no harvest.

The upsurge of wine-growing in New Mexico started in the late 1970s. New Mexico enjoys a very favorable climate for wine-growing with hot days, plenty of sun and cool nights, in desert-like surroundings. The twenty-four wineries of New Mexico, which are spread from Albuquerque, Santa Fe, and the outskirts of Las Vegas in the north to Las Cruces and Alamogordo in the south, produce a range of classic wines using *Vitis vinifera* varieties such as sauvignon blanc, chardonnay, riesling, merlot, cabernet sauvignon, pinot noir, and zinfandel.

In addition to the areas mention in the south and southeast of the USA, wine is also produced in Alabama, Arizona (very promising), Arkansas, Georgia, Louisiana, Mississippi, Oklahoma, South Carolina, and Tennessee.

NORTH-WEST

The Northwest region is better known as Washington State and Oregon. The Columbia and Snake Rivers are of vital importance to the wine-growing in this area which takes place to the southeast of Seattle, on either side of Portland. Wine-growing and production in this area is a relatively modern phenomenon. There were some trials with native varieties of grapes in the nineteenth century but it was not until the introduction of irrigation projects in the twentieth century that wine-growing on a larger scale became possible. The real breakthrough in Oregon came in the late 1970s when the more seriously-minded growers planted European varieties. Pinot Noir from Oregon has now become famous world wide thanks to the investment of several top French companies such as Drouhin of Beaune.

The climate in the northwest of the USA is moderate in but almost arid and hence desert-like in Washington State where reliance on irrigation is total. The winters in Washington State are also colder than in Oregon. The soil varies from loam in Oregon to volcanic subsoil in the state of Washington. The choice of grape is hence of great importance. Various varieties are grown in the two main AVA areas of Washington State (Puget Sound, Columbia Valley, Red Mountain, Yakima Valley, and Walla Walla Valley) and West Pacific (includes Oregon, Willamette Valley, and Umpqua Valley). Oregon is dominated by pinot noir with some chardonnay while Washington State's main varieties are cabernet sauvignon and merlot. The picture is completed in Washington State with chenin blanc, sémillon, and sauvignon blanc, while Oregon produces reasonable to good pinot gris. Of course results vary between winemakers and in Oregon in particular years can vary enormously due to different weather conditions. Despite this the best of the wines from here are truly great wines.

OREGON

OREGON PINOT NOIR

Some Pinot Noir wines from Oregon can hold their own against the best French wines. They are superb in color, have seductive bouquets of red and black fruits such as blackberry, blackcurrant, red currant, and cherry, and touches of herbs and spices, including sweetwood, and a complex and harmonious texture. They are also elegant with a refined taste. There may also be suggestions of truffle, exotic woods, and a good balance between acidity, alcohol, fruit, and tannin, with a prolonged aftertaste. These wines can be kept for at least five to ten years when they develop a nose of plum, mushrooms, humus, leather, and herbs.

Serve this sensual wine while it is still young with beef or poultry in a red wine mushroom sauce, matured wine should be served with mild wild game dishes and semi-mature cheeses. Drinking temperature is 12–14 °C (53.6–57.2 °F) when young and 14–16 °C (57.2–60.8 °F) when mature.

EYRIE VINEYARDS: THREE CENTURIES OF WINE HISTORY IN OREGON

In the mid 1960s nobody imagined it was possible to grow pinot noir in Oregon. The experts considered it was too cold and above all too wet. Perhaps they had overlooked the fact that pinot noir seems to thrive on the edge in conditions where it is just about impossible and yet it does. Such conditions occur in Burgundy and Alsace that are both completely unsuitable for pinot noir and yet...David Lett ignored the advice of the experts and decided to try. In 1975 his Pinot Noir wines proved themselves equal to the grandest Burgundies during the great wine competitions. In 1976 the Eyrie Pinot Noir even achieved second place behind none less than a Chambolle Musigny 1959 during a tasting at Beaune in Burgundy. This was probably the first signal that led to such a well-respected wine house as Drouhin to later decided to set up in Oregon. David Lett was a pioneer of the Oregon wine industry. Many had problems with and disbelieved his visionary approach. Some forty years on David Lett is now regarded as one of the best producers of Pinot Noir in the world. But Lett is not just America's best Pinot Noir specialist, he was also one of the first to believe in the potential of the best American Pinot Noir specialist, he is also one of the first to believe in the potential in Oregon for Pinot Gris. Lett also produces superb Chardonnay, and uniquely for America also non sparkling Pinot Meunier.

Renowned Oregon Pinot Noir from Eyrie Vineyards'

Oregon Pinot Gris'

In addition to the outstanding quality of Eyrie wines I wish to draw attention also to an important feature of the approach of this praiseworthy winery. All Eyrie wines are made from grapes that are organically grown, without the use of herbicides and insecticides. Any disease is dealt with by natural means without application of chemicals. The yield is sensibly low. The vineyards are not irrigated and the vines are propagated in the old-fashioned *marcottage* manner. This all takes time and costs money but for the discerning consumer it is well worth while to know what is in the glass. The quality approach of David Lett also applies to the cellar where the wine does not undergo any rigorous handling other than a light filtration before bottling. Eyrie Vineyards also do not use storage in wood as a means of increasing flavor but as a slow process of maturing the wine. The cask's function is solely to age a basically good wine and not to blur the edges of any faults. The quality of the wine is determined by the grapes and hence it is important to pick them when they are fully ripe. The intrinsic character of the grapes is best revealed with gentle handling and as little pumping and clarification and chilling as possible and without other artificial methods. David Lett and his wife Diana of Eyrie Vineyards have but one rule: to make wine that they enjoy drinking. Eyrie Vineyards produces superb Pinot Noir, Chardonnay, Pinot Gris, and Pinot Blanc. A characteristic of the wines from this domain is the potential for laying down for a lengthy period of wines such as their Chardonnay and Pinot Noir.

WASHINGTON STATE

The first vineyards were planted in the state of Washington at Fort Vancouver on the Hudson's Bay in 1825. In the early twentieth century vineyards could be found throughout Washington State that had been planted by pioneers from France, Germany, and Italy. The original plantings of native hybrids gradually gave way to cultivation of improved varieties. The first officially recognized wine-growing area in the state was the Walla Walla Valley. Irrigation, using water from the run off from the melting ice caps of the Cascade Mountains, is significantly important for the state's wine-growing. The nature of the loose, volcanic soil, combined with warmth and a dry climate are also important. It soon

became apparent that French and Italian varieties of grapes in particular thrived in Washington. The first wineries were established in the Yakuma Valley just before the outbreak of World War I. Prohibition led to a long cessation of activity but the re-emergence after its repeal was very strong. In 1938 there were forty-two wineries in Washington State and the great commercial success of the Californian wine industry led to a lively upsurge in Washington State in the 1960s. The first of the truly commercial wineries was Columbia Crest Winery followed by Château Ste. Michelle. These pioneers opened the way for countless new wineries. In 2001 there were at least 170 commercial wineries in Washington compared with nineteen in 1981. Wine-growing is flourishing and the wines produced are shipped throughout the USA and to some forty countries around the world. Washington State occupies the second spot behind California for the production of quality wines. The area of vineyards planted with *Vitis vinifera* varieties in Washington in 2001 was almost 28,800 acres.

Canoe Ridge Estate Vineyard, Château Ste. Michelle

The future of the Washington State wine industry rests in the hands of consumers. There does not appear to be any apparent limitation to enormous expansion. The choice also seems entirely open as to which grapes can be grown and which sorts of wine can be made according to consumer demands. Everything seems to be possible in Washington State. The dominant grapes in 2002 were: chardonnay, riesling, sauvignon blanc, sémillon, chenin blanc, and viognier for white wines and merlot, cabernet sauvignon, syrah (shiraz), cabernet franc, and sangiovese for reds.

Columbia Valley Merlot

CHÂTEAU STE. MICHELLE – WASHINGTON STATE'S LEADING LIGHT

The Château Ste. Michelle wine domain was established in 1934 and is the oldest winery of Washington State and easily the best. Château Ste. Michelle tested *Vitis Vinifera* varieties right from the start and these proved to thrive in the state. In this northern state the vineyards get two hours more sunshine in summer than California. This provides the grapes with the extra time needed for ripening. With the heat of the long summer days and cool nights the grapes develop a great deal of flavor and aromatic strength, complexity, and fresh acidity. The wines of Château Ste. Michelle are of impeccable quality and provide a pleasing surprise. No wine domain in California has such a high percentage of wines appraised at or above 90 as Château Ste. Michelle. The single vineyard wines of Canoe Ridge and especially Cold Creek are among the very best in the world.

Château Ste. Michelle produces a number of "ranges": Columbia Valley Wines, Single Vineyard Wines, Reserve Wines, and a pair of top wines from a joint venture: Col Solare (with Piero Antinori) and Eroica (Riesling Dry produced in cooperation with the leading German winemaker Ernst Loosen).

Château Ste. Michelle Estate

COLUMBIA VALLEY

Columbia Valley is a mere 187 miles wide and about 20 miles long. It is home to four recognized AVAs: Columbia Valley (generic area name), Red Mountain, Yakima Valley, and Walla Walla Valley (sub-areas). The total area of vineyards amounts to some 15,600 acres.

Columbia Crest vineyards

THE WINES

CHARDONNAY

Chardonnay is the most widely planted variety of grape in Washington State. Unlike Californian Chardonnay, that is often powerful and ponderous, Washington Chardonnay is fresh and elegant. The bouquet is dominated by hints of green apple with background suggestions of vanilla and butter with appropriate cask aging. It is delicious with grilled lobster, fish (salmon and turbot), scallops, or veal (in a white wine, lemon, or vanilla sauce). Cheese lovers should not miss the combination with a delicious Cougar Gold from the Creamery of Washington State University. Drinking temperature is 10–12 °C (50–53.6 °F).

RIESLING

Washington Riesling wines are fairly floral in their bouquet, with other aromas of apricots and peaches. The semi-sweet, ice-wine, and late-harvest wines produced from grapes infected by *Botrytis* are literally fabulous. Most Washington Riesling though is vinified as off-dry. Serve the ordinary off-dry or semi-sweet Riesling at table with crab, chicken, and fruit salads. It is also tasty with soft cream cheeses. The late-harvest and ice-wines are an ideal accompaniment for crâme brulée, sabayon with fresh white or yellow fruits, or dishes with warm peaches. Drinking temperature is 8–10 °C (46.4–50 °F), with coolest temperature for the sweeter wines.

SEMILLON

Sémillon wines from the state of Washington are well known and much loved. Although the best of them can mature superbly to develop a rich honey-like character with overwhelming bouquet of flowers and nuts, most are drunk while young. People are clearly delighted with the broad range of aromas from fresh apple and citrus fruit to melon, pear, and vanilla. The relatively low acidity of the grapes makes them prone to infection with *botrytis*, but this yields superb late harvest wines. Young Sémillon combines well with fresh fruit salads or as an accompaniment for both savory and sweet salads incorporating e.g. chicken, grapefruit, and/or pineapple. The more mature late-harvest wines demand hot food in the form of peaches or apricots, perhaps with a using the same wine. Drinking temperature is 8–10 °C (46.4–50 °F) with coolest temperature for the sweetest wines.

SAUVIGNON BLANC/FUME BLANC

Sauvignon Blanc wines are also sold under the Californian name of Fumé Blanc. These are popular wines that are fresh and possess vegetal aromas from grass to pineapples and grapefruit. Sauvignon Blanc wines may also contain a small amount of sémillon to produce a mellower result. An excellent aperitif but ideal too for picnics and informal receptions. Drinking temperature is 8–10 °C (46.4–50 °F).

CHENIN BLANC

Well-known from French Loire wines from Vouvray and elsewhere, in Washington chenin grapes produce fresh and fruity wines with floral overtones. Generally green apples and apple blossom can be discerned in the bouquet. These wines are mostly delicate and elegant, ranging from dry to off-dry but there are also late-harvest versions. Serve as for Sémillon and Riesling. Drinking temperature is 8–10 °C (46.4–50 °F).

GEWÜRZTRAMINER

Gewürztraminer grapes were popular from the outset in Washington, largely because of their hardiness to winter conditions. The Gewürztraminer wines are characteristic of the grape, with a full flavor and heady aromatic properties suggesting allspice, tropical fruit, citrus fruit, and a hint of rose petals. They can be dry, off-dry, or slightly sweet. Gewürztraminer is delicious with a crab salad, Oriental sweet and sour dishes, but also with pork and poultry. Drinking temperature is 9–10 °C (48.2–50 °F).

For the sake of completeness there are also entirely acceptable Viognier, Pinot Gris, and Muscat Canelli wines produced in Washington, together with some average Müller-Thurgau, Madeleine Angevine, and Aligoté wines.

Columbia Crest Winery

MERLOT

Washington State's Merlot wines possess the same classic characteristics of their like from Bordeaux but are more full bodied and higher in alcohol. On the other hand, because of their northerly position, they are much fresher and more elegant than the Merlot from California. In addition to the classic bouquet of ripe sweet cherries a Washington Merlot also offers hints of redcurrants, mint, cedar wood (cigar box), and spices such as nutmeg and cardamom. This Merlot is multifaceted and combines well with lamb and beef dishes – preferably grilled or roasted – but also with oven-baked pasta and also surprisingly with grilled salmon. Drinking temperature is 16–17 °C (60.8–62.6 °F).

CABERNET SAUVIGNON

The Cabernet Sauvignon from Washington is fairly classic in style, firm, but fruity, and complex. It needs to be given time to mature but despite this is drinkable fairly quickly. Aromas of blackcurrant, black cherry, chocolate, leather, mint, fresh green herbs, freshly-sliced green pepper etc. can all be detected in a Washington Cabernet Sauvignon. The more complex the wine is the greater the range of its bouquet. Many Washington Cabernet Sauvignons are not wholly made with cabernet sauvignon grapes. To make the wine drinkable sooner up to twenty-five percent of merlot and/or cabernet franc is added. For sales to Europe this is restricted to fifteen percent). Serve Washington Cabernet Sauvignon (e.g. Columbia Crest) with pasta, braised or roast pork, *filet mignon* or pepper steak. Surprisingly delicious if a little decadent is the combination of Cabernet Sauvignon with a chocolate mousse of plain chocolate containing not less than seventy-five percent cocoa – very sensual! The best wines (e.g. Château Ste. Michelle) deserve a fine piece of red meat (beef, lamb, or game) from the oven, grill, or barbecue. Another tip for culinary freaks: try some Single Vineyard Cabernet Sauvignon of Château Sainte Michelle with a hard, well-aged sheep's milk cheese rubbed with cocoa from Sally Jackson of Oroville, Washington. Drinking temperature is 16–18 °C (60.8–64.4 °F).

SYRAH

Syrah is fairly new to Washington State but its share of the acreage is growing rapidly. This famous Rhône grape (also known as Shiraz) produces full-bodied and complex wines here that have considerable aromatic properties (pepper, other spices, blackcurrant, sultanas, coffee, and leather). Syrah is an ideal wine for stews of beef, lamb, or game but is also delicious with grilled and roast meat, particularly if flavored with garlic and Provençal herbs. For the adventurous the combination of Syrah with the exciting cheeses of Sally Jackson of Oroville, Washington can yield a pleasurable evening. Try the mixed goat and cow's milk cheese with herbs, mixed goat and cow with jalapeƒo and garlic, the plain aged, the flavored goat's milk (dried tomato, oregano, basil, garlic and dill, garlic and chives), the grape leaf wrapped aged cheese, the flavored cow's milk, the hard, well-aged cheeses, and de chestnut leaf-wrapped sheep's milk cheese! Drinking temperature is 16–17 °C (60.8–62.6 °F).

CABERNET FRANC

Cabernet franc has long been disregarded as a classic grape except for blending. In Washington though their trials with cabernet franc have been very pleasing. Cabernet Franc wines are pleasingly fruity with a hint of spices with coffee and are fresh without dominant tannin, and very elegant. Delicious with all meat, poultry, duck breast, patés, and terrines. Drinking temperature is 16–17 °C (60.8–62.6 °F).

To complete the picture Washington also makes a wide variety of other wines from lemberger grapes, together with excellent Sangiovese, Grenache, Zinfandel, Nebbiolo, and Pinot Noir wines. The output of these wines is very small, making them hard to find.

IDAHO

Geographically Idaho forms part of the northwest region of the USA but few will have heard of Idaho as a wine-producing state. Best known for potatoes, Idaho does however have vineyards. In 2000 these amounted to a mere 1,056. acres, with only 696 acres in production, but it is anticipated that by 2005 this will have grown by sixty percent to 2,040 acres. The number of wineries is also growing (sixteen in 2001) and considerable investment is being made for each winery. If this investments prove successful then a considerable increase in the area of vineyards can be anticipated. Around 48,000 acres are available for planting as vineyards in Idaho.

Idaho's history of wine-growing dates back to the late nineteenth century when the first settlers arrived on the land. Between 1872 and Prohibition wine-growing flourished in Idaho. During Prohibition and thereafter every trace of wine-growing vanished from Idaho and it was not until the 1970s before new interest arose following the success of California and Oregon. The first modern wineries date from this time. The vineyards were planted in the Snake River valley and an area called Sunny Slope. Idaho's climate is cooler than that of California. During the plant's vegetative cycle the days are very hot and the nights are cool, strengthening the grape's aromatic properties, color, and extract. The severe winters and open structure of the volcanic soil help to keep disease at bay. The difference in temperature between winter and summer on the one hand and between day and night on the other ensure the grapes can be harvested when fully ripe while ensuring a good balance between sweetness and acidity.

At present only a limited range of wines have been proven for Idaho wines. These are chardonnay, chenin blanc, riesling, fumé (sauvignon) blanc, pinot gris, sémillon, and gewürztraminer for white wines, and cabernet sauvignon, cabernet franc, pinot noir, merlot, and syrah for red wines. Researchers are busy conducting trials with experimental grapes and new clones to determine which other varieties are most suitable for Idaho. At the present time it seems as if malbec, petit verdot, and dolcetto offer the best potential for red wines. It is far too early to determine what the quality of Idaho wines will be put the potential is enormous.

CALIFORNIA

California is subdivided into six main areas. From north to south these are the North Coast (north of San Francisco, home of Napa Valley, Sonoma, Carneros wines), Humboldt (on the banks of the Sacramento River), Sierra Foothills (at the foot of the Sierra Mountains east of Sacramento), Central Coast (south of San Francisco to slightly north of Los Angeles), Central Valley (a huge area on the banks of the San Joaquin River), and South Coast (between Los Angeles and San Diego).

Franciscan monks from Spain were the first to risk the effort of planting vines here in the eighteenth century. The wine produced was for their own use. A Frenchman from Bordeaux with the rather appropriate name of Jean Louis Vignes saw the possibilities here in 1830 and he imported countless European varieties of grapes. Things really took off though after the Gold Rush. The growers left the south alone and concentrated their efforts in the central and northern areas where there was a ready market with the large city of San Francisco. The first Californian winery was established in Sonoma in 1857 by Count Agoston Haraszthy.

The general quality of those wines was from modest to poor. In those days California made ponderous syrupy wines of little character and freshness. This was the start of the huge American bulk wine industry. Prohibition from 1919 to 1933, which banned the production of alcoholic drink on a commercial scale, was a major blow for the Californian wine trade. It seemed for a long time as though the growers would not survive this crisis. It was not until the 1970s that changes started to take place. Wine making became a recognized profession and people from California went to study at first hand in Europe with the best wine-makers. The result is nothing less than spectacular.

There are still many 'wimpy wines' (plonk) in California, but quality is becoming more important than quantity with both the big business and small wineries. Yet many still regard California as a massive industrialized wine region with its enormous vineyards, wineries like palaces, batteries of high towering stainless steel storage tanks etc. This image has remained, with some of the wine domains in the Napa Valley looking more like "Disney Wine World" than serious wine producers. Despite this the numbers of smaller producers is growing in places like the Sonoma Valley, and Carneros. These growers and makers not only know what they are talking about, they also bring much verve and passion to their wine making.

Hence the massive rows of readily salable Chardonnay and Cabernet Sauvignon are becoming smaller in scale and some even dare to replace them with specialist varieties such as Viognier for white wines and Barbera, Sangiovese, Syrah, and Grenache for reds.

WINE AREAS

The climate in California varies enormously. The coastal climate could be compared with that of the Mediterranean with hot summers and mild winters, the summers in Central Valley are particularly dry and hot, while the regions immediately behind the coast are much wetter and mistier. The temperatures are highest in the Central Valley and most moderate on the coast. The vineyards on the North Coast experience the most rainfall. The soil also varies immensely, due in part to the many earthquakes that have hit the region: from silts and sediments to volcanic sub-layers. However Californians tend to pay little attention to the terrain, usually selecting a grape based on its climatic preferences rather than the soil suitability. In the past, vines were planted in the most fertile ground, just like any other crops, in order to achieve the maximum yield. This, together with the high production explains why the wines were so unrefined and lacking in character. Thankfully the majority of the wine producers have abandoned this policy.

The following guaranteed places of origin are the best known in California:

Mendocino County, Lake County, Sonoma County (includes the famous Russian River Valley and Sonoma Valley), Napa Valley, Los Carneros, Central Valley, Sierra Foothills, Livermore Valley, Santa Cruz Mountains, Monterey County, San Joaquin Valley, San Luis Obispo Valley, and Santa Barbara County.

NEW AVAS FOR CALIFORNIA

In addition to the existing thirteen AVAs of the Napa Valley a fourteenth has been added. This is a small sub-area between Napa and Yountville. The new AVA is named Oak Knoll and it is characterized by a relatively cool microclimate. Only Carneros, which is closer to San Pablo Bay (an inlet within San Francisco Bay) is cooler than Oak Knoll.

At the time of writing a second new Californian AVA was being created: Capay Valley, just outside the northern boundary of Napa Valley, in Yolo County.

A definitive decision appears to have been made concerning the efforts to create a further AVA for the whole coastal strip of California, to be called California Coastal. Contrary to the argument of certain local major producers the government has decided the coast strip is insufficiently distinctive in character to justify a separate AVA.

Oregon Pinot Noir from Drouhin, the famous French wine house

This splendid Pinot Noir could quite easily have come from the Bourgogne

Domaine Taittinger in Carneros

Irrigation is permitted throughout California but is not necessary everywhere. The most popular grape varieties are chardonnay, colombard, chenin blanc, sauvignon blanc, riesling, gewürztraminer, pinot blanc, and viognier for white wines with cabernet sauvignon, pinot noir, merlot, barbera, sangiovese, syrah, and grenache for reds. The classic Californian grape variety of zinfandel is starting to play an increasingly important role.

Ken Brown from the Byron Vineyard and Winery (Mondavil) is one of the best young wine makers in California

Mediterranean wines, such as this "IO" (Byron Winery) are very promising

drawn out and costly law suits in the American courts, the Champagne houses have had to accept that names such as 'Californian Champagne' are legally permitted here. They are however restricted to the domestic markets so that the so-called Californian Champagne must be sold in Europe merely as 'sparkling wine'. American sparkling wines are made in both pink (rosé) and white and from quite dry to sweet. The driest is the Brut, followed by Extra Dry, Dry/Sec, and Demi-Sec, which is the sweetest. Only the highest quality sparklers are made in the USA by the traditional method with secondary fermentation taking place in the bottle. Most are produced by the closed cuve method. This shows that some people still think of wine as a product to be made down to a price. A third method is the transfer method that combines aspects of both the other two.

California has a number of excellent biological wines

WINES

You may encounter thousands of different types of Californian wine because of the great differences in climate, soil, wine making method, yield, and target group for marketing. The "wimpy wines" largely intended for the undiscerning local population and the countless tourists, should be ignored in preference for the "real wines".

CALIFORNIAN CHAMPAGNE (CHAMPAIGN)

The powerful houses of Champagne forbid everyone from using their name outside the designated area of Champagne in France yet you will find the term 'Champagne' used in the USA on other wines. To avoid long

Excellent wines from the Napa Valley

The Zinfandel becoming ever more the face of Californian wine

The results are of better quality than with the ordinary closed cuve method but costs are lower than the traditional method.

Whether white or rosé, some of these wines are well worth discovering. Two of the leading Champagne houses make good 'Champagne' style wines in America. Those of Mumm are good while the Taittinger product is excellent. The Mumm wines from the Napa Valley are livelier and more unruly than those of Taittinger, which come from Carneros, and are more grown-up and full-bodied. Light sparkling wines are excellent aperitifs, with the stronger varieties being highly suitable for accompanying a meal. Drinking temperature is 6–8 °C (42.8–46.4 °F).

CHARDONNAY

Chardonnay is regarded as the best variety of white wine grape in the world. Many people maintain that the best Chardonnay comes from the Sonoma Valley. Certainly there are remarkably good Chardonnays made in California, especially in Sonoma County. Californian Chardonnay is full-bodied, broad, rich, and very aromatic with hints of fig, pineapple, ripe apple, melon, citrus fruit, and honey. The wine is further improved by cask maturing in oak with notes of toast, nuts, vanilla, butter, toffee, and butterscotch etc. These Chardonnays are not cheap but if you choose a good one you will find it is sumptuous. An ideal accompaniment for grilled seafood, (lobster, crayfish) veal and poultry (turkey) as well as with soft cheeses. Drinking temperature is 10–12 °C (50–53.6 °F).

SAUVIGNON BLANC

Sauvignon Blanc wines often possess a light smoky aroma and can be notably vegetal too with hints of green olives, freshly mown grass, dill, and fennel, but generally are also very fruity with fresh fig, melon, and citrus fruit etc. to be discovered. The wine is fresh but not firm like a white Bordeaux. Although most Sauvignon Blancs are dry, you may also encounter some sweeter examples. Serve this white wine with seafood, veal, (with green olives for example), pasta with pesto, or with salads served with baked goats cheese. Drinking temperature is 8–10 °C (46.4–50 °F).

CHENIN BLANC

This grape is highly popular in California, especially in the Central Valley, where it is used to make fresh, fruity, and inexpensive wines. This light, and fruity version is made in Sonoma and is ideal for a 'happy hour' with friends or with light informal lunches. Drinking temperature is 8–10 °C (46.4–50 °F).

JOHANNESBERG RIESLING/WHITE RIESLING

Do not anticipate an elegant and refined Riesling from California, rather a firm white wine that is fresh, fruity (melon) for everyday drinking, perhaps with poultry. Only a handful of winemakers succeed in imparting great elegance that evokes distant memories of the Rieslings of Alsace or Germany. There are also a few good Late Harvest Rieslings. Drinking temperature is 8–10 °C (46.4–50 °F) coolest for sweeter wines.

Wonderful Domaine Carneros Brut from Taittinger

Beringer Chardonnay

Unfiltered Chardonnay from the Napa Valley

GEWÜRZTRAMINER

Most of the local Gewürztraminer is made as sweet wine with floral notes, suggestions of muscat, a hint of spice, and sultry, but Gewürztraminer Dry is becoming increasingly popular. Many Americans drink the sweet or slightly sweet 'off-dry' Gewürztraminer as an aperitif.

I personally prefer this wine as an accompaniment to roast turkey or glazed baked ham. The dry Gewürztraminer is excellent with chicken and oriental dishes. Drinking temperature is 10–12 °C (50–53.6 °F) dry, 8–10 °C (46.4–50 °F) off-dry and 6–8 °C (42.8–46.4 °F) sweet.

1999

ROBERT MONDAVI WINERY

NAPA VALLEY

FUMÉ BLANC

WHITE WINE
PRODUCT OF USA   750 mL 13.5% alc./vol.   VIN BLANC
PRODUIT DES É.-U.

Fumé Blanc or rather Sauvignon Blanc

WHITE ZINFANDEL/BLUSH WINES/WHITE GRENACHE

Zinfandel and grenache are famous blue grapes but there are also white wines made with them. The wine is of course not truly white but a light pink. These are quite recent creations that are mainly aimed at the younger market. Most wines are not entirely dry and some of them are even slightly sweet. They have a nose in which vanilla ice cream with strawberries can be found in the White Zin or red fruit in the White Grenache. These are typical outdoor wines to be drunk at a picnic or out on the patio. A startling wine with cold pasta dishes or rice salads. Drinking temperature is 10–12 °C (50–53.6 °F).

MUSCAT

Muscat grapes yield sultry sweet wines that in addition to their recognizable aroma of fresh muscat grapes also contain hints of apricot, peach, and ripe pear. This wine is too commonly served in California with foie gras, although this is a far from ideal combination. The same is true of its combination with sweet desserts. It is far better to drink this wine with fresh fruit desserts or for itself on a hot and sensual summer's evening. Drinking temperature is 6–8 °C (42.8–46.4 °F).

CABERNET SAUVIGNON

The name is often unceremoniously shorted to 'Cab'. This classic is one of the better wines of California. It is dark colored and very aromatic with grassy and vege-

Famous Cabernet Sauvignon from Beringer (Napa Valley)

tal hints here, plus suggestions of green tea and leaves. The wine is quite full-bodied. The wine can be undrinkable when young through an over-exposure to new wood. After a few years it develops its full beauty with a nose in which cherry, berries, herbs, currant, cedar wood, tobacco, vanilla, mint, pepper, and chocolate can be discerned. It is very much a wine to serve with haute cuisine. Roast lamb or beef, wildfowl, or even with the traditional roast turkey at Thanksgiving. Drinking temperature is 16–17 °C (60.8–62.6 °F).

MERLOT

Somewhat similar to Cabernet Sauvignon but much softer and more rounded. Merlot is approachable much sooner than Cabernet Sauvignon. It is a real seducer with nose of black cherry, plum, toffee, chocolate, orange, mint, cedar wood, green tea, and violets. The structure is full-bodied and rich while the taste is velvet smooth. An excellent wine with delicate red meat dishes but can also be drunk with white meat and poultry. Drinking temperature is 14–16 °C (57.2–60.8 °F).

PINOT NOIR

Pinot noir is able to combine complexity and elegance like no other grape. It requires some courage to plant pinot noir in California but perhaps not in Los Carneros. The desired results will not be achieved every year but when the weather permits, the results are overwhelming. Californian Pinot Noirs are quick seducers that are fresh and fruity (cherry) with a hint of herbs and mushrooms, but also a sensual nose containing coffee and cedar wood. The texture is full-bodied, elegant, complex, and velvet smooth. Ideal with chicken dishes,

RED WINE   PRODUCT OF USA   750 mL 13.0% alc./vol.
VIN ROUGE   PRODUIT DES É.-U.

1998

WOODBRIDGE
Twin Oaks

CALIFORNIA   Merlot

Woodbridge Californian Merlot

especially when prepared in a red wine sauce, mushrooms, and all grilled courses from pork to fresh tuna! Drinking temperature is 14–16 °C (57.2–60.8 °F) 16–17 °C (60.8–62.6 °F or the stronger varieties).

ZINFANDEL

This is the Californian grape. Zinfandel remains recognizable for the suggestions of vanilla ice cream with strawberries or raspberries in its bouquet, whether made as white, rosé, or red wine. The wine is fairly full-bodied, rich and tannic, with a peppery undertone. The whole of America loves its 'Zin' and Europe is also now starting to enjoy it too. An ideal wine for with the American barbecue with large chunks of meat, (prime rib, T bone steak, etc.), or with Italian dishes or American pizzas. The enormous variety and tastes of the Zinfandel means that there is something for everyone. Drinking temperature is 14–16 °C (57.2–60.8 °F).

Outstanding Carneros Pinot Noir from Taittinger

Full, ripe Zinfandel from the Napa Valley

Fascinating Petite Syrah from a smaller winery

IS ZINFANDEL ORIGINALLY FROM CROATIA?

Since the 1960s it has been suggested that zinfandel and primitivo grapes were one and the same. The oenologist and researcher August Coheen of UC Davis was the proponent of this theory. It was suggested that zinfandel and primitivo were related and perhaps also plavac mali grapes of the former Yugoslavia. In 1998 scientists decided to take samples from all the well-known and lesser-known varieties of grapes in the world in order to analyze their DNA. One of these researchers, Carole Meredith, specialized in seeking the true identity of zinfandel. She visited the Dalmatian coast and collected around 150 samples from which she analyzed the DNA back in California, together with her Croatian colleagues, Ivan Pejic and Edi Maletic. At first everything seemed to point to zinfandel and plavac mali indeed being the same variety of grapevine but further research revealed that zinfandel is not the same as plavac mali (which is probably very closely related) but that zinfandel is in fact really the Croatian crljenak variety. This was proven by extensive analysis of the DNA. It remains a possibility that crljenak grapes came to Croatia from Albania. This seemed bad news for all the Italian companies who called their Primitivo wines "Zinfandel" because of its popularity for sale both to the USA and in Europe. The same was also true of astute Californians who sold their "ordinary Zinfandel" as Primitivo.

The ATF (Bureau of Alcohol, Tobacco and Firearms) decided on 16 April 2002 that the names "zinfandel" and "primitivo" are synonymous from a legal standpoint. This means that despite the DNA research which shows that zinfandel and primitivo are not the same variety of grapevine but variants of the crljenak, either zinfandel or primitivo may in future be used on labels. It is even permissible to use both names. The ATF decision was based on an earlier ruling by the European Commission which declared the two grapes identical. Californian producers were not very happy with this decision as they have established zinfandel as a characteristically Californian grape variety. The Italians and other Europeans though argue that there are no reasons to protect the Zinfandel name in view of the world-wide misuse by the Californians of the name Champagne. This story is surely not yet over.

ZINFANDEL ADVOCATE & PRODUCERS (ZAP)

An increasing group of Californians have been engaged on a friendly crusade since 1991 for the recognition of zinfandel as a typical Californian product. You can visit their web site for the latest information about the zinfandel sage at http://www.zinfandel.org.

PETITE SYRAH/SYRAH

These are two different grape varieties which both originate from the French Rhône. Both produce substantial and firm wines that are deeply colored and very aromatic with hints of blueberry, raspberry, fruit jam, pepper, and herbs. This robust, tannin rich wine should be drunk with hearty, well herbed meat dishes or with grilled beef, lamb or wild game. Drinking temperature is 16–17 °C (60.8–62.6 °F).

GAMAY/GAMAY BEAUJOLAIS

This is a very fruity wine that is fresh and mellow with little acidity or tannin. It is ideal for the newcomer to wine, perhaps with chicken or turkey, or just for a relaxing picnic. Drinking temperature is 12–14 °C (53.6–57.2 °F).

THE CENTRAL WINE STATES

Wine is also made in the USA outside the four major zones. Not always on the same scale, and certainly not on a par with California, Oregon, Washington State, and New York State, but this does not necessarily mean quality is lower. The results are not always convincing from everywhere but those pioneering wine-production in these other areas are convinced that they will achieve quality wines. There are certainly wines worth discovering in each of these states listed. Get to know them.

COLORADO

Colorado is a promising wine state. The wonderful valleys of the Rocky Mountains lend themselves perfectly for wine-growing because of the low humidity, hot summers, and cool winters. These are the perfect conditions to make wine with wonderful aromatic properties.

Many of those living in Colorado themselves have no idea that wine has been made in their state for more than one hundred years, leave alone the average American or European. Wine-growing virtually disappeared tough in the previous century as a result of Prohibition. The vineyards were grubbed up and replaced with orchards or other crops. The present vineyards are of much more recent origins. The first of the modern wineries in Colorado was that of Ivancie (Grand Valley) in 1968. The real rebuilding of the wine industry in Colorado though began a little later in 1978, when Jim and Anne Seewald planted their Colorado Mountains Vineyards, now known as Colorado Cellars. Classic European vines have been planted almost wherever possible. The wine from Colorado have enjoyed a fair degree of recognition in national competitions and the best wines are both very delicious and hence more expensive. The quality wines from Colorado that have made a name for themselves are primarily Chardonnay, Riesling, and Merlot.

Colorado's vineyards are sited in high altitude valleys and plateaus at a height of 3,965–7,962 ft! This makes Colorado among the highest situated wine-growing places in the world and the highest situated commercial winery is probably the Terror Creek Winery at an altitude of 7,091 ft. This altitude is necessary to prevent the grapes being damaged by excessive heat. The high position ensures plenty of sunlight and warmth for the vineyards by day together with the ideal cooling at night that ensures the grapes are ripened fully with a high level of sugars, are concentrated, and possess considerable aromatic properties. The night-time cooling also ensures plenty of acidity. Life is not easy though for the growth, blossoming, and harvest must all take place within a period of six to seven months. The severe frosts here make life for the wine-grower very difficult for the rest of the year. The temperature can drop to well below freezing with winds above 100 m.p.h. and hail as big as a baseball that can destroy a crop in a matter of minutes. The microclimates in the river valleys fortunately provide some protection for wine-growing.

Approximately eighty-five percent of the total vineyard area of Colorado is planted with *Vitis vinifera* varieties of grapes. The most widely planted is chardonnay, followed by merlot, which between them account for almost half the total area. Far behind these come riesling, gewürztraminer, sauvignon blanc, viognier, cabernet sauvignon, cabernet franc, pinot noir, and shiraz (syrah). The total area of vineyards in Colorado amounts to 624 acres (a third of which has been planted since 1998). This is shared between more than forty commercial wineries which are mainly small-scale family-run affairs.

There are four wine areas in Colorado: Front Range (around Denver), The Rockies (around Salida and Aspen), Four Corners Area/Delta/Montrose (close to the towns of Cortez and Durango stretching as far as Paonia and Hotchkiss), and the most important on being Grand Valley/West Elks/Western Slope. This last-named area on the banks of the Colorado River also has the greatest concentration of commercial wineries in Colorado. The vineyards are sited on the Grand Mesa tableland in Delta and Montrose Counties. The best Colorado wines originate from this area that possesses the only two Colorado AVAs: Grand Valley (along the Colorado River between Palisade and Grand Junction) and West Elks (along a northern arm of the Gunnison River, around Paonia and Hotchkiss). The Grand Valley AVA is warmer and has fewer days with frost than the West Elks AVA area. Grand Valley is dominated by the Bordeaux varieties of grapes of merlot and cabernet sauvignon but plantings of viognier and syrah in the warmer areas seem promising. Pinot noir gives reasonable results In West Elks but success here mainly relies upon the white varieties of riesling, gewürztraminer, and pinot gris.

THE WINES

The award winning wines of Grande River Winery are highly recommended (Chardonnay, Sauvignon Blanc, Syrah, Meritage), as are Carlson Vineyards' Chardonnay Select and Gewürztraminer, Colorado Cellars' Gewürztraminer, Chardonnay, Riesling, and Petite Syrah, Mountain Spirit Winery's Chardonnay Barrel Select, Trail Ridge Winery's Merlot, and Plum Creek Cellars' Merlot and Riesling.

Colorado wines are ideal in combination with traditional American dishes. Drink a delicious spicy Gewürztraminer for example with a Thanksgiving turkey or with a fruity off-dry Riesling. With baked ham or other roast meat you can enjoy a delicious mellow Merlot or a classic Pinot Noir. With larger joints of roast lamb or beef or the barbecue the best choice is a great Cabernet Sauvignon of course.

In the center of the USA there is wine-growing in the states of North and South Dakota, Iowa, Kansas, Missouri, Montana, Nebraska, Nevada, Utah, and Wyoming.

THE FUTURE OF AMERICAN WINE-GROWING

Never before has the future for American wine-growing and making seemed so promising. In the past thirty years the USA has made good more than a century of lagging behind Europe. If the quest continues to put quality above quantity then it will be a formidable competitor for European wines. Future generations will make wine history...

A new generation, a great future – Cooper Jay Mitchell of Bellpine vineyard, Oregon

MEXICO

Mexico is probably the oldest wine-producing country of the New World. Vines were introduced by the Spanish conquistadors under the command of the famous Hernando Cortez in the sixteenth century. The results were very disappointing though because of the tremendous heat and arid conditions. The Spanish searched for better places to plant the vines further north in California but the results here were also less than satisfactory. It was only in the eighteenth century that Franciscan monks improved the Spanish vineyards and extended them to the once great California. After California was separated from Mexico, wine growing in Baja California (the Mexican part of California) fell into total neglect. Several large American and European wine and drinks companies saw an opportunity in the later twentieth century to establish a wine industry in Mexico in the best locations. Of these companies the Spanish firm of Domecq achieved short-term success with Mexican wine. Because of the very hot and dry conditions it is essential for wine growing to find cooler places so sites were sought on the high plateaus. Hence some vineyards are sited at 3,280 to 4,921 ft. Although there are others companies engaged in the industry, only three are well-known internationally. These are L.A. Cetto, Mission Santo Thomas, and Domecq to a lesser extent in terms of the wine than the name

L.A. Cetto and Domecq have vineyards in Baja California, about 50 miles south of the border with the USA, in the Guadaloupe Valley, and Mission Santo Thomas has them in the Santo Thomas Valley. There are also vineyards in the Baja California of the smaller scale but high quality wine producer of Monte Xanic. Monte Xanic offers a small range of wines, with a sultry and unforgettable Chardonnay and excellent Cabernet Sauvignon. Both wines are very expensive and difficult to get hold of. Domecq sold its best vineyards to L.A. Cetto and appears to be less interested in wine. Mission Santo Thomas has entered into a joint venture with the famous Californian company of Wente and is extremely busy. Their Sauvignon Blanc, Chenin Blanc, and Cabernet Sauvignon are absolute gems. L.A. Cetto makes a wide range of different types of wine from very acceptable cheap ones for local consumption to excellent Cabernet Sauvignon, Nebbiolo, Zinfandel, and Petite Syrah that are mainly intended for export.

Mexican wines, as the taster will soon discover, are long on sensuality and short on finesse. The success of Mexican wine is due to the soft acidity and fulsome, rounded, and warm taste. In addition the wines from producers such as L.A. Cetto are really quite cheap for the quality they offer. Serve these warm-blooded red wines, (Nebbiolo, Zinfandel, and Petite Syrah) with rich red meat dishes or grilled beef or poultry. The excellent Cabernet Sauvignon can be drunk young with lightly grilled meat, red or white. Drinking temperature is 14–16 °C (57.2–60.8 °F) for the Cabernet Sauvignon and 16–17 °C (60.8–62.6 °F) for the other red wines.

SOUTH AMERICA

Shortly after the Spanish Conquistadors of Hernando Cortéz had introduced vines into Mexico in the sixteenth century, wine growing was introduced to other parts of South America. In addition to the Spaniards, Bolivia, Peru, Argentina, and Chile, the Portuguese in Brazil and the Basques in Uruguay have played prominent roles in the wine growing history of South America.

BOLIVIA

As with Mexico, the Spanish Catholic missionaries introduced the first grapevines to Bolivia between 1550 and 1570. In 1600, the Tarija vineyards were planted that are now responsible for the best wines in Bolivia. The first vineyards were less orientated towards quality than they are now, producing a lot of sweet communion wines for the missionaries and their followers. The criolla negra vines were brought in from California (Baja-California, currently Mexican, and California currently American) by the Mexican missionaries. The vines came from Panama and Peru, to Bolivia where they were planted in orchards. Supporting vineyards with the use of trees is an old fashioned way of wine growing (originally the vines were supported by liane) and is a method that was much used by the Spanish missionaries in South America. The majority of these primitive vineyards have now vanished, but not in Bolivia. In the Capinota region, between Oruro and Cochachamba, at the foot of the Andes, there are still 217 acres of vine-

**Fumé Blanc
(Sauvignon Blanc
from Mexico)**

**L.A. Cetto Cabernet
Sauvignon**

**Delicious Petite Syrah
for an attractive price**

yards planted in the old fashioned way. A special feature of Bolivia is great contrast between the warm wet plateaus in the east of the country, (the *llanos*) and the cold mountainous regions in the south west. The higher extremities of the Andes (up to 11,482 ft) are much too cold for wine growing (annual average: 5–10 °C (41–50 °F). The plateaus with their tropical climate are too warm, and more importantly much too wet for wine growing. The best vineyards are located in the mountain valleys at around 5,577–11,482 ft altitude, and where the average annual temperature is the most favorable: 15–25 °C (59–77 °F). Through the day the vineyards are warmed substantially by the tropical sun, and cooled down at night by the mountain winds.

The amount of quality wines produced in Bolivia is very small and the majority of those are only of a moderate quality, with only a handful of companies making quality wines. The best wines come from an old Jesuit mission, La Concepción de Jesús in Tarija. The first vineyards were planted here as long ago as 400 years, but their intrinsic quality potential was not realized until 1980. Sergio Prudencio, a California trained oenologist, then decided to plant noble European vines in the higher reaches of the Tarijadal. These modern vineyards (222 acres) contrasted greatly with those in the lower areas where the vines were still being trained up "molle"- pepper trees – or trellises. Bodega de la Concepción makes wines of a surprisingly high quality with grapes from the highest vineyards in the world. (There are higher vineyards in Nepal, but the grapes are not used to make wine – thankfully!) The white wines of Bodega de la Concepción are pleasant, but it is the red wines that attract the most attention. These full-bodied, rounded and warm red wines including: Cabernet Sauvignon, Merlot and Syrah, combine the fiery Spanish temperament with the untamed Andes and the exuberance of the Californian wines. Sadly these wines are difficult to find outside of the American continent. The low grape yield results in a low total production that has led to the demand being far greater than the supply.

BRAZIL

Brazilian wine growing dates back to the sixteenth century when Don Martin Afonso de Souza, envoy of the Portuguese king, Don Juan III, planted the first vines at Santos El Baballero Brás Cubas. These vines had been brought from the island of Madeira. The Portuguese also took vines to the north east of Brazil and sold the wine to the Dutch who controlled that territory at the time. The arrival of Portuguese wine growers from the Azores in the eighteenth century briefly created a new impetus in the Brazilian wine industry. Because the European varieties were too susceptible to disease, the Brazilians chose North American grapes such as alexander, isabella, catawba, concord, and delaware which are all varieties of *Vitis labrus*. The results of these experiments were not uniformly successful and the arrival of German, Italian, and

Surprisingly nice Bolivian Cabernet Sauvignon Reserva

Bolivian Cabernet Sauvignon

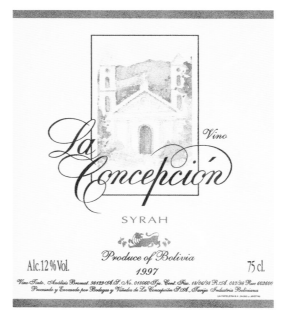

Bolivian Syrah

French immigrants in Brazil brought both better knowledge and vines.

Brazil has three large wine growing regions: Rio Grande del Sur, Nordeste, and Vale de São Francisco. Many of the grapes are still grown as dessert grapes that can be harvested three times each year because of the favorable climate. Slightly less than half of the grapes are destined for wine production. Only about 20 % of Brazil's vines are of the better *Vitis vinifera* varieties, while the others are hybrids and North American varieties, which are used for mass-produced wine. Acceptable to very good wines are made from *Vitis vinifera* varieties such as merlot, cabernet franc, sauvignon blanc. Brazil's potential as a wine-producing country can be shown by the many foreign companies investing in the industry like Moët et Chandon, Mumm, Remy Martin, Martini & Rosso, Domecq, and Seagram. Increasing numbers of Japanese companies are also entering the fray. It is clear that Brazil will soon become one of the major South American wine producers.

Wine quality is getting better year by year. The control of the grape health and quality has been increased, production plants have been renewed all resulting in the present wines being particularly pleasant. A new era is just beginning for Brazilian wine. For those who wish to try Brazilian wine for themselves the Vinicola Miolo of Vale dos Vinhedos at Porto Alegre can certainly be recommended. It is probably Brazil's best wine at the present time.

URUGUAY

While Chile and Argentina have been known as wine producers for some time, Uruguay has been busy in recent years in a spectacular effort to overtake them. Uruguay is relatively small as a country in comparison with its two giant neighbors Brazil and Argentina. Despite this the country has a rich history of wine production. The Spanish Conquistadors introduced vines in the sixteenth century and wine making was in the hands of the Monks for a considerable period of time. Uruguay wine production got a major boost when thousands of immigrants settled from France, Algeria, Germany, Italy, and Switzerland. These brought the noble grapevine *Vitis vinifera* with them. A leading role was played by the French Basque Pascal Harriague who introduced tannat and folle noire to Uruguay in 1870. Tannat is well-known from Southwest France, especially in Madiran where it makes superb wines for laying down from people like Alain Brumon. Meanwhile tannat has become the flagship of the Uruguayan wine industry.

Other noble grape varieties such as cabernet sauvignon, merlot, malbec, and gamay, Spanish varieties such as bobal, garnacha and monastrel and Italian vines like barbera and nebbiolo were planted in the late nineteenth and early twentieth centuries. None of these grapes has managed though to achieve the popularity or quality of tannat.

There are nine producing zones in Uruguay: Norte, Litoral Norte, Noreste, Literal Sur, Centro, Centro Oriental, Suroeste, Sur, and Sureste but most wine is produced in the south of the country around the capital Montevideo. The climate is moderate with sufficient rain to make irrigation unnecessary. The difference be-

tween day and night time temperatures is considerable in the north of the country. The soil varies between loose clay in the south through loose and fertile sediments in the south east, sand and gravel in the center, firm clay in the north east, and gravel in the north.

White wines predominate completely in Uruguay but they are not of the best quality. The best are from sauvignon blanc, chardonnay, pinot blanc, riesling, gewürztztraminer, torrontés and enviognier and are fresh, powerful, and very aromatic.

The reds yielded from cabernet sauvignon, cabernet franc, merlot, pinot noir, nebbiolo, and barbara are carefully made with concentrated bouquets of ripe fruit.

Despite this, Tannat is the more convincing wine. It is full-bodied and deep, very concentrated with firm but not harsh tannin and possesses heady aromas of ripe fruit and spices with a rich, powerful, and rounded masculine taste. It is certainly a wine that can be kept and is ideal with roasted and grilled meat, "a la parilla" (large barbecue) or "a la plancha" (grill). Drinking temperature is 16–18 °C (60–64 °F).

Bear in mind that good Uruguayan wine is not cheap and avoid doubtful cheap examples in supermarkets, seeking out instead better wines such as Tannat RPF of Bodega Pisano, Castel Pujol Tannat of Juan Carrau, Tannat Viejo of Bodega Stagnari, or Don Pascual Tannat Barrels.

A good Brazilian Cabernet Sauvignon from Miolo

A large assortment of Brazilian wines from Miolo

Excellent Chardonnay   **Uruguayan Gewürztraminer**

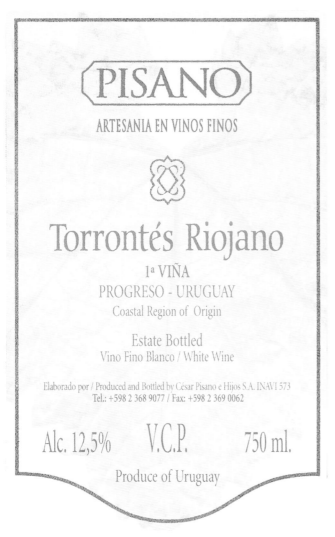

A special Torrentés

A very fascinating Pinot Noir

Cabernet Sauvignon

Merlot

ARGENTINA

The Conquistadors also introduced vines into Argentina in the sixteenth century. The resulting wines were used by Spanish Jesuits for both religious and medicinal purposes. The industry only acquired its present form in the nineteenth century as a result of a flood of European immigrants who brought better vines with them such as cabernet, barbera, and sangiovese for red wines and chenin, riesling, and torrontés for whites. German, Italian, Spanish, and French immigrants established the first independent wine houses. Argentina's vineyards lie at the foot of the Andes, far removed from the pollution of industrial cities. The climate is continental, being very dry and very hot,

A good middle class Tannat

Castel Pujol from Carrau, good old fashioned Tannat

Sublime, forceful Tannat from Pisano

Prince Charles has also discovered the charm of the best Uruguayan wines

– La Rioja/Chilecito which lies just below 30 degrees south. This area is known for its Bodega La Riojana wines.
– Mendoza is undoubtedly the best-known wine area of Argentina. It lies above the latitude 35 degrees south, on the banks of the Rio Mendoza and Rio Tunuyan, and is known for numerous good bodegas such as Etchart, Nieto y Senetiner, Trapiche, Norton, and Flichman.

The wine industry in Argentina is influenced by the Andes

verging on desert. Irrigation with water from pure mountain streams has created the ideal conditions for wine growing.

WINE AREAS

Wine growing is possible along almost half the length of the Andes (between the twenty-fifth and fortieth parallels). The vineyards arise like cooling oases in otherwise desert-like terrain.

It is possible to grow a wide range of varieties of grape here because of the big difference in day and night time temperatures. Argentina has five large wine areas. From north to south, these are:
– Salta/Cafayate that lies just below latitude 25 degrees south, along the banks of the Rio Sali, between the towns of these names. Wines such as Cafayate and those of the renowned Etchart Bodega come from here.

An area within Mendoza is regarded by insiders as the area with the greatest potential for the twenty-first century. This is Lujan de Cuyo to the southwest of the town of Mendoza, which produces outstanding Malbec wines with its own denomination of Lujan de Cuyo, but this area can ensure a spectacular future.
– San Rafael, lies along a latitude of 35 degrees south, between the Rio Diamante and Rio Atuel. Only the wines of Bodega Goyenechea are known to some extent outside of Argentina.
– Rio Negro, the most southerly area, lies just north 40 degrees south on the banks of the Rio Negro. Wines from this area are hardly known outside Argentina.

Trapiche Chardonnay from Mendoza

Trapiche Malbec from Mendoza

WINES

Argentina has been climbing steadily up into the ranks of the top five wine producing countries and in terms of total production has challenged Spain's third position. It is only the past decade or so that wine from Argentina has been discovered in Europe and much of it does certainly not deserve the description of 'quality wine' and at best can qualify as cheap, pleasant slurping wines. But the quality winery of Trapiche Bodega (which is famous for its Fond de Cave Chardonnay and Cabernet Sauvignon) has show the way to other top class Argentine wines. Now wines such as Torrontés and Cafayate Cabernet Sauvignon from the Etchart Bodega have become known along with a number of white and especially red wines from Norton such as Torronté, Syrah, Cabernet Sauvignon, Barbera, and Malbec, together with the outstanding Coleccion Privada.

Finca Flinchman produces the tasteful Syrah and Cabernet Sauvignon together with their superb Aberdeen Angus Malbec and Cabernet Sauvignon.

Nieto y Senetiner is less well known in Europe but is certainly one of the Argentine's best houses with the outstanding Malbec, Torrontés and Chardonnay.

Etchart
Tempranillo-Malbe

Delightful Syrah from
Fnca Flinchman

SAUVIGNON BLANC

Argentina's Sauvignon Blanc (except the cheaper versions that are clumsy and boring) has a pleasing aroma of citrus fruits, peach, apricot, kiwi, and grapefruit with slight vegetative undertones. It is fresh and quite dry, making it a perfect aperitif or it can of course be served with light starters, seafood or fried fish, Best served at 9–10 °C (48–50 °F).

TORRONTÉS

Torrontés is Argentina's white wine specialty. The better ones are greenish-yellow with a hint of gold. The bouquet is never truly exuberant, tending towards subtle floral aromas and a hint of exotic fruit with a clear muscatel nuance. The taste is fresh but never sharply so and is well balanced and harmonious. A fine aperitif or served with fish (casserole) or poultry. Drink at 8–10 °C (46–50 °F).

Etchart
Cabernet Sauvignon

Etchart Malbec

A terrific Malbec from Nieto y Senetiner

CHARDONNAY

Argentine Chardonnay is often pale golden with a green tinge. The bouquet is seductive and reminiscent of ripe apples and hot creamery butter with a hint of wood and vanilla.

The texture is generally full and rounded, complex and broad. A good wine with veal, poultry or strong tasting fish types. Drinking temperature is 10–12 °C (50–53 °F).

The finest Argentine Chardonnays such as Trapiche Fond de Cave retain their elegance despite a luxuriant and heady creaminess. The bouquet is of ripe apple, honey, butter, and spices such as cinnamon. These cracking wines only deserved the best dishes and are therefore recommended with lobster, turbot, or monkfish or allow this wine to gladden your heart with casseroled guinea fowl or a pheasant especially when accompanied by a truffle. Drinking temperature is from 12–14 °C (53.6–57.2 °F).

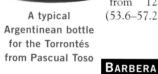

A typical Argentinean bottle for the Torrontés from Pascual Toso

The Torrentés from Toso is sold in Europe in this bottle

BARBERA

This is a deeply colored wine with wonderful aromas of young fruit such as cherries and raspberries. The taste if velvet smooth, harmonious, and elegant. This wine seduces one easily with its combination of fresh acidity and relative high alcohol content. Serve with pasta dishes with a meat sauce, lasagna, roast

Outstanding Chardonnay from Nieto y Senetiner

pork, and braised dishes or at a good barbecue. Drinking temperature is 13–14 °C (55.4–57.2 °F).

MERLOT

This wine is particularly fruity, particularly suggesting plum and bilberry with a hint of blackberry. It harmonious taste a mild tannin make this a pleasant charmer. Ideal with not too strongly herbed red meat dishes, braised dishes, rabbit, guinea fowl, turkey, chicken and other poultry. Drinking temperature is 14–15 °C (57.2–59 °F).

SYRAH

This is a very dark-colored wine with intense aromatic power (spices, pepper, vanilla, toast, and red fruits). It is full-bodied, possesses great strength but is not strongly tannic to the tongue with a rounded and mild aftertaste. Serve this top class wine with grilled or roasted lamb. Drinking temperature is 16–17 °C (60.8–62.6 °F).

CABERNET SAUVIGNON

This a classic wine produced from the wonderful Bordeaux grape but it possesses less tannin than its French

Sultry Barbera from Nieto y Senetiner

counterparts. The bouquet is reminiscent of red and blue woodland fruits with hints of wood and nuts. The taste is soft, full, and rounded with a long and pleasing aftertaste. This wine is great with all types of red meat, small wild game or poultry. Drinking temperature is 16 °C (60.8 °F).

A very fascinating Merlot from Nieto y Senentiner

The better Cabernet Sauvignon wines are aged in wood for a long period as in France. These top wines such as Fond de Cave Cabernet Sauvignon of Trapiche possess greater aromatic power than their younger counterparts. They have a bouquet of cedar wood, tobacco, vanilla, chocolate, and lots of ripe fruit (such as blackcurrant). This wine is recommended as an accompaniment with roasted or grilled beef or lamb. Drinking temperature is 16–17 °C (60.8–62.6 °F).

MALBEC

Together with Torrontés, Malbec is the flagship of Argentine wine. These grapes from south western France thrive here, especially in Lujan de Cuyo. The color is dark red tinged with purple and the bouquet is reminiscent of blackcurrants, raspberries, cherries, and plums. The structure and tannin are both strong but mellow with age to form a superb full-bodied and rounded wine of great complexity. The wine for grilled beef and lamb dishes. Drinking temperature is 16–17 °C (60.8–62.6 °F).

A fine Syrah from Mendoza

MALBEC LUJAN DE CUYO DENOMINACION DE ORIGEN CONTROLADA

This is the apotheosis of Argentine wines. Only the very best wines are permitted to carry this fiercely sought denomination or origin and they must contain at least 80 % malbec, all of which

Excellent Cabernet Sauvignon from Norton

must come from the Luca de Cuyo area. The finest of these is probably the Viña de Santa Isabel Malbec Lujan de Cuyo DOC from the Casa Vinícola Nieto y Senetiner. It possesses an intense ruby red coloring with purple tinges and has a very fresh and fruity bouquet of red fruit, honey, and vanilla with suggestions of chocolate and sweet wood. It is an extremely complex wine that is both refined and powerful, full-bodied and rounded, with great potential for keeping. If this wine is a foretaste of what can be expected from Lujan de Cayo in this new century then let there be more. This wine should be enjoyed with nothing short of the best cut of meat, such as a succulent and tender Argentinean fillet steak garnished with wild mushrooms and truffles. Drinking temperature is 17–18 °C (62.6–64.4 °F).

An especially nice Malbec from Norton

Malbec is sometimes mixed with other types of grapes

CHILE

Chile is a very elongated but relatively narrow country 3,125 miles long and 56 to 250 miles wide, nestling at the foot of the Andes mountains. Grapes are grown here over some 875 miles between the 27th and 39th parallels. An assortment of different soil types and micro-climates ensure quite a diversity in the types of wine. Chile's climate is similar to the Mediterranean, being damp in the winter and spring with dry summers. Chile is blessed with perfect conditions for quality wines with a fairly marked difference between day and night temperatures, with many hours of sunshine, and fairly high humidity from the nearby ocean.

Since the arrival of Spanish Conquistadors in the sixteenth century and despite a surge in quality in the nineteenth century as a result of the

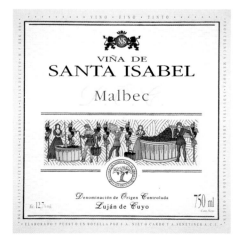

Luján de Cuyo have the best wines that Argentina can offer

arrival of European immigrants Chilean wine had been in a state of almost medieval lethargy until some years ago. The same out-dated methods to make and keep wine had been used for centuries and these were far from hygienic. This changed radically in the late 1970s when the Spanish firm of Torres was the first to establish itself in Chile. The old vineyards were cleared and new vines planted while the wine making installations were either extensively renovated or totally replaced by ultra modern equipment. The old and often dirty wine vats were replaced with small *barriques* of new wood. In spite of these measures it was a surprisingly long time before modern Chilean wines reached Europe in large numbers. Names such as Villard, Santa Rita, Torres, Errazuriz, and Santa Carolina were amongst the first to do so. Chilean wine export started to take off in a big way at the start of the 1990's, following a shift towards democracy in Chile. Big companies like Torres and Concha y Toro (Spain), Lafite Rothschild, Marnier Lapostelle, Pernod Ricard, Larose Trintaudon, Bruno Prat of Cos d'Estournel, and Mouton Rothschild (France) and Mondavi of California are still investing millions of dollars in the Chilean wine industry.

WINE GROWING AREAS

Chile has four large wine regions of which Aconcagua, the Valle Central, and the Region Sur o Meridional are the best. These four are split into sub regions and where necessary also into zones. The most productive areas are Maule, Curicó, Rapel, and Maipo, all located within the Valle Central between Santiago and Cauquenes.

ACONCAGUA

The Aconcagua region is the furthest north Chilean wine growing area and comprises two sub regions of Valle del Aconcagua and Valle de Casablanca. The

Casa Lapostolle (Marnier Lapostolle)

Los Vascos
(Lafite Rothschild)

Almaviv is the result of a joint venture between the French Mouton Rothschild and the Chilean Concha y Toro

Las Vertientes vineyards (Errazuriz) at the foot of the Andes

Aconcagua valley is fairly flat and extends from the Andes to the sea. This long valley is two mile wide at its broadest point and is enclosed by mountains of 4,921–5,905 ft high. The climate is of the Mediterranean type: moderately hot.

The Casablanca valley is smaller but more densely planted than the Aconcagua valley. It lies closer to the sea and therefore benefits from the cooling and moist sea breezes that are prevalent here. The hills extend to a height of no more than 1,300 ft.

The finest Chardonnay comes from the Casablanca valley

Classic Cabernet Sauvignon from the Aconcaguavallei

TERRA ANDINA
CABERNET SAUVIGNON
VALLE CENTRAL
1998

PRODUCT OF CHILE
PRODUCED AND BOTTLED BY
VINOS TERRA ANDINA, CURICO, CHILE

13.0% VOL.75CL.

Cabernet Sauvignon from the Valle Central

VALLE CENTRAL

Running from north to south you first encounter the Maipo valley then the Rappel valley, followed by the Curicó valley, and finally the Maule valley.

The Maipo Valley, called Maipo for short, runs on either side of the river of the same name. This valley stretches from the foot of the Andes to the sea and varies in height from 3,280 ft in the east to 1,640 ft in the west. This difference in altitude and more importantly the oceanic influences in the west have resulted in a big difference in planting from east to west.

The Valle de Rapel or just Rapel is much larger than the Maipo valley and is water by the rivers Cachapoal and Tinguirrica, which run into the Rapel river. The average height is quite low, less than 1,640 ft but some vineyards are sited at up to 3,280 ft at the foot of the mountains. It is more than twice as humid here as in the Maipo Valley because of the moist sea winds that easily enter the valley.

The Valle de Curicó or just Curicó is much smaller than the Rapel valley but is more efficiently and densely planted so that the vineyards useful area is slightly greater than that of the Rapel. This valley does not get its name from the river of the same name but from the

town of Curicó. The vineyards are situated mainly in the central plain but a few are located on the steeper ground at the foot of the mountains. The climate here is quite moist as a result of the nearby ocean.

The Valle del Maul or Maule is the most southerly valley of this central part of the Chilean wine industry.

TERRA ANDINA®
MERLOT
VALLE CENTRAL
2000

PRODUCT OF CHILE
PRODUCED AND BOTTLED BY
VINOS TERRA ANDINA, CURICO, CHILE

13.8% ALC./VOL. 750 ML.

Merlot from the Valle Central

Superior Chardonnay from the Rapel valley

Cabernet Sauvignon from the Rapel valley

It is an enormous area but not necessarily efficiently planted everywhere. Irrigation comes from the Maule and its tributaries. This elongated valley is surrounded by the Andes in the east and the hills behind the coast to the west. Despite this it is a fairly moist area, particularly in winter.

Torres Sauvignon from Curicó

Torres Cabernet Sauvignon from Curicó

A terrific classical red wine from Torres in Curicó

OTHER WINE AREAS

A further two wine areas are situated in the extreme north and south of Chile. Coquimbo region in the north has sub zones of the Elqui, Limari, and Choapa valleys and in the south there are the Iata and Bio valleys. These areas produce a great deal of base wine for the famous Pisco wine distillery. Changes have been taking place here in recent years such as the increased introduction of better grapes.

THE WINES

Chile produces a great deal of Cabernet Sauvignon (about 47 % of the total production) followed by Sauvignon Blanc, Moscatel de Alejandria, Chardonnay, and Merlot (incl. Carmenére) Sémillon and Torontel. Small amounts of Carignan, Malbec, Riesling, Pinot Noir, Syrah, Chenin Blanc, Gewürtztraminer, Cinsault, Zinfandel, Mourvèdre and Sangiovese are also pro-

duced. Chardonnay was originally not so widely planted but has seen explosive growth, with a twenty two fold increase between 1985 and 1997. On the other hand, the country grapes that were used for centuries for making slurping wines are no longer planted and have lost a considerable amount of ground. In the corresponding period, country grape production was almost halved from 74,130 to a little more than 37,065 acres. Semillon is also steadily losing more ground, at the expense of cabernet sauvignon, merlot, carmenére and sauvignon blanc.

SAUVIGNON BLANC

Chilean Sauvignon Blanc varies in intensity and quality from area to area and also from maker to maker. The color of ordinary Sauvignon Blanc is mainly pale yellow

Caliterra wines, a joint venture between Errazuriz and Mondavi

tinged with green. The bouquet is very seductive with fresh aromas of tropical fruit and freshly mowed grass. Some wines have a hint of citrus fruits, gooseberry (Santa Carolina), or flowers (Santa Digna, Torres). The taste is always fresh without being firm. This is an ideal wine with seafood or fresh starters. Drinking temperature is 8–10 °C (46.4–50 °F).

SAUVIGNON BLANC RESERVA ESPECIAL

This wine is cask aged in wood and possesses a characteristic bouquet of wood and vanilla without entirely losing its fruitiness. Less suitable as an aperitif, but perfect with pan fried or deep fried salt water fish or grilled poultry. Drinking temperature is 10 °C (50 °F).

Sauvignon Blanc

SAUVIGNON BLANC LATE HARVEST

This is a rare wine from Concha y Toro that has heady aromas of white fruits (such as peach and apricot), melon and honey. It is a luxuriant and sweet yet fresh white wine with a broad taste and long aftertaste, and should be enjoyed just when you feel like it. Drinking temperature is 8–10 °C (46.4–50 °F).

CHARDONNAY

The taste of Chilean Chardonnay is largely a matter of the wood in which it has been stored and the duration of its storage. The humidity of its place of origin also plays a role. Chardonnay here is generally pale straw yellow with a green tinge. Most wines have a fresh and fruity bouquet with aromas of apple, citrus fruits, grapefruit, pineapple and passion fruit. Those Chardonnays made from riper grapes exude heady aromas more distinctly of honey, butter, mango, cinnamon, apricot, peach, and occasional note of tropical flowers. Those cask aged in good quality wood also acquire a fresh bouquet of oak, hazelnut, toast, and vanilla. These wines are distinguished as in Spain by the additions of the names Reserva and Gran Reserva. All Chardonnays are fresh and mild, creamy, dry but not harsh, rounded, and full in taste. The taste (and price) varies from simplicity to good, broad, complex, and superb. Serve a young Chardonnay as an aperitif or with fish or poultry; the strong and rich with seafood, (lobster, crab), scallops, veal or poultry served in a creamy sauce. Drinking temperature is 10–12 °C (50–53.6 °F) for young wines and 12–14 °C (53.6–57.2 °F) for Reserva and Gran Reserva.

SEMILLON

The ordinary wine of this noble Bordeaux grape here is fresh and intensely aromatic (citrus fruits including grapefruit with occasional hint of vanilla). This dry wine is balanced, rich, full-bodied and strongly alcoholic (13–14%). Its alcoholic strength makes it difficult to combine with food, except perhaps with a strong tasting fish, white meat, or poultry dishes, where the sauce is somewhat creamy without losing its fresh taste. (e. g. poached guinea fowl with a creamy supréme sauce prepared with the same wine). Drinking temperature is 10–12 °C (50–53.6 °F).

SEMILLON LATE HARVEST

The color of these rare wines, including the Viña Carmen tends to golden yellow and has a bouquet reminiscent of honey and overripe fruits (peach and apricot). The taste is velvet smooth, luxuriant, sweet, and rich with high alcohol and a prolonged aftertaste. Share this Semillon Late Harvest with friends. Drinking temperature is 8–9 °C (46.4–48.2 °F).

SPARKLING WINES

Chile produces a number of sparkling wines varying from moderate to excellent.

Choose one of the better ones such as Viña Miguel Torres Brut Nature which has a fresh spring-like aroma of meadow flowers combined with luxuriant white tropical fruits and a fresh but delicate taste of Chardonnay with the full, rich, and rounded taste of Pinot Noir. This is an excellent wine to drink as an aperitif or as a festive accompaniment for any occasion. Drinking temperature is 6–8 °C (42.8–46.4 °F).

CABERNET SAUVIGNON

These wines are classic, elegant, and complex. The ordinary Cabernet Sauvignon is fresh and fruity but it is worth while buying the better wines such as Reserva and Gran Reserva. These offer much richer bouquets and greater complexity. The color is dark ruby red with the occasional tinge of brown. The aroma is reminiscent of plum, blackcurrant, strawberry, mint, and pepper with undertones of vanilla, chocolate, nuts, cedar wood, tobacco, and toast. When young this wine is very tannic but the tannin is more muted after two to three years. This is a terrific wine with pan fried, roasted or grilled red meat (beef). Drinking temperature is 16–17 °C (60.8–62.6 °F).

Cabernet Sauvignon

CARMENÈRE

Carmenére was seen for a long time as a sort of clone of the merlot grape, and was processed accordingly. During a visit by Robert Mondavi to the vineyards of Errazuriz in 1990, the Errazuriz viticulturist Pedro Izquierdo discovered variations in shape and size in the merlot grapes in his vineyards. He offered the grapes for tasting to Robert Mondavi and Eduardo Chadwick, the owner of Errazuriz. The aberrant merlot grapes actually tasted better and more intense. After subjecting the supposed clones to prolonged studies, the French grape specialist Jean Michel Boursiquot finally discovered the true identity of these "deviating" vineyards: they were the remains of a forgotten French grape strain from the Bordeaux region: carmenère or grande vidure. This ancient strain from the south west of France, together with malbec, once formed the foundation for the success of all of the red Bordeaux wines before the arrival of the *Phylloxera*. Cabernet sauvignon and merlot played much less important roles then than now. After the old vineyards were cleared, carmenère vines were not selected for replanting in spite of tremendous history for quality. It was felt that this grape was much to sensitive to frost, rain and a variety of parasitic and fungal ailments, which ultimately resulted in low yields. Preference was given to cabernet franc. Malbac also had to make way largely for cabernet sauvignon and merlot. Just before the *Phylloxera* invasion, French immigrants arrived in Chile carrying young vines amongst their belongings, which they had brought from the south west of France. These vines included cabernet sauvignon, merlot and …carmenère. Some grape specialists believe that these grapes are descendants of the ancient biturica family, of which cabernet sauvignon is also a member. Biturica is said to originate from northwest Spain and to have been introduced to the Bordeaux regions by the Romans or the Celts. Incidentally, the Roman legions took this ancient grape back to Italy, where it can still be found sporadically under the name of "Predicato di Biturica" in a number of regions, including Tuscany.

Carmenère thrives in Chile, where it is not subjected to too much wetness or cold temperatures. Unlike Europe, leaf and grape parasites are extremely rare in Chile due in part to the composition of the soil and the climate. Carmenère is able to totally deploy its supreme quality and tremendous aromatic force here, especially as it enjoys a maturing period of two to three longer than say a merlot. The aroma of carmenère is predominantly vegetal (sliced green pepper) with a lot of fruit (blackberry skins) If the carmenère is harvested fully ripe in a very sunny year, the resulting wines often develop nuances of roasted coffee or cocoa, especially after resting for a time.

Because of their robust structure and ripe taste, Carmenère wines are excellent with fried or roast beef or even wild game, preferably served with a red or a black fruit sauce. This wine also goes surprisingly well with grilled duck breast with say cherries, raspberries or blackberries. Drinking temperature: 15–17 °C (59–62.6 ° F)

MERLOT

This is another classic Bordeaux grape that thrives here. The wine is dark red with some purple tinges here and there. Plum, blackcurrant, blueberry, black cherry, morello cherry, and strawberries can be detected in the bouquet with undertones of pepper, mint, green herbs, wood, and vanilla.

The tannin is mainly mellow and the taste full and rounded. These Chilean Merlots readily charm and are suited for drinking with lighter meat dishes. Drinking temperature is 14–16 °C (57.2–60.8 °F).

Chilean Merlot

BLENDS

This category includes some of the very best wines in Chile, including two absolute toppers Don Maximiano (Errazuriz) and Seña (Errazuriz & Mondavi). The majority of these wines are made from classical blends of (usually) French grapes. These great wines should be rewarded with a beautiful cut of meat, preferably roasted or from the spit. Drinking temperature: 17–18 °C (62.6–64.4 °F).

The Carmenére was discovered in the vineyards of Eduardo Chadwick (Errazuriz)

The best Chilean red wines are often blends of classical French grapes

Australia and New Zealand

Although both countries have made wine for many years the real breakthroughs for Australia and New Zealand have only really occurred within the past twenty or so years. Australian wines in the meantime have become a by-word throughout the world while those from New Zealand are unfortunately still reserved for connoisseurs but that is soon to change.

AUSTRALIA

There is not a New World wine-producing country that has had such an influence on the entire philosophy of wine as Australia, whose wine industry was also established by European immigrants. Australia set about a radical change in wine making techniques so that good wines could be made for a few Australian dollars. The European industry tried for years to protect themselves against these Australian wines but the public proved en masse to prefer the tasty Australian wines that were ready to drink, amenable, comforting, rounded, full-bodied, and warm. What is more they were much cheaper. Countless Australian wine-makers now fly from one European company to another anxious to teach them how to achieve the same kind of results. It was only twenty years ago that aspiring Australian wine makers traveled to France to learn the trade at French

The Australian wine industry is often prejudged by the Europeans.
Not everything there could be referred to as grand. (Brown Brothers winery, Milawa, Victoria)

companies. Nowadays it is the French aspiring wine makers that travel to Australia!

HISTORY

Australia's wine history is certainly not as old as the land itself. The Dutchman Abel Tasman first discovered Southern Australia and this was followed much later by the discovery of Northern Australia by the Briton James Cook. These regions were originally inhabited by the Aborigines, who were certainly not wine drinkers. Sadly there are still too many white Australians that are of the opinion that "their" country's history only began in the late eighteenth century when Australia became a British colony. It was then that the first vines arrived, intended for experimental purposes in a botanical garden. The first official wine growers arrived in the early nineteenth century. The Scot James Busby, with some experience of wine growing and making, acquired in France, successfully planted the first vineyards in the Hunter Valley. Vines were soon growing elsewhere in Australia. Apart from Hunter Valley on the east coast, they were planted in the south, around Adelaide, Southern Vale, and Barossa. The initial wines tasted somewhat like the present day Rhône wines through the excess of sun and too little water, although they were sold somewhat cheekily in London as 'Australian Burgundy' or even 'Burgundy'. The wine industry was given a sudden and unexpected impulse after World War I when thousands of soldiers were suddenly discharged and thrust into unemployment. The government encouraged soldiers to make a new life for themselves by growing and making wine. This proved to be a success, indeed perhaps too successful given the hefty over-production of wine that arose. The growers directed their efforts increasingly towards the production of port and sherry type fortified wines. This gave the growers two ways of getting rid of their surplus. The demand for fortified wines was huge and wine spirit was needed in order to make them. Up until the 1960's most Australians preferred to drink beer or gin to wine. The Australian wines were mainly intended for the local Greek and Italian immigrants and for export. When the Australian government took measures to reduce drinking and driving, the pattern of alcohol consumption began to change. Consumption of wine gradually increased in Australia, both at home and in restaurants, bars, and such places. Although there was a shift towards the better wines, the bulk wine market remained very active. Wine in a can, bag, or box is still widespread here. With a consumption of 40 pints of wine per capita per annum the population of Australia still lags well behind that of most European countries, but a new life style of is clearly evident. The drinking habits of the world consumers changed in the 1970s. Far less sweet wine was drunk, with dry wines becoming far more popular. Australian producers reacted well by seeking out cooler places to grow their grapes such as the Eden Valley and Coonawarra, which are more suitable for grapes like Sauvignon Blanc,

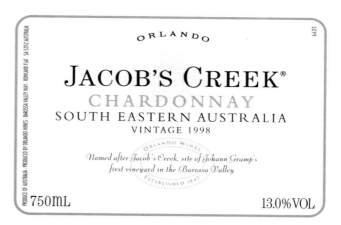

The Chardonnay is still an Australian classic

Colombard, Riesling, Chenin Blanc, and Chardonnay. A similar change also occurred with red wine. Australian wines have now been discovered throughout the world and are placed in high esteem. The explosive growth of the Australian wine industry is set to continue for a long time to come.

WINE GROWING CONDITIONS

Australian wine growing is quite typical of the New World scene with huge vineyards spread across enormous territories between South Australia (Barossa and Coonawarra), Victoria (Yarra), and New South Wales (Hunter), plus hi-tech equipment and methodology and staggering yields. Despite all this Australia is not anywhere near the output of wine-producing countries like Italy, France, and Spain. A large proportion of the potential harvest is destroyed by natural hazards such as hail, rain, extreme heat, fire, kangaroos, foxes, crows, and gray-backed silver eyes.

Considerable government support has been invested developing and extending the local wine industry. Up to the 1970s the most popular wines were mainly sweet rieslings. The plantings of riesling have been decimated since the arrival of chardonnay vines, because the wines from these are more successful in the export market. chardonnay is now the most widely planted grape variety but shiraz is also gaining ground too. Besides these there are also a number of other varieties which are new to Australia that are gaining popularity. Hence in addition to new plantings of shiraz, cabernet sauvignon, cabernet franc, malbec, merlot, pinot noir, and ruby cabernet (cabernet and Cinsault), increasing numbers of sangiovese and barbera vines are also being planted. The white grape that surprises everyone and is gaining popularity at the expense of chardonnay, semillon, riesling, sauvignon blanc, chenin blanc, colombard, muscadelle, and traminer is the verdelho.

Australian wine-makers are often accused of putting more emphasis on the variety of grape than on the aspects related to *terroir*. The criticism is not entirely justified because each wine is a combination of factors: the grape variety, soil, climate, and of course the underground water. Australian wine makers can guarantee their customers constant quality by blending together wines from different areas. This can compensate year in year out for the vagaries of the Australian climate. The result is a superb wine with a distinctive character. Australian wines are almost always produced from a number of vineyards. It is possible for 'single vineyard' wines to be made in Australia, but given the enormous size of many of them, this would lack credibility while also adding unnecessary costs and uncertainty. This would also be contrary to the 'flavor for dollar' policy that has made Australian wines world famous. A 'single vineyard' wine would vary in quality from year to year and this is not what today's consumers want.

It is often essential in Australia to irrigate the vines. This is strictly forbidden in most European countries, even during the most extreme periods of dry weather. New World wine countries though regard irrigation as a perfectly natural occurrence. Their systems are so well refined that the vines can be drip fed at whatever height is required. Spray equipment is installed on both sides of the vines but it is also possible to spray from just one side. This gives the vine a contrasting signal so that the leaves absorb water rather than the grapes in order to maintain a good balance between sun and moisture.

The popular European technique by which the skins are left in contact to extract the maximum possible aromatic and flavor substances in the juice (*macération pelliculaire*), is only used in poor years in Australia. The grapes normally have more than adequate aromatic and flavor substances in them as a result of the good sun/moisture balance. The malolactic fermentation with lactic acids that is used in Europe is only partially used here. Australian wines do not naturally have high levels of acidity, so that it makes no sense, nor is it desirable for a complete malolactic fermentation to take place. The sun also has a beneficial

effect on the growth of the vines. Australian wine makers rarely need to add fertilizer to the soil. Those in favor of organic wine making do not need to ring any alarm bells here as they do in Europe.

Australian wine-makers ideas about cask maturing in wood are also different. In order to provide plenty of flavor at a price they have used wood chips to give cheaper wines a characteristic 'oaked' taste. This is a thing of the past though for today the best Australian companies use huge tanks in which a sort of giant wheel constantly agitates the young wine. This gives the wine regular contact with large oak planks that can be pushed into the tank through special apertures. The length of time that the wine spends in these tanks is determined by the desired strength of the taste of oak required. The eventual result has much greater finesse than the use of oak chips. High-technology therefore can also have its good sides. In this way the top wines are still matured in oak casks, while cheaper ones acquire their oak taste more quickly and efficiently. This system is also more environmentally friendly and considerably reduces the number of oak trees that need to be felled.

WINE REGIONS

Vines are grown in almost every part of Australia but wines are only produced in the cooler southern parts. Australia can be roughly split into seven large regions. From west to east these are Western Australia, Northern Territory, South Australia, Queensland, New South Wales, Victoria, and the island of Tasmania. The regions of primary importance are Western Australia, South Australia Victoria, and New South Wales.

WESTERN AUSTRALIA
The only good wine area of Western Australia lies far to the south of Perth, just inland from the south-western coastal strip.

MARGARET RIVER
Margaret river is an extremely fascinating area that is less well-known outside Australia, but this is likely to change. The climate is strongly influenced by the ocean. The soil is mainly a mixture of gravel and gravel-bearing loam and sand on underlying granite. Margaret River is mainly known for its good Cabernet Sauvignon, but other grapes do well here too.

SOUTH AUSTRALIA
South Australia is known for the following wine areas.

CLARE VALLEY
This is one of Australia's oldest wine-producing areas which has existed since the second half of the nineteenth century. High quality wines, and in particular very aromatic reds and superb floral Rieslings come from the Clare Valley. The climate is predominantly a moderate continental one with big differences between day and nigh temperatures, especially in summer. There is

A Riesling vineyard for quality wine

Vineyards in South Australia

enough rainfall, mainly in the spring, to make irrigation unnecessary. The soil is mainly open calciferous red or brown clay.

ADELAIDE HILLS

The vineyards in this area are sited at heights of 1,312–1,640 ft and are becoming better known thanks to the production of very acceptable sparkling and quality wines. The altitude of the vineyards somewhat mitigates the heat and leads to increased rainfall. Since most of the rain falls in winter though irrigation is still necessary. The soil around Adelaide Hills consists of a fairly infertile mixture of loam and sand.

MCLAREN VALE

McLaren Vale is one of Australia's best wine-producing areas and certainly the best in terms of the varied grapes and types of wine. The area is best known for the power-ful dark and very aromatic reds and mighty whites. Despite the cooling effect of the ocean too little rain falls here and irrigation is necessary. McLaren Vale has many different soil types which explains the diversity of the wine. It is mainly sand and loam on underlying clay and chalk, or sand, or red or black weathered loam.

BAROSSA VALLEY

The Barossa Valley is probably the best-known wine area of Australia, both because of its wines and its rich history. The valley was the first territory of the early German settlers who started the wine industry here. German is still spoken here. The climate is hot, sunny, and with little moisture. Despite this there is little irrigation. The vines are trained low, almost like creepers, and the yield is intentionally kept low. This produces excellent wines, including fortified wines that are very concentrated, full of color and structure. The soil chiefly consists of brown sandy soil or clay to dark sand.

PADTHAWAY

This is a lesser known wine region on fairly level terrain that largely consists of loam or terra rossa with good underlying drainage. The shortage of rainfall here makes irrigation necessary during the summer. This area mainly produces commercial wine but is switching over to quality wines such as those of Hardy.

COONAWARRA

This is an extremely well-known area within South Australia where wine growing started way back in the late nineteenth century. The finest Australian Cabernet Sauvignons originate from this region. The area is situated immediately behind the coastal strip and is favorably influenced by the ocean. The climate here is a moderate maritime one with fairly cool summers (by Australian standards). The loose red terra rossa soil has become a by-word throughout the world. If there is anywhere in Australia where it is possible to speak of the character of the *terroir* then it is Coonawarra.

Jacob's Creek, a by-word in Barossa

Wolf Blass makes fine wines in South Australia

VICTORIA

Apart from the Yarra Valley, the wine areas in the state of Victoria are little known outside Australia. It consists of three sub-regions.

GREAT WESTERN

This area is known for its sparkling wines, which were Australia's first. Great Western resembles an Australian desert-like version of Tuscany, with many gently undulating hills. The climate is dry but fairly cool by Australian standards. The difference between day and night temperatures can be quite high in summer. There is low rainfall and irrigation is therefore usually necessary. The soil consists principally of layers of poor, highly acidic soil with salty undertones which does not simplify the making of the wines from here.

DRUMBORG

This is a fairly unknown area within the hinterland of Portland. The three well-known grapes of pinot noir, chardonnay, and pinot meunier provide the basis for sparkling wines. The area is ideally suited for making sparkling wines because it gets relatively less hours of sun than the rest of southern Australia.

YARRA VALLEY

The Yarra Valley is situated on the outskirts of Melbourne. The soil is a mixture of loam, clay, and sand that is extremely acidic. Some of the better land also has gravel and broken rock. Here too there is insufficient rainfall, making irrigation essential. The climate though is fairly cool, so that the Yarra Valley is able to produce some truly elegant wines.

The cool vineyards at Brown Brothers (Victoria)

NEW SOUTH WALES

New South Wales is a large wine growing area of which the only well-known part is the Hunter Valley.

TUMBARUMBA

Tumbarumba is best known for its top sparkling wines. The area is a fairly difficult one for wine growing with severe winters, excessive rainfall, and cool summers. Despite this the locals manage to produce reasonable to good whites and reds from sauvignon blanc, chardonnay, and pinot noir on pretty acid soil.

GRIFFITH/RIVERINA

This area lies further inland than the previous one. The hot and humid climate in summer makes it ideal here to produce late harvest and botrysic wines, that are mainly made from semillon. The soil is level layers of sand and loam, interspersed with some clay.

YOUNG

The Young area lies inland and to the north west of Canberra. The vineyards are sited fairly high on the hillsides. Although there is fairly substantial rainfall here during the otherwise moderately hot summer, irrigation remains necessary. Despite this the Young area produces reasonable to good wines.

COWRA

Cowra is situated in the hinterland of Sydney. The vineyards are sited on slopes along the local river. The soil is a mixture of clay, loam, and sand that has a fairly high acidity. The climate leans towards continental with hot dry summers. Despite this there is fairly considerable rainfall during the growing period so that irrigation is not always required. Cowra's wines are mainly whites and they are characterized by plenty of taste for little money.

LOWER HUNTER VALLEY

This is one of Australia's oldest wine growing areas, and it is mainly known for its superb Semillon and Syrah. The climate is hot but there is sufficient moisture. The soil on the slopes where the vineyards are situated is mainly sand, which is ideal for white wines.

UPPER HUNTER VALLEY

This too is a white wine area, mainly producing Chardonnay and Semillon. It is somewhat hotter and drier here than in the Lower Hunter Valley. The soil chiefly consists of a mixture of salty and acidic loam and sand. The Upper Hunter Valley is perhaps the most picturesque wine area in Australia.

Victoria produces surprisingly fresh and elegant red wines

AUSTRALIAN WINES

Australia produces and sells many different types of wine. Those that come from one area are characterized by the combination of *terroir* and grape variety. The blends on the other hand are derived from more than one area or region and their style owes much more to the particular winemaker. The type of oak (French, American, or German) used for the casks is also very important. Finally, the price of the wine also has a great bearing on the eventual complexity of the wine but in general every bottle of Australian wine offers value for money or even better.

The following descriptions are intended to stimulate you to do your own research.

Wines from the Hunter Valley are sometimes blended with wines from South Australia

SPARKLING WINES

In view of the remarkably low price it is best to choose a true traditional method sparkler that has undergone a secondary fermentation in the bottle. The white Brut sparkling wines are usually fresh and fruity with occasionally vegetal undertones. Fine as a chic affordable aperitif or as refreshing company with summer fruit. Drinking temperature is 8 °C (46.4 °F).

The Rosé Brut sparkling wines are generally somewhat less dry than the whites. The nose is very fruity with a slight hint of acid drops, strawberry, cherry, and raspberry. Serve these civilized charmers as an aperitif. Drinking temperature is 6–8 °C (42.8–46.4 °F).

CHARDONNAY

This is the success story of the Australian wine industry! The simple, young, Chardonnay that is not cask aged is a nice wine that can be very pleasant but the best ones are cask aged. The wine is fully ripened with an intense color, very complex structure, and wonderful nose containing exotic and citrus fruit with earthy

Exceptional Chardonnay from Jacob's Creek

undertones and suggestions of toast and nuts. Ideal with seafood, (lobster, crab, oysters and scallops), because they often have a taste with light silty undertones. Drinking temperature is 10–12 °C/50–53.6 °F (unoaked) or 12–14 °C/53.6–57.2 °F (barrel select).

SEMILLON

As strange as it may seem this typical Bordeaux grape used in e.g. Sauternes, produces a surprising wine in Australia that closely resembles a white Burgundy. This is why it is often blended with chardonnay.

Semillon is a somewhat strange term in Australia though some areas such as the Hunter Valley call it chenin blanc, crouchen, or even riesling. The bouquet is reminiscent of ripe and sweet fruit with suggestions of citrus fruit and flowers. Serve these rich, well--balanced and lively wines with any treasures that the sea has to offer. Drinking temperature is 10–12 °C (50–53.6 °F).

SEMILLON/CHARDONNAY

These are popular blends in Australia. This aromatic wine smells of fresh citrus fruit, peach, apricot, and tropical fruit. Chardonnay imparts a buttery character and the complexity while semillon and oak provide smoothness and the rounded taste. A little colombard is also often added to this blend to make the wine slightly fresher. Ideal with seafood, braised veal or poultry. Drinking temperature is 10–12 °C (50–53.6 °F).

The Australians are famous for their blended wines

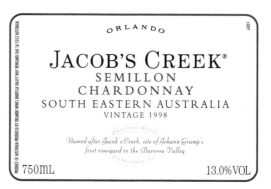

Semillon Chardonnay

SAUVIGNON BLANC

Australian Sauvignon Blanc resembles a good Sancerre rather than a white Bordeaux. Both these French areas grow sauvignon as their basic variety. The wines are very aromatic with characteristic vegetal undertones such as freshly sliced green peppers (paprika). The taste is fresh and lively and less taut than that of a white Bordeaux. This wine is drunk in Australia as an aperitif or with (grilled) seafood or salt water fish without accompanying sauces, and certainly no more than a knob of butter. Drinking temperature is 8–10 °C (46.4–50 °F).

Semillon Chardonnay Colombard

CHENIN BLANC

This variety of grape originates from the Loire Valley in France. Here in Australia it produces an entirely different wine than in Vouvray or Montlouis. These are sultry, full-bodied, rich wines, with a good balance between sweet and sour. These wines go well with creamy toasties or with hearty vegetable pies, poultry and especially with creamy combinations of seafood and avocado. They are also an excellent choice to accompany oriental dishes such as stir fried prawn dishes. Drinking temperature is 10–12 °C (50–53.6 °F).

RHINE RIESLING

This is the true riesling grape, originating from Germany (see remark at Semillon). Various types of wine are made with riesling, which can be dry, off-dry (slightly sweet), or sweet, whether affected by botrytis or not. The latter type of wine is given the name 'Noble', which refers to the noble rot. Riesling produces fresh wines with a nose reminiscent of lemons. The driest Riesling, when young, is fine not only with seafood and fish, but also with vegetable dishes and salads. The full-bodied, dry or off-dry Riesling is excellent with poultry or wildfowl. The Noble Riesling is often served with sweet deserts, but goes much better with goose or duck liver, patés and terrines, or with fresh tropical fruits or perhaps apricots filled with cream cheese. Drinking temperature is 8–10 °C/46.4–50 °F (young), 10–12 °C/50–53.6 °F (aged) and 6–10 °C/42.8–50 °F (Noble Riesling).

GEWÜRZTRAMINER

This is a very popular grape and wine with the Australians, although they have great problems with the name. Australian Gewürztraminers are interesting, exotic wines with fruity and spicy aromas, a full and pro-

longed taste and long finish. Although the Australians love taking this fine wine on their picnics, (with sausages or cheese) it is far more suited to oriental dishes such as softly herbed Chinese dishes or mild Indian curries. Drinking temperature is 10–12 °C (50–53.6 °F).

RIESLING/GEWÜRZTRAMINER

This is an interesting blend that combines the freshness and citrus fruit nose of riesling with the roundness and fresh spiciness of the gewürztraminer. Most wines are off-dry or even medium-dry. This wine is easy to drink and can be recommended with oriental dishes, white meat or poultry in a fruit sauce. Drinking temperature is 8–10 °C (46.4–50 °F).

VERDELHO

This is a very surprising grape that originates in Portugal, and produces good fresh wines with sensual and powerful aromas of tropical fruit. Verdelho is great with seafood, poultry or pork. Drinking temperature is 10–12 °C (50–53.6 °F).

ORANGE MUSCAT

This is the poetical name for the muscat of Alexandria, widely known from the area around the Mediterranean. This grape produces extremely aromatic and tasty late harvest dessert wines here.

FLORA

This grape is used to produce Late Harvest dessert wines with characteristic aromas of ripe fruit and a full and powerful taste. Flora is a hybrid resulting from crossing gewürztraminer and semillon. Orange muscat and flora are vinified separately by the famous Brown Brothers winery as a Late Harvest wine and then blended. This results in a marvelously rich and **Orange Muscat** complex wine with much power. Outstanding with soft blue cheese (Milawa Blue), but also with fresh baking. Drinking temperature is 6–8 °C (42.8–46.4 °F).

GRENACHE/SHIRAZ

Rosé wines are not at all common in Australia. This blend usually results in very fruity wines with a bouquet of fresh strawberry. Ideal

Delightful wine from Orange Muscat and Flora

for picnics and at the barbecue, but also as a table wine with chicken or salt-water fish. Drinking temperature is 10–12 °C (50–53.6 °F).

CABERNET SAUVIGNON

Australia too makes wines that are wholly cabernet sauvignon. Most wines though are blends of cabernet sauvignon and shiraz , or cabernet sauvignon, merlot, and shiraz. The pure Cabernet Sauvignon wines are full-bodied, rich, powerful, and complex. These wines need to be laid down for at least five years to mellow because they are remarkably full of tannin. These are outstanding wines with a nose of plum, blackcurrant, blueberry, and the occasional hints of chocolate, vanilla, tobacco, or cedar wood. Serve this Cabernet Sauvignon with the better meat dishes prepared with fillet of beef or small wild game. This wine will taste even better if the dishes are supplemented with some fried mushrooms or chestnuts. Drinking temperature is 16–17 °C (60.8–62.6 °F).

CABERNET FRANC

Cabernet franc grapes are mainly grown in northeast Victoria and blended with the grapes such as merlot. Sadly, this rather rare red wine is unfortunately some-

Merlot is usually blended with French Cabernet

what underrated in Australia. Tastes terrific with for example lamb Australian style, with a red wine sauce, green peas and fresh mint. Drinking temperature is 14–16 °C (57.2–60.8 °F).

MERLOT/CABERNET FRANC

Merlot is also little used on its own and mainly vinified or blended with the cabernets or even with shiraz. The combination of 65% merlot and 35% cabernet franc that is then cask aged for twelve months is quite common in Australia. This produces a fruity wine with fresh acidity and mellow taste and is especially suited to Provençal style herbed leg of lamb. Drinking temperature is 14–16 °C (57.2–60.8 °F).

Outstanding Cabernet Sauvignon

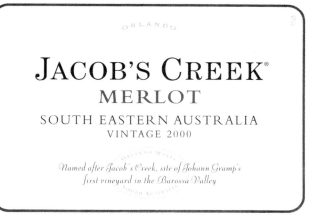

A fairly rare Merlot

PINOT NOIR

This Burgundian grape will be encountered here less widely than in the Bordeaux or Rhône types. Despite this, Australian Pinot Noir is proof of the skill of the successful Australian wine-makers. Anybody can make wine from the idiosyncratic pinot noir but to make good wine requires considerable know-how and plenty of passion. Various styles of Pinot Noir are to be found in Australia, from light, fruity and generous, to full-bodied, sultry, with animal undertones and sometimes a little on the heavy side. The best of them are somewhere in between these two extremes and simultaneously elegant and full-bodied with a seductive nose containing plum and cherry with a rich, almost caressing taste. The lighter types go particularly well with light starters, especially cold meat salads and cold meat. The better varieties are excellent with wildfowl. Drinking temperature is 14–16 °C (57.2–60.8 °F).

SHIRAZ

The Australians use the original name for this grape and not French bastardization of syrah. Australian Shiraz is a sensual tour-de-force with plenty of color, tannin, and acidity but also a wonderful bouquet containing overripe dark fruit such as plum, and spices (e.g. white pepper). Mature Shiraz develops animal undertones with a nose of leather and sable, and occasionally has the smell of freshly roasted Mocca coffee. The perfect partner with roasted or grilled meat and all types of wildfowl. Drinking temperature is 16–17 °C (60.8–62.6 °F).

Shiraz - Cabernet Sauvignon is a very classical Australian combination

SHIRAZ/CABERNET

This is very common blend that produces a wine of intense color with plenty of fruit and a mellow and rounded but fulsome taste. The bouquet mainly evokes thoughts of cherry and blackcurrant with a hint of pepper. Delicious with all main courses comprising of meat, wild game or poultry. Drinking temperature is 16–17 °C (60.8–62.6 °F).

TARRANGO

This is an interesting hybrid resulting from crossing the Portuguese touriga and extremely productive sultana, which is better known as dried fruit. This fairly recent Australian development is causing a major revolution. People who are not accustomed to drinking wine fall for the fruity charm of Tarrango, which can be served at almost any time if chilled. Tarrango wines have been deliberately inserted into international blind

Tarrango, the Australian "Beaujolais"

Shiraz (Syrah) is *the* face of Australian wine

wine tasting to cause confusion because it so closely resembles a French Beaujolais. Serve this wine with fish, cold meat, pasta salads, sliced meat products, fresh goat's cheese or just as a drink with friends. Drinking temperature is 12–14 °C (53.6–57.2 °F).

NEW ZEALAND

Many have made their first acquaintance with New Zealand wines during the past decade. These exceptional wines with their natural elegance and considerable aromatic properties have managed to win everyone over. New Zealand growers have remained sober and modest despite all the praise from both the media and professionals. They put their success down to the richness of their beautiful green country, which they happily call 'God's own country'. The link between man and nature in New Zealand is quite remarkable and it

A special Syrah from the famous French wine maker from Rhône, Michel Chapoutier

Chapoutier also makes this highly exciting rosé from the Syrah

The Australian Syrah produced by Chapoutieris full and powerful.

Chardonnay from New Zealand

is as if man feels at one with nature. This passion for the land is also to be found in the New Zealand wines where the essence of the land and the fruit are overwhelming united.

New Zealand is in the southwestern Pacific Ocean and consists of two main islands and countless smaller ones. North Island and South Island that form the bulk of the country are between them about 937 miles long and 125 miles wide at the broadest point. The majority of the 3,500,000 inhabitants live on North Island, in towns and cities such as Auckland, Hamilton, and Wellington. The main towns of medium size on South Island are Christchurch and Dunedin.

North Island has tempestuous volcanic origins and some volcanoes are still active, especially around Lake Taupo, where there are many geysers and hot water springs. Much of the island is mountainous with several summits above 8,202 ft. The extreme north of the island has gently undulating hills. South Island is dominated by the Southern Alps, dominated by the 3,764 meter high Mount Cook. The center of these Alps are covered with enormous glaciers and ice fields. The south-western coast is characterized by its countless fjord-like sea inlets which were formed by glaciers. The south and east of the island is somewhat flatter and covered with thick layers of fertile alluvial soil.

The climate is fairly mild and moist with rainfall distributed across the year fairly evenly. The difference in temperatures between day and night and between the seasons is insignificant, especially on North Island. Both islands suffer from wet westerly winds but the north-south alignment of the islands and the central mountain ridges means that these only affect the west. Hence twenty times as much rain falls in the west of South Island as in the east. Fortunately the average sun hours here is more than 2,000 hours per year, which is ideal for wine growing.

HISTORY

The Anglican church missionaries were the first to engage themselves in growing and making wine. They were of the opinion that the Maoris must first adapt to the good aspects of civilization before becoming Christians. They were put to work in the vineyards but it was more then twenty years before the first glass of New Zealand could be drunk. French missionaries improved the cultivation of the vines and extended them. This was taken over by English and Spanish immigrants between 1860 and 1870. The conditions at that time with fungus, plagues of insects, and earthquakes were so severe that the market for the wines was limited. Most English immigrants ignored the wine in favor of imported port and sherry. The wine industry came under severe strain around 1900 because of social and church movements that attempted to get a prohibition on alcohol introduced. The movement towards prohibition receded after World War II and the wine industry got fresh impetus from Dalmatian immigrants among others. The demand for local wine grew because of the large influx of wine-drinking immigrants such as those from Greece, Italy, and Yugoslavia. The English immigrants now too began to value New Zealand wines. Australian wine houses such as Penfolds injected the necessary investment to create a real breakthrough. Light, mild, and fruity Müller-Thurgau wines were remarkably popular in the 1970s and during the 1980s these German vines were replaced with French varieties. The results were astonishing. New Zealand Chardonnay, Sauvignon Blanc, Gewürztraminer, Pinot Noir, Cabernet Sauvignon, and Merlot are of excellent quality and the demand for them has grown at record pace, especially in Britain. Within fifteen years New Zealand has managed to become one of the great wine countries and today its wines are valued everywhere.

Sauvignon Blanc from Hawkes Bay

WINE REGIONS

There are nine major wine regions. These are (from north to south): Northland/Auckland (the historical heart of New Zealand wine), Waikato/Bay of Plenty, Gisborne, Hawke's Bay, Wairrapa on North Island, and Nelson, Marlborough, Canterbury, and Otago on South Island. The best wines mainly originate from three main areas.

GISBORNE

Gisborne is probably the best area for Chardonnay in the whole of New Zealand. The Chardonnays here are very full-bodied and rounded because of the mild climate and fertile alluvial soil.

HAWKES BAY

Hawkes bay has the oldest wineries in the New Zealand. The climate is very mild and the soil extremely varied, ranging from fertile alluvial top soil to gravel. This explains the tremendous diversity in styles of the local wines. Hawke's Bay is mainly known for its Cabernet Sauvignon and Chardonnay wines.

MARLBOROUGH

This area is situated in the north of South Island. The finest Sauvignon Blanc wines in the world are made here but the local sparkling wines are also gaining in quality. The climate is more pronounced here than on North Island, with plenty of sun, little rain, and relatively low temperatures. The soil is characteristically rocky with boulders, pebbles, and gravel. In addition to the wonderful Sauvignon Blanc, excellent Riesling and Chardonnay wines are also made here and very acceptable Pinot Noir, Cabernet Sauvignon, and Merlot reds.

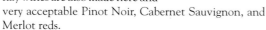

Marlborough
Chardonnay

THE WINES

New Zealand wines stand out not just because of their quality, but also their fairly high prices. The New Zealanders believe the superb quality of their wines will give them the edge and they trust in the healthy understanding of the wine world. Fortunately for them increasing numbers of wine experts have decided that the price of the best New Zealand wines is in proportion to their quality.

What is it that makes New Zealand wines so good? It is a combination of their climate but also their techniques. The traditional know-how of European

Corbans wines are very reliable

wine-makers has been combined with the most modern vinification methods. But New Zealanders would not be the people they are if their wines did not reflect the same respect for nature as the people themselves. Disease and pests are dealt with by natural biological means and no industrial sugar is added. Any stabilizing agents or preservatives to be added to the wine (such as sulfur and citric acid) have been determined by legislation.

CHARDONNAY

New Zealand Chardonnay is made in a variety of styles, with and without cask aging in oak, with and without additional contact with the grape skins during vinification (*macération pelliculaire*), and they are clearly characteristic of the area from which they come. The best Chardonnays are full-bodied and very aromatic (peach, apricot, and apple) and recognized by their fine and elegant acidity. Wonderful with lobster, crab or scallops. Drinking temperature 11–14 °C (51.8–57.2 °F).

SAUVIGNON BLANC

The Sauvignons Blancs are among the best of the world. Nowhere else derives so much power and expressive bouquet from Sauvignon grapes. This is not a mellow Bordeaux type Sauvignon, rather closer to a top-level Sancerre with overwhelming aromas of gooseberry, flint, green pepper (paprika), asparagus, melon, or passion fruit. A New Zealand Sauvignon grabs hold of you and does not let go. Everyone who tastes it is won over by the great strength and fruitiness. This wine is especially suited to dishes that include asparagus, green

MORTON ESTATE

CHARDONNAY
1996

750ml   13.0%   vol

PRODUCED & BOTTLED BY MORTON ESTATE WINES LTD
2 MOUNTAIN RD. EPSOM, AUCKLAND PRODUCE OF NEW ZEALAND

Morton Estate makes world class Chardonnay

vegetables, together with green salads, starters with cold meat and sliced meat products or grilled or deep fried fish. Drinking temperature 10–12 °C (50–53.6 °F).

RIESLING

The Rieslings, especially those of the South Island, are very elegant and aromatic. Some still possess slight residual sugar (off-dry) which is very pleasing. When riesling grapes have been affected by botrytis, the wines are of a very rare quality that is fulsome, rich and sensual, with hints of dried fruit like apricot and also honey in the bouquet. A lovely accompaniment with mild oriental dishes (curries), fish or poultry. Drinking temperature 8–10 °C (46.4–50 °F).

GEWÜRZTRAMINER

Although less well-known than the previously mentioned white wines, New Zealand Gewürztraminer wines are remarkably superb. They are powerful, fulsome and exotically spicy. Excellent with spicy oriental dishes, fresh fruit, semi soft cheeses or simply just for fun. Drinking temperature 10–12 °C (50–53.6 °F).

The New Zealand Sauvignon is extremely aromatic

CABERNET SAUVIGNON/MERLOT/ CABERNET FRANC/MALBEC

The red wines have improved in quality immeasurably in recent years. The best of them are the Cabernet Sauvignon, Merlot, and Cabernet Franc wines, which may have been blended with a little malbec and aged in oak casks. Although these top wines have much in common with a classic Bordeaux wine, they manage to retain a character of their own. These wines are ideal with a lovely piece of grilled or roasted lamb. Drinking temperature 16–17 °C (60.8–62.6 °F).

PINOT NOIR

The production and quality of Pinot Noir wines in New Zealand is on the increase. This wine is full-bodied, rich and bursting with aromas. These wines benefit from a few years aging in the bottle before being drunk. Delicious with small wild game, roast pork, veal and soft cheeses. Drinking temperature is 14–16 °C (57.2–60.8 °F).

SYRAH AND PINOTAGE

Finally wines have been made more recently from Syrah and Pinotage grapes. The Syrah still has some problems of adaptation but the initial results of the Pinotage are encouraging.

A very classical Cabernet Sauvignon

An excellent Merlot

Asia

When we think of wine, Asia is not the first place that springs to mind. It is true that the Asians are known for their thirst for expensive Bordeaux and Burgundy wines, but not exactly for their wine production. There are however four wine producing countries found on the Asian continent, one of which has a very long history of wine production – India. Japan has also been involved in wine making for many years, but is only recently experiencing a revival thanks to the improvement in quality of their native wines. China is probably the most suitable country for new vineyards, however the Chinese wine industry has been placed under enormous pressure by the prevailing political climate. Finally, Thailand started wine production a few years ago.

INDIA

The wine history of India is extremely long, and goes back to the time of the Indus, peers of the Egyptian pharaohs. In old mythological and religious scripts, the name "soma ras" (Indian for wine), the drink from the "soma" plant (wine vine) is regularly encountered. The ancient Indians believed that wine was the spirit of life, and allowed it to flow in abundance at joyous and less happy occasions. The Greeks, who in the time of Alexander the Great were attempting to broaden their outlook on the world, had set up a few settlements in India. They worked together with the people of India to popularize wine, while also helping to improve wine making techniques. The nectar of Hyderabad was well known in the seventeenth century by the world travelers. In the nineteenth century, many new vineyards were planted in order to satisfy the thirst of the occupying troops from England. Sadly, the Indian vineyards were also badly hit by the *Phylloxera* invasion at the end of the nineteenth century. It was almost a century before good wines could once again be produced in India. Thanks to the efforts of a number of companies and

private individuals, India experienced a comeback at the end of the twentieth century. A large number of the Indian vineyards are owned by Sham Chougule, the man who made the rebirth of the old wine region around Maharashtra possible. Very acceptable white and red still wines are made in this region at an altitude of 2460–2788 ft. However the real strength of this area is their sparkling wine, that is made following traditional methods. (e.g. Marquise de Pompadour). These wines, made under the supervision of a qualified wine maker from Champagne, never cease to surprise everybody with their extreme freshness and elegance. This is hardly surprising, as the Maharashtra climate is very similar to that of the Champagne region. Indian wine makers haven generally chosen to follow the traditional French wine making methods, and produce anything but startling wines. The quality of their whites, reds and rosés is moderate to reasonably acceptable. The following grape sorts are used: chardonnay, (also for sparkling wines), chenin blanc, muscat, sauvignon blanc, sémillon, pinot blanc, merlot, cabernet franc, cabernet sauvignon, pinot noir, and pinot meunier for the reds, with two latter being used primarily for sparkling wines. Two special Indian wines are produced in Italy under the official supervision of a well-known Indian oenologist. The characteristic oriental aromas of the white Sahiba and the red Nazraana are a result of lengthy maturing in sandalwood casks. The Sahiba is an excellent accompaniment with fish curries and white meat dishes, while the Nazraana is best suited to meat curries and Tandoori dishes.

THAILAND

Very acceptable white and red wines are produced from chenin blanc and the chenin rouge grapes respectively, harvested from the vineyards of the château de Loei – a 485 hectare wine region in Loei, on the border between Thailand and Laos. This domain is owned by a wealthy Thai businessman and is managed by a French winemake from Bordeaux. The wine production is soon to be supplemented with a second domain, but for the time being the demand for these fine, but more importantly inexpensive wines is by far exceeding the production. Wine production is not expected to meet the demand until 2010. The future of the Thai wine producing industry is be met with great optimism.

CHINA

China has also an abundance of wine producing history, although this has been a source of great mystery for decades. China planted their first vineyards around 2,000 years ago. The first vines were introduced to China by General Chang Ch'ien in 128 BC. They came supposedly from Iran or the Caucuses and were intended as a gift for Emperor Wuti. The first Chinese *Vitis vinifera* vineyards were already in place long before the French started wine production in earnest. The Chinese have actually always preferred stronger drink than wine. A number of old fashioned grape wines can be found in China, and are the legacy of the old Chinese wine production. (China does have a number of rice and fruit wines, but these will not be reviewed in this chapter). The Yantai comes from Shandong, the Red China from near Beijing, the white Shacheng from Hebei and the white Minquan from Henan. The fact that these wines are not in demand in the West has something to do with the vinification method. The grapes are harvested, pressed and the juice is allowed to ferment. The wine is then stored for two years in cement tanks or in large wine casks. Dependent on the desired end result, before or after storage, the young wine is blended with the taste being enhanced with a mixture including older wines, brandy, citric acid, and sugar. The red Yantai is very sweet and has little to offer in the way of aroma. The white wines are often oxidized (they smell and taste like dry sherry) but are somewhat fresher and often less sweet than the red wines. The Minquan is a reasonably fresh and aromatic white wine. I would not recommend the sweet brown red Yantai with Chinese dishes, however the white wines are surprisingly refreshing accompaniments with even the most subtle of dishes.

The majority of Chinese grapes have extremely fascinating names like cock's heart, cow's

Dynasty, French - Chinese wine from Tianjin

udder or dragon's eye. The latter is the only grape of importance to Chinese wine production. The dragon's eye grape or longyan is also used in Japan. About twenty years ago a number of European companies recognized that the Chinese wine industry could develop significantly if the powers that be would give the green light for large scale production. Remy Martin was the first European company to enter into a joint venture with a Chinese wine company. Dynasty, a reasonable to good wine, is produced near Beijing. The Allied Domecq Company signed a similar joint venture deal in 1985 and produces the white quality wines of Huadong Tsingtao. Chardonnay vines are now starting to reach the correct age, and are beginning to produce reasonable wines while riesling grapes are resulting in

中國青島薏絲琳白葡萄酒
11.5% VOL　中外合資華東葡萄釀酒有限公司　　　75 cl.

A very acceptable Chinese Riesling

excellent fresh, aromatic wines. In 1997, the famous Spanish wine maker Miguel Torres became established in China, and entered into a joint venture agreement with China Zhangjiakou Great Wall and the American concern, Montrose International. The new company is called Zhangjiakou Great Wall Torres winery and produces wines bearing the label Jaime Torres. The new off -shoot of the Torres family is in Shacheng, in the province of Hebei. The intention is to build a hypermodern winery in the not all too distant future, which will produce high quality wines from home-grown European grapes. Apart from these three giants from the world of drink, a number of other large multinationals are producing wine in China, including Seagrams, Pernod Ricard and Hiram Walker. All of these wines combine the oriental gastronomy and the western wine culture, and fair is fair, these wines are easier to get used to than the traditional Chinese wines.

JAPAN

Drastic improvements have taken place in the last few years in the land of the rising sun. The first evidence of the Japanese wine making was back in the ninth century when as in China the Japanese Emperor planted his own vineyards. The Emperor's vineyards were maintained by Buddhist monks who had advocated planting of vines on the land. It is not clear whether this was to produce grapes for eating or for wine production. However, one thing is certain the vines were from the *Vitis vinifera* family. The first form of wine production was at the foot of mount Fuji, with the koshu and zenkoji, a grape sort known in China as the longyan or dragon's eye. There was evidence of organized wine production as far back as the seventeenth century, all be it on a small scale. At the end of the nineteenth century young Japanese wine makers were sent to Bordeaux in France to learn the classical French wine making techniques. After returning to Japan these young passionate Japanese laid the foundations for the modern Japanese wine production. Although Japan is favorably placed for wine production, (about the same level as the Mediterranean) wine making is anything but a picnic. The springs and summers are particularly wet and windy, the winters are extremely cold, and the autumn has also usually a few surprises in store. Monsoons and typhoons are the winegrowers biggest enemies. Drastic measures have to be taken to prevent gray rot and total destruction of the grapes during the budding period, the blossoming period, and the period leading up to the harvesting. As in Portugal the vines are trained into a pergola shape, and in addition the vineyards are equipped with a sort of canopy to protect them from hard rain or hail.

Chinese rosé is surprisingly pleasant with sweet and sour dishes

White French - Chinese Wine: an ideal thirst quencher with many Chinese dishes

Mercian quality vineyards

It is extremely difficult for the Japanese wine industry to compete with other wine producing countries, as their production costs by comparison are often as much as five times higher. The Japanese wine consumption is steadily rising, but it is primarily the "cheap" wine countries that are reaping the rewards, such as Bulgaria, Hungary, Greece, South Africa, Australia and Chile. When the wealthy Japanese feel like drinking a "dear" wine, they usually go for a French wine rather than one from Japan.

There are three important names in the Japanese wine industry. The drinks giants, Suntory (also known for their joint venture with Grands Millésemes de France) Mercian and Mars. Apart from these large wine companies there are a number of other large companies together with more than 230 independent winegrowers that produce wines using their own grapes and sell them on to primarily Mercian and Mars. Suntory is the only giant concern that produces wines using grapes from its own vineyards. Officially, there are four wine regions in Japan: Hokkaido, Yamagata, Nagano and Yamanashi.

A typical, trellised Japanese vineyard (Mercian)

White and red quality wine

Sauvignon from Suntory, the Château Mercian Rouge, Shinsu Kikyogahara Merlot, Mercian Yamanashi Rouge and Johohira Cabernet Sauvignon.

The Japanese wine industry is probably faced with more inherent problems than any other wine producing nation, except perhaps Canada. In spite of this the Japanese have been able to produce particularly good wines, especially the red Cabernet Sauvignon and Merlot which are both sublime. Japan has managed to drag itself up to the level of the elite wine producing countries with their considerable knowledge, patience and love of their product.

In order to remove any doubts that may still be lingering about the quality of the best Japanese wines, it is worth mentioning that the now famous Château Mercian won a gold medal at the 1997 Vinexpo in Bordeaux, the most prestigious wine competition in the world.

Château Mercian red, made from classical French grapes

The latter is certainly regarded as the best for quality wine production. The climate is somewhat warmer, which is very favorable for the ripening process of the grapes. Japan has been using their own grapes for centuries, with the Koshu being especially popular. Experiments were later carried out with American hybrids but the results were unsatisfactory. Nowadays the wines are created using a mixture of Japanese and European grapes giving excellent results. Grapes such as koshu, chardonnay, riesling, and semillon are used for white wines, and muscat-bailey A (a Japanese hybrid), cabernet sauvignon and merlot for red.

Both wines initially display a fascinating vegetal undertone, followed by a lot of fruitiness and tremendous freshness. Chardonnay and Semillon are extremely pleasing, but the blended wines such as the Château Mercian Blanc, are absolute top class with their almost explosive aromas. Suntory also makes fairly expensive, but according to reports, a very successful botrytis wine from riesling and semillon. All of the following are excellent red wines in their own right; Lion d'Or Cabernet

Château Mercian white (dry)

Château Mercian white (sweet)

Acknowledgments

The writing of such a complex book would not be possible without help. I would like to thank all those people and organizations which helped with information, bottles, labels, and photographs and especially certain people for their special support, understanding, and patience.

FRANCE:

French Embassy to The Netherlands, Sopexa Pays-Bas Oud Reuchlin & Boelen, Fourcroy-Lenselink, Pernod-Ricard NL, Wijn Verlinden Château Manos (Cadillac), Mouton-Rothschild, Cordier, Didier Michaud CIVR Bergerac, Comte Laurent de Bosredon, Château Pique-Sègue/Dauzan Lavergne (Montravel), Jean & Evelyne Rebeyrolle, La Ressaudie (Montravel), Alain Brumont, Château Bouscassé, Château Montus (Madiran), Etienne Brana (Irouléguy), Cave Cooperative d'Irouléguy, Domaine Nigri (Béarn), Vignerons de Tursan, Cooperative de Fronton, Vignerons de Beaupuy (Marmande), Les Vins du Sud Ouest, Vignerons Catalans, La Cave de L'abbé Rous (Banyuls), Gérard Bertrand, CI Vins du Languedoc, Caves Languedoc Roussillon, Georges Schilperoort (Vilaro), Skalli, Georges Fareng (Val d'Orbieu), Comte Péraldi, Domaine d'Alzipratu, Domaine Leccia (Corsica), Château de Fontcreuse (Cassis); Peter Fisscher (Château Revelette, Provence), Guy Negrel (Mas de Cadenet), Domaine de l'Escarelle (Coteaux Varois), Cave Coopérative Clairette de Die et Crus de la Vallée du Rhône, CI Vins d'A.O.C. Côtes du Rhône et Vallée du Rhône, Château Mont-Redon (Châteauneuf du Pape), Chapoutier (Rhône), J.P. & J.F. Quénard (Chignin, Savoie), Vignerons Foreziens, Rougeyron (Châteaugay), Vignerons de Saint-Pourçain, Corinne Laurent (Saint-Pourçain), Georges Duboeuf (Beaujolais), Joseph Drouhin (Burgundy), Bouchard Père & Fils (Burgundy), Henri Maire (Arbois/Jura), CI Vins d'Alsace, Georges Lorentz, Louis Sipp (Alsace), Laroppe (Côtes de Toul), Lamé Delisle Boucard (Bourgueil/Chinon), Couly-Dutheil (Chinon), Jacques Bailly (Sancerre), Marnier Lapostolle (Château de Sancerre), Château de Villeneuve (Saumur/Saumur-Champigny), François Chidaine (Montlouis), Lisa Heidemanns (Vignobles Germain/Château de Fesles, Anjou), Gérard Bigonneau (Reuilly/Quincy), Philippe Portier (Quincy), Veuve Amiot (Saumur), Cave du Haut-Poitou, Mireille van Château de Mulonnière (Anjou), Champagne De Venoge, Taittinger, Bollinger, Deutz and many others

SPAIN:

ICEX Madrid (Pilar), Vinos de España (Marianne), Sherry Institute (Woudine), ICEX Seville (Isabel), Asociacion Exportadores de Vinos de Navarra (Conchi), Excal, Valladolid, Yolanda Piñero Chacón (Ribeira del Guadiana), Jean Arnaud Tilburg, Intercaves-Koopmans & Bruinier, Oud Reuchlin & Boelen, Castillo de Perelada Amsterdam, Bodegas Antaño (Rueda), Hijos de Antonio Barcelo (Viña Mayor), Marqués de Cáceres, Marques de Riscal, Julián Chivite, Señorio de Sarria, Virgen Blanca, Guelbenzu, Ochoa, Olite; Bodega Nuestra Señora. del Romero, Fariña, Bodegas Frutos Villar, Torremilanos Bodegas Peñalba Lopez, Consejo Regulador Valdepeñas, ICEX Brussels (José), Barbadillo, Fourcroy Lenselink, and many others

PORTUGAL:

Adega Cooperativa Torres Vedras, Oud Reuchlin & Boelen, Zoetermeer; Vinites, Haarlem.

ITALY:

ICE Amsterdam, ICE Rome, Paul Blom (Schermer), Intercaves/Koopmans & Bruinier, Vinites, Margriet Baarns (Incontro Vini di qualità, Nijmegen), Pio Cesare (Piedmont) and many others.

GREECE:

Aridjis De Griekse Wijnhandel (Utrecht)

THE BALKANS:

Du Frêne, W & L Logic Sales (Slovenia), Pernod Ricard NL (Romania)

HUNGARY:

Hungarian Embassy in The Netherlands, Egervin, Euróbor (Bátaapáti), Briljant Holding, Pince Polgár, Pince Bock, Attila Gere, Tiffan's, Vylyan, Hétszölö, Diznókö, István Szepsy, Királyudvar, Henkell & Söhnlein Hungaria; Mihály Figula, András Egyedi (Tokaj Renaissance), Akos Kamocsay (Hilltop), Imperial Wine Buyers (Regina Meij), Godevin (Belgium) and many others.

RUSSIA/GEORGIA:

Pernod Ricard NL (Georgia), Intercaves/Koopmans & Bruinier (Crimea)

AUSTRIA:

Wines from Austria, Vienna, Regina Meij (Imperial Wine Buyers)

SWITZERLAND:

SWEA Lausanne, Marcel Dubois, André Darbellay (Bonvin), Uberto & Cesare Valsangiacomo, Montmollin

GERMANY:

German Embassy in The Netherlands, Promotion Bureau for German Wine, Deinhard

LUXEMBOURG:

Bernard Massard

UNITED KINGDOM:

British Embassy in The Netherlands, Chiltern Valley, Hidden Spring, Sharpharm Vineyard, Lamberhurst Vineyard and many others.

TURKEY:

Kavaklidere, Wanders wine importers (Rotterdam)

THE LEBANON:

Eki International (Château Ksara, Amsterdam), Château Musar, The Lebanon/London

Harvest in the Hungarian Villány

ISRAEL:

Oud Reuchlin & Boelen (Carmel)

EGYPT:

Mercure Hotels Egypt

MOROCCO, ALGERIA, TUNISIA:

Algerian and Tunisian Embassies in The Netherlands, Delta Commerce, Farouk Mechik (ONCV, Algiers), Celliers de Meknès

SOUTH AFRICA:

South African Embassy in The Netherlands, Kaapkelder (Teuge), Guy Hickling, Fourcroy-Lenselink

CANADA:

Canadian Embassy in The Netherlands, Fema Trading (Théo), Château des Charmes, Klaus Reif

THE USA:

The US Embassy in The Netherlands, Wine Institute of California; Fourcroy-Lenselink; Oud Reuchlin & Boelen; Mondavi Europe; Kelly Heitlauf, Kari Leitch & Lynda Eller of Stimson Lane (Washington State); Carry Hay of Columbia Valley Winery Association; Kathleen McArthur Mosher & Sarah Thomas of Biltmore Estate (Asheville, NC); Tania Dautlick of North-Carolina Department of Agriculture and Consumers Services; Linda J. Jones of Michigan Department of Agriculture; David A. Miller of Texas Wine and Grape Growers Association; The brothers and sisters of the Brotherhood of the Knights of the Vine; Doug Caskey of Colorado Wine Industry Development Board; Debbie Hammond, Donniella Winchell & Michelle Widner of The Ohio Wine Producers Association (http://www.ohiowines.org); David Creighton of Michigan Grape and Wine Industry Council; Tareq Salahi of Oasis Winery, Kenneth Haapala; Rachael Rossman of Preston Winery, Oregon; The Oregon Wine Advisory Board; Christine Deussen of Eyrie Vineyards, Oregon; Alan, April & Cooper Jay Mitchell, Territorial Vineyards & Wine Company, Oregon; Kelly Rusk, American Vintners Association and everyone I may have overlooked.

BRAZIL:

Brazilian Trade Bureau in The Netherlands, Adriano Miolo, Gianni Tartari

URUGUAY:

Embassy of Uruguay in The Netherlands, Daniel Pisano, Ing. Javier Carrau and many others.

ARGENTINA:

Intercaves/Koopmans & Bruinier (Trapiche), Ricardo Puebla (Nieto y Senetiner, Mendoza), Pascual Toso (Mendoza), Pernod Ricard NL (Etchart)

CHILE:

Pro Chile NL, Pro Chile Milan, Intercaves/Koopmans & Bruinier, Oud Reuchlin & Boelen, Jean Arnaud, Errazuriz, Casa Lapostolle, Marnier Lapostolle

AUSTRALIA:

The Australian Wine Bureau (London), Phil Laffer (Orlando Wyndham, Barossa Valley), Brown Brothers (Milawa/London), Intercaves/Koopmans & Bruinier

NEW ZEALAND:

New Zealand Embassy in The Netherlands, Quality Wines (Naarden), Pernod Ricard NL

INDIA:

Sahib wines (The Hague), Indage group (India)

CHINA:

Huadong Tsingtao, Pernod Ricard NL, Torres

JAPAN:

Toshio Matsuura (Wands Publishing, Tokyo/Paris), Mercían (Yamanashi)

OTHERS:

Wijn Informatie Centrum, Bossenbroek, Scip Coutellerie de Thiers (Laguiole sommelier fairs), Dutch Museum of Wine, Arnhem

ADDITIONAL PHOTOGRAPHS

Bert de Leeuw, Drent Fotografie Arnhem (portraits of Christian Callec tasting wine);

Philippe Barret photographer, France (photos of Chapoutier bottles France/Australia);

Etienne Sipp (ES), Ribeauvillé, Alsace, France (all the photos of the vineyards of Ribeauvillé, grand cru Kirchberg, and Louis Sipp);

Red Point Studio, Son (pictures of Romania for Pernod Ricard NL).

PHOTOGRAPHIC MATERIAL AND MANIPULATION:

Foto Willemz, Arnhem; Foto Combi Kramer, Arnhem

TRANSPORT:

Autobedrijf Renault Bochane, Arnhem

And all those others I have forgotten to thank...

I also wish to personally thank the following people for their tremendous inspiration and support:

Marianne & Philip Mallard (Pique-Sègue/Dauzan Lavergne), Laurent de Bosredon, Thierry Dauilhiac (Saussignac), Marie Laurence Prince Doutreloux (CIVR Bergerac), Marie Casanave (CIVR Bergerac), Georges Lorentz, Etienne Sipp, Michel Chapoutier, Yves Cuilleron, Claude & Pierre Emmanuel Taittinger, Véronique & Frédéric Drouhin, Bernard Georges (Duboeuf), Georges & Franck Duboeuf, Christian Duport (Val Joanis), Jean Abeille (Mont-Redon), Peter Fischer (Revelette), Guy Négrel (Mas Cadenet), Péter Mosoni (Gödöllö Agricultural College), Attila Domokos (Bátaapáti), János Arvay, Attila Máhr & his son (Aranysárkány Etterem, Szentendre), István Szepsy, Zoltán Demeter, Anthony E. Wang (Királyudvar), Monika & Pál Debreczeni (Vylyan), Tibor Kovács (Hétszölö, Vylyan), László Mészáros (Disnókö), Akos Kamocsay (Hilltop), István Bozóky, Anthony E. Hwang, Marianne Nuberg (Vinos de España NL), José Maria Fernández, ICEX Brussels, Fernando & Mercedes Chivite, Ricardo Guelbenzu Morte, Phil Laffer, Richard Dumas & Sally – does - Kerr (Orlando Wyndham), Piet Rutten, Joop v.d. Kant, Coen Pollaert (Jean Arnaud), Robert Handjes (P.R. Nederland), Ciska Spikker, Dick de Wolf, Jessica van Vliet, Cindy Kneppers, Ellen Bax (Oud, Reuchlin & Boelen), Franka van Unen (Fourcroy-Lenselink), Donders family, Robbers & v.d. Hoogen, Arnhem, Paul Molleman (Wine Institute of California The Netherlands), Robert Leenaers, Hubrecht Duijker, René van Heusden, Karel Koolhoven, Ronald de Groot , Gert Crum and Ton BorghoutsRenate Hagenouw, Textcase.

Finally I wish to thank my dear wife for her eternal patience and understanding.

Bibliography

De wijndruif, Robert Leenaers, Van Dishoeck

Wijn uit de hele wereld, C. Camarra, J.P. Paireault, Rebo

Wijn & Dranken Encyclopedie, Alexis Lichine 1985, Luitingh, publishers

L'histoire de la vigne & du vin, H. & B. Enjalbert, Bordas

Bergerac et ses vins, Éditions Feret

Champagne par Taittinger, Claude Taittinger, Stock.

Le goit juste des vins et des plats, J. Puisais, Flammarion

El vino y su cata, Javier Ochoa, Gobierno de Navarra

Los Mejores Vinos 1998/ 1999/ 2000, José Peñín, Pi & Erre Ediciones

Guía Toyota de los 300 mejores vinos de España

Spain, a matter of taste, Wines guide 1996, Icex

Los vinos de España, Ediciones Castell

Valdepeñas et ses vins, Jestís Martín Rodríguez

Le porto, Chantal Lecouty, Éditions Robert Laffont

The List of DOC and DOCG Wines, XIIIe ed., Enoteca Italiana

La Grèce à travers ses vins, Ditnitri Hadjinicolaou

The wines and vines of Hungary, S. Kirkland, New World publ.

Rohaly's Wine guide of Hungary 2000, Akó Ltd.

Das Tokajerbuch, Michael Sailer

Tokaj-Hegyaljai album, 1867, Szabó & Török

The Wine & Food of Austria, G. MacDonogh, Mitchell Beazley

Connaissance des vins Suisses, OFD Communication & SWEA

The wines of Germany, Andrew Jefford, Deutscher Weinfonds

South African Wines 2000, John Platter, Injectrade

Cape Wines, Body & Soul, Alain Proust/Graham Knox, Fernwood Press

Zuid-Afrikaanse wijn, Willem Arts, De Toorts

De charmante wijnen van Chili, Hubrecht Duijker, Het Spectrum

Wines and vineyards of New Zealand, M. Cooper, Hodder Moa Beckett

Index

Good champagne is a true art!